PAUL
FOLLOWER OF JESUS
OR FOUNDER OF CHRISTIANITY?

PAUL

Follower of Jesus or
Founder of Christianity?

DAVID WENHAM

WILLIAM B. EERDMANS PUBLISHING COMPANY
GRAND RAPIDS / CAMBRIDGE

© 1995 Wm. B. Eerdmans Publishing Co.
255 Jefferson Ave. S.E.
Grand Rapids, Michigan 49503
and
Cambridge, U.K.

Printed in the United States of America

00 99 98 97 96 95   7 6 5 4 3 2 1

Library of Congress Cataloging-in-Publication Data

Wenham, David.
Paul: Follower of Jesus or founder of Christianity? / David Wenham.
p.   cm.
Includes bibliographical references and index.
ISBN 0-8028-0124-2
1. Paul, the Apostle, Saint — Teachings. 2. Jesus Christ — Teachings. 3. Paul, the
Apostle, Saint — Contributions in Christology. 4. Jesus Christ — History of
doctrines — Early church, ca. I. Title.
BS2653.W45 1995
225.9′2 — dc20   95-1071
                                                                CIP

CONTENTS

90840

Preface

A friend who heard that I was writing this book paused and commented "I find Paul difficult." She speaks for many people, and I hope that this book may help a little. I have worked on the question of Paul and Jesus over a period of years, and I have written a number of detailed studies, some quite technical. This is an attempt to offer a broader look at the question for a wider audience. I have been conscious of trying to serve two masters in the book — by reaching for that wider audience and by addressing questions of scholarly debate — and it has been difficult to do so. I hope nevertheless that the discussion, despite its limitations, will be of wide interest.

Many people have contributed to this book directly or indirectly. I would especially like to thank Michael Thompson, Paula Gooder, Peter Ensor, and Idicheria Ninan for reading the manuscript and for all their criticisms and valuable suggestions. I am also grateful to the principal and staff of Wycliffe Hall for allowing me study leave during 1993 to complete the book. I owe much to my family, especially to my wife Clare, who has been a constant support and encouragement.

Wycliffe Hall, Oxford

Abbreviations

AB	Anchor Bible
BJRL	*Bulletin of the John Rylands Library*
BNTC	Black's New Testament Commentaries
CBQ	*Catholic Biblical Quarterly*
EQ	*Evangelical Quarterly*
ETL	*Ephemerides Theologicae Lovanienses*
GNB	Good News Bible
Gospel Perspectives	
I	R. T. France and D. Wenham, eds., *Gospel Perspectives I* (Sheffield: JSOT, 1980).
III	R. T. France and D. Wenham, eds., *Gospel Perspectives III: Studies in Midrash and Historiography* (Sheffield: JSOT, 1983).
5	D. Wenham, ed., *Gospel Perspectives 5: The Jesus Tradition Outside the Gospels* (Sheffield: JSOT, 1985).
6	D. Wenham and C. L. Blomberg, eds., *Gospel Perspectives 6: The Miracles of Jesus* (Sheffield: JSOT, 1986).
H/BNTC	Harper's New Testament Commentaries = Black's New Testament Commentaries
HTR	*Harvard Theological Review*
ICC	International Critical Commentary
Int	*Interpretation*
JB	Jerusalem Bible
JBL	*Journal of Biblical Literature*
JJS	*Journal of Jewish Studies*
Josephus	
Ant.	*Antiquities of the Jews*

War	*The Jewish War*
JSNT	*Journal for the Study of the New Testament*
JTS	*Journal of Theological Studies*
NCBC	New Century Bible Commentary
NICNT	New International Commentary on the New Testament
NIGTC	New International Greek Testament Commentary
NIV	New International Version
NovT	*Novum Testamentum*
NRSV	New Revised Standard Version
NT	New Testament
NTS	*New Testament Studies*
OT	Old Testament
Philo *Leg All.*	*Legum Allegoriae*
RevBib	*Revue Biblique*
RSR	*Revue des Sciences Religieuses*
RSV	Revised Standard Version
SJT	*Scottish Journal of Theology*
TynB	*Tyndale Bulletin*
UP	University Press
WBC	Word Biblical Commentary
ZNW	*Zeitschrift für die Neutestamentliche Wissenschaft*
ZTK	*Zeitschrift für Theologie und Kirche*

1

INTRODUCING
THE QUESTION

Two people dominate the pages of the NT more than any others: Jesus and Paul. These two men were quite different from each other in many ways: Jesus was a charismatic prophetic figure from Galilee, Paul a Greek-speaking intellectual and letter writer. But both played a vital part in the establishment and early development of the Christian movement. The question being addressed in this book is: What was the relationship between these two influential men?

As far as we know, they never met during Jesus' lifetime.[1] But according to the book of Acts, Paul came into contact with followers of Jesus very soon after Jesus' death. He fiercely opposed them at first, but then after his dramatic conversion he joined them and became (in his own words) a "slave of Jesus Christ" (Rom 1:1).

It is commonly assumed that from this point on Paul's relationship to Jesus was that of a faithful follower. As a self-confessed "slave" of Jesus — and like other Christian converts through the ages — he was very interested in the life and teaching of his master. He held Jesus in the highest regard and tried to base his own life and teaching on what he knew of Jesus. So it is supposed.

However, that assumption about Paul has not gone unchallenged. Indeed, in recent years a quite different view has become influential. Far

---

1. Paul was in Jerusalem not long after Jesus' death, and some people have suggested that he must have seen Jesus during his ministry. But there is no indication of this in his letters. When he does speak of having "seen the Lord," the reference is probably to his conversion experience (1 Cor 9:1; 15:8). See Fraser, *Jesus and Paul*, 46, 47.

from meekly following Jesus, it is suggested that Paul was an innovator who brought into Christianity all sorts of ideas and emphases that complicated and spoiled the original, simple religion of Jesus.

This sort of view was put forcefully to the British public in a TV series entitled "The First Christian" in the early 1980s. In the book accompanying the series Karen Armstrong, herself once a member of a Christian religious order, speaks of her admiration for Paul, but at the same time concludes that many of the "unhealthy" and "unpleasant" aspects of Christianity."find their origin in Paul."[2] Among the things for which Paul may be held partly responsible are negative attitudes toward women, sexuality and the human body, and Jews. He also had authoritarian tendencies, and supported (implicitly) the social status quo in regard to slavery. Armstrong comments: "When I turn back to study the life and teachings of Jesus it seems that Paul has not only been an important influence on Christianity, but that in a very real sense he was its founder. He could be called the first Christian."[3]

The fullest and most forceful scholarly presentation of this view in recent years was published in 1986 by the well-known Jewish scholar Hyam Maccoby (who was one of the people Armstrong consulted in preparing her television series). In his significantly entitled book *The Mythmaker: Paul and the Invention of Christianity*, Maccoby calls Paul "an adventurer" and "the greatest fantasist of all"; he explains that "it was Paul who founded Christianity" as we know it today (and, indeed, as it is found in most of the NT). Paul, influenced by Greek ideas and the Greek mystery religions, invented the "myths" of Jesus' divinity and sacrificial death and was also the "creator of the eucharist."[4] He agrees with Armstrong about Paul's other unpleasant contributions to Christianity.

This view of Paul, even though it is stated polemically and in an extreme form by Maccoby, is one with which many less extreme scholars have had and still have sympathy. The view has a long and respectable scholarly pedigree.[5] It was William Wrede, the influential German scholar,

2. Armstrong, *The First Christian*, 12, 13.
3. *Ibid.*, 12, 13.
4. *Mythmaker*, 15, 113, 204, etc.
5. For the history of scholarly discussion of the Jesus-Paul question see Furnish, "The Jesus-Paul Debate"; Wilson, "From Jesus to Paul." Both trace the modern debate back to F. C. Baur, the influential nineteenth-century Tübingen scholar, who postulated a major divergence in the early church between the Jerusalem apostles and Paul. Fraser, *Jesus and Paul*, 9, lays some of the blame for this view on the philosopher Nietzsche, who saw Paul as "the genius of hatred" and as a "morbid crank" who ruined the good news of Jesus the Savior.

who in his book on Paul at the start of this century called Paul "the second founder of Christianity."[6] Many scholars since then have argued that Paul (along with others) turned the Jewish prophet Jesus into a Gentile God and made Christianity what it has been ever since.[7]

It is not only scholars who have argued this. Many ordinary Christians, as well as non-Christians, have found Paul extremely difficult, and feel that Christianity would be very much better off without some of the dogmas that he propounds (e.g., the divinity of Jesus and Jesus' death as a blood sacrifice), not to mention his teachings on sex, women, and slaves. They would be quite happy if we could keep Jesus, but quietly lose Paul.[8]

THE DATA AND THE ISSUES

So was Paul a faithful follower of Jesus or the founder of a new religion? Or is the truth somewhere between those two positions? What evidence is there that will help us answer this question?

Paul's Use or Nonuse of the Stories and Sayings of Jesus

The data

One of the most embarrassing facts for those who see Paul as a follower of Jesus is his failure to refer much to Jesus' life or teaching. In his letters Paul refers very frequently to the death and resurrection of Jesus, but as for Jesus' birth, baptism, miracles, parables, transfiguration, etc., there is a deafening silence. As for the sayings of Jesus, Paul hardly quotes them at all, at least explicitly.

---

6. Wrede, *Paul*, 179.

7. See, among many others, Klausner, *From Jesus to Paul*, 581. More recently Vermes comments in *Jesus and the World of Judaism*, 56-57, that "little by little, the Christ of Pauline theology and his Gentile church took over from the holy man of Galilee." Similarly in *Religion of Jesus*, 212, he asks: "Is it an exaggeration to suggest that oceans separate Paul's Christian gospel from the religion of Jesus the Jew?" It is not only Jewish scholars who have seen things in this way: others who posit a significant gap between Jesus and Paul include Casey in *From Jewish Prophet to Gentile God* and Mack in *The Lost Gospel*. Mack, like Maccoby, uses the language of "mythmaking" when speaking of Christian origins and traces many of the central Christian "myths" to Paul and the Pauline congregations (e.g., pp. 215-22).

8. See Wilson, "From Jesus to Paul," 1, citing *Akenfeld* by R. Blythe.

There are two exceptions to this silence. The first is 1 Cor 7:10, where Paul refers to Jesus' teaching on divorce:

> To the married I give this command — not I but the Lord — that the wife should not separate from her husband . . . , and that the husband should not divorce his wife.[9]

The other is 1 Cor 9:14, where Paul writes:

> In the same way, the Lord commanded that those who proclaim the gospel should get their living by the gospel.[10]

Most scholars agree that Paul is alluding to sayings of Jesus on these two occasions as well as in his account of the last supper in 1 Corinthians 11.[11] Some suspect that he also does so on other occasions. But there is little unanimity on those other occasions, and so the undisputed references to the teaching of Jesus in all of Paul's writings are very few indeed.

Even with the two verses in question, 1 Cor 7:10 and 9:14, it is argued that Paul cites the teaching of Jesus rather freely and without evident enthusiasm: Thus in 7:10 he mentions Jesus' prohibition of divorce, but then proceeds to give his own regulations on divorce in the church. In 9:14 he refers to Jesus' teaching on paying missionaries, but does so in the context of an explanation of why he, Paul, does not accept payment for his ministry.

It is not just the small number of quotations from Jesus that is striking, but specifically Paul's failure to quote from the sayings of Jesus where he might appropriately have done so. For example, in 2 Corinthians 8 and 9 Paul is urging the Corinthians to be generous in contributing to the collection he is making for the Christians in Jerusalem. He uses a battery of different arguments to press his readers to respond, but no use at all is made of the extensive and colorful teaching of Jesus about wealth, poverty, and "laying up treasures in heaven."[12]

---

9. This is taken as an allusion to Jesus' teaching on divorce, which comes in various parts of the Gospels: Matt 5:27, 28; 19:3-9; Mark 10:2-12; Luke 16:18. For full discussion of the sayings in question, see chapter 6 below.

10. This is usually taken to be an echo of Matt 10:10/Luke 10:7, where Jesus says: "the laborer is worthy of his food/hire."* See further in chapter 5 below.

11. The last supper narrative is part of the passion narrative and thus is a somewhat different category from the other teachings of Jesus. In addition, the last supper account has particular liturgical importance, and so Paul's use of it does not necessarily prove anything about his interest in and knowledge of Jesus' pre-passion life and ministry.

12. See Goulder, *Midrash and Lection in Matthew,* 148-49.

Explanations of Paul's silence

What is to be made of Paul's almost total silence in regard to Jesus' teaching and life before his passion? The obvious conclusion, as it has seemed to many, is that Paul was not interested in the pre-passion ministry of Jesus and may in fact have been quite poorly informed about it. This may seem a surprising conclusion. But the argument is logical enough: Had Paul known much about Jesus' ministry and teaching and had they been important to him, he (like modern Christian preachers) would surely have referred to them continually. In fact he does not.

How could Paul have been uninterested in Jesus' life and teaching and yet have called himself a "slave of Jesus Christ"? Paul's faith, it is argued, focused on the death and resurrection of Jesus and then on the risen Lord and his work in the church by his Spirit. It was this Jesus that Paul worshiped and served; what the earthly Jesus said and did was of very little importance to him. So the influential Rudolf Bultmann can say: "Jesus' teaching is — to all intents and purposes — irrelevant for Paul."[13] Commenting on his view S. G. Wilson claims: "One aspect of Bultmann's analysis has won the day: few would now deny that Paul's interest in the person and teaching of Jesus is minimal."[14]

Wilson's concession of victory to Bultmann on this point sounds rather decisive, but it is certainly not the final word on the matter. A significant number of scholars see things very differently, and some indeed offer almost exactly the opposite explanation from Bultmann in seeking to account for Paul's silence. They argue that Paul's explicit quotations from Jesus' teaching are infrequent because he takes knowledge of Jesus' teaching for granted. Paul does not need to quote from it often because he and his readers have been taught it and know it well. In his letters his task is to discuss what is disputed and unclear, not to repeat what is already very familiar.

Using Paul's silence about Jesus as an argument for his knowledge of Jesus may seem rather curious. Wilson comments: "The suggestion that Paul must have known more of Jesus' teaching than he mentions, or that he assumes a common knowledge shared by himself and his readers, are arguments from silence which have never been convincing."[15] However, those who take the

---

13. Bultmann, "Significance of the Historical Jesus," 223.

14. See "From Jesus to Paul," 6, 7. Cf. Fredriksen, *From Jesus to Christ*, 174: "About Jesus of Nazareth Paul evinces little interest."

15. "From Jesus to Paul," 8. See also Bultmann, "Significance," 222: He notes that Paul thought it important to have a word of the Lord in 1 Corinthians 7, which "makes it the more certain that when Paul does not cite such a word where it would be expected, he knows of none." Barclay, in "Jesus and Paul," notes how perilous arguments from

opposite view to that of Wilson argue that the few direct quotations show some knowledge on Paul's part and also that there are numerous possible or probable allusions to Jesus' teaching in Paul's letters, which is precisely what might be expected if that teaching is presupposed. The problem with this last argument is that recognizing allusions can be a very subjective business: Some scholars see allusions everywhere and others fail to recognize them anywhere.

So did Paul have little interest in Jesus and so say little about him? Or did he take for granted considerable knowledge of Jesus? Or are there other possible explanations of the data?[16] The truth could lie somewhere in between the two positions described: Paul's interest in Jesus may not have been quite as lacking as Bultmann and Wilson suggest, and yet it could be that the ministry of Jesus was relatively unimportant to him. This could be simply because Jesus' death and resurrection were theologically so much more important to him; it could be that he found the Palestinian traditions of Jesus not immediately applicable in his Greek-speaking churches;[17] it could even be that some of his opponents in the early church were very keen on Jesus' ministry and that Paul felt himself personally and theologically on much stronger ground when referring to the Lord's death and resurrection than to his ministry;[18] or Paul's nonuse of stories and sayings of Jesus could have arisen from a combination of these factors.

Paul's failure to refer explicitly to the teaching and ministry of Jesus

---

silence are, but suggests that it may be less perilous to infer Paul's ignorance from his silence about Jesus than to infer concealed knowledge (p. 499).

16. It is worth noting that almost all the other letter writers of the NT apart from Paul are equally reticent in referring to Jesus' ministry and teaching. Therefore the issue is not simply a Pauline one, and it may well be that some of the same factors influenced Paul and the other writers.

17. Theissen, *Social Reality and the Early Christians,* 33-59, suggests that there was effectively a censorship in place since the Palestinian traditions reflected a radical itinerant lifestyle that was impracticable in Paul's urban context. He speaks of the synoptic Son of man giving way to the Pauline cosmic Christ.

18. Paul did not have firsthand experience of Jesus' ministry, and there is reason to think that this was held against him by his critics (as we shall see later). It has been argued by various scholars that Paul did not quote Jesus frequently because his critics and opponents made much of Jesus' teaching. See, e.g., Kuhn, "Der irdische Jesus," who argues that Paul's opponents included (1) those who emphasized Jesus' miracles and their own miracles — at the expense of the cross (so 2 Corinthians as explained in Georgi's influential *The Opponents of Paul in Second Corinthians*), and (2) those who were in the "wisdom" tradition represented by the "Q" source (so 1 Corinthians 1–4 as explained by Robinson and Koester; see further in chapter 2 below). Paul thus had a reason for steering clear of the miracle traditions of the Gospels and the "Q" traditions.

may therefore be variously explained. There is no scholarly consensus on the explanation, and the issue deserves continuing attention.

Two Gospels or One?

The question of Paul's knowledge and use of the stories and sayings of Jesus is not the only ingredient in discussion of Paul's relationship to Jesus. There is also the question of the message of the two men.[19] It is taken for granted by many Christians that Jesus and Paul preached essentially the same gospel. However, it does not take a very sharp mind to observe that there are, on the surface at least, quite significant differences between Jesus and Paul.

There are differences in presentation, with Jesus speaking in pithy, pictorial sayings and Paul in sustained and often rather complicated arguments. But there are other differences, too: The center of Jesus' message is the kingdom of God; Paul, however, refers rather rarely to the kingdom, and it is not a central concept in his letters. The center of his message has to do with the death and resurrection of Jesus, and he speaks of people being "justified" rather than of "entering the kingdom." In many other ways Paul is distinct from Jesus: His massive interest in the Holy Spirit and in the Gentile mission, his negative attitude toward the OT law, and his teaching on the church as a "body" all set Paul apart from Jesus (at least as Jesus is described in the synoptic Gospels).

What is to be made of this and other similar data? One obvious possibility, fitting in with the observations we have already made about Paul's failure to draw much on Jesus' teaching, is that he was not trying to follow — let alone to reproduce slavishly — the ideas and teaching of the historical Jesus. His theological vision arose rather out of his experience of the risen Jesus in his own life and in the church, and in developing that vision under the guidance of the Spirit (as he believed) he departed significantly from the religion of Jesus, introducing new ideas and radically reshaping the Christian faith. Whether or not the provocative title "founder of Christianity" is used, many scholars would accept the general assessment of Paul that it represents: He transformed the Jewish religion of Jesus into something very different, and he influenced subsequent Christian thought and belief decisively.

19. Paul could have made extensive and explicit use of Jesus' teaching and yet have come up with a theology having a very different feel and emphasis; on the other hand, he could have made minimal use of Jesus-traditions and yet have proved himself to be theologically very much at one with Jesus.

The opposite point of view is that, despite the surface differences between Jesus and Paul, their theologies are essentially the same. There are certainly differences in how they express their ideas, no doubt due to their different social context. Jesus preached in rural Galilee, Paul in Greek-speaking cities of the Roman world. There is also some development of ideas, particularly in the light of the resurrection. But, it is claimed, there is real continuity between Jesus and Paul: Paul is not an innovator. He brings out things that are implicit in Jesus' teaching, but the main thrust of his teaching is precisely the same as that of Jesus.

So, two gospels or one? Again there is no consensus among scholars on the answer to that question. The answer may be somewhere between the two positions described: Paul may have points in common with Jesus, but also significant divergences. In that case, in order to answer the question "follower of Jesus or founder of Christianity?" we will need to weigh the similarities and differences and to see whether Paul and Jesus are at one in the main points of their theology and in the overall thrust of what they say, or whether there has been a major change of direction between Jesus and Paul.

So we have two disputed questions to consider: (1) How much did Paul know and care about Jesus' ministry (including his teaching)? (2) And how far did Paul agree or disagree theologically with Jesus? The two questions are quite distinct, though not necessarily unrelated.[20]

WHY BOTHER? THE IMPORTANCE OF THE ISSUES

But why does the question of Paul's relationship to Jesus matter? Historically it may be an interesting question, but is it more than that?

The Legitimacy of Pauline and Traditional Christianity

Many people perceive it as very important indeed: The conclusion that Paul was effectively the founder of a new religion may not unreasonably be seen as devastating for Christian faith, since it turns out that the Christian church

---

20. It is probably simpler to think of historical interest in Jesus and theological agreement with him (or lack of interest and lack of agreement) going together than to think of Paul being indifferent to the historical Jesus and yet theologically in agreement or of him being historically interested but theologically in disagreement. But it need not necessarily have been so.

has based its doctrine and life not on Jesus, as it has mistakenly claimed, but on Paul and his misinterpretation of Jesus. On the other hand, such a conclusion has been seen by others as liberating for Christian faith, since Paul is seen as the person who complicated and spoiled the simple religion of Jesus, to which we may now with good reason return.[21]

Both of these positions assume that Jesus has some normative importance for Christianity, and that can hardly be disputed. What may be questioned is any over-simple assumption that any development from the "original" religion of Jesus is necessarily a betrayal or denial of Jesus and what he stood for. Indeed, it is possible to argue precisely the opposite, namely that faithfulness to Jesus has always entailed reinterpreting his religion in and for new contexts.

However, even though the boundary between them may be narrow and sometimes difficult to define, there is an important difference between a faithful and an unfaithful reinterpretation. The accusation sometimes made is that Paul was not trying to be faithful to Jesus — hence his apparent lack of interest in Jesus — and that his is a different religion from that of Jesus, not a legitimate development of it. That accusation certainly has serious implications for Christian faith.

The Nature of Christian Faith

Whether the accusation, if sustained, discredits Christian faith and the Christian church altogether may depend in part on how wide the gulf between Jesus and Paul is seen to be, but also on how important the historical Jesus is seen to be for faith. Many ordinary Christians would consider that the historical Jesus is by definition all-important for Christian faith. But scholars have been less sure: Rudolf Bultmann, as is well known, argued that the historical existence and crucifixion of Jesus are indispensable, but that otherwise the historical Jesus and traditions about him are irrelevant for faith. Bultmann's disciples and successors were not in the end of the day persuaded by this and argued that there must be some continuity between "the Christ of faith" and "the Jesus of history."

It is not the purpose of this book to explore that theological question as such. But study of Paul and Jesus is relevant to how we answer that

---

21. Casey, *From Jewish Prophet*, 178, observes: "If Christianity is to remain a viable option for honest and well-informed people, it should surely undo that process of development, and emerge as something nearer to the religion of Jesus of Nazareth."

question. If it turns out that Paul was not very interested in the historical Jesus, then traditional assumptions about the historical nature and basis of Christian faith are put in jeopardy. Christians traditionally have claimed that the distinctive thing about Christian faith is its historical basis: Its so-called "particularity" lies in its assertion that God's salvation came to humanity in particular historical events — Christ "was handed over to death for our trespasses and was raised for our justification" (Rom 4:25). Christianity is not myth or philosophy or a system of ethics but a historical revelation. If, however, it turns out that Paul, as the first author of the NT and the most influential exponent of Christian faith in the early church, did not see the history of Jesus as especially important, then we will have to conclude that our view of Christian faith was not that of many of the earliest Christians, since Paul was surely not alone in his attitudes.

If Paul, perhaps influenced by the Greek mystery religions, was interested in the proclamation of a dying and rising Christ rather than in the history of Jesus, then we may be forced to conclude that early Christianity was more mythological and less historical than we supposed. This is the sort of conclusion reached by Bultmann, and S. G. Wilson in his article surveying the history of recent Jesus-Paul study finds himself forced by the meager evidence for Paul's interest in Jesus to this theological conclusion:

> Driven by reflection on both the theory and practice of our historical craft to the view that there is little we can confidently assert apart from the mere fact of Jesus' life and death, we are forced to fall back on a mythological figure (the Christ of faith, Pauline or otherwise) and adopt a position which verges on the docetic.[22]

Others come to very different conclusions. If it turns out that there is very strong continuity from Jesus to Paul and that Paul saw himself as very significantly dependent on Jesus, then the traditional view of the importance of history will be a primitive Christian view and to that extent affirmed rather than denied. A. J. M. Wedderburn in his book on *Paul and Jesus* comes to quite different conclusions about Christian theology from those of Wilson:

> While the Spirit of Jesus may lead it into new apprehensions of truth, the Spirit which leads it must remain that of Jesus. Continuity with him remains the touchstone by which all past statements of Christian theol-

22. "From Jesus to Paul," 20.

ogy, including Paul's, must be judged, and is the challenge confronting all present affirmations of Christian faith and its practice.[23]

Our study of Jesus and Paul may enable us to weigh the contrasting opinions of Wilson and Wedderburn.

Light on Gospel Stories and Gospel History

It may also throw light on the history of the gospel traditions. One of the biggest and most controversial questions in NT studies continues to be that of the origin and nature of the Gospels: Two centuries of critical study have clarified some matters, but there is still very wide disagreement as to whether the Gospel accounts are broadly or only marginally historical. Paul is potentially a most important witness in this case.

One view of Paul, as we have seen, is that he was not interested in the historical traditions of Jesus. Jesus "according to the flesh"* — to quote a phrase from 2 Cor 5:16 — was unimportant to him, and he apparently knew little of Jesus' ministry.[24] For Paul it was the living Christ who mattered, the Christ who died and rose and who would one day return. Paul, if he is correctly understood in this way, was not alone in his views. Indeed, it is widely held that the early church generally shared Paul's outlook: Its members were fired by a consciousness of the living Christ and by an eager expectation of his imminent return, not by a backward-looking historical interest. If this picture of the early church is anywhere near the truth, then it may follow that the church is unlikely to have carefully preserved or transmitted the stories and sayings of Jesus; that was not their concern. Our Gospels, therefore, are not based on a historically reliable tradition but on a fluid and relatively haphazard tradition, in which stories of Jesus have become mixed up with all sorts of additional and interpretative material. Such is the conclusion of many scholars, and appeal is made to Paul as an important witness to this process.

The opposite view is that Paul and his readers knew the stories and sayings of Jesus well and that Paul took them for granted in his writings. If this view is correct, then it turns out that, far from being uninterested in Jesus, the church from its earliest days on regarded Jesus and his teaching as of the greatest importance. The Evangelists on this view were heirs, not

---

23. *Paul and Jesus*, 114-15.
24. On 2 Cor 5:16 see chapter 9 below.

to a vague and confused tradition, but to a strong and very early tradition. And Paul is not only an important witness to the gospel tradition as a whole, but also to specific traditions of Jesus that he directly or (more often) indirectly attests. For example, the famous saying of Jesus about Peter being the rock on which the church was to be built is one that only occurs in Matthew's Gospel and has been viewed with historical suspicion by some scholars (Matt 16:16-20). But if Paul indirectly attests this tradition in Galatians 2, then the case for seeing it as an authentic saying of Jesus is greatly enhanced.[25]

Paul is cited by skeptical and conservative scholars to support their view of the gospel tradition. Assessing his evidence is important.

The Unity, Diversity, and Inspiration of Scripture

The traditional Christian view of Scripture as a book that speaks with one voice — God's voice — has been vigorously challenged in recent years. Scripture speaks with many voices, it is said — many different *human* voices, saying significantly different things. The diversity is such that, in the view of many, we cannot speak of *the* theology of the Bible, or even of *the* theology of the NT, since there are different, even contradictory, theologies in the two Testaments. Whether we can continue to speak of the unity of Scripture or even to regard the Bible as the inspired word of God is debated among scholars, with most agreeing that old definitions of the unity and inspiration of the Bible need to be replaced.[26]

This book will not explore the big questions of inspiration and interpretation raised by this discussion as such. But the Jesus-Paul issue is a useful test-case, since there is prima facie evidence of significant diversity here. That evidence needs to be weighed: Is there contradiction or simply

25. On Matthew 16 see chapter 5 below. If it is possible to show that Paul probably knew a particular saying or story of Jesus and that he regarded it as deriving from Jesus, this does not of itself prove that the saying or story in fact goes back to Jesus. The tradition could be pre-Pauline but still post-Jesus. On the other hand, Paul must be regarded as a very important and early witness in such cases, one whose testimony may throw significant light not only on the issue of authenticity but more generally on questions to do with the history and original form of the particular tradition. He is, as it were, an additional witness to consider when discussing the synoptic problem.

26. The most significant recent work on the subject remains Dunn's *Unity and Diversity in the NT.* See also my appendix, "Unity and Diversity in the NT" in Ladd, *Theology of the NT,* 684-719.

divergence and development? If there is a basic unity, there may still be valuable things to learn about the adaptation of the Christian tradition in different contexts from comparison of Paul and Jesus.

SOLVING THE JESUS-PAUL QUESTION: CAN IT BE DONE?

The wide divergence of opinion among scholars about Paul's relationship to Jesus makes it clear that the Jesus-Paul question is complex, to say the least. It is complex for a large number of reasons.

Problems

(1) First, there is considerable scholarly confusion about what, if anything, we can know about the historical Jesus. The Gospel records purport to tell us things, but how reliable they are historically is uncertain. Such uncertainty obviously makes any study of Paul's relationship to Jesus difficult.

It means, among other things, that, if there does seem to be a connection between a story or saying of Jesus found in the Gospels and a Pauline saying, the dependence need not necessarily be from Jesus to Paul, but could be from Paul to the Jesus of the Gospels. Since the Gospels are usually thought to have been written after Paul's letters, it could well be that that the Evangelists have been influenced by Paul or Pauline tradition in their portrayal of Jesus.[27]

Scholars disagree not only on what goes back to Jesus, but also on the interpretation of much of the teaching given by Jesus in the Gospels. Even such a central theme as "the kingdom of God" is understood quite differently by different scholars. Again this complicates the study of Paul's relationship to Jesus.

(2) The uncertainty is not only at Jesus' end of the equation, but also at Paul's, since scholars disagree as to which of the NT letters attributed to Paul actually go back to the apostle. The NT ascribes thirteen letters to Paul, but six of them — Ephesians, Colossians, 2 Thessalonians, 1 and 2 Timothy, and Titus — are regarded as pseudonymous by some scholars.

Scholars also disagree about the interpretation of Paul's theology.

---

27. Goulder argues for extensive use of Pauline tradition by both Matthew and Luke. See *Midrash and Lection,* 153-70; *The Evangelists' Calendar,* 227-40; *Luke: A New Paradigm,* 129-46. Other scholars recognize occasional direct or indirect borrowing.

What is the central theme and focus of Paul's thought? What exactly does Paul mean by "justification"? Scholars disagree on these basic questions.

Such disagreement makes comparing Paul and Jesus difficult. Wilson puts it this way:

> The only certainty is that there is, and can be, no certainty, and that this is as true of our understanding of Paul as it is of our understanding of Jesus. Neither Jesus nor Paul are stable entities and a definitive answer to the Jesus-Paul question, therefore, will always evade us.[28]

(3) Even if, despite Wilson's pessimism, these two rather formidable obstacles are overcome and we feel reasonably confident that a particular saying or idea goes back to Jesus or to Paul, there are still further problems when it comes to showing a connection between them.

It was Samuel Sandmel who coined the expression "parallelomania" to describe the tendency of some scholars to see enormous significance in parallel phraseology found in two different sources, where there may be no significance at all.[29] Two authors may use similar ideas or phraseology entirely coincidentally. We may not assume that if Jesus and Paul have terms and ideas in common (e.g., God's fatherhood or divine judgment) this necessarily proves any connection between them. If there is a connection, it may not be direct: Two authors may well use similar ideas or phraseology because they come from similar backgrounds and have a common literary or social heritage. Jesus and Paul obviously have a very important common Jewish heritage.

And even if all of these difficulties can be overcome and a probable connection discovered between, for example, a saying of Jesus and a statement of Paul, this does not necessarily prove that Paul knew or was consciously drawing on the saying of Jesus. It could be that the saying of Jesus had been assimilated into the teaching of the church and came to Paul as Christian teaching, not specifically as teaching of Jesus.[30] Much the same could be said about particular theological themes and developments: Was Paul a follower of Jesus in any direct sense, or was his theology rooted rather in the teaching of the early Hellenistic Christian community?

---

28. "From Jesus to Paul," 18. See also Drane, "Patterns of Evangelization," 282-83.

29. "Parallelomania."

30. Stanton, *Jesus of Nazareth in NT Preaching*, 98, comments: "Lists of allusions and parallels to the synoptic logia underline their influential role in the primitive church, but they do not reveal Paul's own interest in Jesus of Nazareth."

The Rationale of This Book

The immensity of the problems should perhaps persuade any sane person that to tackle the Jesus-Paul question is a fool's errand or at least a venture that will not achieve much; the most that can reasonably be hoped for is that a case is presented that will prove congenial and helpful to those who share the author's presuppositions and outlook.

But although it would be wrong to minimize the size of the task or the inevitable limitations of a study like this, the sort of pessimism that implies that no progress can be made in tackling difficult historical issues is to be rejected. It may sometimes seem that scholarship has reached an impasse on an issue, but it is usually unwise to declare a final stalemate. There are usually moves still to be made in the game, even if they are not always obvious, and the game can move on constructively, so long as the players are willing to explore the possibilities. The danger in scholarly debate is either too-hasty despair — unwillingness to engage with new ideas and arguments — or too close attachment to existing ways of looking at things — unwillingness to consider radically different approaches.

Different people approach the Jesus-Paul issue, like other issues, with their own presuppositions, and these presuppositions affect their conclusions. But this fact of scholarly — even human — life is not a cause for academic despair or defeatism. Not all presuppositions are equally valid, and the very widely different conclusions reached by different scholars are not all equally supported by the evidence: Some are better supported than others, and, although we need to be aware of our own and others' presuppositions, we must not dismiss others for their presuppositions. Instead, we must test different theories and presuppositions, including our own, against each other and against the evidence.

Although the relation between Jesus and Paul is a big issue with many complicating dimensions, the point should not be exaggerated. Some of the basic questions, such as "Was Paul familiar with the traditions of Jesus or not?" are perfectly straightforward in principle, and it is not being wildly optimistic to hope to throw some light on them.

What Is Distinctive about This Book and Its Approach?

A wide-ranging survey

There have been a number of recent books on Jesus and Paul, notably two collections of essays: *From Jesus to Paul*, edited by Peter Richardson and John Hurd and published in 1984, and *Paul and Jesus* edited by A. J. M. Wedderburn and published in 1989. There have also been several more narrowly focused studies, including Michael Thompson's important study *Clothed with Christ: The Example and Teaching of Jesus in Romans 12.1– 15.13* and Ben Witherington's *Jesus, Paul and the End of the World*, published in 1991 and 1992 respectively. More recently still Victor Furnish has published a brief, though valuable, introduction to the Jesus-Paul question, *Jesus According to Paul* (1993). The present book resembles Furnish's in that it is a broad survey of the subject, but it is a larger study, in which we are able to present the data and the interpretative options much more fully.

It could be argued that the subject is so huge and complex that to try to survey the topic in one book (albeit a substantial one) is suicidal and not likely to be useful. However, we hope that the opposite will be seen to be the case. It is clearly true that a book of this sort will not be able to go into many issues in great depth, but we hope that it will be valuable (a) as an accessible work of reference, bringing together a wide range of data and ideas and drawing on more technical studies, and (b) because a wide-ranging examination of a subject may make things clear in a way that is not possible through more fragmented approaches. It is arguable that one of the weaknesses of some NT study has been — precisely — its piecemeal approach to historical questions: Each piece of tradition has to be weighed, and the evidence is simply insufficient to say anything with confidence. An alternative and sometimes more fruitful approach is to build up a large picture: If the individual pieces of evidence fit well into the large picture, then we may have a case that is much stronger than simply the aggregate of the individual arguments about particular traditions. That is not in any way to demean the importance of detailed study of particular traditions. There will be some detailed study in this book, and we will frequently refer to other more technical and detailed studies, but still the case to be presented here is very much a cumulative argument to which a wide variety of different pieces of evidence contribute.

The influence of recent New Testament study

Scholarship has moved on since any scholar (writing in English) has attempted a comprehensive examination of the Jesus-Paul question,[31] and this book is written in the light of recent discussion of Jesus, Paul, and the synoptic problem.

First, as we have already seen, there continues to be widespread disagreement over the historical reliability of the Gospels and of their portrait of Jesus. Some continue (in the tradition of Rudolf Bultmann) to be highly skeptical; others are much more positive. Some of the most interesting work has been done in recent years by those scholars who have emphasized the importance of Jesus' social and religious context, bringing to bear sociological insights and a fresh appreciation of the Judaism of Jesus' day.[32] Scholars such as Ben Meyer, Geza Vermes, Anthony Harvey, Gerd Theissen, Marcus Borg, Ed Sanders, and more recently Tom Wright have offered particularly interesting perspectives on Jesus, and this book will take account of these scholars and of what has been termed the "third quest" of the historical Jesus.[33]

Second, there has been a significant revolution in thinking about Paul in recent years, associated especially with the name of E. P. Sanders.[34] Sanders and others have offered a strong and sustained challenge to many traditional readings of Paul, seeing Paul not as a Luther-figure wrestling with human guilt, but as a Jewish Christian wrestling with the question of the ingathering of the Gentiles. This and other new perspectives on Paul must from now on influence any discussion of Jesus and Paul.

The synoptic problem — the teasing problem of how Matthew, Mark, and Luke are related — was once thought to have been finally and definitively solved by NT scholars. Mark and "Q," a hypothetical collection of

31. The last substantial study was Fraser's *Jesus and Paul* (1974).

32. The continuing publication of new material from the Dead Sea Scrolls throws important light on Jesus' Jewish environment. See, for example, Eisenman and Wise, *The Dead Sea Scrolls Uncovered*. Their view that the scrolls are Jewish Christian documents is unpersuasive, but it is clear that the early Christians had much in common with the Jewish authors of the scrolls.

33. The term "third quest" was coined by N. T. Wright and used in his various studies, including his useful survey of recent NT study in Neill and Wright, *Interpretation of the NT*, 360-449, and his major work *The NT and the People of God*. For another recent survey and discussion of issues see Charlesworth, *Jesus within Judaism*; also Chilton and Evans, *Studying the Historical Jesus*.

34. Sanders's seminal work on Paul was *Paul and Palestinian Judaism*.

Jesus' sayings, were identified as Matthew's and Luke's sources. The pattern of similarities and differences in Matthew and Luke was explained in terms of their use of Mark, "Q," and their own sources. That "assured result of criticism" is now recognized to be far from sure, and the so-called "two-source hypothesis," even if it is still favored by the majority of scholars, is now competing in the scholarly marketplace with a variety of other views, including the view that Matthew was the earliest Gospel.[35]

The importance of this for the Jesus-Paul question is in its impact on discussion of Jesus-tradition. In discussing Jesus' teaching scholars used to take the two-source hypothesis for granted and assumed that, for example, the Markan form of Jesus' sayings was more authentic than any parallels found in Matthew and Luke. That can no longer be taken for granted. Even those who continue to accept Markan priority are beginning to recognize that Matthew and Luke may have more original forms of wording. This recognition opens up new possibilities for the study of Paul and Jesus, and it is important particularly for discussion of supposed Jesus-traditions in Paul.

Focus on Jesus-traditions in Paul

The final and most distinctive thing about this book is the attention we will give to the question of Jesus-traditions in Paul's letters. Both of the recent collections of essays that I have referred to come to highly pessimistic conclusions about the possibility of detecting echoes of Jesus' teaching in Paul's writings. Thus V. P. Furnish comments: "The Jesus-Paul debate has not ever been significantly advanced, nor will a solution to the Jesus-Paul problem ever be finally achieved, by locating parallel passages in Paul and the Gospels."[36] The quest for allusions is seen as fruitless, and the question

35. Farmer's controversial book *The Synoptic Problem* was perhaps most influential in questioning the consensus in favor of the two-source hypothesis. Farmer advocated the so-called Griesbach hypothesis, according to which Matthew was the first Gospel, Luke second, and Mark third. Scholars have proposed all sorts of other views in recent years — many dispensing with "Q," several postulating multiple editions of Mark and the other Gospels and envisaging a rather complex pattern of synoptic relationships. Among recent scholars who have questioned the two-source theory note Sanders and Davies, *Studying the Synoptic Gospels*, and J. W. Wenham, *Redating Matthew, Mark, and Luke* (see also Ellis, "Making of Narratives"). Significant treatments continuing to defend the theory include Tuckett, *Revival of the Griesbach Hypothesis*, and Catchpole, *The Quest for Q*. For a useful comparison of several differing views see Dungan, *Interrelations of the Gospels*.

36. "The Jesus-Paul Debate," 44. See also Wilson, "From Jesus to Paul," 9.

of theological similarity and dissimilarity is seen as the only fruitful way into the Jesus-Paul question.

This pessimism deserves to be challenged, and indeed it has been challenged, perhaps most notably in Michael Thompson's *Clothed with Christ*, which is valuable not only for its detailed study of Romans but also for its proposals for a rigorous method for identifying echoes and allusions of Jesus' teaching in Paul. Here we will seek to develop and apply more widely the work of Thompson and others.[37]

What to Expect in This Book

Most of this book — chapters 2-7 — is devoted to an examination of the teaching of Jesus and Paul. We will look at the two important questions that we have already introduced: (a) Is Paul dependent on the teaching and traditions of Jesus, directly or indirectly? (b) And is Paul's theological understanding and emphasis similar or dissimilar to that of Jesus? In each chapter those questions will be addressed, though in the opposite order: The first part of each chapter will explore a particular theme of Jesus' teaching as it is recorded in the Gospels and then look at Paul's teaching on the same subject, comparing the two. This comparison will then lead us into the rather more technical second part of each chapter, where we will consider if there is any evidence to show that Paul knew and was influenced by the traditions of Jesus.

Chapter 8 will look at Jesus' life, ministry, death, and resurrection, considering what Paul knew and how he viewed not just the sayings of Jesus, but also the story of Jesus. Chapter 9 will then review and draw together the conclusions of all that has preceded.

---

37. Among recent articles and books identifying Jesus traditions in Paul we note Stanley, "Pauline Allusions"; Brown, "Synoptic Parallels"; Dungan, *Sayings of Jesus;* Fjärstedt, *Synoptic Tradition in 1 Corinthians;* Allison, "Pauline Epistles and Synoptic Gospels"; D. Wenham, "Paul's Use of the Jesus Tradition"; Richardson and Gooch, "Logia of Jesus in 1 Corinthians"; Stuhlmacher, "Jesustradition im Römerbrief"; Dunn, "Paul's Knowledge of the Jesus Tradition," and "Jesus Tradition in Paul"; Kim, "Jesus, Sayings of." Notable skeptics with regard to the quest for allusions include Tuckett, "1 Corinthians and Q"; *idem,* "Paul and the Synoptic Mission Discourse"; *idem,* "Synoptic Tradition in 1 Thessalonians"; Neirynck, "Paul and the Sayings of Jesus."

Method and Assumptions

Preliminary remarks

The Jesus-Paul question is one in which scholars' differing presuppositions and assumptions are influential. For example, on the particular question of Paul's interest in the historical Jesus, there is a tendency among scholars of a conservative bent to minimize the gap between Paul and Jesus, and among more critical scholars to take for granted the view that Paul was not particularly interested in Jesus. However, the issue is not one on which scholars inevitably and always divide according to their theological presuppositions. Thus there are conservative scholars who are quite agnostic (even skeptical) toward the view that Paul knew and made use of much Jesus-tradition, and also more radical scholars who have argued that traditions of Jesus (whether actually going back to Jesus or not) were important in Paul's churches.[38]

This book undoubtedly reflects the author's own background and outlook as a moderately conservative, biblical critic. However, it does not assume that its readers will share its author's presuppositions or prejudices and it makes a serious attempt to weigh the evidence openly and to engage with different points of view.

The Gospel records

We have noted already the continuing confusion among scholars about the reliability of the Gospels and their testimony to the historical Jesus. We cannot take for granted in this study that the Gospels' description of Jesus is historically accurate in all points. We will need to consider the arguments that have been presented for the authenticity and inauthenticity of different stories and sayings.[39]

---

38. E.g., Dungan, *Sayings of Jesus;* see also Robinson, "Kerygma and History." Goulder (see n. 27 above) may also perhaps be cited in this connection: He sides firmly with those who see many significant links between the gospel traditions and Paul, although he thinks that the direction of influence is more from Paul to the Gospels than from Jesus to Paul.

39. So far as the question of Paul's relationship to particular Jesus-traditions is concerned, the crucial issue is not necessarily authenticity but rather the question of the age of the traditions and whether they were regarded as Jesus-traditions when Paul wrote. However, the question of authenticity is still obviously relevant, since a positive answer to the question means that the saying or story in question is one that Paul could have known and used, whereas a negative answer *may* mean the opposite.

We do believe that the extreme skepticism of some scholars (notably in the Bultmann school) has rightly been rejected by many recent scholars, including several of those in the so-called "third quest." Seen in the context of first-century Judaism, the Gospel accounts make more sense historically than has often been recognized, and even sayings and stories of Jesus that have been routinely dismissed by many scholars often deserve a reprieve.[40] But, although this book will presuppose an openness to reconsider all sorts of issues, the presumption is not a naive acceptance of everything in the Gospels as historically beyond question, but a recognition that the Gospel narratives are interpreted accounts of Jesus that must be historically weighed.[41]

The synoptic problem

We have seen that the question of how the Gospels, Matthew, Mark, and Luke, relate to each other is very much an open question once again. This book will not assume a particular solution to the synoptic problem.[42]

40. Mack in his writings, e.g., *Lost Gospel*, represents a radically skeptical approach to the Gospels. He bases his view of the historical Jesus as a Cynic-like preacher on a reconstructed first version of "Q." It is not possible to engage here seriously with his arguments: His dependence not just on the uncertain "Q" hypothesis but on speculative reconstructions of early versions of "Q" makes his whole thesis vulnerable. Perhaps more important, his thesis sets Jesus apart both from his first-century Jewish context (it is the church that turns Jesus into a Jewish eschatological prophet) and from earliest Christianity as it is attested in the NT. (See further below in chapter 2, including the additional note on "Recent Interpretation of Jesus' Kingdom Teaching"; furthermore, my whole discussion of the Jesus-Paul issue raises all sorts of questions for Mack's thesis.)

41. There is no failsafe method of answering questions of authenticity, nor are there criteria that can be simply or automatically applied. The arguments (for example, over how broadly and well attested a particular tradition appears to be in the Gospels or over the coherence of a particular saying or story with what we know of Jesus and his Palestinian context) have to be carefully considered in each case. The literature on authenticity and criteria of authenticity is massive. Two introductory discussions are Sanders and Davies, *Studying the Synoptic Gospels,* and Blomberg, *Historical Reliability of the Gospels.* So far as Paul's knowledge of the Jesus-tradition is concerned, the question of the authenticity of a particular tradition may not be crucial (see previous note), but the question of how widely and well attested a particular saying or story was is extremely relevant: The more widely it was known, the more likely Paul is to have known it.

42. The argument for Markan priority continues to be quite persuasive in my view, but the case for a documentary "Q" source is much more dubious. I will, however, sometimes use "Q" as a convenient label for non-Markan traditions found in both

Declining to adopt one particular solution to the synoptic problem means that whenever we consider a saying or story of Jesus that is found in more than one Gospel we will assume neither that Mark's version is necessarily the earliest nor that it is the source of Matthew's and Luke's versions.

Avoiding that assumption is in any case important: Even if Matthew did use Mark (as is quite likely), it is most unlikely that he only knew or used Mark when retelling Mark's story. It is most unlikely, for example, that, when Matthew came to Mark's version of the parable of the sower, this was the first time he had heard that parable. The stories and sayings of Jesus were, on any view, passed down in the oral tradition of the church, and there is every likelihood that Matthew knew most of what is in Mark before Mark's Gospel had even been thought of! The importance of this consideration has often been neglected by scholars, perhaps because it greatly complicates the synoptic problem: Oral tradition becomes a very difficult joker in the pack; it is much simpler, but quite implausible, to think of Matthew sitting in a sealed room writing his Gospel with no information about Jesus apart from some written sources that have been brought to him.

Reckoning with oral tradition means that, even if the two-source hypothesis is accepted, we cannot assume that Mark's version of any particular story or saying must necessarily be the most original. It could frequently be so, if Matthew had Mark in front of him and was following him carefully, but there is every likelihood that from time to time Matthew slipped into the non-Markan version, which he knew before he ever read Mark. Matthew's version in such cases is independent and may well be more original than Mark's, Matthew having reverted to the older form of words that Mark had modified. The same argument applies no matter what source hypothesis is favored: If Mark used Matthew, for example, he surely had independent oral tradition.

This is not simply a priori very probable; there is a considerable amount of evidence that shows it to be true.[43] Some of that evidence will be explained in the following discussion of Paul and Jesus.

Matthew and Luke. Although unpersuaded of the "Q" hypothesis as such, I do believe that Matthew and Luke had common non-Markan traditions (and not that Luke derived his "Q" material directly from Matthew). See further in the next note.

43. My *Rediscovery of Jesus' Eschatological Discourse* was a sustained argument for the importance of reckoning with "pre-synoptic tradition." Some of the argument was speculative, but the case for Matthew, Mark, and Luke having independent access to common traditions of Jesus' eschatological teaching is very strong. See the discussion in chapter 6 below.

In some ways this consideration may seem to complicate our task very seriously: A simple solution to the synoptic problem would make life altogether simpler when it comes to comparing Jesus and Paul. It turns out that we cannot simply compare the Markan version of a story or saying with Paul's; we have to consider the Matthean or Lukan version as well, and with each tradition we have to weigh what the probable synoptic relationship is. However, although this is a complication, it may also be a liberation. It cannot help any historical research if at the outset the basic parameters are oversimplified; arguably this is precisely what has happened in the past with the Jesus-Paul question (and also other NT questions). Scholars working with an oversimplified view of the synoptic problem have failed to see things that a more open approach would have enabled them to see.[44]

John and other nonsynoptic Gospels

There are other Gospels than Matthew, Mark, and Luke that purport to give us information about Jesus. Most important is the canonical Gospel of John. There is good reason for believing John to contain a considerable amount of early traditions of Jesus, many of them not paralleled in the synoptics.[45]

---

44. E.g., Stanton, *Gospel for a New People*, 330-31 concludes — along with many other scholars who are firmly wedded to the two-source hypothesis — that the sayings of Jesus about mission to Jews in Matt 10:5 and 15:24 derive from Matthew, not Jesus. Vermes, however, being less firmly committed than Stanton to a particular source theory, can speak of the authenticity of the sayings being "well-nigh impregnable" (*Jesus the Jew*, 49). We shall see in chapter 4 (below) arguments (including arguments from Paul) to support Vermes's view. Similarly Goulder, along with many other scholars, sees the saying of Jesus about the church in Matt 16:16-20 as a Matthean addition to Mark: He sees that it has parallels in Paul's letters and explains that there has been Pauline influence on Matthew (e.g., *Evangelists' Calendar*, 232-35). Had he been more cautious about assuming Markan priority in particular contexts, he might have seen that the relationship is quite probably the other way round in this case — with the Matthean saying being primitive and having influenced Paul (see further in chapter 4 below). It is not, of course, wrong for scholars to work with particular source theories (e.g., with the theory of Markan priority), but they should realize that a simplistic application of the theory (such that, e.g., Matthean and Lukan variations from Mark are invariably seen in terms of redaction rather than in terms of non-Markan tradition) is uncritical, and there needs to be an openness to the possibility that Paul may throw significant light on detailed questions of synoptic relationships.

45. Both J. A. T. Robinson, *The Priority of John*, and Hengel, *The Johannine Question*, argue that its author was an eyewitness of Jesus' ministry.

However, there are sufficient scholarly doubts about exactly what sort of history the fourth Evangelist presents to make it prudent in this study (in which we have so many other complicated issues to hold in balance) to use it only as a subsidiary source.

The so-called "apocryphal" Gospels are even more controversial: They are mostly, if not all, significantly later than the canonical Gospels, and despite recent interest in them they have a relatively weak claim to being significant as sources of information about Jesus.[46] They will, therefore, not be given much attention in this study.

Which letters did Paul write?

In comparing Jesus and Paul, Paul's end of the equation is relatively straight-forward, since there is little doubt about the authenticity of most of the Pauline corpus. Perhaps the three most important letters of Paul for our study are Romans, 1 Corinthians, and 1 Thessalonians, and the overwhelming majority of scholars are agreed on their genuineness as letters of Paul, even if there are a few short passages over which questions have been raised.

We could limit our study to the undisputed letters, but the case for also regarding 2 Thessalonians, Colossians, and even (though more hesitantly) Ephesians as Pauline is quite widely accepted in the scholarly community. We believe the arguments to be strong and that we are therefore justified in using those three letters at least to supplement the evidence of the undisputed letters; but it is important to stress that the overall case being presented in this book is in no way dependent on the disputed Pauline letters. The Pastoral Epistles are much more controversial, and, although a good case can be made for viewing them as written by Paul or at his behest, there is so much doubt among scholars about their authenticity as to make it prudent for us to refer to them in passing, rather than to depend significantly on their evidence.[47]

Of course, even if not actually written by Paul, the disputed letters are in a broad sense "Pauline," giving us insight into thinking and teaching that was prevalent in Pauline churches; they are therefore not irrelevant to our investigation. However, if the so-called deutero-Pauline writings were

46. See Meier, *Marginal Jew,* 112-66; Charlesworth and Evans, "Jesus in the Agrapha."

47. On the authenticity of the various disputed Epistles see, among others, Best, *First and Second Thessalonians,* 50-58; Marshall, *1 and 2 Thessalonians,* 25-45; Barth, *Ephesians 1–3,* 36-52; O'Brien, *Colossians, Philemon,* xli-xlix; Kelly, *Pastoral Epistles,* 3-36; Knight, *Pastoral Epistles,* 21-52; also more broadly Johnson, *Writings of the NT,* 255-407.

written significantly later than Paul, their evidence can only be of very secondary importance to this study.

Whatever view is taken on the disputed books, it is worth keeping them in mind in this study, since it could be that a comparison of the use (or non-use) of Jesus-tradition in the disputed letters with its use in the undisputed letters may cast some light on the authenticity question.

How to avoid parallelomania

One of the most important methodological questions is: How are Pauline allusions to Jesus to be recognized? Some scholars seem to see such allusions everywhere in Paul; the most quoted name in this context is A. Resch, who in 1905 published a remarkable book identifying 1158 Pauline allusions to Jesus.[48] Other scholars see hardly any allusions anywhere in Paul's writings. Some see great significance in almost every possible parallel between Paul and Jesus; others are determinedly skeptical. Allusion-spotting seems, thus, to be a highly subjective business. Is there any way of avoiding parallelomania on the one hand or parallelophobia on the other?

Michael Thompson is most helpful here.[49] He first points out the slipperiness or ambiguity of the term "allusion": Do we mean, when using this word of Paul and Jesus, a deliberate reference to Jesus by Paul, which his readers were expected to notice? Or do we mean something much less than that, for example an echo of a saying of Jesus, which even Paul himself may not have been conscious of as he wrote? Thompson makes the following useful distinctions:

> I will use "quotation" to refer to instances in which the writer uses direct quotation with an explicit citation formula (e.g., *gegraptai gar*). "Allusion" will refer to statements which are *intended* to remind an audience of a tradition they are presumed to know as dominical; clear examples by this

---

48. *Der Paulinismus und die Logia Jesu.*

49. See also Fjärstedt, *Synoptic Tradition,* 40-64; Allison, "The Pauline Epistles," 6-10. Thompson, *Clothed with Christ,* 30, correctly observes that how we identify allusions and echoes is not only important for the Paul and Jesus question. The same sort of issues arise in seeking to recognize OT echoes, fragments of early Christian hymns, and other pre-Pauline traditions in Paul's letters. Questions of method have been fruitfully discussed in those connections. (On the OT see, e.g., Hays, *Echoes of Scripture,* 26-32. The parallel is not exact in the case of the quest for pre-Pauline hymns and other early Christian traditions, since we have no control and point of comparison as we do with the Jesus tradition in the Gospels. The OT is closer in that respect.)

definition are 1 Cor. 7.10 and 9.14. "Echo" or "reminiscence" will refer to cases where the influence of a dominical tradition upon Paul seems evident, but where it remains uncertain whether he was conscious of the influence at the time of dictating.[50]

But whether quotation, allusion, or echo, how are we to recognize one when we see it? Various clues may help us.[51]

(1) Sometimes — but not very often — Paul specifically says that he is drawing on Jesus' words; or there are other formal "tradition indicators," as Thompson calls them. Thus in 1 Cor 7:10 Paul specifically introduces the teaching which he is about to give on divorce by saying "To those who are married I command — *not I, but the Lord.*" After discussing that issue, he moves on with "To the rest *I say, not the Lord* . . . ." These phrases function almost like quotation marks around the material between them (though Paul is not actually quoting word for word). In cases like that it is quite clear that Paul intends an allusion to Jesus.

In some other cases the matter is not so explicit, but there is a phrase or a reference to Jesus which may be an oblique hint that he is drawing on a tradition of Jesus, as in Rom 14:14, where Paul comments that "I know and am persuaded *in the Lord Jesus* that nothing is unclean in itself." It is not certain that "in the Lord Jesus" is an indication of dependence on a tradition of Jesus, but that is one reasonable interpretation of this phraseology.

In other places there may be no specific reference to Jesus, but Paul does make it clear that he is drawing on some sort of tradition that he has already passed on to his readers. Thus in 1 Thes 5:1, 2 he comments: "Now concerning the times and the seasons . . . you do not need to have anything written to you. For you yourselves know very well that. . . ." There is no certain implication here that the Thessalonians' knowledge at this point was of teachings of Jesus, but at least it is clear that Paul is referring back to something already known rather than offering new teaching. And if there are other indications that the known teaching comes from Jesus, this "tradition indicator" may well be significant. Much the same may, sometimes at least, be implied in Paul's periodic questioning: "Do you not know that . . . ?" (e.g., 1 Cor 3:16; 5:6; 6:2; 3, 9, etc.).

There are other ways in which Paul may betray his dependence on tradition, for example, stylistically. A simple example of this is his use of

---

50. *Clothed with Christ,* 30.
51. I am again indebted to Thompson here.

"Abba" in Rom 8:15 and Gal 4:5, 6. Why does he suddenly use this Aramaic word when describing in Greek the Christian experience of being a child of God? No doubt because he is drawing directly or indirectly on a tradition of Jesus. A more uncertain example is in 1 Thes 2:13-16, where scholars have been puzzled by the language Paul uses to denounce the Jews. It has frequently been argued that the verses are atypical of Paul, and some scholars have suspected that they are a scribal interpolation. However, another possibility is that Paul is himself using tradition here, and that the language is atypical for that reason.

(2) Another clue is, of course, verbal and formal similarity between a tradition of Jesus and a saying of Paul. Thus with the discussion of divorce in 1 Cor 7:9-11, for example, there is some close verbal similarity between the sayings of Jesus in Matt 19:3-9/Mark 10:2-12 and Paul's teaching, especially the similarity between Jesus' "let no one separate" and Paul's "the wife should not separate from her husband"; the same Greek verb is used.[52] The form of the teaching is also similar, with the discussion moving on from a general prohibition of divorce (Matt 19:6-8/1 Cor 7:10) to comments on whether someone who is divorced may remarry (Matt 19:9/1 Cor 7:11).

Another case of verbal similarity is in 2 Cor 1:17, 18, where Paul is discussing the accusation against him that his word is " 'Yes, yes' and 'No, no.' " We are reminded of the saying about oaths in the sermon on the mount, where Jesus urges: "Let your word be 'Yes, Yes' or 'No, No' " (Matt 5:37). The verbal similarity between the sayings is sufficiently striking to alert us to the possibility of some connection between them.

But we should remember that in the Gospels we have a Greek translation of teaching that Jesus most probably gave originally in Aramaic. So where we find identical wording in the Gospels and Paul, this is not evidence of Paul using the actual words employed by Jesus, but of Paul translating the words of Jesus in the same way as the Gospels or using the same translation of Jesus' words as we find in the Gospels. The linguistic point means that Paul could sometimes deliberately echo Jesus' teaching and yet use different Greek terminology from the Gospels. We have to reckon with translation variants, while also recognizing that some translations are almost inevitable (as with "yes, yes, no, no").

It hardly needs saying that similar wording in itself does not necessarily prove a significant connection between two traditions: The similarity could be coincidental, especially if the general topic under discussion is the same or if the two authors concerned could both be drawing directly or

52. *Mē chōrizetō* in Matt 19:6 and *mē chōristhēnai* in 1 Cor 7:10.

indirectly on a common source, for example, a well-known proverb. However, if there is sufficient in common or if what is common is sufficiently distinctive or unusual, then there is more likelihood of some significant connection.

(3) Another clue indicating dependence of Paul on Jesus may be similarity of thought. In some such cases there may be little verbal similarity, but there may still be a striking similarity of outlook or idea, which is plausibly explained in terms of dependence. In other cases there may be some verbal similarity and also significant similarity of thought. Thus in 1 Corinthians 7 not only are there formal and verbal links between the Jesus-tradition and Paul's teaching, but the views of marriage and divorce expressed are similar and not typical of the Greco-Roman or Jewish worlds of the day. There is no verbal link between Paul's "the Lord commanded that those who preach the gospel should get their living by the gospel" in 1 Cor 9:14 and the so-called "Q" saying "The laborer is worthy of his hire"* (Luke 10:7). But the thought expressed is the same and scholars have generally been happy to make a connection between Jesus and Paul at this point, assuming that Paul is paraphrasing the tradition quite freely.

But again it is worth emphasizing that similarity of thought by itself does not prove any direct relationship: Jesus and Paul were both first-century Jews, whose similar ideas may reflect their common background rather than anything else. It is necessary in each case to consider whether the similarity is distinctive enough to suggest a possible or probable relationship.

It is obvious from what has been said, as well as from the scholarly disagreement, that identifying Jesus-tradition in Paul is a complex task. There are a very few cases, such as 1 Cor 7:9-11, where all three of the clues we have suggested come together: There is a "tradition indicator," some common wording, and distinctive ideas in common. In such cases we can conclude that there is a very high probability of a significant connection of traditions. In 1 Cor 9:14 there is no verbal similarity, but the two other criteria are clearly relevant, and again there is a high probability that there is shared tradition.

In the majority of cases, however, the evidence is much less clear-cut. For example, in 2 Cor 1:17, 18 there is some striking verbal similarity between a synoptic tradition and a Pauline saying, but the ideas being expressed are not so obviously similar, and there is no definite "tradition indicator." Furthermore, whereas with the divorce saying and the saying about the laborer being worthy of his hire scholars are relatively confident about the authenticity of the gospel traditions, with Matt 5:37, a saying only found in Matthew, more questions are to be addressed. In such cases we need to weigh carefully the evidence at both ends of the equation and explore carefully to see if the hypothesis of some link is plausible and illuminating.[53] At that point there is a real danger of the parallelomaniac seeing significance in things that others find quite insignificant, but that danger is no reason for not exploring, since there may be real and not illusory gains to be made. If Paul is in fact drawing on traditions of Jesus at various points in his writings — the hypothesis we are testing — then this must almost certainly be illuminating for our study and understanding of those traditions. One of the tests of the hypothesis will be whether in fact it does prove so illuminating. If it does, then, even if there are no simple and decisive arguments (e.g., clear tradition indicators) to show that this or that Pauline tradition goes back to Jesus, the case may still be a strong one.

We must not — in our enthusiasm for finding out if Paul used Jesus-traditions — forget that, where there is a possible or probable link between Paul and the tradition represented in a Gospel, the relationship may be from Paul to the Evangelist, not from Jesus (or the Jesus-tradition) to Paul.[54]

53. Tuckett, "Synoptic Tradition," 162, warns against a naive use of Pauline evidence. He says, "To point to a possible parallel between Paul and a feature usually regarded as redactional in the gospels, and then to claim both that Paul is alluding to Jesus tradition *and* that the Pauline evidence shows that the gospel material is pre-redactional, is to argue in a potentially dangerous circle." He suggests analyzing the synoptic texts in their own right first and only then bringing in the Pauline evidence. This is wise advice, so long as excessive weight is not put on "usual opinions" (e.g., on the opinion that Matthean and Lukan variations from Mark are almost invariably redactional). If there is a proper measure of openness on the synoptic problem and a recognition that judgments about what is "redactional" are often quite uncertainly based, then Paul's evidence may be of great value and importance, though it should not be used naively in defiance of clearly contrary evidence.

54. There is an apparently attractive simplicity in Goulder's view (see n. 27 above) that, for example, Matthew was written several decades after Paul and that, where there is contact between Matthew and Paul, the relationship is therefore most probably from Paul to Matthew. But Matthew and Luke both claim to be transmitting traditions of Jesus, so their evidence, taken at face value, would in fact reverse Goulder's logic, pointing to Paul's dependence on Jesus. Of course, there are problems with taking any of the Gospels "at face value," but it is important to see that the logic about the relative dates of the documents is not as simple as might appear. Goulder himself allows that Matthew and Luke are using a significant amount of what was thought to be Jesus-tradition, since he argues that Matthew and Luke used Mark and that Luke also used Matthew. Goulder fails to reckon sufficiently with the likelihood that Matthew and Luke

Deciding the direction of the relationship may not always be easy. Sometimes there are possible or probable tradition indicators in a particular Pauline text or passage which make Paul's dependence on Jesus-tradition probable. In other cases there may be features in the respective texts which are more easily explained in one direction than another.[55] In each case the particular evidence must be examined.[56]

In the whole discussion of parallels, there may be some relatively unambiguous evidence, but other cases where the argument is less strong and where the best that can be said is something like: "There is a possible echo of a saying of Jesus here, but the evidence is quite inconclusive." It will be important, as we go along, to recognize different levels of probability. Some previous studies have been easily dismissed because insufficient care was taken to distinguish highly probable and highly uncertain evidence of contact between Paul and the Jesus-tradition.[57]

But, although it is important to distinguish stronger and weaker evidence, it is worth pointing out as well that some of the more ambiguous evidence may look rather different in the light of a broader cumulative argument. If it can be established that there are a significant number of very probable echoes of Jesus-tradition in a particular Pauline context or if it can be established that a particular strand or block of Jesus' teaching (e.g., his eschatological teaching or the sermon on the mount) is quite clearly and frequently used by Paul, then what was only a possibility taken on its own may look much more probable after all.

---

knew and used other traditions of Jesus, and offers instead a brilliant but ultimately unpersuasive interpretation of the non-Markan material in Matthew and the non-Markan/Matthean material in Luke as creative midrash and interpretation.

55. E.g., it is probably easier to give priority to Jesus' parable of the thief, because of its attestation in both Matt 24:42-44 and Luke 12:39-40 and its surprising comparison of Jesus to a thief, and to see Paul's reference to the "day of the Lord" coming like a thief in 1 Thes 5:2 as an allusion to that parable than vice versa. See further in chapter 7 below.

56. If it is concluded that there is substantial dependence of Paul on Jesus-tradition, then it may be reasonable to conclude that the dependence is probably in that direction in some cases where the evidence is ambiguous. But the direction of influence need not be all in one direction: Paul may have used Jesus-tradition and also influenced Matthew and Luke. If the traditional identification of Luke with the companion of Paul is correct, we might expect to find evidence of Paul's influence on Luke from time to time. See also J. P. Brown, "Synoptic Parallels."

57. This arguably happened to Resch's work (Paulinismus) despite its massive erudition. Fjärstedt's work on 1 Corinthians is in the same danger, though it is methodologically far more sophisticated than Resch.

On the wider level too, if all we can do is accumulate a large amount of evidence that is "plausible but not proven," this may necessarily be the verdict on the book as a whole. But, if we can come up with a significant amount of evidence that is highly probable, then the merely "plausible" evidence may take on a different aspect. Not that we can argue simplistically that, because Paul certainly quotes from Jesus' teaching on two occasions, therefore every possible echo and allusion to Jesus' teaching is a probable echo or allusion. That argument could be reversed: Because Paul quotes Jesus explicitly so seldom, it is unlikely that the *possible* echoes and allusions are actually such. But, although a simplistic argument carries no conviction, there is such a thing as a genuinely cumulative argument: Where there is a complex of evidence — some strong, some fairly strong, some weaker but still plausible, some possible — the accumulation of such evidence of different strengths may add up to a very strong case, and the whole thesis may carry more weight than the sum of its individual parts. Furthermore, for such an argument to carry weight it is important not only to show that it is a probable explanation of some evidence, but also to show that it is consistent with other more ambiguous evidence.[58]

How to Read and Assess This Book

Level and limitations

This book is written to be accessible to the nonspecialist, and it looks at the Jesus-Paul question as a whole rather than at some more narrowly defined aspect of the subject. This broad approach has real advantages, but there is, of course, a price to be paid in terms of the thoroughness and adequacy of the treatment given to particular questions. This is especially obvious in the theological comparison of Jesus and Paul in the first part of each of the chapters on the teaching of Jesus (chapters 2-7): To try, for example, to compare Jesus' teaching on the kingdom and Paul's view of justification in little more than half a chapter makes oversimplification unavoidable. It is only possible to offer one possible view, not to interact effectively with widely differing scholarly opinions and approaches.[59] But

58. See Thompson, *Clothed with Christ*, 25.
59. I emphasize this point since readers will undoubtedly find much to disagree with! This book makes no claim to be an authoritative or original work on the teaching of Jesus or of Paul as such. It addresses the question of the connection between Jesus

the overall argument of this book does not depend on the accuracy of every detail in our theological comparison of Jesus and Paul. That comparison will give us a useful framework within which to look at the question of Jesus-tradition in Paul as it is addressed in the second part of each of those chapters.[60]

It is in the discussion of Jesus-tradition that this book has the most to offer; here we do seek to interact with scholarly debate of the issues, and the discussion becomes inevitably more technical. Readers may be conscious of a shifting of academic gears as we move into the second part of each chapter, though we have attempted to keep the discussion accessible to students as well as scholars. The most technical discussion is in footnotes or additional notes.

But even in these more technical parts, there is some inevitable superficiality. If a whole monograph can appropriately be devoted to a study of Jesus-tradition in Romans 12–15 (as it has been by Thompson), it is obvious that any attempt to look at the question of Jesus-tradition in Paul generally will be less thorough. It will not be possible, for example, when comparing Jesus-traditions and Pauline traditions to discuss every question of authenticity in detail or every possible Greek or Jewish literary parallel to the biblical traditions in question.

To do an exhaustive and fully adequate study of the whole question of Jesus-traditions in Paul would require a series of rather technical volumes — perhaps a large series. This book does not pretend to be in any way exhaustive. It is more like a report on ongoing research, bringing together some of the important data and ideas and referring to more technical studies (where they exist). As such it will hopefully be of interest to a wider audience than simply scholars, as well as a stimulus to further research and study.[61]

---

and Paul, and in that context must offer a comparison of their teaching, however provisional and inadequate. But readers will need to look elsewhere for detailed discussion of the many major issues that we have to address quite briefly. We will note other literature, though even the bibliographical references are not exhaustive.

60. Some — perhaps much — of the argument about the relationship of Jesus and Paul and particularly about Jesus-traditions in Paul could stand given a different analysis of their respective theological ideas.

61. My own earlier work in the area, notably *The Rediscovery of Jesus' Eschatological Discourse*, has been more detailed and technical and as a result has not been accessible to many readers. This book builds on and refers back to such earlier work and also interacts with other similarly academic studies, but it is intentionally less technical in its format and argument.

The argument

As well as being a report on research this book does propose a definite thesis, namely that Paul is much better described as "follower of Jesus" than as "founder of Christianity." The argument is a cumulative one of the sort we referred to previously, and it is only by coming to grips with the whole argument of the book that its full force will be appreciated.

One way of writing this book might have been to present the strongest arguments for the thesis being defended in the early chapters and then to fill in gaps in later chapters. But it seemed preferable to offer a more systematic approach to Jesus and Paul, which means that some of the most important evidence comes in later chapters. It is, therefore, important to realize that some of the more tentative conclusions come early in the book and that the full force of the argument will only be apparent later on. Readers should not be prematurely dismissive or despairing, but endure to the end!

To say that the book hangs together as a whole is not to say that the individual parts have no independent worth. This book in fact comprises a whole variety of studies, some of them quite detailed, and, although it may be true to say that the individual parts will not be fully appreciated other than in the context of the whole, it is not the case that everything in the book stands or falls with the overall thesis. Those who at the end remain unpersuaded by the general thesis will hopefully have found much of the particular discussion helpful and persuasive.

This book may therefore be assessed both for its general thesis and for its discussion of particular passages. Quite apart from the value of the conclusions reached, it will hopefully be useful also as a summary of discussion and thus be a handbook to future students of what will remain a vitally important and vigorously disputed subject.

2

THE KINGDOM OF GOD

I. Comparing Jesus and Paul

JESUS' ANNOUNCEMENT
OF THE KINGDOM OF GOD[1]

"The time is fulfilled, and the kingdom of God has come near; repent, and believe in the good news" (Mark 1:15). With these words Mark introduces the ministry and message of Jesus to the readers of his Gospel. The heart of Jesus' message according to Mark is the kingdom of God. Matthew and Luke agree.[2] They agree with Mark that Jesus' parables were kingdom parables: "The kingdom of God/heaven is . . . like a mustard seed . . ." (Matt 13:31/Mark 4:30, 31/Luke 13:18, 19). Matthew and Luke also agree that Jesus' so-called sermon on the mount has to do with the kingdom, not just

1. This discussion of Jesus' kingdom teaching is necessarily a very brief summary, not an exhaustive discussion of the evidence or of different points of view. For more adequate discussion of the subject see among others Beasley-Murray, *Jesus and the Kingdom of God*; Sanders, *Jesus and Judaism; idem, The Historical Figure of Jesus;* Horsley, *Jesus and the Spiral of Violence;* Wright, *Jesus and the Victory of God.* Chilton, ed., *The Kingdom of God,* is a useful collection of essays; also useful as a summary of recent work is Marshall, "The Hope of a New Age."

2. Matthew, being the most Jewish of the synoptic Gospels, prefers the expression "kingdom of heaven," in line with the Jewish practice of avoiding direct use of the sacred divine name. (Compare the words of the prodigal son: "I have sinned against heaven," i.e., God, "and before you," Luke 15:18.) In John's Gospel Jesus only rarely speaks of "the kingdom of God" (3:3, 5); John prefers the expression "eternal life," probably because it seemed a more accessible phrase to his largely Gentile readership.

34

with social or personal ethics as some people mistakenly suppose, hence its opening: "Blessed are the poor . . . for theirs/yours is the kingdom" (Matt 5:3; Luke 6:20). They agree that Jesus' disciples were sent out by the master to proclaim the kingdom (Matt 10:7; Luke 9:2; 10:9).

The evidence is overwhelming, and modern scholars who seem to disagree about almost everything else are nearly unanimous on this one point — that Jesus proclaimed the coming of the kingdom.

But what did he mean? Here the scholarly consensus begins to crack. Very often "kingdom of God" seems best understood in a dynamic sense as referring to God's "reign" or "rule." Thus when Jesus spoke of the kingdom's nearness and told his disciples to pray "Your kingdom come," he was announcing and encouraging them to pray for the establishment of God's rule (Matt 6:10; Luke 11:2).

But Jesus also speaks of the kingdom as something that will be "entered" (or not entered! e.g., Matt 18:3/Mark 10:15). The picture in this case may be that of the promised land, which the Israelites "entered" and "inherited" after their desert wanderings (Deut 4:1; 6:18; cf. Matt 5:5). We may, therefore, think in these texts of the "kingdom of God" as the "realm" of God. But the thought is not of a geographical location so much as of the new order and the new society that God is establishing and in which his rule will hold total sway.[3]

Some scholars believe that the expression "kingdom of God" refers in a rather loose way to God's kingship: Jesus called people to reckon with God as king and with his powerful presence in the world.[4] Most, however, agree that the expression suggests more specifically the coming of the day of divine liberation and of the new society for which Jesus and his contemporaries were longing and waiting. The kingdom of God that Jesus pro-

---

3. For recent discussion of the kingdom of God as "reign" or "realm" see the differing views of Marcus, "Entering into the Kingly Power of God," and O'Neill, "The Kingdom of God." The purely dynamic interpretation of the kingdom as "reign" has been appealing to those who have (quite rightly) been unhappy with a simple identification of church and kingdom; and yet the coming of the kingdom in Jesus' teaching is associated with the gathering of a people and a "family" (e.g., Matt 12:46-50/Mark 3:31-35/Luke 8:19-21; see also chapter 5 below).

4. Norman Perrin speaks of a "tensive symbol" having various symbolic overtones; contrast a "steno symbol" with a specific meaning. The kingdom of God is "a symbol having meaning for people in cultural continuity with ancient Israel and its myth of God acting as king, a cultural continuity in which Jesus certainly stood" (*Jesus and the Language of the Kingdom,* 197). Bruce Chilton paraphrases "the kingdom of God" as "God in strength" in his book of that title.

claimed is, to use a technical term, the "eschatological kingdom" — the kingdom to come in the last days.[5] It is the coming of the divine rule and of the new world order, for which the Jews were looking.

"The Time Has Come . . .": The Theme of Fulfillment

The contemporary context

In order to appreciate this point, it is helpful to be reminded of Jesus' context. Palestine had been controlled and at least partially occupied by the Romans since 63 BC. As foreign imperialists go, the Romans were relatively moderate, but there were all sorts of pressures on the Jews of occupied Palestine. There were, in the first place, economic pressures. Some people did extremely well under Roman rule. But, as some of the wealthy prospered, many others suffered, often losing their land and livelihoods and getting into acute situations of debt. The disparities between rich and poor increased painfully. High taxation was a particular irritant, not suprisingly, and tax collectors were resented, not least because of their own rapaciousness.

More generally Roman rule was irksome, including to those with religious scruples, who saw the presence of the pagan imperial power in the holy land as an affront to the God of Israel and culturally and religiously threatening. There were constant tensions between, on the one hand, the Romans, their client rulers, the Herods, and those who chose to associate with them and their lavish pagan lifestyle, and, on the other hand, nationalistic and

---

5. The eschatological interpretation of Jesus was championed notably by Albert Schweitzer at the start of the century (e.g., *Quest of the Historical Jesus*). Although Schweitzer's view of Jesus as a mistaken disappointed prophet has not so often been accepted, the general point that Jesus understood his ministry in eschatological terms has been widely accepted. See, e.g., Allison, *The End of the Ages Has Come*. See also the additional note below on "Jesus, John the Baptist, and Qumran."

The term "eschatological" is, admittedly, understood in different ways. In speaking of Jesus' understanding of the kingdom as "eschatological," I do not mean that Jesus necessarily expected the end of the world (in the way that some modern Christians expect something like the big bang in reverse). What I mean is that Jesus believed that the "latter days" of God's deliverance of his people were coming. Exactly how Jesus understood this new age is debatable; it would represent a revolution and a new order of things brought about by divine intervention, but Jesus' expectation (like that of his disciples) may have been of a more down-to-earth kingdom than is sometimes supposed.

religious Jews who feared the erosion and destruction of their laws and traditions. These tensions came to the surface from time to time, as in the period just before Jesus' ministry, when the newly appointed Roman governor Pontius Pilate caused great offense. He departed from the policy of his more cautious predecessors and ordered his troops to march into Jerusalem with their regular military standards; these were viewed as idolatrous symbols by the Jews, who were incensed at what they saw as desecration of the holy city. Their protests eventually led Pilate to back down.[6]

Although some well-placed Jews were quite content with the Roman status quo, most resented it, and many looked back to the heroic Maccabean movement of the second century BC. They remembered with foreboding how in 167 BC. Antiochus Epiphanes, the ruler of the Seleucids (who preceded the Romans as the regional superpower) made a concerted attack on the Jewish religion, setting up a pagan altar, the so-called "desolating sacrilege" in the Jerusalem temple. They remembered with admiration how Judas Maccabeus and others conducted a successful three-year guerilla campaign against Antiochus — against all human odds — freeing Jerusalem and reconsecrating the temple. That heroic event was celebrated every year by the Jews in the Feast of Hanukkah (or Dedication). In Jesus' day some hankered after a Maccabean-style campaign against the Romans; Barabbas may have been such a nationalist guerilla. Others, while not advocating such a direct confrontation with the might of Rome, also longed for divine deliverance.[7]

The Old Testament hope

The Jewish hope for divine deliverance was not simply a response to the oppression that they were experiencing, but was fueled by the Jews' religious traditions, and especially by the OT Scriptures. The OT prophets in particular were full of anticipation that God would one day deliver his people. In the book of Isaiah, for example, God promises to exiled Israel: "I will soon lift up my hand to the nations, and raise my signal to the peoples;

6. Josephus, the Jewish historian, describes this and other actions of Pilate that caused great offense to his Jewish subjects, *War* II.169-74, *Ant.* XVIII.55-62.

7. On the Maccabean rebellion (at least as it was perceived by Jesus' contemporaries) see 1 Maccabees 1–4. On Jesus' social, economic, and religious context see among others Goodman, *Ruling Class of Judaea;* Horsley, *Jesus and the Spiral;* Crossan, *The Historical Jesus;* Borg, *Conflict, Holiness and Politics.* Theissen's *Shadow of the Galilean* is an outstandingly vivid picture of the social ferment of Jesus' day.

and they shall bring your sons in their bosom, and your daughters shall be carried on their shoulders. Kings shall be your foster fathers . . ." (Isa 49:22, 23). As for Jerusalem, "in days to come the mountain of the LORD's house shall be established as the highest of the mountains . . . all the nations shall stream to it. . . . Out of Zion shall go forth instruction, and the word of the Lord from Jerusalem. He shall judge between the nations, and shall arbitrate for many peoples; they shall beat their swords into ploughshares, and their spears into pruning hooks; nation shall not lift up sword against nation, neither shall they learn war any more" (Isa 2:2-4). In Jerusalem there was to be a new king from the family of David: "A shoot shall come out from the stump of Jesse. . . . The spirit of the Lord shall rest on him. . . . He shall not judge by what his eyes see, or decide by what his ears hear; but with righteousness he shall judge the poor. . . . The wolf shall live with the lamb, the leopard shall lie down with the kid. . . . They will not hurt or destroy on all my holy mountain; for the earth will be full of the knowledge of the LORD as the waters cover the sea" (Isa 11:1-9). The vision is for a renewed society and for renewal of human life: "Then the eyes of the blind shall be opened, and the ears of the deaf unstopped; then the lame shall leap like a deer" (Isa 35:5, 6); even more than that: "On this mountain . . . he will swallow up death forever. Then the Lord GOD will wipe away the tears from all faces" (Isa 25:7, 8). The vision is not limited to Israel, but is for the Gentiles too: "I will give you as a light to the nations" (Isa 49:6).

Such hopes (and many others from other parts of the OT) were in the Jewish Scriptures of Jesus and his contemporaries. Some of the prophecies had been partly fulfilled in the experience of Israel: They had, for example, been released from the exile in Babylon. But, even allowing for some poetical language and figurative speech, the fulfillment had only been very partial: life under the Romans was not all that the OT had promised for the Jews or for Jerusalem. Indeed, it seemed in many ways closer to the experience of continuing exile in a foreign land than to the salvation of God. For anyone who took the OT seriously — as many did in Jesus' day — there was a massive balance of divine promises still to be realized. Jesus' contemporaries longed for God's intervention and salvation.[8]

But how does this relate to Jesus' message about the kingdom of God?

---

8. On the Jewish messianic hope in the intertestamental period see Vermes, *Religion of Jesus the Jew.* The Dead Sea Scrolls, including those most recently published, make it clear how lively an eschatological hope persisted in Jesus' day at least in some circles of Palestinian Jews.

The OT does not in so many words speak of the coming kingdom (or rule) of God. Indeed, God is spoken of as the one who does already reign: thus the psalmists can proclaim that "the Lord reigns" (e.g., Pss 97:1; 99:1; 146:10). However, although there is one sense in which God is eternally and always reigning as Creator, in another sense God's present reign may be seen as partial and compromised. So the OT can look forward to the time when God will reign completely and over everything. Thus the prophet Zechariah in a vivid passage about the coming day of the Lord speaks of the blessings of that day — no cold, no darkness, no drought — and then says, "And the Lord will become king over all the earth" (Zech 14:9). The book of Daniel also uses the language of kingship and kingdom when looking forward to God's future intervention to save his people: Thus in Daniel 2, where Nebuchadnezzar's extraordinary vision of a massive statue is interpreted by Daniel, he says: "And in the days of those kings the God of heaven will set up a kingdom that shall never be destroyed, nor shall this kingdom be left to another people. It shall crush all these kingdoms and bring them to an end, and it shall stand forever" (v. 44). The same sort of language is used in Daniel 7 in the highly significant passage about "one like a son of man": "To him," it is said, "was given dominion and glory and kingship . . . and his kingship is one that shall never be destroyed" (v. 14). Later, as this vision is explained, we read: "The kingship and dominion and the greatness of the kingdoms under the whole heaven shall be given to the people of the holy ones of the Most High; their kingdom shall be an everlasting kingdom, and all dominions shall serve and obey them" (v. 27).

Jesus announces the day of fulfillment

Given the social and religious context of first-century Palestine, Jesus' announcement of the coming of the kingdom makes sense: He was proclaiming the arrival of the day that so many of his contemporaries longed for. Mark describes Jesus as saying, "The time is fulfilled" (1:15). The sense here could simply be that "the time (or the moment) has come"* (cf. NIV), but the word translated "fulfill" is a very important NT term, associated primarily with the idea of OT prophecy being fulfilled, and it is likely that Mark has that sense in mind. Jesus' ministry marks the end of the time of waiting, the arrival of God's promised day. Thus Mark opens his Gospel in 1:1-3 with a prophecy about the coming of God, and he sees Jesus as the fulfillment of that prophecy.

That Jesus announced and brought the day of fulfillment is very well attested in all strands of the Gospels: Matthew has the famous verse "Do not think that I have come to abolish the law or the prophets; I have not come to abolish but to fulfill" (5:17); Luke has Jesus read the scroll of Isaiah in the synagogue at Nazareth and proclaim to the astonished people, "Today this scripture has been fulfilled in your hearing" (4:16-21); John has Jesus pointing his listeners to the Scriptures because "it is they that testify on my behalf" (5:39). More significantly for those who accept the two-source hypothesis of Gospel origins, the "Q" tradition of Matthew and Luke strongly attests this theme: Thus in Matt 13:16, 17/Luke 10:23, 24 Jesus congratulates the disciples on seeing and hearing and remarks, "Truly I tell you, many prophets and righteous men longed to see what you see, but did not see it, and to hear what you hear, but did not hear it." Also in Matt 11:2-5/Luke 7:18-22, when John the Baptist sends from his prison cell to ask Jesus if he is "the one who is to come," Jesus replies — significantly — by describing his ministry in words taken from Isaiah 35 and 61, "the blind receive their sight, the lame walk, the lepers are cleansed, the deaf hear, the dead are raised, and the poor have good news brought to them." The implication here and in many other Gospel texts is that the day for the fulfillment of God's gracious promises to his people has come.

Even though scholars have raised questions about the authenticity of some of the sayings of Jesus that we have referred to, the weight and variety of the evidence mean that we can be confident that Jesus did see his message and ministry as fulfilling OT hopes and promises. Given his context this is not surprising, and indeed he was not the only religious leader of his day to think in these terms. The Qumran community also understood themselves as living in the last days and in the time of fulfillment, and there were various other prophetic and messianic leaders in first-century Palestine who seem to have seen themselves as eschatological savior figures.[9]

Change of Government!

To say that Jesus announced the eschatological fulfillment of prophecy is not to explain very much about how he envisaged the coming of the

---

9. Although many scholars have been cautious about jumping to conclusions of this sort, the case for linking John the Baptist and Qumran is quite strong, and the case for linking Jesus and John is, of course, much stronger. See the additional note on "Jesus, John the Baptist, and Qumran" at the end of this chapter. On other religious leaders in first-century Palestine see, among others, Webb, *John the Baptizer and Prophet*, e.g., 307-48.

kingdom. The OT vision for the future is diffuse and complex, and Jesus' contemporaries had many different ideas about the future: Some looked for a military and political revolution like that of the Maccabees; others hoped for a supernatural intervention from heaven and a supernatural kingdom. What did Jesus intend?

The Markan words "The time has been fulfilled . . ." are translated by some modern versions as "The time has come" (NIV, cf. GNB), and we are reminded of the slogans of political parties who at election time assure the voters that "the time has come," that is, for a change of government and for their party to take office. This is in some ways not far from the meaning of Jesus' words: Jesus announced the time for a change of government — to the rule of God. Of course, we are not in a democratic party-political context in first-century Palestine; we are in a totalitarian, imperialist state. A change of government in that context will be more like a revolution than a modern election, and indeed Jesus' proclamation of the kingdom might effectively be paraphrased, "The revolution of God is coming" or perhaps, "The revolutionary government of God is coming."[10]

It is easy to see why many of Jesus' contemporaries would have viewed such a message with excitement and enthusiasm, and why others, not least those in power, would have viewed it with great suspicion, especially when Jesus, like his predecessor John, attracted a large and popular following. Jesus' followers appear, not surprisingly, to have hoped that he was about to take power (somehow or other, perhaps by the sword) and that they would have privileged positions in the new order (Matt 20:20, 21/Mark 10:35-37).[11] There seems to have been particular excitement when Jesus came up to Jerusalem (shortly before his death); as Luke puts it, "they supposed that the kingdom of God was to appear immediately" (19:11). However, things did not work out as they hoped, and in fact Jesus was crucified, officially on the charge of fomenting revolution as a self-styled "king of the Jews."

But, although one obvious way of understanding Jesus' kingdom preaching was in terms of a military revolution, there is plenty of evidence that Jesus did not see the kingdom in those terms. Scholarly attempts to

10. R. T. France offers "divine government" as a paraphrase for "kingdom of God" in *Divine Government*. For the kingdom as "the revolution of God" see my *Parables of Jesus*.

11. Such a hope may also be implied in the question of John the Baptist from the disillusioning experience of his prison cell: "Are you the one who is to come, or are we to wait for another?" (Matt 11:3/Luke 7:19).

construe Jesus as a violent revolutionary, who was later whitewashed and even perhaps made into a pacifist by the church, have not been convincing.[12] So what sort of "change of government" or "revolution" did Jesus envisage?

An answer to that question is suggested by his comment on the mission of the seventy described in Luke 10. He sends them out to proclaim the kingdom, and, when they return jubilant over their success, he comments, "I watched Satan fall from heaven like a flash of lightning" (10:18). It is Satan whose power is overthrown as the revolutionary rule of God is established.

The Lukan account of the mission of the seventy raises all sorts of historical questions, but the understanding of Jesus' mission as the overthrow of Satan and Satanic forces is very well attested in the gospel tradition. All three synoptic Gospels give prominence to Jesus' exorcisms: Jesus is portrayed as astonishingly effective in casting out demon-spirits. All three synoptists describe the mission of the disciples as one of preaching the kingdom and casting out demons, and all three include the parable of the burglary of a strong man's house, making the point that Jesus is the one who is tying up the strong man, Satan, and ransacking his possessions (Matt 12:22-30/Mark 3:22-27/Luke 11:14-23). Advocates of the two-source hypothesis argue that these sayings about the strong man were in "Q" as well as Mark because Matthew and Luke have some quite distinctive material, including Jesus' significant comment that "if it is by the finger/Spirit of God that I cast out demons, then the kingdom of God has come to you" (Matt 12:28/Luke 11:20). The fourth Gospel is interestingly silent about Jesus' exorcisms, and yet in a rather typical way the author of that Gospel also expresses the idea that Jesus' ministry represents the casting out of Satan, since he has Jesus say about his coming death, "now will the ruler of this world be driven out" (John 12:31).[13]

Some, though not all, modern readers of the Gospels have great difficulty with notions of demons and of Satan. But those were very familiar notions in the Palestine of Jesus' day, and it is hard to dispute the fact that Jesus saw the coming of the kingdom, as he proclaimed it, as the casting

---

12. Brandon, *Jesus and the Zealots,* saw Jesus as a "zealot" seeking the forcible overthrow of the Romans. See Bammel and Moule, eds., *Jesus and the Politics of His Day* for a collection of essays responding to issues raised by Brandon. Also Hengel, *Victory over Violence; idem, Was Jesus a Revolutionist?*

13. For a synoptic parallel to Satan as ruler of the world, see the Matthew/Luke temptation narrative, where Satan presumes to offer Jesus authority over all the earth (Matt 4:8/Luke 4:5).

out not of the Roman legions but of the Satanic legions (cf. the name of the untamable demoniac in Mark 5:9). The picture is of Satan having hijacked God's world and usurped God's proper authority and of Jesus then casting out the hijacker and restoring the rule of God.

We might conclude from this that Jesus' understanding of the kingdom was "spiritual" rather than political or material. But that would be to offer too narrow an understanding of Jesus' mission (as we shall see, for example, when we consider his healing ministry). It probably reflects also a modern Western tendency to isolate the "spiritual" from other aspects of life. It would be preferable to say that Jesus had a broader and arguably more profound diagnosis of the problem that he and his contemporaries were facing than simply a political diagnosis: He saw the problem as having cosmic dimensions. The problem was not just Rome, but, even more significantly, Satan, and it was Satan's empire that Jesus attacked directly.[14]

Mission of Healing and Reconciliation

Healing

If the coming of the rule of God meant the expulsion of Satan and concretely the exorcism of demons, it also meant much more than that. The Gospels not only describe Jesus casting out devils, but also — and here John is no exception — healing the sick. This is another aspect of the gospel narrative of Jesus that some modern commentators have found difficult historically; but the same comment is in order as with Jesus' exorcisms, namely that modern incredulity about the miraculous was not shared by Jesus' contemporaries. However we today may evaluate claims to healing, ancient or modern, we have strong reason to believe that Jesus was, as some critics have put it, a "charismatic wonder-worker."[15] The Gospels suggest

14. Horsley, in *Jesus and the Spiral*, suggests that in Jewish apocalyptic thought events could be seen as happening "on three 'levels' simultaneously (the spiritual, the social-historical, and the personal), so that happenings on one level constituted evidence for happenings on the other levels." "Jesus was engaged in direct manifestations of God's kingdom in his practice and preaching, and he was confident that God was imminently to complete the restoration of Israel and judge the institutions that maintained injustice" (321).

15. See especially Vermes, *Jesus the Jew*, 58-82, for discussion of other Jewish healers and of the Essenes' interest in healing, also of the Jewish association of Solomon, son of David, with healing. See also Harvey, *Jesus and the Constraints of History*, 98-119.

that Jesus' power was not questioned by his opponents and indeed that they accorded him the doubtful honor of explaining his extraordinary power as the power of Beelzebul, the chief of demons. Later Judaism remembered Jesus as a magician.[16]

The Gospels, as we have seen, associate Jesus' exorcisms with the coming of the kingdom, and the same explanation is — not surprisingly — implied with his miraculous healings. Most significant is the "Q" saying of Jesus in Matt 11:4-6/Luke 7:22, 23, where Jesus tells the disciples of John the Baptist to report the healings to their master in words clearly alluding to Isa 35:5, 6 and 61:1, 2. The implication is that John, who is having doubts about Jesus as the coming one, should recognize that the day of healing promised by the OT has arrived. The rule of God (conversely the overthrow of Satan) is being seen in Jesus' acts of power and healing (see also Luke 13:16).

Sinners welcomed

Another of the most prominent aspects of Jesus' ministry that distinguishes it from the ministry of similar religious leaders was his mixing and eating with sinful people.[17] Scholars who are otherwise extremely cautious about the historical reliability of the Gospels have recognized this as historically authentic. According to the Gospels Jesus' freedom in the company of bad characters, including prostitutes and tax collectors, caused particular offense among his religious critics. His defense of his conduct, as recorded in Matthew, Mark, and Luke, was straightforward: "Those who are well have no need of a physician, but those who are sick. I have come to call not the righteous, but sinners" (Mark 2:17/Matt 9:12, 13/Luke 5:31, 32). This explanation is consistent with the explanation of Jesus' exorcisms and miracles: He is restoring what was satanic, sick, and in need of being brought back under the rule of God. Matthew and Luke both record — rather differently — Jesus' parable of the lost sheep (Matt 18:10-14; Luke 15:3-7);[18] Jesus' ministry is seen as finding the lost and gathering those who

---

16. E.g., Babylonian Talmud, Sanhedrin 107b.

17. There has been considerable debate about who exactly constituted the "sinners." See Sanders, *Jesus and Judaism*, 174-211, and responses to Sanders, including Chilton, "Jesus and the Repentance of E. P. Sanders."

18. It is not necessary at this point to discuss whether Matthew and Luke have a common source here, or whether Jesus used the parable more than once. John's Gospel also attests the shepherd/sheep theme in Jesus' teaching in chapter 10.

are scattered, quite probably in fulfillment of the OT passages that look forward to God shepherding and gathering his people (e.g., Ezekiel 34).

Outsiders and "the poor"

Jesus' mixing with tax collectors was highly controversial, given the social and political situation. If the Gospels are right to state that on several occasions Jesus suggested that the religious leaders of his day were further from God's kingdom than the tax collectors, this must have been especially offensive (e.g., Matt 21:38; Luke 18:9-14).

But it is entirely consistent with the picture of the kingdom of God that we are building up: Jesus was announcing the new day when people would be gathered back into God's family and when old divisions and prejudices would be overcome. Whereas many in his day were emphasizing the need for the Jewish people to maintain their national identity by keeping strictly to their religious and cultural traditions and by separating from Gentiles, Samaritans, and compromised Jews of all sorts, Jesus appears to have been rather relaxed about strict observance of the law (see chapter 6 below) and to have taught and practiced an inclusive holiness, welcoming the outsider (including the Samaritan), loving the enemy, and breaking down the old taboos and divisions that were so strong in his society.[19]

Luke's Gospel is most emphatic about this aspect of Jesus' ministry, with more about Jesus and tax collectors and Samaritans — and women — than the other Gospels (e.g., 8:1-3; 9:51-53; 10:25-41; 17:11-19; 18:9-14; 19:1-10). He also portrays Jesus as someone with special concern for the poor and for material injustice (e.g., 4:18; 6:20; 14:12-14; 16:19-31). But although this is a Lukan "redactional" emphasis, it is not unique to Luke, and there is good reason for supposing that Jesus' understanding of the kingdom was a broad-based view of the day of the Lord as a day of social liberation and reconciliation, as well as of physical healing and spiritual deliverance.[20]

---

19. For OT passages looking for the bringing in of Samaritans and outsiders, see, e.g., Isaiah 56; Ezek 37:15-28.

20. It is interesting to compare John's Gospel, where eternal life is defined in terms of reconciliation with God and fellowship with God and Jesus, but where it also entails love of the brotherhood and Christian unity (17:3, 21-23). Eternal life is two-dimensional, involving love of God and of brother and neighbor (cf. Luke 10:25-27).

Changed attitudes

How were social liberation and reconciliation to be achieved? We suggested earlier that Jesus had a more profound diagnosis of the human problem and of the problems of his society than many of his contemporaries: Satan rather than the Roman Empire was the archenemy. But Jesus seems also to have identified the human problem as having internal dimensions, as residing in the heart. Such at least is the import of the discussion of cleanness and uncleanness in Matthew 15/Mark 7, where Jesus criticizes his Jewish critics' preoccupation with ritual washings and cleanness and explains that "it is what comes out of a person that defiles. For it is from within, from the human heart, that evil intentions come: fornication, theft, murder, . . ." (Mark 7:20, 21). This emphasis on cleanness of heart and inner attitude rather than exterior religion and righteousness is not unique to Jesus. It has many parallels in the OT prophets and elsewhere in Jewish tradition. But it is still a well-attested theme of Jesus' teaching, appearing also in the sermon on the mount, where Jesus warns of the hateful word and the lustful look (Matt 5:21-30), and in Jesus' denunciation of the superficial religion of the scribes and Pharisees (Matt 23:13-32/Luke 11:39-48).

If Jesus' diagnosis of the human problem was in terms of the heart, the implication must be that he saw the coming of the kingdom as the solution to the problem and as bringing inner cleansing. Certainly the idea of inner cleansing and renewal is an important part of the prophetic hope in the OT,[21] and it is likely that, just as Jesus is portrayed in the Gospels as one who brings physical "cleanness," for example, to the ritually unclean lepers (Matt 8:1-4/Mark 1:40-45/Luke 5:12-16), so the kingdom, as he understood it, meant inner renewal.[22]

21. Thus, e.g., Ezekiel speaks of a heart of flesh in place of a heart of stone (11:19; 36:22-28, 37), Jeremiah speaks of a new and effective covenant replacing the old covenant of Sinai with God's commandments written on human hearts (31:31), and Joel speaks of God's Spirit being poured out on everyone instead of just some of God's people (2:28 = 3:1 in Hebrew). These passages are not taken up directly in the tradition of Jesus' teaching, with the important exception of Jeremiah's new covenant passage, which is taken up in the account of the last supper in Luke and 1 Corinthians (on this see chapter 4 below).

22. The implication of a passage like Mark 7 must be that Jesus is not simply offering a diagnosis of the human condition in terms of the heart, but also a solution. Much the same is true of the sermon on the mount. However we interpret it, the sermon certainly does not present a purely theoretical ideal. Obeying the sermon and following Jesus is indeed in one sense quite "impossible," but with God it is possible, and the disciples who are "poor in spirit" and who "hunger and thirst for righteousness" are

Faith/believing in the good news

As for how the renewing, reconciling kingdom comes to people, the Gospels stress both the proclamation of the good news and the attitude of faith. Jesus and the disciples are described in the Gospels as going out to heal and cast out demons, but, most importantly, as announcing the good news of the kingdom (Mark 1:15, 38; 3:14, 15; Matt 10:7, 8; Luke 9:2; 10:9). The kingdom, though powerfully in action in Jesus, comes as an invitation that people may accept or reject, not with compulsion. People are invited to "believe in the good news" and to "hear the word and accept it" (Mark 4:20). Whether the particular phraseology goes back to Jesus or not, it seems likely that Jesus did deliberately refuse to go the way of force, to some people's disappointment and perplexity,[23] relying instead on his healing and preaching ministry and inviting people to identify with him and the good news.

"Faith"/"belief" (representing the one Greek root present in the noun *pistis* and the verb *pisteuō*) is a key term in the Gospel narratives. It is used mainly in accounts of Jesus' healings (e.g., "your faith has made you well," Matt 9:22; Mark 5:34/Luke 8:48; 17:19). But it is also used more generally of the attitude of discipleship (e.g., Mark 1:15; Matt 18:6/Mark 9:42; Matt 21:25, 32). Both in the context of healing and elsewhere it represents the attitude of those who want help and who come to Jesus looking for it.[24]

Now and Not Yet

An issue concerning the kingdom that has absorbed considerable scholarly attention has been its timing. Did Jesus believe that the kingdom *had come* with and in his ministry, or did he believe that it was coming soon? When the Gospels report Jesus as saying that "the kingdom of God has come near" (e.g., Mark 1:15), does this mean that it has come and that it is now near,

---

expected to begin to live according to and in the power of the kingdom of God (Matt 5:3, 6; 19:26). The rich man Zacchaeus may be seen as an example of someone radically changed by his meeting with Jesus (Luke 19:1-10).

23. E.g., Matt 11:3/Luke 7:19; John 6:15.

24. The same sort of attitude is the qualification for entry into the kingdom of God as all the Gospels describe it: it is following Jesus when he calls (Mark 1:17, 18), and being like little children coming to Jesus (10:14, 15); it is being "poor in spirit" (Matt 5:3), and "coming to Jesus" (11:28); it is asking God to "be merciful to me, a sinner" (Luke 18:13) and receiving Jesus into one's house (Luke 19:6; cf. Matt 10:40-42).

if only people will recognize it? Or does it mean that it is near in the sense of nearly here but not quite yet? The preceding words in Mark 1:15, "The time has been fulfilled . . . ,"* suggest that Mark understood the words to mean that the kingdom had arrived with Jesus, and this is probably the most natural understanding of various other sayings, including Matt 12:28/Luke 11:20: "If it is by the Spirit/finger of God that I cast out demons, then the kingdom of God has come to you."

Even if some uncertainty about the interpretation of these verses remains, there is plenty of evidence indicating that Jesus believed the time of fulfillment to have arrived. For example, when he speaks rather mysteriously of John the Baptist as inferior to "the least in the kingdom of heaven" (Matt 11:11/Luke 7:28), the reason seems to be that John for all his greatness belongs to the age of the law and the prophets, whereas Jesus' disciples are in the new age of the kingdom, when the kingdom is "coming forcefully" into the world (cf. NRSV mg. in Matt 11:12).

However, there are also times when the "kingdom" is clearly future, notably in the words of the Lord's Prayer: "Your kingdom come" (Matt 6:10/Luke 11:2), and also where Jesus speaks of who will enter the kingdom — evidently in the future (e.g., Matt 18:3/Mark 10:15/Luke 18:17).

The ambivalence in the Gospels about the tense of the kingdom has been variously interpreted, with many scholars suspecting that we have two conflicting views — Jesus' own view and the view of the church — unresolved within the Gospels. However, there is a strong case for suspecting that the ambivalence was part of Jesus' own view, and that he believed the kingdom had come in one sense (at least by anticipation), but not in another. God's longed-for rule and salvation was breaking in powerfully through the ministry of Jesus, but the new world order in which that rule would be universal and total still lay in the future, albeit in the near future.[25] The new exodus had begun, but God's people were not yet in the promised land.

This view makes sense of several of the parables, especially in Matthew 13/Mark 4/Luke 8, which speak of sowing, growing, and harvesting. It is likely that these parables are concerned with the experience of the kingdom of God in Jesus' ministry. The rule of God was present in Jesus' ministry, as seen in the exorcisms, healings, and so on, but it was present like a growing seed, not yet like the full-grown plant. The parable of the mustard seed speaks of a tiny seed that will grow into a huge plant; the parable of

25. Witherington, *Jesus, Paul and the End of the World,* e.g., 61-62, distinguishes the present experience of the kingdom as a relationship from the future "local" reality of the kingdom as something to be entered or inherited.

the seed growing secretly speaks of a farmer sowing and then apparently doing nothing as he waits for harvest; the parable of the sower speaks of a sowing that has been accomplished, but with mixed results; and the parable of the wheat and the weeds speaks of good seed (of the kingdom) being sown but of weeds continuing to coexist with the wheat. In each case it may be that Jesus is addressing the dilemma of the already and the not yet that Jesus' disciples (in common with modern scholars!) found hard to understand: They hoped for the kingdom to come immediately and in power, but it did not. Jesus explained that he was like a sower and that the harvest would come in the future. (See further in chapter 8 for Jesus' understanding of the future.)

Celebration of Salvation

One of the important features of Jesus' ministry and message that we have not brought out is the strong sense of joy and happiness. The Gospels make it clear that Jesus' style of ministry was celebratory, not ascetic. They record the rather abusive but revealing comment of Jesus' contemporaries that "John came neither eating nor drinking, and they say, 'He has a demon'; the Son of Man came eating and drinking, and they say, 'Look, a glutton and a drunkard, a friend of tax collectors and sinners!'" (Matt 11:18, 19/Luke 7:33, 34). When asked why his disciples did not fast like other religious people, Jesus himself used the analogy of a wedding feast: Can the guests fast while the groom is with them (Matt 9:15; Mark 2:19; Luke 5:34)? The implication is that Jesus' ministry is a time of celebration.

The day of the Lord — the coming of God's kingdom — was associated in Jewish expectation with the judgment of God's enemies, and Jesus' disciples, according to the Gospels, hoped to see that judgment. Jesus did not repudiate the idea of divine judgment; on the contrary, it was an important theme in his teaching. But the judgment of which he warned is associated with the future coming of the kingdom; the present is a time of joy and forgiveness and opportunity for repentance as the blessings of God's rule begin to be experienced and seen. The father in the famous parable of the prodigal son comments: "We had to celebrate and rejoice, because this brother of yours was dead and has come to life; he was lost and has been found" (Luke 15:32).[26] This parable, though found only in Luke, sums up

26. Note the theme of rejoicing in the preceding parables of the lost sheep and the lost coin (15:6, 9) and in the parables of the pearl and the treasure (Matt 13:44-46).

what seems to have been central to Jesus' understanding of the kingdom: The coming of the kingdom was all to do with the restoring mercy and love of God bringing healing, defeating evil, finding the lost, and bringing reconciliation between God, his people, and his world. The OT vision of a new world was being realized. Celebration was therefore very much in order.

The preceding explanation of Jesus' kingdom teaching has been only a brief sketch. However, the main lines of our interpretation have been based on a broad spectrum of Gospel evidence, and, although it has not been possible to defend the positions taken in detail or to interact with all the different interpretations that are possible, the sketch will serve at least as a useful starting point for a comparison of Jesus' teaching with that of Paul.

THE GOOD NEWS ACCORDING TO PAUL

In our equally brief explanation of Paul's teaching, we will look at key themes in Paul, at each point making some remarks of comparison with the teaching of Jesus.

Jesus Christ and Him Crucified

Paul . . .

For Paul the good news is all to do with Jesus: Thus in Rom 1:1-4 he speaks of

> the gospel of God, which he promised beforehand through his prophets in the holy scriptures, the gospel concerning his Son, who was descended from David according to the flesh and was declared to be Son of God with power according to the spirit of holiness by resurrection from the dead, Jesus Christ our Lord.

The centrality of Jesus for Paul arose out of his own dramatic conversion experience, because in that experience "God . . . was pleased to reveal his Son to me" (Gal 1:15, 16); but that centrality was also part of the tradition that Paul received and transmitted to others: "I handed on to you as of first importance what I in turn had received: that Christ died for our sins in accordance with the scriptures, and that he was buried, and that he was raised on the third day in accordance with the scriptures, and that he appeared . . ." (1 Cor 15:3-5). The death and resurrection of Jesus were supremely important for Paul, as is made clear in that summary of the gospel as well as from verse after verse elsewhere in Paul's writings. To take just two examples: In 1 Cor 2:2 Paul tells the Corinthians how "I decided to know nothing among you except Jesus Christ, and him crucified." In Gal 6:14 Paul exclaims: "May I never boast of anything except the cross of our Lord Jesus Christ, by which the world has been crucified to me, and I to the world."

. . . and Jesus

This focus on christology and especially on the cross and resurrection is something that was totally absent from our summary of Jesus' kingdom preaching, and there is prima facie a significant difference between Jesus' gospel of the kingdom and Paul's preaching of Christ.[27] However, it would be premature to make too much of this at this stage, since for organizational reasons we have kept the discussion of Jesus' own self-understanding until the next chapter, and of his death and resurrection to subsequent chapters. It will be important, then, to consider both the content of Jesus' self-understanding and the importance of his "christology" within the overall pattern of his thinking, and then to evaluate the comparison with Paul.

It is not premature, however, to say that Jesus evidently did see that something of decisive importance — namely, the coming of the kingdom — was happening in the context of his ministry and was somehow connected with that ministry. Jesus' experience was Paul's christological conviction: that God's salvation came with Jesus.

Fulfillment of Promise

Paul . . .

Both Pauline summaries of the gospel quoted above, Rom 1:1-4 and 1 Cor 15:3-5, strongly emphasize that salvation in Christ is "according to the Scriptures." This emphasis was probably there in the tradition that Paul received, but is also an emphasis that Paul himself endorses. Paul the Pharisee

---

27. Cf. R. Bultmann's famous comment on the proclaimer becoming the proclaimed in *Theology of the NT,* I, 33.

did not, on his conversion to Christianity (in his own view, at least), discard his Jewish heritage; on the contrary he saw his new-found faith in Jesus as the fulfillment of the faith of Abraham, and he regarded Jesus as the destination and climax of God's purposes for and through Israel (e.g., Romans 4 and 9–11).[28] Even the law, which he had been so zealous to maintain and which was partly responsible for his misguided persecution of the church, is not overthrown, but in some sense fulfilled in Christ (Rom 3:31; 13:10; Gal 5:14). Even the church's mission to the Gentiles, which was so important to Paul, is what the OT prophets looked forward to (e.g., Rom 15:9-12).

. . . and Jesus

This emphasis on fulfillment is clearly something on which Paul and Jesus agree, though the extent to which Paul's thinking about how the OT is fulfilled in Christ corresponds to Jesus' own thinking will only become clear as we go on further.

Now Is the Day of Salvation!

Paul . . .

In referring back to the OT Paul is not saying that Christianity is simply in accord with or in continuity with the OT. On the contrary he sees the gospel as something radically new: Thus he can speak on two occasions of "new creation," and he can comment: "Everything old has passed away; see, everything has become new!" (2 Cor 5:17; Gal 6:15). He does not mean just that things become new for the believer, but that a whole new state of affairs has come with Jesus: God has acted decisively to save his people. The commentator who describes "but now" in Rom 3:21 as "the two most joyous little words in the NT"[29] may seem to be exaggerating the importance of the words, but is not exaggerating the importance of the idea that Paul is expressing. For Paul, God had acted dramatically and decisively in Christ in order to reconcile the world (2 Cor 5:19), and that was indeed the most important and joyous good news.

---

28. See notably on this Wright, *Climax of the Covenant.* As an Oxford colleague and friend, Tom Wright has considerably influenced and stimulated my thinking at various points.

29. W. B. Harris, *Romans,* 94.

Something dramatically new has happened in Jesus for Paul, but this something new is in fulfillment of the OT promise. In other words, we have in Jesus the fulfillment of the eschatological hopes of the OT: The longed-for time has come. As Paul puts it in Gal 4:4, "when the fullness of time had come, God sent his Son. . . ."

The importance of the eschatological dimension in Paul's thinking has been rightly recognized by recent scholars.[30] It has been a commonplace to argue, especially on the basis of 1 and 2 Thessalonians, that Paul, like others in the early church, expected "the end" within his own lifetime. We will have to consider whether this is strictly accurate or not (see chapter 7). What is hard to dispute is that Paul and his converts had a great sense of anticipation and urgency about the future. He could tell the Romans that "it is now the moment to wake from sleep. For salvation is nearer to us now than when we became believers; the night is far gone, the day is near" (Rom 13:11, 12). The reason for such urgency is that Paul believed that the eschatological countdown had begun with the coming of Jesus. The Holy Spirit, the first installment of what is to come, had been given, and so Christians were now longing and groaning for what lay ahead (Rom 8:23). The resurrection of the dead — very much an end-time event — has begun in Jesus, its firstfruits (1 Cor 15:20); the gathering in of the Gentiles, which the OT anticipated, is underway, and Paul has the crucial role to play in this.

. . . and Jesus

Although certain aspects of Paul's eschatological perspective, for example, his emphasis on the Gentile mission, are not prominent in the teaching of Jesus, the exciting sense of the divine moment having arrived is significant, and this they have in common. The Markan phrase "the time is fulfilled" (1:15) is paralleled in Gal 4:4, which speaks of God sending his Son "when the fullness of time had come," as also in Eph 1:10, which refers to God's plan for "the fullness of time."[31] The Lukan description of Jesus' sermon in Nazareth, in which Jesus quotes the verse from Isaiah 61 about "the year of the Lord's favor" (Luke 4:19) and goes on to declare that "today this Scripture has been fulfilled," is paralleled in 2 Cor 6:2, where Paul quotes Isaiah 49 in referring to the "acceptable time" and the "day of salvation"

30. See notably Beker, *Paul the Apostle,* 135-81.
31. The same Greek word for "time" *(kairos)* is used in Mark 1:15 and Eph 1:10, but a different word is used in Gal 4:4.

and goes on to comment that "now is the acceptable time . . . now is the day of salvation."[32]

God's Righteousness Revealed

Paul . . .

In seeing salvation in Christ in the context of eschatological fulfillment of OT promise Paul comes very close to Jesus. But, whereas Jesus speaks of the kingdom of God, Paul speaks rather of "righteousness" and "reconciliation."

"Righteousness" and "justification" are very important concepts in Paul's writings, though to distinguish them as two "concepts" may be misleading, because there is one Greek root, *dikaio-*, behind the two words. It is a limitation of the English language that we cannot easily convey the sense of the Greek with one word group. "Justice" is not an adequate translation of the Greek noun *dikaiosynē*, and there is no English verb "to righteousify" to convey the sense of the Greek verb *dikaioō*, though "put right" might almost do.

"Justification"/"righteousness" has often been seen as the central theme of Paul's whole theology. Not everyone is convinced, however, and it has been observed (among other things) that Paul uses these terms frequently only in Romans and Galatians. From this it has been inferred that the heavy use of this terminology in Romans and Galatians reflects the particular context of his discussion with the "Judaizers," those who insisted that Gentile converts keep the Jewish law rather than the regular shape of his theology. There may be some truth in this view. On the other hand, justification/righteousness terminology does crop up at significant points in letters other than Romans and Galatians, for example, in 1 Cor 1:30; 2 Cor 5:20; and Phil 3:9, and it is at least reasonable to conclude that it was one important Pauline category of thought.

Its importance in the book of Romans is made clear in 1:16, 17. In these programmatic verses Paul offers not a full definition of the gospel — he does not even mention Christ by name! — but an explanation of its importance and of why he, Paul, is not ashamed of it: "It is the power of God for salvation to everyone who has faith, to the Jew first and also to the Greek. For in it the righteousness of God is revealed through faith for faith; as it is written, 'The one who is righteous will live by faith.'"

---

32. See Stuhlmacher, *Biblische Theologie des Neuen Testaments*, 301-2.

What does Paul mean when he speaks of God's righteousness being revealed through the gospel? Commentators have struggled over this almost endlessly. One strong possibility is that Paul means that righteousness *from* God is revealed in the gospel; what is revealed is how we by God's mercy may be righteous (or justified). It speaks for this view that justification is a principal theme of Romans (e.g., in chapters 3 and 4) and that Paul comments on the description of the revelation of God's righteousness by speaking of how we are put right with God: "as it is written, 'The one who is righteous through faith will live.'"[33]

If this view of "God's righteousness" in 1:17 is accepted, as it is by important commentators,[34] there are further questions of clarification to be asked: In particular, if Paul speaks here of our God-given righteousness, how does he understand that? As a *legal* status? There is much to be said for this view, not least because of the emphasis in Romans on the judgment and justice of God (e.g., 1:32; 2:2, 10, 11, 16; 3:4, etc.). On this view Paul sees the death of Christ as securing our acquittal. Or does Paul mean that the gospel brings us into *moral* righteousness? Paul certainly emphasizes the moral effects of the gospel in Romans 6 and 8, though the way he speaks of righteousness being "reckoned" to the believer (e.g., in Romans 4) may suggest that he is thinking primarily of our being granted "right standing" with God rather than moral transformation.

But Paul may mean something quite different in Rom 1:17 when he speaks of God's righteousness being revealed: His point may be, not that the gospel reveals how we may be righteous with God, but rather that God himself is righteous. In other words, the work of Christ demonstrates God's own righteousness. In favor of this view it can be observed (1) that Paul uses two other "of God" phrases in the immediate context of 1:17, namely "the power of God" in 1:16 and "the wrath of God" in 1:18, both phrases referring to attributes or activities of God; (2) that Paul is very concerned to assert the righteousness of God in Romans. Indeed, it has been argued that one of the main motivations behind Romans is that Paul wishes to rebut accusations that his gospel — with its emphasis on the Gentiles and on freedom from law — makes God unrighteous and unfaithful to his promises to Israel.[35]

If this view is accepted, namely, that Paul wishes to assert that the

33. Following the translation in NRSV margin. For a different interpretation of this clause see chapter 8 below.

34. E.g., Cranfield, *Romans*, I, 91-102.

35. See, e.g., Wedderburn, *Reasons for Romans*, 108-25.

gospel demonstrates God's righteousness, there are again several options: Is it God's justice as judge that is demonstrated? Is it God's faithfulness in saving his people in accordance with his covenant? Or is it more broadly his glorious goodness?

It is attractive to suggest that Paul had a broader rather than a narrower intention in using the phrase "righteousness of God," and various commentators have claimed that Paul meant that the gospel reveals both our justification and God's own righteousness. This could sound like scholars trying to transfer their confusion to Paul; however, not only are both ideas important to Paul, but he even has them side-by-side in chapter 3, where he expounds his understanding of justification: The death of Christ was intended "to prove at the present time that [God] himself is righteous and that he justifies the one who has faith in Jesus" (3:26).

A further and probably decisive argument for such a broad interpretation of God's "righteousness" has to do with the background to what Paul says. We have already suggested that Paul sees what God has done in Christ as the eschatological fulfillment of OT promises. When Paul speaks of "the righteousness of God," he speaks of it being "revealed," using the verb *apokalyptō*, which frequently has eschatological connotations; he also immediately supports his assertion by referring back to the prophecy of Habakkuk that the righteous will live by their faith. Given this context, there is every probability that what Paul means is that through Jesus the OT promises of the coming righteousness of God are being fulfilled. In 3:21 he speaks of God's righteousness, which "has been disclosed," as "attested by the law and the prophets."

The OT frequently looks forward to the day when God will establish righteousness — for his people and on the earth. Isaiah 61 is as notable a passage as any and was particularly important to Jesus, to judge from the Gospels.[36] It speaks of the year of the Lord's favor, of the restoration of the ancient ruins, and of the restoration of the people, who will enjoy "the wealth of the nations." Then it goes on to say:

> For I the LORD love justice,
>   I hate robbery and wrongdoing;
> I will faithfully give them their recompense,
>   and I will make an everlasting covenant with them. . . .
>
> I will greatly rejoice in the LORD . . .
> for he has clothed me with the garments of salvation,

36. He quoted it in the Nazareth synagogue according to Luke 4:16-21 (see also Matt 5:3/Luke 6:20; Matt 11:5/Luke 7:22).

> he has covered me with the robe of righteousness,
> as a bridegroom decks himself with a garland,
> and as a bride adorns herself with her jewels.
> For as the earth brings forth its shoots,
> and as a garden causes what is sown in it to spring up,
> so the Lord GOD will cause righteousness and praise
> to spring up before all the nations. *vv. 8, 9-11*

The picture is a very beautiful one — God restoring his people in the context of the nations. This restoration is the manifestation of God's justice, covenant-faithfulness, and righteousness, but also, as part of that, it is the clothing of his people with salvation and righteousness.

This surely is the background to Paul's understanding of the revelation of God's righteousness: He does not mean that God has informed us of an eternal truth about himself, but rather that God has acted powerfully to save his people (Rom 1:16), thus demonstrating and establishing the righteousness that the prophets promised.

Isaiah 61 is only one of many OT passages that speak in this way. The psalmists look to God's intervention to judge the world in righteousness (96:13; 98:9; cf. 85:4-13).[37] Jeremiah speaks of the coming days "when I [the LORD] will raise up for David a righteous Branch, and he shall reign as king and deal wisely, and shall execute justice and righteousness in the land. In his days Judah will be saved and Israel will live in safety. And this is the name by which he will be called: 'The LORD is our righteousness'" (23:5, 6). Later he speaks similarly, but it is Jerusalem that is to be called "The Lord is our righteousness" (33:14-16).

For Paul those promised days have come, and when he speaks of God's righteousness being revealed, the picture is a big one, not a small one: God's righteous character and his faithfulness to his people are vindicated and demonstrated, sin is judged and righteousness is established in the world, people are brought back into a right relationship with God and righteous living. Käsemann speaks attractively of God's righteousness in Judaism having a "field of radiation": So for Paul, as God's righteousness is demonstrated and established in the world, men and women are drawn back into right relationships with God.[38]

---

37. Ps 98:2, "The LORD has made known his salvation, in the sight of the nations he has revealed his righteousness,"* may well be echoed in Rom 1:17, 18; cf. Fitzmyer, *Romans,* 257.

38. Käsemann, *Romans,* 28. Others also emphasize the largeness of the concept. Thus Beker, *Paul the Apostle,* 264: "The phrase 'the righteousness of God' . . . transcends

We conclude that for Paul the righteousness/justification terminology has a broad spectrum of meaning, but that the overarching concept is the idea of God's eschatological righteousness coming into history and into the lives of people through Jesus Christ.[39]

. . . and Jesus

If this understanding of "righteousness" in Paul is valid, then it turns out to be conceptually close to Jesus' understanding of the kingdom. There is a significant difference between Jesus' kingdom teaching and the common Protestant and evangelical interpretation of justification as the acquittal of individual sinners by the divine judge on the basis of the work of Christ. But that narrow interpretation of Pauline justification, though unexceptional as far as it goes, arguably reflects the Lutheran and post-Lutheran experience of personal guilt (reinforced by modern individualism), and in any case does not do full justice to Paul's larger concept with its roots in the OT hope.[40] Seen against that background, Paul's understanding of

---

the category of acquittal and personal relationship because it points to that order of cosmic peace (shalom) and salvation (sōtēria) that has been proleptically manifested in Christ and that discloses itself in our obedience to his lordship. . . ." Ziesler, Romans, 71, comments: "God's righteousness is something into which believers are drawn, so that in their own selves and their own lives, that righteousness which is essentially God's becomes a reality." He goes on to say that the righteousness believers receive is "both their standing before God and a totally renewed life" (p. 72). Wedderburn, Reasons for Romans, 122, argues that the Pauline phrase "righteousness of God" embraces three ideas that we might wish might to distinguish, namely God's righteous character, his righteous action, and a resulting "state of righteousness in human lives and the world." Among the vast literature on justification/righteousness in Paul see also Ziesler, Meaning of Righteousness; Piper, "Demonstration of Righteousness"; Motyer, "Righteousness by Faith"; Stuhlmacher, Reconciliation, Law, and Righteousness, 68-93; Campbell, Rhetoric of Righteousness, 138-72.

39. This is not to say that every use of these words has a broad meaning, but that there is a broad concept of the righteousness of God being revealed with the justification of human beings being an aspect of that eschatological event and reality.

40. A classic statement on this point is Stendahl's "The Apostle Paul and the Introspective Conscience of the West." To recognize the force of Stendahl's argument is not to say that the idea of individual "justification" is not present or important in Paul or Jesus. Farmer, Jesus and the Gospel, 49, observes the strong thematic similarity between Jesus' parable of the Pharisee and the tax collector — the tax collector recognizes his sinfulness and is "justified" (Luke 18:9-14) — and Paul's understanding of sinners being justified, and says that it looks as though the parable was "indelibly burned on Paul's mind."

righteousness and Jesus' teaching about the kingdom come very close together.[41] It is worth noting that the Psalms to which we have referred that
speak of the Lord coming to establish righteousness do so in the context
of reference to the Lord as king: in the ancient world the king is supremely
the upholder of justice, and God's reign and kingdom entail the manifestation and establishment of his righteousness.

Reconciliation

Paul . . .

Whereas some scholars have identified justification as the heart of Paul's
theology, others have looked to the concept of reconciliation,[42] which is, at
least, another central Pauline theme. It is most strikingly expressed in 2 Cor
5:18-20, where Paul comments that God

> reconciled us to himself through Christ, and has given us the ministry
> of reconciliation; that is, in Christ God was reconciling the world to
> himself, not counting their trespasses against them, and entrusting the
> message of reconciliation to us. So we are ambassadors for Christ, since
> God is making his appeal through us; we entreat you on behalf of Christ,
> be reconciled to God.

These words follow immediately from Paul's words about new creation and
about everything becoming new in Christ, and they immediately precede
his description of Christ being "made sin," so that we might become "the
righteousness of God" (5:17, 21). So we are in the same circle of ideas as
before, though the focus is now on reconciliation.

The same theme is also important in Romans, where Paul first ex-

41. R. Bultmann, "Significance of the Historical Jesus," 232, recognized the similar
eschatologies of Paul and Jesus and said of Paul's understanding of the righteousness
of God: "This concept corresponds to the 'kingdom of God.'" Jüngel developed this
argument in *Paulus und Jesus*, e.g., 266-67. But see most usefully Wedderburn, *Paul and
Jesus*, 102-10, who argues that "kingdom" in Jesus and "righteousness" in Paul both have
connotations of powerful divine action, but also of something into which we enter or
which we receive. Thus he comments on "a shared vision in which the often rather
forbidding and menacing ideas of God as king and of the righteous one were transformed by their being invested with predominantly positive and salvific connotations"
(109).

42. E.g., Martin, *Reconciliation*.

plains the work of Christ in terms of justification (chapters 3 and 4), but then proceeds to say in chapter 5 that "since we are justified by faith, we have peace with God through our Lord Jesus Christ" (5:1). He goes on to talk of Christ's death (vv. 8-10):

> God proves his love for us in that while we still were sinners Christ died for us. Much more surely then, now that we have been justified by his blood, will we be saved through him from the wrath of God. For if while were were enemies, we were reconciled to God through the death of his Son, much more surely, having been reconciled, will we be saved by his life.

Paul goes on in the verses that follow to compare Adam and Christ, thus reminding us again of the new creation theme, though not on this occasion using that terminology.

In both passages the emphasis is on the reconciliation of human beings with God. For Paul the heart of the good news of Christ is the bringing of men and women out of enmity and out of slavery — we will return to consider Paul's view of the human predicament — into the freedom of God's children and the experience of God epitomized by the cry "Abba, Father." But there are hints in Paul's language that he sees the reconciliation as not just for humanity but for the whole world, and as not just between God and humanity but also among people.

Thus in 2 Cor 5:19 he speaks of God reconciling "the world," and in Romans he can speak of all creation coming to share "the freedom of the glory of the children of God" (8:21). The new creation is evidently not just for Adam's children but for the whole of creation, which has been "subjected to futility" (v. 20). Paul's vision is for "all things" to be brought into subjection under God's feet and for all God's enemies to be subjugated or, in the case of death, destroyed (1 Cor 15:25, 26).

This vision of cosmic reconciliation is even more explicit in Colossians, which speaks of God being "pleased to reconcile to himself all things, whether on earth or in heaven, by making peace through the blood of his cross" (1:20), and in Ephesians, where "the mystery of [God's] will," "set forth in Christ, as a plan for the fullness of time," is "to gather up all things in him, things in heaven and things on earth" (1:9, 10; cf. vv. 22, 23). In Ephesians the supreme example of this divine peacemaking is the destruction of the barriers between Jews and Gentiles in the church.

> In Christ Jesus you who once were far off have been brought near by the blood of Christ. For he is our peace; in his flesh he has made both groups

into one and has broken down the dividing wall, that is, the hostility between us. He has abolished the law with its commandments and ordinances, that he might create in himself one new humanity in place of the two, thus making peace, and might reconcile both groups to God in one body through the cross, thus putting to death that hostility through it. So he came and proclaimed peace to you who were far off and peace to those who were near; for through him both of us have access in one Spirit to the Father. 2:13-18

This striking statement of the work of Christ in producing reconciliation between people, especially between Jews and Gentiles, is not an innovation in Ephesians: It is one of the most important themes throughout the Pauline corpus, including Romans and Galatians, where the issue of Jewish and Gentile Christians is of special importance. Paul affirms that "there is no longer Jew or Greek, there is no longer slave or free, there is no longer male and female; for all of you are one in Christ Jesus" (Gal 3:28). Paul emphasizes in various contexts that Christians — of whatever background and despite their differences of conscience (e.g., over matters of food and drink) — belong together as parts of the one body and are to live peacefully with all, as far as that is possible (Rom 12:4, 5, 9-21; 1 Cor 7:15; 12–13).

. . . and Jesus

Paul's understanding of reconciliation has obvious antecedents in the teaching of Jesus.[43] We are reminded of the parables of the lost sheep and of the prodigal son by Paul's words about the love of God reaching out to us "while we were still sinners" and "enemies," and even more by the words in Ephesians about "those who once were far off" having been "brought near" (2:13). We are also reminded of Jesus' controversial mixing with sinners.

As for Paul's teaching about barriers being broken down between human beings, this is anticipated in Jesus' own conduct, in mixing, for example, with socially marginalized groups, including tax collectors and women, but also in his teaching about love for enemies and Samaritans. (We will look further at this in chapter 6 below.)

The Pauline vision of cosmic reconciliation is perhaps more difficult

---

43. Stuhlmacher, *Reconciliation*, 1-15, finds the heart of Jesus' ministry to be "messianic reconciliation."

to parallel in the Jesus-tradition.[44] On the other hand, we saw how important the casting out of demons and the healing of disease were in Jesus' ministry: Salvation is not just bringing lost individuals back to God; it is overcoming the strong man and his forces and restoring the physically deformed and diseased.

Paul does not have as overt an emphasis on the satanic and demonic as Jesus does in the Gospels; He does not refer to casting out of devils. And yet Satan is for Paul a reality — a destructive, tempting, deceiving figure of opposition (e.g., 1 Cor 5:5; 7:5; 2 Cor 2:11; 11:14; 12:7; 1 Thes 2:18; 3:5; 2 Thes 2:9; 1 Tim 1:20; 5:15). Paul speaks in 2 Cor 4:4 of "the god of this world" blinding the minds of unbelievers; Ephesians, too, speaks of "the rulers," "the authorities," "the cosmic powers" (6:12). We have here an idea similar to what is expressed in John's Gospel where it speaks of "the ruler of this world" and to the synoptic discussion of Satan's kingdom and portrayal of Satan as the "strong man" (John 14:30; Matt 12:24-29/Mark 3:22-27/Luke 11:15-22). Unbelievers are, according to Paul, in slavery to "the elemental spirits of the world" (Gal 4:3, 9; Col 2:8, 20).[45] Ephesians has a particularly strong stress on the spiritual forces of evil, emphasizing that the Christian's fight is not against human opposition, but against "the spiritual forces of evil in the heavenly places" (6:12). This emphasis may be a reflection of the Ephesian context,[46] but it is paralleled elsewhere in the Pauline corpus, for example in Rom 16:20, where Paul comments that "the God of peace will shortly crush Satan under your feet," and in 1 Cor 15:24-28, where Paul speaks of Jesus' mission being to subdue every ruler, authority, and power and to bring all God's enemies back under his feet.

As for physical healings, Paul does refer to his own apostolic ministry as done "by word and deed, by the power of signs and wonders, by the power of the Spirit of God" (Rom 15:18, 19; cf. 2 Cor 12:12; Gal 3:5; 1 Thes 1:5).[47] But language associated with miracles in the synoptic Gospels seems to be used by Paul mainly in connection with preaching: Thus in the Gospels "your faith has saved you" is used characteristically in connection with Jesus'

44. The Gospel tradition of the nature miracles, e.g., the story of the stilling of the storm, could be of some relevance here; and if Ps 8:4-6 played any part in Jesus' Son of man concept (see below, chapter 3), this could also be relevant (see my article "Kingdom and Creation"). The use of *palingenesia* in Matt 19:28, if it goes back to Jesus, could also be relevant. (I am grateful to Peter Ensor for this suggestion.)

45. On the meaning of *stoicheia* see, among others, O'Brien, *Colossians*, 129-32.

46. See especially Arnold, *Ephesians*.

47. The author of Acts associates Paul with a significant healing ministry, e.g. 14:3, 9, 10; 16:18; 19:11, 12; 20:10.

healings, but in Rom 1:16 Paul speaks of "the gospel" as God's power *(dynamis)* for "salvation" to all who have "faith," and in 1 Corinthians 1 and 2 it is quite emphatically the word of the cross, not signs such as the Jews look for, that is the "power" of God, bringing salvation to the person who has faith.

This emphasis on "the word" and proclamation is not new with Paul; it is a feature also of the Jesus-tradition. But it may be that there has been a shift of emphasis away from miracle and exorcism in the Jesus-tradition to the preached word in Paul as that which brings spiritual liberation to those bound in unbelief by Satan. This shift can be explained by two factors: (1) In both 1 and 2 Corinthians Paul is addressing a highly charismatic church that evidently stressed supernatural signs, and Paul in that context emphasizes the word of the cross, no doubt to balance their one-sidedness in favor of signs and wonders.[48] (2) In the context of Jesus' ministry there was the opportunity to respond directly in faith to Jesus; but for Paul it is through preaching about Jesus that people confront Jesus and may respond to him and come to saving faith. Failure to believe is the supreme satanic enslavement. So the preached word comes to have a prominence and primacy that was not true in Jesus' ministry.

But, although it is true that there is probably a difference between Jesus and Paul at this point, a wholistic view of salvation is shared between them. For Paul salvation is not just individual and spiritual: It leads to resurrection of the body, the redemption of creation, and the final defeat of Satan and of God's enemies.[49]

48. Whether Paul's opponents had a seriously deficient christology in Paul's view — Georgi, *Opponents of Paul,* believes that they saw Jesus as a "divine man" having supernatural power and working miracles — is not certain. What is certain is that they were charismatics and were keen on miracles and spiritual manifestations and that Paul may have wished to correct their one-sided emphasis.

49. Fredriksen, *From Jesus to Christ,* 170-76, finds a much more spiritualized view of the kingdom in Paul than in Jesus: "We search in vain to find Paul praising the future Jerusalem or the eschatological Temple. Images of earthly fecundity or social harmony do not figure in his presentation. The coming kingdom will be 'in the air' (1 Thes 4:16), in the heavens (Phil 3:20) where no flesh can dwell (1 Cor 15:50). The resurrection is *spiritual,* not physical (1 Cor 15)." There may be a grain of truth in what Fredriksen says, but she underestimates the "spirituality" of Jesus' conception and overestimates the "spirituality" of Paul: Paul does, for example, emphasize social reconciliation and believes in the resurrection of the physical body (transformed, of course, by the power of the Spirit). He does not explicitly say that the future kingdom will be "in the air" or even "in the heavens"; his language about the Lord coming from heaven is probably drawn from the Jesus-tradition (see chapter 7 below).

The Human Predicament in Paul

Paul...

Divine reconciliation is necessary, almost by definition, because of present hostility and enmity. For Paul the fundamental human problem is the breakdown of relationships between God and humanity. Thus in Romans 1, as he begins to explain his gospel, Paul starts his classic discussion of the world without God by describing the plight of the Gentile world, and he begins that description by referring to both the "wrath" or "anger" of God and the "ungodliness" of those who reject the truth of God.

Modern commentators have had difficulty with Paul's teaching about God's anger and have tried in various ways to reduce its harshness. However, although it is important to say that God's anger for Paul is nothing like an irrational loss of temper, there can be very little doubt that he, like his Jewish contemporaries, believed in the real, terrifying judgment of God. The theme permeates chapters 1–3 of Romans. Paul, like his Jewish contemporaries, saw God's judgment and wrath as something to be experienced in the future (e.g., Rom 5:9; 1 Thes 1:10; 2 Thes 1:8-10; Col 3:6), but he also saw it as something that was already being revealed in the corruption and degradation of Gentile society.

The fundamental cause of God's judgment, as Paul explains it in Romans 1, is human rebellion against God the creator. The problem is that people "exchanged the glory of the immortal God" (v. 23) for images and lies. Paul has particularly in mind Gentile idolatry, but it is his diagnosis of the human problem more generally, Jews included, that "there is no one who seeks God . . . there is no fear of God before their eyes" (Rom 3:11, 18).

But if this rejection of God is the fundamental human problem, its consequence is moral degradation and spoiled human relationships. In Romans 1 Paul illustrates this with a forthright description of the homosexual practices of the Gentile world. Paul's choice of this example does not, as some have supposed, reflect a bigoted obsession with sex;[50] most probably Paul focuses on this example because sexual perversion was so often associated in the ancient world with idolatry and because homosexual practice seemed to him to exemplify the moral inversions and exchanges that follow from exchanging faith in the creator for substitutes.[51] But Paul

---

50. It may more plausibly be seen as a reflection of his quite accurate appreciation of the importance of sex in human experience.

51. For Paul's view of heterosexual union see below in chapters 5 and 6.

goes on from the particular example to a catalogue of human sins that characterize the unbelieving world and its relationships: "wickedness, evil, covetousness, malice . . . envy, murder, strife, deceit, craftiness . . . , gossips, slanderers, God-haters, insolent, haughty, boastful, inventors of evil, rebellious toward parents, foolish, faithless, heartless, ruthless" (1:29-31).

Paul implies that the Gentile world is trapped in this sort of way of life, knowing it to be wrong but living in a delusion. Three times Paul says, "God gave them up . . ." (1:24, 26, 28). Elsewhere he is quite explicit about the slavery of sin. Sin is not just wrong action, but a power to which "you were slaves" (Rom 6:20). Since "the wages of sin is death" (6:23), those who are in rebellion against God are slaves also to death. The seriousness of sin is described by Paul in Romans 7, where he speaks of its deceitful and deadly effectiveness in preventing "me" from doing what it good; the situation is summed up in the cry in v. 24: "Wretched man that I am! Who will rescue me from this body of death?"[52] The answer to that question is, of course, Christ, and it is for this reason that Paul can speak, for example, in 3:24, of Christ's work as "redemption" — a word meaning liberation, used sometimes of buying slaves out of slavery but also suggestive of the idea of Israel's liberation from slavery in Egypt and from the Babylonian exile.[53] Jesus is not only our peace and our justification, but also our liberation — from sin, from death, and also from the law.

Paul's diagnosis of the Gentile predicament in Romans 1 is followed by his observations about the Jewish predicament in chapters 2 and 3. He argues here that the Jews are in no better situation, despite their privileges: They boast of possessing the law and being God's circumcised people, but Paul finds that they break the law and that they, like the Gentiles, are "under the power of sin" (3:9). He warns that having the law and circumcision will not save anyone and comments that "a person is not a Jew who is one outwardly, nor is true circumcision something external and physical. Rather, a person is a Jew who is one inwardly [literally: in secret], and real circumcision is a matter of the heart . . ." (2:28, 29). Paul speaks of God judging "the secret thoughts of all" (2:16), and he finds that possessing the law, though a valuable gift of God, has not brought salvation to the Jews, but has demonstrated the failure of all. "All have sinned and fall short of the glory of God" (3:23); all are implicated in the fatal, enslaving transgression of Adam (5:12-21). Sin is a most serious reality for Paul.

---

52. See also Eph 2:1-3 for the idea of unbelievers being dead to sin and under God's wrath.

53. See Dunn, *Romans 1–8*, 169.

. . . and Jesus

Paul's denunciation of idolatry and homosexual practice in Romans 1 reflects his Gentile context and has no direct parallel in the teaching of Jesus.[54] Paul's emphasis on the failure of the law reflects both his own personal experience (as a Pharisee on the Damascus road) and his church context, where the issue of Gentile observance or nonobservance of the law was a key issue. But, despite differences, the diagnoses given by Paul and Jesus have important points in common: Thus Paul's comments in Romans 2 on the Jews' misplaced confidence in their Jewishness and their religion and on God looking at the human heart have striking parallels in Jesus' criticism of the piety of Jewish religious leaders and, for example, in the sermon on the mount, where Jesus insists on a higher righteousness than that of the scribes and Pharisees and on purity of heart and motive.[55] As for the wrath of God, we have argued that Jesus' teaching was predominantly good news of salvation rather than bad news of judgment; but so is Paul's. And there is a strong stress on judgment in Jesus' teaching, for example, in his parables on human accountability and on the coming day of judgment, when many will not enter the kingdom.

It may be true that Paul the convert emphasizes more than Jesus the radical lostness of sinful humanity's predicament apart from the gospel, but it is not clear that the picture given by Jesus is essentially different from the Pauline picture. He sees people as sick and in need of a doctor, as lost and in need of being found. The father of the prodigal son in Jesus' parable can say after his son's return from the far country: "this son of mine was dead and is alive again; he was lost and is found" (Luke 15:24); the thought is similar to that of Eph 2:1-5, where the author speaks of God making alive those who were dead in sin and children of wrath.[56]

54. But see Matt 15:19/Mark 7:21, 22 on fornication and adultery.

55. See Matthew 5 and 6. See also the discussion of cleanness and uncleanness in Matthew 15/Mark 7 and Jesus' woes on the scribes and Pharisees in Matthew 23/Luke 11, both of which have been compared to Romans 2 (e.g., Dodd, *New Testament Studies*, 62-65, and see further the discussion below in this chapter). Paul's teaching in Romans 2 may also have a parallel of sorts in synoptic passages in which Jesus speaks of Gentile cities faring better in the judgment than unrepentant Jewish cities (Matt 10:15; 11:20-24; Luke 10:12-15; Matt 12:41, 42/Luke 11:31, 32) and perhaps in the symbolic shaking or wiping of dust from the feet enjoined by Jesus on his disciples, if this was a sign to those Jews who rejected the good news that they were now reckoned as heathen (Matt 10:14/Mark 6:11/Luke 9:5; 10:11; see Davies and Allison, *Matthew*, II, 178). I am indebted to Peter Ensor for this last suggestion.

56. Even if Ephesians was not written by Paul, its second chapter expresses the

Faith

Paul . . .

For Paul there is one way to receive the salvation of Christ, and that is through "faith" or "believing." (This is another case of one Greek root, this time *pist-*, with two different English translations.) So in Rom 1:16, 17 Paul speaks of salvation "to everyone who has faith, to the Jew first and also to the Greek. For in it [the gospel] the righteousness of God is revealed through faith for faith; as it is written, 'The one who is righteous through faith will live.'" The strong emphasis on faith in these verses and elsewhere in Paul's writings is unmistakable: Faith for Paul, along with love and hope, is one of the things that will endure forever (1 Cor 13:13).[57]

Faith for Paul has two dimensions: It involves an element of intellectual belief; thus Paul can say in Rom 10:9, "If you confess with your lips that Jesus is Lord and *believe in your heart* that God raised him from the dead, you will be saved." In 1 Cor 15:1ff. he sets out the key elements of the gospel "through which also you are being saved," the assumption being that these elements have been believed. But faith also involves commitment of life. Thus in Rom 1:5 Paul can speak of his mission of bringing all Gentiles to "the obedience of faith," and in Rom 10:16 of those who have not "obeyed the gospel." In Gal 5:6 Paul refers to "faith working through love."

Both elements are expressed in baptism. For Paul baptism is important (and we will come back to consider it in more detail in due course): What he says about dying with Christ in baptism (Rom 6:3, 4) and of being baptized into the body (1 Cor 12:13) could appear to contradict what we

---

radical Pauline view of the human situation without Christ. It is evocative of the parable of the prodigal son in all sorts of ways: The parable speaks of a sinful son going to "a far country," evidently a Gentile country, of that son being welcomed back and even feted, thanks to his father's extraordinary and undeserved love, of the son being "dead and alive again," and of the father trying to persuade the elder brother to join in the celebration. Ephesians 2 speaks of Gentiles who were far off and dead in sins, being brought back to life and given a place of honor with Christ, thanks to God's grace, whose plan is to make peace and to bring unity to Jew and Gentile. It is not impossible that the author of Ephesians was influenced by the parable (as Resch supposed: *Paulinismus*, 102); but at this point we simply note the parallel ideas.

57. The importance of faith is clear, even if the translation "through faith for faith" is misleading in Rom 1:17 and the phrase actually refers first to the faithfulness of Christ (literally "from faith)" and only then to our faith ("to faith"). See further in chapter 8 below.

have just said about faith being the way to salvation for Paul. But Rom 10:9, which we have just quoted, is very probably a baptismal reference, and we see there that faith and baptism are two sides of the one coin. Baptism is the way a person expresses converting faith, and it includes confession of the Christian creedal conviction that "Jesus is Lord," but also a vivid and practical identification with Jesus.

Faith for Paul is not something for which we deserve any credit. Indeed, C. H. Dodd goes so far as to suggest that faith is "an act which is the negation of all activity," and John Ziesler calls it "almost a non-thing."[58] This is perhaps to go too far. W. B. Harris is nearer the mark when he speaks of the "drowning man who must stop his own struggles . . . and trust himself completely to the other" (i.e. his "rescuer").[59] For Paul faith is indeed a response to the message of God's love in Christ (Rom 10:17), and the necessary condition for such a response is a consciousness of helplessness and need (hence the need for the Jews to experience judgment before they are ready for salvation, as explained by Paul in Romans 11).

. . . and Jesus

There is no emphasis on baptism in the pre-resurrection teaching of Jesus recorded in the synoptic Gospels, though Jesus did have strong links with John the Baptist, as we have seen, and it is much more likely that the Pauline practice of baptism has its roots here than in the Greek mystery religions, as some have suggested.[60]

There is, however, unanimity between Jesus and Paul on the importance of faith. The word "faith" is used in the synoptic Gospels in the context of miracles: "Your faith has made you well"; Paul speaks similarly of miracle-working faith in 1 Cor 12:9; 13:2. But, according to the Gospels of Mark and John at least (Mark 1:15; John 1:12, etc.), "faith" also sums up the appropriate response of anyone to Jesus. That response is, put briefly, to come to Jesus with a sense of need and trust, and the miracle stories typically illustrate that response. Paul's understanding of faith has a christological focus and content that is not explicit in the teaching in the Gospels (except in John); we will consider that difference when we come to christology in the next chapter.

58. Dodd, *Romans*, 16; Ziesler, *Romans*, 69.
59. W. B. Harris, *Romans*, 66-67.
60. We will discuss baptism further in chapter 8 below. On Paul and the mystery religions see Wedderburn, *Baptism and Resurrection*.

Now and Not Yet

Paul . . .

The trusting believer receives, as we have seen, righteousness, reconciliation, redemption, and more besides. For Paul these blessings are experienced in the present, especially through the Holy Spirit; but salvation is also spoken of as something future to be experienced on the Lord's return (e.g., Rom 2:13; 3:30; 5:10; 8:19). This ambiguity is not confusion on Paul's part, but reflects his understanding that salvation has come into the present but has yet to be experienced fully. Thus, as we saw, he can speak of the Holy Spirit as a "down payment" on our future inheritance, that is, as a first, albeit partial, installment of what is to come (2 Cor 1:22; 5:5; Eph 1:14). We know what it is to be children of God now, crying "Abba," but the glory of sonship lies in the future (Rom 8:14-18). We know redemption already, but the redemption of our bodies lies still ahead of us, so that the present is a time of groaning, of conflict between what Paul calls "the flesh" and "the Spirit," and even of frustration (Romans 8). The frustration is evidence of the new life brought by Christ, but also of the partiality of our present experience.

Paul speaks on various occasions of "this age" (e.g., 1 Cor 1:20; 2:6, 8; 3:18), referring to the present godless world or, to be more exact, to the present world, whose god is Satan (2 Cor 4:4). It is precisely to deliver us from "the present evil age" that Christ came (Gal 1:4), and the Christian is instructed by Paul not to be "conformed to this age"* (Rom 12:2). It is clear that the Christian is someone who in one sense does not belong to the present age, though the present age is still present and still a threat. In 1 Cor 10:11 Paul says that Scripture was written for the instruction of those "on whom the ends of the ages have come." The exact force of the phrase is debated, but it is plausibly taken to mean that the Christian lives at the turning point from the old age to the new age; the idea may be of a period of overlap between the conclusion of "this age" and the beginning of "the age to come."[61] It is a case of now and not yet.

. . . and Jesus

The now-and-not-yet of Paul mirrors closely the teaching of Jesus on the present and future kingdom. The exciting day of salvation and fulfillment has broken in, but the consummation lies in the future. If there is a differ-

61. Fee, 1 Corinthians, 459.

ence between Paul and Jesus on this point, it is that Paul focuses on the believer's ambivalent personal experience, whereas Jesus speaks more of the kingdom in society. But that difference should not be exaggerated, since Paul can speak not only of individual experience but also of a growing church and of creation groaning for redemption. Paul's emphasis on the Spirit is not paralleled in the synoptic Gospels, though it is more than an implication that the kingdom that is experienced in Jesus' ministry is "by the Spirit of God" (Matt 12:28; Luke 4:18).[62]

FINAL COMMENTS ON THE COMPARISON

If the sketches we have offered are at least reasonably accurate, then the overall similarity of Jesus' kingdom preaching to Paul's gospel is clear. Both men proclaimed the dawn of God's promised day of salvation. Both believed that God was intervening to bring righteousness, healing, and reconciliation to the world. Both called on people to respond to the good news in faith. Much of what they have in common has Jewish precedent, but the level of agreement in the broad pattern of their respective gospels is striking.

There are differences of terminology, for instance, "kingdom" versus "righteousness," and of emphasis, which to a considerable extent reflect their different contexts. Perhaps the biggest difference is that the kingdom as proclaimed by Jesus is a broadly conceived new age and new society, involving healing, the casting out of devils, the reconciliation of sinners with God, and the reconciliation of people with each other, whereas for Paul everything is focused on belief in Jesus as the center of the good news and on the life of the believing community. This focus is not to the exclusion of the broader vision, but it is noticeable and needs explaining. The explanation will certainly have something to do with Paul's own context: He writes (1) after the resurrection, (2) after his own conversion experience, (3) in the arena of the Roman Empire, not in Palestine, and (4) to Christian communities with particular problems. We shall need to return to this issue as we go along and as we accumulate more evidence.

---

62. On the Spirit see further in chapter 7 below.

II. CONNECTING JESUS AND PAUL

If it is true that there are extensive and substantial similarities between Jesus' teaching and Paul's teaching, what does this prove? Does it prove that Paul has been significantly influenced by the Jesus-tradition? It is worth saying at the outset that some such influence, direct or indirect, must be a possible, even probable, explanation of the similarities. It is striking how some scholars can find Paul in remarkable theological agreement with Jesus and yet conclude that Paul was not interested in the teaching of Jesus.[63] But how then is the theological agreement to be explained? Presumably by continuity of church tradition: In other words, Paul is not interested in Jesus, but is still influenced by him indirectly through the tradition of the church. In that case it is still significant that Jesus' imprint is strong in the Christian tradition.

But can we show that Paul was familiar with the Jesus-tradition? Clearly some of the similarities of thought that we have noted could be explained in these terms. But is it possible to be more specific? A number of pieces of evidence need to be examined.

THE KINGDOM SAYINGS

At first sight Paul's failure to reproduce Jesus' emphasis on the kingdom of God looks like a strong point against him being influenced by Jesus' teaching. However, the kingdom is not in fact absent from Paul's letters. He speaks of it not infrequently, and it is worth recording his usages.

Paul on the Kingdom

In the undisputed letters we find:

> The kingdom of God is not food and drink but righteousness and peace and joy in the Holy Spirit.   Rom 14:17

> The kingdom of God is not in word, but in power.*   1 Cor 4:20

> Do you not know that unrighteous people will not inherit God's king-

63. Bultmann is a case in point.

dom? Make no mistake: neither immoral people nor idolaters . . . nor
rapacious people will inherit God's kingdom.*　　　　　1 Cor 6:9, 10

Then is the end, when he hands the kingdom over to God the Father,
when he eliminates every rule and every authority and power.*
　　　　　　　　　　　　　　　　　　　　　　　　　1 Cor 15:24

Flesh and blood cannot inherit the kingdom of God, nor does the per-
ishable inherit the imperishable.　　　　　　　　　　　1 Cor 15:50

I am warning you, as I warned you before: those who do such things
["the works of the flesh," v. 19] will not inherit the kingdom of God.
　　　　　　　　　　　　　　　　　　　　　　　　　　Gal 5:21

That you are to walk worthily of the God who calls you into his own
kingdom and glory.*　　　　　　　　　　　　　　　　1 Thes 2:12

Elsewhere in the Pauline corpus we find:

Be sure of this, that no fornicator or impure person, or one who is greedy
. . . has any inheritance in the kingdom of Christ and of God.
　　　　　　　　　　　　　　　　　　　　　　　　　　Eph 5:5

He . . . transferred us to the kingdom of the Son of his love.*
　　　　　　　　　　　　　　　　　　　　　　　　　　Col 1:13

These alone are my fellow workers for the kingdom of God.*
　　　　　　　　　　　　　　　　　　　　　　　　　　Col 4:11

[That you suffer] persecutions and afflictions [is] evidence of the righteous judgment of God and is intended to make you worthy of the
kingdom of God, for which you are also suffering.　　　2 Thes 1:4, 5

In the presence of God and of Christ Jesus, who is to judge the living
and the dead, and in view of his appearing and his kingdom, I solemnly
urge you. . . .　　　　　　　　　　　　　　　　　　　2 Tim 4:1

The Lord will rescue me from every evil and save me for his heavenly
kingdom.*　　　　　　　　　　　　　　　　　　　　　2 Tim 4:18

The Argument for a Connection with Jesus' Teaching

Several things are notable about these texts: First, it is clear that Paul is familiar with "kingdom of God" language: He uses it as a sort of catchall phrase to describe Christian salvation — in a way not dissimilar to that of Jesus.[64] Second, he speaks of the kingdom as something present (e.g., Rom 14:17; 1 Cor 4:20) and as something to be inherited and consummated in the future (e.g., 1 Cor 6:9, 10; 15:24, 50) — again like Jesus.[65]

Third, particular sayings are thematically akin to Jesus' kingdom sayings. Paul's association of the kingdom with power and with the Holy Spirit (1 Cor 4:20; Rom 14:17) and his description of Jesus putting down all God's enemies (1 Cor 15:24) are reminiscent of the synoptic teaching on Jesus' miracles and exorcisms (e.g., Matt 12:28/Luke 11:20). Paul's strong association of the kingdom with righteousness rather than with ritual observances (that is, "food" and "drink," Rom 14:17; 1 Cor 6:9, 10) is reminiscent of a broad band of synoptic teaching (not just verses such as Matt 5:20, but much of the rest of the sermon on the mount and other passages). The summary description in Rom 14:17 of the kingdom as "righteousness and peace and joy in the Holy Spirit" picks up a number of key themes from Jesus: "Peace" is associated with the kingdom in the mission discourse of Matt 10:7, 13; Luke 10:5, 6 (cf. also Mark 9:50); "joy" is a significant theme in the parables (e.g., Matt 13:44; Luke 15:6, 9); the Holy Spirit is seen in the Gospels as the power of Jesus and of the kingdom.[66] The description of the kingdom as that into which people are called and for which disciples suffer and work (1 Thes 2:12; 2 Thes 1:4, 5; Col 4:11) evokes the synoptic portrayal of discipleship (Matt 4:18-22/Mark 1:16-20; Matt 9:13/Mark 2:17/Luke 5:32; Matt 5:10, 11/Luke 6:22, etc.).[67]

---

64. See Fee, *1 Corinthians*, 192, who notes the casual way Paul refers to the kingdom in 1 Cor 4:20 and infers that it was part of Paul's usual way of thinking.

65. Johnston, " 'Kingdom of God' Sayings," explains how, having previously seen all the sayings as futuristic, he came to recognize present and future sayings.

66. E.g., Matt 12:28 and by inference Mark 3:28-30. See Dunn, *Romans 9–16*, 822-23. Dunn finds precisely the same eschatological understanding that "the Spirit is the presence of the kingdom" in Jesus and Paul. See also Johnston, " 'Kingdom of God' Sayings," 153-55. The triad "righteousness, peace, and joy" are rather like "faith, hope, and love," both arguably summary descriptions of key themes from Jesus' ministry. Knowling, *Testimony of Paul*, 316, compares the "righteousness, peace, joy" themes in the beatitudes of Matt 5:3-12; cf. Thompson, *Clothed with Christ*, 206.

67. Walter, "Paul and the Early Christian Jesus-Tradition," claims that Paul shows

Fourth, there are some "tradition indicators" suggesting that Paul is referring to known tradition when he refers to the kingdom: "*Do you not know* that unrighteous people will not inherit God's kingdom?"* (1 Cor 6:9, 10); "I am warning you, *as I warned you before:* those who do such things will not inherit the kingdom of God" (Gal 5:19-21). These phrases do not by themselves prove that the tradition is derived from Jesus, but it is interesting that they are used in connection with two rather similar kingdom sayings. Eph 5:5 is another parallel: "Be sure of this, that no fornicator or impure person, or one who is greedy . . . has any inheritance in the kingdom of Christ and of God." We are right to suspect that Paul is working with a traditional saying about unrighteous/immoral people not entering the kingdom.[68]

On two other occasions Paul says: "the kingdom is not *x,* but *y*" (Rom 14:17; 1 Cor 4:20). There are no tradition indicators here. The formal similarity of the two sayings could suggest a common tradition, but though both statements refer to the present kingdom (contrast the statements just

---

no trace of the influence of the "characteristically 'Jesuanic' interpretation of the kingdom of God." He explains (p. 63):

> For Paul the *basileia tou theou* is a (heavenly) "entity" which exists permanently and which can serve as a norm for a way of life corresponding to the will of God; "kingdom of God" is here an appropriate translation. In the message of Jesus, on the other hand, the "reign of God" is that event whose realization commences with and in his appearance.

This generalization may be challenged with regard to both Jesus and Paul: In a significant number of places Jesus speaks of the kingdom as a state or coming realm that one can enter, and the view that these do not go back to Jesus (Walter cites G. Haufe; see n. 68 below) is unpersuasive. Paul has not only the idea of an eternal kingdom to be inherited but also a dynamic idea of it as an active "power" working through the Holy Spirit and an eschatological idea of the conquest of evil forces by Jesus. It is true that Paul does not use "kingdom" as a central category in explaining his theology, but his usages are not out of keeping with that theology or with Jesus' kingdom teaching.

68. Haufe, "Reich Gottes," recognizes that in 1 Cor 6:9, 10 and Gal 5:21 Paul is drawing on a tradition, and he suggests that the sayings derive from a baptismal context (cf. 1 Cor 6:11). He goes on to infer that Gospel sayings such as John 3:5 and Mark 10:15/Matt 18:3 (and then Matt 5:20; 7:21 by redactional development of the form) derive from a similar baptismal context, not from Jesus himself. There could be something in the suggestion about baptismal use of the "inheriting/entering the kingdom" texts, but, given Haufe's own recognition that Jesus did teach about the kingdom, it is simpler to suppose that authentic sayings of Jesus on how to enter the kingdom came to be used in baptismal contexts (perhaps being adapted for that context) than to suggest that baptismal contexts gave rise to the sayings.

mentioned, which speak of inheriting the future kingdom), their content is quite different, and the "not *x* but *y*" form could simply be a convenient way of making a point of clarification.[69]

More broadly, the way Paul seems in all his statements about the kingdom to take for granted the concept of the kingdom, even if he wishes sometimes to clarify and explain it, may well be significant. The "kingdom" terminology is not his preferred way of speaking, but that he still uses it and assumes that his readers know what he is talking about may confirm that it is traditional language.

Fifth, the previous two points (concerning the affinity of Paul's kingdom teaching to that of Jesus and the evidence that Paul is using traditional language) combine together to make it quite likely that Paul has been influenced directly or indirectly by specific sayings within Jesus' kingdom teaching. But is there any more concrete evidence?

The nearest that Paul comes to echoing the actual words of synoptic sayings of Jesus is when on two occasions he emphasizes "righteousness" in connection with the kingdom (Rom 14:17; 1 Cor 6:9, 10), since the same connection is made in two Matthean sayings of Jesus, Matt 5:20 and 6:33. In Matt 5:20 Jesus makes the striking statement that "unless your righteousness exceeds that of the scribes and Pharisees, you will never enter the kingdom of heaven." Paul could well have this in mind when he warns that "unrighteous people will not inherit God's kingdom"* (1 Cor 6:9, 10; cf. Gal 5:19-21; Eph 5:5) and when he emphasizes that "the kingdom of God is not food and drink but righteousness . . ." (Rom 14:17).[70] On the other hand, Rom 14:17 could also be connected with Matt 6:33, where, after telling his hearers not to worry about what to eat, drink, or wear, Jesus tells them to "strive first for the kingdom of God and his [or "its"] righteousness."

69. See Witherington, *Jesus, Paul and the End*, 57 (and more broadly on the kingdom in Paul, 51-58). The two Pauline statements are seen most simply as Paul's application of Jesus' kingdom teaching, which they strikingly resemble; the "not . . . but" form may be Pauline, though it, too, might possibly be derived from the Jesus-tradition (cf. Luke 17:20, 21).

70. Rom 14:17 could well be seen as an application of Matt 5:20 (with its implied criticism of Pharisaic ritualism) to Jewish Christians in Rome who had scruples about matters of food and drink. Sneed, "Kingdom of God," argues that it alludes to Luke 17:20, 21. We have there a kingdom saying with a "not *x*, but y" form, but Sneed's explanation that *paratērēsis* ("observation") in Luke 17:20 refers to Pharisaic observances seems less likely in Luke's context than that it refers to eschatological signs.

There are, however, problems with suggesting that Paul is echoing these specific sayings of Jesus. In the first place, in 1 Cor 6:9, 10; Gal 5:19-21; and Eph 5:5 Paul speaks of "inheriting the kingdom," whereas Jesus in Matt 5:20 and in several other gospel traditions speaks of "entering the kingdom." This is admittedly not a huge difference: The OT speaks of Israel entering and inheriting the promised land (e.g., Deut 4:1; 6:18; 16:20); the concepts are virtually synonymous and interchangeable when applied to the kingdom, and there is evidence of Jesus and Paul using both.[71]

Secondly and more seriously, the word "righteousness" is only found on the lips of Jesus in Matthew's Gospel, and is widely seen as a Matthean term that does not go back to Jesus.[72] Evidence in favor of this view includes Matt 6:33, since the phrase "and his/its righteousness" is absent from Luke's equivalent verse, where the disciples are simply told to "strive for his kingdom" (Luke 12:31).[73] The whole of Matt 5:20 is also often seen as "redactional," that is, as Matthew's interpretative addition to the traditions of Jesus that he was using.[74] Paul, therefore, could not have known it.

71. Paul implies the idea of entering in 1 Thes 2:12 (so Witherington, *Jesus, Paul and the End,* 52). And Jesus uses the language of inheriting the kingdom in Matt 19:29; 25:34 (cf. 5:3, 5). On the interchangeability of "enter" and "inherit" see Haufe, "Reich Gottes," 471.

72. It is possible to argue that Matthew's and Paul's conceptions of righteousness are quite different. But this would not necessarily undermine the argument for common use of Jesus-tradition: It could well be that Matthew developed the Jesus "righteousness" traditions in the light of his particular ethical concerns and that Paul developed it to address in particular the Jew and Gentile issue that he faced. It is in any case interesting to find that the most Jewish of the Gospels and the apostle to the Gentiles agree in attaching importance to "righteousness." Furthermore, it is not as obvious as it may seem that Paul and Matthew disagree radically in their use of the term, especially if Pauline "righteousness" is understood in the broad eschatological sense that we have suggested: Jesus' words to John the Baptist in Matt 3:15 about "fulfill[ing] all righteousness" and perhaps also his instruction to "strive first for the kingdom of God and his righteousness" in 6:33 may well have something like the broad Pauline sense. "Righteousness" does have strongly ethical connotations for Matthew, but then it also does in Pauline statements where a link with Jesus' teaching is most likely, e.g., 1 Cor 6:9, 10. Matthew may not include the Pauline idea of "righteousness" as "justification" given to the believer, but he does have an almost forensic view of "the righteous" being children of the kingdom of the Son of man who will be saved on judgment day (13:43, 49; 25:37, 46).

73. Matt 5:6 is a similar case, since Jesus in Matthew speaks of people hungering and thirsting after righteousness, whereas in Luke 6:21 he speaks simply of those "who are hungry now."

74. Stanton, *Gospel for a New People,* 315, thinks that all seven uses of "righteousness" in Matthew are probably redactional.

But it is by no means certain that this view is correct. Although there is no evidence outside Matthew's Gospel that Jesus used the noun "righteousness," there is some evidence that he used the related adjective and verb (e.g., Mark 2:17; Luke 15:7; 18:14), and it is entirely likely that Jesus used the noun given its importance in Jewish religious thought (including the Dead Sea Scrolls).[75] It is impossible to prove that any of the "righteousness" sayings in Matthew goes back to Jesus. But there is some evidence suggesting that they are not all redactional,[76] and there is nothing intrinsically unlikely in Jesus having said something like what we find in Matt 5:20.[77]

Though we cannot categorically affirm that he spoke those words,

75. See Segal, *Paul the Convert*, 175-77, on the importance of the idea of justification in the scrolls. Stuhlmacher, *Reconciliation*, 30-49, sees Jesus' ministry in terms of a messianic life of righteousness, though he still regards Matt 5:20 and 6:33 as redactional.

76. Luke 7:29, 30, with its slightly mysterious reference to tax collectors and prostitutes "justifying" *(dikaioō)* God ("All the people listening, and the tax collectors, justified God, having been [or being] baptized with John's baptism, but the Pharisees and lawyers rejected God's plan for themselves, not having been [or being] baptized by John"*), may well be an echo of Matt 21:32, where Jesus speaks of tax collectors and prostitutes entering the kingdom of God and explains that John came "in the way of righteousness *(dikaiosynē)* and you did not believe him, but the tax collectors and prostitutes believed him; and even after you saw it, you did not change your minds and believe him." Scholars have been unsure what to make of this Lukan statement, which comes in the middle of a "Q" section but has no parallel in the equivalent Matthean section (Matt 11:7-19/Luke 7:24-35). Perhaps Luke replaced the difficult sayings that came to be in Matt 11:12-14 with his own paraphrase of the parable of the two sons (Matt 21:28-32). See further in the additional note on Luke 7:28-35 at the end of this chapter.

Another small piece of evidence suggesting that "righteousness" in Matthew may not always be redactional comes from Josephus, since Matthew twice uses the word "righteousness" in connection with John the Baptist (3:15; 21:32), and Josephus also associates the word with John (*Ant.* XVIII:116-19). "Righteousness" is such a central and important Jewish concept that it would be hazardous to make too much of such a parallel. Indeed, its centrality as a concept in Judaism and in early Christianity makes it thoroughly likely that it would have been part of Jesus' vocabulary, even if it happens not to be prominent in the Gospels of Mark and Luke.

77. The fact that the saying expresses a thought close to Matthew's heart may explain why Matthew in particular included it in his Gospel, but it does not require the hypothesis that Matthew composed it. If Matthew's only significant sources were Mark and Q, then a verse like 5:20 is likely to be ascribed to Matthean redaction; if Matthew had significant other source material (as is likely), then it could derive from that.

Matthew's evidence may be seen as converging with the evidence that Paul was familiar with a similar tradition. The combination of evidence makes it reasonable at least to suspect that Jesus did associate the kingdom of God and righteousness in something like the way suggested by Matthew, and that Paul was influenced by this bit of Jesus-tradition.[78]

Paul's General Avoidance of Kingdom Language

The evidence for Paul's familiarity with Jesus' kingdom teaching is good, though not conclusive. Given the importance of the kingdom theme in Jesus' teaching, it is likely that Paul would have known of it if he knew anything about Jesus. But the question still to be addressed is why, if Paul was familiar with the kingdom teaching of Jesus, he uses kingdom terminology so much less frequently than Jesus. Various answers to this are possible.

It is possible, first, that the "kingdom of God" language that would have been familiar and intelligible to Jews in Palestine would have been much less intelligible to Paul's Greek-speaking readers. F. W. Beare thus writes that "The kingdom of God, of which Jesus spoke so often, meant nothing to a Greek; and so Paul hardly ever makes use of the phrase when writing to Greeks." He goes on to speak of "the transposing of the gospel into the language and the thought forms of another people, the kind of adjustment that was needed if the gospel of Jesus was to be brought effectually into the Greek world."[79]

It is also possible that "king/kingdom" language, which was sensitive enough in Jesus' rural Jewish context, would have been even more sensitive in Paul's urban Greco-Roman context. His hearers were perhaps more likely to have contacts in high places than Jesus' hearers, and Paul was more exposed

---

78. We could be accused of arguing in a circle, by using Paul's evidence to prove that Matt 5:20 is tradition not redaction, and then Matthew's evidence to prove that Paul is using Jesus-tradition. In fact what we are doing is finding that two uncertain pieces of evidence when put together add up to a significant argument. (In principle it might be possible to argue that, even if the Matthean references to "righteousness" do not go back to Jesus, Paul might still have known the Matthean version of Jesus' teaching. But this would make the so-called Matthean redaction much earlier than most scholars would envisage.)

79. "Jesus and Paul," *CJT* 5 (1959), 79-68, as cited by Johnston, "'Kingdom of God' Sayings," 143. There is a possible parallel in the fourth Gospel, where the Evangelist prefers "eternal life" to "kingdom" terminology, though Mark and Luke in writing their Gospels for Gentiles still keep the traditional wording.

as a visiting foreigner than Jesus working in his home territory. Michael Thompson comments: "We should not expect to find extensive use of kingdom language in the letters of a Roman citizen who was concerned to promote obedience to civil authorities; Paul would want to avoid being misunderstood as a preacher of sedition."[80] For these or other reasons, Paul may have wished to avoid the potential political overtones of "kingdom" language.[81]

And it is possible that Jesus' "kingdom" language had been — in Paul's perception at least — hijacked by some of his opponents and that he was therefore wary of such language. We have observed already that in 1 and 2 Corinthians Paul is responding to the charismatic Christians of Corinth, some of whom were dissatisfied with his teaching and ministry. In 1 Cor 4:8, when discussing his ministry and that of Apollos, he criticizes the boasting and arrogance of the Corinthians and says with strong irony: "Already you have all you want! Already you have become rich! Quite apart from us you have become kings! Indeed, I wish that you had become kings, so that we might be kings with you!" It is not always easy to mirror-read such Pauline texts, but it seems likely that the charismatics in Corinth were boasting of "reigning" with Christ in a way that Paul saw as quite inappropriate.[82] It may well be that Jesus' teaching about "the kingdom" was the basis of their ideas — Paul speaks more of "the kingdom" in 1 Corinthians than in any other letter — and that Paul objects to their theological misuse of Jesus' teaching.[83] Whether, however, Paul would effectively have ceded

---

80. Thompson, *Clothed with Christ*, 205. Acts 17:6, 7 suggests that sedition was a charge that Paul and his companions faced.

81. Compare Wedderburn, *Paul and Jesus*, 112: "Paul may have found it safer politically to avoid references to God's kingdom in his preaching. " It is notable that neither Jesus nor God is referred to as "king" in the Pauline corpus except in 1 Tim 1:17; 6:15.

82. On their over-realized eschatology see Fee, *1 Corinthians*, 171-73.

83. Koester, *Ancient Christian Gospels*, 60, and Patterson, "Paul and the Jesus Tradition," 38, both suggest that *Gospel of Thomas* 2 was influential on the Corinthians: "Let him who seeks continue seeking until he finds. When he finds, he will become astonished, when he becomes astonished, he will be king, and when he has become king, he will find rest" (Koester's translation). But the Corinthians could well have come to their conclusion on the basis of other traditions of Jesus (e.g., Matt 5:3, 6/Luke 6:20, 21; Luke 17:21; Matt 19:28/Luke 22:28-30). Wedderburn, *Paul and Jesus*, 112, comments: "It is likely that the announcement of Christ's present reign, perhaps coupled with heady ecstatic experiences of Spirit-possession, had led to a misplaced confidence which Paul had ironically to rebuke in 1 Cor. 4.8." The Corinthians could have deduced from their charismatic experiences that the future kingdom was already present.

"kingdom" language to his Christian opponents just because they were misusing it may be doubted, but it is possible that a combination of factors has conditioned Paul's choice of language.

Paul's Preference for Other Terms

It is quite likely, not just that Paul negatively had reservations about kingdom language, but also that he saw real merits in using other terminology. Salvation, reconciliation, and peace were attractive concepts for explaining the good news of Jesus. "Righteousness" was an important OT concept that may have been used by Jesus and in any case expressed well Paul's view of the work of Jesus. It was also thoroughly familiar and accessible in the Greco-Roman world.

There may have been other considerations that made "righteousness" a useful term for Paul. We have noted already the suggestion that his opponents may well have accused him of impugning the righteousness of God with his law-free gospel: Not only was Paul, arguably, taking away the basis of morality (moral righteousness) in attacking the law, but he was also denying the faithfulness of God to his covenant and to his covenant people. If this accusation was made, then for Paul to expound his gospel as all to do with the "righteousness of God" was to address the accusation head-on and to contradict it forcefully.[84] It is possible to see a parallel between how the Jewish Christian Matthew and how Paul apostle to the Gentiles respond in their writings to Jewish (and Jewish Christian) anxieties about a "law-free" gospel:[85] Both emphasize "righteousness," albeit in different ways, and draw on relevant Jesus-traditions.[86]

---

84. See Wedderburn, *Paul and Jesus,* 113.

85. Note the interesting contrast in 2 Cor 6:14 between "righteousness" and "lawlessness." See also Wedderburn, *Paul and Jesus,* 100-101.

86. Kim, "Jesus, Sayings of," 480, 484, comments that "kingdom of God" was not a particularly common phrase in Judaism, and that it is significant that Paul uses Jesus' favorite phrase as many as eight times. He suggests that Paul emphasizes justification because of the importance to him of the death of Jesus, understood in the light of Isa 53:10-12, where the servant's sufferings "make many righteous."

1 CORINTHIANS 13:2, 3, 13

There are three possible parallels with synoptic material in 1 Cor 13:2 and 3. The second of the three is the most striking, so we consider it first:

> If I have all faith to move mountains. . . .*   1 Cor 13:2
> If you have faith . . . you will say to this mountain, "Move from here to there," and it will move.   Matt 17:20

> If I . . . know all mysteries and all knowledge*   1 Cor 13:2
> To you it has been given to know the mysteries of the kingdom of heaven/God*   Matt 13:11/Luke 8:10

> If I give away all my possessions. . . .   1 Cor 13:3
> If you want to be perfect, go, sell your possessions, and give to the poor.*
>   Matt 19:21

Faith to Move Mountains

We have already observed how the synoptics emphasize "saving" faith in connection with Jesus' miracles: "Your faith has saved you," whereas for Paul it is the gospel, the word of Jesus, that is "the power of God for salvation to everyone who has faith."[87] The importance of this group of words — power, save, faith — in both the Gospels and in Paul may well be significant. Admittedly there is a difference in the ideas expressed, with Paul applying the terms to the message about Jesus rather than directly to the healing work of Jesus, but we have suggested that this shift is explicable.

1 Cor 13:2 may well be evidence that Paul was familiar with the association of faith with miracles in the Jesus-tradition. The reference to faith moving mountains has an obvious parallel in the synoptic saying of Jesus in Matt 17:20/Luke 17:6 and Matt 21:21/Mark 11:22, 23, which is a typical vivid and pictorial saying of Jesus. Its attestation in both the Markan and "Q" traditions may suggest that it was well known as a saying of Jesus.[88]

---

87. The point should not be exaggerated. We noted that the word "faith/believe" is used more widely than just in relation to healing in the synoptics, as is the word "save" (e.g., Matt 10:22/24:13/Mark 13:13; Matt 16:25/Mark 8:35/Luke 9:24; Matt 19:25/Mark 10:26).

88. Furnish, *Jesus According to Paul*, 61, favors the Lukan version of the saying, which speaks of moving a mulberry tree rather than a mountain, as far as authenticity

In both the Markan and "Q" contexts it is a comment on one of his miracles. The Markan form of the saying is: "Have faith in God. Truly I say to you that whoever says to this mountain, 'Be lifted up and thrown into the sea' and does not doubt in his heart but believes that what he says is happening, it will be done for him."* But it is the "Q" form of the saying that is verbally closest to Paul's wording:

> If I have all faith so as to move mountains. . . .*   1 Cor 13:2

> If you have faith as a mustard seed you will say to this mountain, "Move from here to there," and it will move.*   Matt 17:20[89]

That Paul is echoing the saying of Jesus is suggested by the verbal similarities but also by thematic similarities. In 1 Corinthians 13 Paul is responding to the Corinthians' exaltation of spiritual gifts. In chapter 12 he has affirmed the validity of tongues as a gift and of the even more valuable gift of prophecy, but he now puts the spiritual gifts into the higher perspective of love, asserting that tongues are useless without love (13:1), that prophecy and knowledge are useless without love (v. 2), and then that "faith" is similarly useless without love. In this context, the "faith" referred to is evidently faith to work miracles, which is referred to in 12:9. The mountain-moving faith in the Gospels is similar. Paul's description of faith as able to move mountains could simply have been his own coinage provoked by nothing in particular, but it makes particularly good sense if the Jesus-tradition was familiar to him and the Corinthian church.[90]

It may very well be that the Corinthian charismatics had themselves used this saying of Jesus in relation to their own miracles, which would be the reason that Paul brings it into his discussion. He does not deny the authority of the saying, but he wants it to be seen in perspective. In that case what we have in 1 Cor 13:2 is evidence not just of Paul's familiarity with the Lord's teaching but also of that teaching being more widely used

---

is concerned. But on the history of the tradition and its authenticity, see Telford, *Barren Temple*, 95-119.

89. 1 Cor 13:2: *ean echō pasan tēn pistin hōste orē methistanai.* Matt 17:20: *ean echēte pistin hōs kokkon sinapeōs, ereite tō orei toutō: metaba enthen ekei, kai metabēsetai.* See also Richardson and Gooch, "Logia of Jesus," 46.

90. Paul's failure to pick up "like a mustard seed" does not prove that he was ignorant of the phrase. In the saying Jesus emphasizes that even a little faith is powerful; Paul is emphasizing that even very powerful faith is worth nothing without love.

in the church — and of Paul debating with others about the interpretation of one saying within that tradition of teaching.[91]

The Mysteries of the Kingdom

The synoptic saying about knowledge of the kingdom's "mysteries" has two forms, the Matthew/Luke form as above and the slightly different form in Mark 4:11: "To you has been given the mystery of the kingdom of God. . . ."* Some scholars have doubted that the saying goes back to Jesus, on the grounds that the difficult teaching about parables that the saying goes on to give seems to be at odds with Jesus' own attitude.[92] The reference to "mysteries" has led some to postulate a background for the saying in the Greek mystery religions. But the saying has an excellent Jewish and Palestinian background since the idea of "mysteries" being concealed and revealed is important in Jewish apocalyptic literature, for example, the Book of Daniel, and in the Dead Sea Scrolls.[93] Furthermore, there is reason to believe that Matthew and Luke knew the saying independently of Mark, and indeed that their version may be more original than Mark's.[94]

If Matthew's and Luke's version is independent of Mark's, then the saying was relatively widely known, and as such might well have been

91. See also J. M. Robinson, "Kerygma and History," 128.

92. In my *Parables of Jesus*, 238-45, I discuss the interpretation of Mark 4:10-12, concluding that Mark believed that Jesus' parables were designed to teach and make things clear, but that they only functioned in that way for the disciples who were close to Jesus and to whom he explained parables such as that of the sower (so Mark 4:13-20). To others they remained unexplained and so functioned in judgment, not salvation.

93. E.g., Dan 2:18, 19, 27-30, 47; 1 Enoch 41:1; 52:1-4; 61:5; 63:3; 71:3, 4; 1QpHab 7:4-15.

94. That Matthew and Luke differ from Mark in precisely the same ways, having different word order from Mark, the infinitive "to know," and the plural "mysteries," suggests that they are not dependent solely on Mark in this saying, and indeed there is good reason for thinking that their wording may be more original than Mark's. Matthew and Luke also have an interesting agreement in the echo of Isaiah 6:9 that follows (compare the abbreviated Matt 13:13/Luke 8:10 with the fuller Mark 4:11). On Matthew's and Luke's independence from Mark see Nolland, *Luke 1–9:20*, 377-79; on this and the whole relationship see D. Wenham, "Synoptic Problem Revisited." If the suggestion in the latter about possible Pauline influence on Mark's wording (e.g., singular "mystery" and the expression "those outside") has any truth in it, this adds to the argument for the saying being familiar in Pauline circles.

familiar to Paul and to the Corinthians.[95] The Corinthians might have seen themselves as having the "knowledge of the mysteries" that Jesus had described as the disciples' prerogative. Paul himself claims such knowledge earlier in 1 Corinthians, when he speaks of himself and Apollos as "stewards of God's mysteries" (4:1).[96]

Giving All for the Poor

In the synoptic story of the rich young man, Jesus tells the young man "sell (all) that you have/your possessions and give to the poor"* (Matt 19:21/Mark 10:21/Luke 18:22). The Matthean version of the story (though not Mark's or Luke's[97]) uses the same Greek word for "goods/possessions" *(hyparchonta)* as Paul uses in 1 Cor 13:3 — Paul's only use of the word, though it appears frequently in the Gospels. Luke uses this word in 12:33, where Jesus tells all the disciples "sell your possessions, and give alms." This combined testimony of Matthew and Luke to the clause "sell your possessions" suggests that they were familiar with a non-Markan form of the saying in question, and that it was therefore relatively well known in the church, not simply derived from Mark by the other Evangelists.[98] The starkness and controversial nature of the saying also point to its likely authenticity.[99]

It seems likely that this difficult teaching of Jesus was well known in the church, including Pauline circles.[100] Paul and the Corinthians would thus

95. Matthew and Luke have the Greek verb *ginōskō;* Paul in 1 Cor 13:2 uses the verb *oida,* but then the verbal noun *gnōsis.* There is no word for "know/knowledge" in Mark's version.

96. See chapter 3 for further evidence of Paul's knowledge of similar Jesus-traditions in 1 Corinthians 1–4.

97. In the Markan version the rich young ruler is told to sell "whatever you have" and in Luke "all that you have."

98. Luke 12:33 may have been formulated by Luke on the basis of the invitation to the rich man, Luke betraying his knowledge of the Matthean form of the saying with the use of *hyparchonta.* See Nolland, *Luke 9:21–18:34,* 694.

99. The controversial nature of the saying is suggested by the dialogue that follows it in Matt 19:23-30/Mark 10:23-31/Luke 18:24-30. Gundry, *Mark,* 554-57, speaks of the "explosiveness of the saying," and observes that Jesus' advice to sell one's possessions was in contradiction to normal rabbinic advice; he cites Mishnah *'Arakin* 8:4 and Babylonian Talmud *Ketubot* 50a.

100. Luke's generalizing use of the saying in 12:33 is perhaps suggestive of the importance that he attached to it and may point to its importance in Pauline circles. The

have known it. It might well have been seen as a special act of piety for the rich (like Barnabas in Acts 4–5) to sell and give away their possessions.[101]

In view of (a) this background, (b) Paul's use only in 1 Cor 13:3 of a word that was part of the tradition of this saying of Jesus, and (c) the other possible echoes of Jesus-tradition in 1 Cor 13:2-3, it is very reasonable to see Paul's comment about doling out one's goods as an echo of Jesus' teaching.[102]

Faith, Hope, and Love

If Paul is echoing one or more of the sayings of Jesus in 1 Cor 13:2, 3, he could be thought to be minimizing the importance of Jesus' teaching. But he is in fact doing nothing of the sort: He may be criticizing the Corinthians' use of that teaching;[103] but he is not criticizing the teaching as such so much as contrasting the good with the best. He goes on in 1 Corinthians to refer to that significant triad "faith, hope, and love," affirming the great importance of faith but the even greater importance of love.

This triad occurs in a number of other Pauline passages, including Gal 5:5, 6; 1 Thes 1:3; 5:8; Rom 5:1-5; Eph 4:2-5; and Col 1:3, 4, and also elsewhere in the NT and the Apostolic Fathers (Heb 6:10-12; 10:22-24; 1 Pet 1:3-9, 21, 22; Barnabas 1:4; 11:8; Ignatius to Polycarp 3:2-3.) This widespread attestation suggests that we have here a traditional summary of

---

Acts account of the early church having "everything . . . in common" and of people selling their possessions to finance the support of the poor (Acts 4:32–5:11) may also be associated with this particular tradition.

101. In 1 Cor 13:3 it is associated with spiritual gifts like prophecy and tongues; compare the list of gifts in Rom 12:6-8, which includes sharing and showing mercy. There Paul urges those who share and show mercy to do so generously and cheerfully; so in 1 Corinthians 13 he says that giving without love is useless.

102. Paul goes on in 1 Cor 13:3 to say "if I hand over my body so that I may boast, but do not have love. . . ." If this is the correct reading (rather than "hand over my body to be burned"; see Fee, *1 Corinthians*, 629, 633-35), then there could be a further indirect allusion to Jesus-tradition, since it was Jesus who in Pauline teaching "handed himself over" *(paradidōmi)* to death for us (e.g., Rom 4:25; 8:32; Gal 2:20; Eph 5:2, 25). Paul speaks in 2 Cor 4:10, 11 of himself and others "carrying in the body the death of Jesus," and says: "We are handed over to death, because of Jesus"* (v. 11). This may be in mind in 1 Cor 13:3: Self-sacrifice like that of Jesus is the highest of all spiritual commitments, but is still useless without love.

103. See Tuckett, "1 Corinthians and Q," 609, cited favorably by Neirynck, "Paul and the Sayings of Jesus," 275.

Christian virtues, as does Paul's use of the triad (as persuasively argued by Hunter):[104] "These three," as Paul puts it, appear out of the blue in 1 Corinthians 13 in a context where the focus is on love; Hunter argues that the sense is "the well-known three." In 1 Thes 5:8 Paul echoes the words of Isa 59:17 about "righteousness like a breastplate, and a helmet of salvation," but transforms it by referring now to "the breastplate of faith and love, and for a helmet the hope of salvation." It looks as though he has grafted the traditional triad onto the OT stock.

Hunter proposes that the triad goes back to a saying of Jesus, and he quotes a saying recorded not in the NT but in the fourth-century Homily 37 of Macarius "hearing the Lord saying, 'Take care of faith and hope, through which is begotten the love for God and humankind that gives eternal life.'" To Hunter's question, "Is it rash to find in this uncanonical saying of the Lord the original of the triad?" we may well answer Yes. However, there is evidence (which we will examine later) that suggests that Paul's emphasis on love as well as his eschatological teaching has its basis in the Jesus-tradition. So it seems quite feasible that "faith, hope, and love" represent, if not a particular saying of Jesus, nevertheless an early and widely recognized summary of key ingredients from Jesus' teaching.

THE SAVING WORD: ECHOES OF THE SOWER

We have seen that for Paul "faith" seems to be associated more with the preaching of the gospel than with miracles, but we also observed that the Pauline emphasis on preaching has a precedent in Jesus' teaching. In Col 1:6 Paul speaks of the word of the gospel "bearing fruit and growing . . . from the day you heard it. . . ."[105] The phraseology is reminiscent of Jesus' parable of the sower, especially as the parable is interpreted in the Gospels in terms of "the word" that is "heard" and "bears fruit" (Matt 13:1-23/Mark 4:1-20/Luke 8:4-15).[106] Could Paul be echoing the parable in Colossians (if Colossians is indeed Pauline)?

---

104. Hunter, *Paul and his Predecessors,* 33-35. See also Conzelmann, *1 Corinthians,* 229-31; O'Brien, *Colossians,* 10, 11.

105. "Bear fruit . . . and . . . grow" also appears in 1:10. This combination of clauses has an OT background in the command to Adam and Eve to "be fruitful and multiply" (Gen 1:28), but in Colossians 1 the thought is probably agricultural.

106. Cf. O'Brien, *Colossians,* 13. Mark's version of the parable also includes the verb "grow" (4:8), though this is probably Markan redaction rather than tradition.

Other possible echoes of the parable are in 1 Thes 1:6 and 2:13. Paul speaks in 1:6 of the Thessalonians as "imitators of us and of the Lord, for in spite of persecution you received the word with joy inspired by the Holy Spirit" and in 2:13 of them accepting "the heard word"* (literally "the word of hearing)" as the word of God. The similarity to the parable of the sower, as it is interpreted in the Gospels, is notable: We find in common

- the theme of "the word," that is, the word of God at work in people,
- an emphasis on "hearing" (cf. Rom 10:14-17),
- the idea of "receiving" the word,[107] and
- an association of hearing with both "joy" and "tribulation," the same Greek words being used in 1 Thessalonians and the synoptics.[108]

The parallels are such as to make it possible, at least, that Paul is echoing the parable of the sower in Colossians and 1 Thessalonians, and it could be that Paul's general emphasis on the saving word of the gospel is associated with the parable.

Scholars have suspected that Paul's other "sowing"/"growing"/ "harvesting" language may reflect the influence of Jesus' parables and especially that of the sower. For example, Paul speaks of the "fruit" of the Spirit in Galatians 5. Then in 6:7, 8 he warns that "whatever a person sows, that he will also reap. For he who sows to his own flesh will from the flesh reap corruption, but he who sows to the Spirit will from the Spirit reap eternal life. So let us not grow weary in doing good, for in its own time we will reap if we do not give up. . . ." Paul's language here is evocative of the parable of the sower with the seed falling into good and bad soil[109] and also perhaps of other parables like that of the seed growing secretly while the farmer waits patiently for the harvest (Mark 4:26-29). It even recalls the parable of the wheat and the tares with one man sowing good seed and another sowing weeds (Matt 13:24-30).[110] The problem, however, with making much of such parallels is that agricultural imagery was common-

107. Two Greek verbs, *lambanō* and *dechomai*, are used in both 1 Thessalonians and the synoptics.

108. See J. P. Brown, "Synoptic Parallels," 30.

109. But see Fung, *Galatians*, 295.

110. Other Pauline verses using agricultural imagery that have been linked to Jesus' parables include 1 Cor 3:6, 9; 9:7, 11; and 2 Cor 9:10. See, e.g., Feine, *Jesus Christus und Paulus,* 172; more recently Fraser, *Jesus and Paul,* 94, who also suggests 2 Cor 4:4 as a counterpart to Mark 4:15, and Richardson and Gooch, "Logia of Jesus," 48.

place in the ancient world, not suprisingly,[111] and the similarity needs to be rather specific and distinctive if anything is to be made of it with any confidence.[112]

Despite this caution, the possibility that, especially in Col 1:6 and 1 Thes 1:6; 2:13, we may have echoes of the parable of the sower remains real. Three things tell in favor of this view: First, the prominence and space given to the parable of the sower in all three synoptic Gospels may be a measure of its perceived importance for the Evangelists and so perhaps for the church at large. It is the first parable and is carefully explained to the disciples — in terms of hearing the word.

Second, even if Matthew and Luke used Mark as a source, there is evidence to show that they knew a non-Markan form of the parable and of the interpretation and that both parable and interpretation antedate our Gospels.[113] Therefore it was probably a well-known tradition in the Pauline period.

Third, Luke in his version of the interpretation speaks of the devil snatching the word from the hearts of people "so that they may not believe

---

111. E.g., Isa 55:10, 11 uses agricultural imagery in speaking of the word of God; 4 Ezra 9:31 compares the "law" to seed that is sown. See further Gundry, *Mark,* 208.

112. Stanley, "Pauline Allusions," 34, finds the quantity of rural images striking in the writings of the urban Paul. But the divide between urban and rural was not nearly as great as it generally is today.

113. There is a strong case for seeing Mk 4:11, 12 as inserted by Mark between the parable and its interpretation. A study of Markan style elsewhere suggests that originally a question from the disciples about the meaning of the parable of the sower ("they asked him about the parable"; cf. 4:10) was followed by Jesus' words "Do you not understand this parable? Then how will you understand all the parables?" (4:13). Mark inserted the material in 4:11, 12 between the question (slightly modified to fit) and the answer, using it as a comment on the fact that the parable is given to the crowd, but the interpretation to the disciples only. (Compare the Markan question and answer in 7:14-18 and see my "Synoptic Problem Revisited," 17-20.) If Mark made this insertion, he evidently knew a tradition in which the interpretation followed immediately after the parable.

Furthermore, there are a number of minor agreements of Matthew and Luke against Mark that suggest Matthew's and Luke's familiarity with a non-Markan version, e.g. their simpler description of the seed in good soil (Matt 13:8/Mark 4:8/Luke 8:8), the reference to "the heart" and the use of the participle "hearing" at the start of the interpretation (Matt 13:19/Mark 4:13/Luke 8:11). There is an interesting divergence of wording at the beginning of the interpretation, which is much better explained in terms of a pre-synoptic form of wording known to all three Evangelists ("That which is sown by the path, this is the one who hears . . .") than in terms of Markan priority. (See my "Interpretation of the Parable of the Sower.")

and be saved" (8:12). This very Pauline-sounding clause is not paralleled in Matthew and Mark and may reasonably be seen as a Lukan clarification of the parable's meaning. Whether or not it is, it shows that in the Pauline/Lukan circle the parable of the sower was being used when Luke was written in the context of thinking about the "word" bringing "salvation" to the person with "faith." This is no proof that it was being used in this way at an earlier time, but it lends some weight to the hypothesis.[114]

Against this suggestion that Paul was influenced by the parable of the sower is the widely held scholarly opinion that the Gospel's interpretation of the parable, with its seed = word identification, is inauthentic and derives from the church rather than from Jesus. Scholars taking this view were for many years influenced by the now declining dogma that Jesus' parables were all simple, one-point parables. That was always a most improbable view, given Jesus' social context and the form of some of the parables.[115] However, the case is built not just on that consideration, as is clear from J. Jeremias's very influential discussion of the issue in his *The Parables of Jesus*.[116]

Jeremias offers a plausible array of arguments against the authenticity of the interpretation, but on examination they turn out to be seriously flawed: There is nothing about the form, content, or wording of the interpretation that justifies the conclusion that it does not go back to Jesus. On the contrary the four-section interpretation fits the parable and makes good sense in the context of Jesus' ministry and kingdom preaching (e.g., the importance elsewhere in Jesus' teaching of the themes of persecution and riches).[117] Also, as has already been mentioned, a comparison of the Gospel texts points to the conclusion that the interpretation antedates our Gospels and so goes back very early.

However, so far as the question of Paul is concerned, it does not matter absolutely if the interpretation as we have it goes back to Jesus. Even if it does not, Paul could be reflecting the tradition of interpretation of the

114. Mark's use of the expression "the word" is identified by Jeremias in his *Parables* as a reflection of church usage rather than as going back to Jesus. The argument is quite uncertain. But it is possible that Jesus spoke of "the word of the kingdom" (as in Matt 13:19) and that "the word" does represent the church's shorthand.

115. Recent scholars questioning the older non-allegorical view of Jesus' parables include Boucher, *Parables;* Drury, *Parables;* and most usefully Blomberg, *Interpreting the Parables.*

116. 77-79.

117. For a thorough discussion see Payne, "Authenticity." See also Gundry, *Mark,* 207-11.

sower that was in due course to be enshrined in the Gospels, and he could in that respect at least be drawing on Jesus-tradition.[118]

The case for Paul being influenced by the parable is thus possible, though not proved.

HUMAN TRADITIONS AND CLEANNESS OF HEART

We have noted that Paul and Jesus agree on the importance of the human heart — in the sight of God. Outward religious observance is no substitute. The theme is, of course, not unique to Jesus and Paul; it has a strong OT foundation. But a number of passages suggest that Paul may have been influenced by Jesus-tradition in his teaching at this point.

Things Secret and Public

Secrets made public

In Romans 2, as we have seen, Paul attacks the self-confidence of Jews who believe that their privileged position will protect them from God's impartial judgment:

> God judges the *secrets* of people, according to my gospel through Jesus Christ.*[119]
>
> Rom 2:16

Paul expresses the same thought in 1 Corinthians, speaking of the Lord's coming,

> who will bring to light the *secrets* of darkness and will *make public* the purposes of the heart.*
>
> 1 Cor 4:5

118. This I take to be Brown's view in "Synoptic Parallels," 31. In principle it could be that the interpretation of the parable was formulated on the basis of Jesus' parable and church teaching about the "word" such as we find in 1 Thessalonians 1 and 2, which originally had nothing to do with the parable. On the other hand, if the parable goes back to Jesus and was interpreted in terms of the preached word from an early date, then it is entirely possible that Paul's understanding of "the word" and his use of agricultural language in connection with it reflect that early interpretation.

119. The Greek for "secret" is *krypton;* the verb for "make public" is *phaneroō.*

He uses much the same language later in the letter, but this time of what happens when the unbeliever hears God's word in the church:

> The *secrets* of his heart are *made public.**   1 Cor 14:25

This language and the sort of thoughts that Paul expresses with it have a parallel in the synoptics. In a rather enigmatic saying within the broad context of a chapter about hearing the word of God, Jesus says:

> There is nothing *secret,* except to be *made public,* nor hidden except to be brought into the public arena.   Mark 4:22/Luke 8:17

This saying is found not only in the Markan tradition but also in a slightly different "Q" form in Matt 10:26/Luke 12:2, where the reference is to coming judgment. This double attestation of the saying in the synoptic tradition and the verbal and thematic similarities between Paul's words and the Jesus-tradition make a link possible, though the general and proverbial nature of the saying makes it hard to be certain.

One further point is worth adding: In the first of the Pauline texts just quoted, Rom 2:16, there is a possible "tradition indicator" of sorts in the phrase "according to my gospel through Jesus Christ."[120] Paul could be describing in this phrase the criterion according to which divine judgment takes place, but he is quite likely referring to the simple fact that such divine judgment is part of his gospel message (cf. 16:25).[121] If so, this is not an acknowledgement by Paul of dependence on Jesus-tradition as such. However, it is an assertion that the idea of coming judgment of human secrets is part of what Paul passes on as part of the gospel of Christ — in that sense at least, a tradition.

Public and private piety

Paul explains further in Romans 2 that:

> It is not the Jew *in public* [who is a true Jew], nor is the circumcision *in public* in the flesh [the true circumcision], but the Jew *in secret,* and circumcision of heart in spirit, not letter. . . .*   Rom 2:28, 29

120. Dunn, *Romans 1-8,* 102-3, and others prefer to take "through Christ Jesus" with the verb "judge" rather than as qualifying the word "gospel," though he refers to Schlier as taking the other view.

121. Dunn, *Romans 1-8,* 103, regards the effective difference between the two possible senses as "not substantial"; but on one view the phrase may be a "tradition indicator," while on the other it is not.

We have here the very typical Pauline contrasts between flesh, spirit, and letter along with the contrast of secret and public. In this case the synoptic passage that is thematically most similar is Matt 6:1-19, where the theme is Jewish piety and religious observance and where the contrast is between those who do their piety in order to be *seen publicly* by people and those who pray, fast, and give alms privately before "your father who is *in secret*" (6:5, 6; 6:18). The language and the ideas expressed are similar, though perhaps not distinctively enough to prove anything.[122]

Clean and Unclean Food

The question of Rom 14:14

A much more interesting possible point of contact between Paul and Jesus is in Paul's discussion of questions of food and drink in Romans 14, and in particular in v. 14, where Paul says, "I know and am persuaded in the Lord Jesus that nothing is unclean in itself." Two related questions are raised by this text: Is "in the Lord Jesus" a tradition indicator? And does Paul have in mind the teaching recorded in Matthew 15/Mark 7, in which Jesus discusses the questions of ritual handwashing and more generally of what is clean and unclean, declaring that it is not what goes into a person but what comes out that defiles?

A tradition indicator?

The answer given by many to both questions is No. "I know and am persuaded in the Lord Jesus" is, it is argued, not a quotation formula; it is an appeal to the Lord's authority that Paul claims, but not necessarily an appeal back to something said by the historical Jesus. Paul refers frequently enough in his letters to "the Lord Jesus" without any reference specifically to the historical Jesus, and "I am persuaded" sounds more like an opinion firmly held than a command of the Lord like those referred to in 1 Cor 7:10; 9:14 with a "commanding" verb.[123]

However, although Paul does not necessarily appeal to the teaching of Jesus with this formula, it could well be so that he does. In 1 Cor 7:10,

---

122. Goulder, *Midrash*, 164-65, notes these links and argues for the influence of Romans on Matthew 6 and 23.

123. So among others Räisänen, *Paul and the Law*, 246-48; also Neirynck, "Paul and the Sayings of Jesus," 306-8, noting Phil 2:19; 1 Thes 4:1.

12 Paul speaks of "the Lord" to introduce a teaching of Jesus, and in 1 Cor 11:23 he speaks of "the Lord Jesus" in connection with the last supper. In Rom 14:14 Paul's "I know and am persuaded" is stronger than just "I am persuaded" and could reflect his particular confidence about this controversial matter because of its basis in the Jesus-tradition.[124]

The question then is whether there is evidence of Jesus-tradition here.

The gospel traditions

The closest verbal link between Romans 14 and Mark 7 is between Rom 14:20, where Paul says "all things are clean,"* and Mark 7:19, "cleansing all foods."* At first glance this may look like a highly probable point of connection between Paul and the Jesus-tradition. But the matter is not as simple as it may appear.

In the first place, the Markan phrase here is generally agreed to be Mark's own comment, not part of the original Jesus-tradition. It is absent from Matthew's version of the story. The Gospel narrative is in the first instance about washing of hands, thanks to the disciples' failure to wash theirs, not about food at all, and it has no immediate relevance to the issues of food and drink that Paul is addressing. It is Mark who, through the clause in question, applies it directly to the question of clean and unclean food. Furthermore, it is argued that if the teaching of Jesus had been clearly understood as Mark understands it, then there would have been no problem over the issue in the early church and Paul would have referred more often and more directly to it.[125]

There is some weight to these arguments. However, the observation that it is Mark who explicitly applies the saying of Jesus to clean and unclean food does not rule out the idea that Paul in Romans 14 may be using that same Jesus-tradition to justify his position. Four observations are relevant:

First, although scholars have often assumed that Matthew is dependent on Mark for his version of this story and that he has taken the radical pro-Gentile edge off it, there is good cause for thinking that Matthew here has

---

124. Thompson, *Clothed with Christ*, 196-98, argues plausibly that Paul could hardly have pronounced so confidently on this highly contentious matter to a church that included Jewish Christians and that did not know him personally, if it was simply a matter of his own Christian opinion rather than something with a basis in known tradition.

125. So Räisänen, *Paul and the Law*, 248; *idem, Jesus, Paul and Torah*, 142-43; Neirynck, "Paul and the Sayings of Jesus," 306; Sanders, *Jesus and Judaism*, 266. Responding to Räisänen and Sanders on the authenticity of the Matthew 15/Mark 7 material see, e.g., Gundry, *Mark*, 370-71.

a non-Markan and in some ways more original form of the story than Mark (with some of Mark's interpretative additions, including 7:19b, missing).[126]

Second, the story in Matthew as well as in Mark is definitely and centrally about what is clean and defiling: The word "common/unclean/defiling" is what the discussion is all about, and it is this word that Paul picks up in Rom 14:14.[127]

Third, the story in the Gospels begins with the question of handwashing, but moves on to consider inner and outer purity, the point then being illustrated by the example of food. The question of food is not the focus, but it does come into the discussion in key statements (Mark 7:18, 19).

Fourth, Mark's application of the story to the question of clean and unclean foods shows that this was an interpretation of the story that came to have currency in the early church. This lends plausibility to the suggestion that Paul is interpreting the tradition in this way in Rom 14:14.[128]

Finally, if Paul and Mark are both interpreting the tradition, then the failure of the whole church to recognize the Pauline/Markan logic and even Paul's own failure to use the tradition in some other contexts are both straightforwardly explained: The tradition in itself was not unambiguous,[129] and people could and did take it in different ways.

---

126. See Dunn, *Jesus, Paul and the Law,* 40-44. Although Dunn recognizes the saying behind Mark 7:16 as a primitive saying of Jesus much discussed in the early church (that discussion reflected in Mark 7), he rather curiously fails (in this discussion) to consider seriously that Rom 14:14 may be an allusion by Paul to this saying of Jesus, seeing it simply as a reflection of the discussion arising out of Jesus' saying.

127. The Greek word is *koinos.*

128. Paul could possibly have been responsible, himself or with others, for the interpretation. "I know and am persuaded" — a form of words found only here in his letters — might possibly reflect the existence of a Jesus-tradition of which Paul can say "I know" along with an interpretation of that tradition endorsed by Paul, hence "and am persuaded." But whether the Markan interpretation owes anything to Paul or not, Mark attests what we suspect to be going on in Rom 14:14.

On Rom 14:14 see further Thompson, *Clothed with Christ,* 185-99, who suggests that the Markan interpretation was known in Rome, the traditional location of the writing of Mark, and that Paul accepted the interpretation but immediately went on to to make his apparently rather different point about "walking in love." Dunn, *Romans 9-16,* 818-19, agrees with Neirynck ("Paul and the Sayings of Jesus," 308) that "in the Lord Jesus" is not a citation formula, noting 1 Thes 4:1 as a parallel, and yet he thinks that there is a connection with the tradition of Mark 7, with Mark and Paul representing the same emerging interpretation.

129. It is notable that Matthew and Mark speak of the tradition in question as a "parable" requiring interpretation (Matt 15:15/Mark 7:17).

Other echoes of Jesus in Romans 14

The case for interpreting Rom 14:14 as referring to the Matthew 15/Mark 7 tradition turns out to be quite strong after all, but will be further strengthened if there are other echoes of Jesus traditions in that part of Romans, as is argued strongly by Michael Thompson. Rom 14:17 is one such echo: It is, as has been seen, one of Paul's rather infrequent "kingdom" sayings, which — strikingly — begins, "the kingdom of God is not food and drink. . . ." Paul's use of traditional kingdom language in this very context and his application of it to the question of food and drink strengthen the case for taking 14:14 as a reference to Jesus' teaching.

Additional evidence: 1 Cor 6:12, 13

The case is also strengthened if there is other evidence of Paul's knowledge of the Matthew 15/Mark 7 traditions. One place where such knowledge may well be reflected is in 1 Cor 6:12, 13, where Paul is probably responding to the Corinthians' justification of going to prostitutes on the grounds that "all things are lawful" and that "foods are for the stomach and the stomach for foods."* It seems likely that the Corinthians were appealing to known principles, which Paul accepted and indeed had probably taught to them, namely, that the Christian is free from the law and not bound by the Jewish laws about clean and unclean food. But they were, it appears, drawing a conclusion — that satisfying their sexual appetites with prostitutes was harmless — which Paul found quite unacceptable.

If this is correct, then the first thing to say is that their use of the saying about foods is rather remarkable and suggests that the teaching concerned had special status, even if the way they used it was quite contrary to its original intention. But the second point to be made concerns the actual wording used, that is, *"foods for the stomach."*[130] Jesus in Matt 15:17/Mark 7:19 specifically justifies his statement that nothing going into a person defiles the person on the grounds that "it enters . . . the *stomach*, and goes out into the sewer." It is immediately after this saying that Mark comments on Jesus cleansing "all *foods*." It seems likely that Paul and the Corinthians knew and recognized the authority of these sayings of Jesus — and the sort of interpretation offered by Mark — but that the Corinthians were extending Jesus' logic

130. The respective Greek terms are *brōma* and *koilia*. Barrett, *1 Corinthians*, 146, sees "foods for the stomach" as a quotation from the Corinthians that Paul appears to accept.

about nothing from outside defiling a person, in order to justify their immorality.[131] The evidence fits well with that of Rom 14:14.

Col 2:21, 22

Other evidence includes Col 2:21, 22, where Paul speaks of those who say "Do not handle, Do not taste, Do not touch," and comments that "All these regulations refer to things that perish with use; they are simply human commands and teachings." Three things are notable about this:[132]

- The topic is the question of what may be appropriately touched or tasted and so has some affinities to Matthew 15/Mark 7.[133]
- The reference to "all these things" (NRSV supplies "regulations") as heading for destruction "with use" has some resemblance to Jesus' comment that "whatever goes into a person . . . enters . . . the stomach, and goes out into the sewer."[134]
- The phrase "according to the commands and teachings of human beings"* is taken from Isa 29:13, which is also used in Matt 15:9/Mark 7:13.[135]

131. "Foods" is in the Markan comment on the Jesus tradition; Mark in this case may be influenced by the Pauline/Corinthian interpretation. Resch, *Paulinismus*, 48, makes the connection between the Matthew 15/Mark 7 tradition and 1 Corinthians 6. He less convincingly connects Paul's words in 1 Thes 4:4-7 about each man keeping his own "vessel" in holiness and honor with Jesus' teaching about inward purity (e.g., Luke 11:40, 41). But it is just conceivable that we might here have another case of Jesus' teaching about ritual purity and washings being transferred to the sexual sphere.

132. Note that "as you received Christ Jesus the Lord" in 2:6 could be some sort of "tradition indicator"; see further in chapter 9.

133. It may be that "Do not touch" here can be related to "It is well for a man not to touch a woman" in 1 Cor 7:1, with a similar ascetism being addressed in both contexts. See the discussion above of 1 Cor 6:12, 13 for the linking of food and sex. But see O'Brien, *Colossians*, 150.

134. Note the use of the preposition *eis* in Col 2:22 (literally "all things *into* destruction") and in Matt 15:16, 17/Mark 7:18, 19 ("everything . . . *into* the stomach . . . *into* the sewer").

135. Note also "human tradition" in Col 2:8/Mark 7:8; so O'Brien, *Colossians*, 151.

The common OT background may make postulating any link between Paul and the Jesus-tradition superfluous here, and yet in both cases the Isaiah text is applied to the same sort of issue in a way that may be significant.

The overall similarity is striking, and it looks as though we have in Colossians a parallel use of the Jesus-tradition to that in Rom 14:14, with Paul using the tradition in both cases to respond to those with "weak" scruples over foods and other matters.[136]

CONCLUSION

Only a very brief summary of conclusions reached in the second part of this chapter need be given at this stage. There is significant evidence that Paul was influenced by the Jesus-tradition, some of that evidence being relatively strong, some much weaker.

The case for believing that Paul and members of his churches were familiar with Jesus' teaching about cleanness and uncleanness is particularly strong: That teaching was probably well known, debated, used, and misused (to judge from 1 Corinthians 6). Similarly, they were familiar with Jesus' saying about the mountain-moving power of faith. Again the evidence is strong.

It is probable, though less certain, that they were familiar with Jesus' sayings about the disciples being given knowledge of the mysteries of the kingdom and being called to give up their possessions. It is also probable that Paul was influenced directly or indirectly by Jesus' kingdom teaching, though it is not possible to prove that he knew any particular kingdom sayings. It is likely that Paul's relatively infrequent use of the "kingdom" teaching of Jesus has to do with his particular context, in which he preferred other ways of conveying the Christian good news.

It is quite possible that Paul knew the parable of the sower and other agricultural parables of Jesus and Jesus' sayings about "secret" and "public" things. He may well also have derived the "faith, hope, and love" triad directly or indirectly from the Jesus-tradition. A firmer evaluation of such less certain evidence will be possible only in the light of the chapters that are to follow.

---

136. Less strong evidence of Pauline familiarity with the traditions of Matthew 15/Mark 7 includes Rom 1:29-31, where Paul's list of Gentile vices has been compared with the list of the evils that come from the human heart in Mark 7:21, 22. The problem with this argument is that such vice lists were common in Judaism (see Dunn, *Romans 1-8*, 67), and, although the lists in Mark and Paul have much in common, this does not, certainly by itself, prove much.

ADDITIONAL NOTES

RECENT INTERPRETATIONS
OF JESUS' KINGDOM TEACHING

There have been a number of non-eschatological interpretations of Jesus in recent years, including several by scholars who have associated Jesus with the Cynics, who were a reasonably influential group in the first-century Greco-Roman world. The Cynics had an egalitarian vision of society and expressed that vision by renouncing worldly power and identifying with the poor. The most brilliant exposition of this view of Jesus is probably that of J. Dominic Crossan, who in *The Historical Jesus* portrays Jesus as a Jewish peasant Cynic. Others offering a Cynic interpretation of Jesus include B. L. Mack and Gerald Downing.[137]

The Cynic interpretation of Jesus has some plausibility. However, it is not clear that Cynicism was a significant force in Jewish peasant society,[138] and, although certain features of Jesus' ministry can be explained in Cynic terms, those same features can also be explained in other ways. More significantly, Crossan's Cynic interpretation of Jesus flies in the face of the massive amount of evidence suggesting that Jesus saw something new and dramatic happening in his ministry and that he worked within a thoroughly Jewish, Scripture-based way of thinking. Crossan's Jesus appears rather uninterested in Scripture, and in his non-eschatological Cynicism he differs radically from John the Baptist (though, according to Crossan, he followed John at first) and from the church and the writers of the NT, who have thoroughly misrepresented Jesus. Crossan's evidence for this noneschatological Jesus comes mainly from noncanonical Gospels, such as the Gospel of Thomas. But the value of those Gospels is very much in doubt, and it seems much simpler to see Jesus within the strong Scripture-based tradition represented by the Qumran community, by the Baptist, and by the early church and to see the Gospel of Thomas and the other apocryphal Gospels as representing a Hellenized development and deviation from that tradition.

A quite different interpretation of Jesus' kingdom teaching has been

---

137. Mack, *A Myth of Innocence,* 70-74; Downing, *Christ and the Cynics.* Cf. Theissen, e.g., *Social Reality,* 33-59. For criticism of the Cynic thesis see Witherington, *Jesus the Sage,* 123-43.

138. See Horsley, *Jesus and the Spiral,* 230.

offered recently by G. Vermes,[139] who introduces his discussion with a helpful explanation of OT and intertestamental ideas of the eschatological kingdom (including ideas of the deliverance of Israel and of cosmic renewal). But Vermes discounts various prominent features of Jesus' kingdom teaching (as it is found in the Gospels) that would fit well in this Jewish context, for example, the emphasis on fulfillment, and various sayings about the future kingdom and the coming of the Son of man, which Vermes regards as coming from the church's reflection on Jesus after the crucifixion. Jesus himself appears to have a rather vague idea of a present, though eschatological, kingdom to be received by repentance. This Jesus thus — rather implausibly — has something like a (relatively late) rabbinic view of the kingdom combined with an eschatological urgency typical of Second Temple Judaism and comparable to that found at Qumran.

JESUS, JOHN THE BAPTIST, AND QUMRAN

There is a real possibility that Jesus and his followers had direct or indirect links with the Qumran community, though there has unfortunately been much wild and unhelpful speculation by some scholars proposing such links, which has perhaps made other scholars excessively cautious in the matter. The case for proposing a link can only be summarized here.

The starting point is John the Baptist.[140] The NT is quite open about Jesus' association with his predecessor John the Baptist, though the impression we may get from a rather superficial reading is that John was a relatively minor figure on the stage of first-century Palestine, one who called people to repent but then referred them on to Jesus, allowing himself to fade out. A more careful reading of the NT, as well as of the Jewish historian Josephus, makes it clear that John was a very influential leader in his own right, whose popularity was seen by Herod Antipas as a threat to his position and who had his own disciples, even after Jesus' ministry was well established (see Mark 2:18; 6:29; Josephus, *Ant.* XVIII.116-19).

Jesus' ministry seems in a real sense to have grown out of John's. The synoptic Gospels all begin their account of Jesus' public ministry with his baptism by John, and in different ways they suggest that John and Jesus were closely associated: Matthew suggests that they preached the same

139. *Religion of Jesus the Jew*, 120-51.

140. For discussion of John and for bibliography see Webb, *John the Baptizer*, as well as his "John the Baptist."

message of the kingdom ("The kingdom of heaven has come near") and that their styles of ministry to the marginalized in society were similar (Matt 3:2; 21:32); Luke tells us that their families were connected (Luke 1–2); all three synoptists describe how Herod Antipas identified John and Jesus (Matt 14:2/Mark 6:16/Luke 9:8) and how Jesus himself, when asked about his authority, replied by asking about John's authority (Matt 21:25/Mark 11:30/Luke 20:4); and Matthew and Mark suggest that Jesus connected his own anticipated sufferings with those of John the Baptist (Matt 17:12, 13/Mark 9:12, 13). There is not much evidence in the synoptic Gospels of Jesus and John having contact after Jesus' baptism, except at the time of John's imprisonment, when Matthew and Luke refer to John's disciples being sent by John to Jesus (Matt 11:2/Luke 7:18; in Matt 14:12 John's disciples report John's death to Jesus). The fourth Gospel, however, suggests that John did send disciples of his on to Jesus, and has a particularly interesting description of Jesus having a parallel ministry alongside John in Judea (3:22–4:3); this is the only place in the Gospels where Jesus or his followers are described as engaged in a baptizing ministry, though of course Jesus' followers baptized after the ministry of Jesus.[141]

There is no need to evaluate each of the traditions. But it is worth commenting that the NT has often been seen as betraying some embarrassment about Jesus' close relationship with John, and that there may be more than a grain of truth in this. It is quite possible that there were continuing followers of John the Baptist in the time of the church who claimed John as the Messiah rather than Jesus, and who argued that Jesus was a disciple and follower of John: John the baptizer was greater than Jesus the baptized.[142]

It may be that the Evangelists were directly or indirectly responding to this sort of argument by making it clear that Jesus was the greater one to whom John pointed: This is an especially attractive explanation in the context of the fourth Gospel, where John the Baptist goes out of his way to affirm the superiority of Jesus. For example, in John 1:20 we have a highly emphatic denial: "He confessed and did not deny it, but confessed, 'I am not the Messiah.'"[143] But it may also lie behind the dialogue in Matthew's

141. This Johannine tradition has a particularly strong claim to have a historical basis. See J. A. T. Robinson, *Priority,* 158-89 for discussion. Our argument, however, does not hang on that conclusion.

142. Evidence of a continuing baptist sect is to be found in the second-century pseudo-Clementine writings; evidence of people very much influenced by John's ministry is to be found in Acts 18:24–19:7.

143. The traditional view is that the fourth Gospel was written in Ephesus, and

account of Jesus' baptism where John tries to stop Jesus from being baptized by saying, "I need to be baptized by you, and do you come to me?" (Matt 3:14). It may conceivably also be part of the reason that Matthew, Mark, and Luke fail to mention the baptizing ministry of Jesus in Judea described by the fourth Gospel (if this tradition has a historical basis), since Jesus' ministry here does seem so much like John's.

If there was such embarrassment, this only confirms what the Gospels do not conceal, namely, that there were close links between John and Jesus. E. P. Sanders argues on this basis that Jesus' baptism by John is one of the unquestionable facts of Jesus' ministry.[144]

The relevance of all this to the question of Jesus and Qumran is that there is a reasonable case for associating John with Qumran. Since the discovery of the Dead Sea Scrolls in 1947 it has been tempting to explain Luke's observation that the Baptist "was in the wilderness until the day he appeared publicly to Israel" (1:80) by reference to Qumran. It would be very hazardous to build much on that single reference, intriguing though it is. But there are other considerations: Qumran is quite near the Jordan River, where John baptized; the community made considerable use of ritual washings; it explained its raison d'être in terms of Isa 40:3 — preparing the way of the Lord in the wilderness — precisely the text that is used in all four Gospels to describe John (1QS 8:14; Matt 3:3; Mark 1:3; Luke 3:4; John 1:23); the community was a predominantly priestly community, and John, at least according to Luke, came from a priestly family; and then, last but not least, the Qumran community and John seem to have shared the same sort of eschatological perspective: They were conscious of living in the last days and in the time of fulfillment.

There are, of course, important differences between John and the Qumran community: John's public and inclusive ministry was quite different from Qumran's exclusive ministry. But to say that John left the community and developed his own distinctive emphases is entirely compatible with the view that he was at one time part of the community and that he shared many of their emphases.

If John was connected in this way with Qumran, then Jesus at least indirectly had links with Qumran. But it is possible that he also had more direct links. Various scholars, notably the archaeologist Bargil Pixner, have argued that Jesus and his community had links, not necessarily with Qum-

---

it is interesting that Acts 18–19 attests the presence of followers of John the Baptist in Ephesus. There may be a connection.

144. *Jesus and Judaism*, 91-93.

ran itself, but with the Essene movement. It has been argued that the church lived in the same quarter of Jerusalem as the Essenes and that, for example, their communal style of living, described in Acts, reflects that context.[145]

There are a great many uncertainties about the proposed connections between Jesus, John, and Qumran (including uncertainties about the precise identification of the Qumran community), and nothing hangs on demonstrating any connection, so far as the argument of this book is concerned. The Qumran scrolls in any case show that the sort of eschatological outlook that is ascribed to Jesus in the Gospels was very much part of the first-century Jewish scene.

A POSSIBLE EXPLANATION OF LUKE 7:28-35

We have suggested that Luke 7:29, 30 may be a Lukan equivalent of Matt 21:31, 32.[146] More specifically, we suggest the following about Luke's redaction in Luke 7:

First, Luke in 7:18-35 was following the "Q" tradition much as we find it in Matt 11:2-19, but he departed from that tradition when he came to the difficult saying about the kingdom coming violently and violent people seizing it (Matt 11:12).

Second, Luke 16:16 is the Lukan equivalent of that saying and probably Luke's paraphrase: "The good news of the kingdom of God is proclaimed, and everyone tries to enter it by force." We may conclude from this paraphrase that Luke found the saying as worded in Q difficult, but understood it of people responding to the gospel.

Third, when he came to the saying in its "Q" context, Luke's response to the difficulty of the saying was not to paraphrase it in the way he does later in 16:16, but to draw on the similar parable tradition in Matt 21:28-32. It is not hard to see why Luke's mind went over to that parable: Not only does Luke find the "Q" saying of Matt 11:12 difficult and in need of paraphrasing, but the "Q" tradition that he has been following (Matt 11:2-19/Luke 7:18-35) and the parable recorded in Matt 21:28-32 have several things in common:

145. See Capper, "Interpretation of Acts 5:4." On this and broader questions of the NT and Qumran see also Pixner, *Wege des Messias;* Betz and Riesner, *Jesus, Qumran and the Vatican,* e.g., 125-60.

146. The parallel has been noted by others, e.g., Aland, *Synopsis Quattuor Evangeliorum,* 152.

- Both passages are about John the Baptist;
- both include a parable;
- both parables are about children — two groups of children in one, two sons in the other;
- both parables contrast the receptiveness of the tax collectors and sinners (or prostitutes) with the stubbornness of other Jews; and
- both include the term "justify/righteousness."

The influence of the Matthean parable on Luke may be seen in his use of the word "children" *(tekna)* in 7:35 (cf. Matt 21:28). The relationship between the passages might be otherwise explained, but the argument about Luke's attestation of the word "righteousness" (see p. 77 above) would not necessarily be affected.

3

WHO IS JESUS?

I. COMPARING JESUS AND PAUL

HOW DID JESUS UNDERSTAND
HIS OWN MINISTRY?

"Who then is this?" is the question that Jesus' contemporaries asked about
Jesus and that people have been asking ever since. The Gospels offer a clear
answer: Mark speaks for them all when he opens his Gospel with these
words: "The beginning of the good news of Jesus Christ, the Son of God."[1]
But modern scholars have had serious doubts whether this perception of
Jesus was shared to any extent by Jesus himself or represents just the faith
of Christians living after the time of Jesus and after the experience of his
resurrection. What then may we say about Jesus' self-understanding, if
anything?[2]

It is, as we have seen in chapter 2, almost undisputed that Jesus

---

1. There is some textual uncertainty about the words "Son of God" in Mark 1:1,
but Mark's belief in Jesus as Son of God is unquestioned.

2. We can only sketch out a possible answer to this complex and endlessly debated
issue. Among recent studies of Jesus' self-understanding see Witherington, *Christology
of Jesus*; Wright, *Jesus and the Victory of God*. Other notable studies of NT christology
published in English in the last thirty years include Fuller, *Foundations of NT Christology*;
Hahn, *Titles of Jesus*; Longenecker, *Christology of Early Jewish Christianity*; Moule, *Origin
of Christology*; Sobrino, *Christology at the Crossroads*; Schillebeeckx, *Jesus*; de Jonge,
Christology in Context; Hurtado, *One God, One Lord*; Dunn, *Christology in the Making*;
I. H. Marshall, *Origins of NT Christology*; idem, *Jesus the Saviour*; Casey, *From Jewish
Prophet*.

proclaimed the kingdom of God. By this, very probably, he meant that the day of God's deliverance for his people, a day for the fulfillment of OT promises, was dawning. But how did he see himself fitting into that scene? He could simply have seen his role as that of an announcer of the new day (much as the Gospels describe John the Baptist). But he seems to have connected his own activities — his exorcisms, healings, mixing with sinners, etc. — with the kingdom, and the way in which he did so suggests that he saw himself as more than just a prophet.

Messiah[3]

The Gospels suggest that Jesus saw himself as acting in fulfillment of Scripture. But what scriptural categories did he use to interpret his own role?

Mark identifies Jesus as "the Christ" (i.e., "the Messiah," the anointed one), and the NT as a whole claims that Jesus is the expected king, the son of David, of whom Isaiah and other prophets spoke (e.g., Isa 9:6, 7; 11:1, 2, etc.). But did Jesus see himself as such?

Scholars have had serious doubts. It is pointed out that the messianic expectations of Jews in Jesus' day were not nearly as clearcut as Christians, looking back from their perspective, have often supposed.[4] It should not be imagined that all Jews were looking for "the Messiah" — a royal savior figure from the family of David — and that therefore Jesus must have understood himself in that way.[5] Some did expect such a royal Messiah.[6] Others had different hopes. For example, at Qumran some appear to have been looking for two messiahs, one a king and the other a priest.[7] Others

---

3. The use of christological titles is not the only or even necessarily the best path into the question of Jesus' self-understanding. See, for example, Witherington's quite different approach in *Christology of Jesus*. But it is a convenient way of summarizing some of the important issues and of approaching the Jesus-Paul question.

4. See on the whole question Neusner, Green, and Frerichs, eds., *Judaisms and Their Messiahs*.

5. The term "Messiah" was not a universally recognized technical term for the future royal savior of OT expectation: It is in fact infrequently used in the OT and is not a technical term there for a future royal savior. The term means "anointed one" (*Christos* in Greek), and in the OT various groups of people — notably kings, but also priests and prophets — were anointed for special service (e.g., Exod 30:30-33; 1 Sam 15, 16; 1 Kgs 19:15, 16). "Messiah" is used of Cyrus in Isa 45:1.

6. See, e.g., Psalms of Solomon 17:32.

7. See 1QS 9:11.

again had very little eschatological expectation.[8] Even for those looking to the OT there were other categories than Messiah that could have been utilized to explain Jesus: They could, for example, have seen him as a second Moses (cf. Deut 18:15, 16; Acts 3:22) or as the returning Elijah (cf. Mal 4:5).

It is also pointed out that the evidence in the Gospels that Jesus saw himself as the messianic king is rather meager: Others speak of him in those terms occasionally, but Jesus himself seems to show little enthusiasm for the idea.[9] It has been inferred that, although the church enthusiastically identified Jesus as the Messiah, the potentially embarrassing fact was that Jesus himself did not make the identification.

These points about Jewish expectation and the meagerness of the Gospels' evidence are important, though in both cases it is possible to exaggerate. In the first place, it is true that Jesus and his contemporaries could have explained his ministry in nonmessianic terms, but still the royal savior motif was prominent in the OT and was not forgotten in the pressing sociopolitical situation of first-century Palestine. The most recently published Dead Sea Scrolls have confirmed that the hope was very much alive in at least some Jewish circles: One text speaks of the coming of "the Messiah of Righteousness, the Branch of David, because to him and his seed was given the Covenant of the Kingdom of His people."[10] The reference to the "kingdom" here is notable; messiahship was one obvious available category to use for a person like Jesus, not least when that person was a forceful figure proclaiming the "kingdom" of God.

Second, the meagerness of the Gospels' evidence for Jesus seeing himself as the Messiah is striking given the importance of the category for the early church, but it does not necessarily or even most probably point to Jesus' rejection of the category. Two other explanations are possible: Perhaps the Christian tradition deliberately downplayed the idea because of its political sensitivity in the Roman Empire. Or perhaps the picture in

---

8. So Harvey, *Jesus and the Constraints*, 78-79; cf. Mack, *Myth*, 51.

9. In Mark, Peter confesses Jesus as Messiah in 8:29, but Jesus responds to his confession with no evident enthusiasm; in 12:35-37 Jesus discusses with the scribes whether the Messiah is the son of David, but makes no direct claim; then in 14:62 Jesus agrees with the high priest that he is the Messiah, but then, as in 8:30, proceeds to talk not about messiahship but about "the Son of man."

10. 4Q252, as translated by Eisenman and Wise, *Dead Sea Scrolls Uncovered*, 89; see also the possibly messianic 4Q246, 521. See also Vermes, *Jesus the Jew*, 130-34, on ancient and intertestamental Judaism. Casey, *From Jewish Prophet*, 42, 79, when discussing Jesus argues that there was no general concept of "Messiah" available, and yet when discussing subsequent Christianity he notes the availability of the idea.

the Gospels correctly suggests that Jesus saw himself as Messiah but used the concept cautiously.

In any case the evidence is not as slender as has sometimes been made out. Thus the Gospels are probably correct in recording that the official grounds for Jesus' condemnation and crucifixion were that he seditiously claimed to be "king of the Jews." Given the political situation, it is historically plausible that this was the charge, and it is unlikely that Christians would have "invented" such a politically sensitive charge against their leader.

Of course, the charge could have had no basis at all, but there is considerable evidence that it was not just Jesus' enemies who saw him in this way, but also his friends: The Gospels do not conceal the possibly embarrassing fact that people wanted to make Jesus king (so John 6:15;[11] Matt 21:1-9/Mark 11:1-10/Luke 19:28-40; also probably Matt 19:28-30/Luke 22:28-30; Matt 20:20, 21/Mark 10:35-37). The Jesus of the Gospels rejected many of his followers' aspirations, and yet the story of him riding into Jerusalem on a donkey suggests that he, through this typically symbolic action, accepted the royal claim that others on that occasion made on his behalf, acting out the prophecy of Zech 9:9: "Rejoice greatly, O daughter Zion! . . . Lo, your king comes to you; triumphant and victorious is he, humble and riding on a donkey."[12] At his trial Jesus, according to Mark's Gospel, accepted the designation "Messiah" when questioned by the high priest, apparently thus justifying the charge that was to be made against him (Mark 14:61).[13]

The evidence, as we have seen, is that Jesus' vision of the kingdom was different from the narrow anti-Roman nationalism of many of his contem-

11. John's Gospel may have retained a historical reminiscence here that the synoptics have omitted, possibly because of its sensitive nature.

12. Harvey, *Jesus and the Constraints*, 120-29, argues for the historicity of the triumphal entry, since it is such an "odd" event. He sees it and the cleansing of the temple as prophetic actions, but finds no evidence that Jesus was claiming to be the royal Messiah. He notes a precedent in Simon Maccabeus entering the temple in 141 BC (1 Macc 13:51).

13. Matt 26:64 and Luke 22:67 suggest that Jesus' reply was more guarded than Mark describes, but the implied meaning is the same. Casey, *From Jewish Prophet*, 43, 44, allows that Jesus was crucified as "king of the Jews," but not that the question and answer of Mark 14:61 about his "kingship" are authentic. His comment that "none of his sympathizers were there," that is, at the trial, is hardly a powerful argument against the historicity of the record. Casey allows Jesus' opponents to label him as king and his followers to designate him Christ at a very early date after the resurrection, but he does not believe that Jesus himself, despite his heavy dependence on the OT, might have seen himself as such.

poraries. It makes sense that his understanding of his own kingship, if he had such a concept, might also have been different from theirs. Several Gospel passages have Jesus directly or indirectly drawing on Isaiah 61 to explain his ministry: "The Spirit of the Lord GOD is upon me, because the LORD has anointed me; he has sent me to bring good news to the oppressed [or poor] . . ." (v. 1). Luke has Jesus apply this passage directly to himself in Luke 4:18-21; Matthew and Luke have Jesus allude to it in his reply to the Baptist's question "Are you the one who is to come?" (Matt 11:5/Luke 7:22); and it is quite likely the background to one or more of the beatitudes, notably "Blessed are the poor" (Matt 5:3/Luke 6:20).[14] If this passage was important to Jesus, then that suggests both that he did see himself as "the anointed one"[15] and that he saw his "messianic" ministry as a Spirit-inspired ministry of restoration and his kingship in the sort of terms suggested by Isaiah 61 and Isaiah 11 ("A shoot shall come out from the stump of Jesse. . . . The spirit of the Lord shall rest on him . . . with righteousness he shall judge the poor . . . ," vv. 1, 2, 4), not in more limited nationalistic terms.

The dialogue about the Messiah as the Son of David recalled in Matt 22:41-46/Mark 12:35-37/Luke 20:41-44 is also probably to be understood as Jesus offering a correction to his opponents' understanding of the Messiah as Son of David, not as a rejection of it; Jesus is obviously discussing with his critics something relevant to himself, not just an academic theological point.

The cumulative evidence is quite strong that Jesus saw himself as the messianic king of Israel. The church did not — almost overnight — turn a totally nonmessianic Jesus into a Messiah just because of the resurrection. And it is not obvious why the church should have done so.[16] More likely

14. See Guelich, *Sermon on the Mount*, e.g., 71-72. On Jesus and Isaiah 61 see also Dunn, *Jesus and the Spirit*, 41-62.

15. Anointing was not necessarily a royal ritual (see above). Harvey, *Jesus and the Constraints*, 140, observes the importance of Isaiah 61 in the Jesus tradition and suggests that Jesus was nicknamed "anointed one" because he saw himself as the prophetic figure of Isa 61:1; he was the Lord's servant who was bringing the new age and the good news. This argument is attractive, but there is reason to think that Jesus saw himself also as king, not simply as spiritually "anointed" for prophetic ministry. Isaiah 11 speaks of such a royal figure full of the Spirit. In 1 Samuel 10, Saul is anointed king to save God's people from their enemies, and then God's Spirit comes on him, leading him to prophesy with the prophets: Royal and prophetic anointing come together here; similarly in 1 Sam 16:13 David is anointed, and then the Spirit comes mightily on him.

16. So Harvey, *Jesus and the Constraints*, 137-39. Hengel, *Atonement*, 48, comments: "Easter . . . in no way explains how the alleged 'rabbi' and 'prophet' became Messiah and Son of Man . . . in short how 'the proclaimer became the proclaimed.'"

Jesus himself accepted the designation but used the concept cautiously, even sometimes secretively,[17] probably because of the sort of nationalism popularly associated with it, perhaps because of a Jewish tradition that the Messiah would not proclaim his own identity,[18] and also because his understanding of his own role, as well as of the kingdom, was much bigger than that of his contemporaries.

Son of Man

If there is some uncertainty about Jesus' messianic consciousness, there is little doubt that he spoke of himself as "the Son of man." The sheer number of "Son of man" sayings in the Gospels (the phrase occurs 69 times in the synoptics, 13 times in John) and the infrequent use of the expression to refer to Jesus elsewhere in the NT suggest that, even if scholars have doubts about the authenticity of a good number of the sayings concerned, we can hear in the expression the authentic voice of Jesus.[19]

But what is the significance of the phrase? It is easy for Christian readers of the NT who have gotten used to the expression as a designation of Jesus to miss the force of the Hebraic "son of" idiom. In Hebrew "a son (or daughter) of" something is someone associated with, belonging to, characterized by that thing: A "son of courage" is a brave person or a warrior (1 Sam 14:52); "sons of light and sons of darkness" are those who belong, respectively, to light or darkness; a "son of cattle" is a calf or an ox (Gen 18:7). "Son of man" is, therefore, simply a way of referring to a man belonging to the human species. "The son of man" means simply "the human being." Thus in Ps 8:4 the literal translation is "What is man *(adam)* that you are mindful of him, and the son of man *(ben adam)* that you care for him?" but the meaning is "What are human beings that you are mindful of them, mortals that you care for them?" (NRSV). So "son of man" = man = human being. When the prophet Ezekiel is addressed by God as "son of

17. It is not possible here to go into extensive discussion of the "messianic secret," but there is a good case for thinking that it had a historical basis in Jesus' ministry. For a useful collection of essays see Tuckett, ed., *Messianic Secret;* see also Dunn, "Messianic Secret in Mark."

18. See, e.g., Longenecker, *Christology,* 73, referring to David Flusser.

19. There is a huge bibliography on "Son of man." We cannot even summarize all the arguments and issues. Some of the major contributions include Vermes, *Jesus the Jew;* Lindars, *Jesus, Son of Man;* Casey, *Son of Man;* Hooker, *Son of Man in Mark;* Kim, *"Son of Man" as Son of God;* Caragounis, *Son of Man;* Hare, *Son of Man Tradition.*

man" (e.g., "Son of man, can these bones live?" 37:3, RSV), he is not being given some mysterious or exalted title but is just being addressed by God as "human being" (JB "man," NRSV "mortal").

So when Jesus in the Gospels speaks of "the Son of man," we need to understand it accordingly. For example, Mark 2:10: "that you may know that *the human being* has authority on earth to forgive sins,"* Mark 8:31: "*The human being* must suffer many things,"* and Mark 8:38: "Whoever is ashamed of me . . . , of him will *the human being* be ashamed when he comes in the glory of his Father. . . ."*

But why does Jesus speak of himself in this way?[20] All sorts of ideas have been proposed. The popular Christian assumption is that Jesus spoke of himself as "Son of man" to affirm his human nature. But this is to interpret the phrase in the light of later Christian doctrine and controversy. It is unlikely that Jesus needed to persuade his contemporaries of his real humanity. Various scholars have argued that the phrase was a normal Aramaic way of speaking of oneself or of oneself and others like oneself. But the way the Gospels associate it particularly with Jesus and retain the idiom in translation suggests that it was not normal usage and that, whether or not others used it, Jesus characteristically did.

The most probable explanation, especially in the light of what we have seen about Jesus' kingdom teaching, is that it has an OT background.[21] Possible backgrounds include Ezekiel — Jesus is in some respects at least in the prophetic tradition — and Psalm 8, which speaks in terms reminiscent of Genesis 1 and 2 of "man"/"the son of man" being given dominion over the world — an idea not remote from some of the kingdom teaching of Jesus.

But the most significant and probable background is Daniel 7.[22] In

---

20. There has been massive scholarly discussion about how many of the "Son of man" sayings actually go back to Jesus, with some scholars even doubting if Jesus used the term of himself at all. The weight of evidence for the usage is, however, particularly strong.

21. Casey, *From Jewish Prophet*, 47-54, 70-73, emphasizes how Jewish Jesus was in his thinking, and yet he does not think that Jesus' "Son of man" usage derives from the OT. He recognizes that some of the sayings concerned echo Daniel 7, but he ascribes these to the church, commenting "We cannot explain why the Jesus of history should depart from his normal practice of teaching clearly with authority . . . in favour of indirect references to a scriptural text that he is never said to have quoted" (53). This is a slightly curious statement, especially as Casey himself points to the Danielic background of Jesus' kingdom teaching (though see his fuller *Son of Man*, 157-223).

22. Daniel 7 is in Aramaic, not Hebrew, and so it would have been especially easy

this important chapter Daniel has a vision of four terrible beasts, then of judgment taking place by one who is "ancient of days," and of judgment being given against the four beasts and in favor of "one like a son of man," that is, a human figure, who comes on the clouds of heaven. The vision is interpreted in the same chapter and is a picture of divine judgment coming on the pagan world empires (the four beasts) and of "kingship and dominion" being given to the "holy ones (or saints) of the Most High," in other words, to faithful Israelites, who have suffered oppression but will be saved and vindicated. Jesus in the Gospels alludes clearly to this passage when speaking of himself as "Son of man," for example, in those passages that speak of him coming in future glory with the angels (e.g., Matt 16:27; 24:30; 26:64 and parallels). Some scholars have doubted whether these Son of man sayings go back to Jesus,[23] but there is much to be said for seeing Jesus' Son of man language, like his kingdom teaching, in a Danielic context.[24]

If Daniel 7 is important to Jesus, then in speaking of himself as "the Son of man" Jesus is affirming that in him the promised salvation and "kingdom" of Israel (portrayed in Daniel 7 by the human cloud-riding figure) have come. Psalm 80 is another passage with a rather similar "Son of man" concept: The psalmist prays for God to restore his people — the vine that God planted and that has been burned and cut down — and says, "Let your hand be upon the one [literally: the man] at your right hand, the one [literally: the son of man] whom you made strong for yourself" (v. 17).

---

to link Jesus' Aramaic "son of man" with the Danielic "one like a son of man." The importance of the Book of Daniel in first-century Judaism is clear from Josephus, the Dead Sea Scrolls, and elsewhere. See Goldingay, *Daniel*, xxvi-xxx.

23. Recently, e.g., Crossan, *Historical Jesus*, 227-64. He argues that in the relevant complexes of Jesus-tradition the "Son of man" is only attested in one source. For example, the "Son of man" occurs only in the "Q" form of the parable of the thief, not in Gospel of Thomas 21; 1 Thes 5:2; 2 Pet 3:10; or Rev 16:15. But the absence of the phrase outside the "Q" parable hardly casts doubt on the "Q" wording; indeed, it is usually and plausibly argued that the absence of "Son of man" language outside the Gospels is evidence that it goes back to Jesus. Crossan's way of counting attestation (which includes taking each passage individually and counting Matthew/Mark/Luke parallels as one witness) enables him to minimize the evidence for the coming Son of man motif. But the motif is attested strongly in Mark, as well as in "Q," "M," and "L" traditions.

24. There has been a great deal of discussion of the "son of man" figure in the context of Daniel 7. See, e.g., Dunn, *Christology*, 67-75. It is not vital to our argument to decide whether in Jesus' time the "one like a son of man" was identified with the Messiah or with a supernatural, angelic figure.

It is precisely this restoration of "the son of man," Israel, that is at the heart of Jesus' kingdom message. The psalmist's prayer is being fulfilled in Jesus.

The expression "the Son of man" is thus not exactly a title. It is a somewhat mysterious but highly allusive way of speaking, mysterious because it means "the human being," allusive to those with ears to hear, evoking the OT vision of divine restoration of God's people, but, being mysterious and allusive, not as easily misinterpreted by Jesus' contemporaries as the designation "Christ" would be.[25]

Son of God

Traditional Christian orthodoxy is that Jesus is Son of God, the second person of the divine Trinity. Whether he saw himself as Son of God in any sense, let alone in anything like a trinitarian sense, is highly debatable.

The phrase itself does not necessarily suggest divinity, either in Judaism or in early Christianity. The OT can speak of the king (e.g., 2 Sam 7:14; Pss 2:7, 12; 89:26, 27), of Israel (e.g., Hos 11:14), or of an angelic being (e.g., Gen 6:2, 4) as God's adopted son. The NT can assert that all Christians are sons of God (Rom 8:14). To be a son of God is to be in a special, favored relationship with God, but need not mean anything more.[26]

But did Jesus regard himself as "Son of God" in *any* sense? John's Gospel answers that question with a resounding yes and has Jesus speak constantly of himself as God's Son. But this and many of the synoptic references to Jesus as Son of God have been seen by scholars as read back into the story of Jesus on the basis of the church's post-Easter convictions.

But there is no need to be so skeptical. If the king and Israel could be seen as God's son in some sense, then Jesus, who identified himself as Messiah and as the "Son of man" in whom Israel's salvation was coming, might well have understood himself as God's Son on that basis alone.[27]

---

25. See Horbury's useful article, "Messianic Associations." He comments: "In its aspect of opacity, which the hearer was invited to pierce, it [the expression "Son of man"] resembled the parables."

26. In the Book of Wisdom the "righteous" man is called God's son (e.g., 2:18; 5:5). See also Vermes, *Jesus the Jew*, 205-11, on Jewish charismatics as "sons" of God.

27. One of the newly published Dead Sea Scrolls, 4Q246, has been interpreted messianically. Thus Eisenman and Wise, *Dead Sea Scrolls Uncovered*, 70-71, translate: "He will be called the son of God; they will call him son of the Most High. . . . His Kingdom will be an Eternal Kingdom, and he will be Righteous in all his Ways. He [will jud]ge the earth in Righteousness." There is, however, some doubt about this interpreta-

That he did see himself as God's Son is suggested by significant evidence. Most important for study of Paul and Jesus is the evidence that Jesus addressed God as *Abba*. This Aramaic word surfaces three times in the NT, once on the lips of Jesus (Mark 14:36) and twice in Paul's writings (Rom 8:15; Gal 4:6). The use of this Aramaic term three times in the Greek writings of the NT is striking: Why should Paul and Mark use the term when writing to Gentiles and when there is a perfectly good Greek word that they could employ to mean "father"? The probable explanation is that the term was one that Jesus used and that was, in fact, characteristic of Jesus. Paul almost gives us that explanation in Gal 4:6 when he comments that "God has sent the Spirit of his Son into our hearts, crying 'Abba! Father!'" *Abba* is associated with Jesus.

Abba does not seem to have been a normal way of addressing God in Judaism. It was how children addressed their fathers, and it may well be that Jews felt that it was too familiar an expression to use when addressing the Almighty.[28] If Jesus used the expression, this would have been striking and memorable. It seems quite likely that he used it frequently — not just in Gethsemane as recorded in Mark 14:36 but also on other occasions, including perhaps in the Lord's Prayer, which opens in the Lukan version with the simple address "Father" (11:2).

If Jesus used the term, then this suggests a special consciousness of divine sonship on his part, not necessarily anything like trinitarian convictions, but still a sense of intimacy that is reflected in his innovative usage and that for that reason impressed his followers.

Other passages are even more revealing, even if they are also more controversial. Matt 11:27/Luke 10:22, for example, is a so-called "Q" saying, in which Jesus observes: "All things have been handed over to me by my Father; and no one knows the Son except the Father, and no one knows the Father except the Son and anyone to whom the Son chooses to reveal

---

tion of the text and about whether it is the Messiah or a usurper who is to be called "son of God . . . son of the Most High" (see Vermes, "Qumran Forum Miscellanea I"). Either way the text applies sonship language to an eschatological king (whether good or bad) and goes on to speak of the eternal kingdom in language reminiscent of Daniel 7. See also Fitzmyer, "'Son of God' Document," relating the text to Luke 1:32-33.

28. The point should not be exaggerated: The term is not a childish word like "daddy," and there is some possible evidence of Jewish teachers other than Jesus using it. But the usage seems to have been unusual, and yet characteristic of Jesus. See Jeremias, *Prayers of Jesus*, 10-65, and more recently Dunn, *Christology*, 26-28; Vermes, *Religion of Jesus*, 180-83; Scott, *Adoption*, 183-84; also Witherington, *Christology*, 215-19, responding to, among others, Barr, "'Abbā.'"

him." This saying sounds very much like many of the sayings in John's Gospel, but that is in itself no reason for doubting its authenticity. The one who announced the arrival of God's kingdom, who acted with great personal authority, and who called God *Abba* could well have had such an understanding of his relationship to God.[29]

Another significant passage is the parable of the vineyard, in which Jesus speaks of the vineyard's owner sending first his servants to gather his dues from his tenants, then finally his son (Matt 21:33-46/Mark 12:1-12/Luke 20:9-19). If this parable goes back to Jesus and if the servants of the parable are the prophets and Jesus himself is the son, as seems to be implied, then Jesus was making a startling claim about his status vis-à-vis the great prophets of old.[30]

Similarly in the saying in Matt 24:36/Mark 13:32 Jesus says, "Of that day and hour no one knows, not even the angels in heaven, nor the Son, but the Father only" (RSV). The way in which this saying on the one hand ascribes ignorance to Jesus and on the other hand locates him between the angels and the Father (and closer terminologically to the Father) is striking indeed.[31]

The impression that Jesus saw himself as having a very special filial relationship to God may be confirmed by the immense authority with

---

29. For bibliography on the saying see Davies and Allison, *Matthew* II, 297-302. They refer to Karl von Hase's description of the verse as a "thunderbolt from the Johannine sky," and comment: "This in all likelihood stands the truth on its head. Matt 11:25-27 par. was probably one of the vital seeds from which Johannine theology sprouted." While expressing uncertainty about the origin of the saying, they argue strongly for a Jewish background and in particular for a background in OT traditions of Moses knowing God, e.g., Exod 33:12, 13 and Deut 34:10. On the authenticity of the saying see Witherington, *Christology*, 221-28.

30. Dunn, *Christology*, 28, plays down the importance of the parable by observing that the servant/son contrast "can be fully explained as part of the dramatic climax of the parable." But the parabolic contrast is extraordinary and significant in its implications. Crossan, *Historical Jesus*, 352, denies that Jesus identified himself as the son in the original parable, but he does not offer a persuasive alternative explanation of the parable. On the interpretation and authenticity of the parable see especially Snodgrass, *Parable of the Wicked Tenants*.

31. The authenticity of the saying has been debated, with some arguing that it is most unlikely that the church would have ascribed ignorance of the time of the parousia to Jesus, and others claiming that the church had an interest in ascribing such ignorance to Jesus — either in face of excessive excitement about the second coming or in face of Christian disappointment at the delay of the parousia. See Casey, *From Jewish Prophet*, 45, and for a recent and full discussion Beasley-Murray, *Jesus and the Last Days*, 453-68.

which he seems to have worked. The Gospels agree that this was something striking about him and his ministry (e.g., Mark 1:22/Luke 4:32; Matt 7:29; Mark 1:26/Luke 4:33; Matt 9:8): His teaching had special authority. His interpretation of the law, including the sabbath (in what he said and did), was offensive to his critics, because of his independence of their traditions; it seemed to imply that Jesus was somehow on a par with or even higher than Moses. He healed and cast out devils with great authority, and his claim to bring the forgiveness of God to sinners (by what he said and did) was shocking.[32]

It is not possible in a discussion of this length to explore more fully Jesus' understanding of his sonship; there is a whole host of important and controversial issues involved in the question, not least in relation to first-century Judaism and its understanding of its religious leaders and heroes (e.g., Moses and Enoch). What need not be doubted, given the synoptic evidence, is that Jesus had a sense of great authority and that this went together with a conviction that he was God's Son in some significant way. The evidence suggests that his filial consciousness was much more than that of the righteous man and even than a consciousness of messiahship (see also on "Lord" below). But precise definitions are not possible on the basis of the synoptic evidence.[33]

32. Casey, *From Jewish Prophet,* 44-46, allows that demons may have called Jesus "a son of God," that use of *"Abba"* was distinctive and important to Jesus himself (132, 33), that Jesus worked "with massive personal authority" (68), and that Jesus referred to himself as "the beloved son" in the parable of the vineyard (147-49). Yet, remarkably, Casey rules out the idea that Jesus saw himself as "son of God" in any special sense. He claims, quite unpersuasively, that a saying like Matt 11:27 must derive from a time when Christians, having separated from Jews, wished to assert their own claim to divine truth.

33. The OT looked forward to the coming of the Lord — the coming of God — on the day of the Lord (e.g., Mal 3:1; Isa 40:3). When Jesus announced the rule of God, he was in one sense announcing that coming, and, although scholars have rightly been cautious about reading later Christian theology into the NT, there is a real possibility that Jesus saw in himself (as the Son of God) at least the partial realization of the divine presence. This very Johannine thought may have its roots in Jesus' self-understanding; the synoptic evidence is not extensive, but the identification of John the Baptist as the messenger preparing the way of the Lord is suggestive (Matt 11:10/Luke 7:27; Mark 1:2, 3).

HOW DID PAUL UNDERSTAND JESUS?

In Rom 1:3, 4, Paul introduces his gospel to his Roman readers, and he describes it as

> concerning [God's] Son,
> who was descended from David according to the flesh
> and declared to be Son of God with power according to the Spirit of
> holiness by resurrection from the dead,
> Jesus Christ our Lord.

As we have seen in chapter 2, Jesus was at the center of Paul's theology. His own conversion experience, in which "God . . . was pleased to reveal his Son to me" (Gal 1:16), made that priority inevitable, and in Romans, before he ever comes to discuss the gospel in terms of righteousness and reconciliation, Paul speaks of the good news as "concerning his," that is, God's, "Son."

Some scholars believe, partly because of the unusual vocabulary (e.g., "Spirit of holiness," not "Holy Spirit") that the form of words used to describe Jesus in Rom 1:3, 4 was taken by Paul from some early Christian creed. Whether they were or not, Paul uses them to introduce his gospel in Romans, and we may assume that they express what he wanted to say about Jesus.[34] We will use them as a framework for our consideration of Paul's christology.

What did Paul want to say? These two verses are carefully structured. They start with a statement of Jesus' relationship to God ("his Son")[35] and end with a statement of his relationship to us ("Jesus Christ our Lord").[36] In between we have what may be regarded as a mini-history of Jesus' mission, describing first his descent from David, then his powerful resurrection from the dead.

---

34. On this see especially Scott, *Adoption,* 227-36, questioning the supposed pre-Pauline origin of the verses.   .

35. Rom 1:4, with its description of Jesus being "appointed Son of God . . . by resurrection"* has been seen as adoptionist, that is, as implying that Jesus became Son through the resurrection. But it is impossible that Paul intended that, since he clearly believed that Jesus was the Son when he was sent into the world (Gal 4:4) and even at the time of creation. The sense in Rom 1:4 must be that Jesus, whose life on earth was one of human weakness, was *"declared* Son of God *with power"* by the resurrection (so NRSV). Acts 2:36 has also been understood as adoptionist, but there also the author in whose work it is incorporated does not understand it in that way.

36. Compare the similar combination of ideas elsewhere in Paul, e.g., 1 Cor 1:3; 2 Cor 1:2.

Son of God

Paul . . .

"Christ" and "Lord" speak in different ways of Jesus' relationship to his followers, but "Son of God," for Paul, describes Jesus' relationship to God. "When the fullness of time had come," Paul comments in Gal 4:4, "God sent his Son . . ." (cf. Rom 8:3).

How is this sonship understood? Paul can speak of Christians as children of God, and he refers to God more as "our Father" than as Jesus' father.[37] But, although he does indeed see Christians as brothers of Jesus, it is quite clear that Jesus has a primacy as Son and that believers are adopted by grace into the divine family (e.g., Rom 8:17, 29).

The distinctiveness of Jesus' relationship to the Father is clear from the way that Paul repeatedly and strikingly brackets God and Jesus together in one phrase, as in Rom 1:7: "Grace to you and peace from God our Father and the Lord Jesus Christ." It is a relationship that in Paul's view goes back before time. Thus in Phil 2:5-8 Christ "in the form of God" empties himself and takes human form. Jesus' so-called "preexistence" is affirmed also very clearly in Colossians 1, where Paul speaks of Jesus as the image of the invisible God and as the one in whom all things were created (1:15, 16). Colossians is not always seen as Pauline, but in the undisputed Pauline letters too there are explicit or implicit references to Jesus' preexistent work or glory (e.g., 1 Cor 8:6; 2 Cor 8:9; possibly even Rom 1:3, with "his Son" preceding the history of Jesus).[38]

Most scholars agree that behind at least some of these passages lies the Jewish idea of God's wisdom. In books such as Proverbs, the Wisdom of Solomon, and Ecclesiasticus (Sirach), "wisdom" is spoken of in personal terms, as though it were a colleague working with and alongside God — in creation and afterward. Thus in Prov 8:22-31 wisdom herself speaks: "When he established the heavens, I was there, . . . I was beside him, like a master

---

37. The two ideas are adjacent, though distinct, in 2 Cor 1:2, 3 and Col 1:2, 3. God is "our Father," and "the Father of our Lord Jesus Christ."

38. The structure of Rom 1: 3, 4 is similar to that of Phil 2:5ff., which begins with a reference to Jesus as "in the form of God" and concludes with the reference to him as "Lord" (vv. 5, 11). Cf. R. Pesch, "Das Evangelium Gottes."

Dunn's denial of "preexistence" in Pauline christology is perhaps the least convincing aspect of his magisterial book, *Christology in the Making* (e.g., 114-21, 187-94); the traditional reading of verses such as Phil 2:6 and Col 1:17 continues to be more natural than the readings argued by Dunn.

worker; and I was daily his delight" (vv. 27, 30) [39] Paul and other NT writers probably found this a useful category for explaining Jesus.[40] Jesus was not simply one among many sons of God, but was the eternal agent of God, involved in creation and destined to bring all things under God's feet in the future (1 Cor 15:28). On just a few occasions Paul may actually refer to Jesus as God (Rom 9:5; 2 Thes 1:12; Tit 2:13),[41] but he usually refrains from such language, distinguishing the supreme Father and the obedient Son, but still seeing Jesus as in some real sense divine.

. . . and Jesus

Paul's view of Jesus' divinity and preexistence is paralleled in John's Gospel, even in the words of Jesus himself (e.g., 8:58; 17:5). In his prologue (1:1-18) John reflects the same sort of wisdom thinking as is found in Colossians and elsewhere in Paul.[42]

In the synoptics, however, there is no idea of preexistence, explicitly at least, and in this respect Paul's christology (as also John's) may quite plausibly be thought of as representing an advance on that of Jesus. Paul writes in the light of the dramatic resurrection event — so Rom 1:4 — and of Christian reflection on Jesus (including on Jesus as the preexistent divine wisdom).

But, if the case for a significant gap between Jesus and Paul is as strong here as anywhere, there is also significant continuity. The use of *Abba* is one obvious link, and we have seen that Jesus saw himself as Son of God not in any ordinary sense, but in a particularly authoritative sense. As for preexistence, the way that Jesus speaks of his own "coming" (e.g., "I have come to call not the righteous but sinners," Matt 9:13/Mark 2:17/Luke 5:32)[43] and of having been "sent" by God (e.g., the son in the parable of the vineyard) comes quite close to Paul's thinking about Jesus.[44] Even the

39. See also Wisdom 7 and 8; Ecclesiasticus 24.

40. For wisdom language used in connection with Jesus (though not necessarily related to the Jewish personification of wisdom) see 1 Cor 1:24, 30; Col 2:3.

41. On Rom 9:5; Tit 2:13 see M. Harris, *Jesus as God,* 143-85.

42. The similarity of John 1 and Col 1:15-20 is quite striking, and it may be no coincidence that traditionally John's Gospel has been associated with the area of Ephesus, where Colossae is situated. The authors of the two are both probably addressing christological heresies of one sort or another (see Col 2:8-19; 1 John 2:18-23).

43. See also Matt 20:28/Mark 10:45; Luke 12:49; 19:10.

44. So Ridderbos, *Paul and Jesus,* 115-17. Compare Paul's "sending" language in Gal 4:4; Rom 8:3. We cannot make too much of "coming" and "sending" language: The

association of Jesus with "wisdom" has some parallel in the sayings of Jesus (e.g., Matt 11:19/Luke 7:35; Matt 23:34/Luke 11:49).[45]

Jesus the Human Being

Paul . . .

Paul speaks in Rom 1:3 of Jesus as God's Son "who was descended from David according to the flesh." The word "flesh" often has negative connotations for Paul: He uses it to refer to sinful human nature and experience in contrast to the life of the Holy Spirit. But "flesh" can refer more neutrally to ordinary, human, physical life. This is the sense in Rom 1:3, where Paul introduces his mini-history of Jesus. The first part of that history is Jesus' human life in all its "fleshly" weakness, and the second is the spiritual life of resurrection power. Paul believes in the real humanity of Jesus. He speaks in Gal 4:4 of Jesus being sent by God and being "born of a woman, born under the law."[46]

In several passages Paul speaks directly or indirectly of Jesus as the new Adam. Adam was a figure of great importance in Jewish thought — being the archetypal and original human being. In Romans 5 Paul contrasts Adam's fatal sin, which brought humankind under condemnation, with Jesus' righteousness and obedience, which brought salvation and justification. In 1 Corinthians 15 Paul contrasts Adam's mortality with Jesus' resurrection life. In Philippians 2 there may well be an implied contrast between Adam, who with fatal results was grasping and disobedient, wanting to be equal with God, and Christ, who was the opposite and was highly exalted. Whether or not there is an Adamic allusion in Philippians 2, it is

---

prophets were "sent" (including the servants in the parable of the vineyard), and John the Baptist "came" (Matt 11:18/Luke 7:33). But note the comment of Ninan in *Jesus as the Son of God*, 208: "The son who is sent was the son before his mission."

45. On the texts concerned see, recently, Witherington, *Jesus the Sage*; also Suggs, *Wisdom, Christology, and Law*, 5-61; Deutsch, *Hidden Wisdom*; Laansma, *Use of the Rest Motif*; Davies and Allison, *Matthew*, I, 264-65.

46. In Phil 2:7, where Paul speaks of Jesus in human likeness and form, he does not mean that Jesus only seemed to be human, but rather that he exchanged the divine form for the human form. Similarly in Rom 8:3, where Paul speaks of Jesus being sent "in the likeness of sinful flesh," he is not implying that Jesus' flesh was unreal, but probably that Jesus was human without sinning.

in any case clear that Paul sees Jesus as the new and greater man, as the one who was himself in the image of God and who brings restoration of that image to others (see 1 Cor 15:49; 2 Cor 3:18; Col 3:10), and as the founder of the new and redeemed humanity, the one who has undone Adam's work. We are appropriately reminded of Paul's teaching on Jesus having brought "new creation."

. . . and Jesus

The real humanity of Jesus was, we suggested earlier, not in question to his contemporaries, and Paul knew well that Jesus was a human being, one who had lived and died (by crucifixion) in Palestine.

Paul's "new Adam" teaching has no definite parallel in Jesus' teaching, though Jesus' characteristic self-designation "the Son of man" — that is, "the human being" — is at a superficial level at least a possible parallel (see further, pp. 126-29 below). Jesus' teaching on divorce referred people back to "the beginning" of creation (Matt 19:8/Mark 10:6); if the coming of the kingdom of God was seen as the restoration of creation, then we are arguably not so far removed from Paul's new Adam theology.

The Christ

Paul . . .

When in Rom 1:3 Paul refers to Jesus as "descended from [or "born of the seed of"] David according to the flesh," he is not just giving us interesting information about Jesus' humanity and ancestry, but more specifically identifying Jesus as the messianic king in the line of David.

Admittedly Paul does not make much of this idea in his letters. He never refers to Jesus as "king" and rarely speaks of Jesus reigning. (Such language could have caused misunderstandings in Paul's Greco-Roman urban setting.) However, he does routinely and frequently refer to "Jesus Christ" (so Rom 1:4 and passim). That in itself does not necessarily prove that Jesus' messiahship was important to Paul: It is widely assumed that for Paul "Christ" had become in effect a proper name, with the messianic connotation no longer prominent. But that assumption is uncertain: Paul does speak sometimes of Jesus as "the Christ" (e.g., Rom 9:5), and it is likely that the messianic interpretation of Jesus is almost taken for granted by Paul, so much so that "Christ" has become a name as much as a title —

but without losing its messianic meaning.[47] Paul then does not see Jesus just as Savior of the world in general, but as the Messiah of Israel in particular ("to the Jew first," Rom 1:16), as is clear from all his letters, especially Romans 9–11.

The term "Christ" puts Jesus in the context of Israel, and thus has strongly corporate overtones. It is probably no accident that Paul likes to speak of Christians — the new people of God — as "in Christ." Whereas "Son of God" suggests Jesus' relationship to the Father and "Lord" his relationship to the world and to individuals, "Christ" suggests his relationship to Israel and to the church.

. . . and Jesus

The impression we get from Paul is that Jesus' messiahship is a fundamental given that he accepts without question.[48] We have argued that Jesus probably did see himself as Messiah, even if he was cautious about making royal claims because of the vast potential for misunderstanding such a claim, just as Paul avoided "kingdom" language.

Lord

Paul . . .

If one had to identify Paul's favorite way of describing Jesus, "the Lord" would probably win. *Kyrios,* "lord," was used in a wide range of contexts: It was used of the masters of slaves (as in Col. 4:1; Eph. 6:9), of the Roman emperor, of Greek deities (e.g., 1 Cor. 8:5, 6), and by the Jews, for example, in Greek-speaking synagogues, of Yahweh.[49]

For Paul the term had two major connotations. First, it was a word through which Paul could express his own relationship to Jesus: He saw himself as the "slave" or "servant" of Jesus "the master" (e.g., Rom 1:1; Phil 1:1; 1 Cor 4:1). As the servant it was his task to obey and to give account to his master. It may be significant that, whereas Paul typically speaks of

---

47. On the ongoing significance of *Christos* for Paul see Wright, *Climax,* 41-55.

48. The pervasiveness of the tradition of Jesus as the Christ may tell against the view that it was a post-Easter innovation not rooted in Jesus' ministry.

49. See Marshall, *Origins,* 99, arguing that the usage probably goes back to the NT period.

Christians being "in Christ," when he speaks of the Christian's ethical responsibility he tends to speak of Christians as "in the Lord," perhaps because "lord" suggested one who gives instructions and is to be obeyed.[50]

But Paul did not see Jesus as just a human master. He saw Jesus, as we have seen, as in some sense divine, and the second way in which he uses *kyrios* is to express this conviction. He may have been influenced in this by the Septuagint's use of *kyrios* to represent "Yahweh," the Hebrew name of Israel's God. It is one of the striking features of Paul's letters that from time to time he applies OT statements about Yahweh to Jesus: Thus in Rom 10:13 Paul uses the promise of Joel 2:32 that "everyone who calls on the name of the Lord shall be saved" when speaking of faith in Jesus. And in the great hymn of Phil 2:5-11 Paul speaks of every knee bowing to the exalted Christ, echoing the words of Isa 45:23 about knees bowing to Yahweh; he also refers to Jesus being given "the name that is above every name," and then explains that every tongue will confess that "Jesus Christ is Lord." "Lord" here is that name above every name, in other words, the divine name, which now belongs to the exalted Jesus.

It seems quite likely that "Jesus (or Jesus Christ) is Lord" was the profession of faith made by converts at baptism — thus the first Christian "creed."[51] This is suggested by Rom 10:9, where Paul is speaking of saving faith and says: "If you confess with your lips that *Jesus is Lord* and believe in your heart that God raised him from the dead, you will be saved." It is also suggested by 1 Cor 12:3, where Paul comments that "no one can say 'Jesus is Lord' except by the Holy Spirit": Paul can hardly mean that no one can utter the words except by divine inspiration, but his meaning may well be that no one can come to conversion and baptism except by the Spirit.[52] If this deduction is correct, then "Lord" is clearly a particularly important category for Paul and his churches.

. . . and Jesus

We did not discuss "lordship" in considering Jesus' self-understanding, and it could be that Paul's conviction of Jesus' lordship arose purely out of his Damascus road experience: The Acts traditions have the blinded Paul respond to the heavenly vision with "Who are you, Lord?" (9:5; 22:8; 26:15).

---

50. E.g., Phil 4:1, 2; Col 3:18, 22; 4:7, 17. See also Moule, *Christology,* 59.

51. See, e.g., Dunn, *Christology,* 607-8.

52. Compare the probable baptismal allusion in 1 Cor 6:11: "You were washed . . . in the name of the Lord Jesus Christ and in the Spirit of our God."

It may also be that "Lord" was a term that was especially congenial in the Greek environment in which Paul worked.

However, it is not likely that the usage began with Paul or even with the Greek-speaking church. Paul himself retains the Aramaic phrase *maranatha* ("Our Lord, come!") in 1 Cor 16:22, thereby suggesting that the idea of Jesus as Lord was firmly embedded not just in the baptismal liturgy of Paul's churches but also in the liturgy of the Aramaic-speaking church.[53]

And it goes back further still, since there are references to Jesus as Lord firmly embedded in the gospel tradition. The disciples and others frequently address Jesus as "Lord" or "Master";[54] it may well be that this was one normal, respectful way that the disciples addressed their teacher and leader.[55] More significantly Jesus in a number of well-attested parables speaks of a master with his servants, implying that he is "the lord" to whom his followers are responsible (e.g., Matt 24:45-51/Luke 12:41-46; Matt 25:14-30/Luke 19:11-27). In the story of Jesus' last entry into Jerusalem, he tells the disciples to say "the Lord has need of it" when requisitioning the donkey (Matt 21:3/Mark 11:3/Luke 19:34).

The synoptics come nearest to Paul's idea of Jesus as divine Lord in the dialogue between Jesus and his Jewish opponents about the Messiah as Son of David, where Jesus challenges his critics by arguing from Psalm 110 that the Messiah is not just David's son but also his Lord (Matt 22:41-46/Mark 12:35-37a/Luke 20:41-44).[56] The precise implications of Jesus' question are not spelled out, but there he is evidently making an important christological claim, which at least points in the direction that Paul was to go. It is interesting to note that Paul, in common with other NT writers, uses Psalm 110 in one of his important christological passages (1 Cor 15:20-28).

FINAL COMMENTS ON THE COMPARISON

Moving from the synoptic picture of Jesus, the Jewish prophet from Galilee who announced the kingdom and who spoke of himself as Son of man, to

53. On the meaning of *maranatha* see the commentaries, e.g., Fee, *1 Corinthians*, 838-39.

54. E.g., Matt 8:2, 6, 8, 21, 25; Mark 7:28; 10:51; Luke 22:33, 38, 49.

55. See Matt 7:21, 22/Luke 6:46; 13:25.

56. For discussion of the authenticity of this passage see, among others, Fitzmyer, *Luke X–XXIV*, 1308-14; Gundry, *Mark*, 720-24.

Paul's picture of Jesus the risen Christ and second Adam, the one who was in the form of God at the beginning and through whom God is reconciling the universe, does feel a little like moving from one world of thought to another. But the differences can be exaggerated: Jesus did not see himself as simply a prophet or healer, but as much more,[57] and Paul did not see Jesus simply as a divine figure, but also as a person who lived a human life and died a human death. Furthermore, there are similarities at almost every point between Jesus' teaching about himself (for example, as Messiah, Son, Lord) and Paul's view of Jesus.

The differences between the perspectives of Jesus and Paul are explicable to a considerable extent in terms of their differing contexts. Jesus was constrained by his situation and chose to be allusive in much of his teaching. But Paul wrote after the resurrection and without the constraints of Jesus' situation.[58] Paul's perspective is undoubtedly influenced enormously by his convictions about the resurrection and by his experience of the exalted Christ. But for all the differences, Paul's christology has much in common with Jesus' self-understanding. There is continuity rather than discontinuity.

That Paul was not a radical innovator in the matter of christology may be confirmed by the evidence of Paul's letters dealing with the controversies in which he was involved. His gospel was highly controversial in some circles, but the controversy seems to have focused on his attitudes toward the Gentiles and the Jewish law, and there is no hint that his view of Jesus as Messiah, Lord, and Son of God was seen as inadequate or unorthodox. On this he was in agreement with others.[59]

---

57. Bultmann's "proclaimer becoming the proclaimed" will not do: Jesus saw himself as having a vital role in the coming kingdom; he was himself proclaimer and proclaimed.

58. The difference between the christological emphases of the Gospels and the Epistles is partly a reflection of the nature of the two bodies of literature: The Gospels' focus is specifically on Jesus' earthly life and ministry (though they were of course written with significant hindsight), while Paul sees Jesus in a wider context.

59. This is argued by Ridderbos, *Paul and Jesus*, 52, and especially by Machen, *Origins*, 130-36. Georgi, *Opponents*, suggests that there was christological controversy, with Paul in 2 Corinthians opposing a view of Jesus as a miracle-working "divine man" (note 11:4: "if someone . . . proclaims another Jesus"). There could be some truth in this view, but the evidence (in both 1 and 2 Corinthians) is that the issue involved miracles done by Paul and in the church more than christology. In any case, if Paul was correcting a one-sided christology and so stressing the cross, this does not affect the observation that the christological emphases of Paul that we have discussed in this chapter do not appear to have been controversial.

II. CONNECTING JESUS AND PAUL

But is there any evidence that Paul's christology reflects any direct contact with the Jesus-tradition rather than simply the received doctrine of the church?

ABBA

The most important evidence pointing in this direction must be Paul's use of the Aramaic word *Abba* in Gal 4:6 and Rom 8:15. The term is evidently of great significance for Paul, expressing something essential and central to the Christian's Spirit-given relationship to God. It is quite likely that it was used liturgically by the church, and it could be that Paul derived the term from the liturgy, not directly (or necessarily consciously) from Jesus' usage. However, there is, as we suggested, a very strong probability that the unusual usage goes back to Jesus and that it was specifically recalled as coming from Jesus (thus Mark 14:36). The way that Paul speaks in Gal 4:6 of the Spirit *of God's Son* crying *Abba* within us suggests, as we have seen, that he made exactly that connection. It is significant that early Christian prayer (at this point at least) has its roots in Jesus' own form of prayer.[60]

MARANATHA AND JESUS AS LORD

Maranatha is another Aramaism. It is a Christian prayer *to Jesus* and so presumably not something derived from Jesus directly. It is probably a very early and important liturgical formula (hence its appearance in a context such as 1 Cor 16:22), and thus shows that the idea of Jesus as Lord goes back to the earliest days of the church. Although *maranatha* is thus not a word of Jesus in the same way as *Abba,* it is arguable that the expression of expectant longing for the master's return is precisely what Jesus enjoins in his eschatological parables.[61] There is a strong argument for thinking that those parables, with their portrayal of Jesus as a "master/lord," influenced Paul's thinking about Jesus as lord and himself as Jesus' slave (in, e.g., 1 Thessalonians 4–5 and 1 Corinthians 4). But discussion of this will be reserved until chapter 7.

---

60. See further discussion of *Abba* in chapter 8.

61. *Maranatha* could be seen as a christological version of the petition in the Lord's prayer, "Your kingdom come."

We have noticed that Paul's idea of Jesus as divine Lord is most nearly paralleled within the synoptics in the dialogue between Jesus and his opponents about the Messiah as the son of David, where Jesus uses Psalm 110 to make his point. Paul uses the same psalm in 1 Cor 15:20-28 in speaking of Jesus, and the psalm is used in numerous other places in the NT. Dunn refers to it as "a passage much loved and used in earliest Christology."[62] Its pervasiveness in the NT could reflect its original use by Jesus, and it is possible that Paul was influenced by it in 1 Corinthians 15 and more broadly in his theology.[63]

SON OF MAN AND ADAM

The question of the origin of Paul's idea of Jesus as a new Adam has been widely discussed; scholars have explored all sorts of possible backgrounds, notably in Jewish speculative thought.[64] It may be that it was a combination of OT and Jewish ideas on the one hand and of Paul's own experience of the risen Jesus and his convictions about Jesus as the eschatological savior on the other that gave rise to Paul's Adam christology.

However, it is not impossible that Paul was also influenced by Jesus' "Son of man" teaching. It is intriguing that "Son of man" language, though so significant in the Gospels, is hardly used at all outside the Gospels. The probability is that it was a usage of Jesus himself and that his followers found the deliberately ambiguous "the human being" an inadequate way of referring to the one who in their view had been quite unambiguously raised from the dead.[65] However, it is hard to believe that the early Christians would not have reflected on the significance of this "human being" terminology, if it was anything as important as the Gospels suggest.[66]

The author of Hebrews does use "son of man" language of Jesus when applying Ps 8:4-6 to Jesus (Heb 2:5-8):

62. *Romans*, 503, referring to texts including Acts 2:34, 35; Eph 1:20; Col 3:1; Heb 1:3, 13; 8:1; 10:12; 12:2; and 1 Pet 3:22.

63. See further below on the possible influence of Jesus-tradition on 1 Cor 15:20-28. Bruce, *Paul and Jesus*, 89, sees in the Gospel dialogue about the Messiah a possible clue as to how Paul came to use God-language for Jesus.

64. E.g., Philo, *Leg. All* I.31, 53-65.

65. Also the semitic "son of" idiom was probably less accessible in Greek-speaking circles than in the earliest Aramaic-speaking churches.

66. Even if one were to be very skeptical about Jesus himself, the Gospels make it clear that the title was associated with him and his ministry by the early church.

What is man that you are mindful of him,
or the son of man, that you care for him?
You made him for a little while lower than the angels;
you have crowned him with glory and honor,
subjecting all things under his feet.*[67]

This quotation of Psalm 8 is interesting not only because of its application of "son of man" to Jesus, but also because the phrase that is translated "son of man" in Psalm 8 is *ben adam* and because the language of the psalm is in other ways unmistakably reminiscent of Gen 1:28, where God tells the first created human beings to "have dominion" over the earth. So the author of Hebrews here identifies Jesus as the Adam-like man or son of man, the one to whom God is subjecting all things.

Paul uses the same psalm on at least two occasions — in Phil 3:21 when he speaks of Jesus transforming our humble bodies to be like his glorious body "by the power that enables him to make all things subject to himself," and then also in 1 Cor 15:27, where he speaks of all things finally being subjected to Jesus.[68] In neither passage is the verse from Psalm 8 about "man . . . or the son of man" actually quoted, but it is presupposed. We thus have evidence that Paul identified Jesus with "the son of man" of Psalm 8. Furthermore, in both Pauline passages the thought of Jesus as the new Adam is probably in Paul's mind: Phil 3:21 echoes the Christ-hymn of chapter 2, and 1 Cor 15:27 follows closely Paul's discussion of Christ as the new Adam.

This does not prove that the "Son of man" tradition attested in the Gospels has influenced Paul (or others in the early church, like the author of Hebrews). James Dunn comments, "There is no indication (apart from Acts 7.5b) that a Son of Man christology flourished beyond the limits of the tradition of Jesus' sayings and no evidence for an interaction between Son of Man imagery and the Adam christology we have traced out."[69]

But the following considerations taken together suggest that Dunn is unnecessarily dismissive of any influence of the "Son of man" tradition on Paul:

67. This translation carries the singular "man" and "son of man" of the NRSV's marginal rendering in Heb 2:6 through into vv. 7-8a.

68. See also Eph 1:22.

69. *Christology,* 312; cf. 103-13. Dunn thinks that Psalm 8 came into the christology of the early church by connection with Psalm 110 (where the LORD promises "my Lord" to put all his enemies under his feet).

- the importance of the phrase "son of man" (i.e. "man" or "human being") in the Jesus-tradition,
- the importance of the Adam concept in Paul,
- the evidence that Paul and others in the early church did use and reflect on "the man . . . son of man" in Psalm 8, and
- the fact that both "the son of man" (at least if it is rightly interpreted in the light of Daniel 7) and Paul's second Adam are representative figures.[70]

Given these four points, it seems more likely than not that there is a connection between Jesus and Paul at this point.[71]

Of course, we have argued that the most important background to Jesus' Son of man teaching was probably Daniel 7, where "the one like a son of man" represents "the saints of God." The thought is of Jesus as the new Israel rather than of a new Adam. But this in no way eliminates the possibility of a connection with Paul's Adam christology, for these reasons:

- Although the primary background to Jesus' "Son of man" language may have been Daniel 7, the use of the expression in other parts of the OT (including Psalm 8) may have contributed to Jesus' understanding of the term.
- Paul could have developed Jesus' "Son of man" concept in a direction not necessarily suggested by Jesus.
- It has been plausibly argued that the righteous remnant of Israel represented by the human figure in Daniel 7 is portrayed there as the true Adam, the one who is given dominion over the "beasts." Morna Hooker comments: "There is a very close connection between the figures of Adam and the Son of man."[72] The Israel and Adam themes were, in this view, intertwined well before Paul.
- Paul does not use Daniel 7 directly of Jesus, but his question in 1 Cor

70. So Hooker, *Son of Man*, 198.

71. Stuhlmacher, "Jesustradition," 250, suggests specific connections between Rom 8:34 and Matt 10:32/Luke 12:8 and between Rom 5:15, 19 and Mark 10:45 (note the references to the "many"). Elsewhere, in *Reconciliation*, 18, Stuhlmacher argues that 1 Tim 2:5, 6 is a Hellenized version of Mark 10:45; it is post-Pauline in his view, but his view is interesting since the Timothy text on this view substitutes "the man" for "the Son of man." On Mark 10:45 see the discussion in chapter 6 below.

72. *Son of Man*, 72; see more generally 1-72; also Wright, *Climax*, 23; Moule, *Christology*, 14, 24-26, connecting Psalm 8 and Daniel 7 and noting the importance of Psalm 80.

6:2, "Do you not know that the saints will judge the world?" is probably an allusion to Daniel 7. It thus shows that Paul has reflected on the passage.[73]

- It is possible that in Phil 2:7, where Paul speaks of Jesus being found in form "as a man,"* he is echoing Dan 7:13's "like a son of man," combining Adamic and Danielic ideas.[74]

These considerations, some of more weight than others, combine to make a connection between Jesus' Son of man language and Paul's Adam christology a much stronger possibility than is sometimes recognized.

"I THANK YOU, FATHER . . ."

An interesting possibility is that in his discussion of wisdom and foolishness in 1 Corinthians 1–4 Paul may be echoing the important "Q" verses of Matt 11:25-27/Luke 10:21, 22,[75] where Jesus says:

> I thank you, Father, Lord of heaven and earth, that you have hidden these things from wise and understanding people and revealed them to infants. Yes, Father, for such was well-pleasing in your sight. All things were delivered to me by my Father, and no one knows the Son except the Father, nor does anyone know the Father except the Son and any to whom the Son wishes to reveal him.*

73. See Fee, *1 Corinthians*, 233, on the importance in Judaism of the idea of the saints ruling. 1 Cor 6:2 may itself be related to certain Jesus-traditions, e.g., Matt 19:28/Luke 22:28-30; Luke 12:32 (see Stuhlmacher, *Biblische Theologie*, I, 301). Paul's fondness for referring to the Christians of different churches as "saints" (= "holy ones") could reflect this same Danielic and Jewish tradition.

74. The respective phrases are *hōs anthrōpos* (Phil 2:7) and *hōs huios anthrōpou* (Dan 7:13 LXX). The language of "likeness" in Phil 2:6, 7 may also reflect the Danielic background and perhaps also Ezek 1:26. See Bruce, *Paul and Jesus*, 81, and Stanton, *Jesus of Nazareth*, 104. O'Brien, *Philippians*, 227, like others, argues that an allusion to Daniel's heavenly son of man is out of place in a passage emphasizing Jesus' real humanity and cannot see why the Aramaic "like a son of man" should be rendered "like a man" by Paul. However, "like a man" is an entirely appropriate Greek translation (cf. Marshall, *Christology*, 78 on Paul's "the man" as "the correct equivalent of 'Son of man'"), and it is quite possible that Paul and others might have regarded "son of man/human being" language as having connotations both of glory and of real humanity.

75. For the fullest discussion of this possibility see Fjärstedt, *Synoptic Tradition*, 138-50. Also Richardson, "Thunderbolt."

In 1 Corinthians 1–4 Paul is responding to divisions in the Corinthian church: "Each of you says, 'I belong to Paul,' or 'I belong to Apollos,' or 'I belong to Cephas,' or 'I belong to Christ'" (1:12). He does so by discussing the question of human and spiritual "wisdom." It seems clear that some in Corinth, perhaps the followers of the eloquent Alexandrian Apollos,[76] were making great claims to wisdom. Paul in response emphasizes the foolishness of the cross.

There are a number of arguments for a link between Paul's response and the "I thank you, Father . . ." group of sayings in Matthew 11/Luke 10.[77]

Verbal/Formal Parallels

First, there are a considerable number of verbal and conceptual parallels between the two passages:

Matthew 11/Luke 10	1 Corinthians
you have hidden (11:25/10:21) *(ap)ekrypsas*	hidden (2:7) *apokekrymmenēn*
the wise (11:25/10:21) *sophōn*	the wisdom of the wise (1:19) *tēn sophian tōn sophōn*
the discerning (11:25/10:21) *synetōn*	the discernment of the discerning (1:19) *tēn synesin tōn synetōn*
[you] have revealed (11:25/10:21) *apekalypsas*	God has revealed (2:10) *apekalypsen ho theos*
to infants (11:25/10:21) *nēpiois*	(to) the mature (2:6), (to) infants (3:1) *tois teleiois, nēpiois*
was well-pleasing* (11:26/10:21) *eudokia egeneto*	God was pleased* (1:21) *eudokēsen*

---

76. The description of Apollos in Acts 18:24, 25 as "an eloquent man, well-versed in the scriptures" and as (literally) "boiling in spirit"* is interesting in the context of the Corinthians' interest in wisdom and their charismatic zeal.

77. See Richardson, "Thunderbolt," 96.

no one knows the Father except the
Son (11:27/cf. 10:22)
oudeis (epi)ginōskei ton patera
ei mē ho huios

the world did not know God (1:21)
ouk egnō ho kosmos . . . ton theon
no one knows the things of God
except the Spirit of God* (2:11)
ta tou theou oudeis egnōken ei mē to
pneuma tou theou

The significance of these parallels taken by themselves should not be exaggerated. They are spread out over several chapters of 1 Corinthians and they are not all particularly close or obviously significant. For example, the "no one knows" sayings are in some ways quite different,[78] and Paul's reference to "the discerning" in 1:19 is part of a quotation from the OT (Isa 29:14). It is arguable that verbal parallels are only to be expected in Christian texts with a common subject matter (in this case "wisdom"), and that there is no necessary connection.

Conceptual Parallels

But as well as the verbal parallels there are conceptual parallels. It has been pointed out that although Paul associates "wisdom" with Greeks (1 Cor 1:22) his discussion of wisdom in 1 Corinthians 1–4 seems to reflect a Jewish background, and not primarily a Greek philosophical background. He speaks of the "wisdom of this age," "the rulers of this age," and "the kingdom of God" (1:20; 2:6, 8; 3:18; 4:20). We are in the thought world of synoptic sayings such as the "I thank you, Father" sayings. It has been suggested by a number of scholars that we are in the thought world of the "Q" tradition.[79]

---

78. Note also that the "infants" get a good deal in the synoptic saying, but a poor press in 1 Cor 3:1! On the differences see also Richardson, "Thunderbolt," 97.

79. On the Corinthians and Q, see J. M. Robinson, "Kerygma," and especially Richardson, "Thunderbolt." Richardson argues that some of the Corinthians favored Apollos rather than Paul and that they used the "Q" tradition with its emphasis on (among other things) John the Baptist and "wisdom" — rather than on the cross. Paul responds, using the "Q" thunderbolt tradition (along with related OT texts) to speak of God "destroying" (*apolō* in Greek). There may well be truth in the view that the Corinthian enthusiasm for "wisdom," the Spirit, and perhaps baptism was somehow associated with Apollos and that the Corinthians drew on Jesus-traditions to justify their position, including those that spoke of the disciples having special revelation and a special position in God's purpose. But it is not necessary to postulate the Corinthians' knowledge of the hypothetical "Q" source. (If Matt 13:11/Mark 4:11/Luke 8:10 was one

More specifically Paul's emphasis in 1 Corinthians 1 and 2 on God's choice of the weak and foolish rather than the strong and powerful and on the gospel being hidden from the wise and only knowable by divine revelation is very similar to the emphasis of the "I thank you, Father" sayings.

Other Evidence about the Corinthians

In chapter 2 we saw that there is evidence to suggest that the Corinthians made use of the Jesus-tradition in boasting about their spiritual maturity and knowledge.[80] Some of the evidence is in fact in 1 Corinthians 1–4. Thus the Corinthians may have picked on Jesus' teaching about the presence of the kingdom — note the reference to the "kingdom" in 4:20 — to justify their claim to be spiritually rich and spiritual kings (4:8). They may also have been familiar with the saying in Matt 13:11/Mark 4:11/Luke 8:10 about the disciples being given "knowledge of the mysteries of the kingdom of God,"* claiming that same knowledge for themselves. There is evidence of that in 1 Cor 13:2, as we have seen, but also in Paul's two references in 1 Corinthians 2 to "the mystery of God" (v. 1, cf. v. 7). In language similar to the synoptic saying Paul speaks of the mystery as one that the world does not "know"* (v. 8) and that the Spirit reveals, "so that we know the things given to us by God" (v. 12).[81] Also in 1 Cor 4:1 Paul speaks of himself and Apollos as "stewards of God's mysteries."[82]

Given this evidence, uncertain though it is, it seems very possible that the Corinthians, their mentors, or both picked up on the gospel traditions about the disciples being given divine knowledge and insight.[83] They related

---

of the traditions being appealed to (see chap. 2 above), this is Markan tradition, not "Q.")

80. We will note other possible links between 1 Corinthians 1–4 and the Jesus-tradition in subsequent chapters. For example, see chapter 5 on Jesus as the foundation (1 Cor 3:11), chapter 7 on the stewards who must give account (4:1-5), and chapter 8 on the Jews demanding signs (1:22).

81. Paul uses the verb *ginōskō*, which is used in the synoptic saying, in 2:8 and elsewhere in the passage, but *oida* in v. 12.

82. Compare also Eph 1:10 with its various linguistic similarities to 1 Corinthians 1–4 (wisdom, knowledge, mystery, good pleasure, all things in Christ, steward) and Eph 3:2-4 (stewardship, revelation, knowledge, mystery of Christ, understanding, etc.).

83. Other similar Jesus-traditions have been detected in 1 Corinthians 1–4. Thus the "Q" saying of Matt 13:16, 17/Luke 10:23-24 about the disciples seeing and hearing what previous saints have longed to see is thematically rather similar to 1 Cor 2:9, "What

the teaching to their own charismatic experiences and were proud of their spiritual powers and insight.[84] Paul agrees that it is the Spirit who gives wisdom, but he emphasizes the weakness of those chosen and especially the cross as the epitome of foolishness.[85]

The Christological Saying (Matthew 11:27/Luke 10:22)

Against the view that Paul is influenced in 1 Corinthians 1–4 by the "Q" sayings of Matt 11:25-27/Luke 10:21, 22 might be Paul's failure to pick up

---

no eye has seen, nor ear heard . . . what God has prepared for those who love him." In Luke this saying follows immediately the "I thank you, Father . . ." tradition and so might have been connected with it in the form of tradition known to Paul. The difficulty with this identification is that the overlapping terminology is commonplace — hearing, seeing, eyes — and in 1 Cor 2:9 is almost all found in the OT quotation. But see Richardson, "Thunderbolt," 96.

1 Cor 2:7 has been connected with Matt 13:35, 1 Cor 4:5 with Mark 4:22, and 1 Cor 4:8 with Gospel of Thomas 2 (so Koester, *Ancient Christian Gospels*, 55-62).

84. It is notoriously difficult to be sure what the Corinthians' views about "wisdom" were and where they got them from. It has been suggested that there were Hellenistic "gnostic" influences on the Corinthians. But although it may well be that an emphasis on "wisdom" and "knowledge" was especially attractive in a Greek environment (1 Cor 1:22), it seems quite likely that it was the Corinthians' charismatic experience that was most influential, hence the references to "wisdom" and "knowledge" in the context of discussion of the gifts of the Spirit (1:5-7; 12:8; 13:1, 2; 14:2, 26; note also the use of the word "spiritual" in 2:13, 15; 3:1). Their charismatic experience included particularly speaking in tongues and other claimed revelatory experiences, as well as miracles (see 1 Corinthians 12–14). They probably saw their conversion and baptism as their initiation into the spiritual mysteries (compare the pattern of Christian experience implied or described in Acts, e.g., 19:6; also Gal 3:2). The Jesus-traditions that speak of divine revelation to the disciples were naturally appealing in this context, and the Corinthians interpreted their experience in terms of knowledge of the mysteries — note how Paul himself can speak of tongues as "speaking mysteries in the Spirit" in 14:2 — and of wisdom.

If this is a correct explanation of the situation, then there is not a theological gulf fixed between Paul and the Corinthians: He affirmed their spiritual experience and recognized the Jesus-traditions to which they appealed, but he found their emphasis unbalanced (not least in its triumphalism and its failure to see the centrality of the cross). They in turn found him inferior to other "apostles," including perhaps Apollos, who were in their view more spiritually powerful and experienced (cf. 2 Cor 12:1-13).

85. If they used the "I thank you, Father" saying in relation to their claimed spiritual insight, Paul brings out the emphasis on revelation to the weak and foolish.

the important "sonship" theme in Matt 11:27/Luke 10:22. Paul speaks almost all the time of "Christ" and only once of "the Son" (in 1:9). This may seem odd if Paul has been influenced by the striking "Q" saying.

One possibility is that he knew the saying about the revelation to the foolish and to infants, but not the weighty christological affirmation that follows it in "Q." This is theoretically possible[86] but not a necessary conclusion.

In the first place, Paul's failure to draw on the christological saying with its emphasis on Jesus' sonship is perfectly well explained given the context of 1 Corinthians 1–4. The point at issue is the question of wisdom, not the question of Jesus' identity; so the relevant saying is the one about revelation being given to the disciples, not the one about Jesus as the Son of the Father.[87]

Secondly, there is, in fact, evidence that may point to Paul's familiarity with the christological saying. We have already noted 1 Cor 1:21, where Paul says that "the world *did not know God*"; the phrase is reminiscent of the synoptic "*no one knows* the Father."[88] There is also 2:11: "*No one knows the things of God except* the Spirit . . . ," the form of which is similiar to that of the "Q" saying, and although Paul has "except the Spirit" rather than

---

86. Scholars have had many more doubts about the authenticity of the christological saying than about the preceding saying about revelation to infants.

87. It is true that Paul refers to Jesus as "Son" very little in this passage, or indeed in 1 Corinthians as a whole. It is just possible that this is some sort of reflection on the Corinthian context. It has, e.g., been suggested that Paul prefers a "Christ" christology to a "Son" christology in 1 Corinthians because the latter was associated with the charismatic Corinthian Christianity that he is reacting against (so Richardson, "Thunderbolt," 109). But the opposite might equally be possible: Perhaps the Corinthians emphasized a "Christ" christology and Paul reflects this emphasis (like the emphasis on the Spirit).

However, the absence of an emphasis on Jesus as "Son" is probably not significant for either of these reasons. In fact "Son" is used of Jesus only seventeen times in the Pauline corpus (including one each in Ephesians and Colossians), and eight of those occurrences are in just three chapters (Romans 1 and 8 and Galatians 4); elsewhere the usage is very infrequent. Paul speaks of Jesus as "Son" mainly where he is referring to Jesus in relationship to God the Father, e.g., as "sent" by the Father (Rom 8:3; Gal 4:4). Paul uses "sonship" language relatively infrequently in his letters, preferring "Christ" and "Lord" as designations of Jesus. So 1 Corinthians is hardly out of line, having only two references to Jesus as divine Son (1:9 and 15:28).

88. The phrase occurs in a context where there are several other verbal links with the "Q" sayings we are considering, i.e., "wise," "discerning," and "God was pleased"* (1:19, 21).

"except the Son and anyone to whom the Son chooses to reveal him," the difference is not as great as it may appear, given the very close association of Jesus and the Spirit in Paul's thought.

Outside 1 Corinthians 1–4 the most interesting parallel to the "Q" saying is in 1 Cor 15:24-28. Paul speaks in this passage (unusually) of *"the Son"* and of *"the God and Father"**; he describes the Son as *handing over* the kingdom to the Father at the end, the Father having previously subjected *"all things"* to the Son ("all things" occurs several times in the passage). There are striking parallels between this passage and the "Q" saying: *"All things* have been *handed over* to me by my *Father;* . . . and no one knows the *Father,* except *the Son.* . . ."[89] The Pauline passage has a different focus — defeat of God's enemies at the end — from the synoptic verse, with its emphasis on revelation, but the agreement in the idea of "all things" having been given by "the Father" to "the Son" may well be significant.[90]

There are other possible links between 1 Cor 15:24-28 and the Jesus-tradition: 1 Cor 15:24 contains one of Paul's rare references to the kingdom (in association with the idea of Jesus putting down evil powers). There are also allusions to Psalm 8, the psalm about the Adamic "son of man" having all things put in subjection under his feet (see above on "Son of man"), and to Psalm 110, the psalm (used by Jesus according to the synoptics; see above) in which God speaks to "my lord," promising to put all his enemies under his feet.[91]

The variety of points of contact between the Pauline passage and the

89. Goulder, *Evangelists' Calendar,* 210, notes the links between the "Q" saying and 1 Cor 15:24-28, but offers some rather unpersuasive arguments (use of the LXX in Matthew and Paul and supposedly Matthean vocabulary in Matt 11:25-27) to show that Matthew is dependent on Paul, not Paul on the "Q" saying.

90. In 1 Cor 3:21-23 Paul's comments that "all things are yours . . . and you belong to Christ, and Christ belongs to God." The idea of "all things" belonging to believers and the chain of relationship from Father to Son to believer might also be related to the "Q" saying, even though the emphasis in the gospel saying is on revelation rather than more broadly on spiritual blessings. (For a similar chain see Matt 10:40; 1 Cor 11:3.) Other interesting parallels to the "Q" saying include Gal 1:15, 16, where Paul speaks of God being *"pleased* to *reveal* his *Son"* (see further discussion in chapter 4 below), and perhaps 1 Cor 13:12, where the idea of the Christian's knowledge of God has been compared to that in Matt 11:27 (see Davies and Allison, *Matthew,* II, 284-85).

91. The importance of these psalms in the NT in general suggests that they were widely used in the church, not just by Paul. It could be that Paul reflects this church tradition and that he was not directly influenced by the Jesus-traditions in question. On the other hand, some of the evidence examined (e.g., in connection with the "I thank you, Father" saying) points to the influence of particular sayings of Jesus on Paul.

synoptic christology of Jesus suggests not that Paul is quoting from the Jesus-tradition but that his thought may well have been decisively influenced by that tradition, including by the "I thank you, Father" sayings.[92]

THE PARABLE OF THE VINEYARD TENANTS

If there is a good possibility that Paul knew the Q "Son" saying in Matthew 11:27/Luke 10:22, it is also possible that Jesus' parable of the vineyard (Matt 21:33-44/Mark 12:1-12/Luke 20:9-19), with its description of the vineyard owner sending his son to get the fruits of the vineyard, lies behind the phraseology used in Gal 4:4, "When the fullness of time had come, *God sent his Son* . . . in order to redeem those who were under the law . . . ," and Rom 8:3, "*God . . . sending his own Son* in the likeness of sinful flesh, and to deal with sin, he condemned sin in the flesh, so that the just requirement of the law might be fulfilled in us. . . ."[93]

The parable as it was probably interpreted by the Evangelists portrays

- Jesus as the Son and heir,
- sent as God's last word after God's servants the prophets had been sent,
- to God's tenant-farmers Israel,
- to receive the "fruits" of their obedience,
- being rejected and killed by the tenants in their attempt to seize the inheritance,
- with the result that the vineyard is taken from the original Jewish "tenants" and given to others who will produce the fruits.

At almost every point this picture of Jesus' mission may be said to parallel Paul's understanding. In both the Galatians and the Romans passages, Paul refers to God "sending" "his Son" and in both contexts, especially in Galatians 4, the themes of slavery/slaves and of sonship and inheritance are

92. Another interesting christological parallel is between 1 Cor 8:6, "for us there is one God, the Father, . . . and one Lord, Jesus Christ," and Matt 23:9, 10, "you have one Father — the one in heaven . . . you have one instructor, the Christ." See J. P. Brown, "Synoptic Parallels," 43.

93. For this view see Dunn, *Christology in the Making*, 39-45, referring to Cerfaux, *Christ in the Theology of St. Paul*, 447; Fuller, "The Conception/Birth of Jesus," 43. More recently see Ninan, *Jesus*, 197-209.

important. Gal 4:4 explicitly refers to the eschatological nature of Jesus' coming ("in the fullness of time"), and in Rom 8:3 the purpose of Jesus' coming is said to be to produce "the just requirement of the law," which was impossible under the old regime of the law (cf. fruitbearing in 7:4). In Rom 8:3 implicitly, and often explicitly elsewhere, Paul identifies the death of Jesus as decisively important. Elsewhere he explicitly associates Jesus' coming with judgment on the Jews and with the coming of the Gentiles into Israel's inheritance (e.g., Romans 9–11).

The parallels are not exact, nor are they such as to prove that Paul is echoing the parable of Jesus in the verses in question; other explanations of the idea of "the Son" being "sent" have been proposed.[94] However, there is a good case to be made for the authenticity of the parable, and there is at least a possibility of a connection between the Jesus-tradition and Paul at this point.[95]

CONCLUSION ON THE CONNECTIONS

Paul's use of *Abba* is the one unambiguous piece of evidence linking Pauline christology and the teaching of Jesus. The use of the term was derived from Jesus, and there is evidence that Paul knew that it was.

It is less certain that Paul knew and was influenced by the "Q" "I thank you, Father" group of sayings, but there are sufficient verbal and thematic parallels between the "Q" sayings and various Pauline passages, most notably in 1 Corinthians 1–4, to make it likely that Paul was familiar with the sayings, and indeed that the Corinthians emphasized the teaching of Jesus about the revelation of divine wisdom and mysteries. If this is right, then it is another example of Jesus-tradition being a focus of debate within the church.

Despite the doubts of some scholars, it is at least possible that Paul was influenced by Jesus' Son of man teaching and that it is reflected in his portrayal of Jesus as a new Adam. He may have known Jesus' parable of the vineyard with its portrayal of the owner of the vineyard "sending his son." There may well be a connection between Paul's emphasis on Jesus as Lord and certain gospel traditions, though some of these remain to be examined in a later chapter.

94. Scholars have compared the idea of God sending out his wisdom (e.g., Wis 9:10), as well as the idea of the sending of a second Moses. See the discussion in Scott, *Adoption*, 165-71.

95. On the authenticity of the parable see p. 114 n. 30 above.

4

WHY THE CRUCIFIXION?

I. Comparing Jesus and Paul

JESUS AND HIS DEATH

"May I never boast of anything except the cross of our Lord Jesus Christ . . ." (Gal 6:14). "We proclaim Christ crucified, a stumbling block to Jews and foolishness to Greeks"* (1 Cor 1:23). For Paul the cross of Jesus was absolutely central — central in his own thinking and preaching, but also, and more importantly, in God's world-saving work as Paul understood it.[1]

To what extent, if at all, did Jesus share Paul's view of Jesus' death? It is understandable that Paul and other followers of Jesus should have needed to explain Jesus' death — after the event. It was, indeed, "a stumbling block to Jews," and no doubt had been such to Paul before his conversion; it was "foolishness to Greeks," and the early Christians had to make sense of it. But what of Jesus himself?

---

1. Although it was central, we should not assume from what Paul says in letters like 1 Corinthians or Galatians that the cross was all of Paul's theology. He stresses the cross in Galatians and Romans in face of a Judaizing theology that did not (in Paul's view) take the cross seriously; he stresses it in 1 Corinthians to counter the Corinthian boasting. But in other letters, discussing different issues (e.g., 1 Thessalonians), it is less central.

Did Jesus Expect His Own Death?

The Gospels suggest that Jesus was convinced that his destiny was to die and that he made that conviction clear to his disciples, especially in the latter part of his ministry: "Jesus began to show his disciples that he must . . . be killed" (Matt 16:21/Mark 8:31/Luke 9:22). It is not surprising that the Evangelists portray Jesus foreseeing his death in this way, but did he actually expect it or have they attributed their own convictions anachronistically to him? Many scholars suspect that there has been a significant rewriting of the story of Jesus in the light of experience and that when Jesus predicts his sufferings in some detail (e.g., Matt 20:17-19/Mark 10:32-34/Luke 18:31-34), this reflects the Evangelists' knowledge looking back, not the knowledge of the historical Jesus looking forward.[2]

Against this it may be argued that there is every probability that Jesus would have anticipated his own death. He knew John the Baptist and what had happened to him; he knew the dangers of leading popular religious movements in Roman-occupied Palestine; he could have foreseen his death, even without any supernatural insight.

Still, it is not inevitable that someone who proclaimed and believed in the coming-in of God's kingdom should have expected himself to die before the arrival of that kingdom. Jesus could have gone up to Jerusalem in the way the Gospels describe, aware of some of the risks, but hoping to engineer a coup d'état against the authorities and to establish a new order, or more likely hoping for a supernatural inauguration of God's kingdom and for his own vindication. The story of Jesus' agony in the garden of Gethsemane (Matt 26:36-46/Mark 14:32-42/Luke 22:39-46) has been understood in that way, that is, as a story of Jesus praying urgently for the divine intervention he had been looking for. Jesus' cry on the cross, "My God, my God, why have you forsaken me?" (Matt 27:46/Mark 15:34), has also been understood as a cry of despair on the part of Jesus because of the kingdom's failure to appear.[3]

This sort of reading of the gospel evidence cannot be disproved, but it uses the evidence of the Gospels very selectively, discounting a good number of passages where Jesus speaks directly or indirectly of his coming death (including parables such as that of the vineyard and the story of the

---

2. On the so-called "passion predictions" and more generally on the question of Jesus' attitude to his coming death see especially Bayer, *Jesus' Predictions*. He finds the arguments against the authenticity of the passion predictions unconvincing.

3. For this sort of view see Barrett, *Jesus and the Gospel Tradition*, 46-49.

last supper).[4] It also interprets other material (like the Gethsemane story) in a way that is at odds with the intention of the authors who preserved it for us. Such a revisionist reading can only be justified if there are very good reasons for rejecting a more inclusive and respectful use of the evidence. And in fact the Gospel account makes remarkably good sense.

Why Jesus Was Executed

It may be worth prefacing remarks about Jesus' view of his death with the observation that the Gospels' account of the motivation of those who had Jesus executed makes sense. Pontius Pilate the Roman governor had Jesus crucified as a messianic pretender — as "King of the Jews" (Matt 27:37/Mark 15:26). Whether or not Pilate considered Jesus a real political threat, there was nothing so sensitive to someone in his position as a threat of subversion against the authorities. Passover time was always dangerous from a Roman point of view because of the numbers of people in Jerusalem and because of the nationalistic associations of the feast. The description of Barabbas as involved in "insurrection" along with, quite probably, the reference to the two "robbers/revolutionaries" executed with Jesus (Luke 23:19; Matt 27:38/Mark 15:27), is evidence that this Passover was especially unsettled. Christians may assume that Jesus was purely a religious figure, not a political threat, but in first-century Palestine there was no sharp differentiation between politics and religion, and popular religious leaders like John the Baptist and Jesus were potentially, if not actually, very danger-ous, not least if they proclaimed a new "kingdom" and led their excited followers into Jerusalem in procession.

The Gospels, of course, do not lay the blame for Jesus' execution on Pilate so much as on the Jews who handed Jesus over to Pilate. This blaming of the Jews is not to be explained as simply reflecting Christian hostility toward Jews rather than historical fact. Judaism was a broad church con-taining various theological strands and parties, and little love was lost

---

4. As well as the direct "passion predictions" in the Gospels, there are the more enigmatic sayings of Jesus about his "baptism" and "cup" (Matt 20:22/Mark 10:38; Luke 12:50). In addition to the parable of the vineyard, which speaks of the killing of the son (Matt 21:33-46/Mark 12:1-12/Luke 20:9-19), there are also parables that speak of a master going away and then returning, which suggest that Jesus anticipated "going away" before the coming of the kingdom (on these see chapter 8 below). On the last supper see further in this chapter.

between the different Jewish groups. Groups such as the Essenes made exclusive claims for themselves and were highly critical of other Jewish groups such as the Pharisees. The gospel picture of Jesus coming into sharp conflict with the Pharisees (not least because of his "liberal" views of the sabbath and purity laws) is entirely plausible.[5] To the Jewish hierarchy Jesus was a threat just because he was a popular religious leader who could upset the Romans and the social status quo (so John 11:45-53) and because of the radical kingdom message that he proclaimed. The Jewish authorities would not cheerfully tolerate a leader who made threatening statements about the temple (a very sensitive point in Jerusalem) and who criticized the authorities for their corruption.[6] If he also made the sort of claims for himself suggested by the Gospels, this, too, would have represented an unavoidable challenge to the leadership of others.

The gospel account of the Jewish leaders making common cause with Pilate in seeking to get rid of Jesus is entirely plausible. In discussing the matter with Pilate, the Jews focused on the idea of Jesus as a claimed Messiah. This was a strong card to play with the governor, who was in any case vulnerable to pressure, having mismanaged affairs in the province (particularly Jewish religious affairs) several times already.[7] Whatever doubts Pilate may have had, it was in his interest to go along with the Jewish authorities. Pilate's vulnerability in this sort of situation is interestingly illustrated by Josephus's account of how Pilate eventually lost his job as governor of Judea and Samaria, only a few years after the crucifixion: Faced with another popular religious rising, not in Jerusalem this time but in Samaria, he again acted to put it down, sending in his troops; their brutality was such that protests went to Pilate's superiors, and he was recalled.[8]

---

5. There has been much scholarly debate over the gospel portrayal of the Pharisees, with some such as E. P. Sanders tending to minimize their importance and their likely antagonism to Jesus (see his *Jesus and Judaism,* e.g., 188, 43-58), and others allowing much more credence to the gospel accounts of conflict (e.g., Borg, *Conflict, Holiness and Politics,* 139-43). See generally on the Pharisees Wright, *NT and the People of God,* 181-203. Note also Neusner, "Mr Sanders' Pharisees," on the exclusivism of the Pharisees.

6. Matera, "Trial of Jesus," argues that Jesus was probably not a threat while he was in Galilee, but that his entry into Jerusalem and his "cleansing" of the temple would have been perceived very differently.

7. See chapter 2 above. John's Gospel rather plausibly has the Jews say to Pilate: "If you release this man, you are no friend of the emperor" (19:12).

8. So Josephus, *Ant.* XVIII.87-89. On Pilate and the broad credibility of the Gospels' portrayal see McGing, "Pontius Pilate."

Jesus' View

But if the motivation of Pilate and the Jewish authorities as portrayed by the Gospels makes sense, what of Jesus' own view?

John the Baptist

We have suggested that the association of John the Baptist and Jesus may well have been closer than appears on the surface. If it was, then what happened to John the Baptist is likely to have been of considerable importance to Jesus. The Gospels imply that it was. The synoptics all agree that Jesus' Galilean ministry began "when Jesus heard that John had been arrested" (Matt 4:12/Mark 1:14). Although no explanation is given of this, the implication may well be that John's imprisonment was an important catalyst that led Jesus into the Galilean ministry.[9] The Gospels suggest — interestingly — that Jesus was in touch with John in prison (Matt 11:2, 3/Luke 7:18, 19), and Matthew claims that when John was executed, word was brought to Jesus, who then withdrew into the desert (Matt 14:12, 13). Whether or not Matthew's account is historical at this point, it is obvious that Jesus heard of John's death and inevitable that he reflected on it.

Both Matthew and Mark affirm, in fact, that he did reflect on it, and they claim that he spoke of his own coming sufferings in that connection (Matt 17:10-13/Mark 9:11-13). Such a train of thought makes good sense, not just pragmatically in that Jesus must have realized that John's fate could in due course be his, but also theologically. Jesus would have needed to make sense of John's death within the framework of his own announcement of the kingdom (as the Gospels suggest that he also had to make sense of John's imprisonment), and it is not unlikely that he reflected on his own future in that connection.

The context of the kingdom

If Jesus reflected on John's death and also on his own possible death in the context of his kingdom teaching, two things are likely: First, Jesus probably saw such suffering as fulfillment of the OT (since the "kingdom" was all to do with such fulfillment). Second, he probably saw it as somehow part of the process by which the kingdom was coming.

9. Murphy-O'Connor, "John the Baptist," suggests that Jesus was a follower of John who on John's death took up the cause on Herod's own territory in Galilee.

This is precisely what the Gospels suggest: Jesus' death is seen as necessary for the fulfillment of Scripture and is described in scriptural terms (e.g., Mark 9:12, 13; so also John's death). This could be simply the church's perspective as it looks back, but it is entirely plausible that someone who proclaimed the day of fulfillment and who had experienced the Baptist's sufferings would have looked to the various OT traditions that speak of the righteous suffering, whether the Psalms, or Zechariah with its description of the smitten shepherd, or Isaiah with its famous description of the suffering servant of Yahweh taking on himself the judgment of the people. All these OT traditions are quoted by Jesus in the Gospel narratives (e.g., Zech 13:7 in Matt 26:31/Mark 14:27; Ps 22:1 in Matt 27:46/Mark 15:34; Isa 53:12 in Luke 22:37). Redemptive suffering is an important OT and Jewish concept. For example, the Maccabean martyrs were seen as experiencing God's judgment for Israel's sins.[10]

Jesus' death is also understood as somehow bringing the kingdom. Jesus announced the breaking into history of God's rule, and his death is seen as helping to bring to completion what had begun in his ministry. This is the implication of his remarks at the last supper about not eating or drinking again until the kingdom of God (Matt. 26:29/Mark 14:25/Luke 22:18 and most explicitly Luke 22:15, 16: "I have eagerly desired to eat this Passover with you before I suffer; for I tell you, I will not eat it until it is fulfilled in the kingdom of God"). It may well also be implied by the somewhat mysterious sayings of Jesus about having a baptism to be baptized with (Mark 10:38; Luke 12:50): Jesus must go through the baptism of death before he and others experience the coming kingdom.[11]

Our observations about redemptive suffering make sense here: In proclaiming the coming kingdom Jesus also announced the forgiveness of sins. But on what basis could he apparently bypass the usual Jewish procedures for atonement of sins, namely sacrifice, and simply on his own pronounce people forgiven and fit for the kingdom? He was asked that very question by his critics (Matt 9:2, 3/Mark 2:5, 6/Luke 5:20, 21). The Gospels suggest, plausibly, that Jesus came to see his death as the answer to that question, that is as redemptive suffering for the sins of the people, making possible the kingdom of forgiveness and reconciliation.[12] As we have seen,

10. E.g., 2 Maccabees 7; 4 Macc 17:20-22.

11. It is just possible that we have here a trace of Jesus' reflection on John the Baptist. The Baptist underwent a "baptism" of death; Jesus must do so too.

12. Antwi, "Did Jesus Consider," argues that Jesus operated within a cultic framework of thought, and he connects Jesus' ministry of forgiveness with his final journey

Jesus perceived the kingdom as having come and yet still to be consummated in the future: The disciples could not make sense of this delayed action, but it makes sense given the conviction that something, namely redemptive suffering, must be accomplished before the future consummation.

The last supper narrative and other evidence

We have suggested how Jesus may have related his coming death to his message of the kingdom. But is it possible to be more specific? The Gospels are remarkably reticent when it comes to explaining Jesus' death, and it may be significant that they do not freely import their own theology of cross and atonement into the narrative.

The most important text for understanding Jesus' view must be the last supper narrative (Matt 26:26-30/Mark 14:22-26/Luke 22:15-20).[13] The tradition of the supper is particularly well attested, with Paul himself coming to center stage at this point, since in 1 Cor 11:23-25 he actually describes the supper in very similar terms to the synoptics. (See p. 156 below on the authenticity question.)

There are various, mainly minor, differences among the NT accounts of the supper, some of which we will need to return to.[14] But the synoptic Gospels agree

- that the meal took place in the context of Jesus' final visit to Jerusalem,
- that Jesus and his disciples saw this visit as somehow momentous,[15]

---

to Jerusalem: Jesus comes to Jerusalem and the temple identifying "his role with that of the hitherto given institution of atonement" (27). On Jesus' significant temple sayings see chapter 5 below.

13. On the last supper see the classic discussion by Jeremias, *Eucharistic Words of Jesus;* also Marshall, *Last Supper, Lord's Supper.* I discuss the meaning of the supper in "How Jesus Understood the Last Supper."

14. There is a very important textual question affecting Luke's version of the supper, since a minority of manuscripts omits 22:19b-20 (the second Lukan cup and the words interpreting the bread). Most scholars now agree that the longer text, which reflects something of the shape of the Passover meal (e.g., with several cups), is original and that the shorter text is an abbreviation conforming rather more to the Christian eucharistic pattern. See the discussion in Jeremias, *Eucharistic Words,* 139-59; Marshall, *Last Supper,* 79-80; Fitzmyer, *Luke,* 1387-88.

15. It is Luke who says that the disciples "supposed that the kingdom of God was to appear immediately" (19:11); but all the Gospels suggest that Jesus' followers were

- that the meal was a Passover meal,[16]
- that Jesus interpreted bread and wine in terms of his body and blood and in terms of the "covenant," inviting his followers to eat and drink,
- that the meal preceded his arrest and crucifixion,
- and that he spoke of the coming kingdom (see above).

Even on the basis of this limited information it is possible to suggest the meaning of this acted parable of Jesus. It seems likely that he was giving his disciples a picture and explanation of how he saw that momentous Passover and in particular of how he understood his coming death. His death was

- a liberating event (like the great liberation of Jewish history, the Passover),
- a covenant-making sacrifice having everything to do with the coming kingdom,
- and a sacrifice made on behalf of Jesus' followers, who were invited to participate in it.

Luke and Paul refer to the "*new* covenant" in a phrase reminiscent of Jer 31:31, where God promises a new covenant written on the hearts of God's people. It makes sense in terms of Jesus' kingdom teaching that he should have

---

full of excitement about the entry to Jerusalem, anticipating great things (Matt 21:1-9/Mark 11:1-10/Luke 19:28-40). There is every reason to think that we have a genuine reminiscence at this point, since it is not obvious why the Evangelists should have portrayed the disciples as mistaken in their expectation if they were not. Their excitement, along with Jesus' actions, also helps explain why the authorities acted. If the disciples were full of anticipation, it is likely that they were in some ways at least encouraged in this by Jesus.

16. John's Gospel, which appears to give a different impression, agrees that it was at Passover time. It appears to suggest that Jesus died just before Passover (18:28; 19:14). Some scholars believe that John has altered the original chronology in order to have Jesus die when the Passover lambs are being killed. A surprising number of others prefer John's chronology to the synoptic chronology and assume that the last supper was not a proper Passover. Some have argued that Jesus and his disciples were working with a liturgical calendar different from the official temple calendar; it has been pointed out that the Essenes followed a solar calendar, not a lunar calendar, and that they may therefore have celebrated Passover ·before the official celebration. Others have argued that John's references to Jesus' death being before Passover in fact mean that he died before the sabbath of Passover week. See Marshall, *Last Supper*, 66-75, and commentaries for discussion.

associated the Jeremianic covenant with the kingdom (see chapter 2 above). Matthew and Mark have Jesus speak of his blood shed "for many," a phrase echoing Isaiah 53, where the righteous servant of God gives his life to bear the sins "of many" and to make "many" righteous (vv. 11, 12). It is entirely feasible that Jesus saw his death in these terms, that is, as the redemptive suffering of God's servant on behalf of God's people.[17] His death was to achieve a new exodus and a new release from the judgment of exile.[18]

Such an interpretation fits well with Jesus' kingdom preaching, which had all to do with God's liberating, healing work.[19] Jesus' death is seen in a real sense as the basis for the forgiveness, liberation, and renewal that he offered.

This interpretation also fits in with other teachings of Jesus about his death that are less strongly attested. Matt 20:28/Mark 10:45 is particularly important: "The Son of Man came not to be served but to serve, and to give his life a ransom for many." Two things are particularly striking in this saying: first, "ransom," since this term, suggesting liberation from imprisonment or from slavery, immediately evokes the thought of the Jewish exodus (and exile)[20] and so ties in closely with a Passover interpretation of the last supper. Also striking is the reference to "service" and the occurrence again of "for many." There is good reason here for seeing the saying against the background of Isaiah 53, where the servant lays down his life as a sin offering for many (vv. 10, 11).[21]

17. On the combining of the ideas of Son of man, Messiah, and Servant in Second Temple Judaism see Nickelsburg, "Salvation without and with a Messiah"; Charlesworth, "From Jewish Messianology," 237-41. See further on "the servant" in the discussion of Mark 10:45 on pp. 266-71 below.

18. For Jesus' death as an exodus see also Luke 9:31. For Jesus as the Passover lamb see John 19:36. On Moses typology in general see Longenecker, *Christology*, 32-38.

B. Chilton in *A Feast of Meanings* argues that Jesus said, "This is my body . . . this is my blood," not to refer to his own death, but to assert that the sort of fellowship meal that he and his disciples were enjoying together was the sort of sacrifice that was really pleasing to God. If, however, the words go back to Jesus and have a sacrificial meaning, it is far simpler to accept the unanimous testimony of the New Testament that Jesus was explaining his death in sacrificial terms than to accept Chilton's ingenious proposal.

19. See Beasley-Murray, *Jesus and the Kingdom*, 271-73, drawing on Schürmann.

20. So Hill, *Greek Words*, 49-81: "The field of meaning to which the words point is that of God delivering his people" (81); cf. Hooker, *Son of Man*, 144.

21. On the authenticity and meaning of the saying see, among others, Page, "Authenticity of the Ransom Logion"; Stuhlmacher, *Reconciliation*, 16-29; Kim, *Son of Man*, 38-61; Beasley-Murray, *Jesus and the Kingdom*, 278-83; Witherington, *Christology*, 251-56. Against the "servant" interpretation see Barrett, "Background of Mark 10:45," and especially Hooker, *Jesus and the Servant*, 74-79.

There is also the way Jesus refers to his death as a "cup" that he must drink (Mark 10:38; 14:35, 36). The thought here is almost certainly the OT idea of the cup of God's judgment, which is to be drunk by the wicked (Ps 75:8; Isa 51:17; Jer 25:15, 16). Jesus sees himself as taking that cup for others.

In explaining his death, then, Jesus made use of familiar Jewish concepts — the idea of divine judgment on the people for their sins, the hope of a new exodus, and the idea of a righteous one suffering redemptively for others. Jesus saw his death as righteous suffering on behalf of others, bringing forgiveness, establishing a new covenant betweeen God and his people (now represented by the disciples), and making possible the coming of the kingdom.[22]

PAUL'S UNDERSTANDING OF THE DEATH OF JESUS

The centrality of the death of Jesus in Paul's theological thinking has already been emphasized. But how did the apostle understand Jesus' death?

---

22. John's Gospel lends support to this sort of understanding of Jesus' death. Thus in John 6:51 Jesus speaks of giving his flesh "for the life of the world" and then goes on to say (v. 53): "Very truly, I tell you, unless you eat the flesh of the Son of Man and drink his blood, you have no life in you." Whether the verse should be interpreted in terms of the eucharist is debated among scholars; what is not debatable is that John speaks here of the death of Jesus for the world, which his followers must receive.

John's last supper narrative, as is well known, does not contain the institution of the eucharist at all, but instead describes Jesus' washing of the disciples' feet (13:1-20). In some ways the footwashing is closely parallel to the synoptic eucharist, since it is a symbolic act portraying Jesus' coming death for the disciples (hence the careful introduction to the story in 13:1-3 and Jesus' remark to Peter in v. 8). His death is seen as the supreme humiliation and service, and it is a washing away of evil, which the disciples must receive. The Johannine story is the enactment of the synoptic saying "The Son of Man came not to be served but to serve, and to give his life a ransom for many."

John offers other perspectives on the death of Jesus, most notably seeing it as Jesus' glorification and as the casting out of "the ruler of this world" (12:27-32). The thought is distinctively Johannine, and yet not remote from the synoptic picture of the cross as bringing in the kingdom of God's righteousness and reconciliation.

Eschatology and Fulfillment

Paul ...

Much of Paul's thinking comes together in Rom 3:21-26, and this is a convenient starting point for our discussion. Paul writes:

> But now, apart from the law, the righteousness of God has been disclosed, and is attested by the law and the prophets, the righteousness of God through faith in Jesus Christ for all who believe. For there is no distinction, since all have sinned and fall short of the glory of God; they are now justified by his grace as a gift, through the redemption that is in Christ Jesus, whom God put forward as a sacrifice of atonement by his blood. ...

We notice here, first, the eschatological context of what Paul says about Jesus' death: "*But now* ... the righteousness of God has been disclosed ... ," and also the reference to the law and the prophets: "attested by the law and the prophets." It is a given for Paul that Jesus died for our sins "in accordance with the scriptures" (1 Cor 15:3). For Paul the cross is not an unfortunate accident of history but the key to God's plan for the salvation of the world.

... and Jesus

We have argued that Jesus, too, saw his death in the context of the coming kingdom and in the context of OT and Jewish ideas of judgment and salvation.

Human Sin and Divine Grace

Paul ...

Secondly, in Rom 3:21-26 Paul sees the cross as divine grace dealing with human sinfulness. In Romans 1 and 2 Paul has explained in sometimes colorful detail the human predicament — Gentile and Jew alike are gripped by sin and under God's wrath. This is the backdrop to his teaching about the cross, as he spells out in 3:23: "All have sinned and fall short of the glory of God." The cross is the remedy for this fatal situation. And it is a remedy given by divine "grace as a gift" (v. 24). The cross is the supreme and extraordinary demonstration of God's love: "God proves his love for us in that while we still were sinners Christ died for us" (5:8).

. . . and Jesus

Jesus saw his ministry as the expression of divine mercy for sinners: He was a doctor to the literally, spiritually, and socially sick, and his business was to "seek out and save the lost" (Matt 9:13/Mark 2:17/Luke 5:32; Luke 15; 19:10). His love was seen in practical action, and preeminently in his death. The idea of his death as an act of divine love is perhaps more implicit than explicit in the Gospels, though it is suggested powerfully by the accounts of the last supper, where he gives the disciples the bread and wine and speaks of his death "for you" and "for many." It is also implicit in the description of his death itself, for example, in the Lukan account, where Jesus prays for his executioners and promises paradise to the robber who dies with him (23:34, 43).[23]

Redemption

Paul . . .

Paul speaks, thirdly, of "the redemption that is in Christ Jesus" (Rom 3:24). The word translated "redemption" is related to the word translated "ransom" in Matt 20:28/Mark 10:45.[24] It refers to the action of purchasing someone's — a slave's or a prisoner's — release. Paul could well have in mind the Greco-Roman slave scene and could be picturing the work of Christ as the liberation of slaves from an oppressive master (see Rom 6:14-23 and Gal 3:23–5:1).[25]

But the word also has an OT background, as we have seen, especially in the exodus of Israel from Egypt (Exod 15:13) and Israel's release from exile in Babylon (Isa 41:14).[26] It is probable that Paul has this background,

23. There is some textual uncertainty about Luke 23:34. See also John 13:1 ("Having loved his own who were in the world, he loved them to the end"); 19:26, 27.

24. *Apolytrōsis* in Rom 3:24, *lytron* in the synoptic saying.

25. In Gal 4:5 and 3:13 Paul uses *exagorazō* of Christ's redeeming "us" from the law. Also in 1 Cor 6:20; 7:23 Paul speaks of Christians being "bought *(agorazō)* with a price"; in 7:23 the thought is explicitly of a slave-master relationship.

26. See Dunn, *Romans,* 169.

especially the exodus, in mind, since elsewhere he speaks of Christ's work in these terms. Thus in 1 Cor 5:7, 8 he urges the Corinthians to get rid of "the yeast of malice and evil," explaining that "our paschal lamb, Christ, has been sacrificed." Similarly in 1 Corinthians 10 Paul picks up the thought of the exodus when discussing the Corinthians' misuse of the sacraments: He explains that the people of Israel experienced a baptism when they went down into the Red Sea with Moses and that they had manna as spiritual food, and yet they were destroyed by God for their wickedness. In the light of these passages it seems highly likely that Paul saw the death of Jesus not simply as redeeming the individual from his or her slavery to sin and death, but also as a new exodus event bringing the people of God out of their slavery.[27]

. . . and Jesus

In this respect Paul is in evident continuity with Jesus. Even if there are some questions about the authenticity of the "ransom" saying in Matt 20:28/Mark 10:45, the idea of Jesus' death as bringing liberation and as a new Passover is there in the eucharistic narrative, which, of course, Paul was familiar with.

An Atoning Sacrifice

Paul . . .

But how does Jesus' death bring liberation? Paul speaks, fourthly, of Jesus as the one "whom God put forward as a sacrifice of atonement by his blood" (Rom 3:25). There has been a great deal of dispute about the precise meaning of the word translated "sacrifice of atonement" (Greek *hilastērion*). But what is indisputable is that Paul is speaking here in sacrificial terms. His use of the term "blood," a word so crucial in OT sacrificial contexts and not otherwise a natural way to speak of a person's death, makes this clear.

---

27. Paul can speak of "redemption" as something future, e.g., in Rom 8:23, referring to the redemption of the body, or as something present, as in Col. 1:14. The context in Romans 3 makes it clear that the redemption is for Paul redemption from sin and from its consequences. In Romans 6 and 7 Paul brings out the idea of the Christian's liberation from sin, death, and the law.

For most twentieth-century readers of Paul the notion of animal sacrifice is difficult to relate to; but for Paul and probably most of his contemporaries sacrifice was something that they witnessed frequently and that was of great religious importance in their world. The idea of sacrifice spoke vividly and powerfully to people about divine-human relationships.

But what did it mean to Paul to speak of Jesus' death as a sacrifice? We suggest the following four points:[28] (1) In the OT the worshiper offered sacrifices in order to make atonement for his sin (see, e.g., Lev 1:4; 4–5). Paul sees the death of Jesus as such a sacrifice dealing with sin and bringing forgiveness. Thus in Rom 8:3 he says of that death that thus God "condemned sin in the flesh."

(2) But how were sacrifices for sin thought to work? In OT ritual the worshiper laid his hand on the unblemished sacrificial animal before the sacrifice. The symbolism of this action was either to identify the sacrificial animal as the worshiper's representative, so that the worshiper then offers himself in the sacrifice through the animal; or the picture may be that of the worshiper's sins being transferred to the animal. Either way, the effect was that the animal was punished for the sin of the worshiper. The sin was thus taken seriously and dealt with, and the worshiper forgiven. It was as though there was an interchange of roles between the worshiper and the sacrificial animal: "The implication is that as the sinner's sin was transferred to the spotless sacrifice, so the spotless life of the sacrifice was transferred (or reckoned) to the sinner."[29] This is probably the picture presupposed in several Pauline texts that speak of the death of Jesus, notably Gal 3:13: "Christ redeemed us from the curse of the law by becoming a curse for us," and 2 Cor 5:21: "[God] made him to be sin who knew no sin, so that in him we might become the righteousness of God."

(3) But why the need for the drastic measure of sacrifice at all? The OT picture is of an intensely pure and holy God, whose intolerance of evil is expressed in the punishment of evil. Sin is thus utterly serious, and must be dealt with. But the OT picture is also of a God whose forgiving love for his people is expressed in the provision of a way out of judgment through sacrifice. Similarly for Paul, the human predicament, as explained in Romans 1–3, is that all deserve and face the terrifying "wrath" of God because of sin; but the answer to that wrath is the sacrifice of Jesus.

28. We follow Dunn's helpful treatment here to a considerable extent; see his *Romans,* 172. On the OT sacrifices see, among others, Wenham, *Leviticus,* 48-112.

29. Dunn, *Romans,* 172. For the idea of "interchange" see Hooker's articles "Interchange in Christ," "Interchange and Atonement," and "Interchange and Suffering."

The word used of Jesus' sacrifice in Rom 3:25, *hilastērion,* suggests, in secular Greek at least, precisely the idea of propitiation, that is, of placating someone's anger. Questions have been raised about the meaning of the word in the Septuagint (the Greek version of the OT generally used by the NT writers), but the probability is that Paul does indeed see Jesus' death as a sacrifice taking away the wrath of God. He does not, of course, have a crude notion of God as an angry ogre and of Jesus as an innocent victim; but he does believe in the awful reality of divine judgment and in God sending Jesus to rescue humanity from that judgment.[30]

(4) But the word *hilastērion* may have more to it than simply the idea of propitiation, since it is used more than anything else in the Greek OT (as also in Hebrews) of the "mercy seat" (e.g., Exod 25:16-21; Heb 9:5). The mercy seat was the golden lid of the ark of the covenant and was regarded as the focus of God's presence with his people and as the place above all where the sins of God's people were forgiven and atoned for. It was here that the sacrificial blood was sprinkled on the all-important Day of Atonement. That solemn day with its powerfully symbolic rituals (including the sending away of the scapegoat loaded with the sins of the people into the wilderness) was the one day in the year when the high priest would enter the holy of holies. As the OT put it, "This shall be an everlasting statute for you, to make atonement for the people of Israel once in the year for all their sins" (Lev 16:34). If this is the background to Paul's thinking here, then the thought is that "What was once symbolized in the Day of Atonement ritual (Leviticus 16) is now realized in Christ crucified."[31]

If this plausible suggestion is right, then Paul saw the death of Jesus

---

30. Many scholars have found the idea of "propitiation" difficult theologically or unconvincing exegetically and have preferred the translation "expiation" (with the emphasis on dealing with sin rather than responding to wrath). For discussion of the issues see, among others, Morris, *Apostolic Preaching of the Cross,* 125-85; Hill, *Greek Words,* 23-48; Whiteley, *Theology of St Paul,* 130-51; Ziesler, *Pauline Christianity,* 87-91; Dunn, *Romans,* 171.

31. Hunter, *Interpreting Paul's Gospel,* 31. See also Stuhlmacher, *Reconciliation,* 94-109; Fryer, "Meaning and Translation of *Hilasterion.*" Grayston, *Dying, We Live,* 94-95, comments that the sprinkling of blood on the Day of Atonement was "to secure renewal of sanctity for the priesthood and the sacred enclosure" and concludes that this is an "unsuitable" explanation of Paul's meaning. But broadly understood the day had all to do with atonement for the sins of the people and as such it fits well with Paul's thinking about the death of Jesus. Grayston, like others, objects rather prosaically to the idea of Jesus as the place and means (the blood) of atonement, preferring for *hilastērion* the sense "votive offering" or inducement.

not only as a new Passover bringing "redemption" to the people of God as well as to individuals enslaved in sin, but also as the fulfillment of the day of atonement. He sees Jesus' death, in any case, as an atoning sacrifice for sin, probably as a sacrifice effecting "propitiation" and taking away the judgment of God.[32]

. . . and Jesus

The *hilastērion* group of words is not used in the gospel traditions of Jesus, except in the parable of the Pharisee and the tax collector. Here the tax collector prays "God, *be merciful* to me, a sinner" (Luke 18:13). The Greek verb translated "be merciful" is a cognate with the noun *hilastērion* and may possibly have cultic connotations — and the man is praying in the temple.[33] But the terminology used in this saying could reflect Pauline influence on Luke, and even if it does go back to Jesus it is hardly very informative about Jesus' understanding of atonement. But the idea of Jesus' death having a cultic-sacrificial meaning and taking away the judgment deserved by sinners is quite strongly rooted in the Jesus-tradition. The former is suggested by the "body" and "blood" language of the last supper and perhaps by the whole Jerusalem context of Jesus' death,[34] the latter by the "cup" imagery used by Jesus and by the echoes of Isaiah 53, with its portrayal of the servant taking on himself the punishment of others.[35]

---

32. We do not have to choose between "propitiation" and "mercy seat" as translations for *hilastērion* since the Day of Atonement was certainly concerned with averting and avoiding the judgment of God. Campbell, *Rhetoric of Righteousness*, 130-33, finds Day of Atonement connotations in Rom 3:25, but not propitiation; he seems to underestimate the importance of the "wrath"/judgment theme in Romans 1–3.

33. See Marshall, *Luke*, 680, referring also to Hill, *Greek Words*, 36.

34. See Antwi, "Did Jesus Consider."

35. Paul does not directly quote the Isaianic servant passages when referring to the death of Jesus, but there are possible allusions, as in Rom 4:25 (so, e.g., Hengel, *Atonement*, 35). Johnson, *Writings*, 332, says of Romans generally: "Throughout this letter, full citations or allusions to the latter part of that prophet play an important thematic role. It is clear that Paul has pondered his ministry in the light of a careful reading of Is 49–60." It is very possible that Isaiah 53 was important for Paul's theology of justification through the death of Jesus, since it describes the righteous servant smitten for the transgressions of others: "By his knowledge shall the righteous one, my servant, make many to be accounted righteous" (53:11, RSV).

Dying with Christ

Paul . . .

Our final observation about Paul's understanding of Jesus' death arises not from Rom 3:21-26 but from passages farther on in Romans and elsewhere in Paul's letters. For Paul, Jesus' death was not simply something accomplished by Jesus on behalf of others — even in the place of others — but also something that believers come to share in. It has been argued that this idea of participation is even more fundamental to Paul's thought about the death of Jesus than concepts of sacrifice, propitiation, and the like.[36] Thus in Rom 6:3, 4 Paul comments that "all of us who have been baptized into Christ Jesus were baptized into his death. Therefore we have been buried with him by baptism into death, so that, just as Christ was raised from the dead by the glory of the Father, so we too might walk in newness of life." In Galatians Paul claims that he has been "crucified with Christ" (2:19). Colossians speaks similarly of sharing the death, burial, and resurrection of Jesus (2:8-12).[37] For Paul, then, the Christian does not simply receive the benefits of Christ's work, but is also united to Christ and comes to share in his life and death. The Christian is "in Christ" and dies "with Christ," both in baptism and in an ongoing experience of suffering for the Lord's sake (e.g., Rom 8:17; Phil 3:10).

. . . and Jesus

The idea of participation is a distinctive Pauline emphasis, but the idea of sharing in the death of Jesus is not without precedent in the Jesus-tradition. First, there is the call of Jesus to his disciples to "take up your cross and follow me," which is represented in both the Markan and the "Q" traditions (in different versions). The context in the Markan tradition is quite explicitly a prediction of Jesus' own death, and so the call to the disciples to take up the cross is very nearly, if not quite, a challenge to the disciples to join Jesus in his crucifixion and sufferings (Matt 16:24-26/Mark 8:34-37/Luke

---

36. E.g., Sanders, *Paul and Palestinian Judaism*, 502-8.
37. Colossians also has a particular stress on the cross as victory over spiritual powers rather similar to that in the fourth Gospel (Col 2:15, 20; John 12:31; 16:33). Colossians and John also emphasize the supremacy of Christ in creation (Col 1:15-20; John 1:1-18). The similarity of emphasis may reflect a similar context of christological controversy.

9:23-26; Matt 10:38/Luke 14:27). Second, there is the dialogue between Jesus and the sons of Zebedee, recorded in Matthew and Mark, in which Jesus speaks of the disciples drinking "the cup that I drink" and (Mark only) being baptized "with the baptism with which I am baptized" (Mark 10:38, 39/Matt 20:22, 23). This is not the Pauline baptismal understanding of suffering with Christ, but it is a significant and strong tradition in which Jesus' suffering and death are seen as an experience in which his followers will share.

FINAL COMMENTS ON THE COMPARISON

Some particularly difficult questions are raised by the comparison of Jesus' and Paul's teachings on the cross. But if the sketches that we have offered are anywhere near correct, then they show on the one hand a substantial gap between Jesus and Paul, with Jesus saying rather little about the cross and Paul having a much fuller and more explicit theology of the Lord's death. On the other hand, the main lines of the Pauline doctrine are in almost all cases hinted at in the Jesus-tradition. In some cases there is much more than a hint: The idea of Jesus' death as a redemptive sacrifice bringing in God's salvation is quite explicit in the last supper traditions. But in other cases, notably when it comes to the idea of participation in the death of Jesus, Paul does go well beyond the hints in the Jesus-tradition, though those hints are there (e.g., the "take up your cross" saying).

The differences between Paul and Jesus are explicable to a considerable extent. For Jesus the cross lies ahead, and is in a real sense an unknown and, as the Gospels suggest, almost impossible to explain to his followers in advance. For Paul the cross has happened and is now a massively important datum to be explained; the prominence of it in his thinking is not at all surprising.

His emphasis on participation is something strongly associated with baptism, and it may well be that Paul's distinctive emphasis represents a creative fusion of ideas — bringing together his understanding of the cross as God's way of salvation with the idea of being initiated into salvation and discipleship through baptism. Some have suggested that Paul was influenced by the Greek mystery religions in his concept of dying and rising with Christ. But this hypothesis is unnecessary and unlikely: Baptism is a very Jewish phenomenon, and there is little doubt that it came to Christians directly or indirectly from John the Baptist. For John baptism was very much associated with the advent of the eschatological day of the Lord, and this eschatological dimension continues in Christian baptism. But for Christians like Paul the decisive eschatological events are the death and resurrection of Jesus; it is thus intelligible that baptism as the rite of initiation into the saved eschatological community should come to be associated with Jesus' saving death and resurrection. There is therefore no need to invoke the mystery religions to explain Paul's baptismal teaching.[38] It is, however, possible that the Jesus-traditions that speak of taking up the cross and sharing in the sufferings of Jesus were influential (see below).

II. CONNECTING JESUS AND PAUL

THE SUPPER

Paul explicitly acknowledges his dependence on Jesus' teaching with regard to his own death in the description of the last supper in 1 Corinthians 11, where Paul quotes the eucharistic words of Jesus. Some scholars have questioned the authenticity of those words, suggesting that Paul himself was the real author of the eucharistic teaching and that he introduced sacrificial and sacramental ideas into what was previously a simpler fellowship meal. That position, however, has no probability for these reasons:[39]

38. On the sacraments in Paul and the mystery religions see Wedderburn, *Baptism and Resurrection*.

39. On the authenticity of the supper narratives see Jeremias, *Eucharistic Words*, 173-86, emphasizing the Semitic character of the narratives; also Beasley-Murray, *Jesus and the Kingdom*, 267-73, responding to Bultmann's view of the eucharist as a Hellenistic cult legend. Others questioning the dominical origin of the eucharist include Crossan, *Historical Jesus*, 360-67; Maccoby, "Paul and the Eucharist." Both appeal to the failure of Didache 10 to mention bread and wine. But this is an extremely hazardous argument from the silence of one uncertainly dated text; the author of the Didache may well presuppose knowledge of the central eucharistic words and actions.

Vermes, *Religion of Jesus*, 16, argues that the idea of eating "the body" and drinking "the blood" "strikes a totally foreign note in a Palestinian cultural setting." But Jesus typically uses vivid, almost shocking metaphors (e.g., Matt 18:8, 9/Mark 9:43-48). Furthermore, that the shocking eucharistic words came to be accepted by Jewish Christians (including Matthew) may suggest that they were not quite as unacceptable as Vermes supposes or that they had a strong claim to authenticity, since they would not easily have been accepted if they were not in the Jewish Christian tradition.

- Paul himself specifically claims to be reminding his readers of a tradition that he has received and that ultimately came from Jesus: "I received from the Lord what I also handed to you, that the Lord Jesus on the night when he was betrayed took a loaf of bread . . ." (1 Cor 11:23).[40]
- All four Gospels attest the eucharistic teaching (John indirectly in 6:51-59). It is unlikely that the other Evangelists are all dependent on Mark: The Lukan tradition in particular with its distinctive features (including two cups of wine) is widely recognized as independent of Mark.[41] It is even more unlikely that the Evangelists, and presumably their churches, including the Jewish Christian church of Matthew, have taken their lead from Paul and abandoned the traditional form of the supper for a Pauline innovation.
- The meal, as described by the Gospels, makes excellent sense in Jesus' Palestinian/Jewish/Passover context, as we have seen.[42]

The supper tradition, then, has an excellent claim to authenticity, and the case for Pauline dependence on that tradition is very strong indeed.

There are, however, interesting questions about the precise form of the tradition that Paul knew. In describing the supper Paul's wording is strikingly similar to Luke's, diverging at a number of points from Matthew and Mark:

Matthew/Mark	Luke/Paul
Take(, eat); this is my body.	This is my body, which is (given) for you. Do this in remembrance of me.
Drink from it, all of you./All of them drank from it.	— —

40. When Paul says, "I received from the Lord," he could theoretically have meant that he received the supper tradition by direct revelation from the heavenly Christ; so Maccoby, "Paul and the Eucharist," 247-48, arguing that Paul would otherwise have said, "I have received this account from those present at the Last Supper." But it is much more likely that he meant that the tradition derived from "the Lord" during his ministry in the sense that the words and (in this case) the actions were the Lord's (cf. 1 Cor 7:10, 12). See Bruce, *Paul and Jesus*, 50.

41. So, e.g., Fitzmyer, *Luke*, 1386.

42. For further discussion of the eucharistic words in Jesus' context see, among others, Carmichael, "David Daube on Eucharist," who revives the view of Daube and Eisler that the piece of unleavened bread broken off and set aside in the Jewish Passover, the *afikoman*, originally represented "a longed for redeemer who had not yet appeared" (49). Jesus identifies himself with that redeemer. Carmichael doubts if the cup saying in the Gospels goes back to Jesus, but on this see Casey, "Original Aramaic Form."

This is my blood of the covenant,	This cup is the new covenant in my
which is poured out for many.	blood, which is poured out for you.

The synoptic problem presented by the Gospel and Pauline texts is quite complex. For example, some scholars consider the Lukan/Pauline "This cup is the new covenant in my blood" original and the Matthew/Mark "This is my blood" as a modification made to conform the saying over the wine to the saying over the bread. Others consider the Matthew/Mark saying original and the Lukan/Pauline version as a modification made because of the offensiveness of the idea of drinking blood.[43] Whichever view is correct, the agreement of Luke and Paul is notable.

If Paul agrees with Luke in certain respects, he diverges from all three synoptists in having no equivalent to their saying about the coming kingdom ("I will not eat . . . drink . . . until the kingdom . . . ," e.g., Luke 22:16, 18). This does not suggest that this saying was absent from his tradition, but more likely it reflects the particular situation in Corinth that Paul was addressing. He cites the supper tradition because the eucharist was being celebrated in Corinth in an unseemly and divisive way. For that reason he focuses on two aspects of the supper, its relationship to Jesus' death and its corporate aspect as an expression of unity and sharing. The eschatological aspect of the meal is not so important to Paul in this context, but he does allude to it when he says that with it "you proclaim the Lord's death *until he comes*" (1 Cor 11:26). There is no need to think that Paul was ignorant of the kingdom sayings in the context of the supper.

What seems quite likely is that the Lukan version of the supper broadly represents the tradition used in the Pauline churches.[44] It is possible that Paul himself had some part in shaping that tradition, but the tradition itself is pre-Pauline and probably goes back to Jesus. The very significant understanding of the death of Jesus that it presents — as a sacrifice for

43. The latter view is probably, but not certainly, to be preferred. Both Luke and Paul arguably attest the Matthew/Mark wording. Luke does so in his telltale participial phrase "poured out for you" in 22:20, which goes better after the Matthew/Mark "my blood" than after Luke's "the cup" (though it could simply be that Luke has merged the Markan and the "Pauline" traditions here rather awkwardly: cf. Marshall, *Luke*, 806), and Paul does so in 1 Cor 10:16: "The cup of blessing that we bless, is it not a sharing in the blood of Christ? The bread that we break, is it not a sharing in the body of Christ?" The fourth Gospel also attests the "body/blood" parallelism in 6:53-55 (though the Evangelist has "flesh" rather than "body") and also notes the difficulty of the ideas being presented by Jesus.

44. So Fee, *1 Corinthians*, 547, though noting that Luke has assimilated some Markan material.

Jesus' followers, as a new Passover event bringing redemption and inaugurating the new covenant, and as a kingdom-bringing event — was, therefore, part of Paul's tradition. He was, therefore, influenced by Jesus in one of the most important parts of his theology.

BAPTISM INTO DEATH

We have observed that Paul's participatory view of Jesus' death has parallels of sorts in Jesus' sayings about taking up the cross and sharing his cup and baptism. Is there concrete evidence that Paul was influenced by these Jesus-traditions?

Several observations are relevant:

The Synoptic Texts

Taking up the cross

As we observed, the saying about "taking up the cross" is particularly well attested in the Gospels. It occurs in a so-called Markan tradition:

> If anyone wants to come after me, let him deny himself and take up his cross and follow me.
> For whoever wants to save his life will lose it. But whoever loses his life for my sake will find it.
> For what advantage will it be to a person, if he gains the whole world, but loses his life; or what will a person give in exchange for his life?*

So Matt 16:24-26 and similarly Mark 8:34-36/Luke 9:23-26, which also go on to the saying about being ashamed of Jesus.

The saying about taking up the cross occurs also in a slightly different "Q" form in Matt 10:38/Luke 14:27:

> Whoever does not take his cross and follow after me is not worthy of me/cannot be my disciple.*

Matthew and Luke also have the saying about saving and losing life in Matt 10:39 (after the cross saying) and Luke 17:33 (see also John 12:25).

The sayings then about taking up the cross and losing one's life are thus well attested, and could well have been known to Paul. They are also stark and, given the first-century awareness of the terrible nature of cruci-fixion, almost shocking statements. This strengthens their claim to be authentic sayings of Jesus, since such vivid, pictorial, and drastic statements seem to have been characteristic of him.[45]

The cup and baptism

The idea of Jesus' death as a cup and a baptism that his disciples will share is found in Mark 10:38, 39:

> Are you able to drink the cup that I drink, or be baptized with the baptism that I am baptized with?
> The cup that I drink you will drink; and with the baptism with which I am baptized, you will be baptized."

The saying about the cup has a close parallel in Matt 20:22, 23, and the saying about baptism has a partial parallel in Luke 12:50:

> I have a baptism with which to be baptized, and what stress I am under until it is completed!

It is possible that both Matthew and Luke are dependent on Mark for these sayings, but it is more likely that Luke's rather different saying comes from another source.[46] If so, the idea of Jesus' death as a "baptism" is attested both in the Markan and Lukan traditions. As for the idea of Jesus' death as a cup that must be drunk, this is found not only in Mark 10 and Matthew 20 but also in the Gethsemane story (Matt 26:39/Mark 14:36/Luke 22:42, also John 18:11). This evidence may indicate that the ideas in question were widely associated with Jesus.

45. Luke adds "daily" to Jesus' invitation to his disciples to take up the cross in 9:23, and this very probably reflects Luke's desire to make sense for his readers of the dire demand of Jesus. For other similarly vivid statements of Jesus compare his state-ments about cutting off limbs that offend (Matt 5:29, 30; 18:8, 9/Mark 9:43-48), "hating" family members (Luke 14:26), and not burying the dead (Matt 8:22/Luke 9:60).

Some scholars have argued that the association of discipleship with the idea of crucifixion must have begun after the crucifixion itself and that the sayings cannot go back to Jesus. But see Gundry, *Mark*, 453-54; Nolland, *Luke*, 475-78.

46. It may be that Matthew, who was quite probably sensitive to the idea of Jesus being baptized (hence his 3:14), is responsible for the omission of the Markan "baptism" saying. But it is just possible that Mark, knowing something like the Lukan form of the baptism saying, introduced it in 10:38, 39 alongside the cup saying, perhaps having in mind the sacramental practices of the church.

It is not possible to go into all the arguments for and against the authenticity of the sayings about the disciples sharing Jesus' cup and baptism in Mark 10:38, 39. But there is a significant case for seeing them as genuine. It is, for example, arguable that the pictorial, somewhat enigmatic language is rather typical of Jesus, and that the metaphorical use of the term "baptism" may be easier to understand in the context of Jesus' ministry than in the church, where baptism had become the recognized initiation rite.[47]

What we may reasonably conclude is that the sayings in question could well be Jesus-traditions that Paul might have known. Later we will see further evidence of Paul's familiarity with the rather unflattering story of James and John in which the sayings are found (Matt 20:20-28/Mark 10:35-45).

Baptism into Death in Paul

The Pauline teaching about baptism into the death of Christ is quite distinctive, and the question of its origin has no clear answer. But we have suggested that it represents the coming together of a Jewish and Christian understanding of baptism as initiation into the saved people of God with a distinctively Christian view of the death and resurrection of Jesus as the decisive saving events. This understanding of baptism would have arisen all the more easily if the sayings of Jesus about taking up the cross and about the shared cup and baptism were familiar.

Taking up the cross and losing one's life

The dogmatic, demanding statement of Jesus about discipleship involving taking up the cross had to be made sense of. It could hardly mean that every disciple was bound to be crucified in a literal sense. Luke interpreted it as referring to a daily death to sin.

But there was probably also another interpretation, made appropriate by the aorist tense verbs in the saying, according to which it referred to the decisive act of renunciation and identification with the crucified Jesus in baptism. It is impossible to prove that the saying was interpreted in this way, but it is entirely plausible that, when Paul speaks in Gal 2:19, 20 of having been

47. For a strong argument in favor of the sayings' authenticity and for discussion of their meaning in context see Bayer, *Jesus' Predictions*, 54-89.

"crucified with Christ" so that "it is no longer I who live," he is echoing Jesus' call to deny oneself and take up the cross (Matt 16:24/Mark 8:34/Luke 9:23).[48]

Paul's familiarity with the group of Jesus-traditions attested in Matt 16:24-26/Mark 8:34-36/Luke 9:23-26 may also be suggested by Phil 3:7-11, in which he says:

> Whatever gains I had, these I have come to regard as loss because of Christ. More than that, I regard everything as loss because of the surpassing value of knowing Christ Jesus my Lord. For his sake I have suffered the loss of all things, and I regard them as rubbish, in order that I may gain Christ and be found in him. . . . I want to know Christ and the power of his resurrection and the sharing of his sufferings by becoming like him in his death. . . .

This passage has three striking similarities to the synoptic sayings that we have been examining:

- "Gain" and "loss" appear together in the NT only here and in Matt 16:26/Mark 8:36/Luke 9:25: "What will it profit a person if he *gains* the whole world and suffers the *loss* of his soul?"*[49] These words are not frequently used in the NT; Paul uses "loss" only five times in his letters, three of those in this passage.
- In both we see the thought of renouncing everything that the world offers for the sake of Christ.
- The synoptic saying comes in the context of a prediction of Christ's sufferings with the disciples called to take up the cross and follow; Paul speaks in Philippians 3 of his ambition to share Christ's sufferings and to become "like him in his death."[50]

48. If Paul did interpret "taking up the cross" baptismally, he did not therefore reject the Lukan interpretation of the saying in terms of daily renunciation: He believes in baptismal death to sin but also in a continuing putting to death of sin in conformity to the Lord's death (e.g., Rom 8:13; Phil 3:11).

49. The same Greek verbs for "gain," *kerdainō,* and "lose," *zēmioō* (and the related noun *zēmia*), are used in the synoptic and Pauline texts.

50. On the Philippians passage see especially Thompson, *Clothed with Christ,* 85. J. P. Brown, "Synoptic Parallels," 40, suspects that the synoptic saying is derived from the Pauline metaphors, not vice versa. But it is easier to see how the synoptic discussion of discipleship might have influenced Paul's description of his own conversion than to see that particular Pauline passage (with its unusual vocabulary) influencing the synoptic tradition. Thompson, 222, cites A. Schulz, *Nachfolgen und Nachahmen* (Munich: SANT, 1962), 279, who sees the self-denial motif in Rom 15:3.

Further possible echoes of the same group of traditions are (1) in Rom 1:16, where Paul's comment that he is not ashamed of the gospel has been seen as an echo of the Jesus' saying about "those who are ashamed of me and of my words," which follows the saying about taking up the cross in Mark and Luke (Mark 8:38/Luke 9:26), and (2) in Phil 1:20, where Paul speaks of his expectation that he will not be "put to shame."[51]

Drinking the cup and being baptized

It is also likely enough that early Christians reflected on the sayings of Jesus about "the cup" and "the baptism" that his disciples would share with him. Jesus was clearly referring to literal sufferings and death — and Paul for one was well aware that it is the Christian's destiny to share literally in the sufferings of Jesus (e.g., Rom 8:17).

But it is quite likely that Christians reflected on these sayings in terms of water baptism and eucharist, seeing both sacraments as expressions of sharing in the sufferings of Jesus.[52] The eucharist in any case spoke vividly and visually in those terms — those who partook visibly took the death of Jesus into themselves. It was a "participation" in his death (1 Cor 10:16). Baptism similarly came to be seen by Paul at least as entry into the death. If Jesus' baptism was — in terms of the synoptic saying — his passion, then it was not a long logical jump to see Christian baptism as sharing in the death of Jesus.[53] It is impossible to prove that Paul was influenced by these

51. See J. P. Brown, "Synoptic Parallels," 39. Paul goes on in the following verse to speak of dying for Christ as "gain."

52. Taylor, *Mark*, 441, recognizes that Paul's idea of baptism into the Lord's death may be "a development and an application" of the saying. Anderson, *Mark*, 253, comments: "While the words of verses 38-39 would have reminded the Church of the 'cup' of the Lord's Supper and of the rite of Baptism, and of how the sacaments identified them with Christ in his destiny, we need not suppose they were first formulated in the light of the Church's sacramental practice or theology."

53. It could be that Mark in 10:38 has brought together the "cup" and "baptism" sayings because he saw the sacramental connection. It is interesting, if nothing more, that in 1 Cor 12:13 Paul speaks of believers being "baptized into one body," reflecting the idea of sacramental participation in Jesus, and "being made to drink of one Spirit." Fee, *1 Corinthians*, 604, in keeping with his general tendency to downplay the sacramentalism of 1 Corinthians, dismisses the view of those commentators (including Calvin, Luther, Käsemann, and Conzelmann) who have seen the "drinking" of one Spirit in 12:13 as alluding to the eucharist. He sees the aorist tense as going against that interpretation and observes that there is no hint that the early church understood the eucharist in terms of imbibing the Spirit. This is perhaps surprisingly dogmatic after

particular sayings of Jesus, but it is quite probable that they were at least a catalyst in his thinking.[54]

CONCLUSIONS ON THE CONNECTIONS

The last supper narrative is a particularly convincing example of a Jesus-tradition known to Paul. By itself, however, it does not prove a lot about Paul's familiarity with the story of Jesus in general, since it could have been familiar to him through its use in the church's liturgy. On the other hand, whether liturgically transmitted or not, it is a significant point of theological contact between Paul and Jesus.

It is quite probable, though not provable, that Paul also knew Jesus' sayings about taking up the cross and losing one's life for the sake of the gospel. And it is possible that he knew one or both of the sayings about the disciples sharing Jesus' baptism and drinking his cup. If he did, this may have contributed to the development of his distinctive idea of participation in the death of Christ.

The evidence for Paul's knowledge of the important "ransom" saying of Matt 20:28/Mark 10:45 will be examined in a later chapter.

"spiritual drink" in 10:4 (in a context dealing with baptism and eucharist). 12:13 has some thematic resemblance also to 10:17.

54. 2 Cor 5:14, where Paul says in connection with the death of Christ that "the love of Christ constraineth us" (KJV) has been seen as an echo of Luke 12:50, where Jesus speaks of the baptism he has to undergo and says how he is "constrained" until it is accomplished. The verb in common is striking: It is unusual in Paul's letters (see also Phil 1:23), though not in the Lukan writings.

5

JESUS AND THE COMMUNITY

I. COMPARING JESUS AND PAUL

JESUS, JUDAISM, AND THE MISSION OF THE CHURCH

Apostolic Mission

Jesus had a strong sense of mission. He announced the coming of God's kingdom, and he lived for the coming of the kingdom. He also, according to the unanimous testimony of the Gospels, called others to share his mission. It is the fourth Gospel that describes Jesus as saying to his disciples: "As the Father has sent me, so I send you" (20:21). But the other Gospels agree that Jesus sent out his disciples to preach the kingdom, to heal, and to cast out devils, just as he himself had done.

The Greek word underlying our word "apostle" means literally "one who is sent,"[1] and the Hebrew equivalent was used in Judaism of the representative of a person or a synagogue who went with the full authority of those who sent him.[2] So the disciples according to the Gospels go out with authority — to represent Jesus (see Matt 10:40/Luke 10:16).

Matthew and Mark describe Jesus sending out the twelve, giving them instructions for their mission (Mark 6:6-13; Matt 10:1-42). Luke describes two missions — that of the twelve and that of the seventy (or seventy-two,

---

1. The Greek word is *apostolos*. On apostleship and more broadly on Jesus' mission see Witherington, *Christology*, 118-37.

2. The word is *shaliach*. E.g., Mishnah *Berakoth* 5:5: "A man's agent is as himself."

Luke 9:1-6; 10:1-16). The relationship between the different accounts is complicated: It has commonly been supposed that we have a "Markan" mission discourse (in Mark 6, Luke 9, and Matthew 10) and a "Q" mission discourse (in Luke 10 and Matthew 10). But the matter is certainly not as simple as that. Luke 9, for example, is not purely Markan, but has some things in common with Matthew 10 not found in Mark 6.[3] It is possible in this case that Matthew's account represents the most original in a number of respects and that Mark and Luke are familiar with something like the Matthean tradition.[4] Whatever the precise relationships of the different texts, the probability is that in the mission discourse we have a tradition that goes back very early.

Given Jesus' own urgent sense of a new day of salvation dawning, it is only logical that he should have shared his ministry with others. There is no reason to doubt that the religion of Jesus was a "missionary" or "apostolic" religion from the start.

The Twelve

The Gospels agree that Jesus appointed "twelve" apostles in particular. Despite the questions of some who have made too much of the later Jewish tradition that Jesus had five disciples,[5] there is little doubt that the tradition of the "twelve" is authentic.[6] The unanimity of the Gospels on the point,

---

3. Cf. (1) Luke 9:2, "to proclaim the kingdom of God and to heal" with Matt 10:7, 8, also Luke 9:1 and Matt 10:1, "to cure . . . disease(s)"; (2) the prohibition of a stick in Luke 9:3 and Matt 10:10; and (3) "that town" in Luke 9:5 and Matt 10:14. These agreements may be explained on the two-source hypothesis as due to the influence of the "Q" tradition in the largely Markan Luke 9 (so Marshall, *Luke*, 349). But it is probably preferable to dispense with the Q hypothesis here and to recognize that the discourse was a well-known Jesus-tradition that Matthew, Mark, and Luke were all familiar with and drew on in different ways. See Dungan's particularly important discussion of the texts in *Sayings of Jesus*, 41-75.

4. So Dungan (see previous note). It has often been proposed that Mark — in allowing the disciples to take a stick and to wear sandals — represents a modification of the more stringent Q form of the discourse, in which stick and sandals are prohibited. It is certainly possible that Mark is interpreting the demands of Jesus in and for a different, non-Palestinian context.

5. Babylonian Talmud Sanhedrin 43a. See on this Twelftree, "Jesus in Jewish Traditions," 322-23.

6. See, among others, Jeremias, *NT Theology*, 231-34; Horsley, *Jesus and the Spiral*, 199-208; Witherington, *Christology*, 126-29; cf. also Sanders, *Jesus and Judaism*, 101-2.

even though the twelve do not seem to have played an especially prominent part in the life of the church (at least not in the Jerusalem church — after the earliest days — or in the Pauline churches), tells in favor of this. So do the testimony of Paul in 1 Cor 15:5 (to which we will return), the references to Judas Iscariot as one of the twelve, since the idea of Jesus' betrayer being one of the chosen apostles seems unlikely to have been invented, and, probably, Jesus' promise to the disciples, including Judas, that they would "sit on (twelve) thrones, judging the twelve tribes of Israel" (Matt 19:28/ Luke 22:30), since the church would hardly have created such a promise after Judas's notorious betrayal.

The symbolism suggested by the appointment of the twelve also supports the historicity of the tradition in question. The saying in Matt 19:28/Luke 22:30 associates the twelve apostles with the twelve tribes, and it is likely that this was precisely the symbolism intended by Jesus. His announcement of the kingdom, as we have suggested, was the announcement of the day of fulfillment of promise, and the OT promises are focused on the restoration of Israel. Jesus' kingdom teaching has correctly been called "restoration eschatology" by some scholars,[7] and the appointment of the twelve fits into such a message. Jesus sees his ministry as a gathering in of the dispersed tribes and a restoration of the people of God.[8]

The Lost Sheep of the House of Israel

Matthew makes precisely this point about Jesus' ministry to Israel in two sayings unique to his Gospel. In 10:5 Jesus sends the twelve out, instructing them: "Go nowhere among the Gentiles, and enter no town of the Samaritans, but go rather to the lost sheep of the house of Israel" (cf. also 10:23). Then in 15:24 Jesus explains his initial failure to respond to a Canaanite woman with the words "I was sent only to the lost sheep of the house of Israel." Scholars have frequently declined to accept the authenticity of these sayings — perhaps with some relief because of their apparent insularity. They are not in Mark or Luke, and so, given the two-source hypothesis, it is easy to dismiss the sayings as Matthean compositions.[9] But we have

7. E.g., Sanders, *Jesus and Judaism*, 59-119.

8. There may be an equivalent symbolism in the sending out of the seventy (or seventy-two) in Luke 10, since seventy was traditionally the number of the nations of the world. Does Luke intend us to see the mission of Jesus as one to Israel (the twelve) and to the world (the seventy)?

9. So Stanton, *Gospel for a New People*, 330.

already suggested that it is doubtful if a simple version of the two-source hypothesis will account for the different synoptic traditions of the mission discourse. It is not obvious in this case that the author of Matthew's Gospel, who ringingly affirms the Gentile mission elsewhere, for example, in 28:19, would have added these restrictive sayings of Jesus to his Markan and Q sources.[10] It is, on the other hand, quite likely that Mark and Luke would have left out sayings that could have been perplexing to their Gentile readers.

There is considerable evidence, quite apart from Matthew, that Jesus saw his ministry as directed in the first instance to the Jews. Although Jesus traveled a lot, the Gospels suggest that he worked largely within Jewish territories. When Mark describes Jesus as venturing beyond those territories, he suggests that Jesus did not want to be known where he was. Although he does not have Jesus' telling the Gentile woman that he was only sent to Israel, he does have Jesus' discouraging comment that "It is not fair to take the children's food and throw it to the dogs" (Mark 7:27). Mark prefaces this with Jesus' words "Let the children be fed first," the implication perhaps being that after the children have been fed, then the needs of the "dogs" — the Gentiles — may also be addressed. If this is an attempt by Mark (who is writing for Gentiles; cf. 7:3, 4) to include the Gentiles within the range of Jesus' ministry, it is in the context of an undeniably pro-Jewish and apparently anti-Gentile incident.[11]

Luke similarly is himself thoroughly committed to the Gentile mission of the church, but he does not suggest that Jesus pioneered this mission. His Gospel is focused on Jerusalem, and it is only the church, given a lot of prompting by the Holy Spirit and the pressure of persecution, that starts reaching out systematically to Gentiles. Paul speaks of Jesus as a "servant

10. It is not even very obvious that the author of Matthew would have added them to Mark and Q, had he found them in his own Jewish Christian "M" traditions. It is likely that he knew them in his principal source. Vermes, *Jesus the Jew*, 49, comments: "The authenticity of these sayings must be well-nigh impregnable." Scobie, "Jesus or Paul," argues forcefully that Jesus "confined his mission and that of his disciples to the people of Israel," but still (curiously) ascribes the saying in 10:5, 6 to a "conservative Jewish Christian community that stood in opposition to the outreach pioneered by the Hellenists" (56, 59). Catchpole, *Quest*, 165-71, argues for their presence in Q.

11. It is possible that Mark's interest in Jesus and the Gentiles is expressed in the whole of 7:1–8:10, starting with Jesus declaring "all foods clean" and ending with the feeding of the four thousand in a Gentile area. And it is possible that Luke indicates Jesus' international concerns in his central section, starting from 9:51 (Jesus traveling in Samaria, sending out the seventy, etc.), but the hints are quite muted.

of the circumcised" (Rom 15:8) and of Peter as an apostle to "the circumcised" (Gal 2:7), and there is little doubt that the church, which was to become self-consciously international, was well aware that Jesus' own mission focused almost exclusively on the Jews.

The Church

But how did Jesus envisage his mission to Israel, and did he intend to found "the church"? He clearly did not see it as his mission to replace Judaism with a new religion or, primarily at least, to set up an institution of any sort. He saw himself as announcing God's new day of salvation and as inviting the people of Israel to receive the salvation that they had been promised and were looking for. He saw himself as looking for the lost sheep in order to bring them back into God's fold.[12]

But although Jesus saw himself as having a mission to Israel as a whole, this does not mean that he had no concept of inaugurating a movement with which people could and should identify. On the contrary, he called people to "come after/follow him" (e.g., Matt 4:19/Mark 1:17; Matt 8:18-22/Luke 9:57-62), he spoke of his followers as his family (Matt 12:46-50/Mark 3:31-35/Luke 8:19-21),[13] and he appointed people (notably the twelve) to be his authoritative representatives, to "fish" for people, and to invite others to identify with the movement.

There has been considerable resistance to the idea that Jesus intended to found the church. The two Gospel texts that actually use the word "church" are Matt 16:17, 18 and 18:15-17. In the first Jesus commends Peter on his recognition of him as the Christ:

> Blessed are you, Simon son of Jonah! For flesh and blood has not revealed this to you, but my Father in heaven. And I tell you, you are Peter, and on this rock I will build my church, and the gates of Hades will not prevail against it.

In the second, Jesus gives instructions on dealing with problems among disciples:

12. The picture of gathering in sheep has an important OT background in Ezekiel 34, where God promises to gather the scattered sheep and to give them a new shepherd, "my servant David."

13. Note also the various sayings that speak of disciples as "brothers" (e.g., Matt 5:22, 23; 16:15-35).

If he refuses to listen to them, tell it to the church; and if he does not listen even to the church, let him be to you as a Gentile and tax collector (RSV).

Both texts are found only in Matthew's Gospel, and both have regularly been seen as reflecting a post-Easter perspective rather than Jesus' own perspective. To some Protestant interpreters, with their suspicion of ecclesiastical structure and authority (and especially of a supposedly Petrine papacy), this conclusion has undoubtedly been congenial.

But this conclusion is premature. Whatever questions there may be about the particular Matthean texts — and we have already suggested that some uniquely Matthean texts have a good claim to authenticity despite some source critics' prejudices against the so-called "M" material — it is highly improbable that Jesus called for people to respond to the exciting and urgent good news of the kingdom without explaining how they should respond. Precedents for such response include the Essenes of Qumran — with their clearly defined eschatological community, which distinguished itself sharply from Israel as a whole — and John the Baptist, with whom Jesus was so closely identified, who called people to baptism and who had a body of disciples.[14] Jesus also had disciples, including the symbolically significant twelve, and called people to identify with him. It is likely that he saw his messianic role as one of bringing God's promised salvation to Israel and that he considered those who received and followed him to be the true and saved "remnant."[15]

In this theological context Jesus could very well have spoken of building his community in the way suggested by Matt 16:17, 18.[16] The phraseology — "flesh and blood," "bar Jonah" (transliterated from Aramaic in the Greek), "gates of Hades" — and the thought expressed, namely, the idea of

14. John 3:22; 4:1 suggests that Jesus, in an early period of ministry in Judea, used baptism to enlist people as his disciples, and the early church similarly was a baptizing movement. There is no direct evidence that Jesus baptized during his Galilean ministry, but people could and did "receive" or reject him and his message (Matt 10:14/Mark 6:11/Luke 9:5; Matt 10:40/Luke 10:16).

15. For the OT idea of the remnant see, e.g., Jer 23:3-6: "I myself will gather the remnant of my flock. . . . I will raise up shepherds over them. . . . I will raise up for David a righteous Branch . . . ," and Jer 31:8.

16. In the Septuagint Greek ekklēsia regularly translates Hebrew qahal, which most frequently is used of the "congregation" of Israel. In the Dead Sea Scrolls yahad is often used of the community.

a new Israel and probably of a new temple being "built" by Jesus, are strongly Semitic,[17] and they fit Jesus' context.[18]

As for Matt 18:15-17, the instruction is strongly Jewish in tone ("let him be to you as a Gentile"), and the procedure suggested for dealing with disputes is similar in some ways to what is prescribed in the Dead Sea Scrolls.[19] The passage has parallels in Luke 17:3, 4, and probably goes back very early.[20]

The Temple

The thought of Jesus "building" a community brings us to the question of Jesus and the temple. The Gospels make it clear that the temple featured prominently in the last part of Jesus' ministry — in his teaching as well as in his symbolic act of "cleansing" the temple. They suggest that his attitude to the temple was an important aspect of the charges against him at his

17. Meyer, *Aims of Jesus*, 185-97, sees the background to Jesus' saying in the "master image of the cosmic rock," a rock identified in Judaism sometimes with the temple and also with Abraham; he also develops the idea of the Messiah as the builder of a new temple, linking the saying to the preceding Petrine confession of Jesus as Messiah and "Son of God."

18. The absence of the saying from Mark and Luke is not a major argument against the authenticity of the saying, or even against its authenticity in the Caesarea Philippi context. First, though there is no precisely equivalent saying in Mark or Luke, they do attest the particular leadership role of Simon and that Jesus gave him the name "Cephas" (Mark 3:16/Luke 6:14). They do not explain the name, but that it had symbolic significance is hardly to be doubted. Luke and John also associate Jesus with the idea of a new temple (see below).

Second, there is evidence that could (just possibly) point to Matthew, Luke, and John knowing a non-Markan version of the Caesarea Philippi story: All three agree against Mark in including the genitive "of God" in the Petrine confession (Matt 16:16: "the Son of the living God"; Luke 9:20: "The Messiah of God"; John 6:69: "the Holy One of God").

Finally, it is not impossible that Mark omitted the Matthean saying from this context because he was concentrating in his Gospel on the christological issue (at the expense of ecclesiology) and perhaps because the saying about Peter was controversial in Pauline circles, if not more widely (see discussion below).

On the authenticity question see the particularly important discussion by Meyer in *Aims of Jesus*, 185-97; also Maier, "Church in the Gospel of Matthew"; Witherington, *Jesus, Paul*, 84-94.

19. 1QS 5:24–6:1; CD 9.

20. See Davies and Allison, *Matthew*, 781-807.

trial. Mark describes people accusing him of saying, "I will destroy this temple that is made with hands, and in three days I will build another, not made with hands" (Mark 14:58). At the cross the mockers shouted, "Aha! You who would destroy the temple and build it in three days, save yourself, and come down from the cross!" (15:29, 30).

Mark describes this accusation against Jesus as "false testimony" (14:57), but neither he nor (certainly) the other Evangelists thought it was without any foundation at all.[21] They agree, at least, that Jesus spoke of the coming destruction of the temple (Matt 24:2/Mark 13:2/Luke 21:6) and that he provocatively "cleansed" the temple (Matt 21:10-17/Mark 11:15-17/Luke 19:45, 46). The meaning of that controversial action is debated, but it is presented at least as a protest against the commercialization of the temple, which was supposed to be a "house of prayer." Mark for one sees it as more than that: By locating it within the framework of the story of the cursing of the fig tree, he presents it as an acted parable of judgment on the corrupt sanctuary (11:12-14, 20-26).[22]

There is widespread scholarly agreement that the Gospels are right to suggest that the issue of the temple and of Jesus' attitude to it was historically important in fatally souring relations between him and his opponents. But there is plenty of disagreement about exactly how he viewed the temple and his relationship to it. A number of comments are worth making:

Jesus' opposition to the temple

First, there is no need to doubt the Gospels' suggestion that Jesus, like the Essenes, saw the temple authorities as corrupt and as misusing the sacred house of prayer. Jeremiah warned in his day of those who trusted in the deceptive words "this is the temple of the Lord," but whose corruption was making the temple into a "den of robbers" (7:1-15). There is every likelihood that this is precisely how Jesus saw the situation in his own day — with the temple a massive and proud symbol of great importance in the national consciousness, but built by a corrupt half-pagan king and run by a religiously corrupt and compromised hierarchy.

21. Mark believes that Jesus' opponents misconstrued and misused truths about Jesus, but that they were ironically witnessing to the truth (both at the trial and at the cross).

22. On the cleansing see recently Sanders, *Jesus and Judaism*, 61-76; Witherington, *Christology*, 107-16.

The destruction of the temple

Second, it is entirely credible that Jesus spoke of the temple's coming desecration and destruction. Politically the temple was often the focus of the rather tense relationships between the Jews and their Roman rulers in Jesus' day, and one of the people's worst fears was that the temple, which had been rebuilt by Herod into such a magnificent monument of the faith, might again be attacked. Theologically, to anyone as steeped in the prophets as Jesus was, the temple was inevitably vulnerable to divine judgment: Jeremiah, for example, had warned that the temple, in which people trusted, would become like Shiloh (7:12-15) — and it did. Daniel spoke of "the abomination that makes desolate" being set up before the restoration of the kingdom to Israel, which he portrays as "one like a son of man" (9:27; 11:31; 12:11; cf. 7:13, 27).[23]

The renewal of the temple

But how could such a negative outlook be reconciled with Jesus' positive message of the coming of the kingdom? The prophetic hope was not just — not even mainly! — for the destruction of the temple but for a renewed and purified temple and for Zion restored. For example, Isaiah speaks of the temple mount being established and all the nations streaming to it, saying, "Come, let us go up to the mountain of the LORD, to the house of the God of Jacob; that he may teach us his ways and that we may walk in his paths" (2:2, 3); the same theme is taken up in Isa 56:6-8, where the God who gathers the outcasts of Israel also promises to gather the Gentiles, "for my house shall be called a house of prayer for all peoples." Zechariah also pictures the nations coming up to a temple that has been sanctified, and the author comments (interestingly), "and there shall no longer be traders in the house of the LORD of hosts on that day" (14:16-21). The vision of a restored temple is explicit also in Ezekiel 40–48, and Mal 3:1-4 spells out that such restoration will be through divine intervention: "The Lord whom you seek will suddenly come to his temple. . . . He will purify the descendants of Levi and refine them like gold and silver, until they present offerings to the LORD in righteousness."[24]

---

23. Josephus, *War* VI.300 refers to a later Jesus, son of Ananus, prophesying against the temple in the 60s AD.

24. See Sanders, *Jesus and Judaism*, 77-87, for other evidence of the Jewish hope for a rebuilt and renewed temple.

It seems a priori likely, given such passages as these and given Jesus' conviction that the day of fulfillment — that is, of the kingdom of God — was coming in and through his ministry, that he looked forward to the establishment of a restored temple.[25] He did not see Herod's temple as that eschatological temple; on the contrary, as we have seen, he believed that Herod's splendid building would be destroyed. But it is likely that he looked beyond that destruction to restoration.

The Gospels confirm that he did think in these terms. They confirm that he defined his own relationship to the temple in terms of the OT, both explicitly and implicitly — coming to the temple, casting out the traders, and speaking of the "house of prayer." They also make it clear that the accusation against him was that he spoke not just of destroying the temple, but also of building another "in three days" (Mark 14:58; 15:29).

"I will destroy . . . I will build"

Mark, as we saw, suggests that the accusation was false, but he may mean by this that the interpretation put on Jesus' words by his enemies was false and mischievous, not that there was nothing to the accusation at all.[26] It may well be that he would agree with the author of the fourth Gospel, who unashamedly ascribes the saying quoted in the Markan accusation to Jesus (John 2:19) — except that Jesus says there, "Destroy this temple, and in three days I will raise it up," not "*I* will destroy . . . ," and the Evangelist explains that Jesus was referring to "the temple of his body," as his disciples understood after the resurrection (vv. 21, 22).[27] Whether or not this was Mark's interpretation, it seems quite likely that the enigmatic saying does have its roots in Jesus' teaching — Matthew does not reproduce Mark's comment about the false testimony — and that Jesus was speaking of the eschatological destruction and restoration of the temple.[28]

---

25. Fredriksen, *From Jesus to Christ,* 113, finds the expectation of the destruction and restoration of the temple to be of a piece with Jesus' kingdom teaching: What had happened to Israel before (judgment on the temple followed by redemption and rebuilding) was about to happen again. She cites Tobit 14:5.

26. On Mark see Juel, *Messiah and Temple.* His argument is broadly persuasive despite the extensive critique in Gundry, *Mark,* 898-907. Note also Geddert, *Watchwords,* 113-47.

27. See on this and the "temple" motif in general Sweet, "House Not Made with Hands"; Carson, *John,* 181.

28. Theissen, *Social Reality,* 94-114, speaks of Jesus' "aggression towards" and "identification with" the temple, and sees the saying about destroying and rebuilding

A spiritual temple?

The fourth Gospel interprets the saying about the temple's destruction and rebuilding to refer to Jesus' resurrection and looks forward to the displacement of the era of the physical temple by the era of the Spirit (4:21-24). But how did Jesus himself envision the rebuilding of the temple? "In three days" need not be taken in a strictly chronological sense,[29] but it suggests that Jesus may well have had in mind a supernatural reconstruction of the temple. (Such is probably Mark's interpretation when he speaks of a temple "made without hands.") More specifically, a number of synoptic sayings support the fourth Gospel in suggesting that Jesus thought in terms of a spiritual temple replacing the physical temple.

There is, first, the parable of the vineyard: The story of the tenants' rejection of the son is followed by the quotation from Ps 118:22, 23, which speaks of "the stone that the builders rejected" becoming "the head of the corner." The picture here is of Jesus, the rejected son of the parable, being the foundation of God's new building, and it is quite clear from the context of the story in the synoptic Gospels (following the cleansing of the temple and the cursing of the fig tree) that the building concerned is the temple. The quotation from the psalm has often been seen as a Christian addition to Jesus' parable, bringing into the story the idea of the resurrection. However, there is a good case for regarding the quotation as authentic teaching of Jesus and even as integral to the parable.[30] If it is such, then it is a significant clue suggesting that the supernatural temple that Jesus anticipated was not a building of bricks and mortar but something intimately connected with himself.[31]

Matthew also has significant sayings, including Matt 12:5-7, where Jesus justifies healing on the sabbath by reference to David and the priests and then by his comment that "something greater than the temple is here"

---

as fitting in well with Jesus' eschatological expectations and with the historical context of his journey to Jerusalem. "Jesus like other Jewish prophets goes with his followers to the place where he expects the divine action to take place; it explains why the disciples made Jerusalem their headquarters after Easter; for it was here they awaited decisive eschatological events" (pp. 96-97).

29. The phrase might have a background in passages such as Hos 6:2, speaking of God's restoring and reviving his people.

30. See especially Snodgrass, *Parable of the Wicked Tenants*, 63-65, for a closely argued defence of the integrity of the quotation in the parable; also Bayer, *Jesus' Predictions*, 90-109.

31. If the psalm quotation does not go back to Jesus, its use by the synoptists is evidence of the influence of the idea of a spiritual temple in the early church.

(12:6). We have already discussed Matt 16:16-20 and seen a possible new temple allusion in the saying of Jesus to Peter: "I will build my church, and the gates of Hades will not prevail against it."[32] The old temple is seen to be under judgment, and even the Jewish Christian Matthew can suggest that Jesus' disciples are "free" of obligation to it (17:24-27); Jesus, the new son of David, is building a new temple.[33]

The idea of a spiritual temple was not unthinkable in first-century Judaism. Indeed, this idea and the idea of offering spiritual sacrifices became (of necessity) part of mainstream Judaism after the destruction of Jerusalem in AD 70. But the idea existed already while the temple still stood, not only (very widely) in the NT, but also in the Dead Sea Scrolls.[34] Most striking is the section from the Community Rule to which we referred when considering possible links between John the Baptist and Qumran. It speaks of the council of the community as "a House of Holiness for Israel, an Assembly of Supreme Holiness for Aaron . . . that tried wall, that *precious corner-stone,* whose foundations shall neither rock nor sway in their place." Here we have the idea of the assembly ("the church," as we might translate in Christian terms) as a holy temple and the use in that connection of OT "stone" imagery (from Isa 28:16) to express a thought very similar to what we find in Matt 16:16-20. The scroll goes on to say of the elect members of the community:

> They shall establish the spirit of holiness according to everlasting truth. They shall atone for guilty rebellion and for sins of unfaithfulness that they may obtain lovingkindness for the Land without the flesh of holocausts and the fat of sacrifice. And prayer rightly offered shall be as an acceptable fragrance of righteousness, and perfection of way as a delectable free-will offering.[35]

The language of the scroll (which goes on to speak of the coming of the messiahs and the Prophet) is remarkably reminiscent of various NT

32. Note the "I will build" phraseology here as in Mark 14:58, "I will build it in three days."

33. 2 Samuel 7 speaks of God adopting David's son as his own son and of David's son building a house for God. It also speaks of God building David's house. The passage is important for NT christology (see especially Scott, *Adoption*), and it may be that NT thinking about Jesus as the builder of a new temple, but also as himself the new temple, may have something to do with the "houses" of 2 Samuel 7: The parable of the vineyard describes the master's "son" and then speaks of him as the cornerstone of the temple. (See further below.)

34. Juel, *Messiah and Temple,* 166-67, observes: "In a movement proximate to Christianity in time and place, a community used temple imagery as a self-designation."

35. 1QS 8:5-8; 9:3-5 as translated in Vermes, *Dead Sea Scrolls,* 72-74.

texts that speak of the new temple (e.g., cf. the sacrifices of prayer and righteousness with Heb 13:15, 16; Phil 4:18). Its importance, so far as Jesus is concerned, is that it makes it entirely conceivable that he thought in terms of a spiritual temple embodied in himself and his community.[36]

Not that Jesus' temple theology was identical to that found in the scrolls. He appears to have spoken of the destruction and restoration of the temple, particularly in connection with his own death and resurrection.[37] He regarded his death as marking the end of the old and the beginning of the new: The rejection of the son (in the parable of the vineyard) was the end of the old order and the beginning of the new building. This fits in with what we said in chapter 4 about Jesus' understanding of his death. He saw it as a sacrifice for sin and as a new Passover event, bringing in God's kingdom and establishing the new covenant in people's hearts. It is not a big jump from this to the conviction that from now on forgiveness of sin and the experience of God's presence are to be found in Jesus and his new-covenant community, the new spiritual temple.

The Gentiles[38]

Several of the OT passages that speak prophetically of the temple's restoration refer to Gentiles coming to the temple — to worship and to learn

36. Horsley, *Jesus and the Spiral*, 296, comments: "If Jesus' prophecy against the Temple included the promise of a new 'temple' . . . then the most likely meaning was that God, while about to destroy the Jerusalem Temple, was building his *true* house, the renewed people of Israel." Juel, *Messiah and Temple*, 170-208, suggests that Mark was in a Jewish tradition that associated the Messiah (as son of David) with the building of a new temple or "house" (see 2 Samuel 7). He is agnostic about pre-Markan tradition, but Paul, as we shall see, makes it clear that the idea of the "temple" now identified with the Christian community is pre-Markan. It is entirely possible that Jesus spoke in these terms and saw himself as "building" the new temple.

37. All the sayings about the temple's destruction are connected in the synoptics with Jesus' last visit to Jerusalem. This could be for literary reasons, because Jesus is only in Jerusalem at this point in the synoptic account of his ministry (contrast John 2:19-22, though John also associates the saying with the passion); but it is historically perfectly plausible that he did speak about the temple during his last visit and that this contributed to his arrest and subsequent crucifixion.

38. For a particularly useful discussion of Jesus and the Gentile mission see Scobie, "Jesus or Paul." Earlier important discussions include Jeremias, *Jesus' Promise*; Hahn, *Mission in the NT*; E. P. Sanders, *Jesus and Judaism*, 212-21, arguing that Jesus himself did not express a view about Gentiles, but that Gentile mission was an appropriate extension of his mission of eschatological restoration.

(e.g., Isa 2:2; 56:6-8; Zech 14:16). Such hope for the Gentiles is an important strand in the OT prophetic expectation: Israel will be saved, but as Isa 49:6 puts it, "It is too light a thing that you should be my servant to raise up the tribes of Jacob and to restore the survivors of Israel; I will give you as a light to the nations, that my salvation may reach to the end of the earth."

It is a priori likely that Jesus, given his kingdom perspective, shared this vision. But the Gospels' evidence on this matter is ambivalent. On the one hand, as we have seen, Jesus speaks and acts as though his mission is exclusively to Israel (see above on "the lost sheep"); on the other hand, he speaks and acts in ways that transcend Jewish exclusiveness (e.g., in his attitudes toward Samaritans: Luke 10:25-37; John 4, etc.), and he appears to expect the "gospel" to be preached to all nations (e.g., Matt 24:14/Mark 13:10, etc.).

Several explanations of this ambivalence are possible. It is possible, first, that Jesus himself had no wider vision than for his own people and that the universalism ascribed to him is the post-resurrection perspective of a church that had come to be involved in mission to Gentiles in a way that Jesus never envisaged. This explanation will hardly do: Jesus' revolutionary openness to sinners, tax collectors, and other people on the margins of society (including Samaritans) is well attested, and his view of the kingdom as the restoration of God's world in fulfillment of the OT very probably had a place for Gentiles.[39]

A second possibility is that Jesus did indeed have a place for Gentiles in his vision of God's purposes, but that he saw the gathering of the Gentiles as something that God would accomplish at the end of the age, not as a program to be implemented by himself or his followers.[40] Such a view is possible, and yet the evidence is that Jesus saw the kingdom — in all its revolutionary force — as already breaking through the social and religious barriers of his day, and it is not obvious why he should have included the Samaritans but excluded the Gentiles.

The third possibility is that Jesus saw the kingdom as "for the Jew first, then for the Greek" (to borrow a Pauline phrase), that is, that he saw his own ministry before and up to his death as specifically to the Jews, but looked forward to a future extension of that ministry through his fol-

39. Jesus' ministry to Samaritans, as also his comment to the disciples about their future rule over the twelve tribes (Matt 19:28/Luke 22:28-30), suggests that he was looking for the fulfillment of the OT prophecies that look for the reunification of the twelve tribes of Israel (e.g., Jeremiah 30 and Ezekiel 37). See Scobie, "Origin of the Universal Mission," 53.

40. See the classic discussion of Jeremias, *Jesus' Promise to the Nations*.

lowers.[41] This is, of course, precisely what the Gospels suggest, and it has much in its favor: It makes sense in terms of the OT prophetic perspective, which was focused on Israel but also had a vision for the world;[42] it makes sense in terms of Jesus' kingdom preaching and practice — for example, the way that he limited his ministry to Jews and yet showed notable openness to "outsiders";[43] and it makes sense given the importance that Jesus attached to his own death as marking a watershed, negatively for Jews who rejected him and positively in terms of the salvation that he saw himself bringing. That the early church was slow to implement Jesus' vision for the Gentiles is not a strong argument against this interpretation: Jesus gave his followers a vision, not a mission strategy specifying how and on what terms the Gentiles should be evangelized. Acts is quite credible in suggesting that it was a slow and painful process for the church as it moved out from its Jewish roots into the Gentile world.[44]

JEWS, GENTILES, AND THE CHURCH IN PAUL

To the Jew First and Also to the Greek

Paul . . .

When it comes to the question of Jew and Gentile, we are in a different world when we move to Paul. We are in a Gentile world with largely Gentile churches involved in Gentile mission and facing Gentile problems. And yet this world is not totally different: We have already seen how Paul's theology and eschatology are essentially Jewish, and perhaps the dominant issue in all of his letters is how Judaism and Jewish Christianity relate to Gentile Christianity. That relationship matters.

Paul takes it for granted that in some sense the Jew comes "first" (Rom 1:16; 2:9, 10). His own distinctive ministry is to Gentiles, and he often vigorously defends that ministry from so-called "Judaizers." But he does

41. Compare Schlatter's view of Jesus and the church in *Jesus and Paul*, 36; he argues that Jesus anticipated the gathering of the Christian community after his death.

42. Horsley, *Jesus and the Spiral*, 193-94, argues that the Jewish hope was for the restoration of Israel first, then for the gathering of the Gentiles — hence something of Paul's struggles in Romans 9–11.

43. See Scobie, "Jesus or Paul," 60, on intimations in Jesus' ministry of the future ingathering of Gentiles.

44. See further in Scobie, "Jesus or Paul."

not question the historic claim of the Jews to be the people of God or their privileged position. He knows that Jesus was a "servant of the circumcised" (Rom 15:8) and that Peter (and probably the other original apostles) are commissioned to go to the circumcised (Gal 2:7-9). The Jews are privileged in this respect, and Paul believes that despite their tragic unbelief God has a continuing and important place for them in his purposes (see Romans 9–11).[45]

Despite the Jews' privileges, for Paul the good news is that the Gentiles have been brought in, and that "in Christ Jesus" "there is no longer Jew or Greek" (Gal 3:28; cf. Rom 10:12; Col 3:11). There is equality in Christ, and the old barriers are broken down. That is not to deny the Jews' historical status or privileges: It is into that status and those privileges that the Gentiles have now been grafted (Romans 11). They have become part of the Israel of God through Jesus. They are thus "the saints" (i.e., holy ones) — a term used in the OT of Israel, notably in Daniel 7 ("the saints of the most high"); they are the "congregation of God," the word *ekklēsia* being used in the Septuagint of the people of Israel, though also in secular Greek of an assembly of citizens.

The Gentile mission is, on the one hand, something new. It is in particular a commission and apostleship given to Paul himself, though he was one born out of due time (Gal 1:15, 16; 1 Cor 15:9). On the other hand, it is the fulfillment of OT promise, not a Pauline innovation or invention (Rom 15:9-12).

For all Paul's affirmation of the Jewishness of Christianity, he came into sharp and regular conflict with Jews and Jewish Christians who saw him as betraying the ancestral faith, notably by his refusal to impose the Jewish law and circumcision on Gentile converts. The law was a particularly sore point (to which we shall return in chapter 6). But Paul refused to accept that he was abandoning Judaism. One of his most important projects was the collection that he organized among the Gentile churches for the church in Jerusalem (1 Cor 16:1; 2 Corinthians 8 and 9; Rom 15:25-28). This project could simply be seen as mutual aid among the early Christians. But for Paul it was more than that. It was designed to express and foster fellowship between Gentile Christianity and Jerusalem, not just for pragmatic reasons, but for theological reasons: God's purpose was not just that individuals be saved, but to bring the Gentiles into the family of Abraham. The collection expressed — in Pauline theory at least — something of that

---

45. For Paul's often underestimated Jewishness see Jervell, "Paul in the Acts of the Apostles."

reconciliation between Jew and Greek. Paul may even have seen the collection as a fulfillment of the prophetic predictions of the wealth of the nations flowing to Jerusalem (e.g., Isa 60:4-14; 61:6).[46]

. . . and Jesus

Although Paul's situation is so different from that of Jesus — with Jesus restricting his ministry to Jews and Paul devoting himself to Gentiles — Paul is well aware of Jesus' different missionary priorities. He seems familiar with the traditions of Matt 10:5; 15:24 (or their equivalent). It seems highly likely that Paul's Jewish Christian opponents would have made sure that he was aware of these potentially embarrassing traditions. But Paul is not evidently embarrassed, unless over the Jews' failure to believe in Jesus; this embarrassment arises because his own theology affirms the priority of the Jews.

The Pauline preoccupation with the Gentiles is not paralleled to a significant extent in the Jesus-tradition, but the theological vision expressed in Jesus' boundary-breaking ministry to outsiders is expressed in Paul's ministry to Gentiles.[47] Furthermore, there is reason to think that Jesus looked forward to the gathering in of the Gentiles, even though he did not directly address the difficult practical questions (e.g., circumcision) that were to prove so divisive in the church as it moved out into the Gentile world. Had he done so, such issues would presumably not have become so divisive!

Temple of the Holy Spirit

Paul . . .

If Paul saw his collection for Jerusalem as fulfillment of prophecies about the wealth of the Gentiles being brought to Zion, this does not mean that

---

46. See, e.g., Munck, *Paul and the Salvation of Mankind*, 301-5; Scobie, "Jesus or Paul," 52.

47. If the Lukan version of the parable of the great banquet in Luke 14:15-24, with its reference to the servants going out to the highways and hedges, represents Luke's application of the parable to Gentiles (which is uncertain; see Nolland, *Luke*, 757), then it is evidence of the church's interest in the Gentiles creeping back into the gospel traditions, but also of the fact that Jesus' teaching about the gathering in of the outsiders was seen as relevant to Gentiles.

he saw Jerusalem and particularly the temple as having unchanged significance. He did regard unity between Jewish and Gentile Christians as of
vital importance, and the collection was as much as anything else meant to
express fellowship (e.g., Rom 15:27). But he also believed that a revolution
— new creation indeed — had occurred with the coming of Jesus, so that
conformity to the Jewish law was no longer a necessary mark of the people
of God and the Jerusalem temple was no longer the focus of God's presence.

The Jerusalem temple as such makes at most one appearance in the
Pauline writings, and then in rather unhappy circumstances: In 2 Thes 2:4
Paul speaks of the "lawless one" setting himself up in the temple (see the
discussion in chapter 7 below). But otherwise Paul consistently identifies
the temple with the Christian church. To be more precise, he speaks in two
ways: (1) He refers to the church fellowship as the dwelling place of God's
Holy Spirit: "Do you not know that you are God's temple and that God's
Spirit dwells in you? If anyone destroys God's temple, God will destroy that
person. For God's temple is holy, and you are that temple" (1 Cor 3:16, 17).
Similarly in 2 Cor 6:16 he asks: "What agreement has the temple of God
with idols? For we are the temple of the living God." He goes on to speak
of the need for holiness.[48] (See also Eph 2:21.) It is, then, the "saints" (i.e.,

---

48. 2 Cor 6:16 comes in the middle of a passage (6:14–7:1) that has often been
seen as an interpolation in its context; see especially Scott, *Adoption*, 193-219, for
discussion and questioning of this. The passage is interesting for the way it brings
together the idea of the church as the temple with an echo of 2 Sam 7:14, where God
makes promises to David about his son Solomon: "I will be a father to him, and he shall
be a son to me." As we noted earlier, 2 Samuel 7 speaks of Solomon building God's
house and God building a house (i.e., family) for David. It may well be that this passage
lies behind the Qumran community's view of themselves as God's temple/house (see
4Q176) as well as behind Christian thinking about Jesus as the new son of David and
son of God and the one who establishes a new temple (see also Zech 6:12).

Christian "new temple" thinking has several points of contact with Qumran.
2 Cor 6:14–7:1, with its emphasis on the holiness and separation of the people of God
and its reference to 2 Samuel 7, has links to various texts from the Dead Sea Scrolls,
e.g., 4Q174. Other NT passages taking up the theme of the church as a new temple and
having points of resemblance to the Qumran scrolls include Eph 2:18-22 (with its
inclusive emphasis contrasting with the exclusiveness of 4Q174); 1 Tim 3:15 (e.g., with
its reference to the church as "pillar and bulwark of the truth," cf. 1QS 5:5, 6); and 1 Pet
2:4-6 (e.g., its reference to a royal "priesthood"). I am grateful to Daniel Sefa-Dapaah
for alerting me to some of these links.

If Jesus saw himself as the Messiah and the "son" of God of 2 Samuel 7 and if
he was familiar with the exegetical tradition represented at Qumran, then it is quite
possible that he was himself the originator of what is an important and pervasive NT
tradition.

the "holy ones"), as Paul calls them, who are the temple, and it may be significant that, when Paul makes his great collection, it is quite specifically for the "saints" in Jerusalem (1 Cor 16:1; 2 Cor 8:4; 9:1, 12; Rom 15:25, 26, 31). (2) He also speaks of the individual believer's body as the Spirit's temple.[49] Thus in 1 Cor 6:19 he insists that fornication is not an option for the Christian: "Do you not know that your body is the temple of the Holy Spirit within you?" (cf. also 2 Cor 5:1 on the resurrection body as "a house not made with hands").[50]

. . . and Jesus

Paul's spiritualized view of the temple has some possible precedent in the gospel traditions of Jesus.[51] We have noted that Jesus saw the Jerusalem temple as under God's judgment and destined for destruction. In the enigmatic saying cited against him at his trial, Jesus is said to have promised to build a temple in three days, the implication being that it will be supernaturally constructed and therefore in some sense spiritual. In the sayings of Matt 16:16-20 and 21:42/Mark 12:10, 11/Luke 20:17 there are hints of a temple built on Jesus and his apostles.

The Church "in Christ" and as a "Body"

Paul . . .

Paul speaks of the church as God's temple, but even more characteristically he defines it christologically, as "in Christ" and as the "body" of Christ. It will be helpful to look at Paul's thought here under three subheadings:

"*In Christ.*" This phrase takes us back to Paul's participationist view of salvation, which we have already discussed in connection with the death of Jesus. For Paul the Christian shares in the death of Jesus — not least through baptism and eucharist. But what exactly does Paul mean by the

---

49. In Rom 12:1 he also uses cultic language in urging Christians to present their "bodies" to God as a "living sacrifice."

50. Gundry, *Mark*, 901, wants to take 1 Cor 3:16 and 2 Cor 6:16 individualistically on the grounds of the similarity with 1 Cor 6:19 and because the separation commended in 2 Cor 6:16 is something individual. But the reasoning is not cogent: Paul could perfectly well use temple imagery (like "body" language) flexibly both of the church and of the individual. See Sweet, "A House," 375, 383.

51. And also, interestingly, in the speech of Stephen as recorded in Acts 7.

phrase "in Christ" (or "in Christ Jesus"), of which he is so fond? What does he mean, for example, when he says that "there is therefore now no condemnation for those who are *in Christ Jesus*" (Rom 8:1) or that "as all die in Adam, so all will be made alive *in Christ*" (1 Cor 15:22)? He evidently uses the phrase to refer to Christians, but why this phrase? The matter has been discussed at length by scholars.

The phrase means at least that the Christian is one who has come into the sphere — the eschatological sphere — of Christ's power and saving work,[52] in contrast to the old sinful sphere of Adam. To speak of "spheres of power" is, however, by itself too impersonal a way of describing what for Paul is something very personal.

We perhaps come closer to the meaning of his "in Christ" language by looking to OT figures such as Adam, Abraham, and Moses, who are not just individuals but representative leader figures (even father figures in the case of Adam and Abraham), with whom others are associated, whether by birth, descent, or religious or national allegiance.[53]

Even more relevant for the phrase "in Christ" may be the observation that the king of Israel, and hence the royal "messiah," was a representative leader figure with whom the people were bound together. Even if "Christ" has become, or has almost become, a proper name in Paul's letters, it inevitably continues to have messianic connotations, and to be "in Christ" is to be in the Messiah's people.[54]

But even this explanation may not do full justice to Paul's language — still why "*in* Christ"? — or to his sense of a close personal union with Christ. We come closer to the heart of the matter when we notice that Paul uses the language of the family to refer to Christians: Believers are brothers (and sisters),[55] and not just brothers of each other but brothers of Jesus, crying "Abba" to the Father like Jesus and being fellow heirs with him (Rom 8:17).

The body of Christ. But the personal union between the believer and Christ, as Paul sees it, is more than just shared family membership, and comes most sharply into focus in his portrayal of the church as "the body

---

52. On spheres of power see Ziesler, *Pauline Christianity,* 45-69. Sanders, *Paul and Palestinian Judaism,* 549, speaks of "participationist eschatology."

53. Paul speaks not only of those who are "in Christ" but also of those who are "in Adam" (1 Cor 15:22), of those who were baptized "into Moses" (1 Cor 10:2), and of those who are blessed "in Abraham" (Gal 3:8, quoting Gen 12:3; 18:18).

54. So Wright, *Climax of the Covenant,* 41-55.

55. "Brother" and "son" are regularly used in the Greek of the NT in an inclusive sense to refer to Christian men and women.

of Christ," believers being Christ's limbs (see 1 Cor 6:15; 10:17; 12:12, 13; Rom 12:4; also Col 1:18; Eph 1:22, 23; 4:15; 5:23).

The "body" image is used by Paul, on the one hand, to describe the relationships of Christians to each other within the church: The body is one, yet made up of different, interdependent parts. So there needs to be within the body both love and the exercise and recognition of different gifts and ministries (see particularly the discussion of spiritual gifts in 1 Corinthians 12–14). But the body image is also used, on the other hand, to emphasize the believer's intimate relationship with Christ; thus in 1 Corinthians 6 Paul explains that it is unthinkable for believers who are "limbs" of Christ to have sexual relations with prostitutes, and in Colossians and Ephesians Christ is the "head" of the church (cf. 1 Cor 11:3).

There has been plenty of speculation as to the source of Paul's idea of the "body of Christ." Scholars have compared the Greek idea of the citizens in a particular place as a body, the Stoic conception of mankind as a body, the rabbinic notion that Adam's body contained within it the whole human race, and the Gnostic idea of the world as God's body. That there are so many possibilities points up the fact that the body is a very natural image to use in all sorts of contexts, and so it is not necessary to assume that Paul borrowed it from anyone else.[56]

However, it may be that there was a significant sacramental ingredient to Paul's thinking, since Paul uses "body of Christ" language not only to describe Christ's church but also, of course, in connection with the eucharist. Paul speaks of the eucharist as "a sharing in the body of Christ," and he makes a close connection between that eucharistic sharing and the idea of the church being Christ's body. Thus he says in 1 Cor 10:16, 17: "The bread that we break, is it not a sharing in the body of Christ. Because there is one bread, we who are many are one body, for we all partake of the one bread." It might be that Paul has brought together two originally unconnected ideas here, the sacramental "body of Christ" and the idea of the church as Christ's "body," but it is quite possible that the two ideas were generically connected — with the sacramental picture of the believer receiving Christ's body into himself or herself leading on to the idea of that believer becoming and being a part — a limb — of Christ.[57] If this explana-

---

56. Some scholars have suggested that Paul's Damascus road experience was a catalyst to his thinking, since the risen Christ identified himself with his followers very personally by saying, according to Acts, "Why do you persecute *me?*" (Acts 9:4; cf. Bruce, *Paul the Apostle*, 421).

57. 1 Cor 11:27-29 may lend support, since we have references to the eucharistic

tion of Paul's "body of Christ" language is correct, then it reinforces what was said about the personal nature of the union between Christ and the believer for Paul: The believer is not just a member of a Jesus society, but in the eucharist the Christian takes Jesus into himself or herself:[58] Christ and the Spirit of Christ are within the believer's body and the believer is a part of Jesus' body.

This understanding of the eucharist and of the church as Christ's body fits in also with Paul's baptismal theology. Paul can speak of baptism into both Christ's death (Romans 6) and the body of Christ, the church (1 Cor 12:13). These two ideas may appear to be quite separate. But it seems quite likely that Paul sees baptism as similar to the eucharist:[59] It expresses a sharing in Christ's death, and it is incorporation "into Christ," into his body once given on the cross and now expressed in the church.

The analogy of marital union. Paul's understanding of union with Christ may be illuminated by comparing his understanding of marital and sexual union. More than once Paul himself makes that very comparison. The most famous passage is Eph 5:24-33, where husbands are exhorted to

---

body of Christ in v. 27 and then, as many scholars think, to the church as "the body" in v. 29. "Without discerning the body" in v. 29 is a notoriously ambiguous phrase, and it could be referring to the eucharist, not to the church. But the very ambiguity may be evidence that the eucharistic/ecclesiastical ideas of the "body of Christ" are closely connected in Paul. An objection to the view being proposed is that "receiving" is quite different from "becoming." But this is a rather unimaginative reaction, possibly reflecting Protestant anxieties over crudely literal understandings of the eucharist. But there is nothing crude or very difficult about moving from the idea of taking Christ into oneself to the idea of becoming one with Christ and a part of Christ. It is worth recalling that the Greek word *koinōnia,* which Paul uses when speaking of "sharing/participation" in the body of Christ through the eucharist, often has the very down-to-earth sense of sharing material goods (as in 2 Cor 8:4, 9:13) — it is not a vague "fellowship" word — and that in some contexts at least it suggests the idea of having things in common (as in Acts 2:42, 44).

For the eucharistic explanation of Paul's body language see J. A. T. Robinson, *Body;* E. P. Sanders, *Paul and Palestinian Judaism,* 453-63. See also Ellis, "Traditions in 1 Corinthians," 487-88; *idem,* "Soma in First Corinthians."

58. Paul, if this is his understanding, is not adopting a mechanical or magical view of the sacraments. He warns against false confidence in the sacraments in 1 Corinthians 10. For him the sacraments are an expression of faith on the side of the believer and a spiritual gift on God's side (cf. 1 Cor 10:3, 4: "spiritual food," "spiritual drink").

59. Paul associates the two sacraments (to use our terminology) in 1 Corinthians 10.

love their wives "as Christ loved the church." Paul, if it is Paul who is writing, comments:

> Husbands should love their wives as their own bodies. He who loves his wife loves himself. For no one ever hates his own body, but nourishes and cherishes it, just as Christ does the church, because we are members of his body. "For this reason a man will leave his father and mother and be joined to his wife, and the two will become one flesh." This mystery is profound, and I am saying that it refers to Christ and the church.*

The view expressed here is that marriage brings husband and wife into a union that is described in Genesis 2 as "one flesh" and that means that husband and wife have in some sense a shared and united body — so the husband who loves his wife is loving himself.[60]

Precisely the same theology of sexual union is presupposed in the undisputedly Pauline 1 Corinthians: Thus in ch. 6 Paul rejects the view of those Corinthians who were saying (picking up on Paul's own teaching on Christian freedom from the law) that "all things are permissible for me," including prostitution. Paul disagrees with their claim that sex with a prostitute is as harmless as eating or drinking: "Do you not know," he asks, "that whoever is united to a prostitute becomes one body with her? For it is said, 'The two shall be one flesh.'" Sexual intercourse brings into being a union — a sharing in "one flesh/body" — that makes casual sex with a prostitute unthinkable and that also has implications for husband and wife. Thus in 7:3, 4 Paul explains (in response to the anti-sex teaching of some of the Corinthians) that husbands and wives must give each other their sexual rights, "for the wife does not have authority over her own body, but the husband does; likewise the husband does not have authority over his own body, but the wife does." He goes on to say that husbands and wives should not divorce and remarry, probably presupposing the same "one-flesh" union of marriage (see below).

In 1 Corinthians 6, as in Ephesians, a comparison is made between sexual union and the believer's union with Christ: It is unthinkable, Paul explains, for the Christian to be one with a prostitute and to make his limbs "limbs of a prostitute,"* because the believer is one with Christ and his

---

60. The picture in Genesis, which is of foundational importance for the NT picture, is of Eve being formed by God out of Adam's rib. So Adam can say that she is "bone of my bones and flesh of my flesh." Eve is in a real sense part of Adam, and part of Adam is in Eve. Genesis sees marriage in these terms: Husband and wife are brought by God into an analogous relationship of belonging together.

body is a "limb" of Christ, that is, part of Christ's body. The implication, as in Ephesians 5, is that the Christian's relationship to Christ is comparable to marital union.

The same implication is also present in Rom 7:1-4. There Paul speaks of the legal tie between husband and wife as one that is terminated by death, and then goes on to say: "You have died to the law through the body of Christ, so that you may belong to another, to him who has been raised from the dead. . . ."

Whatever else is suggested by these passages, they make it clear that Paul's understanding of the Christian's relationship to Christ is in terms of a close personal relationship. The Christian church is not just the association of Jesus' followers or even those who have been saved by Jesus and who experience his power. To be "in Christ" is, rather, to be "married" to Christ.[61]

The marriage analogy may also illuminate Paul's "body of Christ" language and his baptismal theology. Marriage for Paul means two becoming "one," so that from now on the body of the one belongs to the other. Similarly baptism for Paul means becoming "one body" with Christ in such a way that the Christian's body is now a "limb of Christ,"* and Christ's body (including his death and resurrection) is now shared with the believer.[62] The Christian receives, shares in, and is part of Christ's body.

. . . and Jesus

There are no close parallels to Paul's "in Christ" or "body" understanding of the church in the synoptic tradition. Paul writes after Jesus' death and resurrection — after the last supper as well — and his thinking arises in part at least out of reflection on Christ's death and resurrection and the last supper.

On the other hand, the Jesus of the Gospels does see himself as gathering God's eschatological people together. He spoke of his disciples as

61. Compare also 1 Cor 11:3; 2 Cor 11:2.

62. It is possible that this is implied in Rom 7:4, where Paul speaks of Christians having died to the law "through the body of Christ." The meaning may simply be that the Christian is free because of the death of Christ, but there may also be here the thought of the Christian being united to the body of Christ in baptism and so coming to share in that body's death.

The marriage analogy, like all parables and pictures, has its limitations. Whereas Paul can speak of husband and wife having mutual "lordship" over each other's bodies, the Christian is in no way lord over the body of Christ in which he or she shares.

members of his family (Matt 12:46-50/Mark 3:31-35/Luke 8:19-21),[63] and there are certainly corporate dimensions to Jesus' christology: The Danielic "one like a son of man" is a representative figure, standing for "the saints of the most high"; if this is the background to Jesus' usage, then Jesus sees himself as in some sense representing Israel.[64] Similarly, as we concluded in chapter 3, Jesus did see himself as "Messiah," another representative figure, and perhaps of decisive importance as background to Paul's "in Christ" language.[65]

If Paul's use of the body as an image for the church owes anything to the eucharistic words of institution, then there is a connection between Paul and Jesus at that point, though not a parallel concept as such. As for Paul's use of the marriage image to describe the relationship of Christ and the church, there is again no close parallel in Jesus' own teaching, but within the gospel tradition Jesus does picture his ministry as a wedding and himself as a bridegroom (e.g., Matt 9:15/Mark 2:19/Luke 5:34; Matt 22:1-14; 25:1-13; Luke 12:36).[66] The Pauline theology of marriage as a relationship of "one flesh" is paralleled in Jesus' teaching: Jesus denies the appropriateness of divorce in Matt 19:5, 6/Mark 10:6-9 by referring to marriage as a divinely created "one flesh" relationship.[67]

---

63. See Witherington, *Jesus, Paul*, 84.

64. If the background is Psalm 8 and Adam thinking, then again we are dealing with a representative leader figure.

65. John's Gospel offers a more direct parallel to Paul's language, notably in the discourse in ch. 15, where Jesus speaks of himself as the vine and of his disciples as the branches, who are to remain "in him." (Compare with this Paul's picture of the olive tree in Rom 11:17-21, where there is also the idea of "abiding" in God's goodness by faith.) John 15 is in many respects very Johannine, but it could be that a parable of a vine and its branches from Jesus underlies the chapter, itself drawing on the OT idea of Israel as God's vine. (There are several synoptic "tree"/vineyard parables, e.g., Matt 13:31, 32/Mark 4:30-32/Luke 13:18, 19; Luke 13:6-9; Matt 21:33-43/Mark 12:1-12/Luke 20:9-19, etc. On the OT background to the "vine" of John 15, note Isaiah 5, as well as Psalm 80, where we find Israel spoken of as the vine and also as "the son of man." For the importance of Psalm 80 see Moule, *Christology*, 24-26.)

66. On Jesus' wedding parables and Paul's thought about the church as Christ's bride, see Donfried, "Allegory of the Ten Virgins," 426, which compares Paul's reference to the church as a virgin whom he is presenting to Christ (2 Cor 11:2) with Matthew's parable of the virgins (25:1-13), which Donfried takes to be describing all Christians awaiting the marriage of the parousia. Stanley, "Pauline Allusions," 36, argues that the virgins actually symbolize the bride.

67. For discussion of this teaching and the comparison with Paul see the next chapter.

FINAL COMMENTS ON THE COMPARISON

So far this chapter has highlighted differences between Jesus and Paul. Thus, whereas for Jesus the focus of mission is on the Jews, with the Gentiles only on the horizon, for Paul the Gentiles are in the foreground and the Jews are rather problematic. The difference is a reflection of different missionary contexts, and yet there is considerable theological continuity, with Jesus looking for a universal kingdom and Paul recognizing the priority of the Jews. Rather similarly with the temple: Jesus in his Palestinian context pays considerable attention to the Jerusalem temple (albeit largely negative attention), whereas for Paul working among Gentiles the Jerusalem temple has effectively been superseded by the church as God's spiritual house. And yet there is continuity with Jesus' anticipation of a new spiritual temple.

Paul's "in Christ" and "body of Christ" language does represent something quite new. The almost mystical language probably arose from reflection on the Lord's death and resurrection as well as out of the sacramental life of the church. But the ideas, though distinctively expressed, are not without any precedent in Jesus' teaching: Jesus may not have seen himself as founding the church as we think of it today, but he did see himself as gathering together the saved people of God.

II. CONNECTING JESUS AND PAUL

In surveying a number of different themes, we have seen various points at which Paul's ideas have parallels in Jesus' teaching, and where there might therefore be a connection with that teaching. His view of the "temple" is an example, and his concept of the church as the "body of Christ" may be linked indirectly at least with the last supper traditions.

But is it possible to argue more specifically for points of connection?

THE MISSION DISCOURSE

There is a particularly good case for thinking that Paul knew and was influenced by the "mission discourse" of Jesus. It is a well-attested synoptic tradition, as we have seen. The evidence for Paul's familiarity with it is principally in 1 Corinthians 9.

The Evidence of 1 Corinthians 9

The broad context in 1 Corinthians 8–10 is the question of what Christians should or should not eat, with special reference to food offered to idols. Having spoken of Christian freedom, but then of the need to restrict one's own freedom for the sake of not causing others to stumble, Paul illustrates the point in chapter 9 by reference to his own apostleship. He is an example of someone who has restricted his own freedom and rights for the sake of the gospel.

In particular he has refrained from taking payment for his apostolic ministry, though he has the right to such payment. In using this illustration, Paul is apparently responding to critics who are questioning his true apostleship and who seem to hold it against him that he does not accept payment from others for his ministry. Paul insists, by way of reply, that he is a properly qualified "apostle," who has seen the Lord (9:1), that he has the "right to our food and drink" (v. 4), but that he has chosen not to exercise that right for the sake of commending the gospel to others (v. 12). He agrees that apostles have the right (or "authority") to eat and drink and that he and Barnabas have the right "to refrain from working for a living" (vv. 4, 6). He gives various examples, including some from the OT, to show that workers (even oxen) have the right to be fed. He refers to those who "work" in temple service and who "get their food from the temple" (v. 13) and comments that "the Lord commanded that those who proclaim the gospel should get their living by the gospel" (v. 14). But then he proceeds to discuss his own policy. He explains that he has chosen to "proclaim the gospel" free of charge, and that by doing so "I have a reward," that reward being to "make the gospel free of charge, so as not to make full use of my rights in the gospel" (vv. 16-18).

What is the evidence that Paul is influenced in this chapter by the mission discourse?[68]

---

68. The most substantial discussions of this chapter are Dungan's *Sayings of Jesus*, 1-80, and Fjärstedt's *Synoptic Tradition in 1 Corinthians*, 66-94.

The saying in 1 Corinthians 9:14

The most important evidence is that of 1 Cor 9:14: "The Lord commanded that those who proclaim the gospel should get their living from the gospel." It is very widely recognized by scholars that this is an allusion to the "Q" saying of Jesus that "the worker is worthy of his food/hire"* (Matt 10:10/Luke 10:7). The wording is not similar in the slightest, but the case is still particularly strong:

* There is an explicit tradition indicator: "The Lord commanded."[69]
* Paul is quoting the tradition against himself and seeking to justify his refusal to accept payment for his work despite the tradition. The implication is that the tradition is a known authoritative saying of Jesus, not, for example, a prophetic word that could have been disputed.[70]
* Although Paul does not reproduce the "Q" wording, the terms "work" and "hire" feature significantly elsewhere in 1 Corinthians 9 (vv. 1, 6, 13, 17, 18).[71]
* Despite the difference in wording,[72] the Pauline description of the Lord's command fits the sense of the synoptic saying.

69. J. P. Brown, "Synoptic Parallels," 37, notes that immediately after the mission discourse Matt 11:1 says, "When Jesus finished *commanding*. . . ."* The same relatively unusual Greek verb, *diatassō*, is used in 1 Cor 9:14.

70. Paul has also quoted the OT as another authoritative tradition in the same vein (vv. 8, 9).

71. The Greek words are *ergon* (compare *ergatēs* in the "Q" saying) and *misthos*. Goulder, *Midrash*, 145, fails to note the use of these words in 1 Corinthians 9, when he argues from the lack of verbal agreement that Paul is not using the "Q" saying. Remarkably (in a passage where Paul speaks of his dependence on a tradition of the Lord and where Matt 10:10/Luke 10:7 is plausibly seen as that tradition) Goulder reverses the usual scholarly view and sees Matt 10:10 as Matthean and as influenced by 1 Corinthians 9.

Another possible echo of the "Q" saying is in 2 Cor 11:13, where Paul is again discussing apostleship, including the question of payment, and where he contrasts his own unpaid ministry with that of the "false apostles, deceitful workers *(ergatai)*, disguising themselves as apostles of Christ."

72. 1 Tim 5:18 does have the saying exactly as in Luke. Holtz, "Paul and the Oral Gospel Tradition," 384, comments: "The deutero-Pauline author of 1 Timothy is unquestionably true to Paul's intentions when he identifies 1 Cor 9:14 with Luke 10:7 or with a corresponding saying in the sayings source."

Of course, the sense of the synoptic saying is only made clear by the context of the mission discourse in which it stands. Taken on its own and out of context the proverbial saying about the laborer would not be problematic to Paul; it is only because he knows that it was applied by the Lord to those "proclaiming the gospel" that it is relevant to his discussion. We may conclude that Paul knew the saying not as an isolated logion but as one specifically applying to Christian missionaries, that is, in an interpretative context such as is provided by the mission discourse.

There is evidence that Paul did know the saying in precisely that context, the evidence being the impressive collection of other possible verbal and thematic links between the discourse and 1 Corinthians 9.

The question of eating and drinking

As striking as anything are the sayings immediately adjacent to the one about the laborer in Luke 10:7, 8. First there is an immediately preceding saying: "Stay in the same house, *eating and drinking what they provide;* for the worker is worthy of his reward (or hire)."* Here the saying about the worker is connected with a saying about "eating and drinking": The worker's "reward" is to have food and drink provided. The same idea is present in 1 Corinthians 9: Paul speaks often of the worker's right to eat (including that of the working ox!). In particular he speaks in v. 4 of himself and Barnabas having the right as apostles to "food and drink" — precisely the thought found in Luke 10:7, 8. (Note also the word "work" in the following verse, 1 Cor 9:6.) Then in v. 13 Paul speaks of those who "work" in the temple service "eating" from the temple, and this leads him directly on to the Lord's command about the preacher of the gospel living by the gospel, which we identified with the saying about the worker being worthy of his reward. The conjunction of ideas in the two contexts can hardly be coincidental. It seems very likely that Paul is familiar with the Lukan form of the tradition.[73]

---

73. Indeed, 1 Cor 9:14 could be a paraphrase not just of the laborer saying but of the preceding saying as well. An alternative possibility, in theory at least, is that the references to "eating" and "drinking" in Luke 10:7, 8 are Lukan, perhaps even that they reflect Pauline discussions of food and drink, and that they were not in "Q."

But (1) Matthew attests the idea of the missionary being fed in "The worker is worthy of his food"* (10:10). His form of words is very probably secondary to the Lukan form, being effectively an amalgamation of Luke 10:7a ("eat and drink . . ."*) and 10:7b ("for the laborer is worthy of his hire"*). (Various scholars have preferred Matthew's wording of the "Q" saying, including Dungan, *Sayings of Jesus,* 69; Crossan, *Historical Jesus,* 343; Goulder, *Midrash,* 145-46; *idem, Luke,* 138-39. The argument that Matthew's

After the saying about the worker Luke goes on: "Do not move about from house to house. Whenever you enter a town and its people welcome you, eat what is set before you" (10:7, 8). The last clause is echoed rather strikingly in 1 Cor 10:27, where Paul recommends, "Eat whatever is set before you."[74] Although 1 Corinthians 10, in addressing the question of food offered to idols, is talking about something rather different from Luke 10, it seems quite likely that we have a further echo here with Paul applying the general instruction to apostles about receiving hospitality (which he has been thinking about) to the specific question facing the Corinthians.

---

wording suggests payment in kind and Luke's payment in cash [or even a salary] and that Matthew is therefore to be preferred is not convincing. Luke's "reward" is explicitly in terms of food, and Matthew's wording is well explained from Luke's. J. P. Brown, "Synoptic Parallels," 38, argues that Matthew put "food" for "reward" to avoid self-styled apostles claiming a salary; he compares Didache 11:6; 13:1.)

(2) It is hard to see how Luke could have gotten his instructions to apostles out of 1 Corinthians 9 (though perhaps he was influenced also by 1 Corinthians 10, where the question of Christians eating Gentile foods is an issue), but it is easy to see how Paul's discussion could have been framed in the light of something like Luke 10.

(3) Since the dependence is from the Jesus-tradition to Paul in the saying about the worker being worthy, it is simpler to find the same direction of relationship in the adjacent texts that are parallel than to postulate also Lukan dependence on Paul.

74. Cf. the Greek in Luke 10:8: *esthiete ta paratithemena hymin*, and in 1 Cor 10:27: *pan to paratithemenon hymin esthiete*. The verb *paratithēmi*, "set before," is common enough in Luke, but not used elsewhere in Paul. On the possible link, see Allison, "Paul and the Missionary Discourse," 373. Räisänen, *Jesus, Paul and Torah*, 134, says that Luke 10:8 could conceivably be "Q" tradition, but that as a radical statement about eating clean and unclean food, it could not go back to Jesus. However, the saying is not unambiguously radical in its "Q" (or Lukan) context: It is a statement about accepting hospitality without picking and choosing (compare the preceding "do not move about from house to house"). It is not explicitly about Gentile mission, though it might in due course have been used by Paul to address questions of Gentile mission (see Marshall, *Luke*, 421). It must be admitted that the history of the traditions in the mission discourse is hard to establish with confidence, and that this complicates the task of relating Paul and the Jesus-tradition (see Neirynck, "Paul and the Sayings," 304-5; for my earlier thoughts on the history of the discourse, see my *Rediscovery*, 243-52). Luke 10:8b is very similar to 10:7a and could be a different version of the same saying. On the other hand, there is arguably a progression from the thought of the appropriateness of accepting hospitality (v. 7a, b) to the thought of not being fussy (v. 7d: "do not move about from house to house," and v. 8b: "eat what is set before you").

Apostleship and authority

All the versions of the mission discourse have Jesus "send" (the Greek is
apostellō) the disciples out (Matt 10:5; Mark 6:7; Luke 9:2; 10:1). The
mission is "apostolic." 1 Corinthians 9 is all about the rights of an "apostle"
and about Paul's apostleship in particular.

The apostles are sent out in the synoptics to preach the kingdom and
to heal and cast out devils (e.g., Matt 10:7, 8/Luke 9:2; 10:9).[75] Paul in
1 Corinthians 9 speaks of his ministry of "proclaiming the gospel."[76] He
does not refer to miracle working, but in 2 Cor 12:12 he shows that he
knows that all "apostles" are supposed to do "signs," and he defends his
own claim to apostleship by affirming that he is quite as good a miracle
worker as those with whom he was sometimes unfavorably compared.

The disciples in the synoptic account are sent out with "authority."
The word is used at the start of the discourse (Matt 10:1/Mark 6:7/Luke
9:1). Although their authority is defined initially in terms of healing and
casting out demons, it becomes clear that their authority is much broader,
as, for example, when they are authorized to give solemn warnings to those
who do not receive them (Matt 10:14/Mark 6:11/Luke 9:5; 10:11). Jesus
comments at the end of the discourse that "whoever listens to you listens
to me, and whoever rejects you rejects me, and whoever rejects me rejects
the one who sent me" (so Luke 10:16; cf. Matt 10:40; John 13:20, both using
a "receiving" verb). In 1 Corinthians 9 Paul is very much taken up with the
question of authority (or rights),[77] including his own apostolic authority
(vv. 4, 5, 6, 12, 18).[78] This is another substantial link between the Pauline
chapter and the mission discourse.

75. Mark 6:7 only refers to casting out demons, but we may infer the dual nature
of the mission from 3:14, 15. Georgi, *Opponents*, 164-70, finds that Mark's mission
discourse emphasizes the miraculous, the "Q" discourse much less so. The distinction
is uncertain and at best a fine one.

76. Luke uses *euangelizomai* in 9:6; the word *kēryssō* is used in Matt 10:7; Mark
6:12; Luke 9:2; and 1 Cor 9:27.

77. The Greek word *exousia*, "right, authority," is also used in the synoptic mission
discourse.

78. Tuckett, "Paul and the Synoptic Mission Discourse," 378, comments that Paul
never relates his apostleship to his being "sent," and so doubts if we can make much of
the parallel between his discussion of apostles in 1 Corinthians 9 and the story of the
"sending" of the disciples in the Gospels. He also finds Paul's concept of apostolic
authority in 1 Corinthians 9 rather different from the authority to cast out demons in
the mission discourse. But (1) there is little doubt that the synoptists all see the discourse
as quite specifically concerning "apostolic" mission. (2) It is impossible to prove that

Elsewhere in his letters Paul speaks of himself as a messenger or ambassador, representing Christ or God (see Gal 4:14; 2 Cor 2:10; 5:20),[79] but most interesting from our point of view is 1 Thes 4:8, where Paul speaks of the authority of his teaching in a way that is verbally and grammatically quite similar to the conclusion of the mission discourse in Luke 10:16:

Luke 10:16   Whoever rejects me   rejects the one who sent me.
1 Thes 4:8   Whoever rejects this rejects not man but God*[80]

Given the other links already noted, it is hard to avoid the conclusion that here again Paul is echoing the mission discourse.[81]

Paul associates his apostleship with being "sent," but he would certainly have been conscious of the etymology of the word, and he certainly believed himself "sent" (e.g., 1 Cor 1:17). (3) It is of interest that Paul refers in 9:5 to his own ministry in connection with the apostles' itinerant ministry. (4) The twelve are given much broader authority in the discourse than to cast out demons and to heal. But, as we have seen, Paul is familiar with the "signs" of an apostle (2 Cor 12:12), even though he focuses on other aspects of apostolic authority in 1 Corinthians 9. Goulder, *Luke*, 190, rightly criticizes Tuckett for making too much of slight differences of sense: "When some associations are being made with both sense and language, others may slip in uncriticized — as happens continually in everyday conversation."

79. See Sanders, *Jesus and Judaism*, 105. He refers to J. O'Neill, *Messiah* (Cambridge: Cochrane, 1980), 90-93.

80. Note in both the similar usage of a verb infrequent in the NT: *ho athetōn . . . athetei.* Tuckett, "Synoptic Tradition in 1 Thessalonians," 163-64, sees Luke 10:16 as the probable "Q" wording of the synoptic saying and notes the parallel in 1 Thes 4:8. But he finds too little in common (e.g., no christological reference in 1 Thes 4:8) to indicate any dependence, and he concludes that we have two "independent adoptions of the shaliah principles." His judgment is understandable if Luke 10:16/1 Thes 4:8 are taken in isolation from the other evidence of Paul's use of the mission discourse traditions. But given that other evidence, it is simpler to postulate Pauline dependence on the Jesus-tradition than coincidental use of a Jewish traditional motif. See Allison, "Paul and the Missionary Discourse," 373-74. Goulder, *Luke*, 142-43, recognizes the link, but argues that Luke has added the clause to Matthew/Q under the influence of 1 Thes 4:8. He could be right, but there is sufficient evidence of Lukan independence of Matthew in the discourse and of Pauline knowledge of the discourse to make it more plausible to see the dependence being from "Q" to Paul.

81. For other possible links between the mission discourse and 1 Corinthians 9 see the discussion of Matt 10:8 below. Fjärstedt, *Synoptic Tradition in 1 Corinthians*, 66-75, and Allison, "Pauline Epistles," 9, note the harvest theme in 1 Cor 9:6-11 and also in the "Q" discourse (Matt 9:37/Luke 10:2, where again we find the term "worker") as well as the fact that Paul's pattern of ministry follows the two-by-two pattern of the discourse (compare Mark 6:7; Luke 10:1 with 1 Cor 9:6 on Paul and Barnabas).

Other Evidence from Matthew

On the basis of the evidence so far adduced, we might conclude that Paul knew something like the Lukan form of the mission discourse. However, there are three further pieces of evidence suggesting Paul's familiarity with features of the Matthean form of the mission discourse. In one case there is again a link to 1 Corinthians 9 (see below on "without payment").

Go to Israel

In discussing Paul's view of Jew and Gentile, we saw how in Gal 2:8, 9 he associates Peter with "apostleship" to "the circumcised." He says about his meeting with Peter, John, and James in Jerusalem: "When they saw that I had been entrusted with the gospel for the uncircumcised, *just as Peter had been entrusted with the gospel for the circumcised*" (v. 7). Peter's responsibility to the Jews seems to be something accepted, not just by Paul but also by Peter himself and by John and James; it is recognized as a commission entrusted to Peter by the Lord.

We may infer from this with some degree of confidence that Paul knew a tradition such as Matt 10:5, 6, where Jesus defines the mission of the twelve in terms of the circumcision: "Go nowhere among the Gentiles . . . , but go rather to the lost sheep of the house of Israel." Admittedly Paul speaks in Galatians 2 of Peter not of the twelve as a whole, but there is a hint that he sees it as a broader commission than just to Peter (thus "*they* to the circumcised" in v. 9), and in any case Paul has reason in Galatians 2 to focus on Peter.[82]

Matthew locates the restrictive saying in the mission discourse. He may be more original than Mark and Luke at this point (see above), and it may very well be that Paul knew a version of the discourse that included the saying.

"Without payment"

Another saying from Matthew's version of the discourse that Paul could have known is "You received without payment; give without payment." (10:8). We have seen how Paul comments in 1 Cor 9:18 that his "reward" is to "make the gospel free of charge," and it could be that he is explaining

82. Note the description of the controversy in Antioch in 2:11-14 and see our discussion of Peter and the twelve below.

his apparent failure to follow one part of Jesus' instruction ("the worker is worthy . . .") by reference to another part of Jesus' teaching.[83]

That Paul knows the saying in question may be confirmed from elsewhere in his letters where he addresses the same issue, his working for a living, and the same sort of ideas and language are used. Thus in 2 Cor 11:7, "I preached the gospel of God to you *without charge,"** the same word as in Matt 10:8 is used. Then in 2 Thes 3:8, 9 we find the word again — though it is used of receiving freely, not giving — together with the idea of an apostolic "right/authority" to eat bread: Paul did not "eat anyone's bread *without paying for it;* . . . not because we do not have that right."[84]

Serpents and doves

It is also Matthew who has Jesus says to the disciples, "Be wise as snakes and innocent as doves" (Matt 10:16), a sentiment possibly echoed in Rom 16:19, where Paul expresses his desire that the Romans be "wise" and "innocent." The word "innocent" is used elsewhere by Paul only once, in Phil 2:15, and is the same word as in the Matthean saying.[85] By itself the

---

83. Interestingly Acts 20:35 portrays Paul as justifying his work with a saying of Jesus, but not, however, with "without payment" but with the otherwise unattested "It is more blessed to give than to receive."

84. On the "without payment" saying see also Brown, "Synoptic Parallels," 37. Dungan, *Sayings of Jesus,* 69, argues that Matthew's saying introduces an alien idea into the discourse in order to curb Christian missionaries demanding a salary; he suggests that Paul in 1 Corinthians 9 and Luke in 22:35-37 are also reacting against the idea of paid apostles. Similarly on Matt 10:8 see McDonald, *Kerygma and Didache,* 118. It could indeed be that Matthew sees the saying as a balance to the following saying about the worker being worthy of his food (note "food," not "reward/hire" as in Luke). On the other hand, (1) "without payment" fits well in its context after the instruction to go out and preach and heal, (2) Matthew does not show himself very embarrassed by the idea of "apostles" being supported in their work (retaining the "worker" saying), and (3) it is not impossible that Mark and Luke could have omitted the saying as superfluous (or even perhaps because they felt the tension with the teaching about the laborer being paid). Theissen, *Social Reality,* 48, comments:

> Healings in the present and eschatological protection — this was "the work per-formed" by the wandering preachers, and it was to be given without payment. "You received without paying, give without pay" (Matt. 10:8). Nevertheless, the work performed was worthy of its proper wage. That it should be paid for in food, drink, and shelter was really a matter of course.

85. See Allison, "Pauline Epistles," 13; Dunn, *Romans,* 905.

parallel proves nothing; in conjunction with the other evidence discussed, it may well be significant.

Summary and Conclusion

We have seen evidence, some stronger and some weaker, that Paul knew various Jesus-traditions that are found in the synoptic mission discourse, including (in the synoptic order):

- the sending of the apostles on itinerant mission (Matt 10:2, 5/Mark 6:7/Luke 9:2/10:1; so 1 Cor 9:1, 5, etc.),
- their authority (Matt 10:1/Mark 6:7/Luke 9:1; so 1 Cor 9:4, etc.),
- to preach the gospel (Matt 10:7/Luke 9:2; 10:9; so 1 Cor 9:14-16, etc.)
- and to cast out devils and heal (Matt 10:1/Mark 6:7/Luke 9:1/Luke 10:9; so 2 Cor 12:12),
- their mission to Israel (Matt 10:5; so Gal 2:8, 9),
- "you received without payment; give without payment" (Matt 10:8; so 2 Cor 11:7; 1 Cor 9:18, etc.),
- "eating and drinking . . ." (Luke 10:7; so 1 Cor 9:4, etc.),
- "the laborer deserves to be paid" (Matt 10:10/Luke 10:7; so 1 Cor 9:14, etc.),
- "eat what is set before you" (Luke 10:8; so 1 Cor 10:27),
- "be wise as serpents and innocent as doves" (Matt 10:16; so Rom 16:19), and
- "whoever rejects me rejects the one who sent me" (Luke 10:16; so 1 Thes 4:8).

The idea that Paul knew an early form of the mission discourse, including what source critics label "M" and "L" material, may seem problematic to some raised on traditional source and form-critical views. However, even if the Pauline evidence is not taken into account, there is good reason for suspecting that the discourse goes back to an early time, that Matthew and Luke knew a non-Markan version, and that they each had independent access to this non-Markan version.[86] Given these conclusions, there is no a priori problem with the idea that Paul was familiar with an early form of the discourse. The evidence suggests that he was.

---

86. See our discussion at the beginning of this chapter. These three conclusions are, as it happens, all quite consistent with the two-source hypothesis.

The evidence also suggests that the Corinthians were familiar with the discourse, since Paul appears to be defending himself against the charge of disobeying the Lord's command that the "worker" should be supported. If Paul was accused of sitting lightly to the Lord's command, he took the charge seriously. He quite strenuously seeks to defend his apparent failure to obey the Lord, not by making light of the Lord's words, but on the contrary by interpreting them (as giving authority, but not requiring wooden compliance) and by explaining his actions in terms of gospel principles and, indeed, in terms of other sayings of the Lord.[87]

THE TWELVE AND PETER

It is not surprising that Paul was interested in traditions about the "apostles," since for him "apostleship" was a matter of acute personal concern. He wished to affirm his own apostleship over against people in the early church who compared him unfavorably with Jesus' original apostles,[88] and he goes out of his way to explain that he was fully qualified as one who saw the Lord and performed signs.

He knows not just of the apostles in general, but also specifically of the twelve (1 Cor 15:5). He also knows of Peter's special position within the twelve and within the early leadership of the church. Thus in Gal 2:7, as we have seen, he speaks of Peter in particular as the one who was entrusted with the gospel to the circumcised, comparing his own commission to go to the Gentiles with Peter's Jewish commission. Peter's position is taken for granted, and Paul is making a striking claim in comparing his apostleship to that of Peter. The same sort of claim may be implied in 1 Cor 15:5-8, where in listing the witnesses to the resurrection he puts Peter first in the list and then himself last.[89]

In referring to Peter's acknowledged position, Paul must have had some particular known tradition (or traditions) in mind.[90] Within the Gospels, Matt 16:16-20, the passage about Peter the rock, is easily the most

87. On whether Paul in 1 Corinthians 9 does indeed sit lightly to the Lord's saying see further in chapter 9 below.

88. Such is the likely background to Galatians 1 and 2, 2 Corinthians 10–12, and indeed 1 Corinthians 9.

89. See, e.g., Jones, "1 Corinthians 15:8."

90. He is not just reflecting on Peter's present prominence. Indeed, in Galatians 2 it seems as though James may be number one in the church, though Peter is historically and traditionally the one entrusted with the mission to the Jews.

explicit narrative elevating Peter to a position of leadership,[91] and there is some reason for believing that Paul has precisely this tradition in mind in Galatians.[92]

The evidence for this is mostly indirect — in Paul's description of his own call and ministry. Paul is quite explicitly comparing himself with Peter, and the phraseology that he uses is like that used of Peter in Matt 16:16-20. Thus:

Matt 16:16-20	Gal 1:15, 16
Simon Peter answered, "You are the Messiah, *the Son of the living God.*" And Jesus answered him, "Blessed are you, Simon son of Jonah! For *flesh and blood* has not *revealed* this to you, but my Father in heaven. And I tell you, you are Peter, and on this rock I will build my church. . . ."	When God, who had set me apart before I was born and called me through his grace, was pleased to *reveal* his *Son* to me, so that I might proclaim him among the Gentiles, I did not confer with *flesh and blood*,[93] nor did I go up to Jerusalem to those who were already apostles before me, but. . . .

In both passages

- there is the thought of a special divine "revelation" to an apostolic figure,
- the revelation is of Jesus, God's "Son,"
- there is a contrasting reference to "flesh and blood" (a phrase found nowhere else in the synoptic tradition, and only twice elsewhere in the Pauline corpus, in 1 Cor 15:50 and Eph 6:12), and
- the revelation is connected with mission ("I will build my church," "so that I might proclaim him").

91. Some have argued that the "rock" on which the church will be built is Peter's messianic confession rather than Peter himself (e.g., Caragounis, *Peter and the Rock*). This exegesis of the Matthean passage is doubtful, but in any case Peter is seen as specially privileged, and it is in connection with his name that the Lord speaks of building his church. It is entirely possible that the passage would have been used to elevate Peter in the church, perhaps at the expense of Paul.

92. For more detailed discussion and for bibliography see my "Paul's Use of the Jesus Tradition," 24-28. Note also Chapman, "St Paul and the Revelation to St Peter"; Dupont, "La Révélation du Fils de Dieu"; Davies and Allison, *Matthew*, II, 609-10.

93. NRSV paraphrases: "any human being."

The parallels are not enormous, and it is arguable that common features and language might be expected in the descriptions of any two revelatory experiences (in a Jewish context).[94] However,

- Paul is quite specifically reflecting in this context on his relationship to "those who were already apostles before me," and it may well be that the question of his relationship to Peter may have been particularly (and painfully) on his mind when he was writing Galatians;[95]
- Paul does seem to have known some tradition about Peter's commissioning, as we have seen; and
- he does specifically compare his call to Peter's in Gal 2:7.

In the light of these considerations the parallels that we have noted may very well be significant.[96] It could be that Paul's critics accused Paul of being a secondhand apostle who was dependent on others and that they contrasted him with Peter, whose revelation was not from "flesh and blood." Paul deliberately uses similar language to assert that he, too, had a divine revelation and to deny that he conferred with "flesh and blood."

Another possible clue confirming this hypothesis may be the use of the Greek name "Peter" in Gal 2:7, 8. Elsewhere Paul always refers to "Cephas," including in Galatians in the verses immediately following (2:9, 11, 14). Why does he quite unusually use the Greek "Peter" when describing the outcome of his and Barnabas's consultations in Jerusalem: "when they saw that I had been entrusted with the gospel for the uncircumcised, just as *Peter* had been entrusted with the gospel for the circumcised (for he who

94. We noted in chapter 3 (above) that Gal 1:16 has some similarity to Matt 11:25-27/Luke 10:21, 22.

95. If Galatians was written, as it can plausibly be argued, when the Antioch incident described in Gal 3:11-14 was recent history and the dispute between Peter and Paul was still unresolved, then the question of Paul's apostleship vis-à-vis that of Peter will have been uppermost in Paul's mind. See Bauckham, "Barnabas in Galatians," and my own "Acts and the Pauline Corpus."

96. It is intriguing, but not obviously significant, that Caesarea Philippi (location of Peter's confession in Matthew) is not far from Damascus and the Damascus Road (location of Paul's conversion); cf. Riesner, *Frühzeit des Paulus*, 213. A.-M. Denis, "L'investiture de la fonction apostolique," 508-10, and Refoulé, "Primauté de Pierre," 17-21, see the connections between Matt 16:16-20 and Gal 1:16, but explain them in the reverse direction, suggesting that Matthew's description of Peter reflects Pauline influence. (See also Goulder, *Midrash*, 381-93.) This is at best a more complicated explanation, given Paul's evident interest in Peter's apostleship in Galatians 1 and 2; more specifically, see Dupont, "La Révélation du Fils."

worked in *Peter* making him an apostle to the circumcised also worked through me in sending me to the Gentiles)."[97] One favored scholarly explanation is that Paul is here quoting from the official protocol that summed up the results of the consultation.[98] There are considerable difficulties with this view,[99] and it may be simpler to suggest that Paul is using the Greek on this occasion because he wants the meaning of the name Cephas/Peter to come over to his Greek readers. Why should he do so on this occasion? Perhaps because he is deliberately alluding to the story of Matt 16:16-20, where the point of the story lies in the meaning of the name. Paul wishes to affirm that his apostleship is comparable to the rock-position that Jesus gave to Peter, according to the gospel tradition.

It may be some support to this hypothesis that Paul in Gal 2:9 refers to James, Peter and John as "those reputed to be pillars."[100] Various observations may be made about this term "pillars": (1) The expression most probably has a background in ideas about the church as the temple.[101] (2) "The pillars" seems to have been an expression used in Jerusalem of the three senior figures in the church, but one about which Paul felt some ambivalence and lack of enthusiasm (so Gal 2:6, 9). We may infer that it was a name used to honor the three, sometimes at the expense of Paul. (3) There is an interesting, if speculative, case for saying that the "pillars" were so-called because of special revelation received from Jesus. We will explore this possibility in chapter 8 below. In each of these three respects there is a parallel or possible parallel with what we have suggested about Paul and the "Peter" tradition of Matt 16:18.

As well as the evidence from Galatians, Paul's fondness elsewhere for "building"/"edification" metaphors when describing the church and Christian ministry could reflect his familiarity with Jesus' saying about "building" the church. Jesus spoke of "building" the church in connection with Peter; so Paul sees his priority similarly (e.g., 1 Cor 14:3, 5, 12, 26; 2 Cor 10:8; 12:19; 13:10).

97. One recent scholar is so impressed at the swapping of names in successive verses that he quite improbably suggests that Cephas and Peter are two different people (Ehrman, "Cephas and Peter"; see also the response by Allison, "Peter and Cephas").

98. See, e.g., Betz, *Galatians*, 97.

99. Paul is certainly not quoting verbatim — note the use of the first person. And would the sort of consultation Paul describes have issued a Greek protocol? Maybe for the sake of Hellenists?

100. See further on this in chapter 8 (below), and for fuller documentation see Wenham and Moses, "There Are Some Standing Here."

101. See, e.g., C. K. Barrett, "Paul and the 'Pillar' Apostles."

Particularly interesting is 1 Cor 3:9-15, where Paul refers to the church as a "building" and goes on to say rather bluntly that "No one can lay any foundation other than the one laid, who is Jesus Christ" (v. 11). This could appear to be in some tension with the Matthean tradition about Peter as the foundation, and so tell against our hypothesis that the tradition was known and recognized even by Paul. However, that does not follow. The Pauline assertion could on the contrary be viewed as a further indirect response to the tradition about Peter the rock: some in Corinth seem to have been preferring Peter to Paul (1 Cor 1:11, 12), and they could well have referred to the tradition of Peter's commissioning by the Lord in that connection. Paul in response emphasizes that Jesus is the real foundation of the church.[102] He need not be seen as denying the truth of the tradition;[103] but he is rejecting any tendency to exalt human authorities like Peter at Christ's expense (compare 1 Cor 1:13).

The suggestion has some plausibility. But there is no need to see Paul's reference to Jesus as the foundation simply as his polemical response to the tradition about Peter as the rock, since the idea of Jesus as the "stone" or the "rock" is widespread and important in early Christian tradition, including in the Gospels themselves. Of particular relevance may be the parable of the vineyard, which concludes with the clearly christological saying about the stone that the builders rejected becoming the cornerstone (Matt 21:42/Mark 12:10, 11/Luke 20:17).[104] There is also the parable with which

102. See Barrett, *1 Corinthians*, 87-88, noting the parallel to the "pillars" passage in Gal 2; also Sweet, "House Not Made with Hands," 373-74.

103. If our argument is correct, he acknowledges the tradition in Galatians 2. The idea of the apostles as foundational is found in the Pauline corpus in Eph. 2:20. It might be that Paul almost always uses the Aramaic "Cephas" because of some unhappiness about how the "rock" tradition was used by others, but perhaps he just prefers to use the name as given by Jesus untranslated.

104. It is just conceivable that 1 Corinthians 3, where Paul speaks of himself and Barnabas as the Lord's servants planting and watering on God's farm and then of God's building with Jesus as the foundation, could be connected to the parable of the vineyard and the following saying about the cornerstone. (So Fjärstedt, *Synoptic Tradition*, 157-60; cf. Kim's interesting discussion of Jesus' temple teaching as known to Paul in "Jesus, Sayings of," 482. Stanley, "Pauline Allusions," 35, 38, links 1 Cor 3:6 with Mark 4:26, 27, and 1 Cor 3:9b with Matt 15:13, but detects the parable of the vineyard in 1 Cor 9:7b.) However, it is wise to be very cautious about concluding too much from common agricultural imagery.

Another interesting "rock" passage is Rom 9:33 (citing Isa 8:14) because of the combination "rock" of "stumbling"; the parallel to Matt 16:18, 23 is striking but does not obviously point to any direct relationship between the texts (compare also 1 Pet 2:7).

both Matthew and Luke conclude their differing and probably independent versions of the sermon on the mount, namely the parable of the wise and foolish builders (Matt 7:24-27/Luke 6:48-49). The man in the parable who builds on the rock is specifically interpreted in both Matthew and Luke of the person who hears and does the words of Jesus. In some ways the parable has more in common with 1 Corinthians 3 than the Peter-tradition of Matt 16:16-20, including the use of the word "foundation," the emphasis on Jesus in this connection (though not Jesus actually as the foundation), the idea of different kinds of building-work, and the warning of coming judgment that will determine whether the building lasts or not (a watery judgment in the parable, a fiery judgment in Paul).[105] One possibility is that Paul is, in effect, playing off the parables of the two builders and of the vineyard against the tradition about Peter the rock, because the Corinthians in his view were misusing the Peter story.

In conclusion, it seems likely that Paul has been influenced by the story of Peter's commissioning, though the evidence is not conclusive; it is possible that he has also been influenced by the parables of the vineyard and of the two builders.[106]

THE TEMPLE

If Paul's building imagery in 1 Corinthians 3 owes something to the story of Peter the rock and perhaps also to the parable of the two builders, another possible influence is the saying of Jesus destroying "this temple" and building another "in three days," which is associated in the synoptic Gospels with the trial of Jesus (Matt 26:61/Mark 14:58; cf. John 2:19). We have found reason to think that the saying went back to Jesus and that its interpretation was a matter for some controversy; so it is not improbable that Paul was familiar with it.

---

105. For the comparison see Fraser, *Jesus and Paul,* 114; Fjärstedt, *Synoptic Tradition,* 161. Allison, "Pauline Epistles," 7, doubts if the parallels are distinctive enough to be significant.

106. Eph 2:18-22 is particularly interesting because of its references to the apostolic "foundation" of the church, to Jesus as the "cornerstone," and to the church as the temple of God.

The Church as the Temple

In 1 Cor 3:16, 17 Paul writes, "Do you not know that you are God's temple and that God's Spirit dwells in you? If anyone destroys God's temple, God will destroy that person. For God's temple is holy, and you are that temple." Here Paul

- suggests that this teaching was already known to the Corinthians ("Do you not know?"), that it was traditional, not a new idea,
- speaks of the church as the "temple of God," using the same Greek word as is used in Jesus' saying about the destruction and rebuilding of the temple,[107] and
- warns against those who "destroy" God's temple, having spoken several times in the preceding verses of "building" the church (vv. 10-15).

The parallelism is not complete. Paul and the gospel saying use different Greek words for "destroy," but this proves little since Paul uses a variety of verbs for the same thought.[108] He also perhaps has a more negative view of "destroying" the temple: for Paul destroying the temple is something terrible, whereas in Jesus' saying the destruction is a prelude to the building of a new one.[109] But this is a thoroughly intelligible difference, since Paul, if he is echoing the saying of Jesus, is using it to speak about the new spiritual temple, which is not to be replaced.

Similar "building/destroying" language is used by Paul in connection with the church and Christian ministry in Rom 14:19, 20 and in 2 Cor 13:10. In Romans 14 Paul urges the believers to work for "upbuilding" and warns against "destroying" the work of God — this time the Greek words are the same as in the gospel saying.[110] In 2 Cor 13:10 Paul

---

107. The NT uses two words for the temple, *hieron* and *naos* (the latter probably referring to the inner sanctuary, not the whole complex of temple buildings; so Juel, *Messiah and Temple,* 127-28). *Naos* is used in all the Gospel versions of Jesus' prediction of the temple's destruction and rebuilding and in all of Paul's references to the church and to Christians as God's temple.

108. In the gospel saying the word is *katalyō*. Paul's words for "destruction" (as opposed to edification) are varied: *phtheirō* in 1 Cor 3:16, 17, *kathairesis* in 2 Cor 13:10. He uses *katalyō* in Rom 14:20; 2 Cor 5:1; and Gal 2:18.

109. But the implication in the gospel saying, as in the eschatological discourse of Matt 24/Mark 13/Luke 21, is that the destruction of the temple is a terrible event.

110. Compare the emphasis on upbuilding/edification in 1 Corinthians 12–14. Cf. also Eph 2:18-24.

speaks of the authority given him by the Lord "to build and not to destroy."*[111]

A rather different use of the same terminology, but also possibly related to the gospel saying, is in Gal 2:18, where Paul says: "If I build again those things that I destroyed, I prove myself a transgressor."* Here Paul approves of the destroying and disapproves of the rebuilding because it is Judaism, not the church, that is in danger of being rebuilt. The context is Peter's siding with the Judaizers and reverting to the regime of law, to which, as Paul explains, Christians have died with Christ (2:19). Peter by his Judaizing is "rebuilding" the edifice of Judaism, which was "destroyed" through the death of Jesus on the cross.[112] He is in effect reversing the process described in Jesus' saying when he (at least in the understanding of the synoptists and arguably of Paul) speaks of the destruction of the old temple and its replacement with the new spiritual temple, associating the whole process with his death.[113]

If this is Paul's train of thought, it is interesting to see how he uses the Lord's saying in different ways: On the one hand he castigates Peter for trying to rebuild the old "temple" of Judaism, which Jesus destroyed through his death; on the other hand, he warns others of the dangers of destroying and failing to build the new temple, that is, the church that is founded on Jesus.

The Individual as the Temple

Paul, as we have seen, speaks not only of the church but also the individual believer as the temple of the Spirit. If a good case can be made for the Jesus-tradition playing a part in Paul's thinking about the church as the new temple in 1 Corinthians 3, an even better case can be made for suggesting this

111. The "build/destroy" contrast by itself proves nothing; there are OT precedents (e.g., Jer 42:10; 45:4). But the connection of this language with temple language in 1 Corinthians 3 suggests a link to the Jesus-tradition.

112. The temple was not literally destroyed at the time of Jesus' death, but for Paul its regime was ended. Compare the likely symbolism of the tearing of the temple veil in Matt 27:51/Mark 15:38, also Acts 7:13, 14. The Jerusalem Christians continued to worship in the temple: It is possible that they interpreted the saying differently or that they (and Paul himself according to Acts) considered it appropriate to meet and pray there even though it no longer had its old authority and significance.

113. I am entirely indebted to Sweet's "House Not Made with Hands," 378-81, for this understanding of Gal 2:18, 19. See his article for further discussion.

with regard to the individual. The two texts that are important here are: 1 Cor 6:19 — "Do you not know that your body is a temple of the Holy Spirit within you, which you have from God . . . ?" — and 2 Cor 5:1 — "We know that if the earthly tent we live in is destroyed, we have a building from God, a house not made with hands, eternal in the heavens." In the latter Paul is speaking of the believer facing death and does not actually use "temple" language of the believer's body. He speaks rather of our earthly "tabernacle" (tent), probably because the tabernacle was temporary and was replaced when the temple was built, which suits Paul's argument in 2 Corinthians 5 about our earthly "tent" and our eternal heavenly dwelling.[114]

Two things are notable about these two verses: First, they both apply the temple language to the Christian's body, albeit differently. Second, both have possible "tradition indicators," "Do you not know?" and "We know."[115] These two characteristics together suggest that there was a Pauline "tradition" associating the idea of the temple and the Christian's body.

2 Cor 5:1

The parallels between 2 Cor 5:1 and the saying about destroying and rebuilding the temple — especially as this is interpreted in the gospel tradition — are striking. In both we have:

- a tabernacle or temple,
- "destroy" and "build" — in this case the same Greek terms in both places,[116] and
- the idea of one building being destroyed and another succeeding it.

Furthermore:

- The saying comes in Matthew and Mark in the context of Jesus' death, with "build in three days" probably being understood of his resurrection, and in John's Gospel that interpretation is made explicit (2:19). Similarly in Paul the passage is about the bodily death and resurrection of Christians, this being quite specifically related in the preceding context to the death and resurrection of Jesus (2 Cor 4:10, 14).

---

114. Ellis, in his valuable discussion "Traditions in 1 Corinthians," 489, observes how in 1 Cor 3:9, 16 "Paul employs the terms 'building' and 'temple' synonymously."

115. Significantly we noted such an indicator also in 1 Cor 3:16.

116. In 2 Cor 5:1 it is the verbal noun "building," not the verb, that is used.

• In both the Markan form of Jesus' saying and in the Pauline teaching the unusual adjective "not made with hands" is used to describe the new building that God gives. Thus in Mark 14:58 Jesus says: "I will destroy this temple that is made with hands, and in three days I will build another, not made with hands."[117]

The Markan "made with hands . . . not made with hands" is not paralleled in Matthew or John, and it may not have been part of the original form of Jesus' saying. But if it is an interpretative addition to the saying (and even if the whole interpretation of the temple saying in terms of Jesus' death and resurrection were similarly not to be traced back to Jesus himself), the fact that the Gospels attest such an interpretation lends weight to the suggestion that Paul is using the saying of Jesus in that way in 2 Cor 5:1.[118] We conclude that there is a particularly strong case for connecting Paul and the Jesus-tradition here, and, if here, then also in 1 Cor 6:19.[119]

Corporate and Individual Temple

We thus have converging evidence that Paul used Jesus' temple saying of the displacement of Judaism and the old temple by Jesus and the new temple, that is, the church, and that he used the same saying of the individual Christian's body, which is "the temple of the Holy Spirit" and which will be raised in the future. Paul thus interprets Jesus' temple sayings both

117. The adjective occurs elsewhere in Col 2:11 in a context that speaks of "putting off the body" and of Christ as the place where God's fullness "dwells bodily." The opposite, "made with hands," occurs somewhat more frequently, including in Acts 7:48; 17:24; and Heb 9:11, 24, all texts speaking in some way negatively of human-made temples.

118. For a valuable explanation of the evidence see Ellis, "Traditions in 1 Corinthians," 488-90. It is conceivable that Mark's "not made with hands" derives from Paul, but it is relatively unlikely that he took the expression from 2 Cor 5:1. It is much simpler to think of Mark and Paul drawing on a common form of the saying (just possibly a form molded by Paul himself) than to have Paul using a simpler form, adding "not made with hands" in his very free application of the tradition in 2 Cor 5:1, and then Mark extracting that interpretation from 2 Cor 5:1 and adding it to the simple form of the saying that he knew.

119. Paul uses the saying of the body in both contexts, but in 1 Cor 6:19 of the Christian's present bodily life and in 2 Cor 5:1 of the resurrection body. As with his corporate use of the temple, Paul uses the saying to different purpose in different contexts.

anthropologically, of the resurrection of the individual, and ecclesiologically, of the building of the church. The probability is that for Paul the ecclesiastical and anthropological belong together, since the death and resurrection of Jesus (specifically of his body) are foundational for both.[120]

Whatever the connection, the combination of evidence adds up to an extraordinarily strong argument for Paul's knowledge and use of this Jesus-tradition. We may conclude that it was such traditions, as Paul and others interpreted them (with the Peter-tradition and perhaps the Ps 118:22 logion as catalysts), that help to explain the remarkable displacement of the Jerusalem temple in Paul's theology, well before the events of AD 70.

CHURCH DISCIPLINE

The cumulative evidence for Paul's familiarity with the "Peter" tradition, which we know through Matthew 16, is significant. It is possible also to argue that Paul was acquainted with the other distinctively Matthean discussion of the church, Matt 18:15-20, which reads as follows:

> If your brother sins against you, go and convict him between you and him alone. If he listens to you, you have gained your brother. If he does not listen, take with you one or two others, so that at the mouth of two or three witnesses every matter may be settled. If he refuses to listen to them, tell the church. And if he refuses to listen to the church, let him be to you as a Gentile and tax collector. Truly I say to you, whatever you bind on earth will be bound in heaven and whatever you loose on earth will be loosed in heaven. Again I tell you truly that if two of you agree on earth about anything they ask, it will be done for them by my Father in heaven. For where two or three are gathered in my name, there I am in the midst of them.*

In this passage on the question of differences/disputes within the church the advice given is:

120. The connection of Christ's body and crucifixion with the temple is reflected on elsewhere in the NT. Heb 10:20 speaks of "the new and living way that he opened for us through the curtain (that is, through his flesh)"; this inevitably reminds us of the synoptic accounts of the death of Jesus, in which his crucifixion (the death of his body) is accompanied by the tearing of the temple curtain (Matt 27:51/Mark 15:38). Whether the tearing represents judgment on the temple or simply the opening up of the holy place, it is associated with the death of the Lord. See also John 2:19-22.

- Any dispute should be sorted out individually with the person concerned, or if that fails within the church (vv. 15-17).[121]
- The offender who fails to repent is to be put out of the fellowship: "Let such a one be to you as a Gentile and a tax collector" (v. 17).
- The judgment of the church has divine authority: What is bound on earth will be bound in heaven. It also has Jesus' authority, as is implied in his promised presence: "Where two or three are gathered in my name, I am there among them" (vv. 18-20).

The Pauline parallels in this case are in 1 Corinthians 5 and 6, where a case of immorality in the church leads Paul to discuss both how a particular dispute and disputes in general within the church are to be handled. It seems that some Christians were taking their quarrels to the secular law courts (6:1). He writes in 1 Cor 5:3-5:

> I, though absent in body but present in spirit, have already judged, as if I were present, the one who has done this thing in this way. In the name of our Lord Jesus, when you and my spirit, together with the power of our Lord Jesus, are gathered, you are to hand over such a one to Satan for the destruction of the flesh, so that his spirit may be saved on the day of the Lord.*

We note what Paul says:

- He insists that disputes are to be handled by the church, not by outsiders (5:4; cf. 6:1).
- He tells the church that they are to "hand this man over to Satan for the destruction of the flesh" (5:5). The implied meaning is very much like Matthew's "and if the offender refuses to listen even to the church, let such a one be to you as a Gentile and a tax collector," though Paul's form of words is understandably more Gentile-friendly!
- Paul understands the church's judgment as having authority: He speaks of "the power of our Lord Jesus" and in 6:2 of the saints having authority to judge the world — that authority being, of course, divinely given. Not only does Paul speak of authority, but, interestingly, he also speaks of presence — not of Jesus' presence "where two

121. The two or three witnesses of Matt 18:16 have an OT background in Deut 19:15 as well as a Pauline parallel in 2 Cor 13:1. Some of the agreement between Matthew 18 and 1 Corinthians 5 and 6 is explicable in terms of common Jewish background, but not all. See also 1QS 5:25–6:1.

or three are gathered" to take a decision, but of himself, Paul, being "absent in body" but "present in spirit" with the Corinthians in their judicial decision (5:3).

The parallelism of thought is striking, and there is also common vocabulary — "brother" (Matt 18:15; 1 Cor 5:11), "church" (Matt 18:17; 1 Cor 6:4), "issue" (Matt 18:19; 1 Cor 6:1), "gather" (Matt 18:20; 1 Cor 5:4), and "in my name/in the name of the Lord Jesus" (Matt 18:20; 1 Cor 5:4). The similarity of wording would not be impressive on its own (though "issue" occurs only once in Matthew and four times in Paul, and "gather" only once in Paul), but the similar ideas and vocabulary do make a connection between the Pauline and Matthean traditions likely, and it must be simpler to see the very Jewish tradition of Matthew as the more original.[122]

If Paul did know something like the Matthean tradition, then his substitution of the idea of his own spiritual presence for the idea of Jesus' presence may seem odd. But he is not, of course, contradicting the idea of Jesus' presence: Indeed, he specifically emphasizes the name and the power of Jesus.[123] What seems plausible is that Paul in wishing to exert his own authority in Corinth has been influenced by the Jesus-tradition and so speaks of his own presence.[124]

122. Dodd in his essay on "Matthew and Paul" in his *NT Studies,* 57-62, says that 1 Corinthians 5 "shows the Matthean regulations, certainly Jewish-Christian in form, at work in Paul's Gentile churches." On the other hand, Goulder, *Midrash,* 154-63, 401, notes *Pirqe Aboth* 3:2 (cf. 6), "Where two sit and there are between them words of the Torah, there the Shekinah rests between them," and argues that the Matthean saying is "an adaptation of the Pirqe Aboth saying to familiar words from 1 Corinthians." He comments that "it is hardly to be believed that Jesus rephrased the rabbis' words to speak of his spiritual guidance of his Church in judgment and intercession after his death." Put like that, Goulder's argument may sound persuasive; but there is no reason why Jesus should not have spoken in this vivid way of his community having his authority while Paul apparently could do so. See Davies and Allison, *Matthew,* II, 790. Though inclined to see Matt 18:20 as post-Easter, they ask: "Was Paul the only one capable of speaking of being spiritually present with others?" The Matthean passage could in theory be post-Easter, but could still have been known to Paul as Jesus-tradition. Catchpole, *Quest,* 135-50, identifies it as "Q" tradition.

123. J. P. Brown, "Synoptic Parallels," 42, says that "in the name of the Lord" (2 Thes 3:6; 1 Cor 5:4) "shows Paul's belief that these materials were genuine *verba Christi,*" but fails to substantiate the claim.

124. It is possible that Paul's understanding of his own apostleship allows him to see his authority as analogous to Jesus' authority (without in any way detracting from Jesus' superiority).

This hypothesis helps explain the Pauline thought at a point where commentators have found his thinking rather elusive.[125] It is interesting that in 2 Cor 2:10, when returning to the issue of church discipline, Paul again speaks of his own endorsement of the Corinthians' decision, but this time refers to the presence (Greek *prosōpon*, "face") of Christ: "Anyone whom you forgive, I also forgive. What I have forgiven, if I have forgiven anything, has been for your sake in the presence of Christ."

It is possible that Paul has been influenced by the traditions of Matt 18:15-20 in one or two other passages.[126] The cumulative case is surprisingly good, but not conclusive.

CONCLUSIONS ON THE CONNECTIONS

This chapter has proved extremely fruitful for the question of the Jesus-tradition in Paul. There is very good evidence that Paul was familiar with the mission discourse traditions. He does not just know one or two of the sayings (e.g., "the laborer deserves to be paid"), but a whole range of different sayings. Interestingly he attests sayings that are found only in the Lukan version of the discourse (e.g., "eat what is set before you") or only in the Matthean form (e.g., "You received without payment; give without payment"). Many of the Pauline echoes are concentrated in 1 Corinthians 9, and it is reasonable to infer that Paul knew not just individual sayings, but actually a form of the discourse.[127] There is evidence that the sayings were a subject of controversy, with Paul's opponents claiming that he was not following the Lord's command about workers being supported, and with Paul responding by interpreting the saying and drawing on other sayings of the Lord.

It is also highly probable that Paul knew Jesus' saying about the destruction and rebuilding of the temple. He uses it in a variety of ways to address a range of questions from the question of church leadership, to the Judaizing issue, to questions of sexuality and resurrection.

125. See, e.g., Fee, *1 Corinthians*, 203-15, discussing, among other things, how to interpret the idea of Paul being "present" and how to construe the phrase "in the name of the Lord Jesus."

126. Dodd, *NT Studies*, 58, 59, compares Gal 6:1 and 1 Cor 9:19-22 (note the word "win/gain" in Matt 18:15); Brown, "Synoptic Parallels," 41, 42, compares the sort of discipline described in 2 Thes 3:6, 14, 15.

127. We have seen that he does seem to have known the "worker" saying in the context of the apostolic mission.

It is perhaps audacious to argue in one chapter that Paul may have known both of Matthew's "church" passages as Jesus-traditions. But the evidence in surprisingly good: The traditions about Peter the rock found in Matt 16:16-20 were probably known to Paul and indeed used by his opponents against him; there is also a good possibility that he was familiar with the instructions about church discipline found in Matt 18:15-20. We have suggested that he may have known also Jesus' parable of the two houses.[128]

128. On the subject of this chapter see, recently, Ellis, "Jesus' Use of the Old Testament." Ellis connects Paul's "eschatological temple" and "corporate Christ" with traditions of Jesus.

6

LIVING IN LOVE

I. COMPARING JESUS AND PAUL

JESUS' ETHICAL TEACHING

The Demand for Perfection

Jesus is associated in many people's minds more than anything with his ethical teaching.[1] A useful way into the question of Jesus' ethics is through his teaching on divorce.

The question of divorce

Matthew and Mark tell how a delegation of Pharisees came to Jesus and asked his opinion on the matter of divorce "to test him" (Matt 19:1-12; Mark 10:1-12). It was indeed a testing question, not only because of the divergent views of divorce among different Jewish groups — with the Pharisees themselves taking a variety of views — but also because of Herod Antipas, ruler of Galilee, and his ambitious partner Herodias. Herodias had been married to Herod's brother, but abandoned him for the more glamorous and politically prominent Herod, who then divorced his first wife. It was a scandalous affair with various repercussions, notably for John the Baptist, who, according to the Gospels, publicly denounced the royal couple. He thus earned the hatred especially of Herodias and was ultimately

---

1. On NT ethics see Schrage, *Ethics of the NT;* also the earlier work of Schnackenburg, *Moral Teaching of the NT.* On Jesus see Harvey, *Strenuous Commands.*

executed in Herod's prison (Matt 14:1-12/Mark 6:14-29).[2] It was therefore a delicate question to ask Jesus, the erstwhile colleague of John.

But Jesus, according to the Gospels, is not intimidated, and his reply is in line with the strictest Jewish outlook, which is also attested in the Dead Sea Scrolls.[3] He refers his questioners back to the story of creation and quotes the words of Genesis about God's creation of male and female and about the two becoming "one flesh." He concludes: "Therefore what God has joined together, let no one separate." Admittedly there was a Mosaic law (in Deut 24:1-4) regulating divorce and requiring the divorcing husband to give his wife a certificate of divorce. But Jesus explains that this regulation was "because you were so hard-hearted." In other words, it was a damage limitation measure and never intended as approval for divorce. He thus denies that a divorce certificate (whether for Herod or for anyone else) could divide those whom God had joined. Indeed, the "one flesh" nature of marital union means that "Whoever divorces his wife and marries another commits adultery against her" (Mark 10:11).[4] According to Matthew, Jesus' disciples were astonished at the stringency of his demand (Matt 19:10).

Radical demands: the sermon on the mount

But Matthew in particular suggests that Jesus' teaching on divorce was only one example of his exceedingly demanding ethic. The so-called "sermon on the mount" in Matthew 5–7 includes the formidable challenge "Unless your righteousness exceeds that of the scribes and Pharisees, you will never enter the kingdom of heaven" and, at the end of the same chapter, the almost unthinkable "Be perfect, therefore, as your heavenly Father is perfect" (5:20, 48). In between Jesus illustrates his meaning by reference to divorce, among other things. He also tells the disciples that it is not just killing or adultery that matter, but even hating or an adulterous look; he denies the appropriateness of using oaths, and he tells them to love not just their neighbors but even their enemies (5:21-47).

There is considerable scholarly debate to what extent the sermon on the mount, as recorded by Matthew, reflects the Evangelist's own Jewish

2. See also Josephus, *Ant.* XVIII.116-19.

3. See CD 4:20, 21.

4. Matthew's version of the saying has his famous "except for unchastity" phrase, apparently qualifying the absoluteness of the demand. On this see n. 67 below. Matthew undoubtedly sees Jesus' teaching as highly demanding (see Matt 19:10 and 5:31, 32 in the context of 5:20).

Christian ethical rigor and to what extent it reflects Jesus' attitude.[5] However, even if there may be doubt about certain particular formulations, there
is a considerable body of evidence suggesting that Jesus was as demanding
as Matthew suggests. Thus Jesus' prohibition of divorce is attested not just
by Matthew and Mark in the dialogue with the Pharisees but also in a
slightly different form in Matt 5:31, 32 and Luke 16:18. And Paul, as we
saw in our first chapter, is familiar with this teaching; we will discuss the
evidence of 1 Cor 7:10, 11 further below.[6] Similarly, Jesus' emphasis on
inner attitude as opposed to outward action has a good claim to authenticity
(as we have seen in chapter 2 in discussing the passage about clean and
unclean things in Matthew 15/Mark 7). So also does the sermon's emphasis
on love, which is well attested elsewhere in the gospel tradition (e.g., Matt
22:34-40/Mark 12:28-34); and the specific call to "love your enemy" is not
just Matthean, but it is present in the Lukan form of the sermon on the
mount (thus presumably in the "Q" source or whatever common source
Matthew and Luke have drawn on) and is most vividly illustrated in the
Lukan parable of the good Samaritan (Luke 6:35; 10:25-37).[7]

Whichever Gospel we look to, a radical ethic is ascribed to Jesus. He
calls his disciples to cut off the offensive (or "scandalous") eye, hand, or
foot in order to get into life (Matt 5:27-32; 18:8, 9; Mark 9:43-48). He insists
on denying oneself and taking up the cross (Matt 10:38, 39; 16:24-28; Mark
8:34-38; Luke 9:23-27; 14:27; 17:33). He calls on the rich man not only to
keep the commandments but also to "sell what you own" and to follow, in
the Evangelists' view not because this man is some sort of special case, but
because this is the radical discipleship that Jesus expects (Matt 19:16-
22/Mark 10:17-22/Luke 18:18-23).[8] Jesus calls all his disciples not to seek
position for themselves, but rather to put themselves last and to serve
others: The radical demand is a radical demand to love others.

5. That there is a parallel, though briefer, sermon in Luke 6:20-49 suggests to
most critics that Matthew's sermon had some basis in tradition. On the interpretation
of the sermon see Kissinger, *Sermon on the Mount*; Guelich, *Sermon on the Mount*
(reviewed by me in *Trinity Journal* 5 [1983/84], 92-108).

6. See the additional note at the end of this chapter on the relationship of the
various synoptic divorce texts.

7. See Piper, *Love your Enemies*.

8. It is clear that for the Evangelists "leaving all things" is part of discipleship.
Note the way the narrative continues in Matt 19:27/Mark 10:28/Luke 18:28 with Peter
commenting, "We have left everything and followed you." Cf. also Matt 13:44-46; Luke
12:33.

Jesus' "Liberalism"

If Jesus' ethical demands seem in some contexts to be stringent, in other contexts he appears to be a liberal, particularly on matters of Jewish ritual.[9] Thus, whereas he appears to push some of the ten commandments (e.g., the prohibitions of murder and adultery) to an extreme, he is accused by his critics of laxity when it comes to the sabbath command. All the Gospels, including the Jewish Christian Matthew (with its high esteem for the OT law), suggest that Jesus' attitude to the sabbath was a sore point (e.g., Matt 12:9-14/Mark 3:1-6/Luke 6:6-11; John 5:1-18). Jesus healed on the sabbath and justified his actions; he also justified his disciples' actions in picking and eating grain on the sabbath (Matt 12:1-8/Mark 2:23-28/Luke 6:1-5). He defied tradition not only on the sabbath question but also on other ritual matters, such as ritual handwashing (so Matt 15:1-20/Mark 7:1-23).[10]

It is clear that these gospel traditions came to be used by the church to justify the Gentile mission and the church's failure to impose Jewish law on Gentiles (see Mark 7:19 and our discussion above). But there is no reason for doubting that Jesus himself did offend his strictly religious opponents by his refusal to go along with many of their traditional practices and interpretations. His mixing with sinners and his disciples' failure to fast were further examples of his offensive liberalism (e.g., Matt 9:9-17/Mark 2:13-20/Luke 5:27-39).

Scholars are not agreed as to whether Jesus' actions actually represented a deliberate breach of the OT law or whether they were more simply a challenge to the narrow and restrictive interpretation of the law offered by some of his Pharisaic opponents.[11] Whichever view is correct, it is striking that Jesus appears to have been a rigorist in ethics and a liberal with regard to ritual.[12] His priorities are accurately summed up in the verse from Hosea "I desire mercy, not sacrifice"* (Hos 6:6; Matt 9:13; 12:7): It is only Matthew who describes Jesus as citing this OT text, but it accurately reflects what is also attested in different ways in the other Gospels, for example, in the parable of the good Samaritan, where

9. To distinguish "ritual" law from other law is convenient for our purposes here, whether or not the NT authors would have recognized the later Christian distinctions between the "moral" laws and the "ceremonial" laws of the OT.

10. Cf. Matt 23:23-26/Luke 11:37-42 on tithing and the description of Jesus touching a leper in Matt 8:1-4/Mark 1:40-45/Luke 5:12-16.

11. See Matt 15:3/Mark 7:9 on "your tradition."

12. Contrast the Qumran community, where ethical and ritual rigor were combined.

the Samaritan who "shows mercy"* is contrasted with the priest and the Levite who fail to do so (Luke 10:25-37).

Jesus and the Law

In Jesus' Jewish world the law of Moses was the acknowledged yardstick for godliness and good conduct. But how does Jesus relate to that law?[13] He seems to go beyond the law in terms of ethical demand and then advocate a relatively relaxed interpretation of its ritual requirements. How did he justify this combination of approaches, and how did he see his own role in offering such an independent interpretation of the divine law?

Matt 5:17-20

Matthew has Jesus define his own role vis-à-vis the law in 5:17-20:

> Do not think that I have come to abolish the law or the prophets; I have come not to abolish but to fulfill. For truly I tell you, until heaven and earth pass away, not one letter, not one stroke of a letter, will pass from the law until all is accomplished. Therefore, whoever breaks one of the least of these commandments, and teaches others to do the same, will be called least in the kingdom of heaven; but whoever does them and teaches them will be called great in the kingdom of heaven. For I tell you, unless your righteousness exceeds that of the scribes and Pharisees, you will never enter the kingdom of heaven.

This passage seems at first sight to represent Jesus as a thoroughgoing conservative so far as the OT law is concerned. It has been seen by some interpreters as a polemical and unhistorical interpretation of Jesus that reflects Christian controversy about the law, with the Jewish Christian Evangelist Matthew deliberately countering Pauline teaching about Christian freedom from the law.[14]

There could be a grain of truth in this position: Matthew may be responding in his Gospel to the antinomianism of some in Paul's churches (as did Paul himself in some of his letters, e.g., 1 Cor 6:12; cf. Rom 3:8;

---

13. See among many others Banks, *Jesus and the Law*; Meier, *Law and History*; Moo, "Jesus and the Authority of the Mosaic Law."

14. On 5:19 as anti-Pauline see, e.g., Manson, *Sayings of Jesus*, 24; 25. Note the comments of Davies and Allison, *Matthew*, I, 497.

6:1). But it is not at all plausible to suggest that Matt 5:17-20 represents a thoroughgoing and conservative Jewish Christian interpretation of Jesus' relationship to the law.[15] Not only is the author of Matthew someone who, though a Jewish Christian, is thoroughly committed to the Gentile mission, but the apparent rigorism of these verses (and of others in Matthew, notably 23:3) needs to be weighed against other passages where Matthew gives a rather different impression: In 11:28-30 Jesus offers his weary listeners an easy and light yoke, and in 17:24-26 he can speak of his disciples being "children" and therefore "free" of the temple tax. Jesus in Matthew, as we have seen, puts "mercy" before "sacrifice" and temple.

The sayings in Matt 5:17-20 must be seen in this broader Matthean context — and also in the context of the verses that immediately follow them and are obviously meant to illustrate them: In vv. 21-48 we have a set of "antitheses" in which an OT law or tradition is set over against Jesus' teaching ("You have heard that it was said . . . but I say to you"). In each case Jesus' teaching is seen to go much further than the letter of the particular law or current interpretation of it went.

Given the context, we may conclude with some probability that the sayings in Matt 5:17-20 are intended to assert very strongly that Jesus' ethical teaching is far higher than that of the scribes and Pharisees. He is not undermining moral standards, as some may have accused him, but rather the opposite. The question of Jewish ritual law is not in view here at all, but the general point is that he has not come to "abolish" the OT but to "fulfill" it.

"Fulfill" is a key word for Matthew, as we have noted before.[16] Jesus is the one who fulfills prophecy, whether in his birth, in his life, or in his death. The "kingdom of heaven," to use the Matthean phrase, is the day of fulfillment, the day looked forward to by prophets and righteous people. In this Matthean context Jesus' attitude to the law makes sense: He himself came to "fulfill all righteousness" and his call to his disciples is that they, too, should live the life of fulfillment — by living lives appropriate to the kingdom of God, where God's will is done "on earth as in heaven." They are to be better than the scribes and Pharisees and to live like "your heavenly Father."

15. See France, *Matthew: Evangelist and Teacher,* 186-97.

16. On the range of possible meanings see Davies and Allison, *Matthew,* I, 485-86. I take it that for Matthew Jesus' mission is to bring the whole of the OT to its eschatological "fullness," achieving God's plan of salvation, bringing in the kingdom, and restoring creation. On the ritual law see further below.

Parallels to Matt 5:17-20

Such is Matthew's likely meaning in 5:17-20. But is it only Matthew's? It is certainly Matthean in style and emphasis. And yet it is not exclusively so. There is a good case for thinking that Luke may have known some at least of the passage.

Luke 16:16-18 reads as follows:

> The law and the prophets were in effect until John came; since then the good news of the kingdom of God is proclaimed, and everyone tries to enter it by force. But it is easier for heaven and earth to pass away, than for one stroke of a letter in the law to be dropped. Anyone who divorces his wife and marries another commits adultery, and whoever marries a woman divorced from her husband commits adultery.

This passage has interesting similarities to Matthew 5:

Luke	Matthew
a saying about the duration of "the law and the prophets" and the coming of the kingdom	Do not think that I have come to abolish the law or the prophets
not a stroke will pass from the law	not an iota or stroke will pass from the law
a saying about divorce, illustrating the principle that has been stated	illustrations of the point (5:21-48), including the example of divorce (v. 32)

Several complex questions can be asked about the precise relationship between these two passages. But the similarities are quite striking,[17] and at least Luke attests one of the key Matthean sayings — that about the (iota and) the letter-stroke.[18] He very probably also knew the saying recorded in Matt 5:17: As well as the evidence of Luke 16:16,[19] there is Luke 24:44, where the risen Jesus says to his disciples: "These are my words that I spoke to you while I was

---

17. E.g., the divorce sayings in Luke 16:18 and Matt 5:32 are formally similar. See the additional note below on the divorce sayings.

18. Luke could, of course, be dependent on Matthew. But there is reason to believe that he has a source independent of Matthew, especially in 16:18 (see the discussion in the additional note on divorce, below).

19. Matthew has a much closer parallel to Luke 16:16 in Matt 11:12, 13.

still with you — that everything written about me in the law of Moses, the prophets, and the psalms must be fulfilled." The risen Jesus here quotes from his own earlier teaching ("that I spoke to you while I was still with you"), and thus we have indirect attestation from Luke of a saying such as Matt 5:17.

This evidence from Luke suggests not only that Matt 5:17-20 is not purely Matthean but also that it may be substantially "Q" material or some equivalent. Furthermore, the ethical understanding that we have proposed for Matt 5:17-20 and for Matthew more generally fits with other aspects of Jesus' teaching that we have already analyzed: The fulfillment theme is one that we have seen to be fundamental to Jesus' kingdom teaching, and it is intrinsically likely that Jesus would have defined his relationship to the law in terms of fulfillment. It is also entirely probable that Jesus' view of the kingdom as the defeat of evil and the restoration of God's people and world would have entailed ethical renewal.

Creation and the new covenant

To be more precise, it seems that Jesus' ethical vision was of a return to the perfection of creation. Thus in the discussion of divorce Jesus refers his hearers back behind the law of Moses (with its provisions for the hardness of human hearts) to creation: He calls for creation standards. The same principle may lie behind the teaching in the sermon on the mount about oaths (Matt 5:33-37): Jesus refers his hearers back behind the law to something more basic still. It may also be involved in his teaching about clean and unclean things in Matthew 15/Mark 7. Jesus' comment that "it is not what goes into the mouth that defiles a person" (Matt 15:11) may simply be a statement of priorities; but it may possibly reflect a perception by Jesus of the cleanness of all foods as created by God. As for the sabbath, Jesus, according to Mark, appealed to creation — more precisely to the creation of the sabbath for humankind — in justifying his conduct (Mark 2:27).[20]

Furthermore, we have already seen some evidence to suggest that Jesus interpreted his mission in terms of the new covenant of Jer 31:31-34.[21] That important passage speaks of the written law being superseded by the law written on the heart. This and other similar OT passages may well be the basis of Jesus' emphasis on righteousness of heart, and they may explain how he, according to Matthew, can call his apparently impossible yoke easy

---

20. Matt 19:28 has Jesus speak of the "renewal" or "regeneration" or "recreation" of the coming kingdom of God.

21. See chapters 2 and 3 above.

and light (11:30). The synoptic Gospels do not have much teaching of Jesus on the Spirit, while the fourth Gospel has a great deal. But it is probable that the synoptics presuppose the same understanding of the spiritual power of the kingdom — as something manifested in Jesus and now available to the poor in spirit and to those hungering and thirsting for the divine righteousness (see Matt 10:20; Mark 13:11; Luke 12:12; Matt 12:28; Matt 12:32/Mark 3:29/Luke 12:10; Luke 4:18; 11:13).

The ritual law

Where does the ritual law fit into this framework of thought? Both the return to creation (before the law) and the Jeremianic vision of the new covenant could have the effect of marginalizing the importance of the written law altogether, while in no way destroying its truth or validity. As for the ritual law, we have already seen some evidence for Jesus interpreting his own mission in terms of ritual sacrifice and looking to the supersession of the Jerusalem temple. It could be that Jesus saw the ritual law as a temporary dispensation that was both fulfilled and made redundant with the coming of the eschatological kingdom through his own sacrificial death.

It is difficult to prove conclusively that this was Jesus' understanding, but the combination of ethical rigor, ritual liberalism, and openness to sinners makes sense in such a context of thought, and the important "Q" sayings of Matt 11:12, 13/Luke 16:16 speak of the law and the prophets being in effect *until* the time of John the Baptist. The implication in both Matthew and Luke is that the age of "the law and the prophets" is giving place to the age of the kingdom. It may well have been Jesus' understanding that in this new age of the kingdom the law and the prophets are no longer needed because the fulfillment has come;[22] the interim ethic represented by various laws (e.g., the laws concerning divorce, oaths, and ritual, including the laws of cleanness and uncleanness) is superseded. But the moral standards of the law are maintained and indeed strengthened as creation is restored and the perfection of the kingdom is inaugurated.

Jesus' authority

One of the distinctive expressions of Jesus seems to have been "Amen, I say to you." All our Greek Gospels attest the phrase, retaining the Hebrew and

---

22. For the idea of prophecy becoming redundant in the new age, cf. 1 Cor 13:8-10.

Aramaic word "Amen" (e.g., Matt 18:3; Mark 13:30; Luke 12:37; John 3:3).[23] The word means "truly" or "certainly," and in using it to preface solemn statements Jesus seems to have been speaking with conscious authority.[24] The Gospels are agreed that Jesus' hearers were astonished at his teaching, "for he taught them as one having authority, and not as their scribes" (Matt 7:28, 29).

Jesus' teaching and conduct were, as we have seen, astonishingly demanding on the one hand (with regard to, e.g., divorce) and astonishingly free on the other hand (with regard to, e.g., the sabbath, touching lepers and corpses, and mixing with sinners). He criticized the traditions of his religious contemporaries (e.g., the Pharisees); even more strikingly he contrasted his teaching with the God-given teaching of Moses. He appears to have had a confidence in the divine authority of his interpretation of God's will and thus could criticize his contemporaries' attitudes, whether, for example, to the sabbath or to divorce, by explaining God's will and plan in creation; he could also suggest that his words would be of decisive importance on the day of judgment (Matt 7:24-27/Luke 6:47-49).

The basis of this confidence must have been in Jesus' consciousness of his own role in the eschatological kingdom: We may surmise that passages like Isaiah 11 (with its reference to the shoot and the branch, on whom the spirit of the Lord will rest — the spirit of wisdom, understanding, counsel, and might) contributed to his awareness of a special spiritual authority. Jesus announced by his words and actions the coming a new society and a new order, based on and around his own teaching and person.[25]

CHRISTIAN LIVING IN PAUL

Four words sum up Pauline ethics: law, Spirit, love, Jesus. For Paul the law of God, given by Moses, was a true expression of the will of God, but for the Christian at least it has been superseded by the coming of the Spirit, who produces love within the believer, in accordance with the teaching and life of Jesus.

23. The double "Amen, amen" is used in John's Gospel.
24. See Jeremias, *NT Theology,* 35, 36; Witherington, *Christology,* 186-89.
25. See also Matt 12:6 for the idea of Jesus' superiority to the temple. On Jesus' authority see Witherington, *Christology,* 59-71. Borg, *Conflict, Holiness and Politics,* 73-199, correctly observes that Jesus offers an inclusive love-based ethic instead of the separation holiness of many of his contemporaries. It was not just an alternative way of looking at things but a reflection of Jesus' conviction that the new age had come.

The Law

Paul...

Paul's teaching on the law is very complex.[26] Scholars have offered all sorts of explanations of the variety of ideas found in his letters — some finding Paul frankly contradictory, others tracing a development from the "early Paul" of Galatians to the "late Paul" of Romans. The difficulty with this second view is that the apparently contradictory ideas surface within single letters. Thus in Romans Paul can at one point say that the Christian gospel means that "we uphold the law" and at another that Christians have died to the law and have been discharged from its claims (3:31; 7:4-6). Or in 1 Corinthians at the one moment Paul can accept that for the Christian "all things are permissible," and at the next recommend "obeying the commandments of God" (1 Cor 6:12; 7:19).

Is Paul frankly confused, or is there some underlying coherence to his thought? It would have been understandable if he was confused: Jewish thinking about the law and about its place in the messianic age was complex enough, and the Christian church found it extraordinarily difficult to decide whether and how the law continued to be valid after the coming of Jesus. It was perhaps the most contentious issue that the first Christians faced. But Paul was probably a lot less confused and more coherent than many of his critics have allowed.

It is important on this issue, as on others, to recall that Paul is responding in his letters to particular problems. The law was a particularly pressing issue for Paul in the context of his mission to Gentiles. The question at stake was not primarily ethical but religious: Should the requirements of the Jewish law, in particular circumcision and the ritual requirements of Judaism, be imposed on Gentile converts? There was prima facie a good case for saying that they should, and many Jewish Christians took that position. But Paul himself was clear that Gentiles should not have the burden of the law imposed on them. He was sharply criticized for his views, inevitably, and he had to define his attitude to the law in response to these criticisms.

But although the issue was initially a question of ritual, the ethical question inevitably came in as well, because the law was not just a religious

---

26. The bibliography on the question of Paul and the law is massive. Excellent summaries of much recent debate are in Westerholm, *Israel's Law;* Moo, "Paul and the Law."

rule of life but also an ethical rule. Paul's critics believed that by undermining the law he was undermining ethics. Paul thus had to explain his ethical principles in relationship to the law and to emphasize that he was not undermining ethical conduct by his gospel.[27] Paul's apparently contradictory statements on the law partly reflect this context: He wants to insist not only on Gentile freedom from the law but also on the ethical nature of his gospel.

Not only is Paul's missionary context important for understanding his view of the law, but so is his own personal history. He had been an orthodox Jew, believing in the law as given by God, zealous to uphold the law,[28] defining "righteousness" by the law. But this commitment to the law led him into rejecting Jesus and persecuting his followers. On the Damascus road he discovered that he, the law-abiding Pharisee, was opposing God, and he discovered salvation not in the law but in the Christ who met him. In a real and vivid sense he discovered the failure of the law at his conversion, and his thought about the law had to make sense of this personal experience.

Given an appreciation of Paul's personal and missionary contexts, his teaching on the law makes more sense than is sometimes appreciated: (1) In the first place, Paul the Christian, as much as Paul the Jew, understood God's plan and salvation within an OT framework of thought; he saw Jesus within that context. Inevitably, or almost inevitably, he therefore recognized — continued to recognize — the law of Moses as given by God, as an expression of God's will, and so as something holy, good, and even glorious (Rom 7:12; 2 Corinthians 3).

(2) But Paul experienced in his own life the "failure" of the law. Instead of finding life through the law, he found himself opposing the Messiah. Similarly in the history of Israel and indeed in the attitudes of his Jewish contemporaries (not least in their failure to believe in Jesus and their negative attitude toward the Gentile mission) he saw evidence of the failure of the law. He could not blame the God-given law as such for this, but he saw the law as having been hijacked by sin and so becoming an ally of sin and an instrument of death.

In Romans 7 Paul vividly illustrates the idea of the law being hijacked, when he describes how "the very commandment that promised life proved to be death to me" (v. 10). It told "me" not to covet, but then sin used the

---

27. See John Barclay's analysis of Galatians, *Obeying the Truth*.

28. In his zeal for the law and the temple in the face of religious compromise or betrayal, Paul was in a good Jewish tradition. See, e.g., 1 Macc 2:27.

commandment to make "me" covet.[29] The law shows me what is good, but I cannot do it, and the paradoxical and frustrating fact is that I end up doing the opposite.

Although this effect is not the fault of the God-given law, it cannot in Paul's theology be an unfortunate accident that God failed to foresee. Paul concludes that the law of Moses was never given to produce righteousness and life; it was given rather to point out sin and to convict us, until the coming of new life and liberation in Christ. Paul uses the picture of the slave who in Graeco-Roman society had responsibility for keeping the children of the wealthy in order until they reached their majority: The law was given to keep us under discipline until the coming of the freedom of sonship in Christ (Gal 3:21-26; Romans 7–8).

(3) For Paul his experience on the Damascus road meant a shattering of his own loyalty to the law and a recognition instead of Christ as Lord. In the same way, but on a broader theological canvas, Paul sees the coming of Christ as a turning point in history and as the end of the era of the law of Moses. "When the fullness of time had come, God sent his Son, born of a woman, born under the law, in order to redeem those who were under the law, so that we might receive adoption as children" (Gal 4:4, 5). Christ's coming, and in particular his death under the curse of the law, brought release from the old heavy-handed slave driver and the freedom of being God's children. "Freedom" is a key word for Paul in Galatians, and in 1 Corinthians Paul can endorse, albeit in a way that is qualified, the Corinthian slogan "All things are permissible"* (6:12; 10:23). Christians are those who have been set free from the law of sin and death (Rom 8:2).

(4) But this freedom from the law, as Paul himself experienced it, was not freedom into a vacuum but freedom into relationship with Jesus. So Paul rejects any idea that his gospel means ethical anarchy. The release from the old life is release into Christ and into the Spirit. And on both counts the result is newness of life, not moral weakness or indifference. Paradoxically the Christian is no longer "under" the law as a master, but by the Spirit the Christian lives in love and so "fulfills" what the law was all about (Rom 8:4; 12:8-10; Gal 5:14). It is no longer a case of the letter of the law, but of the fruit of the Spirit. What we have, as Paul explicitly brings out in 2 Corinthians 3, is the fulfillment of Jeremiah 31, the new covenant in the

---

29. The force of the first person in Romans 7, where Paul speaks of the law and of "my" inability to keep it, may be (partly or wholly) autobiographical. But Paul may be using the first person to speak vividly of human experience generally or of the experience of Israel in particular.

heart replacing the old, written law — which only brought us death. The logic of Paul's remark in Rom 6:14, "For sin will have no dominion over you, since you are not under law but under grace," becomes clear in this context: In the old era of law, sin did have dominion, but in the new era of God's new covenant of grace what was impossible is now possible by God's merciful working in the believer.[30]

And it is not just possible: It is the way Christians should live, because they have been brought by faith and through baptism into this grace — into eschatological righteousness. Paul is under no illusion that Christians automatically will live in this way. He is conscious of the struggle between the old life ("the flesh") and the new life of the Spirit, but he summons Christians to live up to their calling and adoption "in Christ."

. . . and Jesus

Within the Jesus-tradition, there is nothing like the complex Pauline understanding of the law, and Jesus comes across as having a significantly less negative view of the law than Paul.[31] We might characterize the difference by saying that, whereas Paul speaks sharply of the law's failure and does not feel bound by the law, Jesus criticizes those whose law-keeping is hypocritical and advocates a righteousness that goes beyond the law. The difference of emphasis is not surprising, since Paul wrote after the crucifixion, after his own conversion from Pharisaism,[32] and in the context of the Gentile mission. His thinking was profoundly affected by all three of these factors.

But the difference between Jesus and Paul on the issue of the law should not be exaggerated. It is important to remember that much of Paul's teaching on the law in the Epistles is given within a context of controversy and so has a polemical edge to it; there is some reason to think that Paul was not in fact as negative to the law as he sometimes appears.[33] But in any case there are important points of overlap between the views of Jesus and Paul, as we have analyzed them:

30. Cf. Rom 10:4 on Christ as the *telos* of the law. The word can mean — and probably does mean for Paul here — both "end" in the sense of termination and "end" in the sense of goal: Christians are free from the law and yet fulfill it. See, among others, Badenas, *Christ the End of the Law.*

31. Wilson ("From Jesus to Paul," 14) is one of a number of scholars who detects a very major difference.

32. See Schlatter, *Jesus und Paulus*, 24, 25.

33. See, e.g., Jervell, "Paul in the Acts."

(1) There is in Jesus' teaching no Pauline indictment of the law as an ally of sin and a moral failure, but there is a negative assessment of Pharisaic righteousness in Jesus' teaching. This highest righteousness of the time (of which, of course, Saul the Pharisee was an outstanding exponent) is found seriously wanting, and Jesus demands a far higher righteousness, appropriate to the kingdom of God (e.g., Matthew 5, 6, 15, 23; Mark 7, 12; Luke 11:37-54). There are parallels to Jesus' critique of Judaism in Paul's letters.[34]

(2) Jesus' criticism of Pharisaism need not suggest any failure on the part of the law. However, the higher righteousness that he advocates is not presented as something to be achieved by superior law-keeping, but on the one hand as a human impossibility (Matt 19:26/Mark 10:27/Luke 18:27) and on the other hand as an option for the sinners and the spiritually poor, those who are conspicuous failures by Pharisaic standards, those whom Jesus invites to follow him (Matt 5:3-6/Luke 6:20, 21; Matt 11:28-30, etc.). The explanation of this paradox lies in Jesus' belief that a new era is dawning: The era of the "law and prophets" is giving way to the era of the powerful and effective rule of God and the new covenant (Matt 11:12, 13; Luke 16:16). The implication of this is that the era of the law and the prophets was not conspicuously successful in terms of righteousness (cf. Jer 31:32).

(3) This still does not add up to the Pauline idea of the law as a temporary sin-related dispensation. But Jesus' comments on divorce, pointing people back to creation principles and describing certain Mosaic provisions in the law as "for the hardness of your hearts" (Matt 19:8/Mark 10:5), are at least hints in the direction of Paul's ideas both about law and new creation.

(4) Although the law is surpassed in Jesus' ethical teaching, it is not contradicted or destroyed but "fulfilled" (Matt 5:17; Luke 24:44). The Jesus-tradition and Paul agree in using this key term in connection with the mission and salvation of Jesus. It is striking how Paul, who goes out of his way to emphasize Christian freedom from the law, speaks on three separate occasions of the "fulfillment" of the law in Christians. For Paul it is "love" produced by the Spirit within the life of the believer that is the "fulfillment" of the law. Paul's emphasis on love and on the inner life of the believer have parallels in Jesus' teaching (see further below).

(5) As for the ritual demands of the law, Jesus does not address the Gentile issue that faced Paul, but he did believe that the old era of the law

---

34. J. P. Brown, "Synoptic Parallels," 44, compares Gal 2:17 with Matt 23:13 and Rom 2:19, 20 with Matt 23:16; 15:14; Luke 11:52.

(including, probably, its distinctions between clean and unclean) was passing away, and his liberalism toward the ritual law and his vision of a new spiritual temple may well be seen as tending in the direction that Paul eventually took. It is interesting at least that we have in the Jewish Christian Gospel of Matthew the rather curious story of the coin in the fish's mouth, where the idea of the "sons" being "free" (with regard to the demands of the temple) but of the disciples being called to avoid "offense" (making others to "stumble)" is so like the Pauline position on issues such as food offered to idols (Matt 17:24-27; cf. Rom 14:13-23; 1 Corinthians 8).[35]

The Spirit and the Flesh

Paul . . .

The importance of the Holy Spirit for Paul can hardly be exaggerated, not least when it comes to understanding his ethics.[36] For Paul all who are "in Christ" have the Spirit of Christ; conversely, "anyone who does not have the Spirit of Christ does not belong to him" (Rom 8:9). It is the Spirit of God — the Spirit of Jesus — who marks out the believer as a child of God and by whom the believer cries "Abba! Father!" (Rom 8:15, 16; Gal 4:6). The Spirit dwells within the believer, and the believer's body is the temple of the Holy Spirit (1 Cor 6:19).

Not that the Spirit is experienced only individually: The Christian fellowship, the body of Christ, is the temple of the Holy Spirit, and the Holy Spirit inspires the corporate life of the body, giving different gifts to different people for the benefit of all (1 Cor 3:16; ch. 12). It is baptism that brings people "into Christ" and "into the body" and that is associated with the working and giving of the Spirit (Rom 6:3; 1 Cor 12:13). As Paul puts

---

35. See further below on causing "stumbling." Mohrlang, *Matthew and Paul*, does not note the story of the coin in the fish's mouth and finds Matthew significantly less "liberal" on the law than Paul. He does not address the question of Jesus' attitude. So far as Paul is concerned, 1 Cor 7:19 is a fascinating verse: "Circumcision is nothing, and uncircumcision is nothing; but obeying the commandments of God is everything." This does seem to reflect something of Jesus' priorities and possibly even his phraseology (cf. Matt 19:17; 5:18, 19; Luke 10:26, 27). The Pauline emphasis on "freedom" is not paralleled to any significant extent in the Gospels (though compare Luke 17:10-17; John 8:31-36), but Jesus does understand his ministry broadly as bringing liberation (see chapter 4 above on the Passover context of the last supper and on the ransom saying).

36. On the Spirit in Paul and Jesus see especially Dunn, *Jesus and the Spirit.*

it in 1 Cor 12:13, "in [or by] the one Spirit we were all baptized into one body — Jews or Greeks, slaves or free — and we were all made to drink of one Spirit" (see also 1 Cor 6:11).

Paul's understanding of the Spirit is what might today be called a "charismatic" understanding. He is in the OT tradition, in which the Spirit comes on individuals powerfully and visibly to inspire prophecy and mighty actions (e.g., Jdg 14:6; 1 Sam 10:10). Only now this is not restricted to the occasional experience of the few, but is for all who are in Christ. We are reminded of the promise of Joel 2:28-32 (alluded to in Rom 10:13) that God's Spirit would be given to all of God's people, inspiring old and young and even servants, both male and female, to prophesy and see visions.[37] For Paul and his churches the coming of the Spirit is something perceptible and powerful (Gal 3:2), and its presence is manifest in all sorts of ways, including the working of miracles, prophecy, and speaking in tongues (1 Corinthians 12–14; cf. 1 Thes 1:5; 5:19, 20).

Although Paul was in this charismatic tradition, he was not always happy with all that his converts did with his teaching. He was particularly unhappy with the Corinthian Christians, who had divorced their spirituality from ethics, saying "all things are permissible,"* including immorality (1 Cor 6:12-19). For Paul the Spirit is the Spirit of Jesus, whose fruit is, above all, love, and who works in the believer conforming him or her to the image of Christ (Gal 5:22; 2 Cor 3:18).

For Paul the Spirit is contrasted with the law, on the one hand, and with the flesh, on the other. The Spirit is contrasted with the law because the law failed to produce righteousness and led only to condemnation, whereas the Spirit produces love and (paradoxically) fulfillment of the law's ideals. The Spirit is contrasted with the flesh because in Paul's thought "the flesh" most frequently refers to the old sinful nature from which the Christian has been, and is being, released.

Christian living for Paul is living according to the Spirit and not according to the flesh. But, as Paul is well aware (not least from his experience of the Corinthians!), this is not something that happens automatically. He urges his hearers, who have the Spirit, to live by the Spirit; he urges those who are "in Christ" to live accordingly. This is the so-called "indicative-imperative" of Paul's ethics: The Christian is to "be what you are" — to live out the life of the Spirit and the relationship with Christ that was

37. Joel's reference to male and female slaves makes for an interesting comparison with Paul's references to the equality in Christ of slave and free and male and female in Gal 3:28.

entered at baptism. An analogy suggested by Paul himself is marriage: He urges husbands and wives to live out their "one flesh" relationship, which they already possess but must be turned into loving, faithful action.

The present is a time of conflict between the Spirit and the flesh, between the new age and the old age. The Christian belongs to the new humanity of Christ, but is still in this present world, still needing to put to death the "flesh." The Spirit for Paul is the firstfruits of the new life, the eschatological "down payment" that guarantees what lies ahead (Rom 8:23; 2 Cor 1:22; 5:5; Eph 1:14). By the Spirit we already experience being God's children, but that "sonship" will only be fully revealed in the future. By the Spirit we know the Lord already, but only in part; full knowledge lies in the future (1 Cor 13:12).

The background to Paul's emphasis on "knowledge" is almost certainly to be found in the OT (not in Gnosticism or Greek thought).[38] Knowledge of God and of Jesus is what eschatological salvation is all about, knowledge being understood as personal relationship. A key text for Paul is, as we have suggested, Jer 31:31-34, where the promise is of a renewed covenant, in which "they shall all know me, from the least of them to the greatest." The renewed covenant, as Jeremiah explains, will be different from the old written covenant, which Israel broke, because the LORD says, "I will put my law within them, and I will write it on their hearts." Paul specifically relates this passage to the work of the Spirit in the important third chapter of 2 Corinthians, where he contrasts the letter that kills with the life-giving freedom of the Spirit, which is in turn associated with a transforming relationship with Christ, the Lord. If the Joel passage with its emphasis on signs and wonders was the key passage for the Corinthian charismatics, for Paul, on the other hand, Jeremiah 31 was, if anything, even more important, speaking of relationship and of inner ethical transformation. The location of 1 Corinthians 13 in the middle of Paul's discussion of charismatic ministry in the church is no accident or digression, but represents for Paul the most important aspect of the Spirit's ministry.

. . . and Jesus

Paul's emphasis on the Spirit certainly sets him apart from Jesus, at least as the synoptic Gospels describe Jesus. The Gospels themselves offer an explanation of this, since they explicitly (in the case of Luke and John) or implicitly (in the case of Matthew and Mark) suggest that the "baptism" of

38. See O'Brien, *Philippians*, 388, commenting on Phil 3:8.

the disciples in the Spirit took place after the ministry of Jesus. Paul, therefore, writes post-Pentecost[39] and in the light of that experience. But it would be a mistake simply on the basis of statistics concerning the use of the word "Spirit" in the synoptics to assume that Paul is wholly innovative by comparison with Jesus.

First, there is evidence that Jesus saw himself as "Son of God" and as one anointed for ministry by the Spirit (see Luke 4:18 and our discussion of christology in chapter 3 above).[40] It is probably significant that Paul describes the Holy Spirit as "the Spirit of Jesus" and as a Spirit of "sonship": He sees the Christian, the one who has been baptized "into Christ," as having the Spirit of Jesus, as sharing his sonship to God (cf. the baptismal "you are my Son . . ." in Mark 1:11/Luke 3:22) and so as using the distinctive "Abba, Father" in addressing God.

A second and closely connected point is that the kingdom that Jesus proclaims and inaugurates certainly has to do with spiritual power. Though there are only a few references specifically to the Holy Spirit in connection with the kingdom (e.g., Matt 12:28; Luke 4:18-21), the kingdom is evidently the breaking in of a new reality that is seen both in powerful, prophetic words and in powerful, miraculous actions. Despite all the difficulties that Paul has with the charismatics of Corinth, he does not question the validity of signs and wonders or of the Corinthians' prophetic experiences, and we have already seen that he knows of the gospel miracle traditions. But the power of the kingdom in Jesus' understanding not only has to do with signs and wonders but is also to be seen in moral righteousness and renewal. And for Paul the fault with the Corinthians is not their emphasis on prophecy or miracle but their failure to grasp the ethical dimensions of the kingdom, and especially their failure to take the cross seriously.[41]

Moreover, although the synoptic Gospels do not say much about it explicitly, there is evidence that an expectation of future spiritual renewal arose from Jesus' ministry. In the synoptics (as well as in John) it is John

39. It is only Luke who refers to the day of Pentecost as such, but the other Evangelists presuppose some such experience.

40. The Gospels all see Jesus in this way, not least in connection with his baptism. (See also chapter 8 below.)

41. See especially 2 Corinthians 12, where Paul reluctantly speaks of his spiritual experiences but prefers to boast in weakness and the cross. The same preference is expressed in 1 Corinthians 1, where Paul associates the demand for signs with Jews (possibly reflecting the gospel traditions in which Jesus declines to do signs on demand, Matt 12:38-42; 16:1-4; Mark 8:11, 12; Luke 11:16, 29-32; see further in chapter 8 below) and contrasts this with his own preaching of the cross.

the Baptist who looks forward to the coming one who "will baptize you in Holy Spirit"; this is taken to refer to Jesus, but the Evangelists make almost nothing of that striking prophecy: It is almost left hanging in the air.[42] The fourth Gospel, on the other hand, has Jesus himself speaking in his final days before the cross of such a spiritual experience following his death and exaltation. This is often taken to be John's retrospective theologizing, but the synoptics, too, have hints of the same expectation, not only in sporadic references to the Spirit (e.g., assisting the disciples in situations of mission and persecution, Matt 10:20; Mark 13:11; Luke 12:12), but also through the use of the new covenant theme in the last supper, and perhaps in the vision of a new temple and a new spiritual order inaugurated through the death of Jesus. Paul's consciousness of living in the new order of the Spirit does reflect a new context, but it is not out of keeping with the vision of the kingdom that Jesus offered.

Love in Church and Society

Paul . . .

We have already noted the importance of love in Pauline ethics. It is the first fruit of the Spirit in Galatians 5 and the focus of Paul's discussion of spiritual gifts in 1 Corinthians 12–14. Everything is summed up in love, including the demands of the law: "The one who loves another has fulfilled the law" (Rom 13:8).

This love is to characterize life within the Christian fellowship. The church is a "body" within which the different parts are mutually dependent and in which each is to contribute, seeking to build up others (1 Corinthians 12–14). Believers are to welcome Christians who are weak in faith, seeking to avoid offending them (1 Corinthians 8–11; Romans 14–15), putting the needs of others before their own freedoms and rights, subordinating themselves to others in humility (Philippians 2). This way of love is probably what Paul means by "the law of Christ" in Gal 6:2, where Paul urges the Galatians to bear each others' burdens (see further below, pp. 256-61).

But love is also to be directed to non-Christians, even to enemies (Romans 12; Gal 6:10). The Christian is to live "in peace" in the world and in a way that is above reproach (1 Cor 7:15; Rom 13:1-7).

42. Cf. Matt 3:11/Mark 1:8/Luke 3:16; John 1:33. Paul uses precisely the same phraseology in 1 Cor 12:13.

In his teaching on social relationships Paul has often been seen as a social conservative, as one who encouraged Christians to live blameless lives within the status quo without challenging it. Thus in 1 Cor 7:20 he tells the Corinthians: "Let each of you remain in the condition in which you were called," and in discussing social relationships the key word that he uses is "submit, be subordinate." Wives are to submit to their husbands as head because this is the created order, slaves are to obey their masters, church members are to respect church leaders, everyone is to submit to the state since the authorities are God's servants (e.g., Rom 13:1; 1 Cor 16:16; Eph 5:22; 6:5; Col 3:18, 22).

But it is at best an oversimplification to characterize Paul as socially conservative.[43] In the first place, although he does believe in the authority of leaders in church, state, and family, he expects those in Christian leadership to exercise their responsibility with radical and self-sacrificial love and consideration for those in their charge, following the example of Christ.[44]

And there is more to Paul's social ethics than a belief in the benign exercise of authority. The much-quoted Gal 3:28, "There is no longer Jew or Greek, there is no longer slave or free, there is no longer male and female; for all of you are one in Christ Jesus," is not a one-off statement atypical of Paul's theology. It actually sums up a conviction that is fundamental for him, especially in his role as a missionary to Gentiles: God has broken down old barriers in Christ and brought a new day, a new order, and a new freedom.[45]

It seems likely that this radicalism characterized Paul's teaching in the churches that he founded and led to some of the problems that he responds to in apparently conservative ways.[46] Thus in Corinth women who had taken seriously Paul's teaching about equality and freedom in Christ were

---

43. It is misleading to translate *hypotassō* by the rather negative word "submit." It means to "sub-order" oneself, i.e., to put oneself under the authority of another.

44. This is explicit in Eph 5:21–6:4 and Col 3:18–4:1 but implicit also in the undisputed letters of Paul, including where Paul speaks of his own leadership, e.g., 1 Thes 2:5-12; 5:12-14. See further below on Paul's view of servanthood.

45. Cf. the similar statements Rom 10:12; 1 Cor 12:13; Col 3:11. In his letter to Philemon Paul does not discuss the institution of slavery as such, but urges Philemon to receive the runaway Onesimus "no longer as a slave but more than a slave, a beloved brother" (16).

46. Paul's radical teaching was probably quite frequently misconstrued. For example, his teaching that "all things are permissible"* and that "all things are clean" were misconstrued by the Corinthians, and his teaching on the nearness of the Lord's coming was misconstrued by the Thessalonians (see chapter 7 below).

probably praying and prophesying in the church and claiming the right to do so with heads uncovered, like the men, and thereby were causing the offense and unhappiness that Paul has to deal with in 1 Corinthians 11.[47] It may have been that the same women were claiming that sex and marriage had no place in the new order — the issue that Paul has to deal with in 1 Corinthians 7. Paul goes a long way with these liberated Christian women, accepting their right to pray and prophesy and acknowledging the value of celibacy; but he questions aspects of their interpretation, reminding them of the male-female creation order (in ch. 11) and insisting that celibacy is not for everyone (in ch. 7).[48]

The same sort of background may well lie behind Paul's teaching on the state in Romans 13: It may be that Roman Christians and other Christians took very seriously the radical conviction that "in Christ there is neither slave nor free" and believed that those who belonged to the kingdom of God had no obligation to Caesar. Paul, however, while accepting the equality of slave and master, governor and governed, reminds the Romans that those in authority still have a role as God's servants in society.

The mixture of radical and conservative elements in Paul's social ethics may seem confusing. But it is possible to analyze his thinking as having at least three dimensions:

First, he believed and taught that in Christ new creation had come, and he encouraged his converts to live the risen life of Christ. This eschatological conviction was the basis of his and others' radicalism.

Second, others took this to imply that the old created order was a now disposable thing belonging to the sinful past, and that Christians had already arrived spiritually. Paul's eschatology, however, had a strong future dimension. He believed that in the present Christians have only a partial experience — the firstfruits — of the eschatological life; the full experience

---

47. Paul's respect for women, including in ministry, is clear from references to female colleagues, e.g., Rom 16:1, 2, 3, 6, 7; Phil 4:2, etc., as well as from the situation to which he is responding in Corinth. On the attitudes of Jesus and Paul toward women see Klassen, "Musonius Rufus."

48. See below for discussion of this analysis of the Corinthian church. Klassen, "Musonius Rufus," 204, finds the difficult teaching of 1 Timothy 2 on women keeping silence in church clearly and mischievously un-Pauline. It is not obvious, however, that principles very different from those appealed to in other Pauline passages, including 1 Corinthians 7, 11, and 14, are being appealed to in this passage. The appeal is to the creation narratives (though also to the fall narrative), and there is probably a polemic against the sort of spirituality that rejected marriage and childbearing that Paul also criticized in 1 Corinthians 7 (cf. 1 Tim 4:3; 2:15).

is still in the future, albeit imminently expected. The world and the "flesh" are realities with which the Christian still needs to reckon: The "flesh" must be put to death, marriage is a needed antidote to immorality, and the state is needed because of evil in society. The future dimension of Paul's eschatology also meant that for him revolution in the ordering of secular society was not an absolute priority, since the present order is only temporary and will shortly pass away (1 Cor 7:21-31).

Third, Paul's view of marriage and authority was not, however, simply a grudging recognition of them as necessities for the present evil age. He also believed in the goodness of God's creation, including the human body and the marriage relationship: Creation is not something to be discarded, but ultimately to be redeemed and transformed by God (e.g., Rom 8:18-23). And he believed in the value of properly exercised authority in God's world: Above all God's own authority is liberating and makes for harmony; it is not demeaning or oppressive (e.g., 1 Cor 15:28).[49]

. . . and Jesus

In their emphasis on love Paul and Jesus come very close. In Jesus' teaching the priority of love is emphasized directly, as in Matt 22:34-40; Mark 12:28-34; and Luke 10:25-28, where the commands to love God and neighbor are highlighted, with Matthew including the comment "On these two commandments hang all the law and the prophets," and indirectly, as in the so-called golden rule in the sermon on the mount: "In everything do to others as you would have them do to you; for this is the law and the prophets" (Matt 7:12/Luke 6:31). In Jesus' teaching the call is to love and forgive fellow disciples,[50] but also to love one's enemies. Jesus warns against "causing offense" to other disciples (Matt 18:6-9; Mark 9:42-50; Luke 17:1, 2) and calls for an attitude of service, putting oneself last (Matt 20:25-28/Mark 10:42-45; Luke 22:24-27).

So far as social relationships are concerned, Jesus was extraordinarily

49. "Putting oneself under" (Greek *hypotassō*) others makes for a godly order and peace according to Paul in 1 Cor 14:32, 33. See the helpful remarks of Ellis in *Pauline Theology*, 55-65. He comments that "Paul, like the NT generally, holds together quite harmoniously an equality of value and diversity in rank and resolves the problems of diversity in a manner entirely different from modern egalitarianism." He goes on to refer to Christ as the model both of equality expressed in subordination and of leadership.

50. Most clearly in John, but not only there. See further below in the second part of this chapter.

radical. The "no Jew or Greek, slave or free, male and female" of Gal 3:28 probably comes from the Hellenistic church,[51] but the attitudes expressed clearly have parallels in Jesus' ministry. His respectful attitude to women seems to have been distinctive (e.g., Luke 10:38-42),[52] he broke through other social barriers (e.g., toward sinners and Samaritans),[53] and he had a special concern for "the poor," calling on his followers to renounce everything and warning the rich of the dangers of material possessions (e.g., Matt 5:3/Luke 6:20; Matt 19:23-30/Mark 10:23-31/Luke 18:24-30). He also warned his followers against the search for hierarchical status: He spoke of his disciples as "little ones," and he himself welcomed children, "for of such is the kingdom of God" (e.g., Matt 18:1-6/Mark 9:33-42; Matt. 20:20-28/Mark 10:35-45; Matt. 23:9-12; Matt 19:13-15/Mark 10:13-16/Luke 18:15-17).

As for Paul's qualifications of his radicalism, these, too, have parallels in Jesus' teaching. Jesus does not speak of a husband's headship in marriage,[54] but he does refer back to the creation narratives when addressing a different question in regard to relationships of men and women, seeing the creation order as normative for the question of divorce. So far as authority is concerned, Jesus spoke uninhibitedly of the disciples having positions of leadership and authority in kingdom and church, though that authority was to be exercised in a style quite different from that seen in the secular world (Matt 19:28/Luke 22:30; Matt 24:45-47/Luke 12:41-44; Matt 25:21-23; Luke 19:17-19). But even Caesar is acknowledged to have some rights ("the things that are Caesar's"), as Jesus suggested when he refused to prohibit paying taxes to Caesar (Matt 22:15-22/Mark 12:13-17/Luke 20:20-26).[55] The Pauline emphases on "not causing offense" and living "at

51. Gal 3:28 may be an early baptismal formula; see further below, pp. 284-86.

52. On Jesus' attitude in its context see Witherington, *Women in the Ministry of Jesus.* Klassen, "Musonius Rufus," 199, contrasts Jesus' attitude to that found in Jewish texts, including Eccl 7:25-30; Sirach 19:2; 22:3; 42:14.

53. It is an attractive suggestion that the picture in Ephesians 2 of those who were far off and dead in sins being brought near through undeserved grace and of Jew and Gentile being made one is picking up the themes of the parable of the prodigal son (with the younger son being taken to represent the Gentiles, dead and far away from God, and the elder brother being taken to represent the Jews). So Resch, *Paulinismus,* 102.

54. The meaning of "head" as used by Paul in the context of husband/wife relationships is of course keenly debated. It is hard, in my view, to avoid the conclusion that Paul believed the husband to have a position of God-given leadership in the family.

55. Jesus' saying about Caesar was deliberately enigmatic, and scholars continue to debate how positive or negative it is toward Caesar.

peace" with others have their equivalents in Jesus' teaching (e.g., Mark 9:42-50; see further below).

Perhaps the most plausible case for seeing Paul as socially less radical than Jesus is in the matter of money, since the Pauline literature says rather little about poverty and riches until we get to 1 Timothy, where there are strong warnings to the rich, including probable echoes of Jesus' teaching about laying up treasure on earth (1 Tim 6:17-19; Matt 6:19-21/Luke 12:33, 34).[56] It is possible that Paul did not take a particularly strong line on wealth and poverty and that this is a reflection of his context: He is working not in rural Palestine but in the Greco-Roman world among some relatively affluent people, whose homes are used for church gatherings.[57]

However, as usual, the point can be exaggerated: There is, as we have seen, a possible echo of Jesus' teaching about giving away one's goods to the poor in 1 Cor 13:3, suggesting that that strand in Jesus' teaching was familiar.[58] More significantly there is Paul's teaching about his collection for the saints in Jerusalem. In discussing the project, Paul expresses the belief that there should be material "sharing" *(koinōnia)* among Christians as well as spiritual sharing, and indeed that there should be "equality" (see

---

56. The call to be content with "food and clothing" in 1 Tim 6:6-10 may also be compared with the section in the sermon on the mount about not being anxious for food and clothing (Matt 6:25-34/Luke 12:22-32).

57. The "Q" traditions of Matt 6:19-34/Luke 12:22-34 about not being "anxious" about material things but "seeking" the kingdom and about "laying up treasure" in heaven not on earth are just possibly echoed in Phil 4:6 ("Do not worry about anything"); Rom 2:5-7 ("By your hard and impenitent heart you are storing up [treasures of] wrath for yourself on the day of wrath . . . [but] to those who by patiently doing good seek for glory and honor and immortality, he will give eternal life"); and Col 3:1, 2 ("Seek the things that are above, where Christ is . . . set your minds on things that are above, not on things that are on earth"; see Brown, "Synoptic Parallels," who also compares Phil 4:6, "Let your requests be made known," to Matt 7:7, 8/Luke 11:9, 10). If Paul is drawing on these "Q" traditions at these points, then he uses them to make a general point about spiritual priorities rather than to speak specifically of material possessions. On the treasure traditions, see M. Gnanavaram, *"Treasure in Heaven."*

58. See our earlier discussion on pp. 84f. Paul implies that such giving to the poor is one of the highest spiritual actions possible, though in 1 Corinthians 13 he emphasizes that even such sacrifice is valueless without love. We have also seen that it was possible that the Corinthians were familiar with the beatitudes (including "Blessed are the poor") and that they were claiming that the kingdom was theirs (1 Cor 4:8; see discussion in chapter 2 above). There is possible evidence that Paul was familiar with the saying about not serving the two masters, God and mammon; so Brown, "Synoptic Parallels," 28, 29, referring to Rom 6:14, 15; 1 Cor 8:4, 5; 10:19-21; 2 Cor 6:14-18; 1 Thes 1:9.

Rom 15:26-29 and 2 Corinthians 8–9, especially 8:13), though this should be something that is done in love and willingly, not as an exaction.[59] This is in theory at least a very radical doctrine;[60] and Paul's own manner of life seems to suggest that it was not just theory for him (see further in chapter 8).

The Centrality of Jesus

Paul . . .

Paul's Damascus road experience was in one sense a conversion from the law to Jesus, at least as far as Paul's ethical thinking was concerned. The Christian is free from law but "in Christ," and Pauline ethics are well summed up in Col 3:17: "Whatever you do, in word or deed, do everything in the name of the Lord Jesus." Much the same point is expressed in other (undisputed) Pauline verses, such as Rom 13:14: "Put on the Lord Jesus Christ," or Gal 6:2, where the Christian's law is no longer the law of Moses but "the law of Christ" (cf. 1 Cor 9:21).

There has been much scholarly debate about the meaning of "the law of Christ." If it refers to the teaching of Jesus, whether his ethical teaching generally or specifically the love command, this is not the whole of Jesus' significance for Pauline ethics. Paul does refer to Jesus' teaching, as we have seen in relation to the divorce passage, but he also refers to the example of Jesus (Rom 15:3, 7), to Jesus' death and resurrection, in which the believer has come to share (Rom 6:4), and to the future return of Jesus in judgment, when the Christian will have to give account (1 Cor 4:1-5; 1 Thes 5:1-11).

For Paul Jesus is the decisively important reference point. Paul may have been influenced in his ethical teaching by Greco-Roman ethical codes and by the OT. But everything is now seen in the light — through the lens, we might say — of Jesus.

---

59. Feine, *Jesus Christus und Paulus,* 293, notes a parallel between Paul's reference to "need" and "abundance" in 2 Cor 8:13, 14 and Jesus' saying in the gospel story of the widow, which contrasts giving out of one's "abundance" with giving out of one's "need" (Mark 12:44/Luke 21:4).

60. Compare the practice of the early church as this is described in Acts 4:32–5:6.

. . . and Jesus

Jesus' own ethical teaching does not have such an explicit christological focus. And yet Jesus does teach with a sense of great personal authority, with his words being of the highest importance. He calls people to "follow" him in his life and death, the latter being the supreme example of service to others. More generally, the kingdom — present and future — is intimately connected with his person: Jesus' ethics are kingdom ethics and vice versa.

FINAL COMMENTS ON THE COMPARISON

There is much in common between Jesus' ethical teaching and Paul's. Both were critical of "Jewish" righteousness; both spoke of the fulfillment of the law and of a superior righteousness; both emphasized love and had a radical social outlook. At the same time we have noted a number of differences of emphasis, with Paul more negative about the law, more oriented to the Spirit, and perhaps less radical in his social ethics. The differences probably reflect their respective contexts, with Paul writing after the cross and Pentecost in a largely urban and Gentile church setting, as well as in the light of his own conversion experience.

II. CONNECTING JESUS AND PAUL

Paul's ethics and Jesus' ethics have much in common, but are they only similar or actually connected? We have already seen in chapter 2 that Paul is probably alluding to Jesus' teaching in Rom 14:14 where he says, "I know and am persuaded in the Lord Jesus that nothing is unclean in itself." But there are numerous other possible points of connection.

THE MARRIAGE ISSUE[61]

Divorce

There is, as we have seen in our first chapter, very specific evidence that Paul's understanding of marriage in 1 Cor 7:10, 11 is connected to Jesus' teaching. On divorce he says:

> To the married I give this command — not I but the Lord — that the wife should not separate from her husband (but if she does separate, let her remain unmarried or else be reconciled to her husband), and that the husband should not divorce his wife. To the rest I say — I and not the Lord. . . .

Paul very clearly indicates that he is citing the teaching of "the Lord."[62] It is almost as though he puts part of what he says in quotation marks, prefacing it with "not I but the Lord" and following it with "I say — I and not the Lord."[63]

But it is not just his own quotation marks which make it clear that he is drawing on the teaching of Jesus here, but also the wording, form, and content of verse 10, since these have has notable parallels in the synoptic passage where Jesus discusses divorce in response to the Pharisees' question (Matt 19:3-12/Mark 10:2-12). The most striking verbal link is in Paul's expression "let her not be separated,"* which in Greek quite closely re-

---

61. For a detailed discussion of Paul and Jesus on marriage and divorce see Dungan, *Sayings of Jesus,* 83-131; also my "Paul's Use," 7-15.

62. P. Richardson, "I Say, Not the Lord," 70-72, wonders if "the Lord" in 1 Cor 7:10 is the ascended Jesus speaking through a Christian prophet. There is, however, evidence that Paul speaks of traditions of the earthly Jesus as coming from "the Lord" (so 1 Cor 9:14; 11:23), and the synoptic parallels to 1 Cor 7:10, 11 make it almost certain that Paul is referring to such traditions here. Furnish, *Jesus According to Paul,* 46, argues that the wording in 7:12, "I say, not the Lord," may be Paul indicating his deliberate departure from Jesus' teaching. But it is unlikely that he is ascribing authority to the Lord's teaching in one breath and then explicitly setting himself against it in the next. It is much more likely that he is differentiating a matter on which he has teaching from "the Lord" from a matter on which he has no such teaching.

63. "Quotation marks" is slightly misleading in that Paul does not quote verbatim, as we will see. Although Paul does use these quasi-quotation marks, he only slips them in, almost as an afterthought, in the middle of giving his own instructions (in the first person); cf. Richardson and Gooch, "Logia of Jesus in 1 Corinthians," 44. Therefore, we should not assume that when Paul fails to mark a quotation, there is none.

sembles Jesus' instruction, "what God has joined together *let no one separate.*"[64]

The formal similarity lies in the twofold nature of the instruction: In Jesus' teaching and in Paul's there is a general statement against divorce (including the rather similar words about not separating) and then a more specific statement about divorce and remarriage — rather similarly constructed in the two. Thus in Matthew and Mark Jesus makes the broad statement:

(1) "What God has joined together, let no one separate."

Then he says (according to Mark in response to a request for clarification):

(2) "Whoever divorces his wife and marries another, commits adultery."[65]

This compares with Paul's general statement:

(1) "The wife should not separate from her husband,"*

which is followed by his comment qualifying the first statement:

(2) "But if she does separate, let her remain unmarried."[66]

Along with these verbal and formal similarities there is similarity of content, with Jesus and Paul both taking a strongly negative line toward divorce and in particular toward divorce and remarriage.[67]

---

64. The Greek in Matt 19:6/Mark 10:9 is *mē chōrizetō* and in 1 Cor 7:10 *mē chōristhēnai.*

65. Some have seen the second statement as a church modification of Jesus' uncompromising prohibition of divorce in the first statement. But the second statement is well attested (in "Q" as well as in the Markan tradition: so Matt 5:32/Luke 16:16) and at least in its Markan form represents no very significant relaxation of the first statement. It is in keeping with the "one flesh" view of marriage explained in Matt 19:5/Mark 10:6. The evidence is in any case that Paul was familiar with the second statement as a Jesus-tradition.

66. The construction of clause (2) in the synoptics is *hos an* + subjunctive and in 1 Cor 7:11 *ean* + subjunctive.

67. Matthew, of course, has his famous exceptive clause, "except for immorality" (5:32, 19:9), which has been endlessly discussed by scholars. It has often been seen as a

The case for Paul's dependence on the Jesus-tradition that we know from the synoptics is very strong here. Of course there are differences. Paul, for example, focuses on women and divorce, probably because it was some women in Corinth who were advocating celibacy and even divorce as part of Christian holiness,[68] but he strongly attests the synoptic tradition and throws interesting light on the synoptic problem posed by the texts and their variants.[69]

One Flesh

1 Cor 7:10 is evidence that Paul knows more than one of the sayings of Jesus that are preserved in Matthew 19/Mark 10: He knows the general injunction against separating and the particular teaching on divorce and remarriage. In their synoptic contexts these sayings of Jesus are preceded by — and theologically grounded in — Jesus' reference to the Genesis "one flesh" passage: It is because man and woman become "one flesh" in marriage

---

Matthean modification of Jesus' originally unqualified demand, and Paul's evidence may be said to confirm this view. There is a good case, however, for saying that Matthew does not qualify the stringency of the demand significantly: Many scholars have seen Matthew's exception as allowing for divorce in certain rather technical situations (e.g. for marriages contracted under questionable pagan rules); others more persuasively have argued that Matthew's exception permits divorce in cases of immorality, but not remarriage, in which case Matthew is quite close to Paul — in contemplating the need for separation in some cases, but not countenancing remarriage. (See Heth and Wenham, *Jesus and Divorce*.)

There are also questions about whether Paul qualifies the original stringency of Jesus' demand by allowing divorce and remarriage in some cases, e.g., in the case of converts whose partner is not a Christian (1 Cor 7:12-16). He clearly allows separation in such cases, but he never suggests that remarriage is permissible, and it can hardly be argued that he assumes that such separated people will remarry in a chapter where he recommends that some Christians remain celibate (compare also Rom 7:1, 2). Some of the scholars who see Paul as relaxing the teaching of Jesus, e.g., Dungan, *Sayings of Jesus*, 82, have not observed that Paul's "But if she separates . . ." has a parallel in the Jesus-tradition, and so have seen that clause as introducing a significant relaxation of Jesus' absolute prohibition of divorce. (See n. 65 above.)

68. So M. Y. Macdonald, "Women Holy," especially 170-71. See further below in n. 72.

69. See the additional note below on the synoptic evidence. See chapter 9 below on whether Paul modifies or moves away from Jesus' teaching on divorce in 1 Corinthians 7.

that divorce and remarriage are excluded. Paul, as we have seen, uses this Genesis text as the basis of his teaching about sex and marriage; indeed, he uses it in the immediately preceding chapter of 1 Corinthians, in 6:16, and by implication also probably in 7:3, 4, where he speaks of the mutual sexual obligations of marriage. It is probable, given this evidence, that Paul has been influenced by Jesus' teaching more broadly in 1 Corinthians 6 and 7, and not just where he puts what we have described as his quotation marks (7:10, 12).

Celibacy

It is an interesting possibility that Paul's advice on celibacy also derives from Jesus. In Matthew's account Jesus' teaching on divorce and on the "one flesh" basis of marriage is followed directly by the disciples' pessimistic comment: "If such is the case of a man with his wife, it is better not to marry." To this Jesus responds with his enigmatic saying about "eunuchs" (Matt 19:11, 12):

> Not everyone can accept this teaching, but only those to whom it is given. For there are eunuchs who have been so from birth, and there are eunuchs who have been made eunuchs by others, and there are eunuchs who have made themselves eunuchs for the sake of the kingdom of heaven. Let anyone accept this who can.

The meaning of this saying appears to be that celibacy is a worthy calling in the cause of the kingdom of God, but that not everyone is able to go that path, only those so gifted by God. The teaching is very similar to Paul's in 1 Corinthians 7, where he accepts that celibacy is a good vocation for a Christian (v. 8), especially in the light of the eschatological hour (vv. 26, 29; cf. Jesus' reference to the kingdom), but that it is only a vocation for those who have received that gift (v. 7).

Although Paul's teaching is so close to that of Jesus on this matter, he does not attribute it to Jesus, and indeed he appears at one point at least to be offering it as his own opinion (v. 25). This might seem to contradict the suggestion that he is drawing on the Matthean Jesus-tradition.[70]

---

70. In favor of this suggestion see Witherington, *Women,* 128. The fact that the "eunuchs" saying occurs only in Matthew might be thought to put its authenticity in doubt and so to tell against the idea of Pauline use of it. But see Wolff, "Humility and Self-Denial," 152, arguing that rabbinic parallels, the shocking language used, and evi-

However, an interesting possibility is that those in Corinth who were advocating celibacy were themselves drawing on Jesus' teaching and were taking the "eunuchs" saying to mean that celibacy is the highest Christian calling, to which all should aspire. Paul rejects this interpretation and brings out the fact that Jesus specifically said that only some have been "given" the capacity for celibacy; the Corinthians were mistaken and were getting into all sorts of trouble by ignoring this. If this is what lies behind 1 Corinthians 7, then it is obvious why Paul cannot simply deal with the celibacy question by reference to the Lord's word, since the Corinthians were appealing to the same word.[71] Instead he has to dispute their interpretation and offer his own "opinion" of the text as the correct one. The main evidence for this reconstruction of the background to 1 Corinthians 7 is (1) the similarity of Paul's teaching to what is in Matt 19:11, 12, (2) that the teaching on celibacy is adjacent to the teaching on divorce in both 1 Corinthians 7 and Matthew 19, and (3) that Paul is, by his own confession, using the Matthew 19 teaching on divorce. But the case may be strengthened by further consideration of the Corinthian context.

Mary, Martha, and women in Corinth

It has been rather persuasively suggested that the situation in Corinth that Paul is addressing in 1 Corinthians 7 was one in which some Corinthian women were advocating sexual abstinence — even for those who were already married — as a mark of Christian holiness. It is clear from elsewhere in 1 Corinthians that women in the congregation were playing a prominent and controversial part in church affairs (see especially 11:1-16). A small indication that women were at the forefront of the movement in favor of celibacy may be that, in addressing the matter of divorce, Paul says in the first instance that a wife should not separate from her husband (7:10).[72]

---

dence that Jesus himself was celibate warrant the conclusion that the saying goes back to Jesus. Mark's omission of the saying, if it was part of the tradition, is not hard to explain. The obscurity of the saying by itself might have caused him to omit it, but if it was being misused in some Christian circles (see our discussion), then Mark may have preferred to omit it, along with other material (e.g., the strongly Jewish Christian traditions preserved by Matthew and perhaps the tradition about Peter the rock, though Mark's omission there may have as much to do with his christological priorities as with any hesitation he may have had about the Matthean saying).

71. This is the probable answer to Resch, *Paulinismus*, 404, who on this occasion thinks that Paul is ignorant of the Jesus-tradition because he claims to have no command of the Lord on this matter and simply to be giving his opinion.

72. That Paul says that divorcees should not remarry could appear to tell against

The women may have used various arguments in their advocacy of celibacy: For example, those who were married to still-unconverted husbands may well have been worried whether they were compromising their Christian status before God (their "holiness" in that sense) and their children's position, if they failed to "come out from them, and be separate from them" (1 Cor 7:14; 2 Cor 6:14-18).[73]

But the women (and no doubt some men too) probably had an even more fundamental objection to having sexual relations with anyone, Christian or otherwise. They rightly recognized and indeed had experienced for themselves that Christ had brought new life in the Spirit; in this new life in Christ there was no more male and female (as Paul himself taught, Gal 3:28).[74] This was a practically liberating doctrine for the women, who were able to lead the church in praying and prophesying. But the liberating doctrine led some of them to cause offense by breaking with convention and worshiping like the men with their heads unveiled, a matter Paul addresses in 1 Corinthians 11.[75] It also probably led some of them to infer

---

the view that the Corinthians' motivation behind divorce was ascetic. But the dominant issue in 1 Corinthians 7 is clearly the view "that it is good for a man not to touch a woman" (vv. 1, 3, etc.), and it seems likely that Paul's comment on remarriage is almost an aside, perhaps reflecting the influence of the Jesus-tradition on Paul (see above) and perhaps also Paul's awareness of mixed motives among the women contemplating divorce and his consciousness that some of them might sooner or later want to remarry. On the leading role women played in the celibacy issue of 1 Corinthians 7 see M. Y. Macdonald, "Women Holy," noting also the references to "widows" and "virgins" later in the chapter and comparing the references to widows in the Pastoral Epistles (e.g., 1 Tim 5:9-16). See also Wire, *Corinthian Women Prophets,* especially 72-90. Wire plausibly suggests that the problems of 1 Corinthians 6 (i.e., Corinthian men going to prostitutes) may have been provoked by the asceticism of the Corinthian women.

73. Note the interest in holiness in 1 Cor 7:12-14. Whether or not 2 Cor 6:14-18 is an integral part of 2 Corinthians (on this see Scott, *Adoption,* 193-219), it may represent traditional Pauline teaching that could have influenced the Corinthian women.

74. See the additional note below on whether Gal 3:28 is a baptismal text.

75. 1 Corinthians 11 is, of course, a scholarly minefield; we will not attempt to discuss the myriad of different views on its interpretation. But it is possible that the Corinthian women had accepted the sort of teaching that Paul gives in 2 Corinthians 3 about Christians worshiping in the freedom of the Spirit with heads uncovered, seeing the Lord's glory and being transformed into his image. Applying such teaching to their own case, they caused offense and scandal. Paul in 1 Corinthians 11 (picking up the ideas of image, glory, etc.) affirms the women's right to pray and prophesy and the equality of men and women, but argues that sexual differentiation is part of God's creation order and something still to be respected. His spirituality is creation-affirming, not creation-superseding or creation-escaping; thus in other contexts in 1 Corinthians

that there should be no more sex: After all, if the new age has come and there is no more male or female, sex arguably no longer has any place among spiritual people. At least the really spiritual and the really holy should abstain from sexual activity.

They might have reached this conclusion simply on the basis of Paul's "no male/female" teaching. But one real possibility is that they also appealed to Jesus' teaching to justify their position. Had not Jesus taught about the kingdom of God taking priority over family, and had he not even spoken of "hating" one's family (e.g., Matt 12:46-50/Mark 3:31-35/Luke 8:19-21; Luke 11:27; Matt 19:29/Mark 10:23/Luke 18:29, 30; Matt 10:37/Luke 14:26)?[76] Had he not taught that there is no marriage in the age to come (Matt 22:30/Mark 12:25/Luke 20:35, 36),[77] and had not that age arrived through the Holy Spirit — as some of the Corinthians believed?[78]

A particular story that may have been cited by the Corinthian women is that of Mary and Martha in Luke 10:38-42, where Jesus praises Mary for

---

he affirms the importance of the body — in response to the Corinthians' notion that the body was now unimportant (so ch. 6 on prostitution and ch. 15 on the resurrection).

76. See Balch, "Backgrounds of 1 Cor vii," 356-57; D. R. MacDonald, *There is No Male and Female,* 70-71. Balch suggests that the Corinthians appealed to the Hellenistic-Jewish tradition of Moses' vision of God (Exodus 24), according to which Moses' self-purification included refraining from sexual activity. Balch notes the use of Exodus 24 in 2 Corinthians 3.

77. See also J. C. Hurd, "Jesus Whom Paul Preaches," 87. The distinctive Lukan version of the Lord's saying, "those who are considered worthy of a place in that age and in the resurrection from the dead neither marry nor are given in marriage," could be taken to apply to the present and not just to the future. Quesnell, "Made Themselves Eunuchs," and Balch (see previous note) observe that Luke could appear more ascetic, not only in 20:35, 36 but also in 14:26 and 18:29, where his version of the respective sayings speaks of discipleship as involving "hating" and "leaving" wife and family. It could be that the Corinthians knew the Lukan form of the saying and that Matthew and Mark in their editing of the tradition, as well as Paul in 1 Corinthians, seek to correct any misunderstanding. Sneed, "Kingdom of God," 369, notes a possible Pauline echo of Luke 20:35 in 2 Thes 1:5.

78. See our earlier comments on 1 Cor 4:8, 9 (p. 79 above). Was this why they had doubts about the resurrection (cf. 1 Corinthians 15)? Did they believe that they were already experiencing the life to come and that there was no need for resurrection? Compare the Thessalonians (1 Thes 4:13-18).

Walter, "Paul," 70, wonders if Paul's "I say, not the Lord" in 1 Cor 7:12 could mean "I say, departing from a known saying of the Lord," Paul thus distancing himself from those who advocate the dissolution of their marriages on the basis of a saying of Jesus. More likely he is simply differentiating a matter on which there was a clear command of Jesus from a matter on which there was no such clear instruction.

sitting at his feet and listening to his word and says to Martha, the worried homemaker: "Martha, Martha, you are worried and distracted by many things; there is need of only one thing. Mary has chosen the better part, which will not be taken away from her."

It is noteworthy that some of Paul's rather unusual language in 1 Corinthians 7:32-35 is reminiscent of this Lukan story. Thus, in speaking of marriage and singleness, Paul (1) says that he does not want the Corinthians to be *"worried,"** (2) speaks of the desirability of being *"devoted* to the Lord,"* and (3) wants their devotion to be *"undistracted."** Likewise: (1) Martha was *"worried."*[79] (2) The etymological sense of Paul's word translated "devoted"[80] is "sitting well beside." Etymologies are often quite irrelevant, but it could be that Paul uses this unusual word (found only here in the NT) deliberately, with the story of Mary sitting at the Lord's feet in mind. (3) With Paul's "undistracted" (a word used only here in the NT) contrast the description of Martha as *"distracted"* (a related word, also used only here in the NT).[81]

It is tempting to surmise that the Corinthian women had seized on this story to show that the Lord recommended the renunciation of Martha-like domestic "worry" in favor of Mary-like undistracted devotion to the Lord. Had not Jesus said that Martha had chosen the good part, which would not be taken from her (Luke 10:42)?[82] Paul agrees that lack of worry and undistracted devotion is desirable, but he does not agree with the Corinthian women's verdict that celibacy is the way to this goal for everyone.[83]

It is not difficult to see how the Corinthians might have reasoned

---

79. The same Greek verb, *merimnaō,* is used. It is used four times in 1 Cor 7:32-34 (and the adjective *amerimnos* is used once), but only twice elsewhere in Paul's letters.

80. *Euparedros.*

81. The Greek words are *aperispastōs* and *perispaomai.*

82. For the connection see Moule, *Birth of the NT,* 144-52; Fraser, *Jesus and Paul,* 96; Resch, *Paulinismus,* 221-22, who rightly comments that Luke is hardly likely to have created the Mary-Martha story on the basis of the Pauline teaching. Goulder, *Luke,* 136-37, argues on the contrary that Luke is dependent on Paul (see also J. P. Brown, "Synoptic Parallels," 27); he comments that Paul could not be dependent on the Lukan story since "Luke does not even say that Martha was married." This is quite unpersuasive: Martha does not need to be married for the Corinthians to use her as an example, but they might have inferred that she was the wife of the householder (as Goulder himself does!)

83. Barrett and other commentators conclude that Paul argues that singleness produces its worries as well as marriage its worries (*1 Corinthians,* 180-81; also M. Y. Macdonald, "Women Holy," 174); Paul may have been responding to the Corinthians' claim that celibacy was the recipe for lack of worry.

from such passages, including the "eunuchs" saying of Matt 19:11, 12, that Jesus recommended celibacy, at least for the most spiritual.[84] Paul is alarmed at the danger to the morality of the Christian community in Corinth posed by this unrealistic antisexual super-spirituality, and he emphasizes that they have got it wrong and that celibacy is, as Jesus said, only for those to whom it has been given.

Conclusion: sexuality according to Paul

The accumulated evidence for the influence of Jesus-tradition on Paul's teaching about marriage, divorce, and singleness is considerable. 1 Corinthians 7, like 1 Corinthians 9 (with its discussion of the "worker's" rewards) seems to be to a very considerable extent based on teachings of Jesus.[85] As in ch. 9, the parallels are not just between individual sayings: In ch. 7 Paul seems to draw on much of the material that is found in Matt 19:1-12.[86] Also as in ch. 9, it is not only Paul who has been influenced; the evidence suggests that he is debating with the Corinthians about sayings of Jesus which they were familiar with and were interpreting in ways which Paul disagreed with.

ENEMIES, AUTHORITIES, OUTSIDERS

Returning Good for Evil

Romans 12–15 are particularly important chapters for the question of Jesus and Paul.[87] As interesting as any other evidence is that of Rom 12:14-20, where Paul speaks of the Christian response to persecution and maltreatment in terms that are strongly reminiscent of the sermon on the mount.

---

84. Stanley, "Pauline Allusions," 36, 37, speculates that Paul could be echoing the parable of the feast (Luke 14:16-24) in his comments in 1 Cor 7:29-31 on the need for disengagement on the part of those with wives and those selling things.

85. Contra Richardson and Gooch, "Logia of Jesus," 45. The divorce saying is the most weighty piece of evidence, but the cumulative case for the influence of other Jesus-tradition in 1 Corinthians 7 is strong.

86. There is no proof that he knew it in the Matthean sequence, though he does seem to have known the two divorce sayings (Matt 19:6/Mark 10:9 and Matt 19:9/Mark 10:11) in sequence.

87. On these chapters see the authoritative and detailed study by Thompson, *Clothed with Christ*.

Thus in 12:14 Paul urges, "Bless those who persecute you; bless and do not curse them." To this we can compare Luke 6:28: "Bless those who curse you, pray for those who abuse you" (Matt 5:44 has "pray for those who persecute you"). The similarity of idea, wording — "bless," "curse," even "persecute" if we follow the Matthean wording of the "pray" saying — and form — the present imperative followed by the present participle — makes a connection between the traditions very likely.[88]

Establishing a connection does not mean that the dependence must inevitably be from Jesus to Paul. Luke could have been influenced by Paul at this point. But the Lukan section is largely paralleled in Matthew, and it is simpler to suppose that Paul is drawing on a Jesus-tradition that is independently attested by Matthew and Luke than to assume that Luke has for some reason added a Pauline phrase to the Jesus-tradition with which he is working.[89] Paul's repetition of the call to "bless" is, arguably, not just for rhetorical effect, but shows that he has been influenced by the saying of Jesus: Having spoken first of blessing "those who persecute" (that verb being in Paul's mind from v. 13), he picks up the thought of "cursing" from the saying and tells his readers to "bless and do not curse."[90] Paul may well reflect the same saying in 1 Cor 4:12: "When reviled, we bless; when persecuted, we endure."

The thought of returning good for evil is taken forward in Romans 12:17-20, where there are a range of further parallels with the same section of the sermon on the mount:

88. The sudden switch from participles (which Paul has been using from vv. 9-13) to an imperative ("bless") may be evidence that Paul is picking up here the imperatives of the sermon on the mount, though there is also a significant shift of thought at this point (from relationships with insiders to relationships with outsiders) which could account for the grammatical change. See Stuhlmacher, "Jesustradition," 248; Thompson, *Clothed with Christ*, 102-3.

89. The relationship of the Matthew and Lukan texts is complex, but there is good reason for believing that they are independent witnesses to a common tradition. Paul himself may be a witness to this, for example, in his use of "persecute" (paralleled in Matthew) and "bless" (paralleled in Luke). Matthew does not have the Lukan "bless those who curse you," but his saying in his 5:47, "if you greet only your brothers," may well be an indication that he knows the saying. The Lukan phrase is found in Didache 1:3 and Justin, *Apology* 1.15.9. See my "Paul's Use," 15-24, for more detailed discussion of these texts; also Catchpole, *Quest*, 101-34.

90. See Thompson, *Clothed with Christ*, 102-3.

Rom 12:17
Pay back no one evil for (instead of) evil, taking thought for what is good before all people.

Matt 5:38
You have heard that it was said, "Eye for (instead of) eye, tooth for tooth," but I say, Do not resist wickedness.*

12:18, 19
If possible, as far as depends on you, be at peace with all people. Do not avenge yourselves, beloved, but give place to wrath.*

Luke 6:27, 33
Do good to those who hate you. . . . If you do good to those who do good to you, what credit is it to you?*

12:20, 21
If your enemy is hun-
gry, feed him. . . .
Do not be conquered
by evil, but
conquer evil by good.*

Matt 5:39-42 (Luke 6:29)
But whoever slaps you on your right cheek, turn him the other also. And whoever wants to sue you. . . .*

Matt 5:41, 42 (Luke 6:30, 27)
Whoever forces you to go one mile, go with him two. Whoever asks you, give. . . . love your enemies. . . .*

The parallel ideas are interesting, though the verbal parallels are not sufficiently close to prove any connection between the traditions.[91] The most probable echo of the Jesus-traditions is probably Rom 12:17: "Do not repay anyone evil for (Greek *anti*) evil, but take thought for what is noble in the sight of all."[92]

91. There is another possible echo of the same part of the sermon on the mount in 1 Cor 6:7, where Paul castigates the Corinthians for their court cases, and asks, "Why do you not rather accept injustice? Why do you not rather allow yourself to be deprived?"* The phraseology and thought are not far removed from Matt 5:40: "If anyone wants to sue you and take your coat, give your cloak as well." See also 5:25, 26; Resch, *Paulinismus*, 48.

92. Paul repeats this advice in 1 Thes 5:15: "See that none of you repays evil for (*anti*) evil, but always seek to do good to one another and to all." That he uses almost identical phraseology on the two occasions may indicate that the phraseology is traditional. It could be simply Jewish tradition; there are parallels, for example, in Joseph and Asenath (see Tuckett, "Synoptic Tradition in 1 Thessalonians," 164-65). But it may well be that Paul is also and perhaps more directly influenced by Jesus' version of that

Respect for Caesar

Paul proceeds from his discussion about loving one's enemy in Romans 12 to a discussion of the Christian's responsibility to the state in 13:1-7, urging subordination to those in authority, and concluding with the exhortation "Pay to all what is due them — taxes to whom taxes are due, revenue to whom revenue is due, respect to whom respect is due, honor to whom honor is due." The teaching here is closely similar to Jesus' teaching about taxation: "Pay to Caesar the things that are Caesar's and to God the things that are God's"* (Matt 22:21/Mark 12:17/Luke 20:25). There is in both the synoptic and the Pauline passages a specific focus on the Roman authorities and on the issue of tax; there is also in both the broader, and in some ways more noncommittal, idea of paying what is owed to the person to whom it is owed, though in Rom 13:7 there is no mention of "paying" things to God.[93]

The form of words used in the synoptic and Pauline passages is also rather similar:

"Pay" (the same verb in the same tense)
+ accusative ("the things . . . ," "the debts")
+ dative ("to Caesar," "to all").

Paul's word for "taxes" is also used in Luke's version of the question put to Jesus, though not in Matthew's or Mark's.[94]

Jewish tradition, as attested in Matt 5:38, 39, where the command "Do not resist wickedness"* is contrasted with the "eye for (*anti*) eye" attitude, and in Luke 6:27, where the instruction is to "do good [even] to those who hate you." The possibility that Paul is influenced in this way by the Jesus-tradition raises all sorts of questions about the relationships of the Matthean and the Lukan traditions. See further the additional notes below on "The 'Love Your Enemies' Traditions of Matthew 5:38-48/Luke 6:27-36" and "Further Possible Echoes of Matthew 5:38-48/Luke 6:27-36."

93. It is possible to take "pay . . . respect to whom respect is due, honor to whom honor is due" in Rom 13:7 as referring to God; but against this see Cranfield, *Romans*, 670-72; Neirynck, "Paul and the Sayings," 286-91. Paul's failure to reproduce the important clause in the saying of Jesus, "to God the things that are God's," is not hard to explain: Whereas Jesus was making a careful statement in response to a tricky question, Paul is urging the Romans to respect the state, to which they were probably feeling no loyalty. Kim, "Jesus, Sayings of," 479, 481, wonders if Rom 12:1, 2 could be an echo of "to God the things that are God's" (and of Mark 12:29, 30.)

94. Matthew and Mark use the Latinism *kēnsos*. Luke and Paul use *phoros*. The verb translated "pay," *apodidōmi*, is not the obvious verb to use of paying taxes, and

It is at least possible that Paul is echoing Jesus' teaching at this point.

Light and Salt

The question of the Christian in society is addressed in the sermon on the mount in Jesus' comments to the disciples about being the "salt of the earth" and the "light of the world" (5:13, 14). The meaning of the two pictorial images is spelled out in 5:16: "So let your light shine before people, that they may see your good deeds and glorify your Father who is in heaven."* Commentators suspect that some of the wording used here originates with Matthew, but also that Matthew is working with earlier traditions (cf. Mark 4:21/Luke 8:16; 11:33; Mark 9:49, 50/Luke 14:34, 35).[95]

There are two Pauline parallels in this case. First, in Phil 2:15 Paul encourages the Philippians to be "blameless and innocent, children of God without blemish in the midst of a crooked and perverse generation, in which you shine like *stars in the world*." The thought is quite similar to that found in Matt 5:14-16. The wording is also closer than it appears in English translation: "Star" in Phil 2:15 *(phōstēr)* is very similar to "light" in Matt 5:14 *(phōs)*; it is as though Paul speaks of Christians as "light bearers in the world" while Jesus in Matthew speaks of them as "the light of the world."[96]

Second, Col 4:5, 6 instructs the Colossians: "Conduct yourselves wisely toward outsiders, making the most of the time. Let your speech always be gracious, seasoned with salt." The salt imagery is used here very much as in Matt 5:13.

If Matt 5:13-16 is largely an interpretation of Jesus' words rather than Jesus' actual words, then the similarity of the Pauline texts suggests that Paul may be familiar with this interpretation.[97] There is thus at least an indirect link to the Jesus-tradition. But it may be that there are more of Jesus' own words in Matt 5:13-16 than is often supposed and that Paul is thus more directly echoing Jesus-tradition.[98]

Paul uses it quite infrequently for any purpose. He may be influenced by Jesus-tradition in his uses of it in Rom 12:17 and 1 Thes 5:15; in 1 Cor 7:3 he uses it with "debt" *(opheilē)* as its object, as in Rom 13:7.

95. So Davies and Allison, *Matthew*, I, 472-75; Luz, *Matthew 1-7*, 247.

96. Stuhlmacher, *Biblische Theologie*, 302, notes a possible parallel also between Phil 2:15 and Luke 9:41/Matt 17:17.

97. Cf. Dodd, *More NT Studies*, 27, 28, on Matt 5:13 as an application of the Markan "salt" saying drawn from the catechetical tradition of the church.

98. John 8:12 is a striking parallel to Matt 5:14, though it speaks of Jesus, not the disciples. Cf. also 1 Tim 5:23; 1 Pet 2:9, 12 (and see Brown, "Synoptic Parallels," 30).

LOVE ONE ANOTHER

Love for Neighbor as Fulfillment of the Law

After discussing the Christian's responsibilities toward Caesar in Romans 13, Paul proceeds to a more general exhortation to "owe no one anything, except to love one another," continuing (vv. 8-10):

> For the one who loves another has fulfilled the law. The commandments, "You shall not commit adultery; You shall not murder; You shall not steal; You shall not covet"; and any other commandment, are summed up in this word, "Love your neighbor as yourself." Love does no wrong to a neighbor; therefore, love is the fulfilling of the law.

This passage has an important parallel in Gal 5:13, 14, where Paul urges his readers: "Through love become slaves to one another. For the whole law is summed up in a single commandment [*logos*, i.e., "word"], 'You shall love your neighbor as yourself.' " In both passages Paul sums up the law in terms of love for neighbor and explains that such love is the fulfillment of the law.

Both these emphases, love for neighbor as the sum of the law and love as the fulfillment of the law, have important precedents in the Jesus-tradition. The most obvious synoptic parallel to the Pauline passages is in Matt 22:34-40/Mark 12:28-34, where Jesus, having shortly before been asked about paying taxes to Caesar, is now asked about which is the greatest commandment. He replies by quoting the two commandments "You shall love the Lord your God . . ." and "You shall love your neighbor as yourself," and then says, in the Matthean version of the story, "On these two commandments hang all the law and the prophets."

The parallel to the Pauline teaching is not exact. First, Paul does not quote the commandment to love God; he sums up the law only in terms of love for neighbor.[99] But this is entirely explicable: He is talking about the law in relationship to other people and summing up numbers five through ten of the ten commandments, not numbers one through four. When it comes to relating to other people Jesus and Paul agree exactly on how to sum up the law.

Second, the idea of love being the fulfillment of the law is not exactly the same as that of all the law and the prophets "hanging" from

---

99. Neirynck, "Paul and the Sayings of Jesus," 293-94, finds this a significant difficulty.

the love commandments. Furthermore, Mark does not have the Matthean phrase, but more simply "There is no other commandment greater than these."[100]

But although too much should not be made of the particular parallel, the emphasis on love for neighbor is important in the gospel traditions of Jesus.[101] So also is the idea of Jesus' way of righteousness (with its focus on love) as the fulfillment of the OT law, even if this is more often implicit than explicit.[102] It is striking that Paul, who so strongly emphasizes the freedom of Christians from the law, should explicitly and on several occasions speak of the Christian "fulfilling the law."[103] It is tempting to link this with the traditions of Matt 5:17 and Luke 24:24.

Loving One Another: The Law of Christ

The law of love in Paul and John

Paul's exhortations to the Romans and Galatians about love, which we have been considering, both begin with the call to the readers to love "one

100. Scholars following the two-source hypothesis will tend to prefer the Markan wording, though it could be a simplification on Mark's part of the more obscure Matthean form.

101. The commandment "love your neighbor as yourself" features prominently in the Jesus-tradition, though not always on the lips of Jesus himself (see Matt 5:43; Matt 19:19; Luke 10:25-28 and compare the "golden rule" in Matt 7:12/Luke 6:31).

102. We have already noted the fulfillment terminology in Matt 5:17 and Luke 24:44. These synoptic references do not connect fulfillment with "love" — not directly at least. But Matt 5:17 introduces the section of the sermon on the mount discussing the law and Jesus' higher righteousness: As we have seen, the first illustration of this righteousness in Matt 5:21-26 has to do with relationships (hatred and reconciliation), and the final and climactic example (vv. 43-48) speaks of loving even one's enemy. So the fulfillment is in terms of love.

Furthermore, 5:17 has often been seen as bracketing the main section of the sermon of the mount together with 7:12: "In everything do to others as you would have them do to you; for this is the law and the prophets." This so-called "golden rule" is the "love your neighbor" commandment in different words. If 5:17 and 7:12 are rightly connected, then in Matthew the saying about Jesus fulfilling the law and the prophets is explained in the sermon that follows — with its comparison of Jesus' teaching with that of the OT and its strong emphasis on love and with its "love your neighbor" sort of conclusion. Matthew thus ascribes to Jesus a view of fulfillment as coming through love, which at least constitutes a striking parallel to what we find in Paul.

103. Rom 13:8, 10; Gal 5:14. See also Rom 8:3.

another" (Rom 13:8; Gal 5:13). The commandment to "love one another as I have loved you" is very specifically and emphatically ascribed to Jesus in John's Gospel: It is "my *commandment*," Jesus' "new *commandment*" (John 13:34; 15:12, 17; 1 John 4:11). Could it be that Paul knows this tradition that John records?

That he may know it is suggested not just by the similar "love one another" phraseology but also by the evidence of Gal 6:2, where Paul urges the Galatians to "bear one another's burdens, and in this way you will fulfill *the law of Christ.*" There has been a great deal of debate about what Paul means by "the law of Christ." He uses the phrase nowhere else,[104] and it is perhaps a rather surprising usage for someone who so frequently contrasts Christ and the law.[105] But one obvious and serious possibility is that he is referring to the teaching of Jesus. If he is, what specifically does he have in mind?

Bearing another's burdens, which, Paul says, is to fulfill the law of Christ, is quite closely akin to loving another,[106] and it is, of course, precisely the command to "love one another" that John emphatically describes as Jesus' special "commandment" to his disciples. It could be pure coincidence that both Paul and John describe loving one another in terms of "the law/commandment of Jesus/Christ"; but it is more likely that Paul and John know the same tradition. Paul speaks (atypically) of "the law of Christ" because the tradition emphasized that this was *Jesus'* commandment.[107]

104. But cf. 1 Cor 9:21, where Paul speaks of his freedom from the OT law, but then speaks of himself as being "not without God's law but in Christ's law"* (or "not God's lawless one but Christ's enlawed one"*).

105. Räisänen, *Jesus, Paul and Torah,* 182, suggests that Paul got the phrase from his opponents. An alternative is that he got it from the Jesus-tradition. See further below.

106. Gal 6:2 is thematically connected to 5:13, 14 and to Rom 13:8-10; note the idea of helping "one another" as a "fulfillment." This adds weight to the argument that "the law of Christ" is indeed "love one another." Note also Rom 15:1, 2, where the idea of bearing another's burdens leads into the thought of pleasing one's "neighbor." For the idea of bearing or not bearing others' burdens in the Gospels see Matt 23:4. Even more relevant may be Isa 53:4, which describes the servant "bearing" the illnesses of others and is a text related to the healings of Jesus in Matt 8:17; see Dunn, "Paul's Knowledge of the Jesus Tradition," 199; Thompson, *Clothed with Christ,* 210-11.

107. Among the many suggestions made about the meaning of "the law of Christ" in Gal 6:2, some have denied that it is a reference back to Jesus' teaching at all. Whatever view is taken, the phrase must be some sort of "tradition indicator," identifying mutual burden-bearing as somehow commended by Jesus. The "fulfill the law" language suggests some sort of parallel to "the law of Moses," and easily the simplest view is to

Love one another: from Jesus, not just from John

A problem with this proposed connection between Jesus and Paul is that it is only the fourth Gospel that has Jesus specifically command his disciples to "love one another." In the synoptics Jesus urges a love for one's neighbor that is not narrowly defined but that includes even enemies. The apparently inward-looking "love" commandment in the fourth Gospel has been seen as a reflection of the Johannine church situation rather than as something going back to Jesus.[108]

But although the synoptists do suggest that Jesus challenged exclusive and narrow definitions of love, they also imply that Jesus spoke of the disciples having a special responsibility toward their "brothers."[109] Thus especially in Matthew 18/Mark 9:42-50/Luke 17:1-4, a passage where there is reason to believe that Matthew, Mark, and Luke have independent traditions,[110] all three Evangelists have Jesus' solemn words of warning about causing offense to the "little ones." Matthew and Luke speak of forgiving others in the Christian community. Mark has the almost Johannine injunction "be at peace with one another" (9:50).[111]

---

conclude that Paul is describing such burden-bearing as something that Jesus taught. The Johannine evidence makes this conclusion very likely.

Although this argument carries weight, it is worth adding that in John the "new commandment" is to "love *as I have loved you*," so that the law of Christ is what Jesus both commands and exemplifies. Paul may know the tradition in precisely the same form. See Rom 15:7 and cf. Dunn, *Galatians*, 323, who notes the parallel to Gal 6:2 in Rom 15:2, 3 (though not the Johannine parallel) and comments: "We must speak . . . of Christ's self-giving as a paradigm for Christian relationships." See further on "humble serving" below.

108. The repeated and emphatic appearance of the "love one another" commandment in John's Gospel and 1 John might make us hesitate about this conclusion, suggesting that we are dealing with a tradition that was known — as a Jesus-tradition — in the Johannine church (whether or not it went back further than that), not just with a redactional motif.

109. Jesus would not have been unique in emphasizing love for the brotherhood; cf. 1QS 1:9-11 for love of the brothers but hatred of those in darkness. See also R. E. Brown, *John*, 613.

110. Matthew and Luke have material in common not found in Mark, e.g., the "woe" of Matt 18:7/Luke 17:1, and so in terms of the two-source hypothesis we have a Mark/Q overlap.

111. The call to peace is preceded in Mark by the injunction "have salt among yourselves."* The "salt" here may be the salt of the covenant (Lev 2:13), with Jesus thus calling the disciples to live in peace and covenant fellowship (cf. Fleddermann, "Dis-

It is true that Matthew and Luke in other contexts bring out in Jesus'
teaching an emphasis on loving one's enemy and warn against loving just
"those who love you" (Matt 5:46; Luke 6:32). But in Matthew 5 the illustra-
tions of Jesus' higher righteousness start with the question of relationships
with "your brother" — "first be reconciled to your brother" (5:24) — and
end with an exposition of "love of neighbor" including "your enemies"
(5:43-47). It is thus a case of both-and, both love of the brother and love
of the outsider, not of either-or.

We may conclude with some confidence that "loving one another"
was an emphasis associated not only with the Johannine church and that
it probably had its roots in Jesus' own teaching. The pervasiveness of the
idea in many parts of the NT may confirm this. Thus in 1 Pet 1:22 the
author urges love for the brother, using the same phraseology as we find
in John — "love one another." And in the Pauline literature, beyond the
passages we have noted, there are 1 Thes 3:12; 4:9; 5:15; 2 Thes 1:3; Col
3:12-14; and Eph 4:32, all of which speak of loving fellow Christians. In
addition Paul urges Christians to be at peace with each other in 1 Thes
5:13; Rom 14:19; and 2 Cor 13:11.

Further evidence of Paul's use of the tradition

In view of this evidence the identification of the "law of Christ" in Gal 6:2
with Jesus' commandment to his disciples to "love one another" is plausible,
even though that commandment is explicit only in John.

There is a certain amount of further evidence indicating that Paul
was familiar with Jesus' teaching about brotherly love. Thus in 1 Thes 4:9
Paul says: "Concerning brotherly love you have no need to be written to,
for you are all taught by God to love one another."* Paul's language here
is not exactly a "tradition indicator,"[112] but it is a strong statement about
the well-known and fundamental importance of "loving one another"

---

cipleship Discourse," 73; Myers, *Binding the Strong Man,* 264). The idea of brotherly
love may also be implicit in Jesus' teaching about his disciples as his family (Matt
12:46-50/Mark 3:31-35/Luke 8:19-21).

112. But Paul could very well have in mind his own earlier teaching to the
Thessalonians, including teaching of Jesus-traditions; cf. 2:13 on their reception of Paul's
teaching as the word of God, and 4:1, where Paul says: "We ask and urge you in the
Lord Jesus that, as you learned from us how you ought to live. . . ." The phrase "in the
Lord Jesus" could be significant. See also Stanley, "Pauline Allusions," 28; Hurd, "Jesus
Whom Paul Preaches," 85.

within the Christian community. The phrase "taught by God" may have an OT background,[113] and probably ties in with Paul's emphasis on love as the fruit of the Spirit: It is the Spirit who writes the law of love in the believer's heart.

Then in 1 Thes 5:13 Paul says, "Be at peace among yourselves," which is verbally very similar to Mark 9:50, "Be at peace with one another."[114]

Also striking is Col 3:12-14,[115] where Paul says that his readers are to "forgive each other; just as the Lord has forgiven you, so you also must forgive," and then of love as "the bond of perfection."* Forgiving "just as the Lord has forgiven you" is reminiscent of the Johannine "love one another as I have loved you," but perhaps even more of the Matthean parable of the unforgiving servant (Matt 18:23-35).[116] The intriguing description of love as "the bond of perfection"* is conceptually not far removed from the idea of love as the greatest commandment, that which fulfills all the law.[117] It also has

---

113. E.g., in Isa 54:13; Jer 31:33, 34. See Marshall *1 and 2 Thessalonians,* 115. R. Brown, *John,* 614, explains the "newness" of the love command in John's Gospel as having to do with the new covenant of Jeremiah 31. If he is correct, this is a point of contact between the Johannine and Pauline traditions.

114. Allison, "Pauline Epistles," 14, 15, notes that this is one of several Pauline echoes of the material found in Mark 9:42-50. The theme of living "at peace" is important in the Jesus-tradition (see, for example, the beatitude in Matt 5:9 and the missionary commission in Luke 10:5), and it is important to Paul (see also Rom 12:18; 14:19; 1 Cor 7:15; 2 Cor 13:11). Tuckett, "Synoptic Tradition in 1 Thessalonians," 164, thinks that the call to "be at peace" in Mark and Paul may derive from a "common catechetical tradition" (see also Dodd, *More NT Studies,* 26, 27; Neirynck, "Paul and the Sayings," 283-84). He could be right, but it is on balance simpler to think of this Christian ethical tradition as originating with Jesus (as Mark suggests) than to think of it as arising from someone else or somewhere else and then achieving sufficient importance in the church to be read back onto the lips of Jesus by Mark, especially because other sayings in Mark 9:33-50 have a good claim to originate with Jesus.

115. See further on this passage in the additional note at the end of this chapter, "Further Possible Echoes of Matthew 5:38-48/Luke 6:27-36."

116. Compare also the Lord's prayer in Matt 5:12/Luke 11:4; cf. Eph 4:32. Kim, "Jesus, Sayings of," 478, notes Rom 13:8, "Owe no one anything, except to love one another," and suggests that the linking of the ideas of love and debt may be a reflection of Jesus' teaching. Kim notes parallel ideas in the Johannine and Pauline traditions.

117. The Greek terms for fulfillment and perfection (*plēro-* and *teleio-*) overlap semantically. The puzzling *syndesmos,* "bond," surely means something closely akin to what Paul expresses through the verbs *plēroō* and *anakephalaioumai* in Rom 13:9 (and perhaps *telos* in 10:4; see n. 30 above); love brings together all the commandments in perfection. (See O'Brien, *Colossians,* 203-4, though he does not exploit the parallel with Rom 13:9.) It could conceivably be that Paul uses the *teleio-* root in Col 3:14 under the

an interesting parallel in Matt 5:48, where the climactic command to "love your enemies" is followed by the call to "be perfect, therefore, as your heavenly Father is perfect."[118] Colossians continues only two verses later to urge the readers to "let the word of Christ dwell in you richly; teach and admonish one another in all wisdom" (3:16): The "word of Christ" here may simply be a general reference to the gospel of the crucified and risen Christ, but it may well be a broader reference to the Christian tradition of Jesus, including his teaching. This is no proof that the preceding verses are echoes of that tradition, but it is not an unlikely hypothesis.

Jesus emphasized love of the brothers, but also a wider love, including love for enemies. Paul similarly has this double perspective. Thus in 1 Thes 3:12 he prays, "may the Lord make you increase and abound in love for one another and for all." He uses the same phrase in 1 Thes 5:12, urging the Christians to "seek to do good to one another and to all," and in Gal 6:10 he urges his readers to "work for the good of all, and especially for those of the family of faith." The double focus of love is also present in Romans 12, where the instructions about nonretaliation, which we have already discussed, follow the call for "brotherly love toward one another"* (v. 10).[119] The Christian's peacemaking responsibility is similarly directed not just toward fellow Christians but also to those outside the church (Rom 12:18; 1 Cor 7:15).

Caring for the Weak

As well as urging Christians generally to love each other, Paul has much to say specifically about relationships with those who are "weak in faith," that is, with Christians, probably Jewish Christians, who have scruples about what they should or should not eat. In Romans he comes to this issue in chapters 14 and 15 after he has commented on the eschatological hour in 13:11-13, verses with distinct echoes of the Jesus-tradition, and after he has urged the Romans in 13:14 to "put on the Lord Jesus Christ" — reminding

---

influence of the tradition attested in Matt 5:48 (see the additional note at the end of this chapter on "Further Possible Echoes of Matthew 5:38-48/Luke 6:27-36"): His teaching in Col 3:12-14 is not a quotation from one part of the Jesus-tradition, but it may reflect the influence of different Jesus-traditions.

118. The Lukan parallel is, strikingly, "Be merciful, just as your Father is merciful" (6:36).

119. Kim, "Jesus, Sayings of," 481, compares Paul's call for love to be "unhypocritical" in Rom 12:9 with Jesus' sayings in the Gospels criticizing the "hypocrisy" of many of his religious contemporaries (e.g., Mark 7:6).

us of the christological focus of Pauline ethics. In 1 Corinthians he discusses the matter of the "weak" at length in chapters 8–10.

In his discussion of the subject in Romans 14 and 15 there are all sorts of possible echoes of Jesus' teaching. We have already examined Rom 14:14, where Paul expresses his confidence that "in the Lord Jesus nothing is unclean of itself." In addition we note the themes of "receiving," "judging," and "causing someone to stumble."[120]

Receiving, judging, and causing offense in Paul

Thus Paul begins and concludes his discussion in Romans 14 and 15 with an exhortation to "receive" or "welcome" others. In 14:1 he tells the Romans "to welcome those who are weak in faith," commenting on how God has "welcomed them" (v. 3). Then in 15:7 he says, summing up his discussion: "Welcome one another, therefore, just as Christ has welcomed you." This word, "receive" or "welcome," may then be said to sum up Paul's teaching in these chapters, and we notice how in 15:7 the thought is related to Christ as the model "receiver."

After opening his discussion in 14:1 by urging the Romans to receive the weak, Paul continues by focusing on the question of "judging." He introduces the theme in 14:3, where he says that "he that does not eat should not judge him who eats,"* and then he pursues this theme, speaking of the inappropriateness of judging others and of judging days, that is, discriminating between them. He sums up in 14:13: "Let us therefore no longer pass judgment on one another."

In the same verse Paul moves on from the theme of judging (though he will return to it briefly in vv. 22 and 23) and introduces the thought of not putting "a stumbling block or hindrance" in the way of a brother. In the verses that follow (14-21) he develops the thought of not "grieving" or "destroying" a Christian brother, arguing that it is better to forego one's freedom than to destroy the work of God or to cause a brother to stumble. The argument here is paralleled in Paul's discussion of food offered to idols in 1 Corinthians, where he again sides with the logic of the strong about Christian freedom and yet insists that "if food causes my brother to stumble, I will never eat meat, so that I may not cause my brother to stumble"* (8:13).[121]

---

120. The "stumbling" word, sometimes translated "cause of offense," is *skandalon/skandalizō;* cf. English "scandal."

121. See also 2 Cor 11:29 for the combination of the ideas of weakness and "stumbling."

"Receiving" in the synoptics[122]

The theme of "receiving" or "welcoming" is significant in the synoptic traditions of Jesus. Jesus himself is portrayed as one who "receives" others, including children and sinners. This may well be relevant to Rom 15:7, where Paul says: "Welcome one another, therefore, *just as Christ received you*" (e.g., Mark 9:36, 37/Luke 9:47, 48; Matt 19:13-15/Mark 10:13-16/Luke 18:15-17; Luke 15:2).[123] But Jesus also speaks in various contexts about "receiving" Christian disciples (thus in the mission discourse; see Matt 10:14, 40-42; Mark 6:11; Luke 9:5, 8-10; cf. John 13:20) and about receiving children and "little ones," notably in the saying in Matt 18:5/Mark 9:37/Luke 9:47.

This last saying (in Matthew's version: "Whoever welcomes one such child in my name welcomes me," 18:5) is of particular interest from the point of view of the Jesus-Paul question. A number of points are worth noting:

First, the saying occurs in a section of synoptic tradition describing relationships among disciples, where there are several other possible Pauline links (see above on "be at peace" and "forgive one another").

Second, the relationships between Matthew, Mark, and Luke in this section (Matt 18:1-9/Mark 9:33-50/Luke 9:46-50) are quite complex.[124] The very complexity may suggest that we are dealing with traditions of Jesus that were well known and widely used in the church, not with traditions that Matthew and Luke simply took from Mark. Paul, therefore, might well have known them.

Third, although the particular saying is about receiving a child, it is used, as we have said, in all the Gospels in the context of a broader discussion of attitudes to disciples, that is, "little ones" who believe (Matt

---

122. Paul uses the verb *proslambanomai* in Rom 14:1, 3; 15:7 whereas the synoptics use the synonymous *dechomai* in the verses we note. But for a parallel variation compare *lambanō* in John 13:20 with the equivalent synoptic saying in Matt 10:40.

123. See Stuhlmacher, "Jesustradition," 246.

124. E.g., Matt 18:3 is parallel to Mark 10:15/Luke 18:17; Mark 9:41 has a parallel in Matt 10:42; Matt 18:6 has a parallel in Mark 9:42 and Luke 17:2, but 18:7 has a parallel only in Luke 17:1. Various scholars speak of a pre-Markan collection of sayings used by Mark in 9:33-50 (e.g., Davies and Allison, *Matthew*, II, 760-61 on 9:42-47). It is quite likely that Matthew and Luke were familiar with the traditions independently of Mark; certainly there is "Q" material in Matt 18:7/Luke 17:1 and possibly a so-called Mark/"Q" overlap in Matt 18:6/Mark 9:43/Luke 17:2. See also my "A Note on Mark 9.33-42/Matt 18.1-6/Luke 9.46-50."

18:6/Mark 9:42; cf. Matt 10:40, 42). In all three Gospels it follows the disciples' discussion of who among them was the greatest;[125] in Mark and Luke it is followed by the story of the exorcist who was using Jesus' name but was not a disciple (Mark 9:38-41/Luke 9:49, 50). Whether or not the saying about the child was originally used in this context, the significant fact is that the synoptists attest the use of it in connection with "little" and perhaps controversial disciples, that is, in connection with people whom Paul might have called "weak in faith."

Fourth, the saying about "receiving" a child leads on in Matthew and Mark to a warning against causing "one of these little ones" to "stumble" and to other sayings about "stumbling" (Matt 18:6-9/Mark 9:42-47). The coming together of the two themes in the Gospels and in Romans 14 is striking.

We conclude on the basis of these observations that Paul may very well be dependent on the Jesus-tradition when he speaks of "receiving" the weak.

Stumbling in the synoptics

That case is strengthened by further observations about the "stumbling" motif. The reasons advanced for seeing an echo in Paul of Jesus' saying about "receiving" children in Matt 18:5/Mark 9:37/Luke 9:48 in Paul almost all apply equally to Jesus' saying about not "causing one of these little ones to stumble" in Matt 18:6/Mark 9:42/Luke 17:2. The wording of the saying in Matthew is: "Whoever causes one of these little ones who believe in me to stumble, it would be advantageous for him that a mill stone should be placed around his neck and he be drowned in the depths of the sea."*

But in addition to the arguments already discussed in connection with "receiving," three more things may be said about "stumbling": First, the idea of "stumbling" and "causing people to stumble" is well attested in the synoptics. The saying just quoted is followed in Matthew and Mark by the colorful sayings about the need to cut off one's hands, feet, and eyes if they "cause you to stumble" (Matt 18:8, 9/Mark 9:43-45).[126] There is a "Q" woe on anyone who causes another to stumble (Matt 18:7/Luke 17:1), and there is the mysterious story of the coin in the fish's mouth in Matt 17:24-27, where, as we have seen, Jesus speaks of the sons being "free" of the obliga-

125. Dunn, "Paul's Knowledge," 151, compares "the strong" of Paul with the "great ones" of Mark 10:42.

126. See further on these passages below.

tions of the temple, but of the desirability of not causing others to "stumble."[127] The sentiment is very much what we find in Paul's discussions of food offered to idols.

(2) The "stumbling-block, cause to stumble" terminology is rare in secular Greek, though present in the LXX, and the active form of the verb "cause to stumble," which we find in the synoptics and Paul, is especially rare.[128]

(3) In the Jesus-tradition "stumbling" is a very serious matter indeed (see Matt 18:8, 9/Mark 9:43-47 on the fires of Gehenna); causing one's fellow disciple to stumble is therefore to be avoided at all costs (Matt 18:6/Mark 9:42/Luke 17:2). Similarly for Paul it is essential to do nothing that amounts to destroying the brother "for whom Christ died" (1 Cor 8:11; Rom 14:15).[129]

These additional arguments relating to "stumbling" strengthen considerably the case for believing that Paul has been influenced by Jesus-tradition where he urges his readers to "receive" or "welcome" one another and not to cause others to "stumble."

"Judging" in the synoptics

There is a noteworthy parallel in the sermon on the mount to Paul's instructions in Romans 14 about not "judging":[130]

---

127. On the background and history of the Matthean story see Bauckham, "Coin in the Fish's Mouth." See also Bauckham's comment (230) on the possible connection of the story with Paul's collection for the saints in Jerusalem.

128. So Thompson, *Clothed with Christ*, 179, finding only one other example of the active use. For full discussion of the evidence relating to *skandal-* words see Thompson, 174-84.

One small indication that Paul is picking up Jesus-tradition may be the appearance of "or stumbling block" (*ē skandalon*) at the end of the sentence in Rom 14:13 as an alternative to "hindrance" (*proskomma*). *Proskomma* is not as unusual as *skandalon*, and it returns in vv. 20, 21. But in v. 13 Paul adds *ē skandalon*, perhaps because it is an important and familiar word in the Christian tradition. (But note that the two words are also found together in Isa 8:14 as quoted in Rom 9:33 and in 1 Pet 2:8. Cf. also 2 Cor. 11:29.) Paul, of course, uses the *skandal-* root also in 1 Cor 1:23 of the gospel of Christ; this has a possible background in Jesus' "Q" saying to John the Baptist about not being offended about him (Matt 11:6/Luke 7:23); so Thompson, *Clothed with Christ*, 178.

129. Compare the "brother" terminology in Matt 18:15, 21, 35.

130. See also 1 Cor 6:1-8 for Pauline objections to "judging" (especially v. 7).

Rom 14:3:   "Let him not judge"*
Rom 14:13:   "Let us no longer pass judgment on one another"
Matt 7:1:   "Do not judge, so that you may not be judged"
Luke 6:37:   "Do not judge, and you will not be judged."[131]

We notice that the Pauline verses and the synoptic saying (which would normally be seen as "Q" material) have the same verb in the same present tense and imperative mood, governed by the same negative (*mē*, the normal negative with an imperative).

Furthermore, in both contexts the "judging" is criticism of another, specifically a "brother," that is, a fellow Christian (cf. Rom 14:10; Matt 7:3; Luke 6:41). Paul does not have "so that you may not be judged" in so many words,[132] but he does make the point that judging has to do with each person's "Lord" and that we all will stand at the judgment seat of God, each to give his or her own account (Rom 14:10, 12).[133]

The way that Paul circles around the theme, introducing the synoptic-type saying in 14:3, playing with different senses of the word "judge" in vv. 5 and 13, and summing up with a synoptic-type summary in v. 13, may confirm that he is working with a well-known tradition here.[134] It is not possible to prove (here or with the "receiving" and "stumbling" just considered) that he is using Jesus-tradition directly rather than a church catechetical tradition based on the Jesus-tradition. But that he was influenced directly or indirectly by the Jesus-traditions in question seems likely.

Humble Serving

One of the most important themes in the NT is that of service. There is, on the one hand, the thought of Christians as servants or slaves of Christ (or of God). This theme comes out, for example, in Rom 14:4-12, where

131. Rom 14:3 *mē krinetō*
    Rom 14:13 *mēketi oun allēlous krinōmen*
    Matt 7:1 *mē krinete hina mē krithēte*
    Luke 6:37 *mē krinete kai ou mē krithēte*

132. But see Rom 2:1: "When you judge the other . . . you condemn yourself"*; so Resch, *Paulinismus*, 76.

133. See Thompson, *Clothed with Christ*, 161-73, for a fuller discussion of the sayings. Thompson (163) limits his "synoptic" comparison to Rom 14:13; adding 14:3 might have enhanced his argument at that point.

134. Jas 4:11, 12 probably attests the same tradition.

Paul says that it is wrong to judge the "servants of another" and that each must give account to his or her master. The idea is reminiscent of Jesus' parables about masters and servants, to which we will return in the next chapter. But there is also, on the other hand, the thought of Christians being called to serve other people in humility. This idea is at least hinted at in Romans 14 and 15, since in 15:7 Paul grounds his call to "welcome one another" with the comment "just as Christ welcomed you. . . . For I tell you that Christ has become a *servant* of the circumcised. . . ."

The importance of humbly serving others comes out clearly both in the Jesus-tradition and in Paul's writings. In the Gospels there are a number of passages where greatness among the disciples is defined in terms of service. Most notable is Matt 20:20-28/Mark 10:35-45, where James and John's request for the first seats in the kingdom leads Jesus to contrast the style of worldly leadership with servant leadership, and then to his climactic saying: "The Son of Man came not to be served but to serve, and to give his life a ransom for many." This passage has a possibly independent parallel in the Lukan last supper narrative (22:24-27). The story in John 13 of Jesus washing the disciples' feet is thematically very similar, with Jesus' humble action expressing servanthood and anticipating his coming death.

The theme of humility and service is also found in Matt 23:12, "Whoever will exalt himself will be humbled, and whoever humbles himself will be exalted,"* a saying found also in Luke 14:11 and 18:14 and partially in Matt 18:14 (in the context of Jesus' remarks about children). And it is found in Mark 9:35 (again in the context of Jesus' remarks about children; cf. Luke 9:48). It is not necessary to try to unravel the relationships of these different synoptic passages; but the importance of the theme is clear enough.

In the Pauline letters similar themes are to be found. It will be helpful to compare a number of passages:

> Being kind in brotherly love toward one another, preferring one another in honor . . . having the same mind toward one another, not thinking high (exalted) things but mixing with the humble.* (Rom 12:10, 16)

> We ought . . . not to please ourselves. Let each of us please his neighbor for the neighbor's good and to build up the neighbor. For Christ did not please himself. . . . May God . . . grant you to have the same mind among yourselves according to Christ Jesus.* (Rom 15:1-4)[135]

---

135. Note also 15:8 on Christ becoming "servant" of the circumcision.

I have made myself a slave to all, so that I might win more of them. . . . I have become all things to all people, that I might by all means save some. (1 Cor 9:19, 22)

I try to please everyone in everything I do, not seeking my own advantage, but that of *many,* so that they may be saved. Be imitators of me, as I am also of Christ. (1 Cor 10:33–11:1)

We do not proclaim ourselves; we proclaim Jesus Christ as Lord and ourselves as your slaves for Jesus' sake. (2 Cor 4:5)

Did I commit a sin by humbling myself so that you might be exalted . . . ?* (2 Cor 11:7)

Do not use your freedom as an opportunity for the flesh, but through love be slaves to one another.* (Gal 5:13c)

. . . having the one mind, doing nothing from selfish ambition or empty glorying, but in humility counting one another better than yourselves, each not looking to his own interests but to the interests of others. Have this mind in you which is/was also in Christ Jesus. . . . He emptied himself, taking the form of a slave. . . . He humbled himself. . . . Therefore God has highly exalted him. . . .* (Phil 2:2-9)

The recurrence of similar ideas and language is notable, and the similarity of the Pauline teaching to the Jesus-traditions is unmistakable.

Specifically, first, in some of these passages Paul speaks negatively of people pleasing themselves, acting from selfish ambition and empty glorying (so Rom 15:1; 1 Cor 10:33; Phil 2:3, 4; also 1 Cor 10:24; 13:5; Phil 2:21). This may be compared with the synoptic portrayal of the disciples wanting to be the greatest and to Jesus' negative comments on worldly patterns of leadership, though the similarity is hardly distinctive enough to prove anything on its own.

Second, self-glorification is contrasted with an attitude of humble servanthood or slavery. The humiliation versus exaltation theme (present in the Jesus-tradition in Matt 23:12, etc.) is found in differing forms in Phil 2:8, 9 and 2 Cor 11:7 (cf. Rom 12:16).[136] The servant/slave theme (found in the Jesus-tradition in Matt 20:26-28/Mark 10:43-45, etc.) is in Rom 15:8; 1 Cor 9:19; and Phil 2:7.

---

136. The same Greek verbs, *tapeinoō* and *hypsoō* (or derivatives) are used in the synoptic and Pauline texts.

Most interesting as a point of comparison between the Jesus-tradition and Paul is 1 Cor 9:19: "I have made myself a slave to all so that I might win the more."* Here there is an obvious parallel to Jesus' words in Mark 10:44: "Whoever wishes to be first among you must be *slave of all*."[137] But there may be a further less obvious parallel as well in Paul's phrase "that I might win *the more*."* It is not altogether clear why he speaks of "the more," but there is an interestingly similar expression in 1 Cor 10:33, where Paul writes, "I please all people in all things, not seeking my own advantage, but that of *the many*."* The two Pauline verses are thematically very similar:[138] One speaks of ministering to "the more," the other of ministering to "the many." This is probably no accident, and it is arguable that both texts are related to Mark 10:44, 45, since, after speaking of being "a slave to all," Jesus goes on to speak of his ministry as that of the servant who gives his life as "a ransom *for many*." The ministry in both of the Pauline texts and in the saying of Jesus is one of bringing people to salvation. It may clarify the point to put the texts in parallel:

Whoever wishes to be first among you must be *slave of all*. For the Son of Man came not to be served but to serve, and to give his life a ransom *for many*. (Mark 10:44, 45)

I have made myself *a slave to all*, so that I might win *more* of them. . . . I have become all things to all people, that I might by all means save some. (1 Cor 9:19, 22)

I try to please everyone in everything I do, not seeking my own advantage, but that of *many*, so that they may be saved. (1 Cor 10:33)

What seems possible, and even probable, in the light of this comparison is that Paul in 1 Corinthians is deliberately speaking of his ministry in terms of the Jesus-tradition of Mark 10:44, 45.[139]

137. Matt 20:27 has "your slave," not "slave of all," bringing the saying into line with the one in 20:26. Schweizer, *Matthew*, 398, sees Matthew's interest in the community reflected here.

138. Note "all things, all people" and the verb "save" in 1 Cor 9:22 and 10:33.

139. Paul goes on in 1 Cor 9:23 to speak of preaching the gospel to others "so that I may share in its blessings." This may possibly be related to the synoptic suggestion that servanthood is the way to greatness in the kingdom (Matt 20:26/Mark 10:43); see Wolff, "Humility and Self-Denial," 154-56, on the similar eschatological motivation. The reference to "winning" or "gaining" *(kerdainō)* the more in 1 Cor 9:23 is not obviously related to the saying in Matt 20:28/Mark 10:45, unless the financial connotations of

The third thing we notice about the Pauline texts we have cited is the way Paul explicitly relates Christian servanthood and his own servant ministry to Jesus' own servanthood. Thus in 1 Cor 10:33 after speaking of seeking the advantage of "many," he goes on specifically to say "Be imitators of me, as I am also of Christ." The same sort of appeal to Jesus' example is found in Rom 15:1-8 and especially in Phil 2:1-11.

This appeal to Jesus' example would not necessarily indicate anything about Paul's familiarity with particular traditions about Jesus. He could simply be reflecting on the incarnation and death of the Lord, not on particular details of Jesus' life, let alone on any sayings of Jesus. But there is evidence to suggest that he was familiar with traditions of Jesus' life and death (see chapter 8 below). And there is, as we have seen, evidence to suggest that he was familiar with the sayings in Matt 20:27, 28; Mark 10:44, 45; Luke 22:27, where the call to Christian service is specifically connected to the service of Jesus, the Son of man. We have already detected a possible or probable echo of that tradition in 1 Cor 10:33; the fact that Paul follows that verse with a reference to Jesus' example makes it all the more likely that there is an echo. As for Phil 2:1-11, there, too, the exhortation to Christian humility is linked to a description of Jesus becoming a slave and obeying as far as death, which is strongly evocative of Matt 20:27, 28/Mark 10:44, 45.[140] In Philippians 2 Paul does not speak of Jesus' death as being "for many," but he does use precisely that terminology in Rom 5:15, 19, where he speaks of "the many" being justified through Christ, and it is

---

"gain" may be related to the idea of paying a ransom to release people. The verb may come from Jewish missionary vocabulary (see Daube, NT and Rabbinic Judaism, 348-61) or possibly from other parts of the Jesus-tradition, such as Matt 18:15 (Goulder, Midrash, 163, connects these texts and also includes 1 Pet 3:1). The suggestion of Fjärstedt, "Synoptic Traditions in 1 Corinthians," 89, that it comes from the parable of the talents, where the faithful servants "gain" and are given authority over "many," is interesting, but not entirely persuasive.

140. In Phil 2:1-11 we have both "servant" language and the humiliation/exaltation theme; see the combination of ideas in Matt 23:11, 12. On the Philippians passage as appealing to the example of Jesus see especially Hurtado, "Jesus as Lordly Example"; Thompson, Clothed with Christ, 217-22. Hurtado notes the rather similar Johannine story of the footwashing. There is clearly a thematic parallel between that parabolic action of Jesus and Philippians 2 (and both are similar to Matt 20:28/Mark 10:45): In John 13 Jesus, the Lord and Master, portrays his coming death on the cross as humble service by washing the feet of his disciples; Phil 2:5-11 describes the one who was in the form of God taking the form of a servant and going to the cross. Thomas, Footwashing in John 13, 148, suggests that the footwashing story is a relatively primitive Johannine tradition.

arguable that his understanding of the atonement at such points has been influenced by Jesus' teaching.[141]

We conclude that there is substantial evidence suggesting that Paul was influenced by Jesus' teaching on the disciple's vocation to humility and servanthood and in particular by the passage describing James and John's request for prominence in the kingdom, including the saying in Matt 20:28/Mark 10:45.[142]

OATHS

Jesus' statements about retaliation and love of enemies, which we discussed above, come in the so-called antitheses of the Matthean version of the sermon on the mount, in which OT and Jewish tradition is contrasted with Jesus' "But I say to you."[143] The immediately preceding antithesis (Matt 5:33-37) deals with oaths:

> Again, you have heard that it was said to those of ancient times, "You shall not swear falsely, but carry out the vows you have made to the Lord."

141. See, e.g., Stuhlmacher, "Jesustradition," 250. Paul twice speaks of Christians as having been "bought with a price" (1 Cor 6:20; 7:23), the price evidently being the death of Christ. The thought is similar to that in Matt 20:28/Mark 10:45, where Jesus speaks of his death as a "ransom" (or "ransom-price"). Stuhlmacher, Reconciliation, 18, notes 1 Tim 2:5-6 ("the man Christ Jesus, who gave himself as a ransom on behalf of all") as a Hellenized version of the dominical saying, with "the man" substituted for "the Son of man" and "on behalf of all" substituted for "instead of many." Mark parallels "all" in 10:44 and "many" in 10:45.

It is, of course, possible to argue the other way around and, for example, to see Mark 10:45 as influenced by Paul's teaching about servanthood and the atonement. However, this is certainly the more complicated option, not least because of the strong evidence for themes such as that of humble servanthood having a basis in Jesus' ministry and because of Paul's explicit appeals back to Jesus' example.

142. 1 Cor 4:9, where Paul speaks of God exhibiting "us apostles" as "last of all" and "sentenced to death," has been compared to the synoptic servant texts (e.g., Mark 9:35; cf. Matt 19:30; 20:16; Mark 10:31; Luke 13:30, and Feine, Jesus Christus, 292). We have also considered that Paul might have been influenced by Jesus' saying to James and John about sharing his baptism (Mark 10:38); see above in chapter 4. Also see chapter 8 below on hoi dokountes in Mark 10:42.

143. Whether the antitheses are Matthean or pre-Matthean is debated, but there is a good case for suspecting that they were known to Luke (see, e.g., his "But I say to you that listen" in 6:27) and that he has eliminated the polemical form, preferring to concentrate on Jesus' teaching, not on the Jewish teaching with which it was contrasted.

But I say to you, Do not swear at all, either by heaven . . . or by the earth. . . . Let your word be "Yes, Yes" or "No, No"; anything more than this comes from the evil one.

The saying has a parallel in Jas 5:12: "Above all, my beloved, do not swear, either by heaven or by earth or by any other oath, but let your 'Yes' be yes and your 'No' be no, so that you may not fall under condemnation." There is clearly a relationship between this and the saying in Matthew 5, and it has widely (though not universally) been assumed that James is dependent here on the Jesus-tradition.[144]

The evidence for Paul being familiar with the same tradition is in 2 Cor 1:17, 18, where he is commenting on the change in his travel plans and defending himself against the charge of being fickle: "Do I make my plans according to ordinary human standards, ready to say 'Yes, yes' and 'No, no' at the same time? As surely as God is faithful, our word to you has not been 'Yes and No.'" The unusual phraseology used both there and in Matt 5:37 is the strongest argument for some connection between the texts: Not only is there the "yes, yes . . . no, no" in both texts,[145] but there is also the reference in 2 Cor 1:18 to "our/your word being . . . ," which is reminiscent of Jesus' "Let your word be. . . ."

That Paul is quoting here is also suggested by his use of the definite article in 1:17: "*the* yes, yes and *the* no, no." The article probably functions as quotation marks; Paul is referring back to a phrase that is known to his readers.

The formidable difficulty, however, with the view that we have an echo of Jesus-tradition here is that Jesus, according to Matthew, was telling people that they should be "yes, yes, no, no" people (in the context of a discussion of swearing), whereas Paul is saying emphatically that he is not a "yes, yes, no, no" person (in the context of a discussion of his changed plans). Paul's meaning seems to be quite different, even contrary to Jesus' meaning.

Must we then abandon the idea of a connection, despite the striking verbal similarity? It does seem unlikely that Paul would deliberately proclaim his opposition to the tradition of Jesus in question.

But what Paul is opposing is the accusation made against him by some in Corinth that he is a "yes, yes, no, no" person. Paul is not quoting (not directly at least) the saying of Jesus. He is quoting, rather, what was being

144. On the traditions see A. Ito, "Question of Authenticity."
145. The Greek is *(to) nai nai (kai to) ou ou.*

said by his own opponents. This does not necessarily mean the abandonment of the thesis of a connection with the Jesus-tradition. What seems quite plausible is that Paul's opponents had taken the saying of Jesus out of context and used it ironically to accuse Paul of inconsistency: Paul, they observed with sarcasm, certainly takes Jesus' instruction seriously; his word really is yes, yes *and* no, no!

If this is approximately what lies behind 2 Cor 1:17, 18, then we do not have evidence of Paul himself using Jesus-tradition here (directly at least). We have evidence, rather, that this Jesus-tradition from the sermon on the mount was familiar in the Corinthian church, so much so that it could be taken out of context and used against Paul. It might be that Paul himself did not know the saying or did not recognize its origin from Jesus — hence his lack of compunction about appearing to set himself against the teaching of the Lord. However, it is unlikely that he was ignorant of the source of the Corinthian jibe, and his denial that he is a "yes, yes, no, no" person is purely in response to the Corinthians' misuse of the saying and does not suggest that Paul would have questioned the authority of Jesus' word on swearing.[146]

In denying that he himself is a "yes, yes, no, no" person, Paul goes on to affirm that "The Son of God, Jesus Christ, whom we proclaimed among you, . . . was not 'Yes and No'; but in him it is always 'Yes.' For in him every one of God's promises is a 'Yes.' For this reason it is through him that we say the 'Amen,' to the glory of God" (1:19-21). Paul's general point here is clear enough: He is explaining that Jesus was not a yes/no promise-maker and breaker; Jesus was God's utterly positive word to the world. But the way Paul makes the point is striking and unusual.

This is explicable, in part at least, because of the context: Paul is responding to an accusation made against him. But there is almost certainly more to it than that: Paul alludes, for example, to the church's liturgical practice of saying "through Jesus, Amen" (v. 20). "Amen" is the Hebrew equivalent of "yes," as Paul's argument implies. But his reference to "Amen" also brings to mind Jesus' characteristic introduction of solemn sayings with "Amen, I say to you." And it may very well be this that lies behind Paul's comment about Jesus being God's "yes," or, as we might say, God's

---

146. It is doubtful that Paul would have regarded the oath-like formulas that he uses in his letters (calling God as his witness, e.g., 1 Thes 2:5) as contravening Jesus' words against oaths. But it is just possible that his opponents might have accused Paul of ignoring Jesus' prohibition on the one hand and of taking Jesus' injunction to be a "yes, yes, no, no" person too seriously and in the wrong way.

"Amen": Jesus was indisputedly God's yes, because of his affirmative role in God's purposes, as exemplified in his "Amen" sayings. If this is Paul's logic, then he is responding to the Corinthian use of a Jesus-tradition against him with a Jesus-tradition of his own — and a very important and influential one at that.

FLESH AND SPIRIT

Putting to Death the Deeds of the Body

One of the most distinctive things about Paul's ethical teaching, as we have seen, is his use of the flesh-spirit contrast. At first sight it might be thought that this — and especially Paul's usually negative view of "the flesh" — is something that sets Paul apart from Jesus; Paul, it might be supposed, has been influenced by the negative Greek view of the body. Against this last supposition, however, is the strong evidence for Paul's positive and thoroughly Jewish view of the body, for example, in 1 Corinthians 15. It may, in fact, be that Paul's flesh-spirit ideas reflect Jesus' influence as much as Greek influence.

In the first place, there are the sayings in the Gospels in which Jesus advises cutting off the hand, foot, or eye that causes spiritual stumbling (we note this word "stumbling" again). For example, in the sermon on the mount, immediately before the prohibition of oaths, which we have just discussed, Jesus speaks of adultery and divorce and warns against looking at a woman with lust. Then he continues: "If your right eye causes you to sin, tear it out and throw it away; it is better for you to lose one of your limbs than for your whole body to be thrown into hell."* He goes on to speak in the same terms about "your right hand" (Matt 5:29-30). The same sort of warnings are found in Matt 18:8-9/Mark 9:43-47 following the sayings about receiving and not offending little ones (which, we have suggested, were familiar to Paul).[147]

The possible Pauline parallels to these sayings are Gal 5:24, where Paul speaks of those who belong to Christ having "crucified the flesh with

---

147. The relationship of Matt 5:29, 30 to Matt 18:8, 9/Mark 9:43-47 is differently assessed. Davies and Allison, *Matthew*, I, 523, think Matthew is dependent on Mark in both cases, but Luz, *Matthew*, 291-92, sees Matt 5:29, 30 as Q material (with a good claim to authenticity). The differences between the carefully structured 5:29, 30 and the Markan verse would seem to suggest that Matthew has a different source.

its passions and desires,"[148] Rom 8:13, where he speaks of "put[ting] to death the deeds of the body" "by the Spirit," and especially Col 3:5, where he urges his readers to "kill the limbs that are on the earth, immorality, uncleanness, passion, lust (desire) . . . because of which the wrath of God is coming."*

The similarities between this last saying and especially the saying in Matt 5:29, 30 (with its reference to "limbs" in the context of a discussion of immorality and "desire") are striking.[149] It is at least a good possibility that there is a connection[150] and that Paul's striking phraseology here (and in Gal 5:24 and Rom 8:13) has its roots in the vivid parabolic sayings of Jesus. If so, we have an interesting connection between Paul's language about "the flesh" and the Jesus-tradition, though Paul has developed what were characteristically stark parabolic sayings into his characteristically theological way of thinking and writing.

Flesh and Spirit

But the Pauline flesh-spirit antithesis has an even closer parallel in the story of Jesus' agony in Gethsemane as recorded in Matthew and Mark (though not Luke). Jesus urges the disciples to stay awake in prayer "that you may not come into the time of trial; the spirit indeed is willing, but the flesh is weak" (Matt 26:41/Mark 14:38).

There need be no connection between this verse and the Pauline usage: The flesh-spirit contrast is familiar in the OT (e.g., Isa 31:3), and the synoptic usage should probably not be understood in a strictly Pauline

148. Gal 4:15, where Paul speaks of the Galatians' willingness to tear their eyes out on his behalf, is almost certainly irrelevant.

149. O'Brien, *Colossians*, 177, notes the unusual phraseology at this point in Colossians, but finds a difference in meaning between the Colossians verse and the synoptic saying: "Here the practices and attitudes to which the readers' bodily activity and strength have been devoted in the old life is in view." It is not obvious that this is very different from the synoptic meaning. O'Brien fails to notice how close the parallel is, particularly, to Matt 5:29, 30. So does Neirynck, "Paul and the Sayings," 282, who links Col 3:5 to Rom 6:13, 19 rather than to the Gospels. It is possible that there is such a link, but also a link back to the Jesus-tradition.

150. If Matt 5:29, 30 is dependent on and secondary to Mark 9:43-48 (which is not at all certain), the agreements between Matt 5:29, 30 and Col 3:5 may still point to a common interpretative tradition based on the Markan form of the saying (compare Davies and Allison, *Matthew*, I, 523).

151. Taylor, *Mark*, 555.

sense (the Holy Spirit versus the old nature).[151] However, there are some interesting points of contact between the Gethsemane story (including the flesh-spirit phrase) and Paul's teaching about spirit and flesh in Galatians and Romans.

The Gethsemane narrative

Some preliminary observations concerning the Gethsemane story will be helpful:

- The story is attested in all three synoptic Gospels, and also arguably in other parts of the NT (e.g., John 12:27; 18:11; Heb 5:7, 8).[152]
- The portrayal of Jesus' weakness and his desire to be delivered from death and (much more so) of the weakness of three leading apostles points towards the authenticity of the narrative.
- It is in this passage that Mark specifically refers to Jesus saying "Abba" (14:36). The use of "Abba" as a way of addressing God was probably distinctive and characteristic of Jesus (as we have seen in chapter 3), and it may be purely accidental that the only occasion when the Aramaic word itself is reproduced in the Gospels is here. On the other hand, it may well be that this particular prayer in this story was especially important in the memory of the church.
- Matthew and Mark associate this story with Peter, James, and John, the inner circle of three among the apostles (and perhaps "the pillars"; see chapters 5 and 8). This suggests that, rather like the transfiguration, it was seen as a particularly intimate and important revelation of Jesus.
- The story was probably important, not just as a revealing (and perhaps perplexing) revelation of Jesus, but also because of its obvious relevance to the Christian life — with Jesus inviting his disciples to share in his wakefulness and prayer in face of temptation and suffering.[153]

---

152. Schweizer, *Mark*, 310, comments:

There is no reason to question the historicity of Jesus' struggle in prayer in Gethesemane. The essence of it has been handed down also in John 12:27 (cf. 18:11b) and Heb 4:15, 5:7f. Moreover, it does not fit the picture of the Servant of God and is even less appropriate for the glorious miracle-worker and divine Lord.

153. The links between the eschatological discourse and the Gethsemane story have often been noted (e.g., the calls to "keep awake" in Mark 13:37 and 14:34). Jesus'

We conclude from these points that the Gethsemane story was probably early and important tradition in the early church.

Abba in Paul and Gethsemane

What is the evidence that Paul reflected on the Gethsemane story? We know that Paul was aware of a tradition about Jesus being "betrayed" on the night following the last supper (1 Cor 11:23). We do not know what that tradition comprised, but, since his last supper narrative has much in common with the synoptic narratives and since all three synoptic narratives have Jesus betrayed and arrested in Gethesemane, it is a reasonable inference that Paul knew the Gethsemane story. But is there any evidence that he did? Paul's use of "Abba" in Galatians and Romans may be such evidence:

> "When the fullness of time had come, God sent out his Son, born of woman . . . so that we might receive adoption [= sonship]. And because you are children [= sons], God has sent the Spirit of his Son into our hearts, crying, "Abba! Father!" (Gal 4:4-6)

> You did not receive a spirit of slavery to fall back into fear, but you have received a spirit of adoption [= sonship], whereby we cry, "Abba, Father."* (Rom 8:15)

One of the intriguing agreements between these two texts is the use of the verb "cry" in connection with the "Abba" address for God. Paul's use of this verb *(krazō)* has usually been explained as a reflection of the intensity of the Christian's spiritual experience.[154] But it is notable, first, that Paul uses it on both occasions when he refers to "Abba" and nowhere else of Christians praying;[155] this may suggest a traditional link of the verb with use of "Abba." Second, as we have seen, the only occasion where an Evangelist retains the Aramaic "Abba" is in the Gethsemane story (in Mark), and this may be because "Abba" was especially associated with Gethsemane and

---

passion, including his wakeful prayer in Gethsemane, was quite probably seen as the model of Christian suffering in trial; cf. Geddert, *Watchwords,* 89-111. Myers, *Binding the Strong Man,* e.g., 389-92, interestingly but rather improbably identifies Jesus' death with the promised coming of the Son of man of Mark 13:27, but it is just conceivable that Mark saw Jesus' death and resurrection as eschatological events anticipating the destruction of the temple and the glorious return of the Son of man.

154. See Dunn, *Romans,* 453.
155. He uses the verb elsewhere only in Rom 9:27.

because that occasion was especially important in the memory of the church. Third, the Gospels make it clear that Jesus' praying in Gethsemane was extraordinarily intense. And fourth, although the Gospels do not use "cry" of Jesus' prayer, Heb 5:7 does use the word (in its noun form) quite probably with Gethsemane in mind: "Jesus offered up prayers and supplications with loud cries and tears."[156]

It seems possible in view of this that the Gethsemane prayer may somehow be in the background when Paul speaks in Gal 4:6 and Rom 8:15 of the Christian "crying 'Abba.' "[157]

Other evidence of Gethsemane in Romans 8

This has added plausibility in Romans 8, since the reference to the Christian crying "Abba" comes in a passage that speaks of the Christian sharing in the death, sufferings, and resurrection of Christ. Paul has spoken just beforehand of the Christian "put[ting] to death" the deeds of the body and so "living" (v. 13). Then after the "Abba" statement he continues: "The Spirit himself bears witness with our spirit that we are children of God, and if children, then heirs, heirs of God, and fellow heirs with Christ, provided we suffer with him in order that we may also be glorified with him" (vv. 16, 17, RSV).

Not only does the Romans 8 context of the "Abba" cry emphasize the cross and the Christian as sharing in the sufferings of Christ (being reminiscent of Gethsemane in that way); it is also very much taken up with the question of the conflict between the Spirit and the flesh. In the immediate context of the "Abba" statement, as we have seen, Paul speaks of "the deeds of the body" and of the "Spirit" (v. 13), and earlier in the chapter he has

---

156. Hebrews does not say what he cried; it does go on to say that "although he was a Son, he learned obedience through what he suffered," conceivably an indirect allusion to his cry of "Abba."

157. The influence of the "Abba" prayer of Gethsemane in the early church might be confirmed if Riesner, Jesus als Lehrer, 446, is right in suggesting that the clause that occurs in the Matthean Lord's prayer (but not in Luke's), "your will be done" (Matt 6:10), had its origin in the Gethsemane prayer (Matt 26:39/Mark 14:36/Luke 22:42). It is not difficult to see how the Lord's prayer (addressed to the "Father") might have been expanded and explained with clauses from other prayers of Jesus and especially from as significant and sacred a prayer as the one addressed to "Abba" in Gethsemane. (Riesner notes that the other clause found in Matthew but not Luke, "but deliver us from evil," has a parallel in John 17:15, another prayer from the context of the passion, which has indeed been linked to the Gethsemane prayer by some scholars.)

spoken of the conflict of "flesh" and "Spirit" and of the "weakness of the flesh" (vv. 3, 5-9).[158] In the previous chapter, especially in 7:14-25, Paul described graphically the weakness of the flesh in a situation of spiritual conflict: "I can will what is right, but I cannot do it" (v. 18).[159]

So in Romans 7 and 8 these all come together:

- the Abba "cry,"
- an emphasis on Jesus' death and resurrection,
- the thought of the Christian sharing that experience of Jesus,
- the "spirit"/"flesh" terminology, and
- use of that terminology to describe spiritual conflict and weakness.

This all makes for a striking comparison with the Gethsemane story. And we might add:

- an emphasis in both traditions on praying in situations of weakness (Mark 14:38; Rom 8:26).[160]

It seems quite possible, in the light of the evidence, to think that Paul's reflections in Romans 7 and 8 on the Christian's spiritual struggles in the time of suffering before the end have, at the very least, been influenced by the Gethsemane story. It is possible that he sees Jesus' experiences as a pattern for the Christian life: The Christian is called to face suffering and physical death with Jesus; the present is a time of temptation and of conflict between flesh and spirit; the way to face it is, as Jesus did, by prayer through the Spirit to the Abba, Father; the present longing, but also confident expectation, is to share in Jesus' resurrection and the redemption of the body.

---

158. I am grateful to Idicheria Ninan for suggestions at this point. See his *Jesus as the Son of God*, 328-32.

159. In Rom 7:14-25 the terminology is not "flesh" and "spirit" but "flesh" and "mind," thus the conclusion "So then, with my mind I am a slave to the law of God, but with my flesh I am a slave to the law of sin" (v. 25). However, in the very similar Gal 5:16, 17 the terminology is "flesh"-"spirit" and in Romans 8 Paul uses "mind" and "spirit" together. He no doubt deliberately keeps the Spirit until Romans 8, but he could have the Gethsemane contrast between the weak flesh and the willing spirit in mind in chapter 7.

160. Cf. Rom 8:26 ("Likewise the Spirit helps us in our weakness; for we do not know how to pray as we ought, but that very Spirit intercedes with sighs too deep for words") with the Gethsemane story, where Jesus prays intensely to his "Abba" (by the Spirit, as Paul might well say) and calls on his disciples to "keep awake and pray. . . . the spirit indeed is willing, but the flesh is weak. . . ." Cf. Thompson, *Clothed with Christ*, 94. See also 2 Cor 12:7-10 for Paul praying "three times" in "weakness."

The case for this proposal is, however, not certain. In Gal 4:6 the reference to the Christian crying "Abba" does not come in a context of discussion of Christian suffering or spiritual conflict. It does follow a reference to the historical Jesus ("God sent out his Son, born of a woman ...," 4:4), and we do find the idea of the "spirit"-"flesh" conflict later in Galatians (5:16, 17;[161] note also "weakness," "flesh," and "temptation" in 4:13, 14). But the connections are not as neat as in Romans 7 and 8. Furthermore, the absence of the saying "The spirit is willing, but the flesh is weak" in Luke's version of the Gethsemane story could lend support to the views of those who see it as a saying not originally integral to the story.[162] But, even if that quite uncertain view were correct, it would still be possible that Paul knew the Gethsemane story with the saying included.[163]

Conclusion

There is a tiny amount of other evidence that could reflect Pauline familiarity with the Gethsemane narrative. The phrase in Phil 2:8 about Jesus being "obedient up to the point of death"* is reminiscent of the Gethsemane story both conceptually — the idea of obedience — and verbally, since in Matt 26:38/Mark 14:34 Jesus is said to be grieved "to death."[164] Another possible echo of Gethesemane is in Col. 4:2, where Paul urges: "Persevere in prayer, staying awake"*; compare Matt 26:41/Mark 14:38: "Stay awake and pray."[165] This evidence does not add much to the argument. But we can conclude that the case for Paul being influenced by what was probably a well-known (and very striking) story of the Lord is at least a reasonable possibility.

161. There are a number of verbal similarities between Gal 5:16, 17 and the Gethsemane story: As well as "flesh" and "spirit," note "desire" (*epithymeō* in Gal 5:17; *prothymos* in Matt 26:41/Mark 14:38) and "willing" (*thelō* in Gal 5:17 and in Matt 26:39/Mark 14:36).

162. So Schweizer, *Mark,* 310. It could even be that this is a case of a Pauline phrase added to the original story. This, however, is unlikely, as it is not the characteristic Pauline "flesh versus Holy Spirit" contrast that we have in the synoptic narrative.

163. If the saying was not originally in the Gethsemane context, it could still have been a saying of Jesus and one that influenced Paul. In that case Paul and Matthew/Mark may be said to interpret the saying in somewhat similar ways.

164. See Resch, *Paulinismus,* 111. Different prepositions are used, *mechri* in Phil 2:8 and *heōs* in Matt 26:38/Mark 14:34, On the theme of obedience in the context of Gethsemane cf. Heb 5:8, 9.

165. See chapter 7 for further discussion of "keeping awake" in Paul.

CONCLUSIONS ON THE CONNECTIONS

This chapter has been highly productive in showing possible and probable connections between Jesus and Paul. The evidence makes it highly probable that Paul knew Jesus' teaching on divorce and on retaliation.

It is probable that he also knew Jesus' "one flesh" and "eunuchs" sayings, the story of Mary and Martha, much of Jesus' teaching about love — of enemies, of neighbor, and of one another ("the law of Christ") — the saying about paying taxes to Caesar, the words about "receiving little ones" and not "causing them to stumble," and Jesus' prohibition of "judging," his prohibition of oaths, and his teaching on humble service (including the ransom saying).

Paul may also have known the sayings about peacemaking and about "salt" and "light," Jesus' use of "Amen" in introducing his sayings, his words about cutting off limbs that cause offense, the Gethsemane story, and Jesus' words in that story, including "the spirit is willing and the flesh is weak."

Three other things, none of them totally new to this chapter, deserve comment:

First, we have seen further evidence that the Jesus-tradition was discussed and debated in the church, with the Corinthians in particular offering alternative views to Paul on questions of sex and celibacy. They also seem to have used Jesus' saying about not using oaths right out of context in accusing Paul of being a "yes, yes, no, no" sort of person.

Second, we have noticed how there seem to be a considerable number of Pauline echoes of particular synoptic discourses. In particular we have noted a large number of possible echoes of the sermon on the mount (e.g., salt, light, fulfilling the law, cutting off offending limbs, prohibition of oaths, love of enemies, not judging),[166] of the sayings about relationships in the

---

166. We noted earlier other possible echoes of the sermon on the mount, including 1 Cor 4:8 (see p. 79 in chapter 2 above; Schürmann, *Lukasevangelium,* finds a whole range of links or possible links between 1 Corinthians 4 and Luke 6). Goulder, *Evangelists' Calendar,* 229, argues on the basis of parallels to the sermon on the mount in Romans 12–15 that the direction of dependence is probably from Paul to Matthew "since Matthew constructed the sermon thirty years after Paul wrote Romans." Whether Matthew did "construct" the sermon is highly debatable. On the two-source hypothesis there was at least a "Q" substratum, and it may well be that Matthew was (as he, of course, claims) dependent on a primitive "sermon" of Jesus, one that Paul also knew. But our argument concerning Pauline knowledge of the traditions is not undermined if the Matthean sermon is a compilation of originally disconnected ethical traditions: The concentration of parallels to the sermon in Romans 12–15 could reflect common subject matter (as also the parallels between the eschatological discourse and 1 and

church attested in Matthew 18/Mark 9/Luke 9 (e.g., receiving, stumbling blocks, cutting off limbs, peacefulness, salt, forgiveness), and of the sayings about marriage, divorce, and celibacy that are found in Matthew 19. Whether this proves that Paul knew the traditions already collected together in anything like the form we know, or whether it simply reflects the fact that Paul used materials that the Evangelists later gathered together in distinguishable blocks is something that will need to be further considered. It does seem likely that Paul knew the story of Mary and Martha and not just the sayings in that story on their own, and probably that he knew the dialogue-story about divorce.

Third, we have seen a particularly high concentration of echoes of Jesus-tradition in particular parts of Paul's letters, for example, in 1 Corinthians 7, where Paul uses various traditions of the Lord in discussing questions related to marriage, and also in Romans 12–15, where a whole variety of sayings of Jesus are echoed (e.g., "love your enemies" and "judge not," from the sermon on the mount, the "receiving" and "stumbling" sayings from Matthew 18/Mark 9/Luke 9, the "pay to Caesar" saying from the pre-passion controversy stories).

Additional Notes

THE DIVORCE SAYINGS IN THE SYNOPTICS

The relationships among the synoptic divorce texts are complex. This note briefly summarizes the evidence, and offers a proposed explanation.

The texts are as follows:

> But I tell you that everyone divorcing his wife, except for the matter of immorality, causes her to commit adultery [*moicheuō*, used in the passive]; and whoever marries a divorced (woman) commits adultery *(moichaomai)*.* (Matt 5:32)

---

2 Thessalonians). Goulder's suggestion that Matthew is based on a lectionary that included systematic readings of the Pauline Epistles is not required by this sort of evidence and is in any case improbable. (See, among others, Morris, "Gospels and the Jewish Lectionaries.")

Everyone divorcing his wife and marrying another commits adultery
(*moicheuō*), and the one marrying one divorced from (her) husband
commits adultery (*moicheuō*).* (Luke 16:18)

. . . let not (anyone) separate. . . . But I tell you that whoever divorces
his wife, except for immorality, and marries another commits adultery
(*moichaomai*).* (Matt 19:6, 9)

. . . let not (anyone) separate. . . . Whoever divorces his wife and marries
another commits adultery (*moichaomai*) against her. And if she divorcing
her husband marries another, she commits adultery (*moichaomai*).*
(Mark 10:9, 11, 12)

Among the points to note are the different verbs used when Jesus
speaks of divorce entailing adultery — *moicheuō* in Matt 5:32a and Luke
16:18, *moichaomai* in Matt 5:32b; 19:9; and Mark 10:11, 12 — and the
different constructions used of the act of divorce (a participle, "the one
divorcing," in Matt 5:32a; Luke 16:18; Mark 10:12; a subjunctive clause,
"whoever divorces," in Matt 5:32b; 19:9; Mark 10:11). Matthew and Luke
only refer to a man divorcing his wife, but Mark also refers to a woman
divorcing her husband. Paul is addressing women primarily in 1 Corinthians 7, but it may be significant that in citing the Lord's word he refers to
women "being separated" (a passive verb) from their husbands, but to
husbands "divorcing" (an active verb).[167] Matthew has an "exception" to
the divorce stipulation in both 5:32 and 19:6. Paul, like Mark and Luke,
shows no knowledge of the Matthean exception, though we have suggested
that he presupposes a rather similar understanding to Matthew's.

On the basis of this and other evidence the probable explanation is that
there were two quite different traditions of sayings of Jesus relating to divorce.
One of these resembled Matt 5:32a and probably belonged with the antitheses:

I say to you that everyone divorcing his wife, except for the matter of
unchastity, causes her to commit adultery (*moicheuō*).

167. Later Paul can speak of the wife "divorcing" and of the husband "separating"
(middle), and it is arguable that he uses the two verbs interchangeably, also that the
middle of the verb "separate" (*chōrizō*) may have an active force (see Neirynck, "Paul
and the Sayings of Jesus," 318). But it remains the case that when he cites the Lord's
word (and only then) Paul uses the passive "be separated" of the wife in a way that is
consistent with the Jewish tradition, according to which a husband could divorce his
wife but the wife could not divorce her husband, and that may reflect the Jesus-tradition
(see our reconstruction).

The logic here is that when a wife is immoral, she is responsible for the adultery; but when her husband divorces her in other circumstances and she then remarries, then he is responsible for the adultery.

The other tradition resembled Matt 19:9; Mark 10:11; and Matt 5:32b and was the one used by Paul:

> Let not (anyone) separate. . . . Whoever divorces his wife and marries another commits adultery *(moichaomai)*, and whoever marries one divorced from her husband commits adultery.

Each of the divorce texts in the Gospels is well explained on this basis. Mark followed the second of these traditions, but adapted it for Gentiles by referring to a woman divorcing her husband, which was not permissible under Jewish law.[168] In Matthew there has been some cross-fertilization of the two traditions, with 5:32a representing the first tradition and v. 32b representing the second, and with 19:9 representing the second tradition with the "exception" of the first added. Luke has also mixed the traditions.[169]

GALATIANS 3:28 AND BAPTISM

There are rather similar texts to Gal 3:28 in 1 Cor 12:13 and Col 3:11, and it is quite likely that in all three the thought is of Christian baptism, though it is not explicit in Col 3:11.[170] Each text speaks of "putting on" Christ or being incorporated into Christ, of the breakdown of old dualities (between Jew and Greek, etc.), and of unity. Two of the texts allude to the creation story: Gal 3:28 has "no longer male *and* female," echoing Gen 1:27 (contrast "Jew *or* Greek," "slave *or* free"), and Col 3:10 has "putting on the new person, who is being renewed after the image of the creator."* We may infer an association of baptism with the idea of new creation.[171]

It is not difficult to see how, given such baptismal ideas, the Corinthi-

---

168. Walter, "Paul," 69, rightly in my view, sees Mark 10:12 as an expansion of the earlier tradition, but wrongly believes that Paul knew the Markan form.

169. For a detailed explanation of this view and further bibliography see my "Paul's Use of the Jesus Tradition," 7-15. For a recent and full discussion of the history of the traditions (but not including consideration of my view) see R. F. Collins, *Divorce in the NT* (Collegeville: Glazier, 1992).

170. On Gal 3:28 see Fung, *Galatians,* 175, referring also to other scholars. Rom 10:12 is a further comparable text, also probably baptismal.

171. On this see especially Wire, *Corinthian Women,* 123-25.

ans might have inferred that baptism meant the abolition of the old male-female distinction. Paul rejects this inference both in 1 Corinthians 11 when speaking of the ongoing relevance of the created differences between men and women and also in 1 Corinthians 6 and 7 when speaking of the ongoing relevance of the "one flesh" marriage relationship. For him "no male and female" has to do with relationship to Christ and will lead to mutual care and respect (note his emphasis on mutuality in 1 Cor 7:3, 4; 11:11, 12), but does not mean the removal of created differences or created sexuality. It may be no accident that Paul's "no longer male or female" occurs in Gal 3:28, but not in 1 Cor 12:13 or Col 3:11: Was this because of Paul's experience of how the phrase could be misunderstood and misused?

D. R. MacDonald offers a more adventurous interpretation of Gal 3:28 and of how things were in Corinth.[172] He suggests that Gal 3:28 may be connected with a supposed saying of Jesus attested in the *Gospel of the Egyptians:* "When you tread on the garment of shame and when the two become one, the male with the female neither male nor female. . . ."[173] MacDonald argues that this saying was influential on the Corinthians and that baptism in Corinth was a transvestite ritual in which the intitiate was thought to put off the old body and to return to humanity's original androgynous state — "no longer male or female" in that sense. The women cast off their veils in the context of ecstatic worship (1 Corinthians 11) as an expression of this new state.

It may well be true that baptismal ritual and theology were influential on the women of Corinth. For example, baptismal robing might have been taken as an expression of putting on Christ and of the equality of all being baptized, including men and women. But, despite the interest of his analysis, MacDonald's suggestions, both about the saying from the *Gospel of the Egyptians* and about transvestite baptism in Corinth, are quite unlikely.

The position of the Corinthian ascetic women is well explained on the basis of texts from the canonical Gospels that are more plausibly seen as coming from Jesus, whereas the text from the *Gospel of the Egyptians* is not provably primitive or plausibly from Jesus. (MacDonald recognizes that it could not have come from Jesus, though he seems to assume that it was regarded as such from a very early date. He associates the thinking it represents with Apollos.)

Furthermore, it is much more likely that the direction of dependence

172. In *There is No Male and Female.*

173. Quoted in Clement of Alexandria, *Stromateis* 3.13.92; cf. *Gospel of Thomas* 21, 22, and 37; see also M. Macdonald, "Women Holy," 165-66.

was *from* Paul's social understanding of baptism breaking down barriers (a thoroughly Jewish understanding, which Paul had presumably taught in Corinth and which was in continuity with Jesus' own teaching about the kingdom) *to* the Gnostic anthropological understanding of baptism as sexual transformation represented in the saying in the *Gospel of the Egyptians* — rather than in the opposite direction, as MacDonald argues. The Corinthians knew both Paul's teaching and sayings of Jesus, but they were moving in a Gnostic direction under the influence of Greek ideas.[174]

THE "LOVE YOUR ENEMIES" TRADITIONS
OF MATTHEW 5:38-48/LUKE 6:27-36

In my article "Paul's Use of the Jesus Tradition," 15-24, I explore the relationships between the traditions of Matt 5:38-48/Luke 6:27-36, taking Paul's evidence into account. I argue for a presynoptic form of tradition lying behind Matthew and Luke. Although it is not possible always to decide between the Matthean and Lukan wording, I now suggest that the tradition was approximately as follows:

> You have heard that it was said, "Eye for eye and tooth for tooth." I say to you: Do not resist (*or* pay back evil for) evil, but do good to all. To the one who strikes you on the (right) cheek, turn to him the other as well, and to one who wishes to sue you and take your tunic, give your coat as well. Whoever compels you to go one mile, go with him two. To the one who asks give, and do not turn away one who wishes to borrow from you.
>
> You have heard that it was said, "You shall love your neighbor and hate your enemy." I say to you: Love your enemies, bless those who curse/speak ill of you, pray for those who mistreat/persecute you, that you may be children of your Father in heaven, for he makes the sun rise on evil and good and sends rain on righteous and unrighteous. For if you love those who love you, what reward do you have in that? Even tax collectors do the same. And if you greet only your brothers, what do you do that is special? Do not the Gentiles do the same? Therefore, you shall be perfect/merciful. . . .

This reconstruction explains the differences between Matthew and Luke, with Matthew being closest to the original and Luke conflating the two antitheses.

174. See also Wire, *Corinthian Women*, 281; cf. Ellis, *Pauline Theology*, 82-85.

J. Sauer in a major article on these passages proposes a very similar "Q" form,[175] though he accepts with little argument the widespread view that Matthew's antitheses are secondary. Sauer recognizes the parallels in Romans 12 and also argues that Paul is drawing on traditions, but he prefers the relatively complicated view that Paul and "Q" have brought together similar traditional sayings (from Jewish and Hellenistic sources) to the simpler view that Paul was significantly influenced by some form of the "Q" tradition. He doubts that any of the "Q" tradition derives from Jesus himself, claiming, for example, that there is no parallel in the Jesus-tradition to the "love your enemies" commandment — he does not discuss the parable of the good Samaritan — and that Rom 12:14, which he sees as a more primitive form of tradition than Luke 6:28a, cannot go back to Jesus because it presupposes persecution of Christians (he does not explain why Jesus could not have spoken of the persecution of his followers). Perhaps most important for Sauer is the argument that Paul should have cited more of the "Q" tradition than he does if he knew it. But we have seen that Paul typically uses the Jesus-tradition allusively (in, e.g., 1 Cor 9:14 and many other places). He is not quoting Jesus in Rom 12:9-21, but he is probably heavily influenced by the Jesus-tradition there.[176]

FURTHER POSSIBLE ECHOES
OF MATTHEW 5:38-48/LUKE 6:27-36

We have noted the possible echoes of Matt 5:38-48/Luke 6:27-36 in Romans 12. There are other possible echoes in Col 3:12-14 and Eph 4:32, 33.[177] In both passages, whether written by Paul himself or not, the context is one of ethical exhortation, including the injunction to "put off" the old man and to put on the "new man" in Christ. In this context the exhortation is:

> Put on . . . compassion and *mercy,* kindness, humility . . . forebearing one another and forgiving one another if anyone has something to blame another for. Just as the Lord also forgave you, so you, too, should forgive. On top of everything put on love, which is the bond of *perfection.* . . .* (Col 3:12-14)

175. "Traditionsgeschichtliche Erwägungen."
176. See further Thompson, *Clothed with Christ,* 103-4.
177. See J. P. Brown, "Synoptic Parallels," 34.

> Be *kind* to one another, tenderhearted, forgiving one another, as God in Christ has forgiven you. Therefore *be* imitators of God, as beloved *children*." (Eph 4:32; 5:1)

These Pauline texts can be compared with:

> But love your enemies, do good, and lend, expecting nothing in return. Your reward will be great, and you will be *children* of the Most High; for he is kind to the ungrateful and the wicked. *Be merciful,* just as your Father is merciful. (Luke 6:35, 36; Matt 5:48 has "Be *perfect,* therefore, as your heavenly Father is *perfect*")

There are differences between the synoptic exhortation to love one's enemies and the Pauline exhortations to love within the Christian community (albeit in situations of conflict). There are verbal and thematic similarities between the two Pauline passages and the synoptic tradition, notably in the call to imitate God or "the Lord." That these similarities are with both the Lukan and Matthean forms of the synoptic tradition complicates any possible identification of the form of the sayings that may have been known to Paul. For example, did he know "be perfect" or "be merciful," or was he conceivably familiar with both versions and interpretations of the Jesus-tradition, perhaps through differing church catechetical traditions?[178] We cannot move beyond the level of "possibility" with these texts, but it is possible that Paul has been influenced directly or indirectly by the sayings. It could be relevant that Paul refers to "the word of Christ" in Col 3:16, just a couple verses after those we have been considering (see above in our discussion of the "law of Christ").

---

178. Col 3:14 might almost be viewed as either an interpretation of Matt 5:48 along Lukan lines or of Luke 6:36 along Matthean lines.

7

THE FUTURE COMING
OF THE LORD

I. Comparing Jesus and Paul

JESUS' TEACHING

Jesus announced the setting up of a new world government — the kingdom of God. He proclaimed the inauguration of the revolution for which many of his contemporaries were longing — in fulfillment of God's promises. But he disappointed his followers by failing to complete the job in the way they expected, and he had to explain that his own role was like that of a sower — starting the process off — and that the "harvest" lay in the future (Matt 13:1-31; Mark 4:1-32; Luke 8:4-15; 13:18, 19). The kingdom was in one sense present in Jesus' ministry (or at least its effects were already being experienced), but in another sense it was future; so Jesus taught his disciples to pray "Your kingdom come" (Matt 6:10; Luke 11:2).

But how did Jesus envisage that future kingdom?

The Salvation of the People of God

The sowing-harvesting picture suggests that Jesus saw the future kingdom as the completion of what was beginning in his ministry. God's rule was already evident — in healing, the casting out of evil, forgiveness, reconciliation, and so on — and the coming kingdom would be the time when "your will is done on earth as in heaven" (Matt 6:10).[1] There is evidence that Jesus' followers were looking for the salvation of Israel in a very down-to-earth sense, that is, in terms of the defeat of Israel's enemies and the restoration of Israel's sovereignty (e.g., Matt 20:21/Mark 10:37; Luke 19:11; 24:21; Acts 1:6). Jesus related to that expectation: He was carrying out his mission in order to gather "the lost sheep of the house of Israel" (Matt 10:5, 6), and he promised that his disciples would sit on thrones in the kingdom judging the twelve tribes of Israel (Matt 19:28/Luke 21:30). The OT prom-ised the deliverance of God's people Israel, and Jesus saw his mission as fulfilling that promise. But he also shared the wider OT vision for the outsider (such as the Samaritan) and for the nations: The future kingdom would include those at present excluded from the family of Abraham. Jesus was notorious for the way he mixed with "unclean" people, but this was precisely what the kingdom would be like, with people coming from east and west to eat with Abraham, Isaac, and Jacob (Matt 8:11/Luke 7:28, 29). Jesus spoke of the coming kingdom as a feast and anticipated that kingdom by his own conduct, eating with sinners (Matt 22:1-14/Luke 14:15-24; Matt 26:29/Mark 14:25; Luke 22:16, 18).

Coming Judgment

But, even though the dominant note in Jesus' preaching was one of joyful good news, his vision for the future also had a negative aspect to it. His model of the future was not an evolutionary model of a world getting better and better, but a thoroughly Jewish model including the idea of divine judgment on evil and evildoers.[2] The urgency and the joyfulness of the good news of salvation both have to be seen against the backdrop of coming judgment: The good news is of divine deliverance, not of divine tolerance or universalism.

1. Whether or not that Matthean phrase goes back to Jesus (see chapter 6 above), it expresses accurately part of what is involved in the "kingdom" idea.

2. The so-called parables of growth, e.g., the mustard seed, the seed growing secretly, etc., do speak of the kingdom as something that grows to harvest, but it is clear from the parable of the sower (with its categories of soil that fail to produce fruit) and from that of the wheat and the weeds that the picture is not one of evolutionary progress with evil simply withering away and without the need for judgment (see Matt 13:1-31; Mark 4:1-32; Luke 8:4-15; 13:18, 19).

On Jerusalem

The judgment has a narrower and a broader focus. On the one hand, Jesus warned of judgment coming on the temple and the Jewish nation. He had very hard things to say about the emptiness and corruption of the religion of the Jewish leaders of his day, and he warned that the fruitless tree would be destroyed and that the fruitless tenants of God's vineyard would be replaced. Their rejection of his message of the kingdom was the clinching crime against God, and the tragic result would be divine wrath on Jerusalem and the temple in "this generation." This prophetic theme is well attested in the gospel tradition — in both Markan and "Q" traditions, in parables, in Jesus' denunciation of the Jewish leaders, and in his lament over Jerusalem (e.g., Matt 21:10-22/Mark 11:11-26; Matt 21:33-44/Mark 12:1-12/Luke 20:9-19; Matt 22:1-10; 23:29-39/Luke 11:47-51; 13:34, 35).

Most striking is the "eschatological discourse" of Matthew 24/Mark 13/Luke 21, where Jesus speaks of the destruction of the temple and proceeds to describe the temple's desolation. This discourse has been the focus of intense scholarly interest, and it has frequently been asserted that the central passage, which describes the setting up of the "desolating sacrilege" and then the coming of the Son of man on the clouds, is a Jewish or Jewish Christian tract ("the little apocalypse"), not teaching that goes back to Jesus. It has been associated by scholars with the crisis of AD 39, when the emperor Caligula sought to have his statue erected in the Jerusalem temple, and also with the terrible Jewish War of AD 66-70.

There is, however, no good reason for denying that Jesus spoke in these terms, even if some Christian scholars have found it appealing to disassociate Jesus from the rather alien apocalyptic thinking expressed in the discourse.[3] In the first place, the "desolating sacrilege"-"son of man" language is Danielic and refers in Daniel to the terrible events of 167 BC when Antiochus Epiphanes attacked the Jerusalem temple, setting up a pagan altar there and seeking to destroy Judaism. The Book of Daniel and the events associated with 167 BC, including the Maccabean rebellion, were important in the Palestinian context of Jesus, as the people faced the threatening pagan power of Rome.

Secondly, the AD 39 crisis was not the first time the Romans had acted in ways that were perceived as a threat to the sanctity of Jerusalem and the

---

3. For the history of critical study of the discourse see Beasley-Murray, *Jesus and the Last Days.*

temple: Pilate himself offended Jewish sensibilities by bringing pagan symbols into Jerusalem and by commandeering temple funds.[4]

Thirdly, there is good reason to believe that Jesus reflected on the Book of Daniel, deriving his understanding of his own mission as "Son of man" and even perhaps his concept of the kingdom from that source in particular (see chapters 2 and 3 above). There is also reason to believe that he anticipated and warned of disaster to come on Jerusalem and especially on the temple (see chapter 4 above).

Finally, there is strong evidence that Matthew, Mark, and Luke have independent traditions in their respective versions of the eschatological discourse (see further below): The two later Evangelists, Matthew and Luke, do not simply reproduce the traditions of the earliest Gospel, Mark.

We may conclude from all this that there is every possibility of Jesus having spoken of the coming judgment on Jerusalem in "desolating sacrilege" terms.

On everyone

In addition to envisaging a specific judgment on Jerusalem and the temple, Jesus also anticipated a universal judgment, dividing the wheat from the weeds and the sheep from the goats, with individuals giving account of themselves and being included or excluded from the coming kingdom (e.g., Matt 13:24-30; 25:31-46). Matthew's Gospel brings this theme out most strongly and Mark's least strongly. But it is reflected in all the gospel strata. Mark speaks of those who "enter life" or are "thrown into hell" in the discussion of causing offense (9:42-48). Numerous parables in "Q" and passages unique to Matthew and Luke speak of reward and punishment: Some will enter the feast of the kingdom, and some will find themselves excluded (e.g., Matt 7:21-27/Luke 6:46-49 and 13:25-27; Matt 13:24-30, 47-50; Luke 16:19-31; 17:22-37/Matt 24:26, 27, 37-39).

There is nothing surprising about this emphasis, given Jesus' Jewish context. What is different is that in Jesus' teaching, as it is described in the Gospels, the criterion of judgment is frequently defined in terms of Jesus himself and response to him and his teaching. But there is nothing improbable in this, given Jesus' sense of the new age having arrived in his ministry. Jesus' message and that of his disciples is urgent precisely because the moment of destiny is dawning in and through him (see the mission discourses of Matthew 10/Mark 6/Luke 9–10).

---

4. Josephus, *War* II.169-77; *Ant.* XVIII.55-61.

Jesus' future role

Jesus suggested not only that future judgment would be on the basis of response to him and his message, but also that he personally would be an active participant in that fateful day.

The coming Son of man

We have already observed that the Jesus of the Gospels speaks of the Son of man coming "in the glory of his Father with the holy angels" (Matt 16:27/Mark 8:38/Luke 9:26) and "on the clouds" (Matt 24:30/Mark 13:26/Luke 21:27). Such future Son of man sayings are clearly derived from Daniel 7, and the thought is of the coming day of judgment — when each person will be repaid for his or her work (so Matt 16:27), when the Son of man will be "ashamed of" those who have been ashamed of Jesus (so Mark 8:38/Luke 9:26), when the elect will be gathered in (so Matt 24:31/Mark 13:24). In terms of the vision of Daniel 7 it is the day when God's people will be vindicated and delivered and his enemies finally defeated. In terms of the Gospels it is a day of judgment and division between one and another, between faithful and unfaithful servants, between wheat and tares, between sheep and goats.

Scholars, as we have seen, have agonized over which, if any, of the Son of man sayings in the Gospels go back to Jesus. Some have agreed that the future sayings, which are widely attested in the Gospels,[5] do go back to Jesus, but have claimed that Jesus envisaged a figure other than himself coming as Son of man.[6] It is possible to take Mark 8:38, "whoever is ashamed of me . . . of him will the Son of man also be ashamed" (RSV), to support this view, but only by reading the text in a way that was certainly not intended by either Mark or Luke, who have transmitted the text to us.

It is much simpler to suppose that Jesus spoke of himself as Son of man (rather than that the title was transferred from another figure to Jesus in a sense contrary to Jesus' own usage) and that the vision of Daniel 7 was formative in Jesus' thinking. If it was, then it is in no way surprising that Jesus looked forward to the day of vindication described in Daniel and to his own glorification. Just as the kingdom is present, even if only as a

5. As well as in the triple Matthew/Mark/Luke tradition, the idea of the Son of man coming in glory is in the "Q" tradition of Matthew and Luke (e.g., Matt 24:27, 39/Luke 17:24, 30), in Matthew's special material (e.g., Matt 13:41; 25:31), and in Luke's special material (e.g., Luke 18:8).

6. E.g., Bultmann, *Theology of the NT*, I, 5, 28-30.

mustard seed, as well as future, so Jesus himself is Son of man in the present, though a Son of man who must suffer, but also the future glorious Son of man, who comes to judge and to save.

Parables about the Lord's return

In addition to the Son of man sayings, a series of gospel parables speaks of Jesus' future return. Most notable are those that Matthew locates at the end of the eschatological discourse: the thief, the faithful and unfaithful stewards, the wise and foolish virgins, and the talents (Matt 24:43–25:30). All speak of people who are prepared or unprepared for a future coming.

That Matthean series has a parallel in Luke 12:35-48 and would often therefore be designated "Q" material. But there are also echoes of the same parables in Mark 13:33-37, and there is a strong case for thinking that Matthew, Mark, and Luke are all familiar with what might be called a "presynoptic" collection of parables that they have each edited in a different way (see the additional note below on "The Eschatological Parables"). If this view is correct, then we are dealing with a very early and widely known collection of sayings of Jesus about his future coming.

Some scholars have argued that although the parables themselves go back to Jesus they were originally not about Jesus' own future coming in particular, but about the coming day of God. But this probably reflects the critics' own difficulty with the idea of the Galilean teacher Jesus predicting his own powerful return rather than any substantial evidence. The interpretation of the parables in terms of Jesus' return goes back very early, and there is no evidence of any other interpretation. The parable of the thief in particular is unlikely to have been applied first to Jesus by the early Christians, whereas Jesus might well have used such a disreputable image of himself. The parables that speak of a master going away and leaving his servants with tasks to accomplish make good sense as comments of Jesus about his coming departure, but less sense of the coming day of the Lord.

We conclude that there is a good case for the view that Jesus anticipated his own departure from his disciples, their continuation of his work, and his own return to call his servants to account and to bring the kingdom to completion. If Jesus saw his own ministry as inaugurating the feast of the kingdom of God, it is entirely congruous that he also believed that he would finish the task in the future.[7]

---

7. It is notable that Jesus could use the same "feast" imagery of his ministry and of the future kingdom.

Near, and Yet . . .

Imminent action

John the Baptist, according to Matthew and Luke, warned his hearers that "the ax is lying at the root of the trees" (Matt 3:10; Luke 3:9). The picture is of imminent judgment. Jesus' message too had a sense of urgency: The kingdom had come near, the time of fulfillment had come, the eschatological countdown was under way. Like John and the Qumran community, Jesus was conscious of living in the momentous last days.

More specifically the Gospels have a number of sayings of Jesus in which he speaks specifically of things happening soon, notably Matt 10:23: "You will not have gone through all the towns of Israel before the Son of Man comes," Matt 16:28/Mark 9:1/Luke 9:27: "Truly I tell you, there are some standing here who will not taste death before they see the Son of Man coming in his kingdom,"[8] and Matt 24:34/Mark 13:30/Luke 21:32: "Truly I tell you, this generation will not pass away until all these things have taken place." In addition, Matt 23:36/Luke 11:50 speaks of judgment coming on the Jews in "this generation."

At first sight these sayings appear to indicate that Jesus expected the future kingdom to be established very shortly, within the lifetime of his contemporaries. Many scholars believe that this was exactly what Jesus believed. However, it is unlikely that the Evangelists took these sayings to refer to the Lord's return and the end of the age: It is likely, for example, that Mark at least understood the saying about "some standing here" who will not "taste death before they see the kingdom . . ." to refer in the first instance to the transfiguration and the saying that "this generation will not pass away until all these things have taken place" to refer to the setting up of the desolating sacrilege in Jerusalem, which has been described shortly before the saying.[9] But whether the sayings refer to the Lord's return or to

8. Mark speaks of them seeing not the "Son of man" but "the kingdom come with power"; Luke speaks of "the kingdom."

9. As for the saying in Matt 10:23 about the disciples not going through Israel before the coming of the Son of man, Matthew (who knew that the Lord did not return in glory during the original Palestinian mission of the disciples) may have seen this as a reference to coming judgment on the Jewish nation (not to the parousia), or just possibly as a simple promise of Jesus to meet up with the disciples during their mission. But if it is a reference to the parousia, as it may be, it is arguably less a statement of chronology and more an encouragement to the disciples about the continuing opportunities they would have for mission despite opposition. On Mark 9:1 and the trans-

other events such as the transfiguration and the destruction of the Jerusalem temple, it remains true that there is a sense of imminent eschatological action and that this probably goes back to Jesus himself.[10]

The unknown hour

As well as a sense of imminence, there is within the gospel tradition a strong affirmation that the time of the coming of the future kingdom is unknown. Some sayings make the point directly, notably Matt 24:36/Mark 13:32: "About that day and hour no one knows, neither the angels of heaven, nor the Son, but only the Father" (cf. Acts 1:6, 7). The series of parables that we noted before speaks of the Lord's coming and emphasizes its unexpectedness: It will be unpredictable like the coming of a thief; it may happen early or late (the parable of the watchman); Jesus' followers must not be like the steward who mistakenly reckoned on his master coming late, or like the virgins who reckoned on the bridegroom coming soon. Other gospel sayings also emphasize the unpredictability and suddenness of the Lord's coming (e.g., Matt 24:37-41/Luke 17:26-35).

It is possible to see the emphasis on the unknownness of the time of the Lord's coming as deriving from the church as it was faced with the embarrassment of Jesus' mistaken predictions of a near end — the so-called "delay of the parousia," hence the emphasis on delay in some of the parables. But the parables concerned go back very early, and it is entirely possible that Jesus had a sense of living in the last days, an urgent expectation of the coming kingdom, a conviction that judgment was coming on Jerusalem in the immediate future, a consciousness that there was a mission to the nations to be accomplished,[11] and a confidence that the precise timing of the completion of the kingdom was in God's hands.

---

figuration see chapter 8 below. On 13:30 see my "This Generation Will Not Pass," 127-50; also Geddert, *Watchwords*, 223-55. On all these texts (including Matt 10:23) see also Witherington, *Jesus, Paul*, 36-44.

10. It is not very likely that the church would have ascribed such expectation to Jesus without a basis in the tradition.

11. The parables speak of the master going away and leaving his servants with tasks. Matt 24:14/Mark 13:10 speaks of mission to the Gentiles: The Markan text looks rather out of place in its context and has often been seen as deriving from Mark, not his tradition. But it is not altogether clear why Mark should have created this somewhat awkward insertion, and it is more likely that he knew the saying in something like its Matthean position and form and relocated it to follow the saying in Mark 13:9, which he had imported into this context. See my *Rediscovery*, 253-85. On the authenticity of Mark 13:10 see Bosch, *Heidenmission*, 132-74.

Living in the Interim

The servants in the parables are left with specific tasks to accomplish, for example, to administer their master's property profitably (the talents, Matt 25:14-30) or to feed their master's household (the steward, Matt 24:45-51/Luke 12:41-48). The picture is of the servants continuing the master's affairs in his absence, and this ties in with the call to mission, which we considered in chapter 5. The disciples were sent out to continue Jesus' mission in his lifetime; even more so in his absence are they to be his witnesses (Mark 13:9, 10).

The disciples' witness will be given in the midst of suffering and opposition, as the Jesus tradition emphasizes (e.g., Matt 5:10, 11/Luke 6:22; Matt 24:9-14; Mark 13:9-13/Luke 21:12-19). The disciples are called to endure and, as the parable of the watchman in particular brings out, to "keep awake" and to be ready for the Lord's return (Mark 13:34-36; Luke 12:36-40). It is because the time is unknown that wakefulness is important and speculation futile.

In the future the servants will give account to their master for their good and evil actions and will be judged accordingly (e.g., Matt 25:14-30/Luke 19:11-27). Jesus emphasizes that it will not be those who claim to be his followers who will enter the feast of the kingdom, but those who live in practical love and obedience (Matt 7:21-27/Luke 6:46-49; Matt 25:31-46).[12]

PAUL'S VIEW OF THE FUTURE

The Nearness of the Lord's Coming

Paul...

In the middle of his discussion of Christian conduct in Romans 12–15 Paul reminds his readers of "the time" (the *kairos*), "for salvation is nearer to us now than when we became believers; the night is far gone, the day is near" (13:11, 12). This passage makes it clear how important Christian hope was as a motivation of Christian ethics for Paul and how strong a sense Paul had that the time before "the day" was short.[13] He believed that the es-

---

12. For discussion of Jesus' ethics see chapter 6 above.

13. On the eschatological emphasis of Paul's theology see Beker, *Paul the Apostle*, especially 135-81.

chatological countdown was far advanced and that the day of salvation would come soon.

The same impression is given in Paul's other letters, including 1 Corinthians, where he recommends the single state (for those appropriately gifted by God) because "the appointed time has grown short"; this age is passing away, and Christians should live accordingly (7:29-31). Paul goes on to speak of "us, on whom the ends of the ages have come" (10:11), meaning perhaps that we are living in both the dying moments of the old age and the opening moments of the new age, which the Christian is already experiencing through the firstfruits or down payment of the Spirit.[14]

The classic passages for Paul's expectation of a near end are in 1 Thessalonians, one of his earliest letters. It is notable that in 1:10, when describing the Thessalonians' conversion, he speaks of them having turned to God "to wait for his Son from heaven, whom he raised from the dead — Jesus, who rescues us from the wrath to come." The Thessalonians were waiting eagerly for Jesus' return, so much so, it seems, that they were taken aback when some church members died (4:13-18). Apparently they had not reckoned with anyone dying before the Lord's return, and they were afraid that those who had died had missed out on the new age that Jesus was to bring. Paul has to reassure them that the "dead in Christ" will be raised to life when Jesus comes. The Thessalonians' misunderstanding reflected their expectation of a very near end, and it seems probable that they received this expectation from Paul himself: Even in 1 Thes 4:15 he can speak in terms of "we who are alive, who are left until the coming of the Lord." Paul anticipated that the Lord would come soon and thought that he himself would be alive at that time.[15]

Not, however, that Paul is dogmatic about the timing of the Lord's return. Indeed, his specific comment to the Thessalonians on the issue of "times and seasons" is a reminder to them that the day of the Lord will come "like a thief in the night," suddenly, when people are unprepared

---

14. See chapter 2 above on 1 Cor 10:11.

15. Scholars have discussed whether Paul's thought underwent a change as time went on, noting that the hope of the second coming features less prominently in some of Paul's later letters. There is probably a grain of truth in this view: As time went on, Paul must increasingly have reckoned with the possibility of his death preceding the Lord's return. And yet the sense of the nearness of the "day" is present in Romans 13, as we have seen, and there is not much evidence suggesting that Paul went through a radical theological reappraisal on the matter. The point is in any case not important for the Jesus-Paul question since, if there is a distinction between the early and the late Paul, it is the early Paul who is closest to Jesus.

(1 Thes 5:1-3). And although Paul can speak of himself as being alive at the Lord's coming, he can also describe the Lord dying for us "so that whether we are awake or asleep we may live with him" (5:10).[16]

. . . and Jesus

The similarity to the gospel traditions of Jesus is obvious: The combination of a sense of excitement about the nearness of the new age, together with an explanation that the time is unknown and that it will come suddenly and unexpectedly, is present in both. The one significant difference is that Paul writes after the death and resurrection of Jesus, which he sees as decisively important events in the eschatological timetable. It is arguable that Jesus saw them as such as well; thus we argued (in chapter 4 above) that at the last supper Jesus spoke of the kingdom as coming through his death. But still Paul when teaching about the future is a stage further on: Jesus has gone away, and his return is now awaited.

Before the Lord's Coming

Paul . . .

It may be that some of the Thessalonians (like other eschatologically excited people before and since) abandoned their regular work because they thought the new age was so near (1 Thes 5:14; 2 Thes 3:6-13). Paul, however, had a strong sense of a mission to be accomplished before the Lord's return. In particular he believed that he had a mission to the Gentile world, and he was motivated by the conviction that "the fullness of the Gentiles"* must come in before the final salvation (of "all Israel") would happen (Rom 11:24, 25). Paul was, as we noted in chapter 2, working within an OT framework of thought, looking for the Gentiles to be gathered in, and seeing his mission and perhaps also his collection for the saints in that context.[17]

16. Witherington, *Jesus, Paul,* 23-35, argues that Paul reckoned that the Lord *could* come imminently rather than that he *would* necessarily do so. But Witherington also says that for Paul the decisive eschatological events had happened, so that not much was left to happen.

17. As well as Romans 9–11, see Romans 15, especially vv. 19-24, for Paul's ambition to complete his task; also 1 Thes 2:16.

If Paul believed that the Gentile mission must be completed before the Lord's return, he also, according to 2 Thessalonians, believed that a catastrophic evil would precede that day of salvation. In 2 Thes 2:1-11 Paul (if he was the author of 2 Thessalonians) responds to an idea that had caught on in Thessalonica according to which "the day of the Lord is already here" by describing "the lawless one" who must come first, setting himself up as god in the temple, and using signs and wonders to deceive people. Paul says that the lawless one is now being restrained, but will be revealed before being destroyed by the Lord when the Lord comes. The enigmatic language inevitably brings the notorious Antiochus Epiphanes to mind: He was the archetypal lawless one, the one who defiled the temple. Paul thus seems to envisage some comparable disaster in the future.

If this teaching were totally unparalleled elsewhere in Paul's letters, that might strengthen the case of those who see 2 Thessalonians as non-Pauline. But Paul does refer to divine wrath on the Jews in two other places, and they may reflect the same tradition. In 1 Thess 2:16, after speaking of Jewish opposition to the preaching of the gospel, he comments that "the wrath has come upon them finally."* The phrase has greatly perplexed commentators, and it is not possible to be certain of its meaning. However, it seems quite likely, first, that Paul is referring to recent events in Rome and in Jerusalem: In Rome there was rioting in the Jewish community, probably over the new religion of Jesus, and this led the emperor Claudius to expel the Jews from the capital city; in Jerusalem thousands (according to Josephus twenty or thirty thousand) of Jews had been killed by the Roman governor Cumanus after an incident in the temple.[18] Paul could well have seen these setbacks for non-Christian Jews as God's wrath.[19] It

---

18. On the Claudian expulsion see Suetonius, *Claudius* XXV.4; Acts 18:2. It lends considerable weight to this view if Acts is right to say that Paul stayed with people who had been affected by the expulsion, namely, Priscilla and Aquila, at the time when he is thought to have written 1 Thessalonians. On the events in Judea see Josephus, *War* XI.223-31; *Ant.* XX.105-17.

19. The Claudian expulsion affected Jewish Christians like Aquila and Priscilla as well as other Jews, but it was directed to the whole Jewish community, and Paul might well have seen it as punishment for Jewish resistance to the Gentile mission.

It may be significant that Paul, when writing to the Romans, can speak of the authorities as agents of God's "wrath" on evildoers (Rom 13:4, 5). The events of AD 49 may have been part of the background to Paul's teaching on the state in Rom 13:1-7, whether because he is keen to encourage Christians not to antagonize the authorities, as they had done in AD 49, or because some Roman Christians, including some of those who had been expelled, may have doubted if Christians had any obligations toward the

also seems likely that Paul, in using the language of "the wrath" coming on the Jews, was referring to an idea that was familiar to the Thessalonian Christians. It may be that precisely the sort of tradition found in 2 Thessalonians 2 was familiar to them — Paul comments there that he is reminding them of his earlier teaching — and that 1 Thes 2:16 thus confirms that Paul did anticipate "wrath" on the Jews before the end.[20]

The evidence of Romans 9–11 may possibly confirm this, since there Paul discusses the unbelief of the Jews and explains it as a divine hardening — indeed as divine "wrath" (9:22) — which the Jews must experience "until the fullness of the Gentiles comes in"* (11:25). Is this a different Pauline interpretation of the tradition of "wrath" coming on the Jews before the end, which was alluded to in 1 Thes 2:16?[21]

---

pagan state. Paul affirms that the state has a God-given role in rewarding good and punishing evil and that Christians have a responsibility to submit.

On the identification of "the wrath" of 1 Thes 2:16 with the Claudian expulsion see Bammel, "Judenverfolgung und Naherwartung." Some scholars have doubted that the expulsion was on a large scale, suggesting that only the ringleaders of the trouble may have been involved. But neither Acts nor Suetonius suggests this, and it would not necessarily undermine Bammel's view anyway. See Schürer, *History* III/1, 77-78; Smallwood, *Jews under Roman Rule*, 210-16; Riesner, *Frühzeit des Paulus*, 139-80. On the events in Jerusalem see Jewett, "Agitators," 204, 205, arguing that the zealots who provoked the Roman massacre were actively anti-Christian. See further discussion of this below.

20. It is possible that it was Paul's comment about "wrath" having come on the Jews that provoked the excitement about the day of the Lord referred to in 2 Thes 2:1. If the Thessalonian Christians knew a prophecy something like what is in 2 Thes 2:3-12, as Paul implies in 2:5, then his comment may have triggered their excitement. They may have been almost right in their interpretation of Paul: He may have seen in recent events the beginning of "the rebellion" (if *apostasia* in 2 Thes 2:3 is correctly understood in this way, despite many commentators) and of the "wrath on the Jews" — but now in 2 Thessalonians he seeks to cool the situation by pointing out that there are still elements from the Lord's prophecy (the man of lawlessness in the temple) that have yet to be fulfilled. Even if 2 Thessalonians was not written by Paul himself, it represents an early interpretation of Paul's eschatological teaching that could still be instructive about the traditions taught in the Pauline churches and about the meaning of "the wrath" in 1 Thes 2:16.

21. In Romans 11 and 1 Thessalonians 2 the wrath on the Jews is linked to the Gentile mission, though in 1 Thessalonians it responds to Jewish opposition to the Gentile mission, while in Romans it responds to Jewish unbelief and is a catalyst to Gentile mission. It is easy enough to see how Paul's experiences of Jewish opposition could have been seen in both ways (with persecution leading to Gentile mission as well as being a response to it). Witherington, *Jesus, Paul*, 103, 111, notes the parallel between 1 Thes

Related to both the Gentile mission and Jewish unbelief was Paul's experience of suffering. He sees it as the calling of Christians to suffer (1 Thes 3:4). It is part of being "in Christ" to share Christ's sufferings in the present age (e.g., Rom 8:17).

. . . and Jesus

The Pauline vision of mission to the world, judgment on the Jews, and sufferings to be endured by Jesus' disciples matches closely the vision of Jesus as recorded in the Gospels. It is, as we have seen, disputed whether Jesus anticipated the Gentile mission. But there is good reason for believing that he shared the prophetic vision for the world, including the nations. The synoptic eschatological discourse brings together precisely the three ingredients that make up Paul's expectation, with a strong emphasis on suffering and endurance, a specific reference to preaching the gospel to the Gentiles, and a description of judgment on Judea in language borrowed from the Danielic description of Antiochus Epiphanes and Daniel's "desolating sacrilege." We will comment more on these parallels in the second part of this chapter.

On That Day

Paul . . .

For Paul the future day of the Lord will mean (1) the Lord's "parousia" or coming. "The Lord . . . will descend from heaven" (1 Thes 4:15, 16; 1:10; 2 Thes 1:7-10; 2:8, etc.). The day will be (2) a day of disclosure and accounting, when each will be judged and rewarded "according to what he has done in the body"* (1 Cor 3:12-15; 4:4, 5; 2 Cor 5:10; Rom 2:6). The day will be (3) one of terrible judgment on evildoers and on those who

---

2:16 and Romans 11 and accordingly interprets the "wrath" of 1 Thessalonians as the unbelief (i.e., divine hardening) of Israel; see also Steck, *Israel und das Gewaltsame Geschick der Propheten,* 77; Donfried, "Paul and Judaism." This could be right, but Witherington does not note the parallel phrase in Luke 21:23 (which we will discuss shortly), and his view does not seem to do justice to the sense we get from 1 Thessalonians that something has just happened or begun to happen to the Jews. It is more likely that 1 Thessalonians represents one Pauline interpretation of the Jesus-tradition and Romans 11 another.

have not obeyed the gospel. Evil will be destroyed, and all God's enemies finally defeated (1 Cor 3:15; 15:25-28; 1 Thes 5:3; 2 Thes 1:8, 9; 2:8). Conversely, (4) "all Israel" in the sense of all who are in Christ, Jew and Gentile, living and dead, will be gathered to be "with the Lord";[22] they will enjoy face-to-face knowledge of God and the full experience of being his children; they will be glorified and their bodies will be redeemed and raised (1 Thes 1:10; 4:17; 2 Thes 1:10; 1 Cor 13:12; 15:52; Rom 8:17, 23; 11:26, etc.). But (5) this salvation will be not just for individuals but for the whole of God's creation: Creation will be liberated from futility and decay, and all things will be brought together in unity under God's rule (Rom 8:21; 1 Cor 15:24-28; Col 1:16-20; Eph 1:10).

. . . and Jesus

This Pauline vision mirrors the teaching of Jesus quite closely. The idea of creation's redemption is not explicit in Jesus' teaching, but it is implicit. Jesus' vision of the kingdom was not just spiritual or narrowly nationalistic (he healed the sick and welcomed the outsider); the rule of God meant the defeat of Satan and the restoration of creation. The Pauline view of the future kingdom — he uses the word, significantly, in 1 Cor 15:24, 50 — is in line with this.

Another difference in emphasis is that Jesus, according to the Gospels, did not say much about the resurrection of the dead, though he identified with those Jews who believed in resurrection and in the transformation of those raised (Matt 22:23-33/Mark 12:18-27/Luke 20:27-40). Furthermore, he anticipated his own resurrection "after three days."[23] Paul says much more about resurrection because it was an issue in his churches (both in Thessalonica and Corinth, if not elsewhere) and because he was writing in

22. Whether Paul envisaged a final restoration of Jewish Israel after the completion of the Gentile mission is uncertain, though I am inclined to take Rom 11:26 (cf. v. 12) to suggest this. (See Witherington, *Jesus, Paul,* 121-22.) Interestingly, the same uncertainty surrounds the interpretation of Luke 21:24, though once again the implication is probably that Israel will be restored after "the times of the Gentiles" (see also Acts 1:6).

23. On the authenticity of Jesus' predictions of his death and resurrection as recorded in the Gospels see chapter 4 (above) and especially Bayer, *Jesus' Predictions.* Witherington, *Jesus, Paul,* 218-20, finds good evidence in Mark 14:25 of Jesus' expectation that he would share in the kingdom after his death. Witherington argues that the language of the passion prediction in Mark 8:31 indicates that it is pre-Markan and probably goes back to Jesus.

the aftermath of the stupendous event of Jesus' resurrection. It may well be that the question of the resurrection of believers was an issue in Paul's churches precisely because the Christian tradition had not yet paid significant attention to the question of believers who died.

FINAL COMMENTS ON THE COMPARISON

On the basis of the sketch that we have offered of Jesus' and Paul's expectations for the future, we conclude that they have a great deal in common:

- Both have a very strong sense that the last days have come. The eschatological countdown has begun, and the longed-for kingdom of God is excitingly and urgently near.
- Both see Jesus' death and resurrection as key events in the coming of the future kingdom. Jesus looks forward; Paul looks back to the cross and resurrection as the decisively important moments in the eschatological program.
- Both associate the coming kingdom with the future heavenly coming of Jesus.
- Both decline to specify when the future kingdom will actually arrive, but suggest that its coming will be preceded by a period of witness, suffering, and judgment on the Jewish nation.

The differences between Jesus and Paul on the future are not very great, except that Jesus' death is in the foreground of his future expectation, whereas for Paul Jesus' death is in the past. If the critics who suggest that Jesus looked for the coming of the kingdom rather than for his own return are right, then Paul's christological focus represents a significant shift. But there is good reason for thinking that Jesus did, in fact, speak of his own return in connection with the kingdom, and Paul did look for the redemption and restoration of all things, not only for the Lord's return. The difference is at best one of emphasis.

II. Connecting Jesus and Paul

The most important evidence for connections between Paul's teaching on the future and the Jesus-tradition is, not surprisingly, in 1 and 2 Thessalonians.[24]

1 THESSALONIANS 4 AND 5

"The Word of the Lord" (1 Thessalonians 4:15)

In responding to the Thessalonians who were anxious about loved ones who had died, Paul reminds them of Jesus' resurrection and of the Christian assurance that "God will bring with him those who have died." He goes on to say that "This we declare to you *by the word of the Lord,* that we who are alive, who are left until the coming of the Lord, will by no means precede those who have died [literally "fallen asleep"]" (1 Thes 4:14, 15).

Paul's appeal here to "the word of the Lord" is most probably some sort of "tradition indicator": He is not giving his own opinion but quoting the Lord's authority. Some scholars consider this "word of the Lord" as probably a word of the risen Lord given through a prophet, not a traditional saying of Jesus.[25] Perhaps the strongest argument in favor of this view is that there is no saying in the Gospels that says what Paul declares here by the word of the Lord, that is, that the living will not precede the dead. However, there are two possible responses to that point: Paul could be quoting a tradition of Jesus that is not preserved in the Gospels (a so-called *agraphon*), or he could be paraphrasing a gospel saying, as he does, for example, in 1 Cor 7:10, 11; 9:14, interpreting it to make his point.

In favor of the view that he is quoting from tradition rather than from some recent prophecy is the evidence elsewhere in 1 and 2 Thessaloni-

---

24. For more detailed study of the relevant texts and the possible Synoptic parallels see my *Rediscovery;* also Aejmelaeus, *Wachen vor dem Ende.*

25. Neirynck, "Paul and the Sayings," 311, notes OT references to the prophetic "word of the Lord" and concludes that Paul is referring to an oracle originating with himself. But the OT usage is far from conclusive: "The Lord" for Paul is usually Christ, and he uses the title in other contexts to refer to Jesus-traditions (1 Cor 7:10, 12; 9:14; 12:25); so Holtz, "Paul and the Oral Gospel Tradition," 385. If there is evidence of Jesus-tradition in the context, then the possibility that 1 Thes 4:15 is referring to such tradition becomes a probability.

ans that much of his eschatological teaching is tradition that he has already passed on to the Thessalonian Christians. He has, of course, taught them about the Lord's coming, hence the description in 1 Thes 1:10 of them awaiting God's Son; and he makes it clear, for example, in 5:1, 2 when speaking of "the times and the seasons," that he is reminding them of that earlier teaching: Thus "you do not need to have anything written to you. For you yourselves know very well that the day of the Lord will come. . . ." Similarly in 2 Thessalonians there is an explicit statement that the teaching he is giving is a reminder (2:5). Of course, Paul's earlier teaching need not have been based on Jesus-tradition, "a word of the Lord" in that sense. But the fact that Paul's eschatological teaching in 1 and 2 Thessalonians is recalling tradition lends some support to the view that "the word of the Lord" of 1 Thes 4:15 is a tradition of Jesus.

That case is massively strengthened by the similarity of Paul's teaching on the Lord's coming to the synoptic eschatological traditions.[26] For example, in the verses that immediately follow the reference to "the Lord's word" Paul describes the Lord descending from heaven, with the archangel's call and the sound of God's trumpet, and then "we who are alive" being caught up in the clouds to meet the Lord (4:16-17).[27] The picture is strongly reminiscent of the synoptic description of the coming of the Son of man, on clouds, with angels, gathering the elect; even the "trumpet of God" has an equivalent in the "great trumpet" of Matt 24:31,[28] and the catching up of people to be with the Lord resembles the "Q" description of "one taken, one left" (Matt 24:40, 41/Luke 17:34, 35).[29] Even without looking further, we may conclude that Paul is undoubtedly working with what were to become synoptic traditions of Jesus, and it is plausible to take "the word of the Lord" as referring to such traditions.

The problem remains of identifying the tradition referred to in 1 Thes

26. Even if the synoptic traditions were judged not to go back to Jesus, they do go back to an early date, such that Paul could well have known them as teachings of Jesus.

27. Compare other Pauline passages describing the Lord's coming, e.g., 1 Cor 15:52.

28. See the additional note below on "The Trumpet."

29. Gundry, "Hellenization," 166, rightly says that the "snatching" in the synoptic saying is not necessarily snatching upwards to salvation, though it could have been interpreted in that way. If those who are "taken" are taken off to judgment, then those who are "left" are destined for salvation. Paul could in this case be playing on the words and the ideas when he speaks of "we who are left" (ones who are going to be saved) being "caught up" — not to judgment but to be with the Lord.

4:16, which Paul took as including the dead in the eschatological salvation. Various suggestions have been made as to what Paul may have in mind, most of them not entirely persuasive.[30] Is the particular tradition lost to us? We will return to this question a little further on.

The Thief in the Night

One of Paul's reminders to the Thessalonians is in 1 Thes 5:2, where he comments that "You yourselves know very well that the day of the Lord will come like a thief in the night." He goes on a few verses later to comment that the Thessalonians are "not in darkness, for that day to surprise you like a thief" (5:4). Here we have a tradition indicator ("you know very well") and a description of the Lord's coming that is strikingly similar to the "Q" parable of the thief:

> "Know this: if the owner of the house had known at what hour the thief was coming, he would not have let his house be broken into. You also must be ready, for the Son of Man is coming at an unexpected hour." (Luke 12:39, 40/Matt 24:43, 44)

There is an extremely strong case for linking the Pauline teaching and the "Q" tradition here: In both we have the rather surprising comparison of the Lord's coming to that of a thief (though Jesus' parable more daringly compares the thief and the Son of man, whereas Paul compares the "day" of the Lord, not the Lord himself, to the thief), and in both there is the idea of being surprised or not surprised by the thief.[31]

---

30. See the additional note below on "Suggestions about the 'Word of the Lord' of 1 Thessalonians 4:15."

31. It is possible that Paul's "You yourselves know very well that" is not just a "tradition indicator" but itself a verbal echo of the opening of the parable, "(You) know this, that . . . ,"* though the verb is *oida* in 1 Thessalonians and *ginōskō* in Matthew and Luke. Goulder, *Midrash,* 154; *idem, Luke,* 142, claims that Paul's saying is more primitive than the "Q" parable because less allegorically developed. But this argument assumes that what is less allegorical or parabolic is more primitive, a very questionable view, and that in comparing Paul's simile and Jesus' parable we are comparing like with like. But if Paul is simply alluding to the parable, his form is entirely explicable. Dodd, *More NT Studies,* 23, 24, is clear that the passing simile of Paul is drawn from the vivid parable, not vice versa.

Sleeping and Keeping Awake

Paul goes on from his comment about the thief to speak of the Thessalonians as "children of light and children of day. We are not of the night or of darkness. So then let us not fall asleep as others do, but let us keep awake and be sober. For those who sleep sleep at night, and those who are drunk get drunk at night" (1 Thes 5:5-7). These words on wakefulness and sleeping could simply be Paul's reflection on the idea of the thief in the night.[32] But it may be no coincidence that the parable that precedes the thief in Luke 12 is that of the watchman (12:36-38),[33] which is precisely about the importance of keeping awake. The Greek verbs used in that parable are exactly those used by Paul in 1 Thes 5:6.[34] They are not verbs that he uses frequently elsewhere; indeed, he used his more usual verb for sleeping just a few verses before.[35] It is therefore

---

32. Matthew actually refers to the owner of the house keeping awake in the parable of the thief, but this is not in Luke and is probably a Matthean addition under the influence of the neighboring parable of the watchman; so also his "watch" for Luke's "hour." See my *Rediscovery*, 52-54.

33. It also preceded it in presynoptic tradition, as we argue in the additional note below on "The Eschatological Parables."

34. *Katheudō* and *grēgoreō*. The parable of the watchman is found in Luke 12:36-38/Mark 13:34-36 with an echo in Matt 24:42 and perhaps in the Matthean wording of the parable of the thief *(egrēgorēsen, phylakē)*. Putting the different evidence together, we infer that the parable of the watchman originally was approximately as follows:

> It is like a man awaiting his master, when he will return from a feast, so that when he comes and knocks he may immediately open to him. Blessed is that servant whom the master shall find awake when he comes. (Truly I tell you, the master will gird himself, have the servant sit down, and serve him.) So then keep awake, for you do not know in which watch the master of the house comes, whether in the first, or in the second, or in the third, lest coming suddenly he find you sleeping.

For justification of this reconstruction see my *Rediscovery*, 15-47: Luke has preserved the main body of the parable, but makes it plural to link in with his context. Mark has simply taken the exhortation to wakefulness and has used the Roman enumeration of the watches ("late, midnight," etc.).

35. *Koimaomai* (4:13-15). Paul uses *katheudō* only in 1 Thessalonians 5 and Eph 5:14 and *grēgoreō* elsewhere only in 1 Cor 16:13 and Col 4:2. The two verbs are also used in Matthew's and Mark's account of Gethsemane (Matt 26:40; Mark 14:37). We suggested in chapter 5 above that Paul could well have been influenced by that story, including in Col 4:2. But in 1 Thessalonians 5 the links with the eschatological parables are so numerous as to make it most likely that they are the primary influence on Paul in that chapter at least.

quite plausible to suspect that Paul is echoing the parable of the watchman in 5:6.[36]

The other parable about sleeping and waking in the series of eschatological parables attested in the synoptics is that of the wise and foolish virgins, and it is possible that Paul echoes this as well. In the parable the bridegroom arrives in the middle of the night, and there is a cry: "Look! Here is the bridegroom! Come out to meet him." Then the virgins, who have been asleep, rise up and trim their lamps. The wise virgins go "with him into the wedding banquet," but the foolish virgins are left outside pleading, "Lord, lord, open to us" (Matt 25:6-10).[37] There are various parallels in Paul's description of the second coming in 1 Thessalonians 4:

- Paul speaks of the Lord coming "with a cry of command, with the archangel's call" (v. 16); compare the "cry" of the parable.
- Paul speaks of being "caught up . . . to meet the Lord" (v. 17), using precisely the same rather unusual Greek phrase as is used in the Matthean parable: "come out to meet him."[38]

36. Tuckett, "Synoptic Tradition in 1 Thessalonians," 170-73, doubts the connection, arguing that "keeping awake" in 1 Thessalonians 5 is a daytime activity — Christians belong to the day and the light and for that reason are to keep awake — whereas in the synoptic tradition the watchman is to keep awake in the night. Paul's train of thought starts, therefore, with the idea of the "day" of the Lord (not with the synoptic parable); it is this that leads him to mention (using traditional ideas) keeping awake and sleeping. Tuckett is right about Paul's distinctive idea of wakefulness being appropriate for children of light. But Paul's thought about waking, sleeping, darkness, and light develops not directly from reflection on the day of the Lord but from the thought of the day coming like a thief in the night (see 5:2 and especially v. 4, which leads into v. 5). Paul's train of thought, then, is sparked off at this point by Jesus' parable of the thief. Since that parable is connected in the synoptic tradition with the parable of the watchman, with its emphasis on sleeping and wakefulness, and since Paul goes on to talk about waking and sleeping (using precisely the same vocabulary as the synoptics), it seems highly likely that Paul has been influenced by this parable also, even though he introduces his own reflection on people of the day keeping awake.

37. The parable has been seen as a Matthean construct, not as material going back to Jesus; so, e.g., Donfried, "Allegory of the Ten Virgins," 415-28; he notes connections between the parable and Matt 7:13-27 (and its Lukan parallels). See also Gundry, *Matthew,* 497-99. But the parables on either side of this parable are "Q" parables in which Matthew is usually thought to be dependent on his sources. Furthermore, there is evidence of Luke's familiarity with the parable in Luke 12:35, perhaps also in 12:36 (the reference to the wedding) and 13:25. See my *Rediscovery,* 77-95.

38. *Eis apantēsin* occurs only twice elsewhere in the NT, though it is common enough in the Septuagint (cf. Orchard, "Thessalonians and the Synoptic Gospels"). Withering-

- Paul speaks of God bringing the dead Christians "with him," that is, the Lord, to be "with the Lord" (vv. 14, 17), just as the wise virgins go "with him" into the feast, "him" being the bridegroom, whom the foolish virgins call "Lord."[39]
- Paul is speaking of those who have been "asleep" "rising" to be with Christ; the parable speaks of those who were asleep "rising" to meet the master.
- Paul and the parable are concerned with the moment of the Lord's return.

The combination of parallel phrases and ideas is impressive,[40] and it may well be that we have here the answer to the question we have raised about "the word of the Lord" in 1 Thess 4:15. What "word" did Paul have in mind when he spoke of "those who have fallen asleep"* not missing out on the coming kingdom but being raised to be with Christ? Was it the parable of the virgins, of which there are echoes in the immediately following verses, since it speaks of people sleeping and then rising to enter the feast?[41] It is true that

---

ton, *Jesus, Paul,* 155-58, suggests that Paul's picture of the Lord's coming, including "meeting," may reflect the experience of visitations by kings and dignitaries in the ancient world (e.g., Julius Caesar); see also Gundry, "Hellenization," 162-69. It is certainly possible that the use of a term like *parousia* could reflect this background, but it is not very obviously the explanation of Paul's picture of believers being caught up to meet and then be with the Lord in 1 Thessalonians 4.

39. "With" is *syn* in Paul, *meta* in Matthew.

40. Tuckett, "Synoptic Tradition in 1 Thessalonians," 176-77, finds the parallels "particularly weak," but he only takes real note of *eis apantēsin.* It might just be possible to recognize the links between the parable and the Pauline teaching and then to explain that Matthew constructed the parable out of the sort of Christian teaching about the second coming found in 1 Thessalonians. But that would be a complicated thesis. The parable does not very clearly teach Paul's point about the dead being raised — at best very subtly — and in any case we have plenty of evidence that Paul is drawing on tradition.

41. The parable, of course, does not speak of those "who are left" being "caught up." Tuckett, "Synoptic Tradition in 1 Thessalonians," 181, sees these expressions as probably part of Paul's traditional "word of the Lord." What seems quite possible is that Paul has been influenced in his comment on the fate of the Christian dead not just by the parable of the virgins but also by other elements in Jesus' teaching, e.g., by the synoptic picture of the Son of man coming in the clouds and quite possibly by the thought in Matt 24:40, 41/Luke 17:34, 35 of one being "taken" and the other "left." Paul does not reproduce precisely the same ideas as these synoptic traditions, but he uses them creatively to make his point. There is plenty of evidence, as we have seen, of Paul drawing on a variety of traditions.

the parable was probably not intended by Jesus to address questions of death and resurrection. But it is also true that Paul, faced with the question of Christians who died, could have taken the parable as justification from Jesus for the view that Christians who have "fallen asleep," that is, have died, will rise and go to be with Jesus.[42]

Paul may also reflect knowledge of the parable in Rom 13:11, where he comments that it is already "the moment for you to wake [literally "be raised"] from sleep." The passage in Romans is thematically very similar to 1 Thessalonians 5, speaking of the coming day of the Lord and of night, darkness, and light; it is likely that Paul is drawing on the same eschatological traditions in the two passages. If he is echoing the parable of the virgins in Rom 13:11, then here he is using it not to relate to the question of resurrection but more straightforwardly to urge the Romans to wake up for the Lord's coming.[43]

42. The Pauline interpretation of the parable is not as farfetched as it might appear: Whereas the parable of the watchman speaks of the importance of "staying awake" and is naturally applied to those who are alive, the parable of the virgins speaks of those who fall asleep (with justification, because of the passing of time) but are still ready, and this might not unnaturally have been seen as speaking of Christians who die. The one parable speaks of a culpable sleep and the other of a sleep that is not culpable, as does Paul in 1 Thessalonians 4 and 5. Donfried, "Allegory of the Ten Virgins," 424-25, argues that Matthew himself understood the parable of the virgins as referring to death and resurrection. Schenk, in "Auferweckung der Toten," rightly observes the links between the parable and Paul's teaching in 1 Thessalonians 4, but postulates an improbable original form of the parable that had all ten virgins entering the feast at the bridegroom's coming. His reconstruction is unnecessary so far as Paul's point is concerned; it eliminates the note of judgment that is found in other eschatological parables and involves Matthew in a radical rewriting of the parable, which is improbable. (Matthew treats the neighboring parables quite conservatively.) See my Rediscovery, 90.

43. Feine, Jesus Christus und Paulus, 290-91, detects the parable of the virgins behind 1 Cor 4:10 and that of the sheep and goats in 1 Cor 8:12. The second suggestion is slightly more persuasive than the first.

There are other possible echoes of Jesus-tradition in Rom 13:11-14. Paul speaks of knowing the "moment" of salvation being "nearer" than when we believed and of the day being "near" in language that is strongly reminiscent of gospel traditions, including the keynote Markan verse "The moment has been filled up, the kingdom of God has come near"* (Mark 1:14) and, more significantly, of the synoptic eschatological discourse, where in the Markan version Jesus speaks of the eschatological "moment" and in the Lukan version urges the disciples to lift up their heads when "these things" begin to happen, "because your redemption is drawing near" (Mark 13:33; Luke 21:28).

Admittedly Mark 13:33 has Jesus tell the disciples to "keep awake, for you do *not* know when the moment is,"* whereas Paul says that the Romans do "know what time

The Stewards

The argument about echoes of Jesus' eschatological parables in 1 Thessalonians 4 and 5 may be strengthened by evidence that the parables are echoed elsewhere in Paul's letters, as in Romans 13. The parable of the faithful and unfaithful stewards, which is adjacent to the parable of the thief in the eschatological parables of Matthew 24, 25/Luke 12, reads as follows in Matthew's version (24:45-51/Luke 12:41-46):

> Who then is the faithful and wise slave, whom his master has put in charge of his household, to give the other slaves their allowance of food at the proper time? Blessed is that slave whom his master will find at work when he arrives. Truly I tell you, he will put that one in charge of all his possessions. But if that wicked slave says to himself, "My master is delayed," and he begins to beat his fellow slaves, and eats and drinks with drunkards, the master of that slave will come on a day when he does not expect him and at an hour that he does not know. He will cut him in pieces and put him with the hypocrites. . . .

This parable is not clearly echoed in 1 Thessalonians.[44] But there is a probable echo in 1 Cor 4:1-5, where Paul describes himself and Apollos as "servants . . . and stewards" of whom it is required that "they be found faithful."* Paul tells the Corinthians not to "pronounce judgment before the time, before the Lord comes. . . . Then each one will receive commendation from God." We notice several parallels here to the synoptic parable:

- In both the theme is the eschatological day, when "the Lord comes."
- In both the picture is of a master and his servant or steward.[45]

---

it is, how it is now the moment for you to wake from sleep" (13:11). Paul is not denying the Lord's teaching about the unknown hour, but he is presupposing that things have moved on since Jesus' time and that salvation is now near. See Thompson, *Clothed with Christ*, 143-49; he notes the use of "waking-sleeping" language in the Gethsemane narratives.

44. It may be possible to link the "drunkenness" of 1 Thes 5:7 with the drunkenness of the unfaithful steward; so Orchard, "Thessalonians and the Synoptic Gospels," 30. But there is a more plausible link between 1 Thes 5:7 and Luke 21:34-36b. See further below.

45. Paul applies the picture to Christian ministry, and Jesus' parable is quite probably understood by Matthew and Luke to refer to Christian leaders who have responsibility for feeding those in their charge (this being the implication of the question

- In both the question is one of "faithfulness."
- Both refer to the servant being "found" when the Lord returns.[46]
- Both refer to reward, though "praise"* in 1 Cor 4:5 is perhaps more reminiscent of the parable of the talents/pounds ("Well done, good and faithful servant,"* Matt 25:21/Luke 19:17). It may be that Paul's language here, as in 1 Thessalonians, is influenced by more than one parable.[47]

The influence of Jesus' eschatological teaching on Paul in his reflection on himself and Apollos may be confirmed by 1 Cor 3:13, where Paul speaks of "the Day" making clear the value of each person's work and says that it will be "revealed with fire."[48] The possible parallel here is with Luke 17:29, 30, where Jesus is speaking very specifically about "the day" (see 17:24, 26, 27, 29, 30, 31), that is, the day of the coming of the Son of man, which is a day of judgment. Jesus compares the days of Lot, when "fire and sulphur" rained from heaven and "destroyed all of them." Then he comments that "it will be like that on the day that the Son of Man is revealed." The combination of "the day," the "fire" of judgment, and revelation is striking. There are differences between the picture in the sayings of Jesus and the points being made by Paul: Jesus speaks of fire destroying the wicked in Lot's day and of the Son of man being revealed, Paul of people's work being revealed and of the fire testing their work (though he goes on to warn of God destroying those who destroy the temple, v. 17). But it may well be that Paul is influenced by this Jesus-tradition as he develops his own argument about himself and Apollos.[49]

---

that precedes the parable in Luke and, arguably, in the presynoptic form of the tradition also known to Mark, i.e., Luke 12:41); see my *Parables of Jesus*, 78.

46. The verb *katalambanō*, used in 1 Thes 5:4 of the coming day of the Lord, is sometimes used in the LXX to translate the Hebrew word for "find."

47. The parable of the talents may also be reflected in the teaching on different gifts in 1 Corinthians 12–14. In the parable the master sovereignly "gives" different amounts to "each" servant, according to his ability (Matt 25:15; cf. Mark 13:34); in 1 Cor 12:7, 11, the Spirit "gives"/"distributes" gifts and ministries "to each" as he wills. If the parable of the talents does lie behind some of Paul's thinking here, then it is interesting that he uses it to speak of all the members of the church, whereas he uses the parable of the steward to speak particularly of church leaders such as himself and Apollos.

48. This Pauline passage is one in which we have already noted possible echoes from the Jesus-tradition; see chapter 5 above on the "foundation."

49. The Lukan saying about the days of Lot comes in a "Q" passage but is not found in Matthew, so it is possible to regard the saying and also the saying about the Son of man being "revealed" as Lukan and without a good claim to be authentic teaching

The Lord's Sudden Coming

A final point of possible connection between 1 Thessalonians 4 and 5 and the Jesus-tradition relates particularly to 1 Thes 5:3, where Paul, speaking of the "day of the Lord," says: "When they say, 'There is peace and security,' then sudden destruction will come upon them, as labor pains come upon a pregnant woman, and there will be no escape!" The synoptic parallel in this case is Luke's conclusion to the eschatological discourse, 21:34-36:

> Be on guard so that your hearts are not weighed down with dissipation and drunkenness and the worries of this life, and that day catch you unexpectedly, like a trap. For it will come upon all who live on the face of the whole earth. Be alert [= "keep awake"] at all times, praying that you may have the strength to escape all these things that will take place, and to stand before the Son of Man.

We note the following similarities:

- Paul speaks of "the day of the Lord" (1 Thes 5:2), and Luke warns of "that day."
- Paul speaks of "sudden destruction" coming when people think all is peaceful and safe; Luke warns of dissipation and worldly cares, because the day will catch people "unexpectedly" (the same relatively unusual Greek adjective).[50]
- Paul says that the destruction "will come on them," Luke that the day "will come on you,"* with the same verb.[51]
- Paul says that the day will come "as labor pains come upon a pregnant

---

of Jesus. But there is reason to believe that the sayings were in Luke's and Matthew's source. I have discussed these traditions in *Rediscovery,* 150-59, though I would not now agree with all the arguments presented there. I now consider Luke's form of the sayings in 17:26-30 in most respects superior to Matt 24:37-39. Matthew replaces the Lukan references to the "day(s) of the Son of man" with references to the "parousia" in his vv. 37 and 39 (cf. Luke 17:26, 30). Introducing the change in v. 37 forces Matthew to rephrase the sayings about Noah (vv. 37-39, see *Rediscovery*); rather than do the same for the Lot sayings and for the sake of brevity, Matthew omits the Lot sayings, only retaining his version of the conclusion (i.e., Matt 24:39b/Luke 17:30).

50. *Aiphnidios,* used only in these two verses in the NT.

51. *Ephistēmi,* common enough in Luke-Acts, but found only here and in 2 Tim 4:2, 6 in the Pauline corpus.

woman," and Luke speaks of it coming "like a trap" — a different image, but both expressing something sudden and painful and possibly going back to one common Hebrew-Aramaic word.[52]

• Paul says that "they will not escape";* Luke urges prayer "that you may have the strength to escape," again the same verb.[53]

• Paul goes on in subsequent verses to urge wakefulness, sobriety, and the putting on of God's armor, because God has destined us for salvation through Christ (1 Thes 5:6-9); Luke warns against dissipation and drunkenness and urges prayerful wakefulness[54] to be able to escape and to stand before the Son of man. The thought is broadly similar, though in 1 Thes 5:3-9 Paul does not have the emphasis on praying at every moment or on "standing" (and Luke has no armor). But later in 1 Thessalonians 5, and in other Pauline passages, there is an emphasis on persistent prayer (e.g., 1 Thes 5:17; 2 Thes 1:11; Phil 1:4; Col 1:3).[55]

52. Hebrew-Aramaic ḥebel/ḥablāʾ can mean either "rope" (hence trap) or "birth pains." See Hartman, Prophecy Interpreted, 192. Holtz, "Paul and the Oral Gospel Tradition," 388, argues that "escape" fits Luke's "trap" but not Paul's "birth pains." The two Greek words pagis and ōdin are associated in the LXX (e.g., Ps 18:6). In Rediscovery, 111-13, I argue that Paul has substituted ōdin for pagis under the influence of Isa 13:6, 7; Jer 6:14. But he may also have been influenced by Jesus' words about the eschatological birth pains as recorded in Matt 24:8/Mark 13:8. See also the image of birth pains applied to eschatological sufferings in Rom 8:22.

53. Ekpheugō, used three times in the Lukan writings and three times in the Pauline writings.

54. The call to persistent praying does not, of course, only come in the Gospels in Luke 21:36. The sermon on the mount urges disciples to "ask . . . seek . . . knock" (Matt 7:7), and the message of Jesus' parable of the unjust judge is, according to Luke, "about their need to pray always and not to lose heart" (Luke 18:1-8).

55. Eph 6:11-18 is especially interesting in this connection, since there we find (1) the "armor" theme that also occurs in 1 Thes 5:8, 9; (2) a strong emphasis on "standing" and "praying" ("at all times," v. 18) and "keeping awake," all three ideas that are important in Luke 21:34-36 (the same verb for "keep awake" is used in Eph 6:18 and Luke 21:36 — agrypneō, not grēgoreō as in most other Pauline and synoptic contexts); (3) other possible links to the synoptic eschatological traditions, including the exhortation to "gird up your loins" "in readiness"* (6:14, 15; cf. Luke 12:35, 40, etc.). It seems likely that the Ephesians passage is influenced by the same eschatological traditions as 1 Thessalonians 4 and 5 and that both are related to the traditions in Luke 21:34-36. (Note that Rom 13:11-14 also links the wakefulness and armor themes.) For fuller discussion of the traditions concerned see my Rediscovery, 110-17.

Commentators have observed that the language used in 1 Thes 5:3 is not typically Pauline.[56] This, together with the accumulation of verbal and thematic parallels that we have noted, suggests quite strongly that Paul has again been influenced by Jesus-tradition that in this case is attested only in Luke.[57]

2 THESSALONIANS 2

Nothing decisive hangs on the evidence of 2 Thessalonians so far as the thesis of the book is concerned, but, given the strong (though disputed) arguments for its authenticity,[58] it would be foolish to ignore its evidence, even if it should be treated as slightly provisional. As it happens, the evidence of connections with the synoptic eschatological traditions is strong, and in this respect at least 2 Thessalonians is very similar to 1 Thessalonians.

The crucial evidence is in 2 Thessalonians 2, where Paul, if it was Paul writing, teaches about the "parousia of our Lord Jesus Christ and our gathering to him"* (2:1). The teaching concerned is in response to what was happening in the Thessalonian church, with some saying that "the day of the Lord has come"* (2:2).[59] But, as we have noted, Paul explains that

56. Best, *1 and 2 Thessalonians*, 207, notes the impersonal "they say" and unusual words "safety," "sudden," "come on."

57. For a quite different interpretation of the evidence see also the additional note below, "Is Luke 21:34-36 Dependent on 1 Thessalonians 5:3-8?"

In view of the accumulation of echoes of the synoptic eschatological traditions in 1 Thessalonians 5, it is tempting to connect 5:1, 2, "*Concerning the times and seasons* . . . you do not need to have anything written to you. For you yourselves know . . . ," with Matt 24:36/Mark 13:32, "*Concerning that day and hour* no one knows . . . ," and with what is sometimes seen as Luke's equivalent in Acts 1:7, "It is not for you to know *the times or periods* that the Father has set . . ." (see Orchard, "Thessalonians," 26, 27). In view of the similar wording, the reference back to the Thessalonians' prior knowledge, and the fact that Paul knows the parables that follow the Matthew/Mark saying, it may be that there is some sort of echo here. (Even though Paul speaks of the Thessalonians "knowing" rather than "not knowing" — contrast the Gospels and Acts — what they know is that the day comes like a thief, i.e., that they do not know!) But the phrase in 1 Thes 5:1 makes perfectly good sense as Paul's own introduction to the topic he is about to discuss. (See also Tuckett, "Synoptic Tradition in 1 Thessalonians," 169.)

58. See, e.g., Best, *1 and 2 Thessalonians*, 50-58; I. H. Marshall, *1 and 2 Thessalonians*, 28-45.

59. On the meaning of the phrase see Holman, *Eschatological Delay*, 175-85. Paul's comment in 1 Thes 2:16 about "the wrath" having come on the Jews, if we interpreted that phrase correctly, could have been the catalyst that led the Thessalonians to conclude that the day of the Lord had come (see our discussion of 1 Thes 2:16 above).

the teaching he gives is by way of reminder to the Thessalonians of what they had already heard from him, which is thus in that sense at least "a tradition" (2:5). That this tradition was teaching of Jesus is strongly suggested by the string of connections between 2 Thessalonians 2 and the synoptic eschatological discourse.

The very phrase with which Paul opens the section in 2:1, "the parousia of our Lord Jesus Christ and our gathering to him,"* may be significant, with "gathering" *(episynagōgē)* being from the same Greek root as that used in the synoptic description of the Son of man and his angels "gathering" the elect (Matt 24:31/Mark 13:27). And there are more substantial points of similarity.

The Call Not to Be Shaken or Misled

Paul responds to the Thessalonians' idea about the day of the Lord having come by telling them in 2:2, 3 "not to be quickly shaken in mind or excited by either spirit or word, or by letter purporting to be from us, to the effect that the day of the Lord has come. Let no one deceive you in any way."* This opening is closely paralleled thematically and verbally by the opening of the synoptic eschatological discourse, where Jesus says in Mark 13:5-7 (similarly with minor variations Matt 24:4-6; Luke 21:8, 9): "Watch out lest anyone deceive you. Many will come in my name saying that I am (he) and will mislead many. When you hear of wars and rumors of wars, do not get excited. It must happen but the end is not yet."*

Here we notice

- a very similar theme: people announcing the Lord's coming prematurely,[60]
- a warning against being disturbed and excited by the false rumors, including the same Greek word for becoming excited,[61] and
- a similarly phrased warning against deceivers:
  - "watch lest anyone mislead you"* (Mark/Matthew);
  - "lest anyone deceive you"* (Paul).[62]

---

60. Luke 21:8 has them say: "The time is near."

61. *Throeomai* is found in the NT only in Matt 24:6/Mark 13:7; 2 Thes 2:2; and in some manuscripts in Luke 24:37. Luke 21:9 (and other manuscripts of 24:37) have the rather similar *ptoeomai*.

62. 2 Thes 2:3: *mē tis hymas exapatēsē;* Matt 24:4/Mark 13:5 has *mē tis hymas planēsē.*

A Terrible Event Must Precede the End

In countering the false excitement Paul explains that the day of the Lord will not come "unless the rebellion comes first and the lawless one is revealed." He infers that when this terrible event does occur, then the Lord will come, destroying "the lawless one" "by the manifestation of his coming" (2 Thes 2:3-8). The synoptic eschatological discourse similarly describes a terrible event: Matthew and Mark speak of the "desolating sacrilege" and of accompanying distress; they then go on to refer to the Son of man coming to gather his elect "after that suffering" (Matt 24:15-31/Mark 13:14-27; compare Luke's somewhat different 21:20-27).[63]

Paul speaks of this terrible event as the revealing of "the lawless one," the one who opposes every god and sanctuary, setting himself up in the temple and calling himself a god. The picture is unmistakably that of Antiochus Epiphanes, who defiled the Jewish temple in 167 BC, claimed divinity, and who became in Jewish thinking the epitome of lawlessness. In the synoptic eschatological discourse the "desolating sacrilege" evokes precisely the same background of thought: The sacrilege was the pagan altar set up in Jerusalem, and the synoptic passage speaking of terrible distress and of people in Judea fleeing to the hills (as did the Maccabees in 167 BC) thus envisages a rerun of that terrible event.[64]

Misleading Signs and Wonders

Paul speaks of "the lawless one" coming "in the working of Satan" with "all power, signs, lying wonders, and every kind of wicked deception for those who are perishing." The Matthean/Markan eschatological discourse, after describing the "desolating sacrilege," goes on to speak of "false messiahs and false prophets" doing "signs and omens, to lead astray, if possible, the elect" (Matt 24:24/Mark 13:22).[65]

63. Luke's quite distinctive form of the eschatological discourse is explained by some simply in terms of his redaction of Mark, but it more probably reflects Luke's use of independent sources. For detailed discussion of this and of the relationship of the Lukan and Matthew/Mark traditions see my *Rediscovery*.

64. There may be a closer terminological link between the synoptic and Pauline traditions than at first appears, with the terms "sacrilege" and "lawlessness" and "desolation" and "destruction" (2 Thes 2:3) being associated in the LXX. See Ford, *Abomination of Desolation*, 223. See also Burnett, *Testament of Jesus-Sophia*, 327-33; D. Wenham, "Note on Matthew 24:10-12."

65. An important parallel to the synoptic and Pauline traditions is in Revelation's

The parallel between 2 Thessalonians 2 and the synoptic eschatological discourse is not exact. Paul speaks of a "lawless one," the Gospels of a "desolating sacrilege."[66] The ideas are similar, but the language is different. Paul also speaks of someone "restraining" the lawless one; the Gospels have no obvious equivalent notion, unless it is in the reference to the gospel being preached to all nations before the end (Matt 24:14; Mark 13:10), as is possible.[67] But the parallelism of ideas and language is such as to make it virtually certain that Paul is here drawing on the tradition attested in the Gospels.

1 THESSALONIANS 2:15, 16

In 1 Thes 2:14-16 Paul writes to the Thessalonians about their sufferings, and comments on how they are following the example of the Christians in Judea who also suffered acutely at the hands of the Jews. He describes "the Jews" as those

> who killed both the Lord Jesus and the prophets, and drove us out; they displease God and oppose everyone by hindering us from speaking to the Gentiles so that they may be saved. Thus they have constantly been filling up the measure of their sins; but God's wrath has overtaken them at last [or "to the end"].

This harsh denunciation of the Jews for their opposition to the gospel and in particular to the evangelization of Gentiles has often been seen as atypical of Paul — in vocabulary and sentiment — and has so been regarded as an interpolation into the Pauline letter. This view is confirmed if the mysterious reference to wrath having come on them is rightly seen as an allusion to the events of AD 70, as some have proposed, since Paul wrote 1 Thessalonians long before AD 70.

The argument is, however, far from decisive.[68] Not only is there no

---

description of the beast, which is accompanied by a second beast who does misleading signs (Revelation 13; cf. 19:20).

66. But Matthew does refer to the multiplication of "lawlessness" (24:12). See my discussion of this in *Rediscovery*, 256-59. Mark has a masculine adjective, "standing," indicating that he associates the sacrilege with an individual.

67. For useful discussion of the "restrainer" see Holman, *Eschatological Delay*, 203-28. He concludes that God is the one who "restrains" as he works out his plans (including those for evangelization). Compare the two witnesses in Revelation 11, and see Ford, *Abomination of Desolation*, 211-25.

68. See recently Simpson, "Problems Posed by 1 Thessalonians 2:15-16"; Weatherley, "Authenticity of 1 Thessalonians 2.13-16."

textual evidence supporting the interpolation theory, but the unusual features of the verses are at least as well explained by the suggestion that Paul is echoing traditions that he has received.

The Sayings in Matthew 23:29-38/Luke 11:47-51

The traditions that Paul may well be using are seen in Matt 23:29-38/Luke 11:47-51, the part of Jesus' "woes" on the scribes and Pharisees where he speaks about the persecution of the prophets.[69] The most striking parallels to 1 Thes 2:15, 16 are in Matt 23:32, 34-36/Luke 11:48, 49-51:[70]

Matt 23:32 "Fill up, then, the measure of your ancestors."	**Luke 11:48** "You . . . approve of the deeds of your ancestors. . . .
23:34 "Therefore I send you prophets, sages, and scribes, some of whom you will kill and crucify, and some you will flog in your synagogues and pursue from town to town,	**11:49** Therefore also the Wisdom of God said, 'I will send them prophets and apostles, some of whom they will kill and persecute,'
23:35, 36 so that upon you may come all the righteous blood shed on earth. . . . Truly I tell you, all this will come upon this generation. "	**11:50, 51** so that this generation may be charged with the blood of all the prophets shed since the foundation of the world. . . . Yes, I tell you, it will be charged against this generation."

The similarities between 1 Thes 2:15, 16 and these "Q" verses are as follows:

---

69. Matthew and Luke have significantly different versions of the woes, which probably suggests that they were known to both of them independently.

70. Steck, *Israel*, 276, 291, finds the principal links to be between 1 Thes 2:15, 16 and the parable of Mark 12:1-9. The parallels are notable, but less close than with Matt 23:29-36/Luke 11:47-50.

Paul has been speaking of "the Jews" and in particular of the Jewish opponents of Christianity in Judea.	Jesus in the "Q" tradition addresses leaders of Palestinian Judaism.
Paul says that they "killed both the Lord Jesus and the prophets" and "pursued us."*	Jesus speaks of them killing and pursuing "prophets, sages, and scribes" (Matthew) or "prophets and apostles" (Luke).
Paul, after further describing their opposition to the gospel, comments that "thus they have constantly been filling up the measure of their sins."	Jesus according to Matthew says: "Fill up, then, the measure of your ancestors."
Paul goes on to say that "wrath has overtaken them at last."	Jesus speaks of the blood of the prophets being avenged on "this generation."

The similarity of thought and even wording is striking.[71] Admittedly Luke does not have the Matthean "Fill up, then, the measure of your ancestors" (Matt 23:32), which is one of the most impressive parallels to the Pauline text. But Matthew may well have the "Q" wording at this point.[72] In any case the other parallels are enough to make it likely that Paul's language in 1 Thes 2:15, 16 is unusual because he is echoing this Jesus-tradition.[73]

Wrath in 1 Thessalonians 2:16 and Luke 21:23

And there are other interesting parallels to 1 Thess 2:15, 16. Paul says of the Jews in 1 Thes 2:16c that "wrath has overtaken them at last." We sug-

---

71. Goulder, *Midrash*, 165, finds another parallel between Matt 23:13 and 1 Thes 2:16.

72. See further in the additional note below on "Filling Up Sins."

73. Tuckett, "Synoptic Tradition in 1 Thessalonians," 165-67, fails to allow for the cumulative force of the evidence, arguing that each of the parallels is otherwise explicable. For example, he notes that "killing the prophets" is a common Jewish idea, but he fails to bring out the way that in Paul and the synoptics we find killing, pursuing, and "us"/"apostles" together. Goulder, *Midrash*, 165, sees Matthew as dependent on Paul here, but he does not explain the unusual features of the Pauline passage.

gested above when explaining Paul's teaching that he might have had in mind the traumatic events that affected the Jews of the Roman Empire in AD 49, but also that he may have been assuming that his readers were familiar with the thought of "wrath" to come on the Jews. His obscurity could in part be because he was alluding to a tradition that they knew.

Luke in his version of the eschatological discourse describes Jesus as speaking of the coming desolation of Jerusalem and saying (in 21:23): "There will be great distress on the earth and *wrath against this people.*" The possibility that suggests itself is that here we have the tradition to which Paul alludes in 1 Thes 2:16c.[74] If it is, then what we effectively have in 1 Thes 2:15, 16 is a combination of the sayings about the persecution of the prophets (seen in Matt 23:32, 34-36/Luke 11:48, 49-51) with the phrase about "wrath against this people" from the eschatological discourse as recorded in Luke.[75] The combination is thoroughly intelligible, since the sayings about the prophets end with the warning of dire judgment coming on "this generation." Paul has thus interpreted that warning in terms of the eschatological discourse.[76]

This suggestion may sound too ingenious to be likely. However, there is much to be said for it: (1) There is the similarity of the wording about "wrath" in 1 Thes 2:16 and Luke 21:23. (2) It makes good sense of Paul's mysterious warning in 1 Thes 2:16 if he is alluding to a known tradition that was something like the eschatological discourse. He could well have seen in the recent actions of the Romans against the Jews the beginning of the disasters predicted for the Jews and Jerusalem in the discourse.[77] (3) The

74. Paul's use of the phrase about the wrath having come on the people would not on its own point to a connection to the similar Lukan verse. The phraseology could be otherwise explained, e.g., in terms of a parallel in *Testament of Levi* 6:11. But the phrase does take on significance in the context of the other considerations that we note.

75. Note that the verbal parallels of the synoptic "persecuting the prophets" tradition are all in 1 Thes 2:15, 16a, b, whereas the verbal parallels of Luke 21:23 are in 1 Thes 2:16c.

76. Tuckett, "Synoptic Tradition in 1 Thessalonians," 166, criticizes my earlier use of Matthew 23 (in *Rediscovery*) to illuminate Paul's difficult phraseology and says that it is necessary to establish substantial parallelism between texts before using "details of the one to determine the exegesis of the other." I would argue that, although the Pauline text is notoriously difficult to interpret, it is at least plausibly interpreted in a sense that is parallel to the synoptic material, and that the detailed points of similarity between the Pauline and synoptic texts, which suggest contact between them, add to the plausibility of that interpretation.

77. It is easy to see how the atrocities that occurred in Jerusalem under the Roman

interpretation of the "judgment on this generation" sayings of Matt 23:35, 36/Luke 11:50, 51 in terms of the eschatological discourse is attested in Matthew, since Matthew has the discourse (ch. 24) following directly on from those sayings.[78] (4) We have seen other evidence that Paul and the Thessalonians knew the eschatological discourse (see above on 1 Thes 4:16 and 2 Thessalonians 2).

(5) There is other evidence of Paul's familiarity with the distinctively Lukan form of the eschatological discourse. We have already seen echoes of Luke 21:34-36 in 1 Thes 5:3-6. There is also the evidence of Rom 11:25, where Paul says: "A hardening has come . . . on Israel until the fulness of the Gentiles comes in,"* which is intriguingly similar to Luke 21:23, 24, where the reference to "wrath against this people" is followed by a description of Jerusalem being "trampled on by the Gentiles, until the times of the Gentiles are fulfilled."[79] In both texts there is the thought of judgment on the Jews until a period of Gentile victory or salvation is completed.[80]

The interest of the Rom 11:25 evidence from our point of view is not just that it is another possible echo of Luke 21:23, 24 to put alongside 1 Thes 2:16, but that there is a three-way parallelism between the texts:

---

governor Cumanus, as described by Josephus, might have been seen as the beginnings of a new desecration of the temple like the earlier one under Antiochus: The atrocities began with a Roman soldier publicly insulting the temple by an indecent act, continued with a terrible massacre of protestors, and were followed by other outrages against the Jewish law. Even to the modern historian the events of AD 49 may be seen as something like the beginning of the end, so far as Jerusalem was concerned; it was only a matter of time until the outbreak of the disastrous Jewish war of AD 66-70. Compare Kasher, *Jews and Hellenistic Cities,* 253.

78. Note also the linking phrases "all these things," "this generation" in 23:36; 24:33, 34.

79. Luke's reference to "the times of the Gentiles" could be intended negatively to refer to the time of Gentile domination of Jerusalem; if it was so intended, Paul could still have taken the tradition and interpreted it differently — of the Gentile mission to which he was so committed. But Luke's use of the word *kairoi,* "times," and his own interest in the Gentile mission mean that it is quite probable that he understood the phrase positively in the sense of Mark 13:10. See Bosch, *Heidenmission,* 172-74.

80. The Lukan "wrath" and Paul's "hardening" are not identical concepts, but Rom 9:22 uses the word "wrath," and Paul could well have interpreted Jewish unbelief as part of the "wrath." See our discussion of Paul's eschatology above, pp. 299-302.

Luke 21:23, 24	1 Thes 2:16	Rom 11:25
"Wrath against this people. . . . until the times of the Gentiles are fulfilled"	"Wrath has come on them to the end"* in the context of a reference to Gentile mission	"A hardening on Israel until the fullness of the Gentiles come in"*

The parallelism among these texts is not just verbal, but involves ideas as well — with the idea of judgment on the Jews and opportunity for the Gentiles coming together within an eschatological framework moving toward "the end." Furthermore, the verbal parallelism is between Luke 21:23 and 1 Thes 2:16 on the one hand, and between Luke 21:24 and Rom 11:25 on the other hand. The meshing pattern of agreements is such as to make it thoroughly plausible to suppose that the Lukan traditions are being echoed (though interpreted differently) in both Pauline texts.

(6) Finally, the last phrase of 1 Thes 2:16, "at last,"* is literally "to (the) end"* and is paralleled in the eschatological discourse in Matt 24:13/Mark 13:13,[81] "The one who endures *to the end* will be saved."[82] "End" *(telos)* also occurs in the Matthean form of the saying in Matt 24:14/Mark 13:10, "This good news of the kingdom will be proclaimed throughout the world, as a testimony to all the nations; and then the end will come."[83] The ideas found in Matt 24:13, 14/Mark 13:13, 10 of "the end," eschatological "salvation," and proclamation of the gospel to the nations are all paralleled in different ways in 1 Thes 2:16 and Rom 11:25, 26. This may confirm that Paul has been influenced by the traditions of the eschatological discourse in these passages.

There are possible objections to the case we have presented. Many critics, for example, see the section of the Lukan eschatological discourse

81. Luke 21:19 is a paraphrastic version of the same saying.

82. The meaning of *eis telos* in 1 Thes 2:16 is debated. See Witherington, *Jesus, Paul,* who concludes that it probably means "until/unto the end"; Donfried, "Paul and Judaism," 252-53, takes the same view, and compares Romans 11 with its suggestion of judgment lasting on the Jews until the parousia, when God's mercy will be shown. If "until the end" is the correct translation, then it is parallel to the synoptic phrase in meaning. If the more usual translations (e.g., "at last," "finally") are preferred, Paul could still have been influenced by the language used in the Jesus-tradition.

83. There is reason to believe that the Matthean wording may be more original than the Markan wording, Mark having shifted the saying from its original location, which is seen in Matthew, to go with his v. 9. See n. 11 above. J. P. Brown, "Synoptic Parallels," 38, compares Mark 13:10/Matt 24:14 with Phil 1:16; Rom 1:1, 5.

containing the saying about "wrath" as Luke's modification of Mark, written in the light of the events of AD 70. Paul could, therefore, not have known it when writing 1 Thessalonians in perhaps AD 49. This view would not necessarily undermine the whole argument: Luke rewriting Mark after AD 70 would still be a witness to an interpretation of the eschatological discourse in terms of "wrath against this people" that could well go back much earlier and might be reflected in 1 Thes 2:16. But it is by no means certain that the Lukan discourse is a Lukan adaptation of Mark. We have already seen evidence that some of the distinctive Lukan traditions — those in 21:34-36 — were known to Paul, and it may well be that other Lukan elements in the discourse go back equally early and were also known to Paul.[84]

A different objection to what we have proposed has to do with the legitimacy of using not just Lukan, but also Markan and distinctively Matthean traditions, in arguing for the influence of the Jesus-tradition on Paul. We have suggested that in 1 Thes 2:15, 16 Paul may have been influenced not only by sayings found in the Lukan version of the discourse, but also by Matthean and Markan traditions. Are we then to think that Paul knew something like the Lukan form of the eschatological discourse, as well as the Markan and the Matthean forms? This sounds suspiciously like parallelomania.

It is, however, nothing of the sort. In the first place, there is no reason at all why there should not have been different versions of the discourse around when Paul was writing — maybe something like the Matthew/Mark version and also one or more heavily interpreted versions, such as we find in Luke. Paul could perfectly well have known and been influenced by more than one version. In the second place — and this is probably the more significant consideration — there is good evidence that Matthew and Luke,

---

84. Against the view that Luke 21 is a post-AD 70 redaction of what we have in Mark, see my *Rediscovery*, 175-218; Dodd, *More NT Studies*, 69-83. The distinctive features of the Lukan discourse (e.g., the references to armies surrounding Jerusalem) do not, as is sometimes thought, prove that Luke is writing after AD 70: They do not correspond exactly to what happened (e.g., there is no reference to the city being burned in Luke 21); they mostly have an OT background, and, if Luke is using Mark, they are well explained in terms of Luke's desire to clarify the rather obscure Markan description of the "desolating sacrilege" language. But Luke is almost certainly not wholly dependent on Mark. We have seen that Paul was probably familiar with the material found at the end of the discourse (Luke 21:34-36), this therefore being a non-Markan tradition. It may very well be that other parts of the Lukan discourse, including the reference to "wrath against this people," could be early and independent tradition.

though they may well have used Mark, also had independent sources at certain points. The evidence that they had independent access to presynoptic traditions is particularly strong in some of the eschatological sayings, including the eschatological parables,[85] and we have seen reason to think that Paul knew such presynoptic traditions. It is, therefore, not just legitimate but also important to consider Paul as a possible witness to distinctive elements in the different Gospels.

We conclude that the case for Paul being influenced in 1 Thes 2:15, 16 by the traditions of Luke 21:23, 24 is (however surprisingly) a good possibility, especially given the stronger evidence of the influence of the traditions of Matt 23:32, 34-36/Luke 11:48, 49-51 in the same verses.

THE CALL TO SUFFER

The saying of Jesus that "the one who endures to the end will be saved," the phraseology of which may be echoed in 1 Thes 2:14-16, is an exhortation to stand firm in face of persecution and suffering. In all three synoptic versions of the eschatological discourse there is a strong emphasis on coming sufferings — on natural and human-made disasters in the world, then specifically on the sufferings and hatred that Christians will face,[86] and then on the distress and agony that will accompany the desolation of Jerusalem (Matt 24:6-22/Mark 13:7-20/Luke 21:9-24).

Paul speaks in 1 Thes 3:3, 4 of the Thessalonians' faith and says that he sent Timothy to them "so that no one would be shaken by these persecutions. Indeed, you yourselves know that this is what we are destined for. In fact, when we were with you, we told you beforehand that we were to suffer persecution; so it turned out, as you know."

Here Paul is referring back to something he has taught the Thessalonians. Suffering was part of the Pauline tradition. There is no need necessarily to associate this Pauline tradition with the Jesus-tradition; Paul had plenty

---

85. See the additional note below on "The Eschatological Parables."

86. Mark and Matthew diverge quite markedly at this point: Matthew has the material found in Mark 13:9-13 within his version of the mission discourse (Matt 10:17-22), and he has a non-Markan tradition in 24:9-14. The relationship of the differing traditions here cannot be disentangled simply. See my *Rediscovery*, 219-52, for the view that Mark has interpolated the sayings about appearing before sanhedrins and synagogues into the presynoptic form of the eschatological discourse and that Matthew has brought his verses 10-12 into the discourse.

of firsthand experience of suffering. On the other hand, the reference to Christians being "destined" for suffering may suggest something theologically based rather than simply arising out of Paul's experience; Paul uses the same word for "suffering"/"persecution" (here and frequently elsewhere) as is used in the Jesus-tradition (e.g., Matt 24:9, 21, 29; Mark 13:19, 24);[87] and there is, as we have seen, plenty of other evidence for Paul's familiarity with Jesus-traditions that are found in the eschatological discourse. Here again Paul could have been influenced by those traditions.

Of course, the theme of suffering is found elsewhere in the synoptic tradition, notably in the beatitudes of Matt 5:10-12/Luke 6:22, 23, where Jesus speaks of joy in suffering and also of the heavenly rewards of suffering. In Matt 5:10 he promises, "Theirs is the kingdom of heaven." Paul speaks similarly of joy in suffering in Rom 5:3; 2 Cor 7:4; 12:10; and Col 1:24.[88] In 2 Thes 1:4, 5 he refers to the sufferings of the Thessalonians as evidence that God is making them worthy of the kingdom of God (compare Matt 5:10 as well as Rom 5:3, 4 on hope).

It does seem likely that Paul has been influenced by Jesus' teaching about suffering. But the demonstrable connections are not great, and we must categorize this evidence only as "possible" evidence of Pauline dependence on Jesus-tradition.

CONCLUSIONS ON THE CONNECTIONS

There are a remarkable number of parallels between Paul's eschatological teaching and that of Jesus as it is attested in the Gospels. Some of the

---

87. Greek *thlipsis*. The word is very common in the LXX, and the agreement of the synoptics and Paul in use of this word can at the best be a minor supporting argument for a relationship of Paul and Jesus. Paul speaks of "enduring" distress in Rom 5:3; 12:12 (cf. Matt 13:9, 13), and in Col 1:24 he speaks of himself "completing what is lacking in Christ's afflictions *(thlipseis)*." Where Matthew and Mark use *thlipsis* in the eschatological discourse, Luke has *anankē* (Matt 24:21/Mark 13:19/Luke 21:23). Paul speaks of the "imminent *anankē*" in 1 Cor 7:26, quite possibly a reference to the eschatological *anankē* of the last days. He also uses *thlipsis* and *anankē* together in 2 Cor 6:4; 1 Thes 3:7.

88. See Goulder, *Evangelists' Calendar,* 228; also J. P. Brown, "Synoptic Parallels," 30. Brown, p. 38, also notes Pauline parallels to the synoptic promises of the Holy Spirit teaching the disciples what to say when facing authorities; cf. Matt 10:19, 20; Mark 13:11; Luke 12:11, 12 with 1 Cor 2:8, 13; Col 4:3-6; Eph 6:10-20. Stanley, "Pauline Allusions," 31, notes Phil 1:19.

parallels are so close as to demand the conclusion that there is a connection. Others are more uncertain, but given the overall picture they, too, carry some weight.

In the category of "highly probable" connections come the parables of the thief, the watchman, and the stewards and the exhortations with which Luke concludes his eschatological discourse (21:34-36). Other "probable" connections include the parable of the wise and foolish virgins, the desolating sacrilege, the warnings about deceivers, the woe concerning the persecution of the prophets, and the Lukan sayings about "wrath" and "the times of the Gentiles."

The category of "possible" connections includes the sayings about coming sufferings, about enduring to the end, about the gospel being preached, and about Lot and the revelation of the day of judgment (Luke 17:29, 30).

The connections are almost certainly in the direction from Jesus to Paul: There are a few "tradition indicators" that suggest this (notably "the word of the Lord" in 1 Thes 4:15), and it is much easier to conceive of Paul drawing his nonparabolic teaching from the parables of Jesus than the Evangelists composing parables on the basis of sayings such as we find in Paul and then ascribing them to Jesus.

Much of the gospel material concerned has a high claim to authenticity: It can be shown, at least, that it antedates the synoptics. Some of the material, however, is found only in one Gospel; thus we noted that Paul seems to draw on distinctively Lukan tradition from time to time. It is not easy to be certain about the form of the tradition known to Paul: It could be that he knew the sayings of Jesus as discrete sayings and that he gathered them together in 1 and 2 Thessalonians in particular because he was addressing questions about the end; it is an understandable coincidence that the Evangelists also gathered many of the same sayings in their eschatological passages. On the other hand, the evidence of 2 Thessalonians 2 points to Paul having known something like the eschatological discourse, and the evidence of the eschatological parables of Matthew 24, 25/Luke 12/Mark 13 suggests that they were collected together at an early date so that Paul might well have had access to such a collection.[89]

89. In *Rediscovery* I postulate a large presynoptic discourse that Paul could have known, and I argue that much of the eschatological material in Matt 24, 25/Mark 13/Luke 21 and also Luke 12:35-48; 17:20-37 may be derived from this discourse. Beasley-Murray may be right to suggest that I am too ambitious with my thesis (so *Jesus and the Last Days,* 303). But it is interesting that Aejmelaeus in his *Wachen vor dem Ende,* 58-89, comes, entirely independently, to some of the same conclusions about the sayings material known to Paul, while differing from me in other respects.

Additional Notes

THE ESCHATOLOGICAL PARABLES

The evidence bearing on the relationship of the eschatological parables of Matthew 24, 25/Luke 12/Mark 13 is complex, but can be summarized as follows. There are five parables:[90] the thief, the stewards, the virgins, the talents, and the watchman or watchmen. Matthew has all but the watchman, and he has an exhortation that sounds like that parable in 24:42: "Keep awake, for you do not know on what day your Lord is coming."[91] Luke has all of them in chapter 12 except for the talents and the virgins, and he has an equivalent to the talents parable in ch. 19 and an exhortation that sounds like the parable of the virgins in 12:35: "Let your loins be girded and your lamps burning."*[92] Mark has no full parables, but he has probable echoes of the parable of the talents in 13:34 ("It is like a man going on a journey, when he leaves home and puts his slaves in charge . . .") and of the watchman in 13:34, 35 ("and commands the doorkeeper to be on the watch [= "keep awake"]. Therefore, keep awake — for you do not know when the master of the house will come, in the evening, or at midnight . . ."). In addition to all this, a further intriguing partial parallel is between the question that Luke has after the parable of the thief ("Lord, do you say this parable to us or to all?"* 12:41) and the final saying in Mark 13 ("What I say to you I say to all: Keep awake," v. 37).

90. To be precise there are five parables found in at least two Gospels. Luke 12 has an additional parable about a slave in vv. 47, 48, and Matthew has the parable of the sheep and the goats in ch. 25. We have not discussed the parable of the sheep and the goats, but scholars have found echoes of it in, e.g., 1 Cor 8:12 and 2 Cor 5:10 (see Knowling, *Testimony*, 291), though 2 Cor 5:10 has also been associated with Matt 16:27.

91. On the parable of the watchman see *Rediscovery*, 15-49, responding to the earlier discussions of Jeremias, *Parables*, 53-55; Dupont, "Parabole du Maître"; Weiser, *Knechtsgeichnisse*, 123-77.

92. Luke also probably betrays his familiarity with the parable of the virgins in 13:24, 25, where the shift from the idea of a narrow door (v. 24) to that of a closed door (v. 25) is explicable if Luke was familiar with the traditions found in Matt 7:13, 14 and 7:21, 23 as well as with the parable of the virgins: His wording represents a conflation of ideas from the three passages with the idea of the closed door and the wording "But he will say, 'I do not know where you come from'" both coming from the parable of the virgins (cf. Greek *ouk oida hymas*). See my *Rediscovery*, 91-95; also Hoffmann, "Πάντες ἐργάται ἀδικίας."

So to summarize:

	Matthew 24–25 has	Luke 12 has	Mark 13 has
the virgins	yes	an echo	
the watch-man/watchmen	an echo	yes	an echo
the thief	yes	yes	
		"Lord, do you say this parable to us or to all?"*	"What I say to you I say to all: Keep awake"
the stewards	yes	yes	
the talents	yes	(19:12ff.)	an echo

It is not at first obvious how this complex pattern of parallels is to be explained. But the explanation is probably that all the three Gospel writers are drawing on a collection of parables that was as follows:

- **the virgins**
  - Exhortation: "Gird up your loins and keep your lamps lit"
- **the watchman**
  - Exhortation: "Keep awake, for you do not know in which watch the Lord comes"
- **the thief**
  - Exhortation: "Be ready"
  - Peter's question about whether the parable is directed "to us or to all"
  - Jesus' reply: "What I say to you I say to all: Keep awake"
- **the stewards**
  - Exhortation "Keep awake, for you do not know the day or hour"
- **the talents**

Each of the Evangelists has used this collection, retaining, rewording, and omitting different elements. Luke follows the original order most closely in chapter 12, though he picks up the source after the parable of the virgins with the exhortation about girding up one's loins and keeping lamps lit, probably starting at this point because of the sequence of material attested in Matt 6:21, 22 (cf. Luke 12:34, 35). Matthew picks up the source in 24:44 with the exhortation that goes with the parable of the watchman, modifying it to fit his preceding context, and then he brings in the parable of the virgins after that of the steward. Mark does not reproduce any complete parables, but offers his own synthesis of sayings to emphasize the theme of wakefulness. Most strikingly, while Luke retains the presynoptic question "Lord, do you say this parable to us or to all?" it is Mark who gives us the presynoptic answer, "What I say to you I say to all: Keep awake," thus ending the section with the emphasis on wakefulness that he has been developing since v. 33.[93]

I have set out in detail the arguments for this explanation of the synoptic relationships elsewhere.[94] The conclusion is that the parables concerned, together with their accompanying hortatory applications, antedate all the synoptic Gospels and that the three Evangelists all had independent access to the material. And they all regarded the traditions concerned as coming from Jesus.

THE TRUMPET

Tuckett objects to any attempt to make much of "the trumpet" in Matt 24:31 and 1 Thes 4:16 on the grounds that Matt 24:30-31 "is usually regarded" as Matthean redaction of Mark.[95] He is unpersuaded by L. Aejmelaeus that the verses were in Q, as well as by my attempt to postulate a presynoptic discourse form.

I would certainly not wish to make much of the trumpet on its own.[96] But Paul (twice: see also 1 Cor 15:52) and Matthew refer to the heavenly

93. On the question and answer see *Rediscovery*, 57-62; Swete, *Mark*, 319. Beasley-Murray, *Jesus and the Last Days*, 474, notes the striking similarity of content and wording but does not explain it, simply speaking of "a curious coincidence." He also sees that Mark 13:34-36 is quite probably an amalgam of material from the parables of the watchman and the talents, but he does not see that the different pieces of evidence fit together in the way I propose. At one point (p. 299) he mistakenly says that I believe that Matt 25:13/Mark 13:33 was the presynoptic ending of the parable of the watchman, whereas I believe that Matt 24:42/Mark 13:35 was the conclusion to the watchman and that Matt 25:13/Mark 13:33 concluded the parable of the stewards and preceded the parable of the talents (hence the Markan order in vv. 33, 34). Beasley-Murray finds it hard to see why Mark would have omitted the sort of material found now in Matthew 24, 25/Luke 12 (including the parable of the thief), had he known it; and yet he admits a trace of the parable of the talents in Mark 13:34.

94. *Rediscovery*, 15-100.

95. "Synoptic Tradition in 1 Thessalonians," 177-78; see also Goulder, *Midrash*, 166-69.

96. On the familiarity of the trumpet in apocalyptic literature and in Roman imperial life see Gundry, "Hellenization," 163.

trumpet in the context of similar descriptions of the second coming, so some connection between the two is not unlikely. It need not be that Paul was dependent on a Jesus-tradition at this point, but he is dependent on such tradition in other material in the same context (e.g., the thief: see above).

Furthermore, even if the two-source hypothesis is broadly correct (as it may or may not be), Matthew does have some of his own (so-called "M") traditions in his version of the eschatological discourse (e.g., 24:10-12; 25:1-13, 31-46),[97] and he has independent access to some of the traditions that he shares with Mark and Luke (see, for example, the additional note above on "The Eschatological Parables"). So if Matthew has added 24:30, 31 to his Markan source, that does not mean that that material necessarily originated with Matthew.

The "usual" scholarly conclusion may be that the verses are redactional, but that is an inference from the two-source hypothesis, not something otherwise strongly based. Tuckett suspects that I work from a general premise about the Evangelists as highly conservative editors, hence my inclusion of all sorts of traditions in my reconstructed presynoptic discourse. There may be a grain of truth in this. But I suspect that his argument reflects his own adherence to a rather narrowly conceived version of the two-source hypothesis, and that a more open approach would allow him to see the force of my argument.[98]

SUGGESTIONS CONCERNING THE "WORD OF THE LORD" IN 1 THESSALONIANS 4:15

All sorts of suggestions have been made as to which gospel saying or sayings might have been in Paul's mind when he wrote in 1 Thes 4:15 of a "word of the Lord." It could have been the sayings of Matt 24:40, 41/Luke 17:34, 35, according to which "one will be taken and one will be left." Paul in explaining himself speaks of Christians who are "left" being "caught up" to meet the Lord (1 Thes 4:17); the language is similar to the synoptic sayings (though the Greek verbs are different). But these particular gospel sayings hardly seem to address the issue of the dead being raised, which Paul is discussing in 1 Thessalonians 4. They are speaking of some being saved and

---

97. On 24:10-12 see my "Note on Matthew 24:10-12."

98. Stuhlmacher, "Jesustradition," 243, comments that it can hardly be doubted that both "parousia" and "trumpet" in 1 Thes 4:15, 16 came to Paul from traditions behind Matt 24:31, 37, 39.

some not saved, and, if anything, they relate more to Paul's comments on the living ("we who are alive, who are left until the coming of the Lord") than to the question of the dead.

The "word of the Lord" could conceivably have been the saying in Matt 16:28/Mark 9:1/Luke 9:27: "There are some standing here who will not taste death before they see the (Son of Man coming in his) kingdom." From this saying Paul might have inferred that some would, in fact, die and see the kingdom.[99] But it is at best a very oblique hint about the matter Paul is discussing in 1 Thessalonians 4.

Was "the word of the Lord" the saying about the Son of man gathering the elect from the four winds and from the ends of the earth to the ends of heaven (Mark 13:27) or from one end of heaven to the other (Matt 24:31)? The saying speaks of the universal gathering of the elect in a way that could have justified Paul's point about the dead being included. But it does not explicitly address the question of the dead.

Another suggestion is that we should think of the traditions in John 11:25, 26: "I am the resurrection and the life. He who believes in me, if he dies, will live, and everyone who lives and believes in me will not die for ever."*[100] These sayings do quite directly address the question of the living and the dead, but the verses are strongly Johannine (in terms of vocabulary and emphasis) and so would be seen by many scholars as deriving from the Evangelist rather than from Jesus; Paul would not, therefore, have known them as Jesus-tradition.[101] Even if this argument is not conclusive, since there is reason to believe that the fourth Gospel contains a significant amount of historical tradition, Paul's thought in 1 Thessalonians 4 and 5 seems generally much closer to the synoptic eschatological traditions (e.g., with their emphasis on the parousia) than to the Johannine saying.

Yet another suggestion is that Paul had in mind the parable of the wise and foolish virgins. On this see our discussion above.

---

99. See E. P. Sanders, *Jesus and Judaism*, 144-46.
100. See Gundry, "Hellenization," 164-65.
101. See Tuckett, "Synoptic Sayings in 1 Thessalonians," 180-82.

IS LUKE 21:34-36 DEPENDENT
ON 1 THESSALONIANS 5:3-8?

L. Aejmelaeus and C. Tuckett both recognize the connection between Luke 21:34-36 and 1 Thes 5:3, but they argue that Luke has been influenced by Paul, not Paul by the Jesus-tradition as found in Luke.[102]

Aejmelaeus argues that Luke, having used some of Mark 13:33-37 in Luke 12:35-38, offers his own non-Markan conclusion to the discourse in 21:34-36. He suggests that Luke has been influenced in these few verses by Mark 13:33-37, by other traditions that he has used earlier in the Gospel (e.g., Luke 8:12, 14; 12:22, 35-46), by the Septuagint text of Isaiah 24 and Jeremiah 32, and by 1 Thessalonians 5 and Ephesians 5. It is a "veritable meeting-point of different traditions."[103]

Aejmelaeus's argument is impressive in some details, but in the end of the day it is too complicated to be credible. The complexity is compounded when he argues that Luke made use of 1 Thessalonians 5 in composing his replacement for Mark 13:33-37 because he recognized that there were traditions from Jesus in 1 Thessalonians 4 and 5, but that Luke had to rewrite Paul's words in case his readers were confused to find words they knew as Pauline on the lips of Jesus.

Given Aejmelaeus's admission that 1 Thessalonians 4 and 5 do contain a significant number of Jesus-traditions, it is far simpler to suppose that Luke 21:34-36 and 1 Thes 5:3-8 are both based on a common tradition (which was thought to go back to Jesus).

Aejmelaeus does allow that Luke has non-Markan eschatological traditions of Jesus, which Paul may draw on in 1 Thessalonians 4 and 5 (e.g., the "Q" material of Luke 17:24, 26-35), but he does not take seriously the possibility that Luke 21:34-36 may be one such tradition.[104] Aejmelaeus is misled by too readily assuming that Luke 21:34-36 is Luke's redactional replacement for Mark 13:33-37. He fails to reckon sufficiently with the fact that Mark 13:33-37 itself is probably composite and based on earlier fuller traditions, some or all of which were known to Luke (see Luke 12:36-38 and the additional note above on "The Eschatological Parables").

Tuckett's rather subtle arguments in favor of Luke's use of 1 Thes 5:3

---

102. Aejmelaeus, *Wachen vor dem Ende,* 99-136; Tuckett, "Synoptic Tradition in 1 Thessalonians," 173-76.

103. *Wachen vor dem Ende,* 133-34.

104. 21:34-36 is in fact thematically similar to 17:26-35, and I suggest in my *Rediscovery* that they may have belonged together in the presynoptic tradition.

are, first, that Paul drew 1 Thes 5:3, with its negative comment about not escaping, from tradition, but the positive thought in vv. 4-8 about the Thessalonians not being caught is Paul's reflection on that tradition. Luke 21:36, on the other hand, speaks positively of escaping. Tuckett sees it as more likely that Luke has combined the wording of 1 Thes 5:3 with the thought of vv. 4-8 than that Paul has been influenced by the Lukan tradition.

The logic is unpersuasive. Paul's train of thought moves from the negative idea of the thief in the night (1 Thes 5:2) into further "negative" reflection on people being unready (5:3): It is at this point that Paul uses the wording of Luke 21:34-36, drawing out the implied warning in it. ("Lest . . . that day come on you suddenly like a snare"* is a warning about something from which there is no escape.)

Tuckett argues, second, that Paul's progression of thought in 1 Thes 5:3-8 moving from "day" to "night" to "drunkenness" is not easy to get starting from Luke 21:34-36. It is, however, entirely possible to explain Paul's train of thought in terms of his reflection on a variety of Jesus-traditions, starting with the thief.

Tuckett's explanation leaves all sorts of things unsatisfactorily explained: First, he recognizes 1 Thes 5:3 as pre-Pauline tradition. But he does not suggest what sort of tradition it was or where Paul got it from. Since Paul uses it in close conjunction with what is clearly a tradition from Jesus (the thief) and with what is probably another tradition from Jesus (the watchman), it would be attractive to postulate that 1 Thes 5:3 is based on tradition from Jesus even without Luke's evidence. But Luke gives evidence that the tradition was seen as originating from Jesus.

Second, Tuckett does not explain Luke's use of the Pauline material in 21:34: Why does he suddenly diverge from Mark here? Aejmelaeus could be correct in supposing that Luke wants to avoid overlap with what he has written in 12:36-38. But why does Luke turn to 1 Thes 5:3 for his new material? Given that he had non-Markan eschatological traditions of Jesus (e.g., the "Q" traditions of Luke 12 and 17), it is arguably more likely that he is drawing on such traditions than suddenly turning to Paul. (As we noted, Luke 21:34-36 is thematically very similar to 17:22-35.)

It is not absolutely impossible that Luke knew and drew on 1 Thessalonians 5 as material thematically similar to Mark 13:33-37, though it is striking, if he did so, that he did not develop the light-darkness theme. However, Tuckett's analysis, like that of Aejmelaeus, is complicated, if not convoluted — with Paul dependent on Jesus-traditions in 1 Thessalonians 4 and 5 (Tuckett allows that the thief is probably a Jesus-tradition in Paul) and with Luke using some of those Jesus-traditions in Luke 12, then avoiding those traditions when he comes to Mark 13:33-37, and then going back to 1 Thessalonians 5 for substitute material. It is far simpler to argue that in Luke 21:34-36 Luke is making use of (and no doubt redacting in certain ways) non-Markan sayings that were also known to Paul.

Third, Tuckett fails to note some of the other evidence we have advanced (e.g., the parallels in Eph 6:11-18).

"FILLING UP SINS"

The single most impressive parallel that we noted in our comparison of 1 Thes 2:15, 16 and Matt 23:29-36/Luke 11:47-51 is the reference to the Jews "filling up" their sins in 1 Thes 2:16/Matt 23:32.[105] But Luke at this point does not support Matthew. It could be, therefore, that Matt 23:32 is Matthean wording (rather than the "Q" wording) and so unlikely to have been known by Paul.[106]

That view of the synoptic relationships, however, is not certain. It may well be that Matthew has the more original wording here and that Luke has substituted his simple "You . . . approve of the deeds of your ancestors" for the much more obscure "Fill up, then, the measure of your ancestors" (Luke 11:48/Matt 23:32). Paul's evidence probably supports this suggestion, since his agreement in referring to "filling up" of sins in the context of other similarities is unlikely to be coincidental.[107]

105. "Filling up (anaplēroō) their sins" (1 Thessalonians) is not exactly the same concept as "filling up (plēroō) the measure of the ancestors" (Matthew). But the ideas are similar and the usage of the verb in this negative way is without parallel elsewhere in the NT. Steck, Israel, 291, argues that because the idea of filling up one's sins is a common enough Jewish idea, there is no need to associate the Pauline and Matthean phraseology. This may be true, but it is striking to find the parallel phraseology in Paul and Matthew in contexts that have other links.

106. So Tuckett, "Synoptic Tradition in 1 Thessalonians," 166, suggesting that the Matthean form of the saying fits Matthew's emphasis on the guilt of the Jews. This may well be the majority view of the synoptic relationship, but it is at best one viable opinion.

107. This is not a viciously circular argument, but a situation where differing pieces of evidence interlock to point in one direction. This interlocking evidence is

• a number of similarities between the Pauline and the "Q" passages,
• some uncertainty about whether the Matthean or Lukan wording of the particular "Q" saying in the passage is to be preferred, and
• a rather striking parallel between the Pauline passage and Matthew's form of the uncertain "Q" saying.

The inference that Paul probably knew the "Q" passage, including the Matthean form of the uncertain saying, is therefore a reasonable one.

But even if we discount that possibility, the similarity of the texts in other respects (notably in the references to pursuing and killing the prophets) is such as to make the connection a good possibility,[108] and Paul's unusual language in 1 Thes 2:15, 16 is probably better explained in this way than in any other.[109]

108. Paul uses the compound verb *ekdiōkō* ("pursue," "drive out"), Matthew and Luke the simple *diōkō* ("persecute," "drive").

109. Tuckett, "Synoptic Tradition in 1 Thessalonians," 165-67, fails to allow for the cumulative force of the evidence, arguing that each of the parallels is explicable in some other way. For example, he notes that "killing the prophets" is a common Jewish idea, but he fails to bring out the way in which in Paul and the synoptics we find killing, pursuing, "us" (Paul), and apostles/sages (Matthew/Luke). Goulder, *Midrash*, 165, sees Matthew as dependent on Paul here; but he does not explain the unusual features of the Pauline passage.

8

JESUS' LIFE AND MINISTRY

So far we have explored the question of Paul and the teaching of Jesus; now we move on — much more briefly — to the question of Paul and the story of Jesus.[1] What did Paul know of Jesus' life and ministry?[2] What knowledge does he presuppose in his readers and church members? What importance did traditions of Jesus' life and ministry have for him?

THE BIRTH OF JESUS

The logical place to begin is with the question of Jesus' birth and family background. Did Paul know any of the traditions of Jesus' birth recorded in the Gospels?

Many scholars would, almost without thinking, give a negative answer to the question, since it is widely held that the infancy narratives of Matthew and Luke represent a relatively late development in the christological thinking of the early church. Paul's letters are indeed seen as evidence for this view, since Paul, like Mark (usually seen as author of our earliest Gospel), gives no obvious indication of being familiar with the story of Jesus' virginal conception.[3]

1. It is not easy always to distinguish between the narrative and the teaching traditions of the Gospels. Some of what we have already looked at (e.g., the mission discourse, the Mary and Martha story, the last supper narrative) has at least a narrative framework.

2. Much of this chapter overlaps with my "Story of Jesus Known to Paul."

3. The reference to Jesus as "the son of Mary" in Mark 6:3 has sometimes been taken to be an insulting way of referring to Jesus as illegitimately born, and possibly as a hint that Mark is familiar with the virgin birth story. It may more straightforwardly reflect the fact

338

For several reasons, this line of argument should not be too quickly taken for granted. (1) Although the Matthean and Lukan infancy narratives raise all sorts of questions for the critic, not least because they are so different from each other, they have features in common that may well antedate both Gospels.[4] This includes an emphasis on Jesus as Son of God, as a descendant of David, as born of Mary, having been conceived by the Holy Spirit. Both narratives also have a strongly Semitic flavor. So whatever we conclude about the ultimate origins of the traditions and their final form in Matthew and Luke, it is quite possible that they are early Palestinian traditions that Paul might well have known.

(2) Paul does show some interest in Jesus' origins. Thus in Rom 1:3 he speaks of Jesus as God's Son "who was descended from David according to the flesh" and in Gal 4:4, 5 he comments that "when the fullness of time had come, God sent his Son, born of a woman, born under the law, in order to redeem. . . ." The primary interest in these two texts is, respectively, Jesus' Davidic descent and his Jewishness ("under the law") rather than the circumstances of his birth, but it is still significant that the birth of Jesus (and not just his death and resurrection) has theological importance for Paul.

(3) It is notable that what Paul brings out in these two texts are matters also emphasized in the Matthean and Lukan infancy narratives (which are also interested in the theological significance of Jesus' birth as much as in the historical circumstances). Thus:

- Paul emphasizes in both texts that Jesus is God's "Son," and this is a theme strongly emphasized especially in the Lukan infancy narrative (Luke 1:32, 35; cf. Matt 2:15).[5]
- At the same time both Pauline texts presuppose that Jesus had a normal human birth: "according to the flesh" (Rom 1:3), "born of a woman" (Gal 4:4). The Gospels, too, describe a normal human birth from a woman, though the conception is miraculous.[6]

---

that Joseph had died at the time, though the divergence from Matt 13:55 and John 6:42 is interesting. Cf. Gundry, *Mark*, 290-91; Davies and Allison, *Matthew*, I, 452-53.

4. The standard work on the infancy narratives is still R. E. Brown, *Birth of the Messiah*.

5. Hays, *Faith of Jesus Christ*, 88, 89, notes the close parallelism between Gal 4:4, 5 (with its focus on the incarnation) and Gal 3:13, 14 (with its focus on the cross), but observes several differences, including the use of the term "Son" in Gal 4:4 as distinct from "Christ" in Gal 3:13.

6. Paul speaks of Jesus' birth as "according to the flesh" and of his resurrection

- "Born of a woman" in Gal 4:4 gives prominence to Jesus' mother, as do, of course, Matthew's and Luke's narratives.
- In Rom 1:3 Paul speaks of the Davidic descent of Jesus;[7] this, too, is important to Matthew and Luke (Matt 1:1, 17, 20, 21; 2:5, 6; Luke 1:32, 69; 2:4, 11).
- In Gal 4:4 Jesus is said to have been born "under the law"; Luke's Gospel brings this out in his narrative of Jesus' circumcision and presentation in the temple (2:22-24).
- Gal 4:4 says that Jesus was born "when the fullness of time had come," setting the birth of Jesus in an eschatological framework and within the context of OT fulfillment. The Matthean and Lukan infancy narratives portray Jesus' birth in the same way.[8]

The thematic parallels between the two brief Pauline texts and the Matthean and Lukan infancy narratives are striking, and they give the lie to any idea that Paul was unfamiliar with the sort of traditions about Jesus' birth that are found in the Gospels. Paul seems to be working with very much the same sort of ideas.

The parallels do not, however, prove that Paul knew these ideas in the narrative form that the Gospels present. Indeed, it is possible that the gospel stories developed from the ideas rather than vice versa.[9] On the other hand, there may well have been early Palestinian traditions lying behind the gospel infancy stories, and it is quite possible that Paul knew them.

(4) In favor of the view that Paul knew the tradition of Jesus' birth underlying the Gospels' accounts could be the fact that he speaks specifically of Jesus' mother and not of his (human) father.[10] However, it would be unwise to read too much into the phrase "born of a woman" by itself, since

---

as "according to the Spirit" (Rom 1:3, 4). It would be unwise to press this contrast to suggest that Paul did not believe that Jesus' birth was also by the Spirit and that there is therefore a contradiction with the Gospels.

7. On the possibility that Rom 1:3, 4 is pre-Pauline see our discussion in chapter 2 above and Scott, *Adoption,* 227-36, who argues that the theology is fully Pauline and finds other evidence of Paul's convictions about Jesus' Davidic roots (e.g., Rom 15:12).

8. Even the phraseology of Gal 4:4, "when the fullness *(plērōma)* of time *(chronou)* had come, God sent his Son, born of a woman," is paralleled in Luke 1:57: "For Elizabeth the time *(chronos)* was completed [*eplēsthē*, "filled"] for her to give birth, and she bore a son,"* and 2:6, 7: "The days were completed *(eplēsthēsan)* for her to give birth, and she bore her firstborn son."*

9. So Goulder, *Midrash,* 56.

10. He mentions Jesus' brothers in 1 Cor 9:5.

it was a common enough way of referring to human beings. Jesus said that "among those born of women no one has arisen greater than John the Baptist" (Matt 11:11/Luke 7:28) without implying that John had no human father. Paul's point in Gal 4:4 is that God sent his Son as a human being like us. It is true that Paul nowhere mentions any human father of Jesus, but then there is only the one passing and almost incidental reference to his mother.

It is also true that Paul explicitly speaks of God as Jesus' Father, but he would not necessarily have seen any tension between this and the idea of Jesus having a human father. After all, the OT can speak of Solomon as God's son while he is physically David's son, and Paul can speak of Christians as sons of God along with Jesus.[11] Admittedly Jesus is the preexistent son of God for Paul, and so in a different category from either Solomon or Christians. But there is no certainty that Paul would have seen any difficulty in the idea of the divine Son having a human father when he was sent into the world.

(5) But there is one small piece of evidence that may point to Paul's familiarity with the tradition of Jesus' virginal conception. In Rom 1:3 ("*descended* from David"); Gal 4:4 ("*born* of a woman"); and Phil 2:7 ("*born* in human likeness"*), Paul uses the same Greek verb, *ginomai*. This verb was very common and meant (broadly) "become." It was not the most obvious or usual word to refer to someone being born, and it is not used in this way elsewhere in the NT.[12] The usual verb for begetting, giving birth, or (in the passive voice) being born is *gennaō*, which Paul uses five times.[13]

What is perhaps most striking is that in Galatians 4, after speaking of Jesus being "born of a woman, born under the law" (4:4), he goes on in the same chapter of Galatians to speak of Sarah and Hagar giving birth to Isaac and Ishmael (4:21-31). He uses here the same sort of phraseology as he uses to refer to Jesus' birth in Gal 4:4 and Rom 1:3. So, for example, we may compare:

11. On the importance of the 2 Samuel 7 passage for Paul see especially Scott, *Adoption;* also chapters 3 and 4 above (e.g., pp. 112-15, 175-83).

12. John 8:58 is a possible exception, though there is no emphasis on Abraham's birth here.

13. A few manuscripts have *gennaomai,* not *ginomai,* in Rom 1:3 and Gal 4:4 (testifying to the scribes' awareness that *gennaomai* was the verb one might expect), but the overwhelming majority have *ginomai.*

Gal 4:4:	Gal 4:23:	Rom 1:3:
"his Son,	"The one	"his Son,
born (become)	*from the slave girl*	born (become)
from a woman"*	was born	of David's seed
	according to the flesh"*	*according to the flesh*"*

The similarity of ideas and even of grammatical form is clear. But though Paul uses the "become" verb both times when he refers to Jesus' birth, in Gal 4:21-31 he consistently uses the usual verb, *gennaomai*, to refer to the birth of Isaac and Ishmael (vv. 23, 24, 29).[14]

One suggestion as to why Paul does this is that he is thinking of Jesus entering the human state and condition rather than of his birth as such.[15] This may possibly be the correct explanation, but, first, it is quite specifically Jesus' entry into the human state through birth that Paul is referring to ("of the seed of David,"* "of a woman"). Second, it is not obvious that the point about entering the human state would be any less clear with the more common verb, and perhaps it would be more clear. Third, the focus in Gal 4:21-31, where the usual "be born" verb is used of Isaac and Esau, is not on the birth as such, but on parentage and status.

Other scholars give an almost opposite explanation, namely that the "become" verb was sometimes used of "being born" (that is, synonymously to *gennaomai*); so Paul is using a perfectly normal verb for "to be born," without any special significance.[16] This explanation could also be correct, and yet the overwhelmingly common verb for being born in the Septuagint and the NT (including Paul's own writings) is *gennaomai*, so that Paul's choice of the different verb when referring to Jesus remains mysterious.[17]

14. Compare the comments on Sarah and Hagar in Gal 4:23 (*ho men ek tēs paidiskēs kata sarka gegennētai*) and Gal 4:29 (*ho kata sarka gennētheis ediōken ton kata pneuma*) with the description of Jesus in Gal 4:4 (*genomenon ek gynaikos*) and Rom 1:3 (*genomenou ek spermatos Dauid kata sarka . . . kata pneuma*).

15. So Dunn, *Romans 1–8*, 12; *idem, Galatians*, 215; but see Scott, *Adoption*, 237. This view is especially plausible in Phil 2:7, where "becoming in human likeness"* is contrasted with "being in the form of God"* in the preceding verse. Also in Gal 4:4 "becoming from a woman"* is parallel to "becoming under the law"*; it is Jesus' humanness and Jewishness that are emphasized. Also in favor of this view may be the use of the participle *genomenos* in Gal 3:13, 14 of Jesus "becoming" a curse and in Phil 2:8 of him "becoming" obedient to death: Paul thus uses the participle to speak of Jesus "becoming" on our behalf.

16. So Bruce, *Galatians*, 195, referring to 1 Esdras 4:16; Tobit 8:6; Wisdom 7:3; Sirach 44:9; John 8:58.

17. When Jesus speaks of John as one "born of woman" in Matt 11:11/Luke 7:28,

A final and serious possibility is that Paul was familiar with and influenced by the story of Jesus' virginal conception.[18] He therefore avoids the usual verb — with its frequent connotations of male begetting — and uses the less obvious "become" verb instead.[19]

A further observation may be added. There are, in all, four rather similar passages referring to Jesus' birth — Gal 4:4; Rom 1:3; 8:3; and Phil 2:7.[20] Three of them, as we have seen, use "become." The other two speak of Jesus taking human "likeness" (Phil 2:7: "in human likeness"; Rom 8:3: "in the likeness of sinful flesh"). Paul's use of "likeness" does not imply that he thought of Jesus as only apparently human, but it does suggest that he saw some distinction between Jesus' humanity and normal sinful humanity. Commentators usually suggest that he wanted to make the point that Jesus was like us, but "knew no sin" (2 Cor 5:21). Paul's conviction of Jesus' sinlessness need not have entailed a belief in a virgin birth, and yet this conviction and his belief in Jesus as the preexistent Son almost by definition point to a miraculous birth of some sort. Although Paul need not have envisaged that miracle in anything like the way the Gospels describe it, the cumulative evidence suggests that he may have been familiar with their tradition.

JESUS' BAPTISM AND TEMPTATION

It is impossible that Paul, having resided in Palestine in the first half of the first century, did not know of John the Baptist and his ministry. According

---

the verbal adjective used is *gennētos* (which is related to *gennaomai;* cf. Job 14:1; 15:14 in the Septuagint); but Paul in Gal 4:4 uses *ginomai.*

18. See Cranfield, "Reflections"; W. C. Robinson, "Re-Study"; McHugh, *Mother of Jesus,* 274-77. The argument about the verb used is rejected as inconclusive by R. E. Brown, *Birth of the Messiah,* 519. For a survey of opinions see De Roover, "Maternité virginale."

19. It is interesting that Luke uses the usual *gennaomai* in the infancy narratives of the birth of John the Baptist (1:13, 35, 57), but not of Jesus. He uses the verb of Jesus only in Acts 13:33, speaking there of the relationship of God to Jesus. Matthew does use *gennaomai* of Jesus in his infancy narratives, but he is careful to explain that "that which has been begotten in her is from the Holy Spirit"* (1:20).

20. See also Rom 15:8 (somewhat parallel to Gal 4:4 — "Christ has *become* a servant of the circumcised"); 2 Cor 8:9 ("he became poor," this time not *ginomai*) for other possible allusions to Jesus' birth. Knowling, *Testimony,* 333, notes also Col 2:11 on "the circumcision of Christ."

to Acts Paul spoke of John and saw him as Jesus' forerunner (13:24-25; 19:4). There are possible echoes of John's teaching in the Pauline letters: In 1 Thes 1:9-10 Paul describes the Thessalonians as "turning" from idols to God and Jesus as the one who saves us "from the wrath that is coming." This is reminiscent of John's call to "repent" and to "flee from the wrath to come" (Matt 3:1, 7/Luke 3:3, 7). And in Romans 2 Paul's teaching to the professing Jew about repentance, good works, wrath, and judgment is similar to John's warnings to the presumptuous Jews who claimed Abraham as their father (Matt 3:7-10/Luke 3:7-9).[21]

But did Paul know of Jesus' baptism by John?

The Likelihood That Paul Knew of Jesus' Baptism

Jesus' baptism was common knowledge

Various considerations make it likely that he did. Apart from anything else it is probable that John's baptism of Jesus was common knowledge in the early church. All four Gospels refer or, in John's case, allude to it, and there is some reason to think that it was a topic of debate in the early days of the church, with some followers of John pointing to the baptism as an indication of John's superiority to Jesus.[22]

Baptist churches

Paul is unlikely to have been oblivious to all this. He moved in circles where baptism was important. In his own churches baptism (as the expression of faith) was the normative initiation rite. This by itself proves little for the question of Paul's knowledge of Jesus' baptism by John, but the fact that the Christian movement was in many ways so similar to the older Jewish baptist movement of John (and indeed was known to have grown out of that older movement) means that the question of the relationship of the two movements and of their two leaders could hardly have been avoided, at least if the two movements had any contact with each other.

21. On these parallels see Michaels, "Paul and John the Baptist." He notes how the "children of Abraham" theme is important to Paul. The parallels are striking, even if it is impossible to prove direct dependence.

22. See, e.g., Matt 3:14, 15 and our discussion in the additional note on "Jesus, John the Baptist, and Qumran" in chapter 2 above.

Paul's contact with followers of John

We have seen that there is reason to think that the two movements did have contact and were debating the issue of John and Jesus; but there is also evidence that Paul in particular had contact with the followers of John. Thus Acts 18:24-28 describes Apollos as one who knew only John's baptism until he was further instructed about Jesus by Paul's colleagues Priscilla and Aquila. And Acts 19:1-10 refers to Paul meeting and instructing twelve disciples who knew only John's baptism. There has been much scholarly discussion of these two passages, but whatever their historical background, the tradition that Paul had contact with people who were associated with the Baptist and that he was involved in discussion about how Jesus and John were related is thoroughly credible.[23]

So far as Apollos is concerned, 1 Corinthians 1–3 and 16:12 confirm that Paul had contact with the eloquent Alexandrian. 1 Corinthians does not associate Apollos with John the Baptist. But it is an interesting, if unprovable, hypothesis that Paul's slightly defensive comments on baptism in 1 Cor 1:13-17 may have been in response to some of his critics in Corinth who preferred Apollos and emphasized not only "wisdom/eloquence" and "spirituality" but also baptism.[24] It may be that they claimed that Apollos was superior in all these areas;[25] Paul in 1 Corinthians defends himself accordingly. If this hypothesis is correct, then it is all the more likely that Paul was involved in discussions of baptism — of John's baptism, Christian baptism, and the relationship of John and Jesus.

But all the evidence so far has been at the level of probabilities. Is there any more concrete evidence that Paul knew the story of Jesus' baptism as the Gospels tell it?

23. If the traditional Ephesian origin of John's Gospel is accepted, then the case is strengthened, since there are hints there of controversy about the relative greatness of Jesus and John (e.g., 1:20; see the note on "Jesus, John the Baptist, and Qumran" in chapter 2 above).

24. See Richardson, "Thunderbolt," 101-7.

25. Cf. Acts 18:24, 25 with its description of Apollos as a follower of the Baptist, as eloquent, and as "boiling in spirit."* It is possible that 1 John addresses a somewhat similar church situation involving teachers who emphasized baptism ("water"), spiritual anointing, and knowledge, but who failed to give proper emphasis to the cross ("the blood"; 1 John 5:6; 2:27, etc.).

Jesus' Baptism and Christian Baptism

What may well be significant in this connection are the common features in the Gospels' description of Jesus' baptism and Paul's understanding of Christian baptism. Jesus' baptism in the Gospels is

- a baptism with water,
- accompanied by the descent of the Spirit,
- associated with divine sonship — hence the words of royal adoption, "You are my Son.".

For Paul Christian baptism is

- a baptism with water,
- in the Spirit, associated with the receiving of the Spirit, and
- involving adoption of the Christian as a child (or "son") of God.[26]

A key text is Rom 8:15, where Paul comments that "You did not receive a spirit of slavery to fall back into fear, but you received a spirit of adoption/sonship, whereby we cry, 'Abba Father.'"* The verb "you received" (Greek aorist tense) is widely recognized as referring to the occasion of the readers' baptism. If it does, then we have baptism specifically associated with adoption as God's children and with the Spirit in a way that presents a notable parallel to the Gospels' account of Jesus' baptism.[27] Gal 3:26, 27 also bring together sonship and baptism, and in 4:6 sonship and the gift of the Spirit are associated. The "Abba" cry is found in both the Romans and Galatians passages and is evidence that Paul is looking back to the ministry of Jesus (even if the "cry" itself is associated more with Gethsemane than with Jesus' baptism).

There are, of course, differences between Christian baptism according to Paul and Jesus' baptism in the Gospels. For Paul Christian baptism is "into Christ" in a way that Jesus' own baptism could not be. And yet that

26. I take it that Paul is referring to water (or water and Spirit) baptism in texts such as 1 Cor 6:11; 12:13, not just to baptism in the Spirit; cf. Beasley-Murray, *Baptism in the NT,* 167-71; but see Dunn, *Baptism in the Holy Spirit,* 120-32. Even if the texts themselves do only refer to Spirit baptism, there is no question that Pauline baptism involved water. On the connection of baptism and adoption as children of God, see most directly Gal 3:23–4:6 (cf. Romans 8).

27. On Jesus' baptism and Christian baptism and the significance of Rom 8:15 see Scott, *Adoption,* 262-63.

observation may simply be to recognize that for Paul Jesus' experience is primary and Christian experience is derivative from that primary experience.[28] Furthermore, Jesus' baptism, as portrayed in the Gospels, may be seen as "into Christ" in one sense, since "Christ" means "anointed one"; and Jesus' baptism was an "anointing" with the Spirit and as the royal son.[29] Christian baptism may be seen as bringing the Christian to share in that anointed experience of sonship and Spirit and in that way as baptism "into Christ."

Gal 3:26, 27 come close to making that point: "In Christ Jesus you are all sons of God, through faith. For as many of you as were baptized into Christ have put on Christ" (RSV). Baptism here brings the believer into "Christ" and thus into sonship. 1 Cor 12:12, 13 is also interesting: Paul speaks of the one body with many parts, and says, "so it is with Christ. For in the one Spirit we were all baptized into one body. . . ." Baptism is in the Spirit and into Christ. Another significant verse is 2 Cor 1:21, 22, where Paul speaks of God as the one "who establishes us with you in Christ and has anointed us, by putting his seal on us and giving us his Spirit in our hearts as a first installment." There is a play on words here between "Christ" and "anointed" (chrisas), and the thought may well be that in baptism (referred to here as anointing and sealing with the Spirit) we enter into the experience of the one who was himself anointed with the Spirit.[30]

Paul, of course, associates baptism with the death of Jesus (Romans 6). This association is not explicit in the Gospels' narratives of Jesus' baptism. But to recognize this is only to admit that Paul's understanding of baptism is not only based on the story of Jesus' baptism: His post-cross and post-resurrection perspective has enriched his understanding, and, as we have seen, he may also have been influenced by the sayings of Jesus about "taking up the cross" and about his baptism of death (Mark 8:34; 10:39).[31] Baptism brings a person not just to share the Spirit and the relationship of child to God, but also the cross, which for Jesus went with the Spirit and sonship.

If there is some connection between the account of Jesus' baptism

---

28. See Gal 4:6: "Because you are children, God has sent the Spirit of his Son into our hearts. . . ."

29. For Jesus' baptism as his anointing see Acts 10:38 and cf. Luke 4:18.

30. On this interpretation of 2 Cor 1:21, 22 see Scott, *Adoption*, 263. The aorist tenses "anointed . . . sealed . . . gave" suggest a possible reference to baptism. What precedes in 2 Corinthians 1 contains a number of echoes of Jesus-tradition, which makes the suggested connection in these verses the more likely (see chapter 7 above on 1:17-20).

31. See chapter 4 above.

and the Pauline view of Christian baptism, it could be *from* Paul *to* the Gospels, that is, with the Pauline (or pre-Pauline) understanding of Christian baptism shaping, or even giving rise to, the story of Jesus' baptism. But Paul's understanding of the Christian as one who is incorporated into Christ and his experience and his other references to Jesus-tradition in the context (e.g., "Abba" in Rom 8:15) make it more likely that it is Paul who is influenced by the gospel tradition, not vice versa.

There are no definite verbal echoes of the gospel tradition in Paul, though Paul's language in 1 Cor 12:13, "we were baptized in one Spirit,"* is similar to that used of Jesus by John the Baptist in the Gospels, "he will baptize you with the Holy Spirit" (Matt 3:11/Luke 3:15; John 1:33). Paul may be familiar with the Baptist's words, contrasting his own baptism "in water" (cf. 1 Cor 10:2) with Jesus' baptism "in Spirit."

The Temptation

In all three synoptic Gospels, following his baptism, Jesus is led (or driven) by the Spirit into the wilderness to be tempted by the devil. Mark describes Jesus' temptation very briefly (1:12, 13); Matthew and Luke have a more elaborate description of Jesus as Son of God being tempted by the devil in three different ways (Matt 4:1-11/Luke 4:1-11).

Paul nowhere specifically refers to these traditions. He believes in Satanic temptation as a reality in the Christian life (e.g., 1 Cor 7:5; 2 Cor 11:14; 12:7-10; Gal 6:1; 1 Thes 3:5), and he believes that the Christian may overcome such temptation (1 Cor 10:13). But he does not associate these ideas specifically with Jesus.

He does, however, speak of Jesus as one "who knew no sin" (2 Cor 5:21), and he sees Jesus as the specifically righteous one (e.g., Romans 5). It is possible that this emphasis on Jesus' moral perfection has more to do in Paul's mind with Jesus' sacrificial death than with his life or ministry; Jesus had to be sinless in order to be the perfect sacrifice.[32] And yet it is hard to imagine Paul speaking or thinking thus if Jesus' moral uprightness was not part of the tradition of Jesus' earthly life that he knew.[33]

---

32. So Casey, *From Jewish Prophet*, 125.

33. Certainly it is part of the gospel tradition (e.g., Matt 3:13-15; John 7:18; 8:46). Wolff, in "True Apostolic Knowledge," 96, speaks of Paul endorsing "the widespread Christian idea of Christ's sinlessness . . . ; that presupposes a knowledge of a corresponding conduct on the part of the earthly Jesus."

Was this a general impression gained from the story of Jesus, or was it something associated with specific traditions concerning the Lord? The author of Hebrews, when speaking of Jesus as "one who in every respect has been tested as we are, yet without sin," probably had in mind, among other things, the agony of Gethsemane (4:15; cf. 5:7). We have seen some evidence that Paul was also familiar with that story. Whether he also knew something like the "Q" or the Markan temptation narratives is harder to say.

It is just possible that his description of Jesus in Phil 2:5-11 as one who was "in the form of God" but who "did not regard equality with God as something to be exploited, but emptied himself, taking the form of a slave," owes something to the "Q" temptation narrative, where Jesus declines to exploit his status as "Son of God" for his own advantage and refuses the devil's offer of authority over all the kingdoms of the world.[34] It is also possible that the "Q" temptation narrative, which describes Jesus' temptations in terms of Israel's wilderness experiences,[35] has influenced Paul's discussion of the Corinthians' idolatry and immorality in 1 Cor 10:1-13: He speaks explicitly of Israel's temptations in the wilderness.[36] But neither

34. See C. Brown, "Person of Christ," 785. Jesus in the "Q" narrative is tempted as "the Son of God" to exploit his relationship with God by turning stones to bread and by jumping from the pinnacle of the temple; he is also tempted with the promise of all the kingdoms of the earth in return for worshiping the devil. He refuses to grasp for power in that way.

35. In the Q temptation Jesus looks back to Israel's wilderness experience, citing Deut 8:3; 6:16, 13. Israel was God's son who failed; Jesus is the son who succeeds. See, e.g., Gerhardsson, *Testing*.

36. The major thematic link between 1 Cor 10:1-12 and the "Q" temptation narrative is the use of Israel in the wilderness as a negative model. But there are other themes in 1 Corinthians 10, including desire, idolatry, and not testing God or Christ, that have some sort of parallel in the "Q" narrative; thus Jesus is tempted to make bread, to bow down to Satan to win world dominion, and to jump off the temple and so to "test" God. Paul concludes: "No testing has overtaken you that is not common to everyone. God is faithful, and he will not let you be tested beyond your strength, but with the testing he will also provide the way out so that you may be able to endure it" (1 Cor 10:13). It is possible that Paul's exhortation to the Corinthians does arise in part out of his reflection on the "Q" story. But there is no way of proving this; the relationship could be in the other direction with the "Q" story developing out of the sort of thinking found in Paul, or it could be a case of a common Christian exegetical tradition being used independently in the two NT contexts. (There is no reference to Jesus' example in 1 Corinthians 10; "the Christ" is the "rock" in the Israelites' desert, and then is the one who must not be put to the test [10:4, 9].)

Phil 2:5-11 nor 1 Cor 10:1-13 amounts to a very clear or strongly persuasive parallel to the synoptic temptation story.

Romans 8 may be a little more promising. We have already suggested that in 8:15 Paul speaks of Christian baptism in ways that are reminiscent of Jesus' baptism (with references to adoption and the Spirit). But we also find in the same context a reference to the Christian facing moral struggle: "If by the Spirit you put to death the deeds of the body you will live. For all who are led by the Spirit of God are sons of God. For you did not receive the spirit of slavery . . ." (8:13-15, RSV). The combination of ideas here is interesting: Paul speaks of sons of God, adopted in baptism, being "led by the Spirit," and putting to death the deeds of the body. This is all that far removed from the picture presented in the "Q" narrative: Jesus is acclaimed as God's Son in baptism and then is "led" by the Spirit to face and conquer Satan's temptations.[37] It is at least possible that Paul, who goes on in 8:17 to speak of Christians as "joint heirs with Christ," has been influenced by the story of Jesus' baptism and temptations and sees the baptized Christian as following the master's lead in facing temptation.

We conclude that Paul could have known something like the "Q" temptation narrative;[38] but still the evidence is hardly distinctive or strong enough to allow us to assert confidently that he did.

THE MINISTRY, MIRACLES, AND LIFESTYLE OF JESUS AND THE APOSTLES

In the course of discussing Jesus' teaching we have already seen that Paul was probably familiar with various aspects and incidents of Jesus' ministry. It is not necessary to add much to our earlier findings.

Paul was aware that Jesus ministered mainly to Jews (as a "servant of the circumcised," Rom 15:8). He was aware of "the twelve" and that Jesus sent out apostles, and he knew of Peter's special commissioning and that Peter and others were sent particularly to the Jews (1 Cor 15:5; Gal 2:7, etc.).

37. I am indebted to Idicheria Ninan for pointing out that "led by the Spirit" in Rom 8:14 is paralleled in the gospel temptation narratives of Matt 4:1/Luke 4:1. See his *Jesus as the Son of God*, 333.

38. Mark 1:13 describes Jesus being "with the wild beasts" at the time of his temptation, and Paul speaks, probably metaphorically, of "fighting with wild beasts"* in 1 Cor 15:32. But there is probably no connection.

Paul also knew that the apostles were given authority to do miracles, and so speaks of his own working of miracles (2 Cor 12:11, 12; Rom 15:19; cf. also Gal 3:5; 1 Thes 1:5).

Jesus and Miracles

Evidence of Jesus' miracles in Paul

Paul does not specifically refer to Jesus' miracles, but it is entirely probable that he knew of them. His familiarity with the tradition of apostles being sent to do miracles suggests this, since it is highly unlikely that he associated the apostles but not Jesus himself with working of miracles.[39] It is also suggested by 1 Cor 13:2, where, as we argued in chapter 2 (above), Paul echoes Jesus' saying about miracle-working faith moving mountains.

Was Paul's ministry modeled on that of Jesus the healer?

Paul's description of his own ministry also may reflect the traditions of Jesus' miracles. Thus in Rom 15:18, 19, he speaks of "what Christ has accomplished through me to win obedience from the Gentiles, by word and deed, by the power of signs and wonders, by the power of the Spirit of God . . . I have fully proclaimed the good news of Christ." This says nothing directly or necessarily about Jesus' own miracles, but it is hard to imagine Paul speaking thus of Christ working "through me," if he did not believe that Jesus' own ministry of the good news was also a ministry marked by similar powerful signs. Paul's words certainly make particularly good sense if he was familiar with Jesus' miracles.

Phil 1:8 may be another hint pointing in the same direction, since Paul speaks of longing for the Philippians with "the compassion of Christ Jesus." The verb cognate with the noun translated "compassion"[40] is used in the Gospels of Jesus' attitude to those who came to him in need (though not just of his healings; e.g., Mark 1:41; Matt 14:14/Mark 6:34; Matt 15:32/Mark 8:2; Matt 20:34). There is no necessary connection between the Pauline phrase and the gospel traditions, but it may be that here, and

39. Negatively it may also be suggested by the way 2 Thes 2:9 speaks of the "lawless one," referring to his deceptive "power, signs, lying wonders"; if this antichrist figure had such powers, we may assume that Paul believed that Jesus had such powers.

40. Greek *splanchnon*.

elsewhere where Paul speaks of compassion and mercy as prime Christian virtues, he has been influenced by the stories of Jesus.[41]

Weakness/sickness

Yet another echo of the miracle stories of Jesus may be in Paul's teaching about the importance of caring for "the weak" (e.g., 1 Thes 5:14: "help the weak"). Usually by "the weak" he means those who are spiritually weak and whose consciences are tender (e.g., Rom 14:1, 2, 21), though sometimes he uses the word of physical weakness and illness (so 1 Cor 11:30). The Gospels use the same word group of those who are physically sick: Jesus brought healing to "the weak" and told his disciples to "heal the weak" (i.e., the sick: e.g., Matt 10:8; Mark 6:56; Luke 5:15). It is possible that in emphasizing the need to care for "the weak" Paul sees himself as continuing the ministry of Jesus to "weak" people.[42]

A spiritualizing tendency?

If the last suggestion has any weight, then it may be that, as well as a link between Jesus and Paul at this point, there is a significant shift of emphasis from Jesus to Paul with the idea of healing physical "weakness" giving way to the idea of supporting the spiritually "weak." This would fit in with the observations we made in chapter 2 about the ideas of "power," "faith," and "salvation" being associated in the synoptics particularly with Jesus' miracles and in Paul with the preaching of the cross. Has Paul moved significantly away from Jesus at this point? Does he effectively reject the miracle-working Jesus?

But Paul speaks in Rom 15:18, 19 of his own ministry "by word and deed, by the power of signs and wonders, by the power of the Spirit." It is clear from this that there is no contradiction in his mind between the word of the cross that he has expounded in Romans and the working of miracles. The same is clear in the Corinthian letters, where Paul accepts the validity of the miraculous gifts of the Corinthians and speaks of his own exercise of those gifts (1 Cor 14:5, 18; 2 Cor 12:12).

---

41. See also Phil 2:1; Col 3:12. O'Brien, *Colossians*, 198-99, notes the OT and Jewish background to "mercy and compassion," and observes that the verb *splanchnizomai* is used in the NT of God or Christ, in the synoptics of Jesus himself, but also in the parables of the forgiving master, the good Samaritan, and the father of the prodigal son (Matt 18:27; Luke 10:33; 15:20).

42. Cf., interestingly, Acts 20:35.

Nonetheless, he does fault the Corinthians for their one-sided and simplistic emphasis on the miraculous, which fails (most importantly of all) to take seriously the cross and all that it means for the place of weakness in the Christian life. If the Corinthians saw the miracles of Jesus as showing that "weakness" is something to be eliminated by the exercise of divine power, Paul could draw an opposite lesson from the miracles, seeing them as evidence that human "weakness" is precisely the context where God's grace is seen. But more particularly he sees the cross of Jesus as the supreme evidence that weakness is not always something negative, something that God chooses to remove immediately, but something in and through which God exercises his saving power (e.g., 1 Cor 1:23, 24; 2 Cor 12:9, 10; 13:4).

If these suggestions are correct, then we do not have in Paul any repudiation of the gospel miracle traditions. What we do have is an attempt to maintain the dual emphasis of Jesus' ministry on both "word" and "deed" and in particular to interpret the traditions of Jesus' ministry in the light of the cross. For Paul the supreme healing of the "weak" is through the cross (see Rom 5:6).[43] If there has been a shift from the Jesus-tradition, it is more an extension of that tradition in the light of the cross than any radical departure from it.

Sign-seeking

In fact, the Pauline perspective on "signs" has something of a parallel in the gospel tradition, since Jesus himself is seen to be a noted miracle worker who also firmly repudiates the demands of those who ask him for "signs" (both the "Q" and Markan traditions: Matt 12:38, 39/Luke 11:16, 29-32; Matt 16:1-4/Mark 8:13). It is possible that Paul was familiar with this anti-sign-seeking Jesus-tradition. Certainly in 1 Cor 1:22 he specifically describes the Jews as those "who demand signs."

In the "Q" form of Jesus' saying Jesus turns down the request for a sign and says that no sign will be given "except the sign of the prophet Jonah"; he then goes on to speak of how the Ninevites "repented at the proclamation of Jonah, and see, something greater than Jonah is here." He also tells of how the Queen of Sheba came "to listen to the wisdom of Solomon, and see, something greater than Solomon is here." Scholars have

---

43. It is interesting to find Isa 53:4, "he took our weaknesses and bore our diseases,"* used in Matt 8:17 of the healing ministry of Jesus, and the same sort of language used in Rom 15:1 more broadly of the Christian's responsibility to others (with perhaps a particular reference to the cross).

noticed how the ideas expressed here — the rejection of the Jews' seeking for signs, the offer instead of the "preaching" of Jesus (the one greater than Jonah), and Solomon's "wisdom" being surpassed by Jesus — all have parallels in 1 Corinthians 1, notably in vv. 22-24, where Paul speaks negatively of the Jewish demand for signs and of the Greek search for wisdom and offers instead the "preaching" of the cross of Christ and speaks of Christ as the "wisdom" of God.[44] Even the thought of the cross may be connected with the Jesus-tradition in question, since in Matthew "the sign of Jonah" is specifically interpreted in terms of Jesus' death: "For just as Jonah was three days and three nights in the belly of the sea monster, so for three days and three nights the Son of Man will be in the heart of the earth" (12:40).[45]

Whether or not the Matthean interpretation of the sign of Jonah antedates Matthew,[46] the possibility that Paul has been influenced by the "Q" tradition is real. If he was, the case for his knowledge of Jesus' miracles is not directly strengthened; but it is significant that his thinking about miracles is related to traditions of Jesus.

Jesus' Lifestyle and Style of Ministry

There is every likelihood that Paul saw his own apostolic ministry as modeled on that of Jesus, not only in his miracles and in helping the "weak," but in many other ways as well. In 1 Cor 11:1 he specifically says to the Corinthians that they are to be "imitators of me, as I am of Christ"; he is referring in the context to his own style of ministry as a model (see also 2 Thes 3:7, 9), but he sees Jesus as the original and perfect pattern.[47]

We have seen in previous chapters various specific areas in which Paul was probably influenced by Jesus' example: He saw Jesus as the model servant, the one who welcomed others (e.g., Rom 15:7, 8). He was probably influenced in this by what he knew of Jesus' openness to sinners, outsiders, and those on the margins of society, including Samaritans and women (see chapter 6 above).

More generally Paul speaks of Jesus as one who "knew no sin" (2 Cor

44. See J. M. Robinson, "Kerygma and History," 129.
45. See Fjärstedt, *Synoptic Tradition*, 150-52.
46. Whether Matthew's interpretation of the sign of Jonah was shared by Luke is debated; I. H. Marshall, *Luke*, 484-87, argues strongly that it was. For the complex critical questions surrounding the history of the different synoptic traditions see Marshall, Davies and Allison, *Matthew*, II, 351-53, and other commentators.
47. See also 1 Thes 1:6; cf. Schippers, "Pre-Synoptic Tradition," 225-26.

5:21). In 2 Cor 10:1 he refers to "the meekness and gentleness of Christ"; he may have Jesus' incarnation and passion in mind when speaking thus, but he may well be thinking more broadly of Jesus' whole ministry and lifestyle.[48] Paul sees himself as called to follow in Jesus' steps.[49]

Two further specifics deserve particular mention:

The poor

Jesus' ministry, unlike that of most rabbis, was that of an unmarried, itinerant preacher, of whom it could be said that "the Son of Man has nowhere to lay his head" (Matt 8:20/Luke 9:58). He was associated especially with the poor and spoke of his ministry in those terms (e.g., Luke 4:18; 6:20).

Paul also speaks of Jesus as one who "though he was rich, for your sakes became poor" (2 Cor 8:9). This may be a reference primarily to the incarnation (as by definition an act of impoverishment) or to Jesus' death (the supreme act of impoverishment) or to both, rather than a comment on Jesus' social or economic status. But it would not be an obvious way to describe the incarnation, had Jesus been materially rich, and it is not a particularly natural way of referring to Jesus' death. In the context of 2 Corinthians 8, where Paul is discussing down-to-earth financial matters, it seems quite likely that his thought includes the idea of Jesus' literal poverty.

Paul probably also knew of Jesus' celibacy. This is strongly suggested by what he says about the advantages of the single state in 1 Corinthians 7.

Paul may very well have seen his own ministry as modeled on that of Jesus in these respects. He was himself unmarried. He was an itinerant evangelist, and he associated apostleship with itinerant ministry (1 Cor 9:5). He describes how he — as an apostle and minister of Christ — has experienced hunger, thirst, poverty, and homelessness (e.g., 1 Cor 4:9-13; 2 Cor 6:4-10; 11:23-27). It is likely that he saw himself not simply as sharing in

48. See Martin, *2 Corinthians*, 302. The wording of 2 Cor 10:1 is reminiscent of Matt 11:29, "I am gentle and humble of heart" (cf. also Matt 5:5; 21:5), and could be an echo of it. This verse is, however, widely regarded as Matthean redaction; so, e.g., Stanton, *Gospel for a New People*, 369-70. If it is, it is still testimony that Jesus' life and ministry were seen in this way. J. P. Brown, "Synoptic Parallels," 29, thinks that Matthew may have been influenced by Eph 4:2, but fails to note the evidence of 2 Cor 10:1.

49. See Wedderburn, *Paul and Jesus*, 180, who thinks that the descriptions of Christian virtues that we find in 1 Cor 13:4-7 and Gal 5:22, 23 could "stem ultimately from the remembered life of Jesus."

the death and resurrection of Jesus but as working out and reflecting in his ministry the "ways of Christ Jesus" (1 Cor 4:17).[50]

Jesus' faith

A more debatable, but interesting, possibility is that Paul sees Jesus not just as a model for Christian living and ministry but also as a model person of faith.[51] Thus in Rom 3:22 Paul speaks of God's righteousness having been revealed (literally) "through faith of Jesus Christ to all who believe."* "Through faith of Jesus Christ" has usually been interpreted as meaning "through faith in Jesus Christ," Paul's point being that God's justification is received by sinners as they put their trust in Jesus.[52] However, an increasing number of scholars in recent years have argued that in this and other similar "faith of Christ" texts (e.g., Rom 3:26; Gal 2:16; 3:22; Phil 3:9), Paul is not referring to faith *in* Jesus, but to the faith exercised *by* Jesus. This is not to deny the importance of the Christian's faith in the context of justification; it is to say that in texts such as Rom 3:22 Paul sees justification both as the result of Jesus' faith ("through the faith of Jesus Christ") and as received by the Christian through faith ("for all who believe").[53]

On this view "the faith of Jesus Christ" is comparable to "the faith of Abraham," which Paul refers to in Rom 4:16: Jesus is the seed of Abraham, who himself exercised faith like Abraham; Christians share in his sonship and his saving, Abrahamic faith. Jesus may himself be "the one who is righteous" who "will live by faith" (Rom 1:17).[54]

The arguments for this view are not conclusive.[55] Paul nowhere un-

---

50. See especially on this whole point Wolff, "Humility and Self-Denial." It is interesting to compare Paul's remark about Jesus becoming poor to make others rich in 2 Cor 8:9 with his comment in 2 Cor 6:10 on his own ministry — "as poor, yet making many rich."

51. Cf. Heb 12:2.

52. So Cranfield, *Romans,* 203: "The genitive Χριστοῦ expresses the object of faith."

53. For this view see, among others, Hays, *Faith of Jesus Christ,* discussing particularly the Galatians texts. On Romans see Campbell, *Rhetoric,* 58-69, 214-18; G. N. Davies, *Faith and Obedience,* 107-10; B. W. Longenecker, "ΠΙΣΤΙΣ."

54. So Hays, *Faith,* 151-57, referring to A. T. Hanson; see the latter's *Studies in Paul's Technique and Theology,* 42-45.

55. M. D. Hooker, "ΠΙΣΤΙΣ ΧΡΙΣΤΟΥ," argues that the logic of Paul's view of participation is that Christian faith is a sharing in Christ's faith, but she also suggests that we need not set a "subjective" genitive (Christ's faith) over against an "objective" genitive (faith in Christ): Paul's expression "begins always from the faith of Christ

ambiguously refers to the faith of Jesus, nor do the Gospels speak explicitly of Jesus as a person of "faith" or a believer (though he is clearly someone who trusts God totally).[56] But that Paul should have seen Jesus as the model for faith would fit in with what we have argued for concerning Paul's view of the Christian life as a sharing in Jesus' life (his baptism, experience of the Spirit, sonship, etc.).

THE TRANSFIGURATION

In more senses than one the transfiguration (Matt 17:1-9/Mark 9:2-10/Luke 9:28-36) is a high point in the Gospels' accounts of Jesus' ministry. We touched on the question of Paul's knowledge of this mysterious story in chapter 5 in connection with Paul's reference to the "pillars" in Galatians 3. But it is in 2 Cor 3:1–4:6 that we have the most interesting parallels to the transfiguration narrative.

The Evidence of 2 Corinthians 3:1–4:6[57]

In this passage Paul is defending his ministry against his detractors (see 3:1-6; 4:1, 2). He insists that it is God who has made him a minister of the new covenant of the Spirit, and he then compares the old covenant and the new. He takes as the basis for his comparison the story of Moses going up Mount Sinai into the presence of God to receive the law, then coming down with his face shining and having to veil it. Paul makes two points (at least!) on the basis of that story: First, he insists on the far greater glory of the new covenant of the Spirit; second, he emphasizes that "we" have seen the glory of the Lord with unveiled faces. Thus he describes Christians as those who "with unveiled faces, seeing the glory of the Lord as though reflected in a mirror, are being transformed [or transfigured] into the same image" (3:18), and he goes on to comment that Christians have a revelation from God "who has shone in our hearts to give the light of the knowledge of the glory of God in the face of Jesus Christ" (4:6).

---

himself, but . . . includes, necessarily, the answering faith of believers, who claim that faith as their own" (341).

56. See C. D. Marshall, *Faith as a Theme in Mark's Narrative*, 239.

57. On the possible influence of the Jesus-tradition on Paul in 2 Corinthians 3, 4 see further Moses, *Significance*, 234-45.

Three aspects of this enormously rich and complex passage suggest that, although Paul is explicitly expounding an OT text, he may also have the story of Jesus' transfiguration in mind. First, the picture of Moses on a mountain in the presence of God and with shining face is itself evocative of the transfiguration narrative: Jesus goes up a high mountain, his clothes and his face are transfigured, and God speaks.[58] This, however, does not of itself show that Paul has the transfiguration in mind; it could simply be that the same Mosaic motif is being used in a similar, though not identical, way by Paul and in the transfiguration account.

Second, the dominant theme of 2 Cor 3:1–4:6 is "glory" and in particular the glory of God visible in Christ. This particular use of the word "glory" is hardly paralleled elsewhere in Paul,[59] but is, of course, very much the theme of the transfiguration narrative.[60] This again is no proof that Paul has the transfiguration in mind; his emphasis on the glory of Christ could simply be derived from his reflection on the Moses story. On the other hand, it could have been the transfiguration story that stimulated his reflection on the comparative glory of Moses and Jesus.

Third and most interesting is Paul's use in 2 Cor 3:18 of precisely the same unusual verb *"transform/transfigure"* as is used by Matthew and Mark in the transfiguration narrative.[61] Paul admittedly uses it of Christians seeing the glory of the Lord rather than of the Lord himself being transfigured, but then Paul does go on to speak of God shining "in our hearts to give the light of the knowledge of the glory of God *in the face of Jesus Christ*."

The combination of these three observations, none of them decisive in themselves, makes it at least a reasonable possibility that Paul has the transfiguration story in mind.

---

58. On the transfiguration as a new Sinai event see Moses, *Significance of the Transfiguration*. Mark refers specifically to Jesus' clothes shining, not his face. But his general comment that "he was transfigured before them" (9:2) probably implies that Jesus' face was also transformed. Matthew and Luke both refer to Jesus' face being transformed; they may well have an tradition independent from that of Mark, but in any case they show how the story was understood at an early date.

59. Cf. possibly 1 Cor 2:8; Phil 3:21; 2 Thes 2:14.

60. The word "glory" is used only in Luke's account (9:31, 32), but is also found in 2 Pet 1:17.

61. *Metamorphoomai* is used four times in the NT: in Matthew's and Mark's account of the transfiguration, in 2 Cor 3:18, and in Rom 12:1, where again some have suspected a transfiguration allusion (e.g., Resch, *Paulinismus*, 202-3). On "transfiguration" in Paul see Segal, *Paul the Convert*, 22, 111-12.

But why in the context of defending his own ministry does he develop the theme of the glory of the new covenant and emphasize that "we" see the glory of the Lord? Is it simply because Judaizers criticized his gospel of freedom and the Spirit? This would explain his emphasis on the superior glory of the new covenant, but not so obviously the point that "we" see the glory. Or is it perhaps because his critics were elevating Peter and other apostles at Paul's expense by referring to their vastly superior experience of the transfiguration? If so, Paul replies by taking up the theme of the glory of Christ and by insisting that he and others have seen the glory of the face of Jesus.[62] In fact, he says, we are all being transfigured as we see the Lord's glory.[63]

The idea is speculative, but makes sense of Paul's emphases in the passage, and there are other arguments to support the thesis.

Other Observations

Paul and his denigrators

There is no question that Paul found it necessary to defend himself from those who exalted other more "original" apostles and denigrated him. We have seen in chapter 5 above that in Galatians 2 Paul may be claiming to have had as genuine a revelation and commissioning as Peter the rock in response to his critics. It is clear that Paul faces the same sort of questioning of his ministry in the Corinthian church (e.g., 1 Cor 9:1-3; 2 Cor 11:5, 6; 12:11, 12). Indeed, as we have observed, such questioning is the explicit context of his discussion in 2 Corinthians 3 and 4 (see 3:1-6).

The importance of the transfiguration

There is no question that the transfiguration came to be seen in the church as a particular privilege for those who had experienced it and probably as

---

62. 2 Cor 4:6 has often been taken as a reference to Paul's Damascus experience. If it is, then he may be claiming in that experience a revelation quite comparable to the transfiguration.

63. It is interesting to compare Paul's reference in 2 Cor 4:6 to the knowledge of God's glory "*in the face of* Jesus Christ" with his reference in 2 Cor 5:12 to those who "boast *in face*."* Martin, *2 Corinthians*, 125, translates this as "those who boast of what is seen" and he notes as one possibility the view that the reference is to those who attack Paul as one who had inferior knowledge of the historical Jesus.

giving them particular authority and status. 2 Pet 1:16-18, for example, singles out the transfiguration as demonstrating that "we did not follow cleverly devised myths when we made known to you the power and coming of our Lord Jesus Christ, but we had been eyewitnesses of his majesty. . . . We were with him on the holy mountain."[64] The Evangelists also evidently saw the transfiguration in this way; hence Peter's understated remark, "It is good for us to be here," and Jesus' caution about keeping the revelation quiet until after the resurrection (Matt 17:4, 9/Mark 9:5, 9/Luke 9:33). There is some reason to think that Peter, James, and John were the leading triumvirate within the apostolic band in the earliest days of the church, and it may have been the transfiguration more than anything else that was seen as giving them special authority.[65] If it was, then Paul might very well have felt a need to discuss his apostleship in terms of their experience.

Paul, "the pillars," and the transfiguration

It is possible that Paul indirectly confirms the special position of the inner three in Gal 2:9, where he speaks of the "acknowledged pillars," whom he met in Jerusalem. These three leading figures in the Jerusalem church were James, Peter, and John. The James in this case is James the Lord's brother, not James the apostle, who had already been executed, but it is possible that James the brother succeeded James the apostle within the inner three after the latter's death.[66]

It is even possible to link the title "pillars" to the transfiguration narrative, since all the Gospels precede the transfiguration story with the much-discussed saying of Jesus that "there are some standing here who will not taste death until they see that the kingdom of God has come with

---

64. The point is unaffected by questions concerning the authorship of 2 Peter.

65. The Gospels suggest that Jesus himself chose the inner three. Even if there are some scholarly questions about this, that the Gospels portray these three as the inner circle must reflect a perception of their position. Since James was executed at quite an early date, the probability is that they had a leading role in the very earliest days. As it happens, Acts does refer to these three in particular in the opening chapters (Peter and John in Acts 3 and 4, James and Peter in ch. 12), and Paul refers to Peter and John as two of the pillars in Gal 2:9.

66. Acts 12 (especially v. 17) suggests that James the Lord's brother came to prominence at that time (cf. Wall, "Successors to 'the Twelve'"; D. Wenham, "Acts and the Pauline Corpus"). On the idea of James succeeding James as a "pillar" see Bruce, *Galatians*, 123; Wenham and Moses, "There Are Some"; Chilton, *Feast of Meanings*, 81-86, commenting also on the transfiguration and Gethsemane.

power" (so Mark 9:1; Matt 16:28 and Luke 9:27 are slightly different). Scholars have widely divergent views on what the saying means and meant originally, but there is a strong case for believing that Mark at least took it to refer in the first instance to the transfiguration, hence the specific chronological link between the saying and the transfiguration story "six days later." The transfiguration was a notable manifestation of the coming kingdom, one that "some" disciples (i.e., Peter, James, and John) witnessed before the sufferings that Jesus had predicted.[67]

If this was the interpretation of the saying accepted by Mark and others, then it is interesting at least to note that the Hebrew and Aramaic words for "pillar" (*'ammûd, 'ammûda'*) come from the verb "stand" and might literally be translated "standing one." Was it then the saying of Jesus about the transfiguration that spoke of "standing ones" seeing the kingdom that led to Peter, James, and John being nicknamed "pillars"? Just as Simon was called "Peter" as the rock on which the new temple was to be built — on the basis of a saying of Jesus — so he and his colleagues came to be known as "pillars" in the church, which is the new temple.[68] This idea might seem over-ingenious; but it is striking that we have in the gospel tradition a saying about "standing ones" linked to an event featuring the trio of Peter, James, and John and in Galatians a reference to three "pillars" including Peter, John, and a different James.[69]

---

67. If casting out demons was a manifestation of the eschatological kingdom (Matt 12:28/Luke 11:20), how much more the startling event of the transfiguration (including the appearance of Moses and Elijah, both figures associated with the coming day of the Lord). In the story Peter proposes to build booths for the glorious ones, perhaps on the assumption that the eschaton had come. Among recent commentators linking Mark 9:1 and the transfiguration see V. Taylor, C. E. B. Cranfield, J. Gnilka, and R. Pesch. The last comments (*Markusevangelium*, II, 67): "The three disciples, outstanding authorities of the early church . . . experience before their death a vision of the glory of Jesus as the risen one, the one exalted as Son of man."

68. On this see also the comments in chapter 5 above. We note that in Matthew the promise to Simon the "rock" comes in 16:18, very shortly before the transfiguration narrative and the saying about the "standing ones" (16:28–17:8). Matthew also has in the same context (16:24-26) the sayings about "taking up the cross" and "losing/gaining," with which Paul may have been familiar (see chapter 4 above).

69. For this hypothesis see in greater detail Moses and Wenham, "There Are Some Standing Here." Fossum, *Name of God,* 56-58, 120-24, 139-41, brings out the importance of the expression "standing one(s)" in Gnostic and Samaritan texts. God and angels are "standing ones"; more interestingly Moses is God's standing one when he goes up Mount Sinai (Deut 5:31), and *Memar Marqa* (a Samaritan work) 5.3 says, "When he went up to Him and the cloud covered him for six days, his body became holy. . . . He ascended

In favor of this view is the fact that it helps explain the "pillars" title. It may also explain Paul's apparent unease about the title in Galatians 2: He speaks of those "acknowledged" or "reputed" to be "pillars." If the title "pillars" and the associated transfiguration tradition were used by some in the Jerusalem church to exalt the three and to denigrate Paul, then this may explain both Paul's lack of enthusiasm for the title in Galatians 2 and (as we have already argued) his specific insistence in 2 Corinthians 3 and 4 that he and all Christians have in one important sense participated in the transfiguration.

The "acknowledged ones"

A final additional observation strengthens the argument. It looks as though the triumvirate in Jerusalem may not simply have been called "the pillars," but also, by some, *"the acknowledged ones/reputed ones."* This is suggested by Paul's use of that expression three times in Galatians 2 (vss. 2, 6, and 9).[70] Again it is possible to sense some irritation on Paul's part with the title, thus his comment in Gal 2:6: "What they actually were makes no difference to me." It may be that "the acknowledged ones" was another nickname given to the Jerusalem leaders in the early church, and it may again have been derived from the traditions of Jesus, since the relevant verb is used in Jesus' discussion with his disciples about leadership and greatness.

Thus in the Lukan version of the tradition we are told that "there was a dispute among them about which of them should be *acknowledged* as greatest"* (22:24), and in Mark 10:42 Jesus responds to their bickering by speaking of "those *acknowledged* to be rulers over the nations"* and then by speaking of Christian leadership.[71] Mark has precisely the same participle as that used by Paul in Galatians 2, and interestingly the Markan discussion is provoked specifically by James and John. The coincidence of vocabulary and subject matter (apostolic leadership in the church) is striking, and it seems quite likely that we have another play on Jesus' words with people

---

from human status to the status of angels" (as cited by Fossum, 123). It is interesting at least to find "standing one" associated with this OT experience of transfiguration.

70. The Greek here (and in Mark 10:42) is *dokountes*.

71. There is reason to believe that the Lukan and Markan traditions are probably independent of each other, so that the coincidence in the use of the verb *dokeō* ("be acknowledged") is significant. On the Lukan tradition see recently Nelson, *Leadership and Discipleship*.

in Jerusalem elevating the "acknowledged" leaders in a way that Paul reacts uneasily toward.[72]

This last argument, though it has added to the evidence for the importance of Jesus-traditions in the earliest days of the church, has taken us away from the transfiguration. However, it has added weight to the previous explanation of the "pillars" terminology and so to the overall case that the transfiguration tradition and the saying about "some standing here" that accompanies it in the Gospels were well known in the early church, and that Paul also knew them.[73]

THE PASSION

The supreme importance of Jesus' death for Paul's theology is indisputable. But how much of the story of the passion did Paul know? Was it simply the fact of Jesus' death that was important to him, or was the sequence of events also important to him?

We have already discussed Paul's perspective on the last supper and in particular his narrative of institution in 1 Corinthians 11. From 11:23, "I received from the Lord what I also handed on to you, that the Lord Jesus on the night when he was betrayed took a loaf of bread . . . ," it is clear that Paul was familiar not only with the story of the last supper itself but also with its time and context, that is, "the night when he was betrayed."[74] On

72. The Greek for "the acknowledged ones" (hoi dokountes) is a recognized classical usage. But there is a semantically similar Hebrew and Aramaic verb (ḥšb), which is used to translate the Greek term in Mark 10:42 in Lindsey, Hebrew Translation of the Gospel of Mark, 129. For further discussion of the term see Wenham and Moses, "There Are Some Standing Here."

73. J. M. Robinson, "Kerygma and History," 141-42, suggests that Paul in 2 Corinthians may be combating a christology that emphasizes Jesus as a powerful miracle-worker like Moses, with the transfiguration understood as a climactic point (see also Georgi, Paul's Opponents, 170-74). There is, however, little evidence to suggest that Paul is rebutting a Moses christology in 2 Corinthians 3 and 4; the issue Paul is primarily addressing is that of his own ministry and apostleship (so 3:1-6), and it is more likely that he is responding to the use of the transfiguration story to glorify particular apostles than to any christological misuse of the narrative.

74. The Greek verb translated "betray" here is paradidōmi, which is elsewhere used of Jesus' death and is more appropriately translated "hand over" (cf. Gal 2:20; Rom 4:25; also 2 Cor 4:11). For Paul's familiarity with "the night when he was betrayed" see

the basis of this evidence alone we might reasonably infer that Paul knew a passion narrative.[75]

It is not easy to say how much of the story that we know in the Gospels was familiar to Paul. But the following points are worth noting: (1) Paul knows that Jesus died by crucifixion (e.g., Phil 2:8: "even death on a cross"; 2 Cor 13:4: "he was crucified in weakness"). (2) Paul must, therefore, have been aware that Jesus' execution was carried out by the Romans, but (like the Gospels) he pins the primary blame on "the Jews," who "killed the Lord Jesus" (1 Thes 2:14, 15). In 1 Cor 2:8 he speaks of "the rulers of this age" crucifying Jesus in ignorance; whether he has in mind here the Jewish leaders, or (in view of his explanatory reference to ignorance) is thinking of the Romans, or has both groups of "rulers" in mind is not clear.[76]

(3) Paul was well aware that Jesus' death involved real, bodily "sufferings." He sees his own physical sufferings as a participation in the sufferings of Christ (2 Cor 1:5; 4:10; Phil 3:10; Col 1:24).[77] In Gal 6:17 he refers intriguingly to himself carrying "the marks" *(stigmata)* of Jesus in his own body. The word here may refer to brands identifying a slave as belonging to a particular owner, and Paul may simply mean that he is marked as a follower of Jesus by the scars he bears from the beatings and persecution that he has endured. But he may more specifically be alluding to the physical wounds that Jesus received at his crucifixion (the beatings, the nails, etc.)[78] and saying that he, Paul, has been similarly wounded; he has himself been "crucified" for and with Christ (Gal 2:19; 6:14), and his body bears the marks that Jesus' body bore.[79]

---

also our discussion of Gethsemane in chapter 6 (above). Sneed, "'The Kingdom of God,'" 369, notes a possible connection between Col 1:13 and Luke 22:53; it is at best possible.

75. Walter, "Paul and the Early Christian Jesus-Tradition," 62, 63, sees 1 Cor 11:23-25 as an "aetiology for ritual" and not as evidence that Paul knew anything like the synoptic passion narrative. And yet he admits that 1 Cor 11:23 suggests Pauline knowledge of some sort of passion narrative.

76. Stuhlmacher, "Jesustradition," 245, suggests that both are in mind. *Archontes,* "rulers," is used in Rom 13:3 of the Roman authorities. For understanding *archontes* in 1 Cor 2:8 as human rather than demonic rulers see Fee, *1 Corinthians,* 103-6. 1 Tim 6:13 refers specifically to Pontius Pilate.

77. Wright, *NT and the People of God,* 408, comments on 2 Cor 4:10: "In this and the subsequent verses, 'Jesus' refers unambiguously, as elsewhere in Paul, to the human Jesus."

78. Wolff, "Humility and Self-Denial," 156, comments that it is the specific reference to "Jesus" that makes an allusion to the crucifixion clear here.

79. It is just possible that there is significance in Paul's use of the verb "carry/bear"

(4) Paul speaks not only of Jesus' physical suffering but also of the "insults" that fell on him: "Christ did not please himself; but, as it is written, 'The insults of those who insult you have fallen on me'" (Rom 15:3, quoting Ps 69:9). The reference here need not be to the crucifixion: The Gospels describe Jesus being insulted during his ministry (e.g., as the agent of Beelzebul, Matt 12:24/Mark 3:22). But it is likely that what Paul has in mind is the insults and taunts that Jesus experienced during his passion (e.g., Matt 27:44/Mark 15:32).[80]

(5) Col 2:14 speaks of God "erasing the record [literally the "handwriting"] that stood against us with its legal demands. He set this aside, nailing it to the cross." It is just possible that there is here an allusion to Pilate "writing" the accusation that stood against Jesus and attaching it to the cross.[81] What Pilate did in condemning Jesus at the cross is taken as a picture of what God was doing to save humanity through Jesus.[82]

(6) If that is a rather speculative inference, Paul's knowledge of Jesus' burial following his crucifixion is quite explicit. It is striking that in his very brief summary of gospel facts in 1 Cor 15:3, 4 Paul includes the clause "and that he was buried." His highlighting of what might seem to be a relatively unimportant event (as compared to the death and resurrection) may simply be a lead into his following discussion of resurrection. But it quite probably also reflects the fact that the burial featured prominently in the passion traditions that Paul knew, as it does in the gospel narratives.[83]

---

in this context (compare also Gal 6:2; Rom 15:1). It is the verb that is used in John 19:17 of Jesus carrying the cross, in Luke 14:27 of the disciples carrying the cross, and in Isa 53:4 of the suffering servant bearing the sins of others.

80. A reference to the passion in Rom 15:3 may be supported by the references in the context to "bear[ing] the weaknesses of the powerless"* (15:1; see preceding note on "bearing") and to "steadfastness" (15:4; cf. "the steadfastness of Christ" in 2 Thes 3:5). See Thompson, *Clothed with Christ*, 208-36, for detailed discussion of this section of Romans. In 1 Cor 4:12 Paul says "when reviled, we bless," perhaps echoing the language of the sermon on the mount (see chapter 5 above), but perhaps also recalling the sufferings of Jesus. (See our earlier observations about 1 Cor 4:11-13 and cf. 1 Pet 2:23; 3:9.)

81. Cf. O'Brien, *Colossians*, 126.

82. It is also possible that Paul's questions in Rom 8:33, 34 (following his description in v. 32 of God giving Jesus up "for all of us") — "Who will bring any charge against God's elect? . . . Who is to condemn?" — recall Jesus' trial and condemnation.

83. Crossan, *Historical Jesus*, 391-94, considers the burial (like most other ingredients in the passion narrative) inferred by Christians on the basis of scriptural reflection, not on the basis of knowledge. But his assumption that early Christians had no information about the circumstances of Jesus' death (having fled the scene) is extraor-

In Gal 3:1 Paul asks the Galatians how they can be turning away from the gospel he preached to them: "Who has bewitched you, before whose eyes Jesus Christ was publicly portrayed as crucified?" (RSV). Paul implies here, as elsewhere, that the crucifixion was the center of his gospel. That does not necessarily mean that he described the events of Jesus' passion in his preaching.[84] And yet the language used here — "before whose eyes Jesus Christ was publicly exhibited (or placarded)"* — perhaps suggests something more than an unadorned announcement that "he died for our sins."

Similarly, when Paul speaks of the sufferings of Jesus as shared by Christians and as the model to be imitated (Rom 15:3; Phil 2:5; 1 Thes 1:6; cf. 1 Cor 11:1, etc.), he and his readers could in theory have only the general idea of Jesus' crucifixion in mind. But it is more likely that he and they were familiar with a passion narrative, such as the Gospels variously contain.

The evidence for Paul's knowledge of the details of the passion story is not extensive, but in view of his undisputed knowledge of "the night when Jesus was betrayed" and of the resurrection traditions, we may confidently "assume that Paul knew details of Jesus' passion."[85]

THE RESURRECTION AND EXALTATION

1 Corinthians 15:3-9 and the Gospel Resurrection Accounts

Jesus' resurrection was of primary theological importance for Paul, and he was evidently familiar with some stories of the resurrection. The most important evidence here is 1 Corinthians 15:3-9, where Paul introduces his discussion of the Corinthians' doubts about the whole notion of resurrection with a summary of the gospel.[86] He says of the resurrection:

---

dinary. It is incredible, even if they were not in Jerusalem at the time, that they would have searched the Scriptures for information about Jesus' death but not have researched the facts. It would not have been hard to do such research, and the narratives that we have, though confusing in certain respects, make good historical sense given our knowledge of the political situation and Roman legal procedures. (For a recent article with bibliography, see Corley, "Trial of Jesus.")

84. Fung, *Galatians,* 129, takes it to refer to the preaching of the cross.

85. So Wolff, "Humility and Self-Denial," 159.

86. Paul reminds the Corinthians of the tradition that has passed on to them: "I handed on to you as of first importance what I in turn had received." Here there is an explicit "tradition indicator," one that specifically identifies the tradition as one that

... and that he was raised on the third day according to the Scriptures, and that he appeared to Cephas, then to the twelve. Then he appeared to over five hundred brothers on one occasion, of whom most remain until now, though some have fallen asleep. Then he appeared to James, then to all the apostles. Last of all, as to one born out of time, he appeared to me.* (vv. 4-8)

What does this passage indicate about Paul's knowledge of the resurrection when he wrote 1 Corinthians? First, he dates it (as do the Gospels) to the "third day" after Jesus' death and burial. Second, he knows of various resurrection appearances, which he lists apparently in chronological order:[87] to Peter ("Cephas"), the twelve, five hundred brothers, James, and "all the apostles."

How does this account of the resurrection appearance relate to the synoptic accounts? Any correlation is difficult, not least because the synoptic accounts are so different from each other.[88] But the first two appearances that Paul names — to Peter and to the twelve — do correspond quite closely to the Lukan resurrection narrative, since there it is suggested that the first appearance was to Peter (Luke 24:34), though the appearance itself is not described, and the narrative goes on to refer to Jesus appearing that same day to "the eleven and their companions" (24:33, 36; see also John 20:19-23). Paul does not have the Lukan story of the appearance on the Emmaus road.

The appearances to the five hundred and to James have no obvious equivalents in the synoptic narratives,[89] though it is arguable that the rise to prominence of James in the early church (after his apparent unbelief

---

goes back before Paul's ministry in Corinth and probably to the time of his own conversion. (He received it, as the Corinthians did, at the time of conversion.) Unfortunately we cannot be certain how much of 1 Cor 15:3-9 comprises this early tradition: It could simply be vv. 3, 4, where Paul refers to the death, burial, and resurrection of Jesus, not vv. 5-7, where Paul lists the witnesses to the resurrection. But it could be the whole section.

87. Note the repeated use of "then" and Paul's comment in v. 8 on the appearance to him being "last of all."

88. The wide divergence of the narratives convinces many commentators that they cannot be historically harmonized (e.g., Perrin speaks of "glaring discrepancies," *Resurrection*, 2). Others are historically more optimistic, e.g., J. W. Wenham, *Easter Enigma;* Osborne, *Resurrection Narratives.*

89. It may possibly be relevant that in both Matt 28:10 and John 20:17 Jesus speaks of "my brothers," which is usually taken to be a reference to his disciples rather than to family members such as James. The meeting with the five hundred should perhaps be identified with the Galilean appearance foretold in Mark 16:7 and Matt 28:10 ("tell my brothers to go to Galilee . . ."). In favor of this it can be argued

during Jesus' ministry, Mark 3:31) is at least compatible with the idea that
the risen Jesus appeared to him and that this gave him special standing in
the church. The final appearance to "the apostles" could have a parallel in
one or more of the commissioning ("apostolic," we might say) appearances
of Matt 28:16; Acts 1, etc.[90]

Paul's evidence, then, intersects with the synoptic tradition to a
limited extent. His failure to mention various ingredients of the synoptic
accounts has led many scholars to conclude that he was ignorant of them,
in particular the story of the empty tomb and of the women coming to the
tomb. That story has often been judged a relatively late tradition, even
though it is attested in all the Gospels in their rather different accounts. It
is possible to argue from Paul's testimony that the earliest resurrection
traditions were the appearance traditions and even, on the basis of Paul's
inclusion of himself in the list of resurrection witnesses, that the resurrection experience was some sort of visionary experience that only later came
to be described in more concrete and tangible terms.[91]

- that five hundred is a large number of disciples to have gathered together, so that
  such a gathering would more likely have taken place in Galilee than in Jerusalem,
- that it would be an especially significant occasion and so might well have been
  highlighted by Matthew and Mark,
- that such a gathering would have needed to be especially organized, and Matthew
  and Mark suggest that the meeting in Galilee, unlike other resurrection appearances, was specifically convened by Jesus, and
- that the "brothers" language in Matt 28:10 and 1 Cor 15:6 might favor identification of the two occasions.

It is true that Matt 28:16 could suggest that the meeting was only with the eleven, but
it may be that something wider is envisaged (e.g., in v. 17, "but some doubted"); see
J. W. Wenham, *Easter Enigma*, 112-16.

90. The mini-history of Jesus (from birth to resurrection) that Paul gives in Rom
1:3, 4 is followed immediately by Paul's comment, "through whom we have received
grace and apostleship to bring about the obedience of faith among all the Gentiles for
the sake of his name" (v. 5). This makes for an interesting comparison with Matt
28:16-20, where the risen Christ speaks of his authority and then commissions the
apostles to "make disciples of all nations, baptizing them in the name of the Father and
of the Son and of the Holy Spirit, and teaching them to obey everything that I have
commanded you." Luke 24:44-49 similarly has the risen Jesus commissioning the apostles to go "in his name to all nations." It is possible that Paul knew something like these
synoptic resurrection traditions. I am grateful to Idicheria Ninan for pointing out the
parallels with Rom 1:3, 4.

91. For this sort of view see, among others, G. Grass, *Ostergeschehen und Osterberichte*; Perrin, *Resurrection*; Lüdemann, *Resurrection of Jesus*.

However, it is doubtful that Paul's silence can legitimately be understood in this way. He specifically mentions that Jesus "was buried" and then goes on directly to say that "he was raised on the third day," and it is most unlikely that in writing this he imagined anything but a bodily resurrection. As a Pharisaic Jew he would most probably have thought in such terms.[92] As a Christian theologian he emphasizes that Jesus' body was raised (in face of the Corinthian doubts about the resurrection) and transformed (1 Cor 15:35-57; Phil 3:21).[93]

The fact that Paul includes himself in the list of witnesses to the resurrection does not prove that he regarded his experience as identical in character to that of the earlier witnesses. But even if he did, this does not necessarily mean that he saw the earlier experiences as visionary. The opposite inference is arguably more probable, namely, that he did not see his own experience as simply a vision but as something more "objective" and "physical" than the visions that he later experienced and did not categorize as resurrection appearances.[94]

As for why Paul fails to mention the empty tomb, the answer may simply be because he wished to mention the unambiguous evidence (i.e., the seeing of the risen Jesus by eyewitnesses) rather than the ambiguous evidence (the empty tomb, which by itself proved nothing and could be otherwise explained). His account of the resurrection is in any case extremely brief; he could not say everything.

Of course, Paul's list of witnesses of the resurrection differs from the synoptic accounts. The differences between all the accounts, including Paul's, may give the impression of a very confused tradition. However, too much should again not be made of Paul's silences. His list of resurrection witnesses is quite brief and includes

- Peter, then the twelve
- Then more than five hundred people who saw Jesus at one time
- James, then the apostles.

92. See the remarks of Lapide in *Resurrection of Jesus*, 130.

93. A good case can be made for regarding the empty tomb story as primitive tradition (so, cautiously, Perkins, *Resurrection*, 94): All the Gospels attest it, despite their other divergences (which suggest the independence of their accounts), and it is striking that it is women (not male apostles) who find the tomb, given the prejudice in many circles against women. Matt 28:11-15 is a polemical passage, but it suggests that the Jews did not dispute the emptiness of Jesus' tomb.

94. See especially Craig, "Bodily Resurrection."

He also adds himself to the list.

This list seems to be made up of particular key witnesses: first, Peter with the twelve, that is, the original chosen leaders, then James, the leader of the church in Jerusalem when Paul wrote 1 Corinthians, with all the apostles (not just the twelve). Peter and James were perhaps the two most important people Paul had to deal with in the early church (see Galatians 2);[95] his own relationship with these two and more broadly with the twelve and the apostles was a controversial matter of great personal importance to him.

Then it is no accident that Paul ends the list, having referred to all the apostles, by adding his own name and referring to himself as an apostle. The list thus may have an almost polemical purpose for Paul as he includes himself in the band of properly qualified apostles.[96] And yet in the context of 1 Corinthians 15, where the question of resurrection is the issue being discussed, it is most likely that the names mentioned, together with the huge crowd of more than five hundred, are meant primarily to emphasize that the resurrection was well attested, whether by known authorities or by a very large group of people. In view of this, there is no need to conclude that Paul intended the list to be exhaustive[97] or that he was necessarily ignorant of other resurrection appearances.

Jesus' Exaltation

For Paul the "story" of Jesus moves from the incarnation to the cross, then from the cross to the resurrection and to Jesus' exaltation at God's right

---

95. Compare Bruce, *Paul and Jesus,* 50.

96. It is not entirely clear why he should give such a list in the context of 1 Corinthians 15, where the issue is resurrection, not the legitimacy of his apostleship. This may suggest that the list is the tradition as Paul passed it on at an earlier date and in a different context. On the other hand, questions of his apostleship are addressed earlier in 1 Corinthians, e.g., in chs. 1–4 and 9 (where significantly we find Peter, the Lord's brothers, and other "apostles" mentioned and compared to Paul and Barnabas). On the structure and legitimizing function of 15:5-8 see Lüdemann, *Opposition to Paul,* 46-51. Lüdemann's suggestion that v. 5 was a formula legitimizing the leadership of Peter and the twelve and that v. 7 was a later, competing formula legitimizing James and a wider group of apostles is a rather unlikely speculation.

97. It is instructive that Luke mentions a few selected resurrection appearances in his ch. 24 (the Emmaus road, the appearance to Peter, and the appearance to the apostles), but indicates in Acts 1 that there were many other appearances that he does not describe.

hand.[98] In Phil 2:5-11 Paul tells the story from beginning to end, though he does not mention the resurrection as such, speaking simply of Jesus being "highly exalted." In Rom 8:34 Paul speaks of the Christ who died and rose, "who is at the right hand of God, who indeed intercedes for us."

It is not possible from these texts (or from the references to "ascension" in Eph 1:20; 4:7-10; 1 Tim 3:16) to be sure how Paul understood the relationship of Jesus' resurrection and his exaltation to God's right hand. It is possible that he simply identified them, even though the concepts are quite distinct. But it is also possible that he knew something like the Lukan tradition, in which the ascension is distinguished from the resurrection, but follows it closely (Luke 24:50, 51; Acts 1:6-11). Paul certainly thinks in terms of the resurrection appearances lasting for a limited period of time (in the way suggested by Luke) and coming to an end; he thus has to justify his own claim to have seen the risen Lord. The appearance of the Lord to him is the "last" resurrection appearance in Paul's view, but is itself a chronological exception, presumably because it took place well after the end of the original appearances (1 Cor 15:8).

CONCLUSIONS

This chapter has, like its predecessors, been necessarily sketchy, skating rapidly over some highly controversial matters. But it has brought together a variety of evidence showing that Paul may well have been familiar with much of the gospel "story" as we know it. He certainly knew resurrection traditions, very probably a form of the passion narrative, and also traditions of Jesus as a miracle-worker. He probably knew about Jesus' baptism, about his style of ministry and life, and (a little less certainly) about the transfiguration. He may have known stories of Jesus' infancy similar to those found in Matthew and Luke, the story of Jesus' temptation, and possibly an ascension story.

Some of the evidence, if we have correctly understood it, points again to the traditions concerned being common knowledge and a source of controversy — with the meaning of the miracles and the transfiguration being particularly debated by Paul and his critics. What both sides of that debate appear to agree on is that the Jesus-traditions have some normative

---

98. Hays, *Faith*, 85-137, identifies the Pauline "story" of Jesus in Gal 3:13, 14 and 4:4, 5 as including the incarnation and the cross. Rom 1:3, 4 and Phil 2:5-11 have close parallels to the Galatians texts, and take the story forward.

significance. Paul thus justifies himself and his apostleship in terms of the Jesus-tradition, denying that he is inferior to those who saw the Lord either at the transfiguration or at the resurrection. It could be that Paul by arguing in this way is simply meeting others on their own ground; but the evidence suggests that he entirely accepts the appropriateness of the appeal to the ministry and person of Jesus while disputing the interpretation given thereto by some of his critics.

9

THE QUESTION OF
PAUL AND JESUS

Was Paul a follower of Jesus — really? Or was he the founder of a new religion? In the preceding chapters some of the data bearing on these questions has been assembled and some of the differing scholarly views have been described and discussed. In this chapter we will attempt, quite briefly, to draw the threads of the argument together.

SUMMARY OF CHAPTERS 2-8

It may be helpful to summarize the preceding chapters where the data has been presented and particular conclusions have been reached.

In *chapter 2* we described Jesus' teaching about the kingdom of God: Jesus announced the day of fulfillment, the coming of the government of God, and the casting out of the Satanic ruler of this world. Jesus healed the sick, welcomed sinners and outsiders, and spoke of the need for changed human hearts. He called people to have faith. The kingdom, as he understood it, had come, but it was still to come in its fullness in the future. Paul's message, on the other hand, was focused on Jesus himself and particularly on Jesus' death and resurrection. But like Jesus Paul believed that the time of fulfillment — God's new day — had come. He spoke of God's righteousness and reconciliation having been made manifest, to be received through faith and baptism. Paul's teaching may have differed from that of Jesus not only in its focus on Jesus' death and resurrection but also in placing greater emphasis on the preached "word" than on miracles. Paul used different terminology from Jesus, preferring "righteousness" and "reconciliation" to

373

"kingdom" language, but the same underlying concept of God's new day of salvation having arrived is present in both.

As for points where Paul has probably been influenced by traditions of Jesus, his "kingdom" sayings, though few in number, do seem to be traditional; he can assume that his readers "know" them. But he prefers "righteousness" language (which may itself have a root in the Jesus-tradition) probably because of his social context. Paul knows the saying of Jesus about faith moving mountains, and his comments in 1 Cor 13:1-3 about "knowing mysteries" and "giving one's goods" to the poor are also possibly echoes of sayings of Jesus, as is his characteristic emphasis on "faith, hope, and love." He may have derived his teaching about the saving "word" from Jesus' parable of the sower. He and his churches were probably familiar with the teaching of Jesus about things clean and unclean and with other teachings about God seeing the secret things of the heart.

Chapter 3 asked "Who is Jesus?" and argued that Jesus did see himself as the anointed Messiah of Israel, though he preferred the mysterious expression "Son of man" (having Daniel 7 especially in mind). He was conscious of a special filial relationship to God, his Father. Paul saw Jesus as the preexistent Son of God (going beyond the synoptics in this respect) and at the same time as a real human being, the new Adam. But he also saw himself as the Christ and as the divine "Lord," again going beyond what is explicit in the synoptic Gospels, though the idea of Jesus' lordship is attested in various gospel sayings.

As for points of contact between Paul and Jesus-traditions, Paul's use of the expression "Abba" is one of the clearest examples of Jesus-tradition that has come down to Paul. It may be that Paul's new Adam concept has links with Jesus' "Son of man" language. There is also some evidence to suggest that in 1 Corinthians 1–4 Paul is echoing the christologically weighty "Q" sayings of Matt 11:25-27/Luke 10:21, 22. Paul may perhaps have known Jesus' parable of the vineyard.

Chapter 4 argued that Jesus anticipated his coming death, seeing it as somehow instrumental in bringing the coming kingdom. The last supper narratives suggest that he saw his death as redemptive suffering that would bring liberation to his followers. Paul saw the death of Jesus as bringing God's redemption to sinful humanity and as an atoning sacrifice; he also saw it as something in which believers participate.

The connections between Paul and Jesus are especially clear here since Paul knows of and has taught the Corinthians about the last supper. Paul is closest to the Lukan form of the eucharistic narrative. But it may be that Paul's idea of baptism into the death of Christ also has its roots in Jesus' teaching about the disciples taking up the cross and drinking his cup and sharing his baptism.

Chapter 5 examined the mission of Jesus. Jesus sent out the twelve (representing the twelve tribes of Israel) and focused his mission on Israel. He expected his followers to be a community (or "church") and gave Peter a particular position of leadership. He spoke of the destruction of the Jerusalem temple and looked forward to the establishment of a new temple, quite probably in the community of his followers. He did not see mission to Gentiles as his task, but he did demonstrate a revolutionary opennness to sinners and outsiders and looked forward to the gathering of the Gentiles.

Paul, by contrast, is deeply involved in Gentile mission; he is aware that this is a new development from the more limited Jewish mission of Jesus and the apostles. For Paul the temple where God dwells is now the church, though his favorite way of speaking of the church is as "the body of Christ" — perhaps a development of his eucharistic thinking. Paul's understanding of union with Christ is comparable to his understanding of marriage as a one-flesh relationship.

We found strong connections betweeen Jesus and Paul in this chapter. Paul's knowledge of the teaching found in Jesus' mission discourse was extensive, including not just the saying about the laborer being worthy of his hire but a variety of other sayings, some only attested in Luke (e.g., "eat what is put before you") and in Matthew ("freely you have received, freely give"*). Paul knows of the twelve and of Jesus' congratulation of Peter as "the rock," though he probably also knows Jesus' parable of the wise and foolish builders. Paul is familiar with Jesus' prediction of the destruction and rebuilding of the temple, and probably also with his instructions about church discipline.

Chapter 6 looked at the ethical teachings of Jesus and Paul, beginning with Jesus' radical teaching on divorce. We found that Jesus called for ethical perfection and yet was liberal with regard to the ritual demands of the OT law. He saw himself as "fulfilling" the law, restoring the creation order, and bringing the new covenant. Paul offers a more elaborate explanation of the law: He sees it as having had a negative role in the purposes of God and he sees Jesus as having brought a new era of freedom in the Spirit. Paul has a much fuller doctrine of the Spirit than is found in Jesus' teaching (at least in the synoptics): The Spirit gives gifts for ministry and the inward knowledge of God and his law. For Paul love is the Christian priority (as it was for Jesus) and the "fulfillment of the law." Paul is socially radical ("no slave or free") and yet his radicalism is tempered by his belief in the "not yet" aspect of salvation. For him the person of Jesus is the center and focus of Christian ethics.

There are all sorts of detailed connections between Paul's ethical teaching and that of Jesus. Paul knows Jesus' teaching about marriage and divorce and probably other related traditions, including the saying about "eunuchs for the kingdom of heaven" and the story of Jesus visiting the home of Mary and Martha. Paul's teaching on returning good for evil echoes the Jesus-tradition that Matthew has in the sermon on the mount. "Love one another" is the law of Christ for Paul, but he has also learned from Jesus the importance of loving the outsider and the idea of love as the fulfillment of the law. Other themes — paying taxes, receiving others, not causing little ones to stumble, not judging, service, humility as the way to exaltation — all echo teaching of Jesus. Paul may have been known the sayings about salt and light and the "yes, yes . . . no, no" saying about oaths in Matthew 5 (which seems to have been used by Paul's opponents against him), as well as Jesus' characteristic "Truly I say to you. . . ." It is possible that Paul's injunction to his readers to put to death the deeds of the body echoes Jesus' teaching about cutting off parts of the body that offend, and even that Paul's flesh-spirit contrast may have connections with the Gethsemane story.

In *chapter 7* we noted how Jesus looked forward to the final salvation of God's people but also spoke of coming judgment, including judgment on Jerusalem. He spoke of himself going away and returning, and he suggested both that things would happen imminently and that the time of God's final salvation was unknown. Paul, too, had a strong sense of the nearness of salvation, and yet he believed that things (including the Gentile mission and judgment on the Jews) must happen before the end. He looked forward to "the day" when the Lord would return, when judgment would take place, and when God's people would be saved.

Paul specifically identifies some of his teaching as a "word of the Lord" and as tradition that he passed on to the Thessalonians, and his teaching is closely parallel to that of Jesus at various points. Paul echoes the parable of the thief in the night, and probably other parables, including the watchman, the wise and foolish virgins, and the stewards. There are notable parallels between Paul's description of the Lord's return and Jesus' eschatological teaching, notably in Luke 21:34-36. 2 Thessalonians 2 is parallel to Jesus' eschatological discourse, and 1 Thes 2:15, 16 has clear connections with Jesus' eschatological teaching.

In *chapter 8* we left the teaching of Jesus and looked at the gospel narrative tradition, finding evidence (some strong, some more tenuous) that Paul may have known traditions of Jesus' infancy, his baptism, his miracles, and the transfiguration. He probably knew of Jesus' lifestyle, including his poverty and his singleness. He had a considerable amount of information about Jesus' death and resurrection, and he may even have known the story of Jesus' ascension.

THE THEOLOGIES OF JESUS AND PAUL

What, then, has emerged for the question of Paul and Jesus? We will consider first the question of the theologies of Jesus and Paul, then the question of Paul's knowledge and use of Jesus-traditions.

Overlap

The first thing to emerge from the admittedly very limited comparison of Jesus' teaching and Paul's theology that we have presented is that there is massive overlap between the teaching of the two men.[1]

At the heart of Jesus' teaching and of Pauline theology is the conviction that God has intervened and is intervening to save his people and the world. This divine intervention is the fulfillment of OT promises and is associated particularly with Jesus' own coming and sacrificial death. God's salvation is not just for the religious or the righteous, but is for sinners and outsiders. They are gathered into the restored Israel — the community of those who receive the word and have faith in Jesus. That community is God's new temple and is called to live in perfect love, thus fulfilling and

---

1. It is worth reemphasizing the necessary limitations of a study of this sort. As we saw in chapter 1, anyone attempting to compare the teaching of Jesus and the teaching of Paul faces a hugely complicated task, both because of the nature and extent of the relevant NT texts and also because of all the critical questions that scholars have asked about the texts. There are questions about the Gospels as historical sources and questions about Paul. (It is important, among other things, to remember that the letters of Paul are only occasional letters, so that we do not get a full or total picture of Paul's theology from them. Different aspects of Paul's theology are emphasized in different letters, according to the church situations. Had it not been for the problems in Corinth we would have known virtually nothing of Paul's sacramental theology; had it not been for the Thessalonians we would have had a very partial picture of Paul's expectations for the future.) In this study it has not been possible to address all the critical questions or to describe all the possible scholarly views. We have, rather, only offered a possible sketch of the main lines of Jesus' and Paul's theology, taking into account some of the historical and critical discussion of the texts.

surpassing the OT law, and in expectancy of the Lord's return to judge and to complete his saving work.

Some of the agreement between Jesus and Paul could be explained simply in terms of their common Jewish heritage, and there are parallels between their teaching and, for example, the teaching of the Dead Sea sect. But many of the points of agreement (e.g., the openness to sinners, the command to love even enemies, and the proclamation that the day of messianic salvation has arrived) are distinctively Christian and no coincidence.

Differences

Although the overlap is great, there are, of course, differences. There are differences of terminology, the most obvious being between Jesus' "kingdom" language and Paul's "righteousness" language. But that particular difference, though striking, turns out to be one of terminology, not of substance.

There are other more substantial differences: Thus Paul has a strong and distinctive christological focus in all of his theology; not only are the death and resurrection of Jesus the vital saving events for him, but Jesus is the cosmic preexistent Lord. Paul's theology emphasizes the Gentiles more than that of Jesus. The Holy Spirit features more explicitly in Paul's thinking than in Jesus' teaching (at least in the synoptics), whereas the law gets a rather negative treatment. Paul has a more developed doctrine of the church (e.g., as the body of Christ), and his theology is perhaps more "word," "cross," and "church"-based, whereas Jesus has more emphasis on the physical (i.e., healing), on the material (i.e., money), and on social relationships in general.

Although these differences are important, they do not represent any fundamental divergence of outlook. In each case the Pauline emphasis has a possible, or probable, root in Jesus' teaching, and it represents a development within the broad framework of their shared view of God's saving action in fulfillment of OT hope. In no case is it obvious that Paul diverges from the theology of Jesus in a way that comes near contradiction.

The divergences that are there reflect in all, or almost all, cases the differences between Jesus' situation and Paul's. First of all, Paul writes after the death and resurrection of Jesus, which are toweringly important events for him and the starting point of much of his theological thinking. There is good evidence that Jesus also saw his death as decisively important in

God's redemptive plan, but his death and resurrection lay in the future during his ministry and so the perspective is different from Paul's.[2] Jesus and the disciples experienced the coming of the kingdom of God practically in the casting out of demons and the healing of the sick, and the cross was a shadowy future prospect; for Paul the crucifixion was hard, recent fact, and the cross and resurrection were eschatological events of the first importance, putting everything else to do with the coming kingdom into the shade.[3]

Secondly and similarly, Paul writes after Pentecost and the start of the Gentile mission. Whereas the eschatological coming of the Spirit on all flesh and the gathering of the Gentiles were probably part of Jesus' future expectation, for Paul Pentecost had happened and the Gentile mission was under way. Both Jesus and Paul operate with an already–not yet theology and with an understanding that the kingdom of God is in the process of coming; but things have advanced significantly between Jesus and Paul, and Paul is farther along the already–not yet line. He works and writes in and out of the new context: The experience of the Spirit in the church and the mission to the Gentiles, which were only in prospect for Jesus, are dominating parts of Paul's present experience, and this is reflected in his theology.

Not only have positive new things happened, but, of course (thirdly), Jesus is no longer present when Paul is ministering, and so the relationship that his followers were able to have with him during his ministry is changed. So for Paul preaching about Christ becomes of special importance; it is through this preaching that people come to faith in the Lord and hear the Lord. The sacraments, too, become important as ways of relating to the Lord. "Taking up the cross and following" Jesus is now expressed baptismally, and the eucharist is a participation in Christ. Some of Paul's distinctive participationist theology (e.g., the idea of the church as the body of Christ) may arise out of the sacramental life of the church. If it does, then we have something with its roots in the ministry of Jesus, but undergoing development in the new situation of the church.

Fourthly, Paul is absorbed with practical questions and issues of church life (Jew-Gentile questions, the charismatic experience of the

2. Jüngel, *Paulus und Jesus*, 268-73, comments that for Jesus the present was qualified by the future, whereas for Paul the present was governed by the past, which itself pointed to the future. Kim, *Jesus, Sayings of*, 483, speaks of the promise of Jesus' kingdom teaching being realized in the cross and resurrection and so involving continuity and necessary change.

3. For Paul, looking back on it, it is the cross, rather than the miracles, that is Jesus' supreme healing work.

church, church divisions generally, the homosexuality of the Gentile world, etc.), which were not issues for Jesus in the same way. Paul's theology has to address these issues, going beyond what Jesus taught (even if starting firmly with what Jesus taught). Paul's situation has also no doubt been influential on his language: Thus Jesus preaching in rural, Jewish Galilee may speak of "the kingdom of God," but Paul working in an urban, Gentile environment prefers other ways of describing the intervention of God through Jesus. More generally, his situation is often one of sharp controversy, and this inevitably affects both what and how he writes.

The fifth and final difference of context has to do with Paul's own conversion experience. It was undoubtedly extremely formative and important for Paul,[4] molding his attitude to Judaism and the law and making christology the absolute priority and focus of his theology. Paul writes after the resurrection and after his own meeting with the risen Christ, so it is not surprising if his Christ is unambiguously and majestically Lord of the cosmos. Jesus, by contrast, while speaking of himself and of his mission with authority, seems quite deliberately to have chosen the path of humble service, not of self-glorification. It is hardly surprising if master and grateful convert have a different emphasis. We have seen in this study real continuity between Jesus' self-understanding and Paul's understanding of Jesus, but Paul writes from his post-Easter, post-conversion standpoint, and it shows.

JESUS-TRADITION KNOWN TO PAUL

If Paul's theology seems to be in very definite continuity with that of Jesus, how has this essential unanimity come about? The answer must be that directly or indirectly Paul has been influenced by the teaching of Jesus. What evidence is there, then, of Paul knowing the sayings and stories of Jesus?

This question brings with it a number of methodological problems, as we saw in chapter 1. It is important, apart from anything else, not to assume naively that any and every parallel idea or phrase in the Gospels and the Pauline letters is an indication of a direct relationship between them, let alone to assume that the relationship must be one of Pauline dependence on Jesus (rather than, for example, of Pauline influence on the Gospel writers). In our survey of the evidence, although we have not been able to offer an exhaustive evaluation of the texts in question, we have tried not to jump to conclusions prematurely and we have sought to differentiate

---

4. See his own comment in Gal 1:12; also Kim, *Origin of Paul's Gospel*.

between places where the evidence for a particular relationship between the texts is stronger and less strong.

What conclusions, then, have we reached? In brief, our findings have been that there is massive evidence of Pauline knowledge of Jesus-traditions. Some of the evidence is relatively weak — a parallel idea or phrase, but no really strong argument for Pauline dependence on the parallel Jesus-tradition (at least when that piece of evidence is seen on its own rather than within the context of a broader cumulative argument). However, there is also a good quantity of much stronger evidence — places where Paul indicates that he is drawing on tradition or where the wording used or idea expressed is so similar as to make a connection likely.

It may be helpful to try to summarize the evidence roughly according to the strength of the evidence, starting from the relatively uncontroversial evidence.[5]

Highly Probable Connections (and Associated Material)[6]

(1) Paul's familiarity with the story of the last supper is clear from 1 Corinthians 11: He says that it is a tradition that he received, and his description of the supper is very similar to the synoptic accounts. He is closest to Luke in certain respects. The way that he introduces his description of the supper suggests some knowledge of the historical context of the supper ("the night when he was betrayed"). It is difficult to be sure how much of the passion narrative he knew, but there is some evidence to suggest that he probably knew quite a lot.[7]

(2) Similarly Paul's familiarity with the resurrection stories is clear enough from 1 Cor 15:3-5: Again Paul speaks of tradition that he has received and passed on, and again he has interesting points of contact with the synoptic tradition, especially with Luke. Negative arguments about Paul's failure specifically to mention the empty tomb or the women's visit to the tomb were seen to be quite inconclusive.[8]

5. We will not give all the biblical references in this summary section. For references and discussion of the positions taken see the earlier chapters.

6. In this section we consider the most certain echoes and allusions to the Jesus-tradition in Paul, but we will also note some of the associated material where the connections are less certain. The borderlines between what we will categorize as "highly probable," "probable," and "plausible" are in any case often fuzzy.

7. On the last supper and the death of Jesus see chapters 4 and 8 above.

8. On the resurrection see chapter 8 above.

(3) Paul is dependent on Jesus' teaching on divorce in 1 Corinthians 7. This has been widely recognized by scholars, and Paul indicates such dependence. What has not always been observed are the specific verbal and formal links between 1 Cor 7:10, 11 and the traditions of Matthew 19/Mark 10. Paul knew not just one or two sayings of Jesus but probably the whole dialogue described in Matthew/Mark, including the important "one flesh" saying, and possibly, even plausibly, the Matthean saying about eunuchs for the kingdom of God.[9]

(4) Paul specifically refers to the Lord's teaching about preachers being paid for their work; he has in mind the saying about the "laborer being worthy of his hire"* (so 1 Cor 9:14/Matt 10:10/Luke 10:7), as has often been noted, but also probably much of the rest of the mission discourse. He knew of the twelve and of the apostles being sent out with authority, including authority to heal. He probably knew that they were restricted by Jesus to mission among Israel (so Matt 10:5; Jesus also so restricted himself). He may well have known specific sayings such as the Lukan "eat whatever is put before you" and the Matthean "freely you have received, freely give"* (Luke 10:8; Matt 10:8). He also probably knew of Jesus' healings and of his saying about mountain-moving "faith."[10]

(5) Paul speaks of a "word from the Lord" about the second coming (1 Thes 4:15), and although some have seen this as a reference to a Christian prophecy, there is a strong argument for saying that Paul is drawing on sayings of Jesus in much of his eschatological teaching. He knew the parable of the thief in the night, and probably the parables of the watchman, the stewards, and the wise and foolish virgins (the evidence that these parables were known independently to all three synoptic Evangelists suggests that the parables go back very early). If Paul wrote 2 Thessalonians, he knew the eschatological discourse of Matthew 24/Mark 13/Luke 21, including its warning of the desolating sacrilege preceding the return of the Son of man. Paul knew some of the distinctively Lukan traditions — including the exhortation to be awake for the Lord's sudden return (21:34-36) and (less certainly) the saying about wrath coming on the Jews (21:23). He knew other sayings of Jesus about judgment coming on Jerusalem and the Jews, including Jesus' saying about the temple being destroyed and rebuilt, which he echoes in several contexts.[11]

(6) Paul's ethical teaching seems heavily dependent on that of Jesus. We have noted already his teaching about marriage. His teaching about

9. See further in chapter 6 above.
10. See further in chapter 5 above.
11. See further in chapters 5 and 7 above.

nonretaliation is strongly reminiscent of Jesus' teaching in the sermon on the mount about love of enemies and turning the other cheek. His emphasis on love as the fulfilling of the law echoes the teaching of Jesus, and "the law of Christ" in Gal 6:2 is probably a "tradition indicator" to be linked with the Johannine new commandment "love one another as I have loved you" (of which there are also important traces in the synoptics, including the Markan saying about having "peace among yourselves," 9:50).[12]

(7) Paul's statement that "I know and am persuaded in the Lord Jesus that nothing is unclean" in Rom 14:14 is, despite some scholarly doubts, very probably a Pauline allusion to the traditions of Matthew 15/Mark 7. Paul echoes these traditions on more than one occasion, and Mark attests the same interpretation of the saying that we find in Paul.[13]

(8) Paul's references to the Christian crying *Abba* are an allusion to Jesus' own usage, as Paul almost says (when he speaks of the Spirit of Jesus crying out in the believer).[14]

Other Probable Connections

There are a considerable number of places where Paul is probably influenced by the teaching of Jesus, even though the evidence is less conclusive than in the cases noted already.

(1) It is probable that Paul knew of Jesus' baptism by John the Baptist (and possibly some of John's sayings), and that he saw Christian baptism (into sonship by the Spirit) as following in Jesus' steps. But he quite probably also knew the sayings of Jesus about taking up the cross (and losing and saving one's life), and perhaps about drinking his cup and sharing his baptism, these being reflected in his teaching about dying with Christ in baptism.[15]

(2) He probably knew of the commissioning of Peter, "the rock," and also of Jesus' transfiguration. It is likely that these traditions were used by Paul's critics to glorify the apostles and to denigrate Paul and that he is responding to this in the way he describes his own spiritual experiences. He probably knew the story of James and John's request for high seats in the kingdom and of Jesus' words in reply about servant-leadership and about the Son of man as a servant and ransom. The story may be reflected

12. See further in chapter 6 above.
13. See further in chapter 2 above.
14. See further in chapters 3 and 6 above.
15. See further in chapters 4 and 8 above.

in Paul's atonement theology, in his teaching about his own servant-ministry, and in his reference to the "acknowledged" leaders in Jerusalem.[16]

(3) Paul knew of Jesus' kingdom teaching. He probably knew the parable of the sower (which appears to have had special prominence in the church's tradition), as well as many sayings about Christian living — the warnings about "judging" others and about causing "little ones to stumble" and cutting off offending limbs, the words about "peacemaking," and the advice about paying taxes to Caesar and (to the rich man) about giving one's goods to the poor. Paul's opponents used the "yes, yes, no, no" saying of Jesus as a stick to beat Paul with; Paul responded with a possible reference to Jesus as the "Amen," having in mind Jesus' characteristic way of introducing his solemn statements.[17]

(4) Paul was probably familiar with Jesus' saying about the revealing of the secrets of the kingdom to the disciples, and with the "Q" saying about Jesus as revealer and Son.[18]

(5) Paul was familiar with Jesus' negative statements about the piety of some of the Jewish leaders, including with the "woe" against those who persecute the prophets and complete the tally of the ancestors' misdeeds.[19]

(6) And Paul was familiar with (and himself reflects) Jesus' positive attitude to sinners, to the marginalized like the Samaritans, and to women. The story of Mary and Martha was familiar to people in Corinth and no doubt to Paul. The sayings of Jesus about renouncing one's family and about the resurrection life involving no marriage or giving in marriage may also possibly have been known and influential. Paul may well have known of Jesus' poverty, homelessness, and singleness.[20]

Plausible Connections[21]

There are many other places where there is an interesting thematic or verbal parallel between Jesus and Paul, which could well be significant — even

16. See further in chapters 5, 6, and 8 above.
17. See further in chapters 2 and 6 above.
18. See further in chapter 3 above.
19. See further in chapter 7 above.
20. See further in chapters 6 and 8 above.
21. We use the word "plausible" here as a slightly more positive word than "possible" to refer to places where there is evidence that may reasonably be interpreted as an echo of the Jesus-tradition. Paul could "possibly" have known all sorts of things without our having any evidence to show that to be the case.

highly significant — but where the evidence (seen on its own) does not add up to more than a reasonable possibility.

Paul may have known traditions of Jesus' birth (including the virginal conception), perhaps the story of Jesus' temptation (certainly he believed that Jesus was sinless), and several of the sayings found in the sermon on the mount, including the beatitudes on the poor and the persecuted, the sayings about salt and light, and the parable of wise and foolish builders. He may well have known Jesus' "Son of man" language, which appears to be picked up in Paul's teaching on the new Adam, and he may have known the dialogue with the Jews about the Messiah as son or lord of David. He may have known Jesus' teaching about the "righteousness" of the kingdom, about church discipline and about suffering and not being ashamed, as well as the saying about the days of Lot, and the parable of the prodigal son. He may have known the parable of the vineyard tenants and the story of Gethsemane, including Jesus' saying about the spirit being willing and the flesh weak, and even possibly an account of the ascension.

Gospel Traditions Known to Paul

The cumulative argument

The sheer quantity of evidence assembled is impressive. Indeed, if Paul knew all the gospel traditions which we have noted, then he knew most of the story of Jesus as the Gospels present it (at least in content, if not in order) — from the infancy of Jesus to his baptism, his ministry, and on to his death, resurrection, and ascension.

Of course, the evidence is not all equally strong. However, the cumulative effect of the argument, when the different pieces of evidence are taken together, is to add weight to the case for seeing particular parallels between Paul and Jesus as Pauline echoes of Jesus-traditions. What seems only plausible or probable when evaluated on its own may seem probable or highly probable when seen in the light of the whole argument.[22]

The point about the cumulative effect of the argument may be illustrated by an analogy: If we wished to ascertain whether a modern author

22. This could sound like the sort of scholarly sleight of hand by which ideas that are first introduced as "possible" later without any justification become "probable" or even surer than that! But in this case we are not surreptitiously upgrading the probability rating of particular traditions but offering a serious cumulative argument.

was familiar with and influenced by the writings of Shakespeare, we would not be impressed if there were very few possible echoes of Shakespeare's writings in the modern writer's poems; we might well dismiss the possible echoes as accidental and insignificant. If, on the other hand, we found many possible echoes and some echoes that were very probable (because of the extent of the linguistic similarity or even because the author indicated that he or she was quoting), the picture would be different. Similarly, if we found in a particular poem of the modern author several possible echoes of Shakespeare, perhaps of different plays, in a short space, or if we found the same possible echo occurring in different poems of the modern poet, then the case would be strengthened, and we would be inclined to see the possible echoes as much more probable than we might otherwise have supposed.[23]

This is the sort of situation that we have found with the question of Jesus-traditions in Paul.

(1) There is the sheer quantity of evidence. If there were only a few possible echoes of Jesus, then we could — and perhaps should — dismiss them as coincidental and insignificant. In fact, there are many, many pieces of evidence pointing in the same direction, and they add up significantly and reinforce each other.

(2) Although some of the evidence points rather weakly and uncertainly in the direction of Paul's knowledge of Jesus-traditions, there is also a considerable amount of very much weightier evidence, where Paul's use of Jesus-tradition is confirmed by the presence of "tradition-indicators," by the high level of similarity, or by both.[24] In the light of this more certain evidence, the less certain evidence takes on a different complexion.

(3) In addition to the overall quantity of possible echoes of the

23. The view that the relationship might be the opposite, i.e., that the Gospels have been influenced by Paul rather than vice versa, may have some plausibility in a few cases — we have noted possible influence in, e.g., Mark 4:11; Luke 8:12; 18:13, 14; 22:17-20 — but the evidence is so strong that Paul is using Jesus-tradition as to make it much more likely that the dependence in the overwhelming number of cases is from the Jesus-tradition to Paul than the other way around. Fjärstedt, *Synoptic Tradition*, 77, says, apropos of the mission discourse: "It is easier to think of Paul's freer and more extensive exposition of the theme as being built on a rather fixed piece of tradition than it is to imagine that Luke sorted out certain theme words from a longer passage to build such a concentrated and well-constructed story." What he says is true not just of the mission discourse but much more widely. It is almost always easier to think of Paul alluding to the gospel tradition than of the Evangelists building their parables and other stories out of material gleaned from Paul's letters.

24. In terms of Thompson's distinctions (discussed in chapter 1, pp. 25f. above) there are clear "allusions," but also many less clear "echoes."

Jesus-tradition, we have quite frequently found several possible echoes of the Jesus-tradition together in Paul's letters: Thus in 1 Cor 13:2, 3 we find three quite different echoes of the Jesus-tradition together ("understand all mysteries," "faith, so as to remove mountains," "give away all my possessions"). That these possible echoes come together in this way may confirm that Paul here has been influenced by the Jesus-tradition in this context. Similarly in a short passage in 1 Thessalonians 4 we found possible echoes of several of Jesus' eschatological parables (the thief, the watchman, the wise and foolish virgins). The combination of evidence confirms that we are right to detect the influence of the Jesus-tradition. More broadly in Romans 12–15 there is a mass of echoes of Jesus-traditions, and it is not always easy to say which of several Jesus-traditions has influenced Paul in a particular context (e.g., in Rom 15:1-3 we have possible echoes of the passion, of the "love your neighbor" and "servant" traditions, and the idea of "building up" others); Paul seems in such contexts to be working very much within a framework of broad reflection on various Jesus-traditions.

(4) Not only does Paul seem sometimes to be drawing on a variety of Jesus-traditions within the same context, but he also uses the same tradition in different contexts. We noted, for example, how Jesus' saying about destroying and rebuilding the temple is echoed or possibly echoed in 1 Cor 3:16, 17 (in connection with building up the church), in 2 Cor 5:1 (in connection with the resurrection of the body), and in Gal 2:18 (in connection with Judaizing destruction of the gospel). Taken individually, these different possible echoes may be only moderately persuasive; taken together they add up to something significant. Much the same can be said about Jesus' saying that "nothing defiles a person. . . ."

A related point comes from the way that different elements from one synoptic story seem to surface at different points in Paul. Thus Jesus' discussion of things clean and unclean in Matthew 15/Mark 7 is variously echoed in Rom 14:14; 1 Cor 6:13; and Col 2:21, 22. Similarly, the story of James and John asking for top seats in the kingdom (Matt 20:20-28/Mark 10:35-45) has surfaced at various points in our discussion in relation to Paul's understanding of the atonement (compare the ransom saying), his teaching about servanthood (e.g., in 1 Cor 9:19, 20), and his somewhat derogatory references to "the acknowledged ones" in Gal 2:6, 9. Our confidence that a parallel is an echo of a Jesus-tradition is considerably increased when there is evidence of that tradition being used elsewhere by Paul.

The cumulative argument is very important. There is a web of evidence, some strands being quite weak, some strands very strong, and some in between, and the overall result is a very strong argument. The cumulative argument is not such as to "prove" that every possible echo is an actual echo, since there may, of course, be coincidental (or otherwise explicable) parallels between Jesus and Paul; but it is such as to increase the probabilities considerably.

The form of the traditions

It is not possible to be certain about the form of the traditions of Jesus known to Paul.[25] But it is notable that he echoes a good number of sayings from some of the gospel discourses, notably the sermon on the mount, the mission discourse, and the eschatological discourse, and that there are sometimes clusters of echoes of the same synoptic discourse in one Pauline context — for example, there are a number of possible echoes of Jesus' teaching on marriage and divorce (Matt 19/Mark 10) in 1 Corinthians 6 and 7; there are also numerous echoes of Jesus' eschatological teaching (Matthew 24, 25) in 1 Thessalonians (and 2 Thessalonians, where chapter 2 resembles the synoptic discourse in form).

It would be unwise to make too much of this, as though it necessarily proved that Paul knew these discourses and not just the individual sayings that make up the discourses. It could be an entirely intelligible coincidence that the Gospels and Paul gather together sayings of Jesus on a particular topic when dealing with that topic. On the other hand, there is good evidence for thinking that some of the material found in the discourses was gathered together at a very early date (e.g., the eschatological parables). Furthermore, we have seen at least a few indications that Paul knew the teaching of Jesus not as an entirely fragmentary tradition but already gathered together to a greater or lesser degree. Evidence of this is seen in

25. It should, of course, not be supposed that the traditions of Jesus of which there are traces in Paul are all that he knew. His letters are occasional letters (see n. 1 above), and the topics that they discuss (and so the traditions that they echo or allude to) are determined by the particular needs of the churches to which they are addressed. Were it not for the Corinthians and their problems concerning the Lord's supper we would have no knowledge of Paul's eucharistic theology, and we might — entirely erroneously — conclude that he knew nothing of the institution of the supper. Much the same is true of the resurrection. It has thus been said that what we see in the Epistles is only the tip of an iceberg (see Allison, "Pauline Epistles," 16). It might be more accurate to say that the tip is unmistakably visible, but that a lot more of the iceberg is probably visible, even if the view is sometimes rather misty, and that a lot more again is no doubt hidden below the surface!

2 Thessalonians 2; 1 Cor 7:10, 11, where Paul uses together Jesus' two sayings about not "separating" and not divorcing; and in 1 Cor 9:14, where Paul's reference to Jesus' saying about the laborer deserving his hire presupposes an appreciation of something like its context in the mission discourse.[26]

If Paul did know Jesus-traditions not just singly but already collected together in some way, what form did these collections take? Did he know anything like a whole Gospel, or only various collections of the traditions of Jesus, or both?[27] It is not possible to answer this with any confidence, but there is more to be said for the view that Paul may have known a gospel-like narrative than might be supposed.[28]

As we observed in chapter 8, Richard Hays has argued that Paul knew an outline story of Jesus and that this is reflected in verses like Gal 4:4, 5 ("When the fulness of time had come, God sent his Son, born of a woman, born under the law, in order to redeem. . . .)" and 3:13 ("Christ redeemed us from the curse of the law by becoming a curse for us . . ."). Hays suggests that such an outline story may have been a catalyst to the development of the Gospel form.[29] His argument about Paul's knowledge of a "story" of Jesus is persuasive, and may be supported from other Pauline passages including Phil 2:5-11 and Rom 1:1-5.

The Romans passage is especially interesting. Paul here speaks of:

26. See our earlier discussion of 2 Thessalonians 2 in chapter 7, of 1 Corinthians 7 in chapter 6, and of 1 Corinthians 9 in chapter 5.

27. Allison, "Pauline Epistles," notes particularly heavy use by Paul of certain synoptic traditions, including Mark 9:33-50 and Luke 6:27-38, and of the mission discourse. He thinks Paul knew a version of these blocks of tradition and a passion narrative, some conflict stories, several isolated sayings, and other traditions of which we have no evidence. He could be right, but I have argued that there is evidence for Paul's use of a wide range of other traditions in addition to those identified by Allison. Furthermore, I am not persuaded that Paul necessarily knew the sayings in Mark 9:33-50 in anything like their Markan form. These sayings are paralleled in various places in the synoptic tradition, and it could be that the person(s) who collected Mark 9:33-50 (whether Mark or a predecessor) did so because they seemed to be particularly important sayings of Jesus relevant to church life. And it could be that Paul's heavy use of the same traditions reflects their importance. It could also be that Paul knew something like Matthew's equivalent passage (Matthew 18).

28. By "gospel-like narrative" I do not mean anything written, but more probably a developing oral tradition. On the other hand, the possibility that there were very early written narratives cannot be ruled out.

29. See his *Faith of Jesus Christ*, 257, and the discussion in chapter 8 above.

"the gospel of God,

(1) which he promised beforehand through his prophets in the holy scriptures,

(2) the gospel concerning his Son,

(a) who was descended from David according to the flesh,

(b) and was declared Son of God with power according to the spirit of holiness by resurrection from the dead, Jesus Christ our Lord,

(3) through whom we have received grace and apostleship to bring about the obedience of faith among all the Gentiles for the sake of his name."

What is interesting about this is how Paul's explanation of "the gospel" corresponds in form to the Gospels, and especially to Matthew and Luke, who

(1) set the story of Jesus in the context of OT history and expectation,[30]

(2) tell the story of Jesus, the Son, from

(a) his birth in the family of David to

(b) his resurrection, and

(3) speak of the authoritative risen Christ sending out his apostles in his own name to preach the gospel to all nations.

The parallels are striking,[31] and certainly seem to lend support to Hays's argument that Paul was familiar with an outline of the "story" of Jesus as well as to Hays's suggestion that there may be some connection between the Pauline story and the Gospels. He could well be right in thinking that our Gospels represent a development of something like the semi-creedal Pauline story.

What cannot be taken for granted, however, in view of all the evidence that we have produced for Paul's wide knowledge of Jesus-traditions, is that the only "story" of Jesus known to Paul took the form of a brief creedal statement. He could, in theory, have known only the briefest outline of Jesus' life and also many individual traditions of Jesus; but it is entirely possible (and perhaps more likely) that the gospel story or stories that he knew already included much of the detail. If they did, it could still be that

---

30. Matthew does so through the genealogy in 1:1-17 and heavy use of OT citations. Luke sets the scene for Jesus' birth by first describing the birth of John the Baptist, putting both quite explicitly in the context of OT expectation (chs. 1 and 2).

31. Cf. Ninan, *Son of God*, 176-78.

the creedal statements were the seed out of which the gospel narratives grew, or it could be the opposite way around, with the creedal statements representing summaries of gospel narratives.[32]

Gospel sources

If there were early accounts of Jesus' life and teaching and if Paul knew them,[33] then it might be expected, given the consensus of the source critics, that those accounts looked most like Mark or "Q" or both. However, what is interesting about the evidence we have examined is that although there are plenty of Markan and especially "Q" traditions echoed in Paul, he also rather frequently echoes what the critics call "M" and "L" sayings, that is, material recorded only in Matthew or Luke (e.g., Matt 10:5; 16:16-20; 18:15-20; Luke 10:38-42; 21:34-36, etc.). Paul's agreements with Luke may not be unexpected, since, whatever view is taken of the tradition that Luke was written by a companion of Paul, the author of Luke is clearly interested in Paul and might reasonably be thought to come from the same theological-ecclesiastical stable, with its particular stream of Jesus-traditions. Paul's echoes of Matthean traditions are less expected, since Matthew is usually thought to represent that Jewish Christian strand of Christianity from which Paul differed most sharply. However, it was precisely with Jewish Christians that Paul was frequently in dialogue, and it may not therefore be surprising if he was familiar with their traditions of Jesus.[34]

But to identify these traditions as "*their* traditions" is to speak on the basis of modern scholarly differentiation of "Markan," "Q," "M," and "L" traditions. In Paul they seem to be used indiscriminately, and it is probable that although the Jesus traditions were sometimes used differently (and often polemically) by different groups of Christians, they were recognized as a common inheritance and resource, not as the traditions of one or another party.[35]

It is clearly of great importance for the gospel critic if it turns out that much "M" and "L" material is primitive and part of the pool of

32. See further below on Paul's gospel.

33. Luke's reference to his predecessors in Luke 1:1, 2 is of interest. See also the remarks of Bauckham, "The Study of Gospel Traditions," 370-72.

34. It has also been interesting to note some evidence of "Johannine" traditions of Jesus in Paul (e.g., the "new commandment" of John 13:34), though we have deliberately not sought out such evidence. The whole question of Paul and the Johannine Jesus is an important one that deserves attention.

35. See also Allison, "Pauline Epistles," 19-21.

Jesus-traditions that was known to Paul. If Matthew and Luke were drawing on such traditions, their importance as independent sources of information about Jesus is greatly enhanced.

PAUL'S USE OF THE TRADITION

Where and How Does Paul Use It?

Particular concentrations

Paul echoes the sayings and stories of Jesus very frequently and in all his letters. There is a high concentration of echoes in 1 Corinthians: It seems that the Corinthians themselves were very familiar with traditions of Jesus and were using them in ways that Paul strongly disagreed with (for example, in justifying their immorality, on the one hand, and in advocating Christian celibacy, on the other). Some at least of these traditions had been taught to the Corinthians by Paul himself, as he explicitly says (for example, about the last supper and the resurrection, 1 Cor 11:23 and 15:3);[36] he therefore takes them back to what he has taught them, supplementing it and correcting their misinterpretations of it.[37]

Similarly in 1 and 2 Thessalonians Paul is constantly drawing on the teaching of Jesus. Here again he explains that he is reminding the Thessalonians of teaching that he has already given them, and again he is correcting misunderstandings.[38] In Romans the most notable concentration of Jesus-traditions is in the section of ethical exhortation at the end of the letter.[39]

36. It might be possible to argue that the Corinthians were interested in Jesus-traditions because they had been taught not just by Paul but also by Apollos and maybe Cephas (who would, of course, have been uniquely well-placed in this matter). But Paul does speak of traditions that he has passed on, and there is not a great difference in the matter of Jesus-tradition between 1 Corinthians and parts of Romans.

37. The Corinthians' slogan "all things are permissible" (1 Cor 6:12; 10:23) may well represent their version of Paul's teaching about freedom from law, including his exposition of Jesus' teaching about nothing being unclean. See further on Paul's debate with the Corinthians on the Jesus-tradition about cleanness and uncleanness in chapter 2 above.

38. It was quite likely Paul's teaching about the nearness of the Lord's coming that caused some of the worries that he addresses in 1 Thes 4:13-18. Then it is possible that the problems addressed in 2 Thessalonians 2 arose partly out of misinterpretation of 1 Thes 2:16. See further discussion of the Thessalonian letters in chapter 7 above.

39. Davies, *Paul and Rabbinic Judaism*, 137-40, notes also the concentration in Colossians.

Paraphrase

Paul rarely quotes the traditions of Jesus directly. Even when there is a tradition indicator, it is not an exact equivalent of our quotation marks, since Paul typically paraphrases the relevant teaching of Jesus, applying it to the question he is discussing. Thus in two of the least disputable allusions — the discussion of divorce in 1 Cor 7:10, 11 and the saying about mission in 1 Cor 9:14 — he clearly has sayings of Jesus in mind and wants the Corinthians to recognize the allusions, but he very freely paraphrases Jesus' meaning. Thus "the laborer is worthy of his hire"* (Luke 10:7) becomes "those who proclaim the gospel should get their living by the gospel." Paul is not ignorant of the precise wording, and indeed it surfaces from time to time, but he can and evidently does presuppose a high level of familiarity with the tradition on the part of his readers. That he uses the traditions of Jesus in this way in almost indisputable allusions is worth bearing in mind when other less clear echoes or allusions are in question.

One particular feature of Paul's paraphrastic use of Jesus-traditions is that he picks up ideas from the stories and sayings of Jesus without reproducing the stories themselves. Thus he makes use of the imagery from various parables, for example, the thief, the two builders, the wise and foolish virgins, and the sower, but he does not retell the stories.[40] He echoes the story of Mary and Martha, but he does not refer directly to the two women or to the incident.[41] He is, we might say, "deparabolizing" the parables (and other stories), replacing the storytelling technique of Jesus and the Gospels with less colorful theological discourse. But this should not necessarily be seen as a feature of Pauline style in general; it can as easily be seen as a reflection of what Paul is doing in his letters, namely, alluding to traditions that he can presuppose knowledge of, sometimes paraphrasing and discussing them. He is not reproducing the traditions as such, and he does not need to.[42]

Reapplication

We have said that Paul applies Jesus-traditions to the questions in hand. This sometimes involves quite creative exegesis on his part. Thus Jesus' saying

40. See chapters 2, 5, and 7 above.
41. See chapter 6 above.
42. See further below. Farmer, *Jesus and the Gospel*, 48, 49, argues that parables were more appropriate to Jesus' spoken preaching than to Paul's letter writing and that Paul does not reproduce the parables because they were framed in terms of Palestinian life and culture.

about nothing from outside defiling a person was not originally a comment on the question of clean and unclean food, but Paul uses it in the context of discussing Gentile Christians eating food offered to idols; the Corinthians used it (even more creatively!) to justify prostitution.[43] Paul, however, refutes their view by bringing Jesus' "one flesh" teaching to bear on the question, though that, too, did not originally address the question of prostitution. Paul also uses Jesus' instruction to his apostles to "eat what is set before you" to address the question of Christians eating "unclean" food.[44]

Paul's versatile exegesis is perhaps most clearly illustrated by the ways he echoes Jesus' saying about the destruction and rebuilding of the temple, since he uses it in three very different ways: of ministers who threaten to "destroy" the temple of God, that is, the church; to criticize Christians who by their reinstatement of the law want to rebuild the old temple of Judaism; and of the death and resurrection of the temple of the body (1 Cor 3:17; Gal 2:18; 2 Cor 5:1).[45] In each case Paul's use of the text may be said to be a serious interpretation, not an irresponsible misuse of Jesus' saying; but he uses the text flexibly and creatively.

Dialogue

One of the important things that has come up repeatedly in this study is that Paul is often in dialogue with others about the Jesus-tradition. He is in dialogue with Jewish Christians associated with Jerusalem who appeal to the particular revelations granted to Peter and other disciples and find Paul lacking as an apostle; they may well also be criticizing his law-free gospel as encouraging unrighteousness.[46] He is in dialogue with people in his own churches: Thus, as we have seen, some men in Corinth were probably using Jesus' teaching about inner cleanness to justify going to prostitutes, and some women used various sayings of Jesus (e.g., Jesus' saying to Martha) to justify their pro-celibacy, anti-sex line.[47] Some in Corinth may have criticized Paul for his tentmaking (or leather working) on the grounds that it was contrary to Jesus' command to his apostles to accept support for their labor.[48] The Corinthian pneumatics were probably

---

43. See chapter 2 above.
44. See chapter 5 above.
45. See chapter 5 above.
46. See chapters 2, 5, and 8 above.
47. See chapters 2 and 6 above.
48. See chapter 5 above.

using the idea of the kingdom having come to justify things that Paul firmly rejected.[49] In due course some used the "yes, yes, no, no" saying as a stick to beat Paul with when he changed his mind about his planned visit to Corinth.[50] The Corinthians quite probably learned these teachings of Jesus from Paul himself (or in the course of his mission), but they were now turning them back on him.

The picture that emerges is of a continuing and sometimes controversial discussion of Jesus and his teaching, with Paul's opponents quoting a text in one way, and with Paul coming back on them with other texts and other interpretations.[51] What is clear is that the traditions of Jesus were a very important given, over which it was possible and worthwhile to argue.

Where Did Paul Get His Knowledge of Jesus?

It is possible to argue that much of what Paul has in common with Jesus came to him as part of the general Christian tradition rather than specifically and distinctly as teaching of Jesus. Thus he need not have been conscious, for example, that his teaching on nonretaliation or suffering with Christ came from Jesus (any more than most Christian readers of Paul are conscious that his teaching comes from Jesus!).

This could in theory be the case; certainly some of the ideas and emphases are common to the NT tradition as a whole. But it is at least an open question whether in the earliest days that tradition might have been clearly understood to comprise — more than anything else — traditions of Jesus. And so far as Paul himself is concerned, he sufficiently frequently indicates that a particular tradition has something to do with Jesus himself as to make it likely that he was quite conscious of his dependence on Jesus (as in Rom 14:14; 1 Cor 7:10, 11; 9:14; 11:23; 1 Thes 4:15). Thus he could, of course, have been familiar with the *Abba* prayer through the church's liturgy, but the way he specifically describes it as the cry of those who have

---

49. See chapter 2 above.

50. See chapter 6 above. The dialogue seems most evident in the Corinthian correspondence, and this could have something to do with the fact that there had been other teachers than Paul there, including Apollos and perhaps Peter. But there is a more muted dialogue going on elsewhere, for example, in Galatians (the question of Paul and Peter) and in 1 and 2 Thessalonians.

51. So J. P. Brown, "Synoptic Parallels," 46, 47, on the Corinthian liberals quoting "nothing is unclean" and Paul countering with "don't judge" and "don't set stumbling blocks."

the Spirit of Jesus makes it virtually certain that he knew of its origin; he would in any case have reflected on the Aramaic used. Since it is clear that he taught traditions of Jesus, it is simplest to suppose that he was influenced directly by such traditions rather than to explain his agreements with Jesus via the third party of church tradition that was not specifically Jesus-tradition.

But how did Paul learn so much about Jesus? The obvious answer would be that he learned it largely from those who were Christians before him. But Paul's assertion in Gal 1:11, 12 that "the gospel that was proclaimed by me is not of human origin; for I did not receive it from a human source, nor was I taught it, but I received it through a revelation of Jesus Christ," seems at least to put a question mark against that obvious answer. In the context of Galatians Paul is specifically rebutting the charge that his gospel and his apostleship are secondhand, and so he asserts his exclusive dependence on divine revelation so far as his gospel is concerned. This could be taken to mean, quite literally, that he learned all that he knew of the Christian faith directly from heaven. But this is an unlikely interpretation, given the opportunities he had before, at, and after his conversion to learn from others about the faith and given his open acknowledgement in other contexts (notably 1 Cor 11:23; 15:3) of tradition which he received.

What is much more likely is that Paul means that the essence of his gospel of God's grace (including for the Gentiles — the point at issue in Galatians) was divinely given to him when he was converted on the Damascus Road. In that conversion experience Paul, who had been a law-loving Pharisee persecuting the church of God, learned in a dramatic way that keeping the Mosaic law did not bring salvation but potentially damnation, that Jesus was alive and was Lord, that salvation was a matter of God's undeserved love, coming through Christ, that salvation was not for law-abiding Jews as such but for sinners, and, perhaps, that Jesus' death was not proof of his guilt (as Paul had previously thought) but God's way of salvation.[52] It was this divinely revealed gospel that Paul saw being challenged by the Judaizers in Galatia, and he insists that this was no second-hand gospel, but as firsthand as the gospel received by any other apostle.

But Paul does not mean that he learned nothing from anyone else. Indeed, the evidence is that he learned a huge amount about Jesus and his sayings from others. It is entirely probable that he learned much in dialogue

---

52. See Furnish, *Jesus According to Paul*, 12-13, on this. But the distinction he makes between the "gospel" and the traditions that were handed on (pp. 28-30) is quite unpersuasive: The "good news" of 1 Cor 15:1-3 is precisely what Paul handed on.

with those Christians whom he persecuted before his conversion. The Book of Acts implies that Paul was associated in Jerusalem with the Greek-speaking synagogues, out of which the Hellenist Christians like Stephen came. It may be inferred that Paul was one of those involved in heated dialogue with Stephen and his colleagues (see 6:9; 8:1, 3; 9:29). The Acts account is plausible in this respect. Some of the particular Pauline emphases (his critique of the law and the temple) seem to have been anticipated in the Greek-speaking Christian community, and it is likely that it was through that community that Paul had his first significant introduction to the traditions of Jesus, though he at first rejected their interpretation of Jesus fiercely.[53]

Then after his conversion he was, according to Acts, with the Christians of Damascus for some time, including, notably, Ananias (Acts 9:10-23). Scholars have questioned the Acts story of Ananias ministering to Paul, arguing (among other things) that Paul says in Gal 1:17 that after his conversion, "I did not confer with any human being."[54] But to take Paul's words to mean that he had no significant contact with any Christian after his conversion is to press them much too far: He means that he had no official consultation or briefing with any of the apostles (or anyone equivalent), not that he lived somehow in isolation from the Christian community in Damascus. There is every likelihood that he was instructed as a new convert and took every opportunity to learn of Jesus from his fellow Christians.

A little later Paul met and stayed with Peter, having ample opportunity then to fill out his knowledge of Jesus (Gal 1:18).[55]

What Was Paul's Attitude to the Jesus-Tradition?

It is one thing to show that Paul was familiar with many of the stories and sayings of Jesus; it is another to show that they were important to him. It is possible to argue that Paul shows some impatience with the Jesus-tradition, as though he does not see it as of binding or primary importance, and that it was peripheral rather than central to his thinking.

---

53. On the theology of the Hellenists the primary evidence is the Acts account of Stephen and his speech (6:8–7:53). See also the discussion in Hengel, *Earliest Christianity*, 71-80; Räisänen, *Jesus, Paul and Torah*, 149-202; Wedderburn, "Paul and Jesus: Similarity and Continuity," in *idem*, ed., *Paul and Jesus*, 117-43.

54. E.g. Betz, *Galatians*, 73.

55. Cf. Drane, "Patterns," 284-87, commenting on, among other things, the much-discussed verb *historēsai*.

Was he critical of the Jesus-tradition?

Paul's infrequent quotation of Jesus-traditions could be seen as support for this. But specifically it has been argued that he sits lightly to Jesus' teaching in both places where he admits quoting from the Lord: Thus in 1 Corinthians 7 he knows of Jesus' prohibition of divorce, but goes on to speak of situations in which he sees divorce as permissible. And in 1 Corinthians 9 Paul quite specifically defends his failure to do what Jesus commanded, that is, to accept support when on mission.

But neither example proves the point. It is true that in 1 Corinthians 7 Paul has to address a particular issue that Jesus did not address (Christian converts with non-Christian spouses), and he says that in such cases divorce is permissible (vv. 12-16). But he has started with Jesus' teaching about divorce and remarriage and sees it as the general principle governing even this situation (vv. 10, 11). Furthermore, in allowing divorce in such situations, he appeals to the principle of living at "peace," quite possibly drawing on Jesus' teaching for that principle (e.g., Mark 9:49). And he does not say that remarriage is permissible in such cases (though some commentators have assumed that) and so does not retreat from Jesus' basic "one flesh" principle.

In 1 Corinthians 9 Paul does not question Jesus' teaching about the laborer being worthy of his hire/reward, and indeed he speaks of his own "reward"; but he does not see Jesus' saying as an invariable rule to be applied woodenly in any situation (as though a Christian worker *must* ask others to support him) so much as a right that it is legitimate to waive in the service of the gospel.[56] Paul sees his policy of working with his hands so as not to burden others as in keeping with Jesus' other saying about "giving freely," and he sees the waiving of his rights as in keeping with Jesus' teaching about leadership through humble service (compare 1 Cor 9:18, 19 with Matt 10:8; Mark 10:44, 45).

Another case where Paul has been seen as critical of a Jesus-tradition is in 1 Cor 13:1-3, where he says that faith to move mountains (such as Jesus had spoken of) is worth nothing without love. But here Paul is not at all denying the importance of miracle-working faith (or of giving to the poor or speaking in tongues, which he speaks of in the same breath): His

---

56. Kim, "Jesus, Sayings of," 475, argues that Jesus' instruction to the apostles about accepting payment for their labors was intended to free them for preaching the good news and that Paul's refusal to accept payment was to further his preaching, thus — paradoxically — in keeping with Jesus' intention.

point is that the greatest gifts of the Spirit, such as faith and speaking in tongues (both of which he has spoken positively about), are worth nothing in the absence of the Spirit's greatest work, which is love. Paul is in no way denigrating the teaching of Jesus: Indeed, his emphasis in 1 Corinthians 13 on faith, hope, and love, with the primacy given to love, is an emphasis of the Jesus-tradition. What Paul is doing is to interpret the tradition, bringing out its priorities, as he sees them, in response to the Corinthian charismatics, who may also have quoted the Jesus-tradition, but in a way that was, in the end of the day, a distortion rather than a faithful representation of Jesus' meaning.

Central or peripheral?

But is the Jesus-tradition really central, or is it peripheral in Paul's thinking? At first sight some of the major themes of Paul's theology may appear to be quite different from the themes of Jesus' ministry.[57] But on closer inspection we have found, first, that the overall structure of Jesus' and Paul's theology is the same — with the emphasis on Jesus having brought the promised day of fulfillment and salvation for God's people;[58] second, that major terminological differences prove to be just that rather than differences of substance, so that, for example, Jesus' "kingdom" teaching and Paul's justification/righteousness teaching are much closer than may at first appear; and third, that some of the other key Pauline ideas, for example, participation in Christ — in his body and his death, Paul's Adam christology, his flesh-spirit dualism, and his faith-hope-love triad, all may be seen as deriving from the Jesus-tradition, even though some of the application (e.g., of the body language to the practicalities of church life) is distinctively Pauline.

Far from being peripheral, it is arguable that Jesus-tradition is central to Paul's theology.[59] The OT is clearly the background to Paul's thinking, but his focus is on Jesus. Jesus, specifically in his death and resurrection, is the center of God's saving plan, and the Christian life is essentially living in relationship to Jesus, living in union with him, following his example, obeying his teaching, and looking for the future that he promised.

---

57. So Walter, "Paul," 63.

58. See Farmer, *Jesus and the Gospel*, 49, arguing that much of Paul's deepest thought may reflect Jesus' teaching in parables.

59. It was vital to others as well, including to Paul's opponents who decried him precisely because he was not deemed a first-class apostle with firsthand information; contrast the "pillars." (Note the possible play with the very words of the Jesus-tradition.)

It is widely accepted that participation in Christ is a key concept for Paul, but that has often been seen rather narrowly as a mystical or sacramental concept. The importance of the sacraments for Paul is quite clear, but it is arguable that for Paul baptism brings the believer to share not just in the death and resurrection of Jesus, but in his whole story:[60] The Christian life, starting from baptism, is life in union with Jesus and thus is to be a retelling of Jesus' story, living as children of God by the Spirit, overcoming sin, "imitating" Jesus' example of faith and service, suffering, but looking forward to resurrection. Jesus is the new Adam, and the Christian life is a life of being conformed to his likeness; we are no longer under the law of Moses' but, to use Paul's phrase in 1 Cor 9:21, we are "enlawed" to Christ. In this context the story and teachings of Jesus are vitally important: They are in a real sense the text of the Christian life.

The story and teachings of Jesus are important for the Christian life in general, but also for Paul's view of his own ministry: Although his call came to him on the Damascus road, his own apostleship is defined in terms of apostleship as Jesus inaugurated it during his ministry, and his eschatological expectation, which gave urgency and purpose to his ministry, derived from Jesus. He (and indeed his converts) were eagerly looking for the fulfillment of Jesus' vision for the future.[61]

2 Cor 5:16

Before leaving the question of the importance of Jesus for Paul, we must note the much-discussed verse 2 Cor 5:16, where Paul comments that "although we once knew Christ according to the flesh, now we know him thus no longer."*[62]

Paul's words were taken by Rudolf Bultmann to mean that Paul once had an interest in the Jesus of history (Christ according to the flesh), but that as a Christian he no longer had any such interest.[63] Paul is now

---

60. So Hays, *Faith,* e.g., 250.

61. See chapter 7 above for the suggestion that Paul in 1 Thes 2:16 and elsewhere was explaining current world events in terms of Jesus' eschatological teaching.

62. Paul is speaking in the context of his ministry, which is impelled on by the love of Christ, who "died for all." He continues (literally) (vv. 16, 17): "So from now on we know no one according to the flesh. Even if we knew Christ according to the flesh, now we know him thus no longer. So if anyone is in Christ, there is new creation. . . ."*

63. Bultmann, *2 Corinthians,* 155-56: "The Χριστὸς κατὰ σάρκα is Christ as he can be encountered in the world, before his death and resurrection. He should no longer be viewed as such. . . ." See also Robinson, "Kerygma," 142-43.

interested in the Christ of faith — in the good news of Jesus who died and rose — but not in Jesus' human life.

But this interpretation of 2 Cor 5:16 is unacceptable.[64] It is clear from the context that when Paul says that he once knew Christ according to the flesh, the phrase "according to the flesh" qualifies the verb "we knew," not the noun "Christ," and that what Paul means is that as a non-Christian he viewed Christ in a limited, fleshly way; but now he sees Christ with the eyes of faith.[65] Paul's comment about knowing Christ follows his comment about knowing "no one according to the flesh": His point is that he has a new perspective on where everyone stands, thanks to the death and resurrection of Christ. It is this "new creation" perspective that is the basis of his evangelistic ministry (vv. 14, 15, 19, 20). There is no implication that he used to be interested in people's human lives and is so no longer; but he now sees people in the context of God's saving work. So with Christ, Paul is not implying that he has lost interest in the historical Jesus, but that as a Christian he sees Jesus in a new light.[66]

2 Cor 5:16 cannot then be taken to mean that Paul is uninterested in the Jesus of history. Nor indeed does Paul make a distinction between the Jesus of history and the exalted risen and returning Christ.[67] For him the

64. See Wolff, "True Apostolic Knowledge"; Wright, *NT and the People of God*, 408, commenting on how important the historical "Jesus" (note the name) has been in the context of 2 Corinthians 4–5, especially in 4:7-15. Earlier discussions include Fraser, *Jesus and Paul*, 46-62, and Blank, *Paulus und Jesus*. Although Paul is not denying the importance of the historical Jesus, it is just possible that his choice of phrase in 2 Cor 5:16 could reflect his critics' emphasis on their firsthand knowledge of Jesus and that he could (indirectly) be reacting against their boasting of special knowledge (while in no way denigrating the historical Jesus).

65. Wolff, "True Apostolic Knowledge," 92, speaks of "the spiritual hermeneutics by which Paul interprets the early Christian Jesus-tradition."

66. In the context of Paul's remarks about his ministry to "all" (vv. 14, 15), Paul's specific point could be that he had previously thought of Jesus in very limited Jewish terms (as an Israelite and descendant of David; cf. Rom 1:3), but that now he sees Jesus as for all people. Compare the slightly different view of Wright, *NT and the People of God*, 408: "According to the flesh" is Paul's usual way of referring to Jewish attitudes. The Jews' aspiration was for a nationalistic Messiah; Paul knows of Jesus as a different kind of Messiah, whose "flesh" died and rose again.

67. Paul can use "the Lord" of the earthly Jesus and also of the risen Christ (see Furnish, *Jesus According to Paul*, 64, citing 1 Cor 14:37). To recognize this, however, is not to accept that Paul made no distinction between words of the earthly "Lord" and prophetic words of the risen "Lord." We have seen considerable evidence (not least in 1 Cor 7:10-12) that suggests that the words of the earthly Jesus had an unquestioned status quite different from words of prophecy, which needed to be tested, and from Paul's own words.

story is a continuity beginning with the preexistent Son, proceeding on through the incarnation to the supremely important cross, resurrection, and exaltation, and leading finally on to the Lord's return and the handing over of the kingdom to the Father. The whole story is a unity, and the whole story is important for Paul.

Why Does Paul Refer to Jesus' Life and Ministry So Seldom?

But if Jesus and the traditions of Jesus are so focal for Paul, why does Paul not more frequently refer to them?[68] Why does he more frequently quote the OT explicitly? A number of points may be made in response to these important questions.

The quantity of echoes

First, Paul does in fact, as we have seen, echo and allude to the teaching of Jesus very extensively, and in a significant number of cases he expects the allusion to be recognized.

The presupposition of familiarity and the nature of Paul's gospel

Second, there is evidence that the stories and sayings of Jesus were taught in the churches, including in Paul's churches and by Paul himself. Paul can therefore, and does, presuppose knowledge. He does not often need to quote directly or explicitly from what is common knowledge to him and his addressees.[69] (With the OT he may be able to presuppose much less knowledge.)

The way Paul paraphrases Jesus-traditions supports this view: He expects people to pick up the allusions. He does not always need to mark

---

68. See on this especially Thompson, *Clothed with Christ*, 70-76.

69. It is striking how many of Paul's uses of the phrase "Do you not know?" and to a lesser extent "You know" can be related back directly or indirectly to gospel traditions. See 1 Cor 3:16 (related to Mark 14:58); 5:6 (possibly, though not necessarily, related to sayings of Jesus such as Matt 13:33/Luke 13:21; Matt 16:6-12/Mark 8:15/Luke 12:1); 6:2, 3 (cf. Matt 19:28); 6:9 (cf. Matt 5:20); 6:15, 16 (cf. Matt 19:5); 6:19 (cf. Mark 14:58); 1 Thes 3:3, 4 (cf. Mark 13:9-13); 4:2 (perhaps cf. Mark 7:21, 22); 5:2 (cf. Matt 24:43, 44); and perhaps 2 Thes 2:6 (cf. Mark 13:10).

allusions or echoes with quotation marks (or "tradition indicators").[70] His readers can see how fundamental Jesus-traditions are to Paul's teaching without being told.[71]

The way Paul seems to be responding from time to time to other people's use of Jesus-traditions points in the same direction. The impression we get is that there was a vigorous discussion going on, with Paul and others quoting and counter-quoting sayings and stories of Jesus. The sayings and stories were common property.[72]

The view that Paul could presuppose knowledge of the stories and sayings of Jesus may be confirmed by reflection on the likely nature of Paul's own gospel preaching. It seems sometimes to be assumed that "the gospel" that Paul preached was something like 1 Cor 15:3, 4, that is, a brief declaration of the fact that Jesus died and rose for our salvation. But it is certain that 1 Corinthians 15 is only an extremely compressed summary of some of the main points that Paul preached, quite probably also a selective summary focusing on the point at issue in 1 Corinthians 15, namely, Jesus' resurrection.[73] What else did he teach to potential or actual converts?

He could simply have passed on to them traditions of Jesus' passion. Paul speaks in 1 Corinthians 15 of Jesus' death and resurrection (and perhaps also the resurrection appearances) as part of the tradition that he has already "passed on" to the Corinthians and that they have "received"; he uses similar language of the last supper (1 Cor 11:23). But did he only pass on such passion traditions? We have found reason to believe that Paul knew a much wider "story" of Jesus, a story that included a reference to Jesus' birth (Gal 4:4).[74] It may well be that Rom 1:1-5, which we commented on above, can give us a clue as to the shape of Paul's gospel.

Paul also speaks of ethical traditions that he passed on (1 Cor 11:2; 1 Thes 4:1; 2 Thes 3:6),[75] and we have seen that some at least of his ethical

---

70. In chapter 6 we noted the way Paul slips in "not I, but the Lord" in 1 Cor 7:10 almost as an afterthought.

71. Contra Richardson and Gooch, "Logia of Jesus," 45, who fail to see how much Paul's authoritative teaching is based on Jesus-traditions.

72. Dunn, "Jesus Tradition in Paul," 178, argues interestingly that allusive reference to a shared tradition has a bonding effect on a community. "To force . . . the web of allusion and echo into the open may strengthen the explicit authority of a particular exhortation, but it also weakens the bonding effect of a particular discourse."

73. So Stanton, *Jesus of Nazareth*, 114.

74. See chapter 8 above.

75. The "traditions" of 1 Cor 11:2 could be Paul's instructions about "no male and female" in the church. It is not so obvious which Jesus-traditions might be behind

ideas were derived from Jesus. Thus he can speak of living "in accordance with Christ Jesus" (Rom 15:5) and can instruct his readers to "put on the Lord Jesus Christ" (13:14).[76] More generally, in Col 2:6 we read of "receiving" Christ: "As *you have received Christ Jesus the Lord,* walk in him."* "Receiving" is the word used elsewhere of reception of tradition (e.g., 1 Cor 11:2, 23; 15:3).[77] It is not fanciful to infer that the "tradition" that Paul passed on and that others received included stories about Jesus and ethical teaching from Jesus.

Later the Colossians are urged to "let *the word of Christ* dwell in you" (Col 3:16). Rather similarly Paul writes in 1 Thes 2:13 of *"receiving the word of hearing"** (the same "receiving" verb),[78] and in 1 Thes 4:1 he says: "We urge you *in the Lord Jesus* that, as *you received* from us how you ought to walk. . . ."* In Rom 10:17 he speaks of being saved through hearing *"the word of Christ."*[79] What does Paul mean by such phrases? What does he mean when he refers to Christians becoming slaves to *"the pattern of teaching to which you were handed over"** (Rom 6:17)?[80]

Scholars have been amazingly reluctant to think that Paul may have in mind the stories and sayings of Jesus and that these comprised the heart of his "gospel."[81] This reluctance may arise in some cases from a modern

---

1 Thes 4:1 and 2 Thes 3:6, though we have connected Paul's sexual ethics with Jesus' teaching (see, e.g., Matt 5:27-31; Matt 15:18, 19/Mark 7:21, 22); in both Pauline contexts there is an interesting reference to "the Lord Jesus (Christ)."

76. Dunn, "Paul's Knowledge," 198, suggests that to "put on Christ" most likely means in this context to model one's life on that of Jesus.

77. Cf. Eph 4:20, 21: "You did not so learn Christ, if indeed you heard him and were taught in him, as the truth is in Jesus. . . ."*

78. See Schippers, "Pre-Synoptic Tradition," 225-29, for the view that "hearing" (*akoē*) is used in 1 Thes 2:13 of tradition, that which has been heard. The same word is used in Rom 10:17.

79. Compare "the word of the Lord" in 1 Thes 4:15; we argued in chapter 6 that Paul is referring here to the traditions of Jesus. In several places where he is drawing on tradition he uses the word "Lord" (cf. Rom 14:14; 1 Cor 7:10; 9:14; 11:23), but it does not follow that "the word of Christ" may not also refer back to Jesus' ministry.

80. "Handed over" here is the verb used elsewhere of the passing on of traditions of Jesus (1 Cor 11:23; 15:3). Here it is probably the picture of a slave being handed over to a master, but there may be a hint of the passing on of tradition; see Dunn, *Romans,* 343-44, and "Paul's Knowledge," 196, where Dunn argues that "pattern" *(typos)* is used almost always in Paul of an example to be followed (e.g., Phil 3:17; 2 Thes 3:9; 1 Cor 10:6; 1 Thes 1:7).

81. See the comment in chapter 8 above on Gal 3:1 with its reference to Christ crucified being placarded before the Galatians. O'Brien, *Colossians,* 105, helpfully de-

theological agenda: Salvation comes through the simple proclamation of Jesus' death and resurrection, not through knowledge of the broader story of Jesus. But in other cases the reluctance is there probably because people have perceived Paul as so little dependent on the stories and sayings of Jesus. If in fact he was heavily dependent on those stories and sayings, then that the "gospel" that Paul handed on included very much the same sort of ingredients as we find in our written Gospels, that is, an account of Jesus' life, teaching, death, and resurrection, becomes a strong and attractive possibility.[82]

Luke's testimony in the Book of Acts would certainly point in this direction. He portrays the twelve as "witnesses" to the life of Jesus (from John the Baptist to the ascension) and as "ministers of the word" (1:8, 21, 22; 6:4). He does not explain what the "word" was that they ministered, but it is reasonable to infer that the "witness" and the "word" go together, and that Luke intends us to think of the apostles as doing precisely what he has done in his Gospel, namely, telling and explaining the story of Jesus to the growing church.[83] Luke goes on to portray Paul as someone who taught about the "kingdom of God" (19:8; 20:25; 28:23, 31), thus also as someone who taught the sort of traditions that he, Luke, has presented in his Gospel. He could, of course, be anachronistically making Paul and the apostles in his own image. But the evidence that we have presented lends credence to Luke's account.

If the suggestions we have made about the nature of Paul's "gospel" are correct, then the importance of Jesus-tradition to Paul is all the clearer; even if they are not all correct, the argument about Paul's presupposing his readers' knowledge of Jesus-traditions still remains.

The purpose of the Epistles

The whole point of the Pauline letters was to clarify what was unclear or disputed. It was not necessary, usually, to retell the stories of Jesus, since they were well known.[84] What was necessary was to clarify their interpreta-

---

scribes the traditions passed on by Paul to his churches under three headings: "(a) a summary of the gospel, particularly the death and resurrection of Christ, expressed as a confession of faith (1 Cor 15:1-5; 1 Thess 2:13); (b) various deeds and words of Christ (1 Cor 11:23-26; 7:10, 11; 9:14); and (c) ethical and procedural rules (1 Cor 11:2; 1 Thess 4:1; 2 Thess 3:6)." He does not observe how all of these categories may belong together and be related to Jesus' life and teaching.

82. See the additional note below on "The Form of Paul's Gospel."

83. Cf. Luke 1:1-4, with its references to eyewitnesses and ministers of the word.

84. One might say that, from our point of view, it is a rather "hit or miss" business as to which Jesus-traditions do surface in the Epistles. Paul echoes or explicitly alludes

tion and application, not least because of the misleading interpretations held by some in the churches to which Paul was writing. In other words, we have two very different things in the Gospels and in the Epistles:[85] The Gospels are essentially traditions of Jesus being handed on (albeit interpreted); the Epistles are explanatory. It is notable that in the Book of Acts the one speech of Paul that is addressed to established Christians (20:17-35) is quite different from the evangelistic sermons described by Luke.[86] The Gospels are neither evangelistic nor pastoral sermons, but it is likely that explaining the story of Jesus was an important part of the evangelistic process quite distinct from the task of the letters.

It is also notable that the NT Epistles not written by Paul (e.g., James, 1 Peter, and 1 John) also have little explicit citation of Jesus-traditions, though there is often reason to believe that their authors knew a good quantity of such traditions.[87] Like Paul these writers echo the traditions without ascribing them to Jesus. There is a common pattern here, and the explanation is more probably that the authors all presuppose knowledge of the tradition than that they are ignorant of it or not interested in it.[88] They expect the echoes and allusions to be recognized and heard by their

---

to certain traditions because they were relevant to the particular problems of the church to which he was writing; other traditions may have been equally well known, but he has no cause to mention them. See n. 25 above.

85. Cf. Goppelt, "Jesus und die 'Haustafel' Tradition," 103-4, who contrasts the preaching of Jesus in the Gospels and the call to conversion with the parenesis of the Epistles. Dunn, "Paul's Knowledge," 206, is misleading in this respect, when he suggests that we see in Paul's use of the Jesus-tradition *"precisely the way in which the Jesus tradition was retained and used."*

86. So Stanton, *Jesus of Nazareth*, 110-11. Whether or not the speeches of Acts are seen as historically reliable, the fact is that Luke sees a significant difference between Paul's proclamation of the kingdom to nonbelievers and his speech to Christian leaders. The speech to the Ephesian elders has a number of similarities to Paul's letters.

87. On James, for example, see Davids, "James and Jesus"; on 1 Peter, see Maier, "Jesustradition im 1. Petrusbrief?" On the general point see Thompson, *Clothed with Christ*, 37-63. Stanton, *Jesus of Nazareth*, 113, notes also that Acts is reticent in its use of Jesus-tradition and comments that if we had only Acts and the Johannine letters "we might conclude that neither Luke nor the Johannine community had much interest in the sort of material the Gospels contain."

88. B. Gerhardsson uses the silence of the Epistles as evidence against the form-critical view that the gospel traditions were passed down piecemeal in the preaching and teaching of the church, and he argues that the evidence points to the stories and sayings of Jesus being passed down as a tradition in their own right. See Gerhardsson, "Path."

readers, just as the author of the Book of Revelation expects his readers to recognize his vast number of allusions to the OT, even though he at no point explicitly indicates that he is using the OT.[89]

Paul's new context

All that we have said about Paul's interest in, even dependence on, the Jesus-tradition should not be taken to suggest that differences between Paul and Jesus were almost nonexistent.[90] In fact the vocabulary and style of Paul's letters and the topics that he discusses are different from what we meet in the Gospels (as indeed the ordinary Christian reader recognizes), and, as we have seen, Paul's theology does represent a significant development of Jesus' teaching.

The reason for this is not just that we are dealing with two very different men, but it is also, perhaps even more, because of their differing social and theological contexts. Paul writes, as we have mentioned, after Jesus' crucifixion and resurrection, after Pentecost, after his own conversion, after the Gentile mission has gotten under way, in a church context where the sacraments are celebrated and are important, and to churches whose situation and problems are miles away (literally and metaphorically) from the situation addressed by Jesus in his teaching. It is not surprising in view of all this that Paul's letters are very different from the Gospels: He is in a new situation with (in many ways) a new agenda. It is also not surprising if some of these new realities have come to dominate his thinking, overshadowing other things.

In particular the death and resurrection of Jesus are the supremely important facts about Jesus for Paul. They are theologically of overwhelming importance in bringing God's liberation to the world. Everything else (e.g., the miracles of Jesus, even the teaching of Jesus) is secondary by comparison, though not for that reason unimportant.[91] The Lord's death

89. Cf. Fjärstedt, *Synoptic Tradition*, 55. On the use of the OT and Jesus-traditions in Revelation see Beale, "Use of Daniel."

90. A good part of this book has been given over to an examination of parallels and possible parallels between Jesus and Paul; the quite mistaken impression could be gained that everything is parallel and that Paul and Paul's teaching are slightly modified versions of Jesus and Jesus' teaching!

91. Kim, "Jesus, Sayings of," 489, comments: "For Paul, Jesus is significant primarily not as a teacher but as the *Christ* who died and rose again for the salvation of humankind! Hence the meaning of Jesus as the risen Lord for Paul is essentially different from that of a rabbinic or a philosophic teacher for his pupil."

and resurrection were also the events to which Paul came closest personally: He was not a witness to the events of Jesus' lifetime — his knowledge was secondhand at that point — but he was witness to the resurrection of Jesus from the dead (by his own account). His much greater stress on Jesus' death and resurrection than on his life and ministry makes sense both in Paul's theological context and in his personal context.[92]

One more doubtful suggestion is that the traditions of Jesus' ministry had almost been hijacked by Paul's opponents, so that he refrained from referring frequently to them. There may just be a grain of truth in the idea: In certain controversial contexts he may have preferred to stress that which he had firsthand knowledge of rather than that for which he was dependent on others and in which he could justly be accused of being an inferior apostle.[93] When it came to quoting Scripture, he was on equal terms with others; when it came to quoting Jesus-traditions, he could be supposed to be at a disadvantage.

On the other hand, the evidence is not that Paul was particularly reticent in his use of Jesus-traditions, rather the opposite. There is no good reason for thinking that Paul had effectively opted out of the traditions of Jesus' ministry (or ceded them to his opponents); there is every reason for thinking that those traditions continued to be of great importance for him, even if they were overshadowed by the overwhelmingly important events that followed the ministry.

FOLLOWER OF JESUS OR FOUNDER OF CHRISTIANITY?

What has this book achieved? It has attempted to give an overall view on the question of Paul's relationship to Jesus. It has been inevitably sketchy in its discussion of all sorts of issues and ideas, but I hope that at least it has opened up the subject in a fresh and sometimes controversial way and that it will stimulate others to explore more fully and adequately the questions that have been raised.[94] But where has it brought us in ad-

92. Cf. Kümmel, *Heilsgeschehen und Geschichte*, 83, 84, though I would not accept the "either-or" implied in his view that Paul saw himself as the disciple of the risen Christ, but not of the earthly Jesus.

93. Stuhlmacher, *Biblische Theologie*, I, 303, notes the possibility but raises against it the fact that the letters of James and 1 Peter are similarly reticent.

94. If the conclusions reached in this book are correct, then all sorts of questions need to be reopened. Some of the older works on the subject (such as Feine, *Jesus*

dressing the question of Paul — follower of Jesus or founder of Christianity?

Paul's contribution to the development of Christian thinking and church life was stupendous. He, more than anyone else, molded the church's thinking about how the Palestinian stories and sayings of Jesus should be interpreted in the wider context of the Gentile world and the urbanized Roman Empire and in the post-Easter situation. He lived at the beginning of a process that has gone on ever since — of Christians wrestling with the meaning of the traditions of Jesus. In face of all sorts of different situations and conflicting interpretations, he worked out an interpretation that was perceived by the church to express the truth of Jesus in a way that was faithful both to Jesus and to the new context in which he was working.

All sorts of other interpretations were being canvassed: Some interpreted the sayings and stories of Jesus to justify prostitution or to advocate celibacy for all Christians (anticipating later Gnostic interpretations); some insisted on a very literal, even simplistic, interpretation of Jesus' words, for example, about the apostle being paid for his work; and some put certain leaders on a pedestal despite Jesus' teaching about servanthood (even taking the expression "the acknowledged ones" out of context to exalt their leaders).

By contrast, Paul's own interpretation of the Jesus-tradition was flexible. He did not, for example, feel bound by the letter of Jesus' command that evangelists should be paid for their work. His interpretation was imaginative, as when he applied Jesus' instruction to his apostles about eating "what is set before you" to the question of eating food offered to idols. But his interpretation was also impressively faithful to the spirit and intention of Jesus. He maintained Jesus' perspective and priorities, and he could with justification claim that "we have the mind of Christ" (1 Cor 2:16). His interpretation may justifiably be said to be a model in terms of method, and to have maintained the church in the faith of Jesus.[95]

For all the importance of his interpretation, Paul would have been horrified at the suggestion that he was the founder of Christianity. For him

---

Christus; Knowling, *Testimony;* even Resch's massive *Paulinismus,* despite its weaknesses) may also deserve reevaluation, having been too quickly dismissed in the past. Davies, *Paul and Rabbinic Judaism,* 137, judges Resch's argument to be overstated but still very impressive.

95. This is not to say that all of his interpretation is easy either to understand or to accept. But we hope that some of the explanation that we have offered in the book, e.g., of his teaching about sex and about women, will have helped make sense of Paul.

the fountain of theology was Jesus: first, the Jesus whom he met on the Damascus road; second, the Jesus of the Christian tradition. He of course identified the two. Paul saw himself as the slave of Jesus Christ, not the founder of Christianity.[96] He was right to see himself in that way.

The importance of this conclusion, if it is broadly correct, is great. It has implications for our understanding of the gospel traditions, for our understanding of early Christianity, and for our understanding of Paul. If the primary text that Paul is expounding in his writings is the text of Jesus, then instead of reading Paul's letters in isolation from the Gospels, it will be important to read them in the light of the Gospels — not falling into naive harmonization, but recognizing that Paul was above all motivated by a desire to follow Jesus.

96. Even Paul's description of himself as a "slave of Jesus Christ" may well reflect the influence of Jesus' teaching (i.e., the parables about masters and servants).

ADDITIONAL NOTE: THE FORM
OF PAUL'S "GOSPEL"

If Paul did teach the story and sayings of Jesus, what form did that teaching take? It is often assumed uncritically that the mass of stories and sayings circulated without any organizing framework for many years; but it seems very likely that the materials were gathered into a framework (or into various different frameworks) from a very early date, if only for teaching purposes.

Scholars have suggested that there were early collections of traditions, for example, the sayings that we now find in Mark 9:33-50, the controversy stories found in Mark 2:1–3:6, etc. This is certainly possible, though it is not all that easy to imagine how such collections would have been used. It is in many ways very much easier to think of Paul and others passing on traditions within a narrative framework. We have seen that Paul seems to have had just such a framework, a story outline of Jesus' life and ministry. It is possible then that Paul's "gospel" of Jesus was something quite similar to our present Gospels.[97]

If it was, then the common assumption that our written Gospels are compilations of earlier more fragmented traditions may need to be questioned. The real state of affairs may in fact be the opposite, namely, that our written Gospels represent distillations of fuller oral traditions (such as Paul and others passed on).[98] We have seen some evidence that could confirm this, notably in Mark 13:33-37, where Mark has preserved very brief extracts of a fuller tradition, but also in the Matthean and Lukan versions of the eschatological parables, where each Evangelist has preserved some but not all of the underlying tradition (see chapter 7 above). Mark 9:33-50 might be similarly explained, that is, as a brief distillation of a broader tradition.[99]

---

97. Whatever the form of the tradition known to Paul, the Gospels themselves are testimony to the interest of people in the early church in the stories and sayings of Jesus; the idea that Paul and his churches were somehow immune from this interest has been shown to be highly improbable.

98. See Fjärstedt, *Synoptic Tradition*, 174-75.

99. It could be that Matthew 18 represents something like the fuller form of the tradition.

WORKS CITED

L. Aejmelaeus, *Wachen vor dem Ende. Die Traditionsgeschichtlichen Wurzeln von 1. Thess 5:1-11 und Luke 21:34-36* (Helsinki: Finnische Exegetische Gesellschaft, 1985).

K. Aland, *Synopsis Quattuor Evangeliorum* (Stuttgart: Würtembergische Bibelanstalt, 1965³).

D. C. Allison, *The End of the Ages Has Come* (Philadelphia: Fortress, 1985).

————, "Paul and the Missionary Discourse," *ETL* 61 (1985) 369-75.

————, "The Pauline Epistles and the Synoptic Gospels: The Pattern of Parallels," *NTS* 28 (1982) 1-32.

————, "Peter and Cephas: One and the Same," *JBL* 111 (1992) 489-95.

H. Anderson, *The Gospel of Mark* (NCBC; London: Marshall, 1976).

J. Antwi, "Did Jesus Consider His Death to Be an Atoning Sacrifice?" *Int* 45 (1991) 17-28.

K. Armstrong, *The First Christian: Saint Paul's Impact on Christianity* (London: Pan, 1983).

C. E. Arnold, *Ephesians: Power and Magic* (Cambridge: CUP, 1989).

R. Badenas, *Christ the End of the Law: Romans 10.4 in Pauline Perspective* (Sheffield: JSOT, 1985).

D. Balch, "Backgrounds of I Cor. vii: Sayings of the Lord in Q; Moses as an Ascetic θεῖος ἀνήρ in II Cor. iii," *NTS* 18 (1971/72) 351-64.

E. Bammel, "Judenverfolgung und Naherwartung. Zur Eschatologie des ersten Thessalonicherbriefs," *ZTK* 56 (1959) 294-315.

E. Bammel and C. F. D. Moule, eds., *Jesus and the Politics of His Day* (Cambridge: CUP, 1984).

R. Banks, *Jesus and the Law in the Synoptic Tradition* (Cambridge: CUP, 1975).

J. Barclay, "Jesus and Paul," in G. F. Hawthorne, R. P. Martin, D. G. Reid, eds. *Dictionary of Paul and His Letters* (Downers Grove/Leicester: IVP, 1993) 492-502.

————, *Obeying the Truth* (Edinburgh: Clark, 1988).

J. Barr, "'Abbā Isn't Daddy,'" *JTS* 39 (1988) 28-47.

C. K. Barrett, "The Background of Mark 10:45," in A. J. B. Higgins, ed., *NT Essays* (Manchester: MUP, 1959) 1-18.

————, *A Commentary on the First Epistle to the Corinthians* (H/BNTC; London: Black/New York: Harper and Row, 1971²).

————, *Jesus and the Gospel Tradition* (London: SPCK, 1967).

————, "Paul and the 'Pillar' Apostles," in J. N. Sevenster and W. C. van Unnik, eds., *Studia Paulina* (Haarlem: Bohn, 1953) 1-19.

M. Barth, *Ephesians: Introduction, Translation and Commentary on Chapters 1–3* (AB; Garden City: Doubleday, 1974).

R. J. Bauckham, "Barnabas in Galatians," *JSNT* 2 (1979) 61-70.

————, "The Coin in the Fish's Mouth," *Gospel Perspectives* 6, 219-52.

————, "The Study of Gospel Traditions outside the Canonical Gospels: Problems and Prospects," *Gospel Perspectives* 5, 369-403.

H. F. Bayer, *Jesus' Predictions of Vindication and Resurrection* (Tübingen: Mohr, 1986).

G. K. Beale, "The Use of Daniel in the Synoptic Eschatological Discourse and in the Book of Revelation," *Gospel Perspectives* 5, 129-53.

G. R. Beasley-Murray, *Baptism in the NT* (London: Macmillan/Grand Rapids: Eerdmans, 1963) 167-71.

————, *Jesus and the Kingdom of God* (Grand Rapids: Eerdmans/Exeter: Paternoster, 1984).

————, *Jesus and the Last Days* (Peabody: Hendrickson, 1993).

J. C. Beker, *Paul the Apostle* (Philadelphia: Fortress, 1984).

E. Best, *A Commentary on the First and Second Epistles to the Thessalonians* (H/BNTC; London: Black/New York: Harper and Row, 1972).

H. D. Betz, *Galatians* (Hermeneia; Philadelphia: Fortress, 1979).

O. Betz and R. Riesner, *Jesus, Qumran, and the Vatican* (London: SCM, 1994).

J. Blank, *Paulus und Jesus* (Munich: Kösel, 1968).

C. Blomberg, *The Historical Reliability of the Gospels* (Leicester: IVP, 1987).

————, *Interpreting the Parables* (Downers Grove/Leicester: IVP, 1989).

M. Borg, *Conflict, Holiness and Politics in the Teachings of Jesus* (New York: Mellen, 1984).

D. Bosch, *Die Heidenmission in der Zukunftsschau Jesus* (Zurich: Zwingli, 1959).

M. Boucher, *The Parables* (Wilmington: Glazier, 1981).

S. G. F. Brandon, *Jesus and the Zealots* (Manchester: MUP, 1967).

C. Brown, "Person of Christ," in G. W. Bromiley, et al., eds., *International Standard Bible Encyclopedia* III (Grand Rapids: Eerdmans, 1986) 781-801.

J. P. Brown, "Synoptic Parallels in the Epistle and Form-History," *NTS* 10 (1963) 27-48.

R. E. Brown, *The Birth of the Messiah* (London: Chapman/Garden City: Doubleday, 1977).

———, *The Gospel according to John* (AB; Garden City: Doubleday/London: Chapman, 1966, 1971) lxvii-lxix.

F. F. Bruce, *The Epistle of Paul to the Galatians* (NIGTC; Exeter: Paternoster/Grand Rapids: Eerdmans, 1982).

———, *Paul and Jesus* (Grand Rapids: Baker 1974/London: SPCK, 1977).

———, *Paul: Apostle of the Free Spirit* (Exeter: Paternoster, 1977) = *Paul: Apostle of the Heart Set Free* (Grand Rapids: Eerdmans, 1977).

R. Bultmann, *The Second Letter to the Corinthians* (Minneapolis: Augsburg, 1985).

———, "The Significance of the Historical Jesus for the Theology of Paul," in *Faith and Understanding: Collected Essays* (London: SCM, 1969) 220-46.

———, *Theology of the NT* I (London: SCM, 1952).

F. W. Burnett, *The Testament of Jesus-Sophia: A Redaction-Critical Study of the Eschatological Discourse in Matthew* (Washington: University Press of America, 1981).

D. A. Campbell, *The Rhetoric of Righteousness in Romans 3.21-26* (Sheffield: JSOT, 1992) 138-72.

B. Capper, "The Interpretation of Acts 5:4," *JSNT* 19 (1983) 117-31.

C. Caragounis, *Peter and the Rock* (Berlin: de Gruyter, 1990).

———, *Son of Man* (Tübingen: Mohr, 1986).

D. B. Carmichael, "David Daube on Eucharist and the Passover Seder," *JSNT* 42 (1991) 45-67.

D. A. Carson, *The Gospel according to John* (Pillar; Leicester: IVP/Grand Rapids: Eerdmans, 1991).

M. Casey, *From Jewish Prophet to Gentile God* (Cambridge: Clarke, 1991).

———, "The Original Aramaic Form of Jesus' Interpretation of the Cup," *JTS* 41 (1990) 1-12.

———, *The Son of Man: The Interpretation and Influence of Daniel 7* (London: SPCK, 1980).

D. R. Catchpole, *The Quest for Q* (Edinburgh: Clark, 1993).

L. Cerfaux, *Christ in the Theology of St. Paul* (New York: Herder/Edinburgh: Nelson, 1959).

J. Chapman, "St Paul and the Revelation to St Peter, Matt. XVI,17," *Revue Benedictine* 29 (1912) 133-47.

J. H. Charlesworth, "From Jewish Messianology to Christian Christology: Some Caveats and Perspectives," in Neusner, Green, and Frerichs, eds., *Judaisms and Their Messiahs*, 225-64.

———, *Jesus within Judaism: New Light from Exciting Archaeological Discoveries* (Garden City: Doubleday/London: SPCK, 1988).

J. H. Charlesworth and C. A. Evans, "Jesus in the Agrapha and Apocryphal Gospels," in Chilton and Evans, *Studying the Historical Jesus*, 479-533.

B. Chilton, *A Feast of Meanings: Eucharistic Theologies from Jesus through Johannine Circles* (Leiden: Brill, 1994).

————, *God in Strength* (Linz: Plöchl, 1979).

————, "Jesus and the Repentance of E. P. Sanders," *TynB* 39 (1988) 1-18.

————, ed., *The Kingdom of God* (London: SPCK, 1984).

B. Chilton and C. A. Evans, eds., *Studying the Historical Jesus: Evaluations of the State of Current Research* (Leiden: Brill, 1994).

R. F. Collins, *Divorce in the NT* (Collegeville: Glazier, 1992).

H. Conzelmann, *A Commentary on the First Epistle to the Corinthians* (Hermeneia; Philadelphia: Fortress, 1975).

B. Corley, "Trial of Jesus," in J. B. Green, S. McKnight, and I. H. Marshall, eds., *Dictionary of Jesus and the Gospels* (Downers Grove/Leicester: IVP, 1992) 841-54.

W. Craig, "The Bodily Resurrection of Jesus," *Gospel Perspectives I*, 47-74.

C. E. B. Cranfield, *The Epistle to the Romans* I (ICC; Edinburgh: Clark, 1975).

————, "Some Reflections on the Subject of the Virgin Birth," *SJT* 41 (1988) 177-98.

J. D. Crossan, *The Historical Jesus: The Life of a Mediterranean Jewish Peasant* (San Francisco: Harper, 1991).

D. Daube, *The NT and Rabbinic Judaism* (London: Athlone, 1956).

P. H. Davids, "James and Jesus," *Gospel Perspectives 5*, 63-84.

G. N. Davies, *Faith and Obedience in Romans* (Sheffield: JSOT, 1990).

W. D. Davies, *Paul and Rabbinic Judaism* (London: SPCK, 1980[4]).

W. D. Davies and D. C. Allison, *The Gospel according to Saint Matthew* (ICC; Edinburgh: Clark, 1988, 1991).

M. de Jonge, *Christology in Context: The Earliest Christian Response to Jesus* (Philadelphia: Westminster, 1988).

A.-M. Denis, "L'investiture de la fonction apostolique par 'Apocalypse.' Étude thématique de Gal. 1,16," *RevBib* 64 (1957) 334-62, 492-515.

E. De Roover, "La maternité virginale dans l'interpretation de Gal 4:4," in *Studiorum Paulinorum Congressus Internationalis Catholicus* (Analecta Biblica 17-18; Rome: Pontifical Biblical Institute, 1963) II, 17-37.

C. Deutsch, *Hidden Wisdom and the Easy Yoke: Wisdom, Torah, and Discipleship in Matthew 11.25-30* (Sheffield: JSOT, 1987).

C. H. Dodd, *The Epistle of Paul to the Romans* (MNTC; London: Hodder, 1932).

————, *More NT Studies* (Manchester: MUP, 1968).

————, *NT Studies* (Manchester: MUP, 1953).

K. P. Donfried, "The Allegory of the Ten Virgins (Matt 25:1-13) as a Summary of Matthean Theology," *JBL* 93 (1974) 415-28.

————, "Paul and Judaism: 1 Thessalonians 2:13-16 as a Test Case," *Int* 38 (1984) 242-53.

G. Downing, *Christ and the Cynics* (Sheffield: JSOT, 1988).

J. W. Drane, "Patterns of Evangelization in Paul and Jesus: A Way Forward in the Jesus-Paul Debate?" in Green and Turner, eds., *Jesus of Nazareth*, 281-96.

J. Drury, *The Parables in the Gospels* (London: SPCK, 1985).

D. Dungan, *The Sayings of Jesus in the Churches of Paul* (Oxford: Blackwell, 1971).

————, ed., *The Interrelations of the Gospels* (Leuven: LUP, 1990).

J. D. G. Dunn, *Baptism in the Holy Spirit* (London: SCM, 1970).

————, *Christology in the Making* (London: SCM, 1989²).

————, *A Commentary on the Epistle to the Galatians* (BNTC; London: Black/Peabody: Hendrickson, 1993).

————, *Jesus and the Spirit* (London: SCM, 1975).

————, *Jesus, Paul and the Law* (London: SPCK/Louisville: Westminster/John Knox, 1990).

————. "Jesus Tradition in Paul," in Chilton and Evans, *Studying the Historical Jesus*, 155-78.

————, "The Messianic Secret in Mark," in Tuckett, ed., *The Messianic Secret*, 116-31.

————, "Paul's Knowledge of the Jesus Tradition: The Evidence of Romans," in K. Kertelge, T. Holtz, and C.-P. März, eds., *Christus Bezeugen. Festschrift für Wolfgang Trilling* (Leipzig: St. Benno, 1988) 193-207.

————, *Romans 1–8* (WBC; Waco: Word, 1988).

————, *Romans 9–16* (WBC; Waco: Word, 1988).

————, *Unity and Diversity in the NT* (London: SCM/Philadelphia: Westminster, 1990²).

J. Dupont, "La Parabole du Maître qui Rentre dans la Nuit (Mc 13,34-36)," in *Mélanges Béda Rigaux* (Gembloux: Duculot, 1970) 89-116.

————, "La Révélation du Fils de Dieu en faveur de Pierre (Mt 16,17) et de Paul (Ga 1,16)," *RSR* 52 (1964) 411-20.

B. D. Ehrman, "Cephas and Peter," *JBL* 109 (1990) 463-74.

R. Eisenman and M. Wise, *The Dead Sea Scrolls Uncovered* (Shaftesbury/Rockport: Element, 1993).

E. E. Ellis, "Jesus' Use of the Old Testament and the Genesis of New Testament Theology," *Bulletin for Biblical Research* 3 (1993) 59-75.

————, "The Making of Narratives in the Synoptic Gospels," in Wansbrough, ed., *Jesus and the Oral Gospel Tradition*, 310-33.

————, *Pauline Theology: Ministry and Society* (Grand Rapids: Eerdmans/Exeter: Paternoster, 1989).

————, "Soma in First Corinthians," *Int* 44 (1990) 132-44.

————, "Traditions in 1 Corinthians," *NTS* 32 (1986) 481-502.

W. R. Farmer, *Jesus and the Gospel* (Philadelphia: Fortress, 1982).

————, *The Synoptic Problem* (London: Macmillan, 1964/Macon: Mercer UP, 1976).

G. D. Fee, *The First Epistle to the Corinthians* (NICNT; Grand Rapids: Eerdmans, 1987).

D. P. Feine, *Jesus Christus und Paulus* (Leipzig: Hinrichs, 1902).

J. A. Fitzmyer, "4Q246: The 'Son of God' Document from Qumran," *Biblica* 74 (1993) 153-74.

————, *The Gospel According to Luke (X-XXIV)* (AB; Garden City: Doubleday, 1985).

————, *Romans* (AB; Garden City: Doubleday, 1993).

B. Fjärstedt, *Synoptic Tradition in 1 Corinthians: Themes and Clusters of Theme Words in 1 Corinthians 1–4 and 9* (Uppsala, 1974).

H. Fleddermann, "The Discipleship Discourse (Mark 9:33-50)," *CBQ* 43 (1981) 57-75.

D. Ford, *The Abomination of Desolation in Biblical Eschatology* (Washington: University Press of America, 1979).

J. E. Fossum, *The Name of God and the Angel of the Lord* (Tübingen: Mohr, 1985).

R. T. France, *Divine Government* (London: SPCK, 1990).

————, *Matthew: Evangelist and Teacher* (Exeter: Paternoster, 1989).

J. W. Fraser, *Jesus and Paul* (Appleford: Marcham, 1974).

P. Fredriksen, *From Jesus to Christ: The Origins of the NT Images of Jesus* (New Haven: Yale UP, 1988).

N. Fryer, "The Meaning and Translation of *Hilasterion* in Romans 3:25," *EQ* 59 (1987) 99-116.

R. H. Fuller, "The Conception/Birth of Jesus as a Christological Moment," *JSNT* 1 (1978) 37-52.

————, *The Foundations of NT Christology* (London: Lutterworth, 1965).

R. Y.-K. Fung, *The Epistle to the Galatians* (NICNT; Grand Rapids: Eerdmans, 1988).

V. P. Furnish, *Jesus according to Paul* (Cambridge: CUP, 1993).

————, "The Jesus-Paul Debate: From Baur to Bultmann," in Wedderburn, ed., *Paul and Jesus*, 17-50 = *BJRL* 47 (1964/65) 342-81.

T. Geddert, *Watchwords: Mark 13 in Markan Eschatology* (Sheffield: JSOT, 1989).

D. Georgi, *The Opponents of Paul in Second Corinthians* (Philadelphia: Fortress, 1986/Edinburgh: Clark, 1987).

B. Gerhardsson, "The Path of the Gospel Tradition," in P. Stuhlmacher, ed., *The Gospel and the Gospels* (Grand Rapids: Eerdmans, 1991) 75-96.

————, *The Testing of God's Son* (Lund: Gleerup, 1966).

M. Gnanavaram, "*Treasure in Heaven and Treasure on Earth: A Traditio-*

Historical, Redactional and Exegetical Study of a Biblical Tradition, with Special Reference to Its Socio-Economic Setting" (Ph.D. Thesis, Coventry University, 1994).

J. Goldingay, *Daniel* (WBC; Waco: Word, 1989).

M. Goodman, *The Ruling Class of Judaea: The Origins of the Jewish Revolt against Rome AD 66-70* (Cambridge: CUP, 1987).

L. Goppelt, "Jesus und die 'Haustafel' Tradition," in P. Hoffmann, ed., *Orientierung an Jesus* (Freiburg: Herder, 1973) 93-106.

M. D. Goulder, *The Evangelists' Calendar* (London: SPCK, 1978).

————, *Luke: A New Paradigm* (Sheffield: JSOT, 1989).

————, *Midrash and Lection in Matthew* (London: SPCK, 1974).

G. Grass, *Ostergeschehen und Osterberichte* (Göttingen: Vandenhoeck und Ruprecht, 1962).

K. Grayston, *Dying, We Live: A New Enquiry into the Death of Christ in the NT* (London: DLT, 1990).

J. B. Green and M. Turner, eds., *Jesus of Nazareth: Lord and Christ: Essays on the Historical Jesus and NT Christology* (Grand Rapids: Eerdmans/Carlisle: Paternoster, 1994).

R. A. Guelich, *The Sermon on the Mount: A Foundation for Understanding* (Waco: Word, 1982).

R. H. Gundry, "The Hellenization of Dominical Tradition and the Christianization of Jewish Tradition in the Eschatology of 1-2 Thessalonians," *NTS* 33 (1987) 161-78.

————, *Mark: A Commentary on His Apology for the Cross* (Grand Rapids: Eerdmans, 1993).

————, *Matthew: A Commentary on His Literary and Theological Art* (Grand Rapids: Eerdmans, 1982).

F. Hahn, *Mission in the NT* (London: SCM, 1965).

————, *The Titles of Jesus in Christology: Their History in Early Christianity* (London: Lutterworth, 1969).

A. T. Hanson, *Studies in Paul's Technique and Theology* (London: SPCK, 1974).

D. R. A. Hare, *The Son of Man Tradition* (Minneapolis: Fortress, 1990).

M. Harris, *Jesus as God: The NT Use of Theos in Reference to Jesus* (Grand Rapids: Baker, 1992).

W. B. Harris, *A Commentary on the Epistle of St. Paul to the Romans* (Madras: CLS, 1964).

L. Hartman, *Prophecy Interpreted* (Uppsala: Gleerup, 1966).

A. E. Harvey, *Jesus and the Constraints of History* (London: Duckworth, 1982).

————, *Strenuous Commands: The Ethic of Jesus* (London: SCM/Philadelphia: Trinity, 1990).

G. Haufe, "Reich Gottes bei Paulus und in der Jesustradition," *NTS* 31 (1985) 467-72.

R. B. Hays, *Echoes of Scripture in the Letters of Paul* (New Haven: Yale UP, 1989).

————, *The Faith of Jesus Christ: An Investigation of the Narrative Substructure of Galatians 3:1–4:11* (Chico: Scholars, 1983).

M. Hengel, *The Atonement* (London: SCM, 1981).

————, *Earliest Christianity* (London: SCM, 1986)

————, *The Johannine Question* (London: SCM, 1989).

————, *The Son of God: The Origin of Christology and the History of Jewish-Hellenistic Religion* (London: SCM, 1976).

————, *Victory over Violence* (London: SPCK, 1975).

————, *Was Jesus a Revolutionist?* (Philadelphia: Fortress, 1972).

W. A. Heth and G. J. Wenham, *Jesus and Divorce* (London: Hodder, 1984).

D. Hill, *Greek Words and Hebrew Meanings* (Cambridge: CUP, 1967).

P. Hoffmann "Πάντες ἐργάται ἀδικίας: Redaktion und Tradition in Lc 13 22-30," *ZNW* 58 (1967) 188-214.

C. Holman, *Eschatological Delay in Jewish and Early Christian Apocalyptic Literature* (Ph.D. thesis, University of Nottingham, 1982).

T. Holtz, "Paul and the Oral Gospel Tradition," in Wansbrough, ed., *Jesus and the Oral Gospel Tradition*, 380-93.

M. Hooker, "Interchange and Atonement," *BJRL* 60 (1978) 462-81.

————, "Interchange and Suffering," in W. Horbury and B. McNeill, eds., *Suffering and Martyrdom in the NT* (Cambridge: CUP, 1981) 70-83.

————, "Interchange in Christ," *JTS* 22 (1971) 349-61.

————, *Jesus and the Servant* (London: SPCK, 1959).

————, "ΠΙΣΤΙΣ ΧΡΙΣΤΟΥ," *NTS* 35 (1989) 321-41.

————, *The Son of Man in Mark* (London: SPCK, 1967).

W. Horbury, "The Messianic Associations of 'The Son of Man' Sayings," *JTS* 36 (1985) 34-55.

R. A. Horsley, *Jesus and the Spiral of Violence: Popular Jewish Resistance in Roman Palestine* (San Francisco: Harper and Row, 1987).

A. M. Hunter, *Interpreting Paul's Gospel* (London: SCM, 1954).

————, *Paul and his Predecessors* (London: SCM, 1961[2]).

J. C. Hurd, "'The Jesus Whom Paul Preaches' (Acts 19:13)," in Richardson and Hurd, eds., *From Jesus to Paul*, 73-89.

L. Hurtado, "Jesus as Lordly Example in Philippians 2:5-11," in Richardson and Hurd, eds., *From Jesus to Paul*, 113-26.

————, *One God, One Lord* (London: SCM, 1988).

A. Ito, "The Question of the Authenticity of the Ban on Swearing (Matthew 5.33-37)," *JSNT* 43 (1991) 5-13.

J. Jeremias, *The Eucharistic Words of Jesus* (London: SCM, 1966).

————, *Jesus' Promise to the Nations* (London: SCM, 1958).

————, *NT Theology: The Proclamation of Jesus* (London: SCM/New York: Scribner, 1971).

————, *The Parables of Jesus* (London: SCM, 1963²).

————, *The Prayers of Jesus* (London: SCM, 1967).

J. Jervell, "Paul in the Acts of the Apostles: Tradition, History, Theology," in J. Kremer, ed., *Les Actes des Apôtres. Traditions, rédaction, théologie* (Leuven: LUP, 1979) 297-306.

R. Jewett, "The Agitators and the Galatian Congregation," *NTS* 17 (1970/71) 198-212.

L. T. Johnson, *The Writings of the NT* (Philadelphia: Fortress/London: SCM, 1986).

G. Johnston, "'Kingdom of God' Sayings in Paul's Letters," in Richardson and Hurd, eds., *From Jesus to Paul*, 143-56.

P. R. Jones, "1 Corinthians 15:8: Paul the Last Apostle," *TynB* 36 (1985) 3-34.

D. Juel, *Messiah and Temple: The Trial of Jesus in the Gospel of Mark* (Missoula: Scholars, 1977).

E. Jüngel, *Paulus und Jesus. Eine Untersuchung zur Präzisierung der Frage nach dem Ursprung der Christologie* (Tübingen: Mohr, 1967³).

E. Käsemann, *Commentary on Romans* (Grand Rapids: Eerdmans/London: SCM, 1980).

A. Kasher, *Jews and Hellenistic Cities in Eretz-Israel* (Tübingen: Mohr, 1990).

J. N. D. Kelly, *A Commentary on the Pastoral Epistles* (H/BNTC; London: Black/New York: Harper, 1963).

S. Kim, "Jesus, Sayings of," in G. F. Hawthorne, R. P. Martin, and D. G. Reid, eds., *Dictionary of Paul and His Letters* (Grand Rapids/Leicester: IVP, 1993) 474-92.

————, *The Origin of Paul's Gospel* (Grand Rapids: Eerdmans, 1982).

————, *"The 'Son of Man'" as the Son of God* (Tübingen: Mohr, 1983).

W. S. Kissinger, *The Sermon on the Mount: A History of Interpretation and Bibliography* (Metuchen: Scarecrow, 1975).

W. Klassen, "Musonius Rufus, Jesus, and Paul: Three First-Century Feminists," in Richardson and Hurd, eds., *From Jesus to Paul*, 185-206.

J. Klausner, *From Jesus to Paul* (London, 1946).

G. W. Knight, *The Pastoral Epistles* (NIGTC; Grand Rapids: Eerdmans/Carlisle: Paternoster, 1992).

R. J. Knowling, *The Testimony of St. Paul to Christ* (London: Hodder, 1905).

H. Koester, *Ancient Christian Gospels: Their History and Development* (London: SCM/Philadelphia: Trinity, 1990).

H.-W. Kuhn, "Der irdische Jesus bei Paulus als traditionsgeschichtliches und theologisches Problem," *ZTK* 67 (1970) 295-320.

W. G. Kümmel, *Heilsgeschehen und Geschichte* (Marburg: Elwert, 1965).

J. Laansma, *The Use of the Rest Motif in the NT, with Special Reference to Matthew 11 and Hebrews 3 and 4* (Ph.D. thesis, Aberdeen University, forthcoming).

G. E. Ladd, *A Theology of the NT* (Grand Rapids: Eerdmans, 1993²).

P. Lapide, *The Resurrection of Jesus: A Jewish Perspective* (London: SPCK, 1984).

B. Lindars, *Jesus, Son of Man* (London: SPCK/Grand Rapids: Eerdmans, 1992).

R. L. Lindsey, *A Hebrew Translation of the Gospel of Mark* (Jerusalem: Dagith, 1971).

B. W. Longenecker, "ΠΙΣΤΙΣ in Romans 3:25: Neglected Evidence for the 'Faithfulness of Christ'?" *NTS* 39 (1993) 478-80.

R. N. Longenecker, *The Christology of Early Jewish Christianity* (London: SCM, 1970).

G. Lüdemann, *Opposition to Paul in Jewish Christianity* (Minneapolis: Fortress, 1989).

————, *The Resurrection of Jesus* (London: SCM, 1994).

U. Luz, *Matthew 1–7: A Commentary* (Minneapolis: Augsburg, 1989).

H. Maccoby, *The Mythmaker: Paul and the Invention of Christianity* (London: Weidenfeld and Nicholson, 1986).

————, "Paul and the Eucharist," *NTS* 37 (1991) 247-67.

D. R. MacDonald, *There is No Male and Female* (Philadelphia: Fortress, 1987).

M. Y. Macdonald, "Women Holy in Body and Spirit in the Social Setting of 1 Corinthians 7," *NTS* 36 (1990) 161-81.

J. G. Machen, *The Origin of Paul's Religion* (London: Hodder, 1921).

B. Mack, *The Lost Gospel: The Book of Q and Christian Origins* (New York: HarperCollins/Shaftesbury: Element, 1993).

————, *The Myth of Innocence: Mark and Christian Origins* (Philadelphia: Fortress, 1988).

G. Maier, "The Church in the Gospel of Matthew," in D. A. Carson, ed., *Biblical Interpretation and the Church* (Exeter: Paternoster, 1984) 45-63.

————, "Jesustradition im 1. Petrusbrief?" in *Gospel Perspectives 5,* 85-128.

T. W. Manson, *The Sayings of Jesus* (London: SCM, 1949).

J. Marcus, "Entering into the Kingly Power of God," *JBL* 107 (1988) 663-75.

C. D. Marshall, *Faith as a Theme in Mark's Narrative* (Cambridge: CUP, 1989).

I. H. Marshall, *1 and 2 Thessalonians* (NCBC; London: Marshall/Grand Rapids: Eerdmans, 1983).

————, *The Gospel of Luke* (NIGTC; Grand Rapids: Eerdmans/Exeter: Paternoster, 1978).

————, "The Hope of a New Age: The Kingdom of God in the NT," *Themelios* 11 (1985) 5-15 = *Jesus the Saviour* (London: SPCK, 1990) 213-38.

————, *Last Supper, Lord's Supper* (Exeter: Paternoster, 1980).

————, *The Origins of NT Christology* (Leicester: Apollos, 1990²).

R. P. Martin, *Reconciliation* (Atlanta: John Knox/London: Marshall, 1981).

————, *2 Corinthians* (WBC; Waco: Word, 1986).

F. J. Matera, "The Trial of Jesus: Problems and Proposals," *Int* 45 (1991) 5-16.

J. I. H. McDonald, *Kerygma and Didache* (Cambridge: CUP, 1980).

B. C. McGing, "Pontius Pilate and the Sources," *CBQ* 53 (1991) 416-38.

J. McHugh, *The Mother of Jesus in the NT* (London: DLT, 1975).

J. P. Meier, *Law and History in Matthew's Gospel: A Redactional Study of Matthew 5:17-48* (Rome: Pontifical Biblical Institute, 1976).

————, *A Marginal Jew: Rethinking the Historical Jesus* (Garden City: Doubleday, 1991).

B. Meyer, *The Aims of Jesus* (London: SCM, 1979).

J. R. Michaels, "Paul and John the Baptist: An Odd Couple," *TynB* 42 (1991) 245-60.

R. Mohrlang, *Matthew and Paul: A Comparison of Ethical Perspectives* (Cambridge: CUP, 1984).

D. Moo, "Jesus and the Authority of the Mosaic Law," *JSNT* 20 (1984) 3-49.

————, "Paul and the Law in the Last Ten Years," *SJT* 40 (1987) 287-307.

L. Morris, *The Apostolic Preaching of the Cross* (London: IVP, 1955).

————, "The Gospels and the Jewish Lectionaries," in *Gospel Perspectives III*, 129-53.

A. D. A. Moses, *The Significance of the Transfiguration in Matthew's Gospel Seen in Its Jewish and Early Christian Context* (Ph.D. thesis, Westminster College, Oxford, 1992).

S. Motyer, "Righteousness by Faith in the NT," in J. I. Packer, ed., *Here We Stand* (London: Hodder, 1986) 32-56.

C. F. D. Moule, *The Birth of the NT* (London: Black/San Francisco: Harper and Row, 1982³).

————, *The Origin of Christology* (Cambridge: CUP, 1977).

J. Munck, *Paul and the Salvation of Mankind* (London: SCM, 1959).

J. Murphy-O'Connor, "John the Baptist and Jesus: History and Hypotheses," *NTS* 36 (1990) 359-74.

C. Myers, *Binding the Strong Man: A Political Reading of Mark's Story of Jesus* (Maryknoll: Orbis, 1988).

S. Neill and N. T. Wright, *The Interpretation of the NT 1861-1986* (Oxford: OUP, 1988).

F. Neirynck, "Paul and the Sayings of Jesus," in A. Vanhoye, ed., *L'Apôtre Paul* (Leuven: LUP, 1986) 265-321.

P. K. Nelson, *Leadership and Discipleship: A Study of Luke 22:24-30* (Ph.D. thesis, Trinity College, Bristol, 1991).

J. Neusner, "Mr Sanders' Pharisees and Mine," *SJT* 44 (1991) 73-95.

J. Neusner, W. S. Green, and E. S. Frerichs, eds., *Judaisms and Their Messiahs at the Turn of the Christian Era* (Cambridge: CUP, 1987).

G. W. E. Nickelsburg, "Salvation without and with a Messiah: Developing Beliefs in Writings Ascribed to Enoch," in Neusner, Green, and Frerichs, eds., *Judaisms and Their Messiahs*, 49-68.

I. Ninan, *Jesus as the Son of God: An Examination of the Background and Meaning of "Son of God" in Paul's Christology with Particular Reference to Romans 8* (Ph.D. thesis, Coventry University, 1994).

J. Nolland, *Luke 1–9:20* (WBC; Waco: Word, 1989).

———, *Luke 9:21–18:34* (WBC; Waco: Word, 1993).

P. T. O'Brien, *Colossians, Philemon* (WBC; Waco: Word, 1982).

———, *The Epistle to the Philippians* (NIGTC; Grand Rapids: Eerdmans, 1991).

J. C. O'Neill, "The Kingdom of God," *NovT* 35 (1993) 130-41.

J. B. Orchard, "Thessalonians and the Synoptic Gospels," *Biblica* 19 (1938) 19-42.

G. R. Osborne, *The Resurrection Narratives: A Redactional Study* (Grand Rapids: Baker, 1984).

S. H. T. Page, "The Authenticity of the Ransom Logion (Mark 10:45b)," in *Gospel Perspectives I*, 137-62.

S. J. Patterson, "Paul and the Jesus Tradition," *HTR* 84 (1991) 23-41.

P. B. Payne, "The Authenticity of the Parable of the Sower and Its Interpretation," in *Gospel Perspectives I*, 163-208.

P. Perkins, *Resurrection* (London: Chapman/Garden City: Doubleday, 1985).

N. Perrin, *Jesus and the Language of the Kingdom* (Philadelphia: Fortress/London: SCM, 1976).

———, *The Resurrection according to Matthew, Mark and Luke* (Philadelphia: Fortress, 1977).

R. Pesch, "Das Evangelium Gottes über seinen Sohn Zur Auslegung der Tradition in Röm. 1,1-4," in K. Kertelge, T. Holtz, and C.-P. März, eds., *Christus Bezeugen. Festschrift für Wolfgang Trilling* (Leipzig: St. Benno, 1988) 208-17.

———, *Das Markusevangelium* (Freiburg: Herder, 1977).

J. Piper, "The Demonstration of the Righteousness of God in Romans 3:25, 26," *JSNT* 7 (1980) 2-32.

———, *"Love your Enemies": Jesus' Love Command in the Synoptic Gospels and the Early Christian Paraenesis* (Cambridge: CUP, 1980).

B. Pixner, *Wege des Messias und Stätten der Urkirche* (Giessen: Brunnen, 1991).

Q. Quesnell, " 'Made Themselves Eunuchs for the Kingdom of Heaven' (Mt 19,12)," *CBQ* 30 (1968), 335-58.

H. Räisänen, *Jesus, Paul and Torah* (Sheffield: JSOT, 1992).

———, *Paul and the Law* (Tübingen: Mohr, 1983).

F. Refoulé, "Primauté de Pierre dans les évangiles," *RSR* 38 (1964) 1-41.

A. Resch, *Der Paulinismus und die Logia Jesus* (Leipzig: Hinrichs, 1905).

P. Richardson, " 'I Say, Not the Lord': Personal Opinion, Apostolic Authority and the Development of Early Church Halakah," *TynB* 31 (1980) 65-86.

———, "The Thunderbolt in Q and the Wise Man in Corinth," in Richardson and Hurd, eds., *From Jesus to Paul*, 91-111.

P. Richardson and P. Gooch, "Logia of Jesus in 1 Corinthians," in *Gospel Perspectives 5*, 39-62.

P. Richardson and J. C. Hurd, eds., *From Jesus to Paul: Studies in Honour of Francis Wright Beare* (Waterloo: Wilfrid Laurier University, 1984).

H. N. Ridderbos, *Paul and Jesus* (Philadelphia: Presbyterian and Reformed, 1958).

R. Riesner, *Die Frühzeit des Apostles Paulus* (Tübingen: Mohr, 1994).

————, *Jesus als Lehrer* (Mohr: Tübingen, 1981).

J. A. T. Robinson, *The Body* (London: SCM, 1952).

————, *The Priority of John* (London: SCM, 1985).

J. M. Robinson, "Kerygma and History in the NT," in J. P. Hyatt, ed., *The Bible in Modern Scholarship* (Nashville: Abingdon, 1965) 114-50.

W. C. Robinson, "A Re-Study of the Virgin Birth of Christ," *EQ* 37 (1965) 198-212.

E. P. Sanders, *The Historical Figure of Jesus* (London: Penguin, 1993).

————, *Jesus and Judaism* (London: SCM, 1985).

————, *Paul and Palestinian Judaism* (London: SCM, 1977).

E. P. Sanders and M. Davies, *Studying the Synoptic Gospels* (London: SCM/Philadelphia: Trinity, 1989).

S. Sandmel, "Parallelomania," *JBL* 81 (1962) 1-13.

J. Sauer, "Traditionsgeschichtliche Erwägungen zu den synoptischen und paulinischen Aussagen über Feindesliebe und Wiedervergeltungsverzicht," *ZNW* 76 (1985) 1-28.

W. Schenk, "Auferweckung der Toten oder Gericht nach den Werken, Tradition und Redaktion in Matthäus xxv 1-13," *NovT* 8 (1966) 223-34.

F. Schillebeeckx, *Jesus: An Experiment in Christology* (London: Collins, 1979).

R Schippers, "The Pre-Synoptic Tradition in 1 Thessalonians II 13-16," *NovT* 8 (1966) 223-34.

A. Schlatter, *Jesus und Paulus* (Stuttgart: Calwer, 1961³).

R. Schnackenburg, *The Moral Teaching of the NT* (Tunbridge Wells: Burns and Oates, 1965).

W. Schrage, *The Ethics of the NT* (Philadelphia: Fortress/Edinburgh: Clark, 1988).

E. Schürer, *The History of the Jewish People in the Age of Jesus Christ* III/1, revised by G. Vermes, F. Millar, and M. Goodman (Edinburgh: Clark, 1986).

H. Schürmann, *Das Lukasevangelium I* (Freiburg: Herder, 1969).

A. Schweitzer, *The Quest of the Historical Jesus* (London: Black, 1911²).

E. Schweizer, *The Good News according to Mark* (London: SPCK, 1970).

————, *The Good News according to Matthew* (London: SPCK, 1976).

————, *The Lord's Supper according to the NT* (Philadelphia: Fortress, 1967).

C. H. H. Scobie, "Jesus or Paul? The Origin of the Universal Mission of the Christian Church," in Hurd and Richardson, eds., *From Jesus to Paul*, 47-60.

J. M. Scott, *Adoption as Sons of God: An Exegetical Investigation into the Background of* ΥΙΟΘΕΣΙΑ *in the Pauline Corpus* (Tübingen: Mohr, 1992).

A. Segal, *Paul the Convert: The Apostolate and Apostasy of Saul the Pharisee* (New Haven: Yale UP, 1990).

J. W. Simpson, "The Problems Posed by 1 Thessalonians 2:15-16 and a Solution," *Horizons in Biblical Theology* 12 (1990) 42-72.

E. M. Smallwood, *The Jews under Roman Rule from Pompey to Diocletian* (Leiden: Brill, 1981²).

R. Sneed, " 'The Kingdom of God Is within You' (Lk 17,21)," *CBQ* 24 (1962) 363-82.

K. Snodgrass, *The Parable of the Wicked Tenants: An Inquiry into Parable Interpretation* (Tübingen: Mohr, 1983).

J. Sobrino, *Christology at the Crossroads: A Latin American Approach* (London: SCM, 1978).

D. P. Stanley, "Pauline Allusions to the Sayings of Jesus," *CBQ* 23 (1961) 26-39.

G. N. Stanton, *A Gospel for a New People* (Edinburgh: Clark, 1992).

———, *Jesus of Nazareth in NT Preaching* (Cambridge: CUP, 1974).

O. H. Steck, *Israel und das Gewaltsame Geschick der Propheten* (Neukirchen-Vluyn: Neukirchener, 1967).

K. Stendahl, "The Apostle Paul and the Introspective Conscience of the West," *HTR* 56 (1963) 199-215 = *Paul among Jews and Gentiles and Other Essays* (Philadelphia: Fortress, 1976) 78-96.

P. Stuhlmacher, *Biblische Theologie des Neuen Testaments. I: Grundlegung von Jesus zu Paulus* (Göttingen: Vandenhoeck und Ruprecht, 1992).

———, "Jesustradition im Römerbrief?" *Theologische Beiträge* 14 (1983) 240-50.

———, "Das neutestamentliche Zeugnis vom Herrenmahl," *ZTK* 84 (1987) 1-35.

———, *Reconciliation, Law, and Righteousness* (Philadelphia: Fortress, 1986).

J. Suggs, *Wisdom, Christology, and Law in Matthew's Gospel* (Cambridge: Harvard UP, 1970).

J. Sweet, "A House Not Made with Hands," in W. Horbury, ed., *Templum Amicitiae: Essays on the Second Temple Presented to Ernst Bammel* (Sheffield: JSOT, 1991) 368-90.

H. B. Swete, *The Gospel according to St Mark* (London: Macmillan, 1909³).

V. Taylor, *The Gospel according to St. Mark* (London: Macmillan, 1963).

W. Telford, *The Barren Temple and the Withered Fig Tree* (Sheffield: JSOT, 1980).

G. Theissen, *The Shadow of the Galilean* (London: SCM, 1987).

———, *Social Reality and the Early Christians* (Edinburgh: Clark, 1992).

J. C. Thomas, *Footwashing in John 13 and the Johannine Community* (Sheffield: JSOT, 1991).

M. Thompson, *Clothed with Christ: The Example and Teaching of Jesus in Romans 12.1–15.13* (Sheffield: JSOT, 1991).

C. M. Tuckett, "1 Corinthians and Q," *JBL* 102 (1983) 607-18.

————, "Paul and the Synoptic Mission Discourse?" *ETL* 60 (1984) 376-81.

————, *The Revival of the Griesbach Hypothesis* (Cambridge: CUP, 1983).

————, "Synoptic Tradition in 1 Thessalonians," in R. F. Collins, ed., *The Thessalonian Correspondence* (Leuven: LUP, 1990) 160-82.

————, ed., *The Messianic Secret* (London: SPCK, 1983).

G. H. Twelftree, "Jesus in Jewish Traditions," in *Gospel Perspectives 5*, 289-341.

G. Vermes, *The Dead Sea Scrolls in English* (London: Penguin, 1987³).

————, *Jesus and the World of Judaism* (London: SCM, 1983).

————, *Jesus the Jew* (London: SCM, 1983²).

————, "Qumran Forum Miscellanea I," *JJS* 43 (1992) 299-305.

————, *The Religion of Jesus the Jew* (London: SCM, 1993).

R. Wall, "Successors to 'the Twelve' according to Acts 12:1-7," *CBQ* 53 (1991) 628-43.

N. Walter, "Paul and the Early Christian Jesus-Tradition," in Wedderburn, ed., *Paul and Jesus*, 51-80.

H. Wansbrough, ed., *Jesus and the Oral Gospel Tradition* (Sheffield: JSOT, 1991).

J. A. Weatherley, "The Authenticity of 1 Thessalonians 2.13-16: Additional Evidence," *JSNT* 42 (1991) 79-98.

R. L. Webb, "John the Baptist and His Relationship to Jesus," in Chilton and Evans, *Studying the Historical Jesus*, 179-229.

————, *John the Baptizer and Prophet: A Socio-Historical Study* (Sheffield: JSOT, 1991).

A. J. M. Wedderburn, *Baptism and Resurrection: Studies in Pauline Theology against Its Graeco-Roman Background* (Tübingen: Mohr, 1987).

————, *The Reasons for Romans* (Edinburgh: Clark, 1988).

————, ed., *Paul and Jesus: Collected Essays* (Sheffield: JSOT, 1989).

A. Weiser, *Die Knechtsgleichnisse der Synoptischen Evangelien* (Munich: Kösel, 1971).

D. Wenham, "Acts and the Pauline Corpus, II: The Evidence of Parallels," in B. W. Winter and A. D. Clarke, eds., *The Book of Acts in Its First Century Setting. I: The Book of Acts in Its Ancient Literary Setting* (Grand Rapids: Eerdmans/Carlisle: Paternoster, 1993) 215-58.

————, *Gospel Perspectives 4: The Rediscovery of Jesus' Eschatological Discourse* (Sheffield: JSOT, 1984).

————, "How Jesus Understood the Last Supper: A Parable in Action," *Churchman* 105 (1991) 246-60.

————, "The Interpretation of the Parable of the Sower," *NTS* 20 (1974) 299-319.

————, "Kingdom and Creation: From Jesus to Paul," *Theology in Green* 3 (1992) 27-38; 4 (1992) 32-39.

————, "A Note on Mark 9.33-42/Matt 18.1-6/Luke 9.46-50," *JSNT* 14 (1982) 113-18.

————, "A Note on Matthew 24:10-12," *TynB* 31 (1980) 155-62.

————, *The Parables of Jesus: Pictures of Revolution* (London: Hodder/Downers Grove: IVP, 1989).

————, "Paul's Use of the Jesus Tradition: Three Samples," in *Gospel Perspectives 5*, 7-37.

————, "The Story of Jesus Known to Paul," in Green and Turner, eds., *Jesus of Nazareth: Lord and Christ*, 297-311.

————, "The Synoptic Problem Revisited: Some New Suggestions about the Composition of Mark 4:1-34," *TynB* 23 (1972) 3-38.

————, "'This Generation Will Not Pass . . .': A Study of Jesus' Future Expectation in Mark 13," in H. H. Rowdon, ed., *Christ the Lord* (Leicester: IVP, 1982) 127-50.

————, "Unity and Diversity in the NT," in Ladd, *Theology of the NT*, 684-719.

D. Wenham and A. D. A. Moses, "'There are Some Standing Here . . .': Did They Become the 'Reputed Pillars' of the Jerusalem Church? Some Reflections on Mark 9:1, Galatians 2:9 and the Transfiguration," *NovT* 36 (1994) 146-63.

G. J. Wenham, *The Book of Leviticus* (New International Commentary on the OT; Grand Rapids: Eerdmans, 1979).

J. W. Wenham, *Easter Enigma* (Exeter: Paternoster, 1984).

————, *Redating Matthew, Mark and Luke* (London: Hodder, 1991).

S. Westerholm, *Israel's Law and the Church's Faith: Paul and His Recent Interpreters* (Grand Rapids: Eerdmans, 1988).

D. E. H. Whiteley, *The Theology of St Paul* (Oxford: Blackwell, 1964).

S. G. Wilson, "From Jesus to Paul: The Contours and Consequences of a Debate," in Richardson and Hurd, ed., *From Jesus to Paul*, 1-21.

A. C. Wire, *The Corinthian Women Prophets: A Reconstruction through Paul's Rhetoric* (Minneapolis: Fortress, 1990).

B. Witherington, *The Christology of Jesus* (Minneapolis: Fortress, 1990).

————, *Jesus the Sage: The Pilgrimage of Wisdom* (Edinburgh: Clark, 1994).

————, *Jesus, Paul and the End of the World* (Downers Grove: IVP/Exeter: Paternoster, 1992).

————, *Women and the Genesis of Christianity* (Cambridge: CUP, 1990).

————, *Women in the Ministry of Jesus* (Cambridge: CUP, 1984).

C. Wolff, "Humility and Self-Denial in Jesus' Life and Message and in the Apostolic Existence of Paul," in Wedderburn, ed., *Paul and Jesus*, 145-60.

————, "True Apostolic Knowledge of Christ: Exegetical Reflections on 2 Corinthians 5.14ff.," in Wedderburn, ed., *Paul and Jesus*, 81-98.

W. Wrede, *Paul* (London: Green, 1907).

N. T. Wright, *The Climax of the Covenant* (Edinburgh: Clark, 1991).

————, *Jesus and the Victory of God* (London: SPCK, forthcoming).

————, *The NT and the People of God* (London: SPCK/Minneapolis: Fortress, 1992).

J. Ziesler, *The Meaning of Righteousness in Paul* (Cambridge: CUP, 1972).

————, *Pauline Christianity* (Oxford: OUP, 1983).

————, *Paul's Letter to the Romans* (London: SCM/Philadelphia: Trinity, 1989).

Index of Biblical References

Index of Modern Authors

Index of Subjects

Abba, 27, 60, 69, 113, 125, 184, 233, 276-80, 346, 383, 395-96
Abraham, 52, 171, 180, 184, 290, 344, 356
Acts of the Apostles, 62, 85, 102, 405-6. *See also* Index of Biblical References
"Acknowledged ones," 362-63
Adam, 60, 65, 119-20, 126-29, 184, 185, 187, 189, 383, 400
Age, 69, 223, 224, 232, 248, 298
Allusions and echoes, 6, 25-26, 30, 381, 393, 402-3, 406-7
Amen, 223-24, 273-74, 384
Ananias, 397
Antiochus Epiphanes, 37, 291, 300, 318, 323
Apocryphal gospels, 24, 98
Apollos, 79, 130, 132, 133, 285, 312-13, 345, 392, 395
Apostle(ship), 133, 165, 180, 191, 192, 195-96, 198, 200, 202, 204, 212, 350-51, 355, 368-70, 382, 396-97, 400, 405
Aramaic, 27, 110-11, 113, 123, 129, 170, 315, 396
Ascension, 370-71, 383
Atonement, 150-53, 271. *See also* Cross; Death of Jesus
Authenticity
    of gospel traditions, 20, 84, 89, 109, 111, 114, 134, 156-57, 161, 171, 303, 313-14

    of Pauline letters, 13, 24-25, 236, 316, 319-20
Authority, 2, 100, 114-15, 195-96, 198, 211-12, 223-24, 235, 237-38

Baptism, 3, 67-68, 99-101, 122, 143, 154-56, 160-64, 188, 230, 232-33, 284-86, 343-48, 350, 377, 379, 383, 406
Birth of Jesus, 3, 338-43, 385
Blood of Christ, 150, 153, 156
Body, 2, 61, 153, 156, 183, 185-89, 208-9, 230-31, 234, 248, 303, 369
Brothers, 117, 169, 184, 212, 258-59, 265-66, 340, 367
Build/building, 174-77, 203-4, 206, 208

Caesar. *See* Rome
Celibacy, 236, 245-50, 355, 382, 384, 394
Charismatic gifts/charismatics, 43, 63, 79, 112, 130, 133, 231-32, 399. *See also* Gifts
Christ. *See* Messiah
Church, 12, 35, 165-213 (including 169-71, 180, 182-83, 206-7), 394
Clean, unclean, 46, 92-97, 194, 222, 383, 387, 394
Collection for Jerusalem, 4, 180-81, 239-40
Corinth/Corinthians, 79, 82, 158, 194,

447